Cœur de Lion; or the Third Crusade; a poem, etc.

Eleanor Porden

Cœur de Lion; or the Third Crusade; a poem, etc.
Porden, Eleanor
British Library, Historical Print Editions
British Library
1822
2 vol. ; 8°.
994.h.25.

The BiblioLife Network

This project was made possible in part by the BiblioLife Network (BLN), a project aimed at addressing some of the huge challenges facing book preservationists around the world. The BLN includes libraries, library networks, archives, subject matter experts, online communities and library service providers. We believe every book ever published should be available as a high-quality print reproduction; printed on- demand anywhere in the world. This insures the ongoing accessibility of the content and helps generate sustainable revenue for the libraries and organizations that work to preserve these important materials.

The following book is in the "public domain" and represents an authentic reproduction of the text as printed by the original publisher. While we have attempted to accurately maintain the integrity of the original work, there are sometimes problems with the original book or micro-film from which the books were digitized. This can result in minor errors in reproduction. Possible imperfections include missing and blurred pages, poor pictures, markings and other reproduction issues beyond our control. Because this work is culturally important, we have made it available as part of our commitment to protecting, preserving, and promoting the world's literature.

GUIDE TO FOLD-OUTS, MAPS and OVERSIZED IMAGES

In an online database, page images do not need to conform to the size restrictions found in a printed book. When converting these images back into a printed bound book, the page sizes are standardized in ways that maintain the detail of the original. For large images, such as fold-out maps, the original page image is split into two or more pages.

Guidelines used to determine the split of oversize pages:

- Some images are split vertically; large images require vertical and horizontal splits.
- For horizontal splits, the content is split left to right.
- For vertical splits, the content is split from top to bottom.
- For both vertical and horizontal splits, the image is processed from top left to bottom right.

CŒUR DE LION.

VOL. I.

CŒUR DE LION;

OR

THE THIRD CRUSADE.

A POEM,

IN SIXTEEN BOOKS.

By ELEANOR ANNE PORDEN,
AUTHOR OF
"THE VEILS," "THE ARCTIC EXPEDITIONS,"
AND OTHER POEMS.

Richard that robb'd the Lion of his Heart,
And fought the Holy Wars in Palestine.—*Shakspeare.*

IN TWO VOLUMES.

VOL. I.

LONDON:
PRINTED FOR G. AND W. B. WHITTAKER,
AVE-MARIA-LANE.
1822.

LONDON:
PRINTED BY COX AND BAYLIS, GREAT QUEEN STREET,
LINCOLN'S-INN-FIELDS.

TO

HIS MOST EXCELLENT MAJESTY

GEORGE THE FOURTH,

KING

OF THE

UNITED KINGDOM

OF

GREAT BRITAIN AND IRELAND,

&c. &c. &c.

THE ENLIGHTENED PATRON AND PROTECTOR

OF

ENGLISH LITERATURE,

𝔗𝔥𝔦𝔰 𝔓𝔬𝔢𝔪

IS,

WITH HIS MAJESTY'S MOST GRACIOUS PERMISSION,

HUMBLY INSCRIBED

BY HIS MAJESTY'S

MOST DUTIFUL AND DEVOTED SERVANT,

ELEANOR ANNE PORDEN.

ODE

TO THE

KING'S MOST EXCELLENT MAJESTY.

RULER of a happy Land!
England's far-descended King!
Sprung from Him whose dreadful band
Fought beneath the Raven's wing:
Whom his Cimbrian galleys bore
To found on Neustria's yielding shore,
Beneath serener skies, a wider reign;
Till, slighting realms so cheaply won,
His brave Descendant launch'd anew, to gain
Fair Albion for his Bride, and fill her Island Throne.

Sprung from those whom Britain's call
    Summon'd in an earlier age,
When her violated wall
    Felt the Pictish spoiler's rage—
Soon a milder, purer creed,
    Changed to white their sable steed;
Soon in one orb the sevenfold rays combined;
    Her vanquish'd foes confest the flame,
And England with her budding laurels twined
Beyond the reach of Time, the wreath of Alfred's fame.

Mourn not, if their mutual force
    Oft the plains in crimson dyed;
If the Saxon's generous Horse
    Stoop'd beneath the Lion's pride.
Thus two mountain springs descend,
    Thus their meeting waves contend:
Long the fierce waters foam, and clash, and roar,
    Till to their strife the channel yields,
Green turf and fragrant blossoms clothe the shore,
And the broad tranquil stream spreads plenty through the fields.

With the broomy garland crown'd
    See the conquering Henry shine!
PLANTAGENET! that lofty sound,
    Blends the boast of either line.
See the Silver Cross display'd
    O'er th' impetuous RICHARD's head!
On Syria's holy plains to win or bleed,
    Pours his devoted host along,
While he, triumphant on his Cyprian steed,
Scatters like morning clouds the misbelieving throng.

MONARCH! him I dare to sing!
    Him! thy kindred Henry's son.
From his gallant warriors spring
    They who late thy battles won.
England now, from fields of strife
    Guards her Sovereign's sacred life,
Yet still aloft her star of glory shines;
    For He that late her Trident bore,
And he to whom thy hand her Sword consigns,
Shall mate with Arthur's peers, and RICHARD's knights of yore.

Though no Cross their bosoms seal'd,
 Their march no mail-clad Prelates led;
Sacred be each laurell'd field!
 In a hallow'd cause they bled.
England's thunders swept the sea
 That her brethren might be free;
Nor for herself were fruitful regions gain'd:
 She the trampled fought to raise,
And of a rescued world alone retain'd
The honour of the strife, th' imperishable praise.

 Beneath Italia's purple heaven
  Two gifted Sons of song divine
 To Immortality have given
  Thy parent Esté's princely line;
 And ever when pale Cynthia pours
  Her radiance on its summer shores,
Along the Adriatic's listening waves
 Still sings the merry gondolier;
His glistening oar to Roland's glory laves,
Or with Rinaldo woos some new Armida's ear.

Long may they sing—but shall not He
    Whom England proudly calls her own,
Whose deeds of song and chivalry
    Once gave new lustre to her throne,
One mellifluous strain inspire,
Or rouse one warrior's latent fire;
Even as Himself could erst the gales invite
    To waft his bark to Syrian plains,
Or call'd indignant from Trivallis' height
His lingering peers to loose their King's ignoble chains?

Say not Chivalry is dead;
    That her spirit charms no more—
Noble souls still love to tread
    Paths of legendary lore:
She speaks from every craggy steep,
    Yet crown'd with some embattled keep,
Or stream that lave the Convent's ruin'd cells,
    And in the Minster's aisles of pride,
Still many a sculptured Hero proudly tells,
For her he bravely fought, for Heaven and England died.

She lives, while England is a name;
    While native in her sons shall spring
That heaven-born zeal, that loyal flame
    Which binds her People to her King;
That zeal all selfish thoughts above
Which lives but in its country's love,
Which seeks for Honour in the front of war;
    Which, as it stamps the Tyrant's doom,
Spreads with her rule the light of Truth afar;
While Justice guides her sword, and Virtue guards her home.

    MONARCH, hold that spirit dear!
        Prize the Muse that gives it fame!
    So, to some future Sovereign's ear
        Shall Bards unborn thy worth proclaim;
Or pausing on thy Father's reign,
Own their loftiest numbers vain,
To picture one in every virtue blest;
    Who firm amid the tempest stood,
Friend of the friendless, Champion of th' opprest,
Thine and thy People's Sire—the Glorious and the Good!

Or how thine own majestic hand,
    Ending works so well begun,
Led to an exulting land,
    PEACE, by noble daring won.
    Which long—but let not man presume
    To lift the veil of years to come,
Suffice it that Eternal Wisdom sways.—
    That we to Heaven our eyes may cast,
    For present good our grateful anthems raise
And wish that future years may but reflect the past.

    To THEE, of Arts and Song the Friend,
        Fearless the Bard her tribute bears,
    With vows for all that Heaven can send
        Of lengthen'd reign and prosperous years!
    And pardon Her whose minstrelsie
        Ambitious dwells on themes so high,
Though haply she in vain the Muse may woo,
    And to thy footstool only bring
A heart in every pulse to England true,
True to her equal Laws, her Altar and her King.

PREFACE.

The greatness of an enterprize, while it increases the diffidence of an Author, almost destroys the right of apology. If, in attempting to celebrate the heroic achievements of RICHARD CŒUR DE LION in Palestine, and the events of the Third Crusade, I have ventured beyond my strength, I can only say that my fancy was captivated by the chivalrous and romantic spirit which breathes from every page of their history, and that in the wish to see them poetically treated, I forgot my own deficiencies, and also that much of the necessary information was to be derived from sources almost inaccessible to a female.

The character of RICHARD has, I think, been a little unfairly delineated; and especially as respects his engagement in the Holy War. It is absurd to try the justice or the prudence of the Crusades by the feelings and opinions of the nineteenth century, and it is almost impossible to estimate what were or were not the advantages which Europe ultimately derived from its consequent intercourse with Asia. Every page of our old chronicles bears record of the darkness and ignorance which then enveloped even the most civilized nations of the West. Fanaticism and valour were the ruling spirits of the Middle Ages; and while we deplore the myriads of human victims that were sacrificed for the temporary possession of a narrow territory in Asia, we ought to remember that many of them would otherwise have fallen in feudal and intestine war, and that when the sword of bigotry reposed for a moment from the task of exterminating the followers of Mahommed, it was never without an object of persecution among the heretics of Europe. If RICHARD drained his kingdom of its bravest warriors and richest treasures to lose them both in Palestine, in a contest which neither advantaged himself nor his realm, we must not forget that it was for the attainment of all which was then believed most precious; in obedience to an authority which he was taught to consider infallible; and to the still stronger voice of universal enthusiasm, which pointed out the pilgrimage to Palestine as the atonement for the greatest crimes; the certain path of salvation. The bravest Princes of Christendom were his comrades and his rivals, and had He only remained in Europe, his contemporaries would not have applauded his prudence, but have reproached him as a coward, and as a traitor to his honour and his God. He has been accused of shewing more of the brutal courage of a soldier, than the skill of a leader; but personal prowess was then esteemed as the noblest quality of a hero, and in that, RICHARD excelled not only his companions, valiant as they were, but almost all the genuine warriors of antient days, and the Paladins of romance. It was not till after the departure of Philip Augustus from Acre, that RICHARD became the leader of the Crusaders, and even then each independent chieftain arrayed his followers with more regard to his own interest and glory, than to the common good; yet the march to Arsouf, and the battle of Jaffa, are evidences that he both possessed and could exert the talents of a general; and the brief period of his stay in Palestine is almost the only page of the Crusades which can be read without horror, as it is the only one which is free from distresses and disasters of the most dreadful kind, and brought on by the most childish want of forethought and discipline.

With regard to his personal character. There are but two of the leaders of the Crusades that will bear the test of time. Godfrey of Bouillon, who was equally exemplary as a private soldier, a general, a monarch, and a christian; and Tancred, the perfect model of chivalry. Hume, in his History of England, has stigmatized RICHARD as a bad son, a bad husband, and a bad king; but let us compare him with his contemporaries. The stains of rebellion, of rapacity, perfidy, and cruelty, are strong upon the names of his brother John, of Alphonso of Arragon, of Leopold of Austria, and Henry the sixth of Germany. While we condemn his rebellion to his father, let us not forget his provocation and his repentance; as a husband, his history is at least unstained by the cold and inexplicable cruelty with which Philip Augustus treated for a number of years the most beautiful and accomplished Princess of her time; and if the indulgence of his martial genius impoverished his subjects, it endeared him to their hearts, and made the name of CŒUR DE LION the pride of England and the terror of Asia. A blind admiration of the Great of former ages, has been so often ridiculed, that we are now apt to run into an opposite extreme; they are like the fossil plants which we sometimes discover far beneath the surface; we know that our soil and atmosphere would not now support them, yet they once flourished there in appropriate use and beauty.

France was the cradle of the Crusades; and we have, till very lately, left it to the French to write their history. It has been remarked that the Monarchs of France and England never fought together in one cause, except at the Siege of Acre; and though the martial achievements and magnificence of RICHARD be more congenial with the general taste of our Gallic neighbours, than the cool calculating policy of Philip Augustus, it cannot be matter of surprize that this circumstance should have peculiarly excited the feelings of national rivalry, to deepen the darker shades of his character, and to pass lightly over many traits of generosity and magnanimity. The jealousy of his comrades occasioned the Crusade to fail in its principal object of the re-establishment of the kingdom of Jerusalem, and their treachery rendered it a source of misery and civil conflict to England; but I cannot help thinking that had a longer life been permitted to him, he would have triumphed over his enemies, consolidated his power, and in the maturity of years and reflection, would have become one of the greatest monarchs in our annals.

The Latin kingdom of Jerusalem maintained itself not quite one hundred years. Of the multitudes that accompanied Godfrey, few contemplated a permanent expatriation, and when the object of their pilgrimage was accomplished in the redemption of the Sepulchre, they returned to Europe, leaving him to defend it with very inadequate forces. Yet the single year of his reign was a course of victory, and the code of laws which he caused to be compiled, has been considered as the best example of feudal jurisprudence. On his death, his brother Baldwin was called from the principality of Edessa to the vacant throne, and though the territory which he quitted was richer and more extensive than his new dominions; these were advantages not to be compared with the glory of reigning over the Holy City, and he cheerfully resigned his conquest into the hand of his cousin Baldwin du Bourg.

The avarice and ambition of the first Baldwin, had been a source of constant dissension among the Crusaders, and retarded the completion of their enterprize, but from the time of his accession, the brother of Godfrey proved himself not unworthy of his relationship. During a reign of eighteen years, with forces that seemed scarcely sufficient for the defence of his little state, he made it formidable to the Saracens of Syria and Egypt, and increased it to an extent which his successors were unequal to maintain. He died childless, and Jerusalem again looked to Edessa for a ruler, while Baldwin du Bourg, was succeeded in the principality by his cousin, Josceline de Courtenay.

The new king spent nearly the two first years of his reign in captivity among the Infidels; but the honour of his kingdom was maintained by his vassals, and with the assistance of the Venetians, he afterwards captured the important city of Tyre. As he had no son, he determined to chuse among the nobles of Europe a husband for his daughter Melesinda, and an heir to his crown. His choice fell upon Fulk, Count of Anjou; the father, by a former wife, of the House of Plantagenet; and who had already distinguished himself in a pilgrimage to Palestine. Fulk accepted the invitation of Baldwin, who expired after a reign of twelve years; and in him his subjects wept over the last of the companions of Godfrey, in whom they could find no fault, but that he was more of a saint than a hero. About this time arose the Knights Hospitallers, or Knights of St. John, and the Knights Templars, afterwards the strongest defence of Jerusalem. But the power of the Christians was already beginning to decline; the virtues of Fulk were esteemed, but his faculties were enfeebled by age, and he left his sceptre to a minor.

The kingdom had hitherto subsisted through the weakness and disunion of the Saracens; they were now beginning to be united under formidable leaders, and in the reign of the Third Baldwin, Edessa was torn from the degenerate heir of Josceline de Courtenay, by Zenghi or Sanguin, Sultan of Aleppo, and his son, the celebrated Noureddin. The news of this disaster revived the enthusiasm of the West. The Emperor Conrad the Third of Germany and Louis the Seventh of France, accompanied by his wife Eleanor of Guyenne, (afterwards married to Henry the Second of England, and mother of RICHARD and John,) led a force of seven hundred thousand warriors to the Holy Land. More than two-thirds of this immense armament perished through the ignorance and disobedience of its chieftains, the treachery of the Greeks, and the hostility of the Turkish Sultans of Iconium. The remnant besieged

Damascus, but their valour was rendered vain by the jealousy of the Syriac Christians; and the Second Crusade was without one glorious action to atone for the appalling waste of human blood, or to vindicate the promises and exhortations of St. Bernard, which had tempted such multitudes from the bosom of their families. Soon after, in the midst of a succession of victory, Baldwin the Third died by poison, and was succeeded by his brother Amalric. A brave soldier but an imprudent king, he often purchased peace from the Saracens by the cession of some of the strongest bulwarks of his dominions, and then as foolishly violated the treaty bought so dear, whenever the arrival of a few straggling pilgrims from Europe held out the hope of obtaining some trifling advantage. He suffered himself to be involved in the domestic broils of Egypt, and afterwards sacrificed the interests of his kingdom to the chimerical hope of conquering that rich country.

The wars of Egypt were indeed fatal to Jerusalem, for it was in them that Saladine first learnt the duties of a soldier; and it is remarkable that Noureddin with difficulty compelled into the path of military renown, the man who was shortly after to pluck the sceptre from the hands of his son, and to become one of the greatest monarchs of the East. At his first campaign the unambitious son of Ayoub reluctantly quitted the pleasures of Damascus, and the toils and perils of war were so little to his taste, that even the distinction which he acquired by the successful defence of Alexandria could not vanquish his disgust; and when the Sultan again ordered him to the banks of the Nile, he went, according to his own confession, with the despair of a man conducted to death. But after he had once fairly tasted the cup of glory his thirst became insatiable. The desire of empire and the triumph of the Koran annihilated every other passion, and the voluptuous youth became remarkable for the simplicity and even austerity of his life. His religious feelings were gratified by the deposition of the heretic Caliph of Cairo, and the restoration of Egypt to the orthodox faith of Islam. During the life of Noureddin, Saladine was contented to govern in his name; but at his death he raised the standard of revolt, won province after province from his children and his emirs, and then advanced to subdue Jerusalem, a city almost equally sacred in the eyes of a Moslem and a Christian. Gibbon has remarked that the successes of Saladine were prepared by the circumstances of the times, and that he was seldom victorious when opposed by equal forces. It is also worthy of observation that he was unable to sustain the frowns of fortune. The loss of a battle or a friend sunk him into a state of despondency, from which he was only to be roused by the remembrance, that, according to the doctrine of his Prophet, all was predestined, and that it was impious to murmur at the will of Alla. His character has derived a singular colouring from the mixture of severe devotion to a bigotted and cruel faith, with the feelings of a heart unusually generous and humane.

Jerusalem was a victim ready for sacrifice: Amalric left his crown to his son, a leper and a child, who died just as he was beginning to shew that he possessed talents worthy of dominion. His infant nephew survived him but a few months, and the kingdom, weakened by intestine broils, and exposed to a powerful enemy, remained in the insufficient hands of his sister Sybilla, and her husband, Guy de Lusignan, who had not even the prudence to conciliate those whom he pretended to govern, or the good faith to observe a treaty with Saladine, which might have delayed for a few years the ruin of his power. He lost his army and his liberty at the battle of Tiberias; and Jerusalem, after a short resistance, submitted to the Soldan. The circumstances of its capitulation, and his generosity to the conquered, are detailed in the notes to the poem. Tyre was soon the only city of Palestine which remained to the Christians, and it was saved from sharing the fate of the rest by the opportune arrival of Conrad of Montferrat, with a few brave followers.

In the mean time the loss of the Holy City spread dismay in Europe. Some years previous, the Patriarch Heraclius had endeavoured to stimulate the potentates of France and England by the recital of its dangers; but the misfortunes of the Second Crusade were not then forgotten, and his intemperate harangues and infamous character were injurious to his cause. The venerable Archbishop of Tyre was more successful; and when he related the sad events of which he was afterwards to write the history, the brave and pious wept at the idea of the Saracens trampling on the Tomb of their Redeemer. Philip Augustus and RICHARD sheathed on the field of battle the swords which were drawn for mutual warfare, and vied with the Emperor Frederic Barbarossa in their preparations for its rescue. Myriads hastened to take the cross, and to defray the expense of their equipment, the memorable tax of the

Dixme Saladine, or the tenth part of their rents and moveables, was imposed on all who remained behind. In the meanwhile the Soldan had released Lusignan from captivity, and as the hatred of Conrad had caused the gates of Tyre to be shut against him, he collected the few friends which still remained to him, and began the siege of Acre. Saladine advanced to its relief; successive bands of Christians, whose less splendid preparations had enabled them to outstrip the three great monarchs of Europe, arrived to reinforce the army of Lusignan, while that of the Soldan was continually recruited from Egypt, Damascus, and Aleppo; and the siege had continued nearly three years at the time when the Poem commences.

In this brief abstract I have merely attempted to recall to the memory of the reader a few of the principal events which preceded the action of the Poem. The recent publication of Mr. Mills's History of the Crusades, has rendered more minuteness unnecessary. It is needless to say, that in a poem, much of fiction is necessarily blended, but where I have drawn from history, I have endeavoured to be correct. For one great anachronism I must throw myself on the mercy of the critic, but it seemed to me otherwise impossible to preserve any unity of story without omitting the most romantic part of RICHARD's life.

It only remains for me to express my thanks to those friends who have assisted my labours. To Mr. Gifford, for the benefit which I have derived from his friendly criticism; and to Mr. D'Israeli, and Messrs. Longman and Rees, for the loan of many valuable books.

CŒUR DE LION.

BOOK I.

THE SIEGE OF ACRE.

ARGUMENT.

THE SIEGE OF ACRE.

The Poem opens in the evening after the defeat of the Christians before Acre—Debate of the impious Genii on Mount Carmel—Death of Sybilla, Queen of Jerusalem—Contest of the crusading Princes for the vacant throne—Violence of Conrad, Prince of Tyre—Appearance and death of Raymond—The contending parties are appeased by Hubert, Bishop of Salisbury—Meeting of Conrad and Isabella, sister to the deceased Queen—Battle with Saladine; Stratagem of Omar—Success of the Christians—The intoxication of success, and reverse of fortune—The danger of Conrad, and his rescue by Lusignan—Arrival of King Philip, who joins the Battle—Complete rout of Saladine's army—Death of Eudon—Reflexions of Lusignan and Hubert.

CŒUR DE LION.

While Britain's annals shine with many a name,
   Her loftiest Poets might contend to sing;
While British bosoms feed poetic flame,
   Why should Her Lyre with foreign praises ring?
Not for my own, but for my country's fame,
   Oh! make me worthy of my theme, and bring,
Sweet Muse! thy noblest numbers, while I dare
To blazon Richard's deeds, and Richard's Holy War.

In Honour's fountain steep my Lyre, and give
    The great of distant ages to mine eyes,
With all their martial pomp the dead revive,
    Heroic deeds and holy extasies;
That they through long futurity may live,
    And breathe o'er unborn heroes as they rise
The courteous grace, the spirit wild and high,
The warm, romantic glow, of genuine Chivalry.

For, Britain! not in this thy noon of fame,
    Hast thou a son to noble hearts more dear,
Than He, the terror of the Moslem name,
    Who on the deep thy White-Cross dared to rear
And spread in Palestine, till it became
    The Christian's day-star, and th' Apostate's fear,
Who mix'd with martial deeds the minstrel lyre,
He of the Lion-heart, the dauntless soul of fire.

CŒUR DE LION.

BOOK I.

THE SIEGE OF ACRE.

On Carmel's brow, and Acre's placid tide,
The crimson Evening's latest radiance died;
Warn'd by the thickening gloom of awful Night,
The weary hosts suspend th' unfinish'd fight,
Each fainting Christian to his tent retires,
And counts on either side the hostile fires,
That from the towers of leaguer'd Acre shine,
Or (stretch'd around,) the camp of Saladine.*

---

* On the eastern coast of the Mediterranean is a small bay, of which Mount Carmel forms the southern extremity, while that to the north is occupied by the city of Acre. The plain, on the south, is watered by

Since Salem's exiled King begirt her wall,
Since Asia's Lord obey'd his people's call,   10
For three long years, in doubtful conflict tried,
The scale of Victory bow'd to either side,
Yet ne'er the sun on such a fatal field
Had set, or saw so far the Christians yield;
The Moslems sallied from th' unconquered town,
From Kaisan's heights the Soldan thunder'd down,
In vain they strove to stem the tide of fate,
And crowds of Martyrs throng the heavenly gate;
A strange mysterious terror seiz'd on all,
Alike the feeble and the valiant fall;   20

two rivers; the Belus, whose sands were sought from a great distance for the manufacture of glass, and the "ancient river, the river Kishon;" but like most of the Syrian streams, they roll a torrent in the Spring, and nearly disappear in the Autumn. Acre, washed on two sides by the sea, is protected on the third by strong walls, and a succession of massy towers. The Christians, at the commencement of the siege, pitched their camp on the hill of Turon, to the north-east of the town; but this camp being enlarged by the arrival of successive bodies of Crusaders, it extended gradually from Belus to the sea, and almost matched the city in the strength of its ramparts. To the south-east, and a little more remote, but still *within* the Belus, is a conical hill, called Mahumeria, or the Hill of the Mosque, and by some writers, the Tomb of Memnon. Here were the head-quarters of Saladine; but much of his army seems to have been encamped on the heights of Kaisan, and in winter it retired to the yet remoter mountains of Kharouba. Acre was therefore enclosed by the Christian army, which, in its turn, was enclosed by that of Saladine.

Nine slaughter'd ranks the purple plain o'erspread,
And every rank contain'd a thousand dead.*

The anxious warders in the camp below
Mark'd a dense cloud on Carmel's lofty brow,
Portentous lightning flash'd; a sullen sound
Of mutter'd thunder roll'd the mountain round,
And lo! a sanguine meteor fires the air,
Cleaves the dark mass and shrouds its brightness there;
While the dun vapours and the clamorous din
Declar'd that still it fiercely blazed within.   30
With horror seiz'd, they tremble at the sign,
And breathe in pious prayer the name divine.

Well might they tremble—there in close debate,
A dark divan of hellish Genii sate.
On that vast mount where in his lone abode
The wrapt Elijah communed with his God,
Where, when a crowd of impious Priests, in vain,
With harpings loud and steam of victims slain,
Invok'd their slumb'ring Baal from morn till even,
The Prophet's voice drew down the fire from heaven;

* " Neuf rangs de morts couvraient le terrein qui s'étend entre la colline et la mer, et chaque rang était de mille guerriers."—*Michaud from Bohaheddin.*

In after times, Alkarmel's Altar rose—
Alkarmel, fellest of Messiah's foes;^a
Though ne'er in walls his vot'ries dared enshrine
His horrid vastness, or his form define.
But hence expell'd, by Mary's vestal choirs,
His sanguine orgies ceas'd and impious fires,
Till now again he treads the hallow'd ground,
And blasts the vines, and calls the Genii round;
All that to punish or to prove mankind,
Direct the plague, the earthquake, or the wind, 50
Gild with false rays th' Arabian Prophet's name,
Or bow before the fount of living flame;
All that against the Son of God combine,
To foil the Champions of his Holy Shrine.
On flying columns borne of whirling sand,
Speeds dark Demroosh from Zara's burning land;
From Libanus the snowy tempest brings
The hideous Ullah on its icy wings;
And like a vapour from the foaming tide,
Rose stern Mordash, Maimoune at his side; 60
On a light cloud her lovely limbs reclin'd,
Her sable locks a starry wreath confin'd;
Shame, Guilt, and Fear had darken'd every face,
But her's had yet a beam of heavenly grace;

What though no more it vies with Eden's rose,
Nor in her eye angelic rapture glows,
Who could behold her pensive charms, and seek
A smile more brilliant, or a ruddier cheek,
Could think that guilt deprest that gentle eye,
Or endless torture breath'd so soft a sigh? 70
Aw'd by her beauty, as a thing divine,
From their dark thrones the Genii half incline;
Then while his frame in fiendish transport shook,
Alkarmel rose, and thus in thunder spoke:

" Woe to the Gospel! to the Koran joy!*
On yonder plain ten thousand Christians lie.
Joy! for this night the Queen Sybilla[b] dies,
And fierce contentions round her bier arise.
Fools! for a name, a realm yet unsubdued,
Hark to their clamour! may it end in blood! 80
May fiercer strife succeed this war of words,
And Christian do the work of Moslem swords!
Sing, till our Pæans reach the realms below,
Joy to the Koran! to the Gospel woe!"

* Michaud, vol. ii. p. 70, in speaking of the Turkish mode of warfare in their inroads on the kingdom of Jerusalem, says, that when successful, they returned to their country loaded with spoil, and singing these words:
—" The Koran is plunged in joy, the Gospel in tears."

"Joy!" cried Demroosh, while fill'd with sudden ire,
From his dark eye-balls flash'd vindictive fire.
"What joy is ours? such joy as traitors feel,
Nail'd to the cross, the gibbet, or the wheel;
Or birds that, spell-bound by the serpent's eye,
Perceive their doom, yet lose the power to fly.   90
Go! credulous, and shout your Prophet's name,
Till all his mosques are lost in Christian flame.
In vain is Salem yours, in vain ye swore
To chase the Cross from this contested shore;
In vain whole hosts of vanquish'd martyrs bleed;
Like waves on waves, devoted hosts succeed.
Though due to British worth, yon ramparts know
Their fated strength, nor fear a meaner foe,
Already RICHARD comes—his fleet has past
The Cyprian isle, and we are foil'd at last."   100

" 'Tis well," Mordash began, " for Islam's sake,
While thou art slumbering, that her guardians wake;
I rais'd the storm; on Cyprus rocky coast
Is RICHARD's gallant fleet dispersed or lost.
Vers'd in the counsels to his father's dear,
The faithless, fatal policy of fear.

That Turk and Christian hates alike, and pays,
Feeds, clothes, enriches both, and both betrays,
The Cyprian sceptre base Comnenus sways.^c
The Lion King shall struggle in the toils; 110
Not Demons match Comnenus' race in wiles;
Not all our arts have served the Faith so well,
Or sent such hosts of Christian dogs to Hell.
Philip may come—to-morrow's sun may bring
His vaunted fleet—we fear not Gallia's king!
To war and Ullah we his troops consign;
The harder task of RICHARD's bane be mine;
Caught in their snares whom Godfrey learn'd to curse,
Their hatred deadly, but their friendship worse."

" Nor scorn a softer spell," Maimoune said, 120
" His daughter's smiles Comnenus' craft shall aid.
E'en now, or all my wonted arts are vain,
Evanthe strives with Love's insidious pain;
Fair as her Island's Queen, her pensive charms
Shall lure the King from Berengaria's arms,
Inglorious flowers shall wreathe his idle sword,
And his stern knights deplore their recreant Lord."

Contempt and malice Ullah's smile exprest.
" How ill thou know'st these warriors of the West!

Go! spread for Asian Youth thy tempting spells, 130
In Knighthood's breast a loftier spirit dwells:
Shrined in each bosom reigns one peerless fair,
And true to her, as to the Cross they wear,
Strong in their faith, through fields of death they move,
For only Glory wins the smiles of Love;
No second beauty lures their constant eye—
Maimoune's charms might pass unheeded by."

" Nay!" said the Peri, " look on yonder plain,
And own, my philtres are not always vain."

" Aye, look on yonder plain! behold how near 140
My busy fiends besiege each princely ear!"
Alkarmel shouted. " Look, Demroosh! and own
That Godfrey's faith and Tancred's zeal are flown;
Those trusting zealots served their God too well,
We found no vantage, and the city fell.
But these are brave in vain—their hearts are ours:
Ha! floats our standard not from Sion's towers?
Have we not crush'd Imperial Conrad's host?[d]
And Gaul's gay troop at proud Damascus crost?
We bade the Earthquake towns and towers destroy
We hurl'd red meteors through the flaming sky!
We sear'd the grain! we dried the crystal springs!
We fill'd with leprosy the courts of kings![e]

Look on yon plain, Demroosh! thou can'st not fear
Each spotted Conscience will be wash'd so clear,
That not one fiend shall win his entrance there.
Not Richard's soul is pure—on Asia's shore,
Soon shall the Christian name be heard no more,
The Soldan's dying voice shall warn in vain,
And Guilt and Rapine claim their licens'd reign." 160

"But," the stern Afrit said, "what arts are ours
To check the course of Frederic's conquering powers?
Young Angelus Comnenian craft has tried,
But proved alone his weakness and his pride:
For Frederic's valour had too bold a spring,
To brook the trifling of a powerless king;
On Stamboul's faithless towers his flag was spread,
The treacherous Turks before his army fled.
And proud Iconium's Sultan found too late,
Who trifles with his friendship, sports with fate."ᶠ 170

"Fear, doubt, alarm from Frederic's might is o'er,
His army baffled, and its chief no more!"
Thus spoke the fierce Moozallil, as he came,
Swift as a hurricane, and wrapt in flame.
"Twice warn'd, that spot shall Suabia's Princes shun,
Erst fraught with ill to Philip's godlike son.

Where Conrad droop'd, a king without a host,
Now Frederic's myriads mourn their leader lost;
For as he bathed in Saleph's frigid tide,
Amid its poison'd waves he sunk and died.*   180
Was it not well? I hover'd o'er the brink
His latest breath of agony to drink,
His people's cries, his son's unceasing tears,
His moans, sweet music to Moozallil's ears!"

They shout applause; the meaner Demons round,
Hovering like birds obscene, prolong the sound.
Delight through either Moslem host it spread,
And chill'd the Christians with spontaneous dread.

"Hail, Mighty Spirit! thou whose powerful soul,
Fruitful of ill, nor ruth nor fears control!   190
Most dire, most hateful—yet my lips decline
A rival's praises—would the deed were mine!"
Alkarmel spoke, "but see, a warning dye
Of feeble purple streaks the eastern sky;
Hence let us haste, ere Angels purge the ground,
With heavenly dews and fragrance sprinkled round,

---

* The Emperor Conrad the IIId. of Germany lost his army, by the treachery of the Turks of Iconium, in the mountains of Armenia. Frederic Barbarossa overcame the Turks, but perished near the same place in the river Saleph, believed by some writers to be the Cydnus, whose icy waters had nearly proved fatal to Alexander the Great.

Lest here enthrall'd we pine in hated light,
And yon vile Christians prosper in our sight.
I go to taint the bosoms of the brave,
And wake new tumults round Sybilla's grave;   200
Thou, Ullah! steep these fields in sudden rains,
And thou, Demroosh! on all the humid plains
Breathe thy hot gales, till clouds of venom rise,
And famine follows, and yon army dies.
Mordash with storms shall RICHARD's fleet detain,
And fair Maimoune twine her flowery chain;
For thee, Moozallil! who shall dare confine
Such bold invention, and such power as thine?
Go where thou wilt, for in thy baleful breath,
Where'er thou art, are treachery, woe, and death."

 He spoke, and like the thousand sparks that fly
From the sprung mine, and fade amid the sky,
The Genii vanish'd, ere in golden pride
The sun rose glorious from the tranquil tide.

 The Christians watch'd not for the dawning light,
Nor blest the day that call'd them forth to fight.
Theirs the sad task their slaughter'd friends to shield
From ravenous birds that hover o'er the field,

And wolves and shakals, that would rob the brave
Of their last hope, an honourable grave. 220
Nine mighty mounds arose, gigantic tombs,
For every mound a thousand dead inhumes,
While scarce distinguish'd from the general plain,
One scanty pile conceal'd the Moslem slain.

But not their labour foil'd, their bravest lost,
So fills with grief and fear the anxious host,
As Queen Sybilla's death; beside her sate
The widow'd Lusignan, her princely mate,
Graceful in grief, his locks of waving gold
Neglected o'er his regal mantle roll'd, 230
He thought with what fond faith Amalric's heir,
Twice made herself, and once her realm, his care.
Ah, from his grasp that short-lived power was fled,
And she was cold, and hope itself was dead.
But while he mused, with brows of thick'ning gloom
Indignant Geoffrey rushes to the room.

"Weak fool! will tears recall Sybilla's ghost,
To give again the kingdom thou hast lost?
Oh! that a brother I had never known,
Or found in him a spirit like mine own! 240
Yet come, nor tamely see thyself bereft,
Of all of power that war and fate have left.

From thy weak heart its fruitless sorrow fling,
And guard, what yet thou hast, the name of King!"
  The King one moment on the senseless clay
Fix'd his fond gaze, then dash'd his tears away;
" And must we part, ere I to earth resign
These fair cold relics? yet the gift was Thine—"
  With folded arms and aching brows he went
Where met the nobles in the regal tent,   250
(Arm'd save their casques), and mounts the golden throne
Conspicuous rais'd, and long esteem'd his own,
And scarce he mark'd, that 'mid the princely crowd
No chieftain rose, no head respectful bow'd;
" Shame on you, Lords!" cried Geoffrey, " whence can spring
This cold neglect of Sion's hapless King?"
  "And who is Sion's King, but he who reigns
" In Sion's Kingdom?" cried the bold Avesnes.*
" Her Lord again should Lusignan appear,
Again I bend; but stand his equal here—   260

---

* James, Lord of Avesnes and Guise, was one of the most renowned captains of his age, and emulated the fame of his ancestor Gerard D'Avesnes, who had gained honour in the first Crusade.—*Maimbourg.*

Go! scent his hair, and wreathe his fragile blade,
Not for hot fight, but courtly pageant made.
Hast thou not mock'd him oft, and said that she
Who made Him King, should make a God of thee?*
Scarce while she lived a forced respect we gave,
Our freedom rises from Sybilla's grave.
Let female eyes his beauteous form admire,
Our northern souls a hardier chief require.
Not his an arm the Soldan's might to bend,
And win a realm he knew not to defend." 270

Pride check'd the tears that fill'd the Monarch's eye,
And fiery Geoffrey struggled for reply;
When Thoron thus his mild reproof addrest,
Of Syria's Counts the bravest and the best,
Above ambition, pious, liberal, sage,
For wisdom honour'd, though unbent by age.

"Ungenerous Chiefs! to poison thus the dart
That grief has planted in a Monarch's heart;
Come ye, like vultures, darkening all the sky,
Ere the first burst of hopeless grief be dry, 280

* When Geoffrey de Lusignan heard that Sybilla had made his brother Guy King of Jerusalem, he replied, with more of frankness than fraternal affection, "If she have made Him King, she would have made a God of me."

Ere on the long-loved form the earth shall close,
To tear the garland from his widow'd brows?
When, at her brother's death, her peers implored,
From sad Sybilla's choice a warrior lord,
Though then, perchance, by erring fondness led,
To bind the fillet on her husband's head,
If she could yield those rights by birth her own,
Still Lusignan must fill the sacred throne,
If not—to doubt his claim is mine alone.*
'Tis mine the throne with Isabelle to share,   290
Amalric's younger child, and now his heir."

"Thy rights! as well might base-born kites aspire
To rule the eagle!" cried the Prince of Tyre.[g]
"We leave at leisure, Lusignan and thee
To settle points of legal courtesie,
Thanks to your prowess! we may waive them now,
Or I could tell him of a broken vow,
That when a captive he his realm resign'd—†
But that were nought, nor oaths compell'd can bind,

* Isabella, married to Humfrey Count of Thoron, was the daughter of Amalric by his second wife, Mary, sister to Isaac Comnenus.

† Before Saladine released his royal prisoner, he bound him by an oath to resign all future pretensions to the throne of Jerusalem; but Lusignan was no sooner at liberty than his desire of vengeance awakened, and

So say those Priests that Heaven's high dictates scan;
And chain or loose the ready faith of man.
But for his Queen—Oh! could my brother know
His widow'd bride would dare to stoop so low!
Or when her warlike peers no more obey'd [h]
Her minion's rule, the solemn farce she play'd!
The feign'd divorce, the pledge from morn till even
To seek in prayer the guiding hand of Heaven.
All day she pray'd, and music's loftiest sound,
And spicy clouds, the fatal drama crown'd;
Gull'd by her words, her nobles waited round 310
As Heaven should bid to pay their ready vow;
She rais'd the regal circlet from her brow
And placed on Lusignan's, but did a voice
Of man or angel rise to bless the choice?
They bow'd in silence, duped as all shall feel
Who trust a woman with a nation's weal.

" Doubtful of all that arms or counsel bore,
And worse, his own weak powers mistrusting more,
How did he reign? how many months were flown
Ere Asia's sovereign fill'd his conquer'd throne? 320

Heraclius made no difficulty of freeing him from his vow, declaring, not only that compulsory engagements could not be considered as binding, but that it was meritorious to break such as were made with infidels.

Say! where were Lusignan? and even now,
But for the arm of Conrad, where wert thou?
A dungeon's damp had chill'd this lust of power,
And not one Christian breath'd on Syria's shore.
Now hear my will, and should not words avail,
Beware! my sword has weight to turn the scale;
Mine is the right, the power, I ask the name!
And if Amalric's child must aid my claim,
Despite thine angry curse or martial pride,
I make thy vaunted Isabelle my bride,   330
Nor dread to hear the Roman thunders roar—
They spare the sinner that extends their power!
Or while thou liv'st, if she respect her vow
To wed a *widow*, all our laws allow—
And think ye, Lords! too boldly I aspire?
My fleet now guards you—shall it sail for Tyre?
Or—yon brave foe a warrior's worth can feel,
And more than Salem would reward my zeal."

 Bold Thoron's answering falchion quits the sheath,
Frowns dark Avesnes, and Geoffrey threatens death,
While by the side of Conrad, fierce and bold
Like some strong tower, stood Austrian Leopold.[i]
When rose the King, and even that lawless throng
In silence heard a Chief obey'd so long.

"Oh! let not weapons that should stream alone
With impious blood, be sullied by our own;
And blame not me, if niggard Nature gave
A form unwarlike, though my soul be brave.
Yet ah! can those whom Hope's gay dreams beguile,
Whose names are honour'd, and whose fortunes smile,
Thus for the shade of vanish'd power contest,
Desert their God, and crush a bleeding breast?
By Him who came in meekness, He whose name
Should soothe our spirits, while his wrongs inflame,
Oh! cease this strife, nor be his champions found
In vain contention for an empty sound!"

"What dar'st thou, dastard! call an empty name?
I give it value, if I deign to claim!"

"Pause!" cried a voice that every bosom froze,
And 'mid the hall a ghastly man uprose. 360
The grave's white vestments form'd his wild attire,
His glazed eyes glimmer'd with unearthly fire;
On high his lean and wither'd arms he spread;
Is that the hand that Moslem hosts have fled?
They doubt if those sepulchral accents came
From Raymond's spectre, or his living frame.
"Stop, impious and insensate!—Lo! I come
Ev'n from the very borders of the tomb,

Once more your guilty fury to restrain,
Once more to warn you, and to warn in vain. 370
Cowards! to taunt the fallen with his shame!
And who that hears me has the right to blame?
Not you, his subjects, rebels to his power,
And false to Sion in her dangerous hour;
Not you, ye Templars, who the strife renew'd,
Your robes polluting with a Herald's blood;[k]
Not Eudon, scorning my prophetic word,
Who forced a fatal counsel on his Lord.
'Twas then the Soldan girt Tabaria's wall—
But I was deaf to wife and offspring's call; 380
I wept for Sion, I besought him yield
Their fate to Heaven, and be his Sion's shield—
In vain! he flew to guard the leaguer'd town,
He could not save it: and he lost his crown.
This was his crime! and that my honest zeal
To all I loved preferr'd the public weal,
That when my voice was scorn'd, destruction came,
Ye call me traitor! I retort the name.
Is this the meed for acts so great and bold
As should have lived in everlasting gold? 390
This warp'd my brain, this foul reproach has riven
The bonds of life, this pains my sires in Heaven.'[l]

Woe, woe for Sion! for her hearths profaned,
Her murder'd children, and her temples stain'd;
Oh recreants! traitors to the Cross ye bear!
Whom fury, avarice, lust, alternate share,
Still must your half-heal'd feuds again begin,
And scorn and rancour blast the wreaths ye win.
Know ye, whose madness all the good deplore,
Know! heaven respects that great Barbarian more,
Whose soul untaught in virtue yours exceeds,
Than ye, apostates not in name, but deeds."

He spoke; his eyes a ghastlier lustre fired,
It flash'd like lightning, and like that expired;
Through all his frame a strong convulsion past,
One startling shriek he gave, it was the last;
With that his mighty spirit burst away,
And cold and rigid fell the lifeless clay.

Awe, shame, and sense of past ingratitude,
Chain'd every tongue, and every heart subdued; 410
But Conrad frown'd; "Are we, that even now
Raged like the winds on Thabor's stormy brow,
Hush'd to such stillness that we hear the call
Of the changed guard on Acre's distant wall—
Heroes! so prompt to scorn the Soldan's sword,
Yet cow'd and trembling at a maniac's word,

Hence I conjure! in peaceful halls recline,
Leave me to martyrdom, or Palestine.
I need not dread to bear the war alone,
Or lose one soldier, when ye all are gone." 420

But moved by heaven to curb his fiery mood,
Rose Sarum's pious Prelate, great and good;
Though he had laid his saintly garb aside
For the dark hauberk and the helmet's pride,
He deem'd it duty; nor that warrior-age
Disdain'd to blend the soldier and the sage,
But lauded Hubert's martial pilgrimage.^m

"Ye Franks and Syrians, Knights and Princes, hear.
Hear for his sake whose sacred badge ye wear;
Has the keen sabre swept whole ranks away, 430
Has Death permitted, struck a royal prey,
Even in your sight his last dread warning dealt,
And is the awful lesson yet unfelt?
Perjur'd, if here your swords ambition draws,
Traitors, if arm'd to fight a Saviour's cause,
Alike this senseless strife some Demon fires,
And your rash folly mocks your own desires.
Oh Conrad! I would see thee falter now,
There is no manhood in that scornful brow;

Long shall these realms a female reign deplore, 440
But let not Sion mourn thy valour more—
Flush'd with the conquest of the sacred town,
Heroic Godfrey shunn'd her proffer'd crown,
Nor where his Saviour felt the torturing thorn,
Would he with gold his humble brows adorn.*
Art thou more pure that thou thy head canst rear,
And bid the God of Empires fix it there?
Oh! think on Antioch—vain was valour's sword
Till contrite hearts appeas'd the offended Lord.ⁿ
Even now two powerful Sovereigns stem the tide, 450
Let Philip, let Plantagenet decide;
Meanwhile let sabres clash, and lances shine,
Rush all to war, but war with Saladine.
He deems us baffled, by defeat deprest,
Haste! let our trumpets break his scornful rest;
If all unite, we yet may brave his host,
And Heaven again restore our glory lost."

* After the taking of Jerusalem, the crown was offered to Godfrey of Bouillon; but that pious leader declined it, saying, "that he would never wear a crown of gold in the place where his Saviour had worn a crown of thorns." The title of first King of Jerusalem, which he bears in history, was bestowed on him by his comrades, but, I believe, never assumed by himself.

He spoke, and stubborn age and fiery youth
Smooth'd the bent brow, and own'd the voice of truth.
Again in peace the jarring chiefs unite, 460
And marshal all their various bands for fight.

Yet not for this the Demon's art was foil'd,
Not yet Alkarmel's venom'd shaft recoil'd.
With wounded pride consumed, and smother'd ire,
He marked fierce Conrad and his friend retire,
And while his arts a deeper gulf prepare,
Exults to see them rushing to the snare.
In Conrad's tent in suppliant guise was seen,
A graceful woman with majestic mien;
Veil'd were her features, but his Tyrian band, 470
Respectful own'd her accent of command;
" Conrad!" she said—the wondering chieftain turn'd,
And on his cheek indignant crimson burn'd;
For in that age when heroes loved to own
Their deadliest peril in their lady's frown,
Her smile the dearest guerdon of the brave,
His was the boast to live no woman's slave.
" Conrad, attend! I brook no careless ear,
What I shall say, thou well may'st deign to hear."

Even as she spoke her veil embroider'd fell, 480
He knew the wife of Thoron, Isabelle.
Yet while a sister's corse her tears should claim,
While life's last warmth yet lingers in her frame,
What means that purple robe, that regal air,
That diamond wreath that binds her sable hair?
But Conrad silent stands, amaz'd to trace
The calm, proud grandeur of that lovely face,
Amazed to feel a woman's words control,
A woman's glances awe his fiery soul.

" Lend, on thy vassal faith, a duteous ear; 490
Tis Salem's Queen that stands a suppliant here.
What means that frown? be proud that I require
A warrior's aid, and choose the Prince of Tyre.
I know thy daring hopes, thy bold design,
Obey me, and those daring hopes are thine;
But pause, and I with Lusignan unite,
And who but arms to guard a female right!
Thou know'st my claims; howe'er thy fiery mood
May feign to scorn the sacred rights of blood,
Thou know'st Judea's crown is mine alone, 500
A ravish'd crown! a kingdom to be won!
Oh! how my soul is panting to unite
A conqueror's glory with a sovereign's right;

But Thoron's timid breast can never glow
With those high thoughts that nobler natures know.
Fate to his form a kindred spirit gave,
And did but mock him, when she made him brave.*
My eager hopes with listless mind he hears,
And melts at Lusignan's unmanly tears.
Think not I come in passion; unprepared; 510
He shall not keep the rights he will not guard.
In youth's first dawn, ere reason learned to guide,
My mother gave me, an unwilling bride;°
Edessa's Priest shall free me from my vows.
So thou my interests and myself espouse,
Together we our claims, our arms combine,
I give the right, the martial fame be thine."

 Amaz'd he listen'd; humbled, gratified;
While joy with anger strove, and shame with pride.
Yet his proud knee has prest the wondering sand,
He kiss'd with deep respect the proffer'd hand.
Own'd it his dearest glory to obey,
And vow'd allegiance where he meant to sway.

<small>* The Count of Thoron must have been brave, since he is often spoken of in battle, and prudent, since he was frequently employed as an Ambassador; yet it is difficult to conceive how a man of any spirit could submit to the indignities which were put upon him.—Maimbourg says that he was extremely boyish in his person and manners.—Such a husband was not likely to suit with the high spirit of Isabella.</small>

Then as the Queen retired, and louder round
The war-cries thicken, and the trumpets sound.
O'er his dark brow his sable helm he drew,
Mounts his stout charger, and to combat flew.

    Already, eager for the conflict, shine
On Acre's plain the troops of Saladine,
Already on her towers th' intrepid foe   530
Whirl the long sling, and bend the stubborn bow;
Between, with massy walls and trenches bound,
The Christian camp the heights of Turon crown'd.
The gates unfold, and forth the warriors pour,
From Belus' banks to Ocean's sloping shore;
First, on the right, amid a chosen throng
Of knightly guards, the STANDARD mov'd along;
Six snowy steers, that sable housings bear
Since Sion's capture, drew the milk-white car,
Where on a turret, from a Cross of gold,   540
The spotless banner of her faith unroll'd;
Beneath, and veil'd in silk from eyes profane,
Four reverend priests the BOOK OF LIFE sustain.
Near it rode Lusignan (whose vest display'd
The hue of grief), and Gallia's troop array'd

With those brave knights, not more for arms re-
    nown'd
Than tender skill to heal the burning wound.*
On Ocean's verge the Prince of Tyre commands
His own, the Lombard and Venetian bands;
The wealthy Pisans, and Thuringians bold   550
Move in the centre, led by Leopold.
Apart, to watch the battle's doubtful fate,
With Gueldres' Duke the white-rob'd Templars wait,
While Geoffrey, to protect the camp, retains
The Count of Flanders, and the stout Avesnes.
Cold was each Christian's heart, as he beheld
His comrade's sepulchres o'ershade the field;
But when on high that sacred STANDARD rose,
Through all their veins a brisker current flows,
New hopes, new strength, inspire the pious throng,
" 'Tis HEAVEN'S HIGH WILL," they shout, and rush
    along,†
And Conrad cries, exulting in his powers,
" Stand neuter, Heaven, and Victory is ours!"‡

  * The Knights of St John, or Knights Hospitallers.

  † *Deus id vult*, or *Dieu le veut*, the spontaneous burst of popular feeling at the Council of Clermont, and afterwards the well known war-cry of the Crusaders.

  ‡ " Que Dieu reste neutre et la victoire est à nous." *Michaud* and others.

In close array from Belus' banks advance
The men-at-arms, and archery of France,
Where Omar's voice the Soldan's left commands
An arrowy tempest thins the Moslem bands;
That ardent Chieftain whom the fiends inflame
With deadliest hatred of the Christian name,
Who in Tabaria's field its guards subdued   570
And dragg'd through dust and gore the "HOLY ROOD."
Skill'd in the wiles of war, a moment eyed
The field of blood and "Fly, my Friends!" he cried,
" By feign'd disorder rash pursuit invite,
But wait the foe on Kaisan's rocky height.
And thou, brave Selim, bid the Soldan know,
I but retreat to strike a heavier blow;
Let all his warriors, marshall'd on the plain,
Close on the Franks, and drive them to the main,
While in yon dells again I raise the spear,   580
And on th' assailants turn the storm of war."*

 The warriors heard, and at their Chief's command,
A well feign'd terror spread through all the band;
To Kaisan's ridge with broken ranks they flew,
And wild in thoughtless haste the Franks pursue.

* Histoire de Saladin.

Already Selim in the Soldan's ear
Begins his tale, but Lusignan was near;
His whizzing javelin pierc'd the Arab's side,
And on his lips th' important tidings died.
Meanwhile the Soldan, by his death betray'd,   590
Sends his best forces to his Nephew's aid,
But Omar's flying squadrons spread despair,
And the feign'd panic grew to real there.
Like frighted deer on every side they fly—
While thundering comes the Christian Cavalry;
Without a blow the trembling caitiffs yield
And thousands dead or dying strew the field.

 Now to the Moslem Camp the Christians sped,
Assail'd the ramparts, heap'd the fosse with dead.
In vain the gates, in vain the guards oppose,   600
Their feeble force against the conquering foes,
They through the camp with madding fury flew,
Trod down the Crescent, and the tents o'erthrew,
The wealth disclosed rapacious thoughts inspires,
That quench the warrior's rage, the zealot's fires.
Now near a Bedouin's tent they seiz'd a steed
Of far descended fame, and matchless speed,
A fatal prize!—Now dainties lure the eye,
Fezzan's rich date-bread, fruits of Araby,

And marble vases fill'd with iced sherbet, 610
The temperate banquet for the Soldan set.
Elate they bid the cooling beverage flow,
And while they drain the bowl, the fight forego.
Inebriate all, such idle pranks they play'd,
As prov'd the snare by fell Alkarmel laid.
Some their rude limbs in Persian robes enfold,
One seiz'd a turban stiff with gems and gold,
Round his brown helmet winds the starry coil,
Mounts the divan and portions out the spoil.
On Mahumeria's height the Count of Bar, 620
From Saladine's pavilion views the war,
Mounts the Muezzin's consecrated tower,
And calls with scoffing dissonance the hour;
His laughing troops beneath the frenzy share,
In mock ablutions mix'd, and mimic prayer.*

 Meanwhile the Soldan speeds o'er all the plain,
Entreats, commands, exhorts, and threats in vain.
Five dauntless Mamlukes, in his palace bred,
Alone remain to guard his sacred head;
As Eudon and his Red-Cross knights advance, 630
For him they spread the shield, and point the lance,

---

* This whimsical instance of the delirium of success is historical.

And, careless of their lives, protect alone
Their generous Lord, too careless of his own.
But forth Moheddin flew, his powerful blade
By Selim's corse the pious Azo laid,
(Pleas'd in his Saviour's cause to yield his breath,
And fill'd with holy hope he smiles in death,)
Then as he saw Seiffeddin speeding by,
" And can," he cried, " the King of Mosul fly?
Can souls like thine inglorious safety prize,   640
And flee from peril, while the Soldan dies?"
He spoke, the proud Seiffeddin waved his hand,
But swifter sped to call his scatter'd band.

 " But hark! yon drum; to end th' unfinish'd fight,
Another army stands on Kaisan's height.
Be Allah prais'd! 'tis Islam's flag of gloom,
'Tis Mosul's youth, 'tis Omar's yellow plume!"
The keen-eyed Soldan spoke, new hope succeeds,
Behind a hill his little troop he leads;
Again resounds the royal Atabal,   650
And routed Islam rallies at the call.
His four fair dwarfs, insensible of fear,
Who bore the Koran through the ranks of war,
Haste to their pious Lord and round him raise
The calm but joyful chaunt of prayer and praise.

Scarce seem'd these elfin forms the sons of earth;
Born in one hour, one mother gave them birth.
Their little limbs in just proportion shew,
Graceful their walk, their voices sweet and low;
Untouch'd by sorrow, as unknown to guile,   660
Nor anger rais'd a frown, nor mirth a smile,
Nor in their hearts had love or hate a share,
Each thought was heaven's, their whole existence prayer.
Though they unmoved through fields of slaughter ride,
To swell their veins no living creature died,
Nor while the Sun dispens'd his golden light
Think they of food, but when he sets in night
The Camel's milk, or heaven's ambrosial dew,
Or Asia's nectar'd fruits, their strength renew.
In yellow robes, as slaves of Saladine,   670
These infant forms on downy cushions shine.
Four sable mules their fairy hands obey;
Between, on yellow silk the Koran lay
In sable folds (the hue of Islam), bound ^p
With studs of pearl, and clasp'd with silver round.
Unharm'd they stem the battle's fiercest tide
And Moslems deem that angels guard and guide;
Perchance 'twas pity turn'd the sword aside,

Or He whose mercies human thought exceed,
Approves their blameless lives, forgives their erring
  creed.   680

 Thus while the Chief his faithful band array'd,
And hush'd the drum, and form'd his ambuscade,
Sage Karacous from Acre's lofty walls
Observes the battle, and on Mestoc calls;⁹
His colleague hears, a chosen troop they wait,
Then burst, a torrent, from the Patriarch's gate.
At that dire moment—'twas some Demon's deed—
The cord was cut that held the Bedouin steed,
Snorting he bounds away, his guards pursue,*
Their comrades deem it flight and follow too—   690
But soon recoil, for where they late subdued
The hostile host, the strength of Acre stood.
Confusion reigns; encumber'd with the weight
Of useless spoil, they ill may fly or fight,

---

* The Latin historians ascribe the defeat of the Crusaders to this singular occurrence, and the confusion which it occasioned. The Arabians say, that the horse got out of one of the vessels, and was pursued. He took shelter with the Musulmans, who presented him to Saladine, which was regarded as an evil omen. See *Michaud, Morin, &c. &c.*

One casts aside the load that checks his speed,
Another seizes, but alike they bleed,
This by the sabre, that the swift Jerreed.
Not, tempest-tost, the Mariner descries
The distant port with such desiring eyes,
As they their camp, whose walls, whose massy towers,
Like some strong town, might mock th' assaulting
    powers;
There is the press, there battle's clamorous cry,
There groan the wounded, there the mighty die.
Before the gate th' intrepid Templars stood,
Their snowy surcoats dyed with impious blood,
For Omar comes again—Great Eudon calls
To close the valves, but as he speaks he falls;
Of all his warriors first in worth and name,
Till one rash deed obscured his splendid fame.
The Templars tremble—Omar rushes on,   700
Bounds o'er the corse, and shouts, "the Camp is won."
Brave Andrea saw the dreadful conqueror near
And hurl'd at Omar's heart his powerful spear,
But Omar tore it guiltless from his vest,
And plunged its mortal point in Andrea's breast:

"Oh save me, Erard!" was his dying cry;
Unheeding Erard pass'd his brother by;
And great Avesnes, in his impetuous course
Borne down, encumber'd by his slaughter'd horse,
Had died, but swifter than a beam of light   710
He sits, remounted by the Emerald Knight.
The Emerald Knight?—alike to all unknown,
Seldom his voice was heard, his features shewn.*
First in the van his milk-white Jennet flew;
Last from the breach his lingering steps withdrew.
Plain was his shield, but Islam's fears confest
His warlike worth, and rescued Tyre had blest,
What time with Conrad from her batter'd towers,
In shameful flight he drove the Soldan's powers;
Yet when his casque was rais'd, his pensive look   720
Of sorrow more than martial fury spoke.

* The Green Knight, "*Le Chevalier aux armes vertes,*" seems to have excited no less interest by his valour, than by the mystery in which he was enveloped. He distinguished himself particularly in the defence of Tyre, under Conrad of Montferrat. " Lui seul, disent les vieilles chroniques, il repoussait et dispersait des bataillons ennemis; il se battit plusieurs fois en combat singulier, terrassa les plus intrépides des Musulmans, et fit admirer de Saladin sa bravoure et ses faits d'armes." *Michaud, Hist. des Croisades.* James of Avesnes would certainly have perished in this battle, but for the assistance which was promptly afforded to him.

And once a wanderer in the moonlight grove
Heard a soft voice that plain'd of slighted love,
And saw surpris'd, a Knight in armour green,
With streaming eyes and silver mandoline,
Who breath'd his sorrows in so sweet a strain,
All nature seem'd to share his amorous pain;
But now his mind far other thoughts engage,
Fierce as the famish'd tyger's direst rage,
He rush'd to check the Arab Chief's career,   730
And through his other arm impell'd the spear.
Where still the Templars, prodigal of life,
With hearts unshrinking bear th' unequal strife,
The grey-hair'd Gerard dies; but while the foe
Bent o'er the slain, repeats the murderous blow,
Smote by that Knight Unknown, the Turk expires,
And Omar bleeding, from his sword retires.

 But not since first arose the shout of death
Had Austria's Duke or Conrad paus'd for breath.
Brothers in arms as by their race allied,   740
On sable steeds they combat side by side;
First in pursuit o'er dying crowds they flew,
Nor now retired when Fortune's smiles withdrew,
Brave as twin Lions, still they smite, they slay
On every side, and half redeem the day.

But Tyre's proud Prince by high ambition wrought
To prove him worthy of the crown he sought,
And mad to lose a battle gain'd, exceeds
His kinsman's* fame, his own exalted deeds.
Where numbers bled by Omar's biting sword, 750
He hastes to succour Altaripa's Lord.†
Where late the Knight Unknown infix'd the wound,
Tight o'er his arm his scarf the Arab bound,
And close he prest his priestly foe, the smart
Firing to keener rage his savage heart.
But Conrad's lance his better shoulder tore,
And death had follow'd with the spouting gore
Save that some fiend forbade; his shield he threw
O'er the torn limb, and glaring rage, withdrew.

Next from where Nilus' ample waters pour 760
O'er craggy cliffs, and deafen with their roar,
Came the black Melkos; wide his shoulders spread,
A crimson shawl thick wrapp'd his giant head.‡

---

* Frederic Barbarossa.

† Ralph, or Radulph of Hauterive or Altaripa, Archdeacon of Colchester. He exerted himself nobly in the defence of the Camp against the attack of Omar.

‡ Vinsauf speaks of a savage nation who fought in this battle, with bodies as deformed as their minds were ferocious, black, of enormous stature,

By his huge club fair Castelluno's pride
Guido the bold and gentle Lovel died;*
Pierc'd through his Panther's hide, the mightier hand
Of Conrad stretch'd the Ethiop on the sand.

 Next Ismail bled; belov'd by Asia's Lord,
Who own'd a kinsman in the noble Kurd.⁵
Where mountain streams the rapid Tigris fed, 770
Sprung from one tribe, and in one valley bred,
The morn of life in rival sports they led;
And, side by side, had since in battle fray
For glory labour'd many a dreadful day.
Long in the strife he Conrad's rage withstood,
But sunk at last his victim, drench'd in blood:
Not all his own; the Prince was taught to feel
Through his stout mail, brave Ismail's trenchant steel.
Infuriate Conrad lopp'd his head, and sought
Where near the ocean strand the Soldan fought, 780
Yet, not unmindful of a leader's care,
With prompt, decisive wisdom, rul'd the war.
" Behold thy Friend!" the savage victor said,
Then at his feet he cast the gory head.

---

stature, having red shawls on their heads instead of helmets, and bearing clubs set with fragments of iron.

 * Guido, of Castelluno, and Lovel his brother.

The Soldan knew the long-lov'd face, the dart
Uprais'd to pierce the young Anselmo's heart,*
Down dropp'd—a deathlike darkness o'er him came,
Moheddin's arm supports his tottering frame.
On press'd the Prince, " Let Asia weep," he calls,
" By Conrad's arm her vaunted Ruler falls ;" 790
But Asia lov'd her Lord—an arrow flies,
Pierced in the spine his German War-horse dies,
And Hassan, while he struggled on the ground,
In Conrad's side inflicts another wound;
Where now that boastful spirit that denied
The help of Heaven, and on itself relied?
Not wholly fled—he rais'd him from the plain
And as the Chief revived, impell'd by pain
Forward he sprung : " Defend thee, Saladine !
If fate resume a gift so nearly mine, 800
I scorn to die by meaner hands than thine."
Moheddin's massy shield received the stroke,
The shield was shiver'd, but the falchion broke.
What now can save him? weaponless he stands
Alone and wounded 'mid th' infuriate bands;
But Lusignan his rival's danger saw
And rancour fled at Nature's mightier law;

* Anselmo, Lord of Karac and Montroyal.

He call'd for aid, th' illustrious Glanville came,[u]
Hoary with years, yet still of vigorous frame,
He plies his dreadful mace that ne'er in vain   810
Smote the crush'd foe, nor needs to smite again.
Awhile the troops recoil—the King with speed
Uplifts the fainting Conrad on his steed,
Then through the fighting throng retreating slow
Wards with his buckler every hostile blow.
Not so the Norman, he whose youth had led
A Scottish King in chains, whose manhood sway'd
The sword of Justice, and who first bestow'd
On England's Isle her law's collected Code,
Who mourning o'er his royal patron's loss   820
Would serve no second King, and took the Cross,
By stern Moheddin's vengeful javelin dies,
And low in dust the noble veteran lies.

  Nor had the King the Camp in safety gain'd,
But Geoffrey, who with Flander's Earl sustain'd
Lulo,[w] and Karacous, and Mestoc's might,
Flies to his aid, and guards him through the fight.

  Thus mix'd in conflict, neither host descried
The Christian vessels darkening all the tide;

The heaven descended Oriflamme unfold 830
Its crimson banner from the lance of gold.
Yet now has France, amid the yielding sand
Driven her firm prows, and Philip springs to land.
Far off he sees the tumult of the field,
The Moslems conquer, the Crusaders yield;
And like a steed that knows the trumpets sound,
Scarce stays to call his brave RIBALDI round;*
(That valiant band, then great in worth and fame,
Though base opprobrium now defile the name.)
He heads their charge; on Sion's impious foes 840
His lance, his sword, avenge their long repose.
The bands of Karacous, dispersed, o'erthrown,
Fly to the hills, or seek the sheltering town.
And where with Gueldres' Duke the Templars fought
Like powerful succour Montmorency brought;†
The Soldan, still in danger undismayed
Cheer'd his brave army, and again arrayed,

* The Ribauds or Ribaldi were, as Marin expresses it, the Mamlukes of Philip Augustus; his body guard, composed of young men of family and of acknowledged valour. Throughout the Siege of Acre, they seconded every enterprize of their Monarch, and were foremost in every assault; but the memory of their dissolute habits survived their martial fame, and *Ribald* has long been a term of reproach.

† Josceline de Montmorenci.

But when stout Joinville, Courcy and Champagne,
Drogo and Alberic heap'd the field with slain,*
When Otho flush'd with hope and glory pours 850
His brave Burgundians from the neighbouring shores,
He flies—while reckless now of scar or wound,
New hope, new strength the routed Christians found;
Again they rush'd impetuous where afar
Their STANDARD floated from its lofty Car,
And loyal in th' unhoped advantage won,
Call on their slighted King to lead them on.
He heeds them not, for 'mid a crowd of slain
He mark'd a waving hand and heard the groan of pain.
The Templars' Chief, the noble Eudon there 860
Ebb'd out his life, yet ere he rose to share
A martyr's crown, his fleeting soul implored
For conscious crime forgiveness from his Lord.
" O Lusignan! most injur'd, yet most kind,
I dare to call, I know thy generous mind.
Forgive me that by interest sway'd, and pride,
The Mountain Herald by my dagger died;
Forgive what follow'd from that guilty day—
Of deeds disloyal to so mild a sway.

---

* Drogo of Amiens, and Alberic Clement, the first who bore the title of Maréchal of France. Of the celebrated Hangest de Courcy, more will be said hereafter.

I go where all our earthly passions cease, 870
And my repentant soul would part in peace."

"Oh! Eudon, that my prayers could life recall,"
He said, " as freely as I pardon all.
Yet, Eudon, thou mayst joy in strength renew'd—
Trust me, my skill can stanch the welling blood."

The Templar faintly smiled—his panting breath
Grew thick and heavy with approaching death,
And his weak frame, half rais'd upon his hand,
Fell back a lifeless burthen on the sand.

" Alas !" the monarch murmur'd, " day by day,
Our best, our bravest, wisest, melt away.
What crowds since morn have found their earthly goal,
And thine is fled to Raymond's kindred soul!
In vain these zealous Gauls your place supply,
Too soon by famine, war, disease, to die;
Oh! when again shall Heaven's full favour shine
On its once loved, now wretched Palestine?"

He felt a friendly grasp—beside him stood
Hubert, his blade in Moslem gore embrued,
And even his silver plumage wet with blood. 890
But as he turn'd, the smiles of peace assuage
On the mild prelate's brow the warrior's rage.

" Nay, blush not, Prince! thrice honour'd every tear
That falls from thee on noble Eudon's bier;
Nor is the life by thee to Conrad given,
On Earth unhonour'd, or unblest in Heaven.
Yet turn and see what countless galiots sweep
With crowded sails triumphant o'er the deep;
Nor Raymond warn'd, nor Eudon fell in vain,
But their glad spirits smile on Acre's plain." 900

He look'd, and saw the foe in rapid flight,
Stay'd only on Kharouba's distant height,
While, their red crosses glittering in the sun,
The eager Franks pursue th' advantage won;
He look'd again, where Ocean blacken'd o'er,
Still floats unnumber'd vessels to the shore,
From each stout galley springs its armed freight,
And the glad seas feel lighten'd of their weight.[x]

" Behold the power of Faith!" the Prelate cried;
" No more by famine and by fraud destroy'd, 910
Weaken'd by toil, with frames, with hopes decay'd,
From Europe comes an inefficient aid.
Faith leads our warriors on, she stems the seas,
Defies the current, and controls the breeze,
The Soldan's courage quails before her power,
And trembling Acre dreads her funeral hour."

Then laying as he spoke his helm aside,
With lifted Cross and saintly smile he hied
O'er all the field, the doubting soul to save,
To dew with tears the contrite sinner's grave,   920
And while, St. John! thy pious brethren bind
The gaping wound, he heals the tortur'd mind,
Holds mercy's pledge before the closing eye,
And bids the parting soul ascend to joy.

END OF BOOK I.

CŒUR DE LION.

BOOK II.

THE CONQUEST OF CYPRUS.

ARGUMENT.

THE CONQUEST OF CYPRUS.

Voyage of King Richard to Acre—The Storm—Danger of Berengaria—Appearance of a Demon—his defeat—Vision of Richard—Arrival at Cyprus—Embassy to Isaac—Escape of Albert, and Discovery of Isaac's treachery—Evanthe—Berengaria—Return of Richard's Ambassadors—Richard descends on Cyprus—Defeat of the Greeks—the meanness of Isaac, and supplication of Evanthe.

CŒUR DE LION.

BOOK II.

THE CONQUEST OF CYPRUS.

But England's King becalm'd on treacherous seas,
Remote from Acre, mourns the failing breeze;
His martial band, to toil and strife inured,
Ill the dull languor of repose endured,
And envied Frederic's host, though fraud and force
And famine, mark'd its long laborious course.
Day after day, upon the glassy main
Rose the broad sun, and crost, and sunk again;
Night after night, the moon unclouded shone
On waves detested, under stars unknown. 10

Oh! for some rock, some island's distant form;
Oh! for the change, th' excitement of the storm.
It comes!—the storm—clouds darken all the heaven,
The raging billows roar—the sails are riven;
From every point the winds contending meet,
Disperse, destroy, or whelm the struggling fleet.
Alone the regal bark with steady prow,
In crimson splendour scorns the waves below;
Proud of her freight, she bends not to the blast,
And her red flag flows freely from the mast. 20
That power divine which guards the life of Kings,
Spreads o'er the vessel its protecting wings.

 Fix'd on the beak, the monarch's anxious mind
Watch'd a light Galliot, tost by waves and wind,
With streamers gay, as form'd alone to bear
On summer lakes the courtly and the fair.
Frail as it is, its painted sides contain
The best and fairest of his princely train,
Matilda, less in blood than love allied,
And Berengaria, his affianced bride.[a] 30
He hears their cries amid the tempest's roar,
He sees them kneeling, him and Heaven implore;
But as he gazed, to shroud them from his eyes,
The sky sinks down, the foaming waters rise;

On boiling waves a giant phantom stands,
Spread o'er the heaven, the lightning arms his hands;
His head is veiled in darkness, but his form
Reveals the Demon that excites the storm.
Where'er he moves, oars, rudders, sails are lost,   40
And helpless barks in circling eddies tost;
He strikes a mast—it falls—one dreadful cry
Bursts from the Ship, one shriek of agony;
In rush the roaring waves, the breakers sweep
O'er the low helm, and bear it to the deep.

  Again his lightnings fly; sublimely dire
The fated Galley shines, a sheet of fire;
Now here, now there, by foaming surges cast,
Its blazing fragments scattered on the blast,
The dark heavens blush above, the sea below,
And terror sits upon the flaming prow.   50
So late robust with winds and waves to fight,
But now a spectre-ship of paly light,
Sudden its golden hue grows dull and dark,
And hissing ocean closes o'er the bark.
Awe struck, each rower drops the useless oar,
Looks on the tempest, and contends no more:
But RICHARD raises to the sunless sky
His calm sad gaze: "Oh! Thou that rul'st on high!

"Just are thy judgments, yet if Thou disdain
This arm unworthy, spare my guiltless train!"   60
  To whelm the regal bark, dilating wide,
Now moves the Demon o'er the troubled tide,
But Heaven forbids—commission'd from on high
The bolt of vengeance cleaves the flaming sky,
It strikes the phantom form, loud thunders sound,
He flies in mist and pours a deluge round.
Then soon the storm is hush'd, and broad and bright,
The level sun beams forth his parting light:
But where the bridal ship? the King in vain
Strains his keen sight, it floats not on the main;   70
And where his princely galleys? far away,
Dispers'd or lost is half that proud array;
The rest with shatter'd masts and canvas torn,
Are but the wrecks of those he rul'd at morn—
O'erspent with toil, when danger threats no more,
Soon each tired rower slumbers on his oar:
But what benignant spirit charms to rest
The griefs contending in the royal breast?
He sleeps! serenely sleeps!—and not a trace
Of deeper care than on an infant's face.   80
Nor of that ship he dreams, nor of the storm,
Nor Berengaria, nor Matilda's form,

But one that seem'd more fair; a nymph unknown,
Whose azure eyes in softest lustre shone.
Her cross of virgin gold, her purple vest,
Her christian faith and royal birth attest:
And now the restless deep is spread with flowers,
The amorous birds sing sweet in myrtle bowers;
While airy hands the rich pavilion drest,
And dancing youths bring in the gorgeous feast; 90
While tapers flame and incense breathes around,
And silver citterns yield a sprightly sound;
On seats of painted velvet they recline,
And quaff from glittering bowls the amber wine.
And now she sings, and never waking ear
Such strains of melting harmony shall hear,
In ever varying bliss the moments fly,
And his delighted spirit swims in joy.

 Startled he wakes—and is the vision true?
The clear waves shine with morning's saffron hue, 100
And all around him, like an emerald zone,
Stretch'd the fair harbour of some isle unknown.
The blossom'd shrubs, regardless of the breeze,
Hang their rich clusters o'er the rippling seas,
While 'mid the classic plane's sublimer shade
Shines the proud temple, and the long arcade,

The vast rotunda of imperial Rome
And Islam's minaret and pigmy dome.
Eternal summer seems to linger there,
The vivid flowers attest the balmy air, 110
And every gale voluptuous fragrance pours,
Soft odours, strangers to our northern shores.

   The wanderer, long by winds and currents driven,
Finds earth a garden, every port a heaven;
Can hail Muscovia's rocks and gelid gloom,
Though stripes and slavery be the stranger's doom:[b]
Then in this eager host what raptures rise
As morn unfolds an earthly Paradise.
" Prais'd be the Virgin! or what gracious power
Hath been our pilot to so fair a shore. 120
Yet," cries the King, " by these delicious gales,
'Tis Cyprus woos us to her smiling vales.
My Lord of Pembroke, be it thine to bear
Our royal greetings to Comnenus' heir;
We come as friends, to free the sacred shrine,
But find his waves are leagued with Saladine!
Say that we crave, by their rude fury crost,
Aid for our barks, refreshment for our host,
Yet wait his princely sanction ere we pour
An armed nation on a foreign shore." 130

The day wears on; while anchor'd by the port,
He waits his herald from th' imperial Court,
Six noble galleys, from the storm secure,
Hail the red flag, and near their sovereign moor.
The night descends—again the morning shines,
But brings no envoy, and the host repines,
Condemn'd, like fabled Tantalus, to bear
The sight of pleasures which it cannot share.
Nor more the King approves his herald's stay,
" And whence," he said, " this long, this strange
  delay? 140
Methinks Byzantium's exiled Lords retain[c]
Their fathers' pride, though not their fathers' reign.
Our shatter'd state demands a speedier aid,
Nor thanks that love which lingers for parade."

" Perchance, my liege," a youthful Noble cried,
" Far from the shore the Cypriot Chiefs reside."—

" Perchance, Earl Leicester! but my father's coast
Was still a haven to the tempest tost;[d]
Ill rules the Sovereign, where a servile train
Dares wait his royal leave to be humane. 150
Our Irish Kernes, Barbarians though they be,
Might teach these polish'd Grecians courtesie.

We stay till morn—if no respect they shew,
The King who came a friend may land a foe."

He ceas'd, and silent sate from all apart,
With darken'd brow and agonizing heart;
Now seem'd to count the waves, or on the sky
Impatient glanced, but still the sun was high.
Of his lost friends he thought, or those more dear
Whelm'd in the waves, or rack'd with equal fear; 160
Yet ever and anon, a vision fair,
A Syren's voice seem'd floating on the air,
And mix'd unbidden with the mournful theme,
The lovely form that lured him in his dream.

Now bath'd in crimson earth and ocean glows,
Now coldly fair the silver moon arose;
Bright fell her beams on Amathusa's shore,
Where round the cliffs eternal breakers roar.
A fitful light appears—one warrior braves
That stormy cape, and dares contending waves. 170
Now hid by rocks, now tost by angry tides,
Near and more near his little skiff he guides,
Till o'er the royal deck his arms he flings,
And to his Monarch's feet exulting springs.

" My gallant Albert! but thy news declare,
Swift! for thy smiling front bespeaks them fair."

" Blest be that Saint, my gracious Liege, that gave
Thy bark to dance so gaily o'er the wave,
When others founder'd—doubly blest the care
Which now has sav'd thee from a deadlier snare." 180

" Amen! Lord Albert; but what snares are here?
From Christian Prince can Christian Pilgrim fear?"

" A Christian Prince! Oh no! my generous Lord,
By Isaac's soul is Asia's God ador'd;
With Saladine eternal faith he swore,
They lanced their veins, and drank the mingled gore.ᶜ
But I have happier tidings—proud to bear
Kind greetings from thy Lady of Navarre,
And England's Princess—moor'd in safety near,
For thee alone they pray, alone they fear." 190

" Ye bounteous heavens! then am I doubly blest,
But these are riddles—speak, explain the rest."

"Torn from our friends, the storm," said Albert, "bore
My bark and Harcourt's to this hateful shore,
Wreck'd on the rocks, with many a treacherous smile,
The artful natives hail'd us to the isle;
On to the fort our dripping troop they led,
As guests we enter'd, but as captives staid.

Foodless, and chain'd within a dungeon's gloom,
Alone I pin'd, and curst my lingering doom; 200
At length a slave appear'd—his scarf he wound
Tight o'er my eyes, and next my limbs unbound.
He led me forth—a length of cavern shed
Chill damps around, and echo'd to our tread,
Till breath'd the gales of heaven, serenely sweet,
And the cool herbage rustled round my feet.
He loos'd the bandage—under citron bowers
Refreshing fountains fell in lucid showers;
Alone, and shelter'd by a rich arcade
Stood, like the Paphian Queen, a Grecian maid. 210
A gold tiara wreath'd her tresses round,
A golden zone her purple tunic bound,
Nor e'er the Goddess wore so sweet a smile,
Nor seem'd her tender dove so void of guile.

" Approach" she said, " no foes are ambush'd here,
Thy faith, thy country, to my heart are dear,
And every morn before the Virgin's shrine,
I pray for those that fight in Palestine.
Alas! while yet I speak, thine eyes upbraid;
But how may I, a weak and erring maid, 220
Unvers'd in state or policy, presume
To blame those laws that fix the stranger's doom!

Yet ah! if Kings must chase each kindlier thought
By Heaven self-planted, or Religion taught,
Oh! may this frame the breath of life resign,
Untimely withering, ere the crown be mine.
Stranger! if erring pride my soul mislead,
Oh pray with me that Heaven absolve the deed;
To save the helpless from a fatal snare,
To save my sire from guilt, his wrath I dare.   230
Two royal dames are anchor'd nigh, and one
To whose lost spouse that parent ow'd his throne,*
But if they touch this inauspicious shore
Or life or freedom may be theirs no more.^g
So speak my fears—but haste, the task is mine
To fill this vase with Commanderian wine,
That wine unmatch'd beneath the bright abodes,
Which Pagan Bards might challenge for their Gods.
With proffers fair are fraudful envoys sent,
They perish if no friendly voice prevent;   240
To me their speech is strange, write thou the scroll,
And with a sacred warning wreathe the bowl."

* The Princess here alludes to the circumstance mentioned in the note to line 141. That Isaac had been assisted in his attempt on Cyprus by Margaritus, Admiral of William King of Sicily, whose widow, the Matilda of the Poem, accompanied the Queen Berengaria. His exploits had gained Margaritus the surname of King of the Sea, *ou le nouveau Neptune.*

I wrote, o'erwhelm'd with new excited fear,
" Fly, royal dames! for danger waits you here."
Then as the graceful Princess waved farewell,
And call'd the slave to lead me to my cell,
" Have I but breathed these gales of balm," I said,
To quit Elysium for the Stygian shade?"
" Alas!" she answer'd with a pitying sigh,
" Powerless to grant, with anguish I deny."   250
   Yet had her words the path of freedom shewn—
Blindfold again, my gaoler led me on;
I watch'd the time, when all seem'd still and lone,
To burst my bonds, and rushing on the slave
Disarm'd and bound him, but his life forgave;
I bribed his silence (powerful gold had moved
A Grecian's faith, had Isaac been beloved),
Then hid my sable mail and knightly crest
In his high cap and loose embroider'd vest.
'Twas on yon peak, where once a splendid pile   260
Rose to the Goddess of this favour'd isle:
Some columns yet a broken frieze sustain
Sad with the tale of Cytherea's pain;
The Phrygian hunter, and the fatal boar,
And that pale flower now purple with his gore.

No longer hid in clouds of spicy gloom,
And cypress boughs, and wreaths of roseate bloom,
The rest in beauteous ruin strew the ground,
Chok'd with rank weeds, or clasp'd with ivy round:
There too the myrtle, faithful to her Queen,   270
Veils her fallen statue with perennial green.
A mournful theme, but mine were raptures then;
On either side I viewed the boundless main;
Oh! with what joy thy crimson sails were seen,
But ah! too distant, and the town between.
Nearer, and anchor'd in the Paphian bay,
West of the Cape, thy lovely Consort lay.*
I ran, I mingled with th' Imperial band,
I mount the ready bark that leaves the land,
And near my Queen, unmark'd, unknown, I stand.
A slave was there, from crafty Isaac sent
With tempting fruits and courtly compliment.
A golden vase of ample size he bore,
Much for the metal prized, the sculpture more:

* Albert has already been mentioned as having doubled the Cape of Amathus, on which I believe some relics of the famous Temple of Venus are yet remaining. It is a bold promontory, on the southern coast of Cyprus. Limisso, near which RICHARD anchored, is to the west of the Cape; and Baffa, or Paphos, on its eastern side, and somewhat nearer. This tract is the most fertile part of the Island, which is on the whole mountainous.

It shew'd, contending in th' Idæan grove,
The blue-eye'd Pallas, and the spouse of Jove,
And matchless in her charms the Queen of Love.
Etherial rapture fills her conscious eyes,
As from the royal swain she takes the prize,
And seems to say, with looks of soft regard,   290
" Who honour beauty, beauty shall reward."

With folded arms, and meek submissive look,
The envoy placed the splendid vase, and spoke:
" Imperial Isaac of Comnenus' race
Greets you, fair Queens! of Western climes the grace.
Soon may your Lord in Sion's ramparts sway
And at your feet the conquer'd orient lay:
Yet wearied with the voyage, the angry blast,
In this blest isle some happy moments waste;
And while your mariners prepare again   300
Your shatter'd bark for combat with the main,
Taste Nature's lavish bounty, nor decline
To pledge our friendship in our island's wine."
The Queen received the vase; her glowing hue
Changed, as her eyes the awful warning knew:
'Twas but a choice of ills, for ne'er again
Her fragile bark may tempt the dangerous main;
Yet soon recover'd, she with pensive air,
Her fears dissembling, speaks the envoy fair—

"Wealth, power, and fame Comnenus' days attend, 310
The Grecian glory, and the stranger's friend.
But let him pardon, if opprest by fear
For our loved Lord, we hide our sorrows here.
It were discourteous, with these looks of care
To mar the pleasures that we cannot share."*

The Cypriot train retired, I need not say
With what delight I flung disguise away,
And told them all; or with what grateful joy
They heard of thee, and love, and vengeance nigh."

"Tis well!" the King replies, " and if again 320
Thou dar'st, my friend, to tempt yon boiling main,
Say *that* just vengeance sleeps not; be it theirs
To aid my blows, and combat with their prayers:
And tell my love, her sacred cause shall warm
With tenfold zeal, and nerve her champion's arm."

The morning dawns, the eager warriors stand
Arm'd on the decks, and eye the hostile land.

* This fraudful embassy is spoken of by Vinsauf. He says that "Isaac sent presents of provision and Cyprus wine (whose like is not to be found in any other land) to the Queen, trying to persuade her to disembark. But she suspected his treachery, and refused, alleging her anxiety respecting RICHARD: otherwise she would have been imprisoned."

With such unequal force will RICHARD tread
An unknown shore, a powerful realm invade?
Yes! were the Cypriots thick as Autumn's rain, 330
As leaves on trees, or billows on the main,
No doubt had England's dauntless sons confest,
While the White Cross is glittering on their breast,*
And he, that still the coyest victory won,
Their King, their Lion RICHARD, leads them on.
Yet one, a priest, whom age had taught to fear,
With cautious counsels vex'd his Sovereign's ear.
" Most reverend Clerk!" the impatient Chief replies,
" Read o'er thy Scriptures, there we hold thee wise,
But know the sword is ours; yet pause—in haste 340
A boat puts off—'tis Pembroke comes at last."[h]

 He climbs the arduous deck, and climbing speaks,
"Descend, O King! and crush these treacherous Greeks,
That outrage Heaven and man—Dread Monarch, see
Thy friendship spurn'd, thyself despis'd in me.
The mean usurper boasts thy Queen detain'd,
Unknightly deed! thy shipwreck'd friends enchain'd;

---

* At the Council of Clermont, which led to the first Crusade, all the crosses were red; but it was afterwards found convenient to have some national distinction in a war where all the nations of Christendom were mingled. The French, who had been foremost in the Crusades, retained the Red Cross. The English wore it white, the Austrians blue, the Germans yellow, the Flemings green.

His Seneschal, who dar'd the act arraign,
Reft of his ears, will scarce offend again.[i]
Thou shalt not land! so Isaac swears in scorn,   350
Thou dar'st not land! but is he not forsworn?"

"Aye, my brave Earl! preventive of thy zeal,"
His King replies, " behold us sheath'd in steel—
But don thy casque, that not an arm be lost,
We need them all, if his yon glittering host."

He ceas'd—the trumpets sound; in fair array
Row the swift galleys up Limisso's Bay,
While from the castled prow the archers pour
Their shafts, a dreadful tempest, on the shore.
There stand their foes; in many a rainbow vest   360
The fair form'd mule or foaming steed they prest:
As spring the Knights to land, they strive in vain
To pierce their mail, or hurl them in the main.
On RICHARD speeds, while hate and vengeance pour
Fresh force in breasts where valour reign'd before;
Nor needs the progress of the fight be said,
From Europe's strength voluptuous Asia fled.
For her slain sons in vain Limisso calls,
Nicotia trembles in her distant walls;
In vain Comnenus mounts a fresher steed,   370
In vain attempts his rallying friends to lead.

From such can Richard fly? can reptiles prove
The Lion's match, can eagles fear the dove?
But hark! from Paphian hills a joyful shout!
Back on his sword returns the flying rout:
'Tis Turnham's well known banner shines on high,
'Tis Harcourt's word of battle rends the sky.^k
Where late they languish'd in a dungeon's gloom
And shameless Isaac will'd a felon's doom,
Urg'd by despair, that fires the noble mind,   380
They burst their fetters and their murderers bind;
Three bows were theirs that miss'd their gaoler's ken,
One Bosco seiz'd, for knighthood scorn'd not then
The woodsman's skill; at every shaft he sends
Some hostile bosom bleeds, and death attends.
The Greeks recoil, then first compell'd to know
The cloth-yard shaft, the force of England's bow.
Brave Harcourt seiz'd a steed: "Our fortunes bloom
In hope no more, the favouring hour is come^l."*
So spoke the Knight, his vassals took the word   390
And snatch'd from slaughter'd foes the dart or sword.
Meanwhile the Queen addrest her little band:
"Those shouts announce the war—my friends, to land!

* The incidents of this battle have the authority of Vinsauf. Harcourt is meant to allude to his family motto, " *Le bon temps viendra.*"

Fear not for me, I have a guard on high,
Safe if my RICHARD win, and if he die
My doom is fix'd—the ruthless conqueror's chain.
Now you may save, but could not aid us then."
  Soon on the shore round noble Albert shine
The gallant Robert, heir of Grosvenor's line;
Talbot and Wyndham, following from afar   400
The din of battle, soon they join the war.
Press'd on all sides the wretched Cypriots bleed;
Who runs from Albert's lance, with fruitless speed,
Becomes the monarch's prey, and he who flies
From RICHARD's axe, by Harcourt's falchion dies.
Thus when some Eastern despot seeks the chase,
His numerous train select a woodland space,
With shouts and fires the narrowing circuit close
Till, forced, th' invaded game affronts the foes;
The wolf, the tiger, pard, or tusky boar,   410
By common peril link'd, are foes no more,
Each, once the monarch of his sylvan reign,
Bleeds, by a random dart ignobly slain;
On every side the ambush'd hunters strike,
On all they turn, and bleed on all alike.

Thus fall the Greeks—they glut the weary sword,
Or, loth to perish in a cause abhorr'd,
They yield their weapons, and renounce their Lord.
Short was the conflict, and one summer's sun
Beheld a war commenced, a kingdom won. 420
That eve on Isaac's throne the conqueror found
The Queens beside him, and his Knights around;
Beneath, in silken robes were captives seen,
Fair polish'd caskets, but no gem within;
For conquest trod so oft that tempting shore,
That change seem'd gain, defeat was shame no more.
Contemptuous sneers and scowling looks they cast,
On one, their mightiest once, but now the last,
The setting moon, so late their idol, scorn,
And turn adoring to the rising morn; 430
Not his to find, when fortune's smiles are flown,
Above her reach, in every heart a throne.

Unhappy Prince! if e'en by pomp opprest,
(Like some rude clown for kingly pageant drest,
Who struts his hour of borrow'd state, and then,
Stripp'd of his robes, to nothing sinks again),
At thine own throne a slave, and grovelling low
To one thy pride had forced to be thy foe,

How poor, how less than little art thou grown,
Mean in all eyes, and meanest in thine own.   440

    But Richard speaks : " Behold one fleeting hour
Has chang'd the scene, has turn'd the tide of pow'r;
And now, Usurper, what shall bid me spare?
Not e'en that self-distrust, that kindred fear,
That Monarch's feel when lawful Kings transgress,
And curse the regions Heaven had bid them bless.
Speak—why should I withhold the shameful yoke?
Why save thee, tyrant, from the headsman's stroke?"

    Low kneels the humbled Greek, with terror pale,
While avarice, shame, and hate, by turns prevail; 450
Now wishes that his glance had power to slay,
Now turns, as from some basilisk, away;
Fearful of guile, yet ignorant in sooth,
How best to force unwonted lips to truth,
Through his dark mind, a crafty maze, he tries,
But follow's guilt's instinctive course, and lies.
Speaks of his grief for wrongs to knighthood shewn,
Or highborn dames, their race and claims unknown;
Professes deep respect, extols his zeal
For Britain's godlike King, and Salem's weal;   460
But reading ill the scornful smile that now
Half melts the sable cloud on Richard's brow,

Dares proffer terms of amity—and then
Recoils to see the gathering cloud again;
Owns all's his guilt, but craves a living doom,
The strictest chains, the dungeon's darkest gloom,
The hardest labour, or in triumph borne
To drag his conqueror's car, the public scorn.
But spare his life! he offers weight of gold,
And costly cups, and gems, and wealth untold. 470
Here spoke stern Richard: " Would'st thou then resign
Part of those spoils, by conquest wholly mine?
Or think'st thou, if my will decree thy death,
That gold or fawning words shall buy thy breath?
Oh! worthy offspring of a treacherous race!
The curse of Cyprus, and our faith's disgrace,
Vanquish'd, dar'st thou on terms or truce presume,
Or blame thy sentence if I speak thy doom?"

 He ceased; to Isaac present death appears—
Prone on the ground, no more he feels or hears; 480
When now the doors unfold, a lovely band
Of Cypriote maids before the conqueror stand.
Yes! still the Nymphs of Venus' favourite isle
Boast her soft glance, her walk, her chastened smile,

Fair as the Ocean foam from whence she sprung,
And honey flows from each melodious tongue.
They love to wander in Idalian bowers,
And wreathe their golden locks with virgin flowers;
Or as they strip them from the vernal grove
To bid the senseless blossoms whisper love.^m   490

But she who, as in birth, in form transcends,
Before the throne, a beauteous mourner, bends,
And drops her veil; still humble, meek in power,
Her gentle spirit rose in danger's hour.
The cedar thus, when halcyon summer shines,
Graceful to earth its pendant boughs declines,
But when on Libanus the snows descend
To meet the weight its rising branches bend;
And thus Peruvia's bridge of lattice frail,
That shakes with every step and every gale,   500
Uninjur'd stands where stone, or stubborn wood
Were but the mockery of the foaming flood.
While RICHARD starts to see the vision'd form
In beauty beaming, in existence warm;
" O King!" she speaks, " the glory of the West,
With native rule, and foreign victory blest,
By Him who pleads for erring man above,
Whose word is mercy, whose behest is love,

Nay, by the conquest beaming round thy head,
By all the tears these captive virgins shed,   510
In pity to a wretched daughter, hear!
And learn of heaven its attribute, to spare.
I would not bid thee think 'twas I that braved
A father's wrath, or tell thee whom I saved,
But that affrighted conscience says too late,
That act, tho' guiltless, was my father's fate.
'Tis said thy heart, inflamed with youthful fire,
Was once rebellious to a regal sire,
Oh! if repentance ever waked a sigh,
To pity grant, what justice might deny."   520

 Swift from his throne the generous King descends,
To raise the fair with courteous grace he bends:
" Rise sweet Evanthe, rise; thy fears resign,
At least I war not with a soul like thine."

 Cheer'd by these accents, though commanding, sweet,
She looks on him her eye had fear'd to meet;
How different from the foe her fancy drew,
Horrid with blood, or foul in shape and hue.
Tall was his stature, and his auburn hair
Curl'd round a face, in youth perchance too fair, 530

But war and toil now lent a ruddier glow;
A gracious smile relaxed his awful brow,
While like that jewel which by turns can shed
The softest azure and the flaming red,
His large dark eye which kindled in the fight
Through the long lash now beamed a dewy light.
Free flow'd his robes, the sceptre graced his hand
As heaven itself had mark'd him for command,
While regal pride was veiled in courteous ease,
A wish at once and conscious power to please.   540
Thus granite rocks a softer outline show
When their sharp peaks are lost in fleecy snow.

"Think not," he said, "that, aliens to our creed,
We joy in blood, and bid a brother bleed:
Thy sire is safe, and know, PLANTAGENET
Ne'er brook'd an insult, nor forgot a debt;
And if my heart should measure what I owe,
The vast amount not Cyrus could bestow.
I may not, dare not, loose thy father's chain,
Ask for thyself, thou shalt not ask in vain."   550

Entranced she stands; her cheeks with pleasure glow,
The dreaded conqueror seems no more a foe.
Still in her breast unspotted peace had shone
And Love with all his woes was yet unknown;

Yet if her fancy wander'd to the theme
Such was the hero of her virgin dream,
Valour and truth, and mercy's angel smile,
But not the languor of an Asian isle.
Her grateful soul his gentle speech inhales,
And dreads no venom in the fragrant gales.   560
Perchance Maimoune hover'd near, to dart
The subtle poison deeper to her heart.

" What should I ask," she answered, " what require?
My boon is granted, thou hast spared my sire.
And for myself—to knighthood's sure defence
Fearless I trust my maiden innocence;
Yet if thy bonds my parent must detain,
Let me, who shared his grandeur, soothe his pain.
Then in my prison's solitary shade,
When on my knee reclines his weary head,   570
And to the moon my solemn vespers flow,
I'll bless the power that sent so mild a foe;
So valiant, that it scarce was shame to bend,
So generous, that he seem'd almost a friend."

" Ah, no! fair Princess, different far must be
The cell, the fetters, fate assigns to thee,

BOOK II. THE CONQUEST OF CYPRUS. 79

'Twere sacrilege so fair a form to bind
Or shroud in solitude a fairer mind ;
His prison gates shall open at thy will,
And thou in name shalt be my prisoner still,   580
But in my Court, where soon those locks of gold
In stronger chains thy conquer'd slaves shall hold.
See either Queen her gracious arms extend,
With theirs thy pursuits and thy thoughts shall blend,
A captive call'd, but honour'd as a friend."
He ceased; the Queens embraced the weeping maid
With kindly words that half her woes allay'd;
When spoke her Sire, from dread of death relieved,
Now pride inflam'd his soul, and avarice grieved:
" And shall, Oh, Monarch, no respect be shewn   590
To one whose fathers fill'd Byzantium's throne ?
Shall iron fetters, such as vex the race
Of common churls, these regal limbs disgrace?"

" Nay, if thou wilt, each silver link shall shine
Rich with the splendours of the Indian mine;*
Thou wilt but tempt some fool to end thy pain
And take thy life, that he may win thy chain.

* Some writers say that RICHARD honoured Isaac with silver chains, in mockery of his avarice; others that he asked for them. I have tried to combine the two accounts.

Thine be whate'er may soothe thy useless years,
Thou harmless snake, unworthy hate or fears;
Whose secret venom wants the fangs to kill,   600
Curst with the wish, without the power of ill.
But thank thy better stars that I withhold
The Persian Tyrant's doom; to starve on gold."ⁿ

He spoke: the Greeks with smiles obsequious hear,
And mock the Tyrant they no longer fear.

END OF BOOK II.

CŒUR DE LION.

BOOK III.

THE NUPTIALS OF RICHARD AND BERENGARIA.

ARGUMENT.

THE
NUPTIALS OF RICHARD AND BERENGARIA.

Arrival of Lusignan and his Brother with Thoron at Cyprus—The Marriage of Richard and Berengaria—Emotion of Evanthe—Character of Matilda—The Coronation of Richard as Emperor of Cyprus—The Marriage Festivals—Threat of Maimoune—Description of Hermesind—The Serenade and Combat—Feast in Richard's Palace—History of Raymond of Toulouse, Bertrand de Born, Pardo, Ricardo, Albert, and others—Conversation of the King and his Peers—The Minstrel Vidal—Lusignan relates the Conquests of Saladine, his own imprisonment and liberation—King Richard institutes the Order of the Garter.

CŒUR DE LION.

BOOK III.

THE NUPTIALS OF RICHARD AND BERENGARIA.

Three setting suns have shed a roseate glow,
Three dawns in purple bath'd Olympus' brow;*
A Pisan bark the fourth returning day
Brought either Lusignan to Paphos' bay;
And Thoron, flying from a sight abhorr'd,
A faithless wife, that weds a second lord;
For Philip favours Conrad's lawless will,
And Asia's shameless priests his hopes fulfill;

* The highest mountain in Cyprus bears the name of Olympus.

While o'er their tarnished fame the good repine,
And loathe the day, and fear the wrath divine.   10
  The wanderers view'd with wonder and delight
St. George's banner stream from every height,
With hopes new kindled to the shore they spring,
And through fair Cyprus seek her new made King.
  Within a fane whose light Corinthian grace
Once well beseem'd the goddess of the place,
The conqueror stands, to claim in peaceful state
Th' Imperial Crown his valour won so late.
There throng the Greeks, by braided tresses known,
The fair straight forehead, and the sweeping gown, 20
Or by the graceful lip, contemptuous curl'd
At those " Barbarians" of the western world,
Who gird a King ador'd, and need not there
The bloody axe, or crest of nodding hair,
To prove, if Greece such warlike hosts had sway'd,
That Greece had triumph'd still, and Rome obey'd.
  Yet two appear'd amid the festal show
Whose hearts reflected no congenial glow;
The Cyprian Princess mourns her father's fate,
And Salem's Sovereign his degraded state;   30
With tend'rest sympathy he turns to trace
The placid sorrow of Evanthe's face.

Oh, Lusignan! scarce yet thy frequent tear
Dries on the turf that hides Sybilla's bier;
Unwither'd on her modest urn remain
Thy votive wreaths, and canst thou love again?
Oh, had she smil'd, had pleasure warm'd her eye,
Evanthe's charms had fail'd to wake a sigh.
He lov'd the grief her downcast looks exprest,
And every pang was answer'd in his breast.　　　40
Weak Prince! too weak for martial souls to prize,
Too good to fear, too generous to despise,
Sad was the hour which made thee King, that hour
Most sad which call'd thee to defend thy pow'r.

　And why, sweet maid, while timid glances seek
The generous Victor, does a brighter streak
Now dawn, now fade upon thy beauteous cheek?
Love round thy heart has twined a subtle snare,
If Hope already cling so fondly there.
Yes, he was kind, but pity gave alone　　　50
That softer cadence to a conqu'ror's tone;
Not only art thou call'd to see him shine
In regal honours once expected thine,
A trial waits thee: see yon white robed throng
That scatter roses as they dance along,
And raise to heaven the hymeneal song.

She comes, the Princess of Navarre, to join
Her conqu'ring hero at the sacred shrine;
For RICHARD vows that she no more shall brave,
Far from his aid, the dangers of the wave.   60
" Henceforth alike we share in joy or pain,
One fate shall meet us, and one bark contain.
Nay, our own Peers in " Cupid's Court" might prove
Us recreant, should we quit this Isle of Love.
Now when he laughs on all the blossom'd plains,
And jocund May is dancing in our veins,
Nor to its Queen her lawful homage pay,
But careless fling the offer'd rose away."*

   While pious awe in Berengaria strove
With maiden bashfulness and holiest love,   70
Matilda, second in that princely scene,
With rapture hail'd her sister and her Queen.
Alas! how different was *her* bridal hour!
In earliest youth, to swell her father's pow'r,
Compell'd to change her cloisters' peaceful life,
For regal duties and domestic strife:

---

   * " And because Cyprus by antiquity was celebrated as the seat of Venus, that so it might prove to him, in the joyous month of May, he solemnly took to wife his beloved Ladie Berengaria."—*Fuller's Holy Warre*, p. 121.

But pure Religion rul'd her gentle breast,
With snares beset, with jealous rage opprest;
That spirit which in RICHARD's ardent soul
Wak'd the soft lyre, or urged to glory's goal,   80
Fenced her from all that thoughtless dames allure,
And gave that highest courage, to endure.
Dear were the hours that she might spend apart,
And ease with book or lute her lonely heart.
Of suffering virtue, Queens whose bland control
Check'd half the fierceness of a tyrant's soul,
She read delighted, ponder'd oft and long,
And, meekly duteous, verified the song.
King William died: she watch'd his parting breath;
She could not love him, yet she wept his death;   90
Wept it in chains, till RICHARD's awful power
From Tancred forced her freedom and her dower.[a]
Now calm in joy, as when her placid brow,
Like some still lake, conceal'd the griefs below,
She look'd around, she met a kindly eye,
Felt on her glowing cheek a deeper dye,
And turn'd from Raymond's gaze her conscious sight
To where, completed every nuptial rite,
The pious King devoutly kneeling down
To England's Primate gave the Cyprian Crown.[b]   100

With loyal tears the aged Baldwin shed
The sacred chrism; next placed on RICHARD's head
Th' imperial gold, and gave to either hand
The orb of empire and the royal wand.
Then to the Lord of Hosts preferr'd his prayer,
"Oh, make this monarch and his realms thy care!
Twice has thy servant heard his regal vow,
Twice fix'd the precious garland on his brow.
Strong in thy might, may he on Syria's plain,
Or Sion's hill, sublimer wreaths obtain!   110
Wreaths that shall flourish in unfading bloom
When Cyprus sinks beneath the general doom;
When earth and all its glories melt away,
And like a scroll the shrivell'd heav'ns decay."
Then, smiling on the Queen, with many a gem
Enrich'd, he plac'd the nuptial diadem.
" To thee, illustrious Virgin, we consign
A nation's hopes, and be its blessings thine!
From thee the matrons of a virtuous land
The bright example of their lives demand,   120
So vice and shame thy radiant sphere shall fly,
Loathe their own foulness, and neglected die;
Thy worth a grateful nation shall proclaim,
And with thy Lord's entwine thy lasting fame."

How fares Evanthe now? a sudden start
Has to herself reveal'd her treach'rous heart;
Instant she droop'd her lovely head, and drew
Her azure veil to hide her changing hue;
Speechless and motionless: yet some had guest
By the convulsive heavings of her breast,　　　130
She wept in anguish o'er her alter'd lot,
And mourn'd for honours, in her grief forgot.
Yet when she rais'd her veil with calmer air,
Mild beam'd her eye, no ling'ring tear was there.

It needs not here the bridal sports to tell;
What knights in tilting or Castilles excell;[c]
How oft the pageant foe was forced to run,
How oft in sport was mimic Acre won;
What minstrel's harp best pleas'd the warlike throng,
Or how the gen'rous King repaid the song;　　　140
What princely presents waited every guest,
What gay profusion graced the bridal feast;*
Even royal eyes were dazzled to behold
The martial pomp, the blaze of gems and gold;[d]

* At these feasts it was usual to lay a present on the plate of every guest, proportioned to the respect in which he was held.

There ev'ry luxury England deem'd her own,
Or Asia prized, to England then unknown,
Invite the taste; the stag, the brindled boar,
The swan, the pheasant, all that swim or soar,[e]
Or range the hill, the forest, and the field;
With every fruit that Cyprian gardens yield;   150
On massy chargers piled, with myrtles green,
And loveliest flowers in fragrant groups between.
A thousand Chiefs, in ermined robes arrayed,
With each a noble dame or high-born maid,
Surround the board, and each distinguish'd pair
From the same plate partake their mutual fare.*
While squires of gentle lineage train'd to serve,
To fill the jewell'd goblet, and to carve,
Present the spicy pigment, flaming wines
Press'd from the golden grapes of Cyprian vines,[f] 160
Clairette in fuming beakers, and the juice [g]
Th' industrious bees from Paphian flowers produce.
Soon through the festive throng commingled rise
Convivial sounds, jests, laughter, gay replies,

* To eat on the same trencher or plate with any one was considered as the strongest mark of friendship. At great entertainments, the guests were placed two and two, and only one plate was allotted to each pair. In the romance of Perceforest it is said, " *There were eight hundred knights all seated at table, and yet there was not one who had not a dame or damsel at his plate.*"—See Way's Fabliaux, vol. i.

Confused, not inharmonious; Mirth that hour
Ruled with despotic, unresisted power;
And though unshrined, the Queen of gay desire
In each soft bosom wak'd her former fire;
Love from a thousand eyes elanced his dart,
While broken sighs reveal'd the conscious heart, 170
And valour, vanquish'd by superior arms,
A willing captive bow'd to Beauty's charms.

   No words can paint the changes of the scene,
And each fantastic interlude between.[h]
Now on the board, with martial trophies graced,
A troop of Fauns a stately laurel placed,
A myrtle, gay with flowers of bridal white,
And last a rose, sweet emblem of delight;
While gaudy birds, as in their native bow'r,
Sing from the blossom'd shrub and fragrant flow'r. 180
When now that God for whom such flowers are worn,
Who gives to life its sweetness and its thorn,
Springs from the rose, and with his dart of gold
Strikes on the myrtle, lo! its boughs unfold!
And Venus with her favourite jasmine crown'd,
The table circling with a frolic round,
The prize of beauty she receiv'd of yore
On Ida's mount to Berengaria bore.

Now brays the trumpet; the vast laurel heaves
With labouring throes, and shakes through all its
    leaves;   190
The clang of arms is heard, the courser's neigh,
The rush of fight, the shout of victory;
When from the opening branches sternly strode,
Sublime in burnish'd arms, the Warrior-God,
Bears to the King the palm to valour due;
Then, while the clarions shrill their notes renew,
Again the involving boughs the Gods invade,
And jolly Fauns remove the mystic shade.

Now sprightlier music sounds; to dance and song
Life's sweetest hours, the hours of eve belong. 200
A spacious bower receiv'd the princely throng:
High rose the pillar'd roof, the stems around
The wanton vine her graceful foliage wound,
And on the trellaced arches over head
With love's own woodbine wreath'd, her tendrils
    spread,*
And all seemed nature, save the lamps, which hung
Like trembling stars the fluttering leaves among.

    * " But those who wear the woodbine on their brow,
      Were knights of love who never broke their vow."
                                              The Flower and the Leaf.

There, hid in clouds of fleecy white, that came
From cedar, myrrh, and aloe's fragrant flame,
Maimoune hovering nigh, beheld with pain   210
Her spells, by heavenly influence render'd vain;
The dream forgot, the monarch's mighty mind
Wholly to love, but lawful love, resign'd;
And pale Evanthe, sorrowing yet serene,
With zeal unfeigned attend her beauteous Queen.
"Think not," the Peri cries, with bitter smile,
" Thy feeble soul Maimoune's arts can foil:
The poison slumbers now, but thou may'st feel
Some wounds are deadliest when they seem to heal."
Threat'ning she fled, her heart with sorrow fill'd, 220
Her lucid form in dewy tears distill'd.
Etherial tears! When morning breezes blow,
They wake in flowers, yet not such flowers as know
The nectar-seeking bee, for theirs is empty show.

The dance is hush'd, the harp no longer fires
The languid limb, the sated troop retires;
And sinks in silent streets the jovial cry
Of homeward guests beneath the moonlight sky.
Fairest of Berengaria's maiden train
Was Hermesind, an orphan child of Spain.   230

Wide were her lands, her parents' only heir,
Early they left her, and their dying care
Chose for her home the Court of high Navarre.ⁱ
Fleet in the dance, and like the lark in song,
Through life's young hours she bounded light along;
Proud to behold of knights a gallant train,
Slaves of her charms, but heedless of their pain,
Nor thought, by flatt'ry's inward glass betray'd,
That she might feel them, or that youth could fade.
Th' Idalian jasmine cluster'd o'er the bower   240
Where, in the coolness of the midnight hour,
While the bright moon her silver radiance threw
O'er Paphian groves, and ocean's boundless blue,
She sate revolving looks, and words, and sighs,
And all the fancied victims of her eyes;
The warmth of Lusignan's imagined glance,
The crowds that watch'd her thro' the mazy dance,
And why young Pardo, dear to England's King,
Should first to her the spicy pigment bring,
While sad Ricardo saw with jealous gaze   250
The plumy fan she dropp'd, another raise.
So deep she mused, a solitary skiff
Had shot unmark'd from high Colosso's cliff;*

---

* Colosso is a projection on the Cyprian coast, to the west of Paphos.

Veil'd in a mantle dark, a form was seen,
That touch'd with tuneful skill the mandoline;^k
Too well she knew the voice whose mournful strain
Now breathed prelusive o'er the Cyprian main:
Oh! none in Sancho's court with happier aim
Could pierce the ring, the raging bull could tame;
For princely race, for manly virtues known,   260
And for a heart that felt for her alone.
For years with patience her disdain he bore,
At length he vow'd to wear her chains no more.
None knew his fate, but weeping maids believ'd
That Arga's stream th' unhappy youth receiv'd.*
Grief for her victim spread through Ebro's vale,
While the proud beauty feign'd to scorn the tale.
Yet through her heart a secret pleasure ran,
As thus with steady voice the Knight began:

    Lady, thou hast thought me dead—   270
        Did one pang thy heart discover?
    Deign'd thine eye one tear to shed
        O'er thy fond, thy wretched lover?

* The river Arga traverses the kingdom of Navarre, passing close by Pampeluna, and falling into the Ebro, which separates Navarre from Old Castille.

If the scorn of long past hours
    Be in that cold breast remaining,
Glory in thy beauty's powers!
    Pride thee in thine art of paining!

Pride thee that I love thee still,
    That my heart from thee must borrow,
As thy frown or smile shall will,   280
    All its rapture, all its sorrow!

Pride thee! for thine empire flies—
    Thou no more shalt hear my story,
In the grave affection dies;
    Palestine has tombs of glory.

Yet, and Lady, for thy sake,
    Hope would nurse the precious blossom,
Now, if better thoughts awake,
    Now if pity warm thy bosom;

This fond breast to Hope restore,   290
    Time nor chance our love shall sever;
Trifle with my pain once more,
    And my tongue is dumb for ever.

Her victim lives! from unacknowledged grief
E'en Hermesind's light heart confest relief;
But pride revives—another owns her power,
And wakes the echoes at this silent hour
With equal sweetness. Fir'd by deadliest rage,
The jealous rivals in their skiffs engage;
Brightly the weapons flash'd in Cynthia's ray, 300
And Ocean's ruffled waves expect their prey,
When the coy maid, rous'd by the clash of arms,
Threw back the lattice: " Why these rude alarms?
Whence, and who are ye, warriors; what the cause
That to this spot your midnight fury draws?
Respect a virgin's rest, respect the night,
And strive on shore, or wait the dawning light."
" Oh, fairest Hermesind!" Ricardo said,
" Too well thou know'st—but be thy will obey'd.
Alas! when night is in her awful noon, 310
And all is slumb'ring, save the pitying moon
That hears my woes, must I no longer breathe
My secret sighs, thy sacred bower beneath?"

" Know thee!" exclaim'd the unrelenting fair,
" Hence, madman, hence, lest royal RICHARD hear,
Or I arouse the guard; and from my view,
Thou, muffled stranger!—do I know thee too?—"

"Yes! scornful Hermesind, thou know'st me well,
As conscience oft in lonely hours shall tell;
Long hast thou known—but I no more endure   320
Taunts still renew'd, I thank thee for my cure.
Behold this glove, which, more than empires dear,
I long have worn, and ever thought to wear;
Now from this relic of my shame I part,
And with it fling the giver from my heart.
And thou, young stranger, break like me her chain,
The yoke's inglorious, its reward is pain.
Thou know'st me not, but I like thee have lov'd,
Like thee been flatter'd, courted and reprov'd;
Been scorn'd like thee, till ev'ry hope was gone, 330
And injur'd reason totter'd on her throne.
Like me, but oh! with less of pain, be wise,
I cannot love the being I despise;
Or crouch like Persian satraps round a throne,
Opprest, and kept for vanity alone.
For her lost victim let her now deplore,
But living never shall she see me more."

He ceas'd, his bark shot swiftly from the bay;
Ricardo staid, to softer thoughts a prey:
He marvell'd at the tongue which thus reprov'd, 340
Nor saw a blemish in the maid he lov'd;

Ling'ring till she the jealous lattice drew,
And Heaven appear'd to vanish from his view.

Eight suns on laughing Cyprus rose and set,
And RICHARD linger'd in the island yet.
Though wing'd with new delight the hours advance,
The chase, the joust, the banquet and the dance;
And he the foremost of the martial throng,
Alike directs the galliard, or the song,
Affronts the boar, or shares with lance and shield 350
The mimic warfare of the listed field:
Yet, as the magnet constant, RICHARD's soul
Through all these seeming wand'rings sought its pole;
His galleys, long of winds and waves the sport,
Now ride triumphant in the crowded port.
New laws he frames, he checks each nascent wile,
And in his sway confirms the wavering isle;
While Cyprian vales the graceful plane resign,
Her hills the oak, the ash, the tap'ring pine;
To frame huge engines, whence his ambush'd powers
May spring on Acre's walls, or dreadful show'rs
Of stones and fire assail her haughty towers.¹

With no gradations of declining light,
That wed the day so softly to the night,

No clouds that borrow, while they veil his rays,
Ethereal hues that vary as we gaze,
Sunk the broad sun, the shades of night extend
O'er all the isle, and cooling dews descend.
Tired of the bow, the hunt, the martial play,
Tired of the lighter sports that closed the day,   370
With mirth, with Cyprus' luscious wines opprest,
In tent or bower the warriors sink to rest.
Not so their Chiefs—the feast, the minstrel's song,
Eve's fleeting hours in RICHARD's hall prolong;
And should once more our long-lost Arthur reign,
Or spells recall the Knights of Charlemagne,
Scarce should those vaunted Paladins be found
Of princelier rank, or more in arms renown'd.
The injured Count, and exiled monarch there
The highest seats with noble Raymond share.*   380
Where fair Toulouse in distant prospect sees
O'er olive groves the snow-crowned Pyrenees,
He ruled, from that heroic leader sprung
Whom Godfrey honour'd, and whom Tasso sung.

* Raymond Count of Sanctus Egidius, *Gallice* St. Gilles, was a descendant of the Raymond de St. Gilles who accompanied Godfrey to Palestine, and whose son became the first Count of Tripoli. He was consequently related to that Raymond of Tripoli whose death was described in Book I.

His gentle soul at Acre hopes to find
A kinsman's welcome from a kindred mind,
Nor knew, by grief and base reproaches torn,
His reason warp'd, his life untimely shorn.
Next sullen Bertrand, whose imperious sway
Strong Hautefort's towers and Perigueux obey; 390
By heirship one he held, (the castled height),
And one by force usurp'd, his brother's right.
His scowling brow and glassy eye confest
Despair and rancour brooding at his breast.
Yet who so ardent in the desperate fight?
Whose mirth was louder on the festal night?
Or who of all that struck the minstrel lyre
In loftier numbers breathed Tyrtæan fire?[m]
Yet downcast now in RICHARD's sight he sate,
And moody silence veil'd his deadly hate. 400

   Far other thoughts three gallant youths inspire,
Who loved the generous monarch as their sire.
Young Pardo first, his birth in mystery veil'd,
Nam'd from the leopards that adorn'd his shield:
On that same shield, in splendid robes array'd,
Before King Henry's gate the babe was laid;
When RICHARD pass'd, its infant smiles engage
The youthful prince—he train'd him for his Page.

Then pleas'd to find his vigorous soul aspire
To deeds of glory, bred the favourite Squire; 410
And scarce three happy moons had waned away
Since by his valour in Messina's fray
The gilded spurs he gain'd, and right to wield
That mystic blazon in the martial field.
To all was Pardo dear—in RICHARD burn'd
A father's love, with equal love return'd.

  Nor less Ricardo felt the grateful flame,
Nor less his generous thirst of martial fame:
Yet would he oft the social feast refuse,
In secret shades to court the wayward muse; 420
In gayer hours the mirth that lit his eye,
Was like the sunbeam from a wat'ry sky.
High was his birth, his sire and lovely bride
On Ceuta's shore in Moorish bondage died;
Left almost in the hour that gave him breath
In barbarous hands, and doom'd to bonds or death,
The good Justinian heard, his ready sword
To Christian lands his brother's child restor'd;
By RICHARD in his father's rights install'd,
He from himself the noble orphan call'd, 430
But (for the youth from southern Poitou came)
His vassals to Ricardo changed the name.

Nor less Northumbrian Albert; firm and bold.
His mind, his form from Nature's fairest mould,
With youth's frank cheerfulness sedate and sage,
His was the wisdom of maturer age.
The last blythe May had deck'd with odorous flowers
His bridal revel in the Cestrian towers,
And RICHARD heard the holy vows unite
Cyveilioc's daughter and th' enamour'd knight.* 440
The bride had borne, to crown the nuptial feast,
The peacock proud in gaudy plumage drest,
With Eastern spices rich, and gems of price,
Placed on a golden dish of rare device.°
To greet the royal bird, with naked sword,
The King had risen from the festal board:
Each eye expectant watch'd his thoughtful brow,
Each heart revolv'd the meditated vow;
When from without a plaintive cry was heard,
" Vengeance, brave Monarch! by that honour'd bird,
By him who reigns above!" a troop was seen
In pilgrim garments, but of martial mien;
Lame, blind, and seam'd with many a dreadful scar,
The sad remains of unsuccessful war.

* Hugh Cyvcilioc Earl of Chester.

"Behold the relics of a faithful train,
Who fought for Palestine, but fought in vain!
We vow'd to tame the Soldan's impious pride,
And free that region where Emanuel died.
Behold us now! Oh King, avenge our doom!
Arm! England, arm! redeem the sacred tomb." 460

   Each lady's eye with pious tears was fill'd,
Each manly breast with martial ardour thrill'd;
But most the King's—when Pandulph's holy words
Charm'd to their sheaths his own and Philip's swords.
Long since he took the cross, but wars oppos'd
And civil strife: till now, his realm compos'd,
His stores prepar'd, the injur'd wretches came,
By heaven inspired to rouse the latent flame.
" Before the Peacock and the Dames I swear,
Nor thought of earthly power, nor regal care,   470
Nor my near nuptials, shall delay me now;
Too long has Heaven arraign'd the slighted vow:
Now be it paid! my gallant Peers arise—
Now by this royal bird, your ladies' eyes,
Your fame, your faith, whoe'er would share my heart,
In arms complete at once with me depart."

   He spoke; his vassals caught the martial glow,
And with fantastic fancies bind the vow.

Albert was last; awhile he paus'd and sigh'd,
Then took the oath which tore him from his bride. 480
    Next sate D'Arselles, and high St. Valery's heir,[p]
And stout St. John,[q] and Arnulph of St. Clair;[r]
Harvey, whose axe was never rais'd in vain;[s]
And Nevile, skilful on the troubled main.[t]
Spencer,[u] whose name was to his office due,
And Ferrars'[x] valiant Earl; and Fortescue,[*]
Sprung from that RICHARD, who on Hastings' field
Before Duke William bore the guardian shield.
Grosvenor,[y] whose house held kindred with the Dane,
That won by daring arms his Norman reign;   490
And him more great, the last that e'er shall claim
From England's prostrate strength a CONQUEROR's name:
By Deva's wizard stream, the noble race
Awake her echoes with their sylvan chace;
Yet foremost now in Sion's cause advance,
And change the boar-spear for the sterner lance.

    [*] Sir Richard *Le Forte* was a man of extraordinary strength and courage, in the time of William the Conqueror. At the battle of Hastings he bore a strong shield before the Duke, and contributed greatly to his preservation, he being often in imminent danger and having three horses killed under him. From this circumstance arose the motto with a double meaning, " FORTE *scutum, salus* DUCUM," and the addition to the name Fort-escu. A shield is also the family crest.

Then Leicester's Earl, than whom no braver Lord*
E'er couch'd a spear: his filial grief deplor'd
A noble sire; like him the cross he wore,
But in Romania died, nor reach'd the sacred shore.
The brave de Vaux,^z in arms a mighty name;
And Roland, who from stout Belasius came;^{aa}
And veteran Talbot, who in Aquitain,
When Sarum's regent Earl by fraud was slain,
To find his heiress, then a blooming maid,
In minstrel garb his martial limbs array'd;
Mid hills abrupt, and woods, and valleys green,
Where winds, with isles begemm'd, the placid Seine,
To Neustria's hinds of sylvan game he sung,
Or told of war her warlike Knights among,   510
Had lays of love to win a lady's ear,
And lighter jests, the menial throngs to cheer.
At length by Eu's romantic cliffs he came,
Where her false guardians hid the lovely dame,
Heiress of Rosmar's lands and Ewrus' fame.

* Robert Fitz Parnel, Earl of Leicester, son to Robert, who died on his pilgrimage. Fitz Parnel received intelligence of his father's death during his stay with RICHARD at Messina. He first unfolded his paternal banner at the battle of Arsouf, where he was much distinguished. Indeed his exploits in Palestine, in England, and Normandy, were second only to those of his Sovereign.

Nor long he harp'd in vain : 'twas his to bring
The rescued Ela to his generous King ;
Who sooth'd her griefs, and with her father's land
Gave to a princely spouse her willing hand.
His brother, born in that mysterious bower   520
Which Henry framed, to shun his consort's power,
With Dædalean art for beauty's fairest flower.^{bb}

Next, nor unmindful of his sister's shame,
De Clifford* sate, himself of spotless fame ;
Firm, agile, brave, though now in life's decline ;
And Curzon's pride, the youthful Giraline.^{cc}
Three Saxons next, fair-hair'd and azure-eyed ;
Stourton, whose Patriarch pour'd Sabrina's tide
O'er the rich vales, and guarding Avalon,
Peace, safety, honour, from the CONQUEROR won.† 530
Compton,‡ whose grandsire, doubting Harold's claim,
Withheld his feudal aid when William came ;

---

* Walter de Clifford, brother to the Fair Rosamond.

† Botolph Stourton, who when the Conqueror entered into the West, was among those who broke down the sea walls of the Severn, and entering Glastonbury, guarded the pass by land till the Conqueror granted what they required.

‡ Turchil, son of Alwyne, was a powerful noble under Edward the Confessor. On the Norman Invasion he gave no assistance to Harold, although

And Harley,[dd] sprung from that victorious Thane,
In Saxon days the terror of the Dane;
With Godfrey's twined his grandsire's laurels bloom,
Who took monastic vows, a Champion of the Tomb.
The noble Harcourt[ee] next, in whom combine
The Saxon, Danish, and Burgundian line;
Himself a Briton, to his brethren yields
His Norman honors and paternal fields. 540
Berkeley and Pembroke, who with Strigulph share
The conquer'd spoils, and fame of Erin's war.[ff]
Two brothers next—on Audley's crimson shield
Still Lydulph bears the golden fret reveal'd;
But Adam claims, since Stanley's lands he gained,
The silver stags upon an azure bend.[gg]
Then high-born Alan, joyful to retain
With Percy's name the Lion of Lorraine;

although he was then Earl of the County of Warwick, and hence grew into high favour with the Conqueror, who left him in possession of his lands, namely the Lordship of Compton, and forty-seven other manors. Turchil assumed a sirname in imitation of the Normans, and adopted Norman manners in every particular. Under Rufus he took that of Arden (from Arden in Warwickshire), which title descended to Siward his eldest son, while the second took that of Compton.

In barbarous times, ere Rollo's daring sails
His raven banner spread to British gales, 550
The Norman name ere vanquish'd Neustria bore,
Had Danish Mainfred aw'd the Gallic shore.
His brave descendants to our fairer isle
Pass'd with the CONQUEROR, and partook her spoil;
But William, to his royal namesake dear,
Would with no Norman bride his honours share,
But wedded her who should have been their heir;
Hence, when he bravely fell in Palestine,
Allow'd to see, but not to reach, the Shrine,
His weeping Squires to widow'd Emma bore 560
His faithful heart, and where it touch'd the shore
She rais'd St. Hilda's fane, a mighty tomb,
And wept her cheerless days in cloistered gloom;
Yet oft to heaven her grateful eyes would raise,
When trumpets spoke her youthful Alan's praise.
Seven sons were his, all courteous, pious, brave,
Alas! their valour won an early grave,
And Peers and Princes hasten'd to demand,
Percy's last hope, their sister Agnes' hand.
Wisely she chose the gallant Josceline; 570
Nor he, though brother to the English Queen,

Though sprung from one allied with Charlemagne,
The powerful Duke of Brabant and Lorraine,
And kin to him who conquer'd Sion's throne,
Disdain'd to make their lofty name his own.
In Whitby's pile they sleep, his brother's care
Now guards their Alan's bride, and infant heir.
He sails, by pious zeal to Syria driven,
His name renown'd on earth, his "Hope in Heaven."[hh]

    Next the proud Norman, Perceval was seen,   580
Rapacious, cruel, arrogant of mien:
Fit heir of her, who when her castle spread
Its walls complete, struck off the builder's head;
Who dared in arms against her husband stand,
And fell, the victim of his vengeful hand.
Fit heir of Ascelin, whose dreadful crest
(A gaping wolf) his nature half exprest;
Who with a hand of steel, and heart as hard,
Dire pains for Bretevil's captive Earl prepar'd.
Perchance the influence of a milder age   590
In their descendant curb'd ancestral rage,
Yet hated, fear'd, alike by friend or foe,
His look appall'd, and death was in his blow.[ii]

Next Rodney—start not, Britain, at the name!
" From timid doves the Eagle never came."*
That name which taught thy stubborn foes to yield
Thy rightful empire o'er the azure field,
Was known to fame, o'er traitorous billows bore
A Norman victor to thy white-cliff'd shore.

But pause, oh Muse! nor thus thy strain prolong,
All cannot share, though all deserve the song.
And ye, blest Spirits, if ye now behold,
Where crown'd with palms ye fill your thrones of gold,
Your once lov'd England; if that gen'rous glow
Which urg'd to fame on earth, inspire ye now,
Forgive your Bard, whose plumes too vent'rous grown
Melt in the sunlight of your high renown;
Propitious hear! the mists of time unroll,
Pour your forgotten glories on my soul,
So yours (nor less your proud achievements claim) 610
Shall vie with Roland or Rinaldo's fame.

* In reversing the classical motto of Lord Rodney, " non generant aquilæ columbas," so as to give it a prospective rather than a retrospective sense, I trust not to have been thought to violate its true meaning. The Rodneys seem to have been settled in England before the Conquest. Sir Henry Rodney was Steward to the young King Henry (son of Henry IId). His son, Sir Richard Rodney, was the one who accompanied his royal namesake to Palestine.

And hark the King, " Alas! the promised land
Near, yet not ours, for angry seas withstand;
Fate frowns malign : in vain we pant to share
The harvest Philip reaps already there.
Say! shall we then these sultry moons beguile
In these green bowers, this cool-delicious isle,
Or launch our frail and shattered keels again,
Mid all the terrors of an adverse main?
Methinks the rose is richest of perfume   620
Though Fame's dark leaf outlive its fleeting bloom."

" Can Richard speak of pausing?" Raymond cried,
" Or spoke his accents what his heart denied?
Like thee we love, when fortune's gales are bland,
To win her odorous wreath from pleasure's hand,
And snatch each jewel from her shining store,
Like thee we court her smile, but Glory more.
Reluctant Fame already weeps to twine,
On brows less brave, the honours meant for thine;
Reviving Acre breathes, her tottering wall   630
Again is firm, till thou shalt doom its fall."

" Behold!" cried Pardo, " where these groves have dew'd
My crimson'd arms—they should be stains of blood.

Will Asia's fervid suns unnerve us more
Than the soft joys of this voluptuous shore?
Let Ocean rave, and summon every blast,
So he but waft us to our port at last;
So Acre's towers resign their scornful boast,
And learn that RICHARD is himself an host."

"Brave though it be, young warrior," Bertrand said,
" The host you prize but wields a single blade;
And though its owner scorn to pause for breath,
A single blow but gives a single death.
Ill can I brook delay, or stoop to fear,
Yet would not leave this isle unguarded here;
'Tis but the rash that think not of defeat,
The prudent, ere they fight, ensure retreat.
The Vampyre fans the sleeper into death,
But mine, thank heav'n! is not a flatterer's breath;
Not one brave arm a victory can decide." 650

" No! by my troth!" the laughing King replied,
" Or thine to conquest were unerring guide.
Thanks for thy love of RICHARD, generous youth!
Thanks, noble Bertrand, for thy love of truth!
If to my arm superior strength be given,
'Tis Heaven's, I lift it in the cause of Heaven;

Yet, Count, of all that pledge this cup with me,
I least had dreamt such sage advice from thee!
With pride, my friends, I find your spirits high,
Unbending brook this enervating sky;   660
Up! Vidal, up! why sleeps thy martial lyre?
Strike the bold strings, and fan the noble fire."

 From proud Toulouse the favourite minstrel came,
A hand of iron, and a soul of flame.
Of mean descent, with Prince and Peer he vied,
Some wayward planet craz'd his brain with pride;
While love, which wiser souls of sense has reft,
Usurp'd the little light conceit had left,
And oft his slave to wilder pranks betray'd
Than Mancha's Knight, or mad Orlando play'd. 670
He vaunts himself all human worth above,
Each warrior's fear, and every lady's love.
The youthful Knights, whose mirth such folly bred,
By turns his wand'ring fancy mock'd and fed,
And late, when RICHARD's nuptial bonds were tied,
They joined the minstrel with a *royal* bride,
By faint and distant lineage link'd with one
That sway'd, or claim'd, Byzantium's fickle throne.
Nor needed more, he grasps the glittering bait,
Assumes a throne, and apes imperial state. 680

Yet his no madness of the vulgar mind;
With flame divine, like sad Cassandra's, join'd,
Proud of his tuneful art he swept the strings,
Taught faith to nations, government to kings.
Not wintry torrents roll a flood so strong,
Nor night's sweet chantress pours so rich a song.
Each willing sense was wrapt when Vidal sung,
And wondering wisdom warbled from his tongue.[kk]
Of Arthur's pomp, and Carduel's towers he told,
The Christmas feast, and deeds of Gawaine bold; 690
What giants for his lady's love he slew,*
What castles storm'd, what valiant knights o'erthrew.
Or, 'mid th' insidious dangers of the feast,
How his tried courtesy withstood the test;
One word that breathed refusal or command,
Had been a signal to the murderer's hand.†
Entranced the warriors hear; the song inspires
The soul of war, and kindles all their fires;
But when the minstrel quits the field of arms
For Gawaine's happy love, his lady's charms, 700
Then RICHARD spoke: " No more pursue the strain,
Lay down thy harp, or sing of arms again.

* See Ellis's Fabliaux—The Mule without a Bridle.
† See Ellis's Fabliaux—The Knight and the Sword.

Those bursting sighs, and downcast looks attest
Thy power too well, in pity spare the rest;
While distant thus through dang'rous climes we roam,
Thou must not lead our truant fancies home.
Nay, Lords! I merit neither smile nor sneer,
Though newly join'd in bliss, my bride be here,
Not from the fondest lover in my band
Can ENGLAND's name a deeper sigh demand;   710
And SHE perchance, my first affianc'd spouse,
Now blames my wand'ring steps and slighted vows."

"Nay, my lov'd Liege! in vain would England blame
While here thy conqu'ring arm asserts her fame,"
Ricardo spoke; " but just thy care, to chain
Th' unheeding minstrel in his amorous strain.
Proud of his airy *empire*, he controuls,
Without remorse, our weak plebeian souls.
See where brave Albert, lost in trance profound,
With some ideal image paints the ground: 720
Yet here I rush on rocks; he ill can bear
That prying wit should note his changing cheer."

Proud Albert's heart the rising pang supprest,
And with a guarded smile retorts the jest.
" Methinks a bride so fair, and left like mine,
Might wake a sigh from any breast—but thine!

Enjoy the quiet of a loveless heart,

Laugh, while thou canst, at those who feel the smart;

Yet some have dreamt that thou hast chang'd thy cheer,

And vail'd thy crest when Hermesind was near." 730

    Breath'd by what voice soe'er, that magic name

Still o'er Ricardo like an icebolt came;

Died on his quiv'ring lips the gay reply,

Droop'd his sad head, and sunk his lively eye;

And, conscious of the laugh, he tries in vain

To find his wonted cheer, and laugh again.

When Pardo rose, he held the goblet high,

And mirth shone graceful in his eagle eye.

"Health! lovers, health! may all your hopes be crown'd,

Your happy heads with wreaths of myrtle bound, 740

But be the laurel mine—my eager sword!

While victory guides, and youth and health afford

Sound sleep by night and spirit at the board,

I covet not to lie long nights awake,

And fast or perish for my lady's sake;

Of pleasing pains the mystic charms repeat;

I would not mix the bitter with the sweet.

Let some soft smile your martial rage inspire,

In me my monarch wakes as proud a fire;

Though sighs and tender tears inflame your zeal, 750
His glance as deep shall urge my thirsty steel.
Oh! for that hour, when Acre's tott'ring pride
Shall see our rival prowess fairly tried."—
He spoke, the Monarch with a smile replied:
" Pardo, we know thee brave, yet think not thou
That Albert's riper fame to thine shall bow,
Till stoops thy soul to sov'reign beauty's right;
A loveless warrior is but half a Knight,
A moving statue, wise or brave in vain,
An empty nut, a head without a brain. 760
But this is sport:—Avignon's shadowy ease
Were fitter scene for idle themes like these.
T'were meet that now our brother King declare
The Moslem strength, and state of Asia's war;
Say, Lusignan, for on our distant shores
Wild, wond'rous tales fallacious Rumour pours.
What is this mighty man, this Saladine,
The Asian boast, and scourge of Palestine?
Some paint an Ogre, drunk with Christian blood,
A giant, foul in form, and fierce in mood; 770
While some employ the rainbow's softer hues,
One that by mercy, more than arms subdues,
A godlike soul, that angels weep to lose.

Say, must we as to hunt some beast prepare,
That claims no common courtesy of war?
Spurn pleading mercy, yield the reins to rage,
Or fight as men with fellow men engage?"
 He ceas'd, and deep the exiled Monarch sigh'd,
One moment prest his burning brow, to hide
The rush of painful thought, and then replied: 780
" There was a time, my torn and tortured mind
Could scarce believe him sprung of human kind,
But youth's wild heat is past; to heav'n I bow,
And own him worthy to be RICHARD's foe.
Not more to others than himself severe;
Patient of toil, unboastful though austere:
No cottage falls to swell his shining hoard,
No peasant starves to pile his groaning board;
Nor lust of spoil nor love of power inspires,
But bigot zeal his restless fury fires; 790
This zeal in youth the Fatimite subdued,
This zeal in age is fed with Christian blood."
In Antioch's towers thy mother's eye could find
In him a spirit form'd to rule mankind;*

---

* When Eleanor of Guyenne accompanied her first husband, Louis the VIIth of France, to the Holy War, she resided some time at Antioch, and is there said to have made acquaintance with a young Turk of the name of Saladine, and it has been supposed by some writers that this youth was the same with the great Saladine.

Though then a boy, no thirst of fame he shew'd,
And pleasure's smile with boyish heat pursued.
But as the tiger cub, once flesh'd in gore,
Disdains the proffer'd dug, and thirsts for more,
His latent greatness burst th' ignoble spell,
He join'd his uncle, and Kahira fell. 800
Noureddin's slave, but traitor to his son,
Egypt he seiz'd, and next Damascus won;
His brother conquer'd Yemen's flow'ry land,
And Mosul's lord was vassal of his hand;^{mm}
And Palestine—Ah! bid me not proclaim
My fatal reign, my sorrow and my shame."ⁿⁿ

Here RICHARD hastes to speak: "O! Monarch! cast
Thine eyes before, nor sorrow o'er the past.
Conquest, in hostile blood already dyed,
Floats o'er our van, and spreads our banner wide. 810
Thus blest by Heav'n, bid cank'ring thought depart,
And yield that best return, a cheerful heart.
Yet say, for thou wert in the Moslem yoke,
How was thy life preserved, thy bondage broke?"

" That eve which closed Tabaria's fatal strife,
I lived, a wretched captive, doom'd to life;
I and Chatillon—to the Soldan's tent
They led us bound, unknowing where we went,

He press'd a plain divan, by which was set
His plainer meal, dried dates and iced sherbet.   820
To me his hands the cooling bowl extend:
Fearless I drank, and pass'd it to my friend.
But then the Soldan's rage in thunder broke,
' Drink not, Chatillon, drink not Thou !' he spoke ;
' To Thee that pledge of safety I deny,
Thou perjur'd Knight, renounce thy faith or die.'

 ' I have not courted danger, liv'd in strife,'
The Knight return'd, ' to barter Heav'n for life ;
And for the broken truce, if guilt there be,
'Twere worse to league with infidels like thee.'   830

 " The Monarch brook'd no more, he snatch'd his blade,
And at my feet down dropp'd Chatillon's head. ^{oo}
I saw and shudder'd—then in Ascalon
For many a moon my wretched life crept on.

 ": Meanwhile, deserted Sion strove in vain—
Compell'd at length to own the Soldan's reign ;^{pp}
Nor was he stern—he spared the prostrate foe,
And fix'd the price of liberty so low,
That, but protracted conflict drain'd the land,
Her poorest sons had paid the mild demand.*   840

---

 * Ten pieces of gold for each man, five for women, and two for children. Those who could not ransom themselves were to remain in slavery.

Then rose through all her streets a fearful cry,
As these lament to stay, and those to fly:
Friend clung to friend; one wail'd his captive doom,
One eyed with ling'ring looks the Sacred Tomb.
From David's gate the conquering Chiefs look'd down *
On the sad pomp slow winding from the town.
Silent the exiles pass'd, nor dared to raise
To their deserted homes their tearful gaze;
But from within discordant wailings rose,
And wilder grief, till pity touch'd their foes. 850
A thousand captives generous Adel freed,
And Mestoc hastes to emulate the deed;
Till Saladine, still prompt at pity's call,
Bids wide the jealous gates unfold for all;
To want and age extends a prompt relief,
And gifts and kindness dry the tears of grief.†

" Now came in sable stoles a female train,
Who wept their wedded lords enthrall'd or slain:
And one was there of more exalted mien,
Supreme in grief, my dear, my wretched Queen. 860

* All the gates of the city were closed except this one, and Saladine, surrounded by his Emirs, waited on the outside of the walls, till the city should be evacuated.

† This trait of generosity is historical.

Though woman's countless charms in vain had shone
To change a heart where honour rul'd alone,
He who but once refus'd a woman's prayer,*
With manly sorrow felt her mute despair;
' Weep not! thy lord has shar'd the bowl with me,
And the twelfth moon,' he said, ' shall find him free.—' "⁹⁹

Here RICHARD, kindling, cries, " And such a deed
Atones Chatillon's blood!—may fortune speed
Our arms to mutual proof—my friend, proceed."

"Those moons roll'd on, and to my gloomy cell 870
Came my sweet Sybill', and my fetters fell.
I flew to Tyre—but saved by Conrad's sword
From Moslem rule, it spurn'd its former lord;
To Acre then my little band I drew—
To guard the town the wary Soldan flew—
My doom seem'd near, when all at once descried,
Three Christian fleets mov'd proudly o'er the tide.†
First mid an English, Norman, Frison train
Came thy brave nephew, Henry of Champagne;

---

* The daughter of Noureddin, when she solicited the Soldan to forego his conquest of the kingdom of Mosul. See note on Almahide to the eighth book.

† These were all in sight at once, and arrived on one day.

Next Austria's haughty ruler sprung to shore;　880
The third small fleet the fervid Conrad bore.
Ev'n then had Acre fall'n, but Egypt's train
With arms and food supplied her from the main.
Two winters now the lingering siege had view'd,
And the third spring had dyed the plains with blood,
When Philip came; yet still her ramparts stand,
Nor yield to less than English RICHARD's hand."

He ceas'd! but RICHARD spoke not; lost in thought,
A wond'rous plan his mighty spirit wrought;
Then smiling, from his pilgrim purse he drew　890
Bright leathern thongs of ether's deepest blue:
"The knight," he cried, "who seeks this badge to bear,
Must never shrink from toil, or stoop to fear;
This round his knee, a proud distinction, worn,*
Let France deride, or Islam feign to scorn,
Soon one with dread, with envy one shall see,
And yield the palm to English Chivalry.
This when the sabre lops the princely crest,
And one deep red obscures th' emblazon'd vest,
Despite the close-barr'd vizor, shall proclaim　900
In breach or desperate field our England's fame.

* See note on the Origin of the Order of the Garter, at the end of the volume.

Yet not to all I give—his happy lot
Who gains may bless; nor he who gains it not,
May deem his worth disgrac'd, his deeds forgot.
Let him that wears it, combat to maintain,
And him that wears not, emulate to gain:
So shall our foes, like timorous sparrows flee,
And Acre fall, and Palestine be free.""

 He spoke, each bosom felt the proud appeal,
Beat high with hope, and glow'd with generous zeal;
Then first to Pembroke (as their years demand),
And Clifford's Earl, he gave the purple band;
Harcourt and Harley next, with ardent eyes,
And noble Percy, glory in the prize;
Leicester and Ferrars then, and Talbot share
The envied badge; then Berkeley, Stourton wear;
Nevile, and Grosvenor, Percival, St. Clair;
Albert, St. John, and noble Fortescue,
And Rodney next, receive the glorious blue.
It adds fresh grace to Spencer's antient name,   920
To Roland's pride and youthful Stanley's fame.
Harvey, De Vaux, with warmer zeal inspires;
And last, not least, the noble Audley fires.

Bright emulation springs in every mind,
While these exult to wear, and those to bind;
And Pardo, as on Albert's knee he prest
The radiant GARTER, thus his friend addrest:
" I will not envy, but by yonder moon,
E'er thrice she wane, thou wear'st it not alone."

Twice twelve, around their valiant Monarch stand,
Matchless in arms, an azure-cinctured band,
And HE the loftiest yields without controul
To that high impulse all his regal soul.
" Vidal! thy harp!"—and, touch'd with minstrel fire,
His rapid fingers struck the trembling wire.
Swift to the pillar'd porch he led the way;
The landscape glitter'd in the moon's bright ray,
And through the light acacia's feathery shade,
As through a veil of gauze, her radiance play'd,
While the tall palm-trees rear'd their trunks on high,
And wav'd their dusky plumes against the sky.
Before them, Ocean's bright expanse was spread,
Behind, Olympus rear'd his snow-capp'd head.
Here mid his Peers, the Monarch pour'd along
The mingled tide of harmony and song.

" Fair Regent of the summer sky!
  How oft, when all was still and mute,
  In thy clear ray my tender lute
Has wak'd soft strains of love-sick melody;
  How oft, when from th' unfinish'd fight   950
  The sun withdrew his envious light,
I bade thy fickle beam the day supply,
And forced from wond'ring Night reluctant Victory.

" Bright Queen of Heaven! I come not now
  To breathe the amorous sigh, or stain
  With blood and death thy silent reign;
I hail thee witness to a lofty vow—
  Courage, and Hope, and Constancy,
  Enduring Faith and Honour high,
And all that should inspire the loyal breast,   960
Which with its holy sign, approving Heaven has blest.

" It comes! th' auspicious hour I hail!
  Once more upon the sparkling brine
  We launch our barks for Palestine,
And spread the golden Lions to the gale;
  Expectant angels, even now,
  Watch from proud Carmel's blossom'd brow;
Weep, weep, ye faithless! smile, ye faithful train!
Sad Sion, lift thy head, thou shalt be Queen again!

"Thou azure badge, not soon to fade, 970
   Ev'n from this night thy glories rise!
   Proud as those palms that to the skies
In the pure light their giant foliage spread;
   Eternal as those hills of snow
   Or yon vast ocean's sullen flow,
Thou shalt be Virtue's highest meed, and worn
'Mid undiscover'd worlds, and nations yet unborn.

"Nor does fallacious Hope inspire;
   Nor is it daring Pride that sings—
   A Cherub's plume has swept the strings, 980
And nobler numbers warble from the lyre.
   More clear yon vivid orb on high
   Moves slowly thro' the purple sky,
In whose dark realm the stars assembling bright,
Mock Europe's dusky heav'n, her pale and cloudy night

"O Thou, who gav'st those orbs to roll!
   If where for Man a Saviour bled,
   Diviner, purer light, they shed,
Now pour the living lustre through the soul!
   Mean as we are, but breathing dust, 990
   Exalt our hope, revive our trust,
Oh! guide our swords—at least accord the prayer
To reach the sacred shore, and fall or triumph there!"

Low to the earth was bowed each noble head,
Each fervent vow in solemn silence paid;
Departing then they sink in peaceful sleep,
Till morn should rouse to plough the foaming deep.

END OF BOOK III.

CŒUR DE LION.

BOOK IV.

THE MEDIAN FIRE.

ARGUMENT.

THE MEDIAN FIRE.

The arrival of fresh forces to Saladine—Philip Augustus assaults Acre—Bravery of Karacous—Defeat of Saladine—His despair—Appearance of Demroosh, and recovery of Saladine—Adventures of Aladin and Moheddin—Zorayda's story—New assault of Acre—Defeat of the Christians by Saladine—Repulse of Philip and Leopold—Destruction of the Christian machines and of the fleet—Heroism of the Count of Bar.

CŒUR DE LION.

BOOK IV.

THE MEDIAN FIRE.

Cautious and calm, meanwhile the Soldan views
The hostile army, and his own renews.
From Egypt's strand (his delegated reign)
He summons Adel to the Syrian plain,
And while his brother ploughs the watery way,
His numerous bands disposed in long array;
Warriors of every race, and every soil,
Sons of the mount, the desert, and the isle;
From Cashmere's flowery vales to Nubia's sand,
From Mocha's sultry coast to Zamarcand.   10

The half-clad Ethiop wields his dreadful flail,
The Syrian clasps his imbricated mail;
The blue-eyed Georgian from his mountain lair
Hurls with Circassia's tribe his slender spear;
The Bedouin comes, with keen and restless eye,
Spare sinewy form, and turban's crimson dye,
Whose home is wheresoe'er his tent may rise,
Or the red banner of his chieftain flies;
Whose only treasure is his faithful steed,
His patient camel, and his sure jerreed; 20
Inured to pain, he mocks the burning scar,
For want and thirst have keener stings than war.[a]
The Persian, cradled in a happier clime,
Of lighter hue, and stature more sublime,
Whose mighty limbs bright flowing silks enfold,
Whose sabre shines with gems, whose robe with gold;
Mahommed's interdicted cup he drains,
And Shiraz' vine flows purple in his veins.
Full in the front of war he loves to wield
His glittering steel, and thunders to the field. 30
The Turk, not yet to opiate drugs a prey,
In stupor lost, and dreaming life away;
Proud of that strength which Persia's lion fled,
And Rome's degenerate eagles learn'd to dread.[b]

And Tartar tribes, whose names not oft are heard
Beyond those valleys where their steeds are rear'd;
They fight, they bleed, yet History shuts her page,
Nor their fierce broils our Western thoughts engage
More than those ants, whose busy nations toil,
And war, and die, beneath the quiet soil. 40
Save when some mightier Khan unsheaths the sword,
O'er wondering Asia pours his barbarous horde,
Bows half the East beneath his iron reign,
Flames like a meteor, flames, and fades again.

But first in rank, in courage and in grace,
To combat train'd, and cull'd from every race,
In radiant yellow clad, the Mamlukes shine,
The household slaves, the guard of Saladine.*
Would you their parents or their home inquire?
He was their home, their country, and their sire; 50
In arms resembling sheath'd, in conflict known
By the rich vest or pictur'd shield alone:
Yet some were there, or they their sires belie,
Whose eyes first open'd on a milder sky,
Perchance were born the heirs of wealth and fame,
And lisp'd with infant tongues a Saviour's name.

* See note on the Mamlukes, book i.

Perfidious Venice! guard thy jealous reign,
Chase each presumptuous rival from the main;
Chain thy sad captives to the gilded oar;
Be misery theirs, but on a Christian shore.   60
Sell not to impious hands the wretched slave,*
Nor let thy hatred reach beyond the grave.

In robes that with no splendid jewels shone,
The placid Soldan fill'd his simple throne.^c
Five youthful chiefs, and each a monarch's heir,
Their vassal aid to Asia's ruler bear:
Prince of Aleppo, ardent Ghazi stands;
Zeineddin, leader of Arbelia's bands;
Osman from eastern Omar's rocky isle,
And Zenghi, lord of Sandjar's burning soil;   70
And Aladin, whom youth's warm hopes inspire,^d
(Seiffeddin's glory), joins his raptur'd sire;
His sire, who sees his early honours bloom,
And dreams of conquest and of power to come;

---

* This odious traffic is the indelible disgrace of Venice. It existed as early as the time of Charlemagne. The Pope interfered, and forbade at least the trade in Christian slaves; but while the markets of the Levant offered a ready sale, the captive and the kidnapped, of either sex, found his anathemas but a feeble defence.—*Heeren, " Sur l'Influence des Croisades," &c.*

When Mosul shall no more to Syria bow,
But claim that tribute which she renders now.
Yet hopes like these he hid, while still the youth
The gen'rous Soldan serv'd with zeal and truth;
And like the infant bird, who sees in air
Its parent soar, and longs her flight to share,   80
In fight he watch'd him, learn'd from him to reign,
And loved the greatness he aspired to gain.

    While near the throne each princely leader stands,
In radiant columns pass their subject bands;
Slow move their steeds, thick clouds of dust arise,
And " Alla Acbar" echoes to the skies!

    His force repair'd, the Soldan on the plain
Provokes the battle, but provokes in vain;
Four rising suns the marshall'd ranks beheld,
And night reluctant to their tents compell'd.   90
He rides round Turon's adverse camp—he calls
The Franks to war—they stir not from the walls!
With growing numbers rich, with conquest warm,
What breeds this sudden fear, or feign'd alarm?
But lo! those towers—such towers has story told
'Gainst Sion's ramparts Godfrey rear'd of old—
Such vast machines can human force repell?
Or Acre stand their shock—when Sion fell?

Three days wear on—while higher yet and higher,
Far o'er the wall those lofty towers aspire; 100
The axe and hammer ring with ceaseless sound,
And Carmel's rocks th' appalling din rebound.
For one vast blow the hosts of Christ prepare,
And knightly hands the glorious labour share.

A fourth bright morning dawns—the gates unfold,
On levers rais'd, on wheels unnumber'd roll'd,
And thickly hemm'd by ranks of chosen powers,
The labouring steers drag on the ponderous towers;^e
With all those pests of war, the mining Sow,
The Cat which clings, and guards the troops below,*
Petraria, Catapult, and Mangonell,
For Heaven employed though first devis'd in Hell.
The clarions bray, while borne in state along
Before the noblest of the noble throng,
The Oriflamme in sanguine splendour flew,
And to the morning sun Montigny threw
The royal lilies on their field of blue.
Last mov'd that banner, victory's holy sign,
The sacred portrait, traced by hands divine,
Where shone the saint, who not less good than brave,
To shivering want his own rich mantle gave;^f

* " Great names, but hard in verse to stand."

Though boiling pitch, and darts, and sheets of flame
Pour on their heads in many a scorching stream,
With earth, with stones collected from the plain,
With ghastly bodies of the gasping slain,
The Christians heap the moat—vast shields on high
Protect their ranks, an iron panoply.
Th' observant Soldan, at their force dismay'd,
Draws forth his host, and flies to Acre's aid;
But Otho leads his brave Burgundians on,   130
The Red Cross Knights, and Brethren of St. John,
And joined by Leopold, in firm array,
Compel the conflict, and obstruct his way.

  The moat is fill'd—beneath the torturing goad
Again the steers urge on their groaning load:
O'er the rough plain slow moves each giant weight;
They reach the walls, and match those walls in height.
Three stages rear'd, the Ram with ceaseless blow
And brazen head, assaults the town below;
Thick bales of wool in vain its fury break,   140
The stones are crumbled, and the ramparts shake;
Midway the rapid sling impells the stone,
And javelins pour, and flaming darts are thrown.
With maces arm'd, an hundred knights aloof
Securely fight beneath the solid roof.

Where Satan's fort the northern shore commands,
'Gainst bold Champagne great Aboul Hagia stands;
While Alberic and brave Montmorency pour
Where Mestoc guards the Patriarch's western tower;
Th' Accursed fortress in the midst ascends: 150
There Philip storms, and Karacous defends,
There mutual valour wakes the fiercest strife,
And the cold thirsty steel drinks deep of life.

  High o'er his peers th' intrepid monarch stands,
And pain and death show'r dreadful from his hands;
While Karacous beholds where'er they fly
The fearful tremble, and the valiant die.
" Ye sons of Islam, yield not thus!" he cried;
" Those threat'ning towers will vanish when defied.
Behold this urn, this urn of liquid flame,   160
Which steel resists not, nor can ocean tame;
When on their heads the fiery storm shall burst,
Well may they call this fatal tower " Accurst."
Accurst as when (for so their legends tell)
It forged the coin through which their Prophet fell.*
All ye, whose trust in Alla rests alone,
All ye, whose music is a Christian groan,

---

* The Accursed Tower is said to have owed its ill omened name to the circumstance that within its walls were coined the thirty pieces of silver for which Judas betrayed his Lord.

Behold, the vengeance from my hands I pour,
Behold, themselves, their castles are no more!"

   Vaunting he spoke, while eager to devour,   170
The lambent flames run swift along the tower;
The Moslems bend to hail th' expected fire,
But lo! they fade, they flicker, and expire.
While high to Heaven the Christian shouts are heard,
Confused, astonish'd, they beheld and fear'd.
Again, again, their boasted fires they try;
Again, again, those fires innocuous die;
The tempered beams the liquid flame repel,
And other arts oppose the arts of Hell.
When from the castle now its drawbridge falls,   180
Lets down its iron hooks, and grasps the walls.
The Franks press on, and none their rage oppose,
Hope nerves their arms, and terror chills their foes.
When Karacous: " Shall yon red banner wave
On Acre's height? shall Magic daunt the brave?
Mahommed sees, and but permits their power
Till yon bright sun unfold the destined hour.
Eternal torments wait the wretch that flies;
But for the brave, his death is paradise!"

   He spoke—his troops again around him close,   190
And to their tower drive back the rising foes;

Their bucklers lock'd present an iron wall,
And ranks behind succeed to those that fall.
But in their triumph, unobserved below,
The Ram relentless urged the fatal blow:
The tottering height a fruitless warning gave,
One moment, and its ruins are their grave;
Down, down, in silent state the weight descends,
Falls with loud crash, earth shakes, and smoke ascends.
In feeble moans it drowns their dying cry!—   200
But Karacous, who clung unhurt on high,
Springs to the breach—the Gallic King defies,
And walls and warriors to the town supplies.
Curved like the moon, he waves his Syrian blade,
While Philip's hand his keen francisque displayed;
Behind, with rage his bold Ribaldi flame—
But Karacous, though short his awkward frame,
(For Nature form'd him in some wayward hour
Of limbs misshapen, but gigantic power);*
Though in his scarf the bristling lances shine   210
Thick as the quills on " fretful porcupine,"
Or the keen arrows of the polar frost,
Shakes off the dreadful hail, and stems an host;

---

* Karacous was so much deformed as to have given his name to a kind of Punchinello, which still continues to amuse the people of the Levant.

While like some mountain peak he braves the storm,
The remnant of his train behind him form;
Careless of death, again in fight they close,
And hand to hand, and steel to steel oppose.

On either side, where Philip's warriors led
The fierce assault, alike the battle bled:
The batter'd walls the dreadful Ram attest;   220
Death stalks abroad, and stills the brave to rest.
While these for glory and for Heaven contend,
And those their country and their homes defend;
Nor mark'd they how the sands of time had run,
Till darkness follow'd on the sinking sun;
The Christians then unwilling quit the fray,
And slowly drag their huge machines away.

Nor was the fight with less of fury waged,
Where to the left, with Saladine engaged,
The Templars, raging at their late defeat,   230
Back to their tents the astonish'd Arabs beat.
Rinaldo, now by vote their leader made,
Appeas'd with ample offerings Eudon's shade,
While for disabled Conrad's every wound,
The Austrian stretch'd a Moslem on the ground.

James of Avesnes, and Otho, side by side,
O'er heaps of slain like vengeful angels ride;
Zeineddin, Osman, Aladin, in vain
With knightly gore their virgin sabres stain,
Condemn'd to see their friends around them die, 240
And by the flying throngs compell'd to fly.
But Saladine, who feels a leader's cares,
Hastes o'er the field, and every danger dares,
Careless his life from showering darts to save,
That seem'd respectful of a breast so brave.
At first he strives to change the doubtful field,
Then bows to fate, and but contends to shield;
Yet oft to Heaven he turns th' upbraiding eye,
And calls the lingering darkness from the sky,
Rejoiced when night with all her shadows came, 250
To save his warriors, or conceal their shame.

Deep in his tent, remote from every eye,
Cast on the ground in breathless agony,
He loathes his food, he seeks his grief to hide,
Nor dare his sons approach their father's side;
Deaf to affection's voice, to pity's tone
He moves not, speaks not, lives to pain alone.[h]

'Tis night's chill noon, yet rest his bosom flies—
Still in his tent, exhausted, pale, he lies;
He starts, he groans, cold dews suffuse his frame, 260
And hoarse and low his painful accents came.

" O Thou, to spread whose glory I resign
Health, peace, whate'er of earthly good were mine,
Thou who hast forced on my reluctant brow
The plumes of empire, wilt thou leave me now?
Oh! had I Ali's strength, or Kaled's sword,[i]
No morn from rest should rouse that race abhorr'd—
Yet thou permitt'st their triumph!—Thou hast arm'd
Their hands with terror, and their engines charm'd!
Twice twenty seasons cold nor burning heat 270
Have seen me cast the slippers from my feet,
If e'er when thy black banner brav'd the wind,
I shrunk in luxury and in sloth behind,
Or e'en in fight forgot the hour of prayer.
Let Acre fall, I merit not thy care;
But if in thee I place unbroken trust,
Sleeps Islam's Prophet?—Is her God unjust?"

With entrance unannounc'd, abrupt and rude,
Before the Chief a turban'd stranger stood;

Dark were his giant limbs, and on his face   280
A mass of evil thoughts had left their trace,
Yet could not quench a wild and awful grace.
Rough, deep and loud, his voice attention bound,
Yet sweetness blended in its sternest sound;
His presence sunk the heart with sudden chill,—
Not shunn'd, though dreaded, and respected still.

  " Fear is for vulgar souls, but not for thine,
Rise, son of Ayoub! conquering Saladine!
Can a slight breeze thus shake a soul so great?
And is it not thy creed, that all is fate?   290
'Mid those lone sands, ere sprung thy race of clay,
Where prostrate Genii hymn'd the living ray,
In later days where many a festive throng
And royal pageant led the hours along;
Where Iran's dark-eyed daughters wont to sing,
While scattering roses of the earliest spring,
And Zoroaster's priests in vesture white
With solemn music hail'd the orient light;
And magic fountains of self-kindled flame
Burst from the earth in many a burning stream: 300
There, 'mid her roofless columns, Istakar,
True to her God, still meets his beam afar;

Still her lone terraces gleam o'er the waste,
Sublimely sad, and speak of ages past,
And still that wond'rous fount's mysterious blaze
Pours its full tribute of eternal praise.
Know, mighty Prince, the mortal who shall dare
To dwell in solitude and silence there,
What time the naptha's pale and livid light
Burns with more splendour through the moonless night,
And, slaves of fire, the mighty Genii lave
Their horrid bulk amid the burning wave,
May view their uncouth orgies, and compel
From their slow utterance many a potent spell:
Command the wealth in caves of ocean barr'd,
That flames encircle and that dragons guard;
Those wond'rous apples, poison half, half sweet,*
And basilisks, whose glance 'tis death to meet;
The Carbuncle that burns, self-pois'd in air,
And Talismans, that e'en the Demons fear, 320
And jewels precious as the vase long hid,
His Genii workmen brought to Giamschid,ᵏ
Whose azure depths were privileg'd to shine
With the first beverage of the purple vine;

* The celebrated apples of Istakar, which are said to be sweet on one side and bitter on the other.

While all around the " charming poison" quaff'd,
The Monarch drain'd the blushing bowl, and laugh'd.

" Prince, not less wond'rous is the vase I bear;
A wave from that mysterious fount is there.
Those Christian towers that mock at other fire,
Once touch'd by this, shall like a dream expire." 330

He spoke, but doubtful still the Soldan stands,
And from the vase averts his pious hands.
" I hate the Christians—live but for their bane,
But Alla's curse is breath'd on arts profane.
Unhallow'd hands that turquoise vase have wrought,
From springs unblest that burning stream is brought."

" Fool !" cried the stranger, while his eyeballs glare
With rage that quench'd each gleam of sweetness there,
" Think'st thou that human voice at Istakar
Hath told thy loss, or borne me thence so far, 340
Ere the gold vessel in thine Imaum's tower
Thrice emptied, thrice hath told the changing hour?*
Prince, know me for Demroosh, and know me one
Of those bright spirits that adore the sun,
Who, but thy Prophet bids, would rather see
Thy race destroyed, than waste one spell on thee."

* The Eastern nations made use of Clepsydra or water-clocks.

He spoke, and his dilated form became
A vast terrific mass of whirling flame;
Still as it grew, his features shrunk from sight,
And vanish'd in a pyramid of light.[1]   350

   The Soldan clapp'd his hands, th' attendants ran,
And the loud trumpet calls the full Divan.
Wond'ring the Princes came, and find their Lord
To health, to all his mighty self restored.

   " Shake off this cloud of grief, my sons," he cries,
" Nor weep for those that wake in Paradise.
Behold the sacred pledge of conquest given,
The gracious promise of approving Heaven;
Not framed by man, or brought by mortal powers,
It holds destruction to the Christian towers.   360
Oh! who but courts th' emprize, the glory rare,[m]
Even through yon camp to Karacous to bear
Our Acre's safety, and her foe's despair?"

   His cheerful words heroic ardour shed,
All court the honour, nor the danger dread;
When from the throng the Prince of Mosul burst,
In years the youngest, but in zeal the first;
While modesty with hope impetuous blends,
Glows in his speech, and on his cheek contends.

L 3

" Not for my own, but for my father's fame, 370
Let Asia's ruler grant his servant's claim;
Not yet on me her smile has glory shed,
Or stoop'd her purple pinions on my head;
While Chiefs are round, so circled with her rays,
This single deed were lost amid the blaze.
Be mine the hazard, give my youth a right
To wage thy wars, their fellows in the fight."

 Though grave his mood, the generous Soldan smiled,
" Seiffeddin hear, and glory in thy child!
Yet to thy realms, as to his valour just, 380
I not alone the daring warrior trust;
Go thou, Moheddin! prove how high I rate
His budding worth, who give him such a mate."

 They doff their robes—the armour that he tore
From a stout German, brave Moheddin wore;
While Aladin a Spaniard's mail assumes,
And quits the turban for the nodding plumes;
His scymitar, that knew its youthful lord,
Alone he chang'd not for th' Iberian sword,
But o'er the turquoise vase with reverence threw 390
His scarf, adorn'd with many a glowing hue.
 Cleans'd with ablutions meet, with silent speed,
In circuit large they urge each foaming steed,

Their clattering hoofs, while yet they skirt the plain,
Unheard amid the murmurs of the main.
'Twas dark—and scarce the watch-fires' feeble gleam
Reveal'd the winding Belus' placid stream,
Whose upward course they trace, and flinging now
Their lengthen'd reins across an alder's bough,
On foot they pass the bridge*—before them frown'd
The leaguer'd town, and danger hems them round,
For, lest their foes some nightly succour gain,
The Christians here a chosen guard maintain;
Yet now their fires are dim, for each had quaff'd
To Philip's health, till slumber check'd the draught.
Rous'd by the tread, they raised their eyes with pain,
Saw Christian armour gleam, and slept again.

Two hostile rows of drowsy guards are pass'd,
The anxious Saracens approach the last,
Where one more wakeful than his comrades stood, 410
To rouse the dying fire with piles of wood;
Then starts, as, by the springing blaze confest,
Shone Aladin's rich mail, and eagle crest.

" St. James preserve us! Lopez, see'st thou there
My master's ghost! by Heaven I saw him fair.

* This bridge is frequently named in Vinsauf, and was the scene of many skirmishes.

Nay mock me not, shake off this rebel sleep,
He comes to blame the careless watch we keep."
But pierced by Aladin, he owns too late
A living arm, and sinks beside his mate.
" The foe! the treacherous foe!" aloud he cries, 420
Waves faintly his expiring brand, and dies.

 Haste, Prince, secure thy charge! for all around
The armed Franks spring furious from the ground,
Close on Moheddin, scan his swarthy brow,
And through the thin disguise the Moslem know.
Oh, shall he leave him vainly to contend,
His charge endanger, or desert his friend?
'Tis Nature's voice prevails; his left arm prest
The precious cup still closer to his breast,
While with his right the thickening ranks he cleaves,
And these of limbs, and those of life bereaves.
He sees Moheddin falter in the strife,
And swords ignoble threat his valued life;
By danger's self inspired, he dares to raise
Its azure cover from the mystic vase,
Blazed like a beacon light that wond'rous fire!
Confus'd, appall'd, the trembling crowds retire.
" Speed!" cried the Prince. He closed the cup again,
And sprang through flying numbers to the main.

"See, see, my friend! kind Alla lends the bark, 440
Our foes are scattered, and the night is dark."

Screen'd by a rock, not then in story known,
But call'd in after years " the English stone,"[a]
With desperate strength they push her from the shore,
Unfurl the canvas, and employ the oar,
And unmolested reach the ancient fort,
Which, rais'd 'mid chafing seas, protects the port.
Moheddin now his purpos'd signal tries,
A ball of light, which high in ether flies,
Breaks into stars, and fades amid the skies. 450
The summon'd guard his well-known voice delights,
And quells the fear his Christian mail excites.
To Karacous, who through the weary night
Still toil'd, expectant of the morning fight,
The envoys give the fatal vase, and then
Guide their light galiot o'er the deep agen.

The dawn to Acre's shores that vessel brought,
With corn and wine for Genoa's pilgrims fraught,
And when young Aladin its flag unroll'd
Deep blush'd the Cross amid a lake of gold. 460
With smiles he spoke, " may Alla now dispose
Our friends to fly—we need not fear our foes.

But near those rocks, Moheddin, dost thou mark
How the rough surges toss a founder'd bark?
And lo! some wretch—I see his signal wave—
Clings to the relic—let us haste to save!"

   He plung'd amid the deep, and snatch'd from fate
A Knight, just sinking with his armour's weight.
One arm sustain'd the load, one stemm'd the tide,
Till safe at last, he mounts the vessel's side,   470
And aids Moheddin, active to reclaim
The life yet lingering in the senseless frame.
They raise his helm, and gaze an instant there
On a pale face, for manly strength too fair,
And dripping locks of long and sable hair;
   At length his eyes unclose—that flag alarms
Returning sense, and starting from their arms,
While o'er his livid cheek the crimson broke,
And his weak frame with frenzied terror shook:
" Oh, cruel chance! oh, luckless hour!" he cried, 480
" And ye unblest, that snatch'd me from the tide!
That Cross, those helms, your Christian lineage shew,
And should be dear, for I am Christian too;
Yet lead me not to Philip's camp, for there
Are eyes whose gaze my brain would burst to bear.

Take me to Saladine, or I again
Will seek that ocean whence ye snatch'd in vain."

"Unhappy Knight! may all thy sorrows fade
Like this false fear," his young preserver said.
"What, though these arms our Eastern race belie, 490
See, as the purple sunrise paints the sky,
I turn to Mecca's holy shrine, and lave
My hands obedient in the cleansing wave.
Behold a Chief long wont in arms to shine,
The Christian scourge, the friend of Saladine;
Thy western climes have heard Moheddin's name."—
"And thine brave youth?"—"As yet unknown to fame,
The humble Aladin begins but now
To seek those wreaths that grace the warrior's brow."

They pass the Christian lines, and row to land, 500
Where the stout Moslems guard the jealous strand.
Who soon Moheddin's swarthy features know,
And hail a comrade, where they fear'd a foe.

Still in his hall, and anxious for their fate,
Amid his chiefs the watchful Soldan sate;
While Mosul's King, whose wily heart confest
A parent's fears, the keener pang supprest.
But when the warriors came, with triumph crown'd,
When Aladin springs forward with a bound,

Proceeds th' adventures of the night to shew 510
And half, in haste, forgets th' obeisance due;
Then, as it needs his own success to speak,
Finds his words fail, and hides his glowing cheek.
The generous King his youthful hero clasp'd,
His conscious hand the happy father grasp'd;
And, as the Monarch's praise delighted flows,
With wary tongue his cold applause bestows,
Fearful too bright his dangerous fame might shine.
Yet ill he read the heart of Saladine;
Who, while no guilt disturb'd his stable throne, 520
Could prize his vassal's glory as his own.

Moheddin now, his graver mission sped,
To Saladine the rescued stranger led;
Slight was his stature, but his noble mien
Shew'd one familiar with such courtly scene.
"Whence, stranger, dost thou come, and what design?
What hopes a Christian Knight from Saladine?"
" From realms as distant as the orient main
Whence springs the sun, to where he sets again,
I come, in virtue's specious name betray'd, 530
Against my Christian foes to seek thine aid.
Yet mine no vulgar grief—to thee alone,
And those that sav'd me, let its source be shewn."

  He paus'd—th' assenting Soldan wav'd his hand,
And from the tent retired th' obedient band.
His cuirass now the stranger knight unbrac'd,
A knight no more—the woman stood confest.
" Prince, if your Prophet, as 'tis said, have driven
Our weaker sex from his voluptuous heaven,
Or but assign'd us there the tasks he gives   540
To poor imprison'd beauty, while she lives,
How strange, how monstrous, must this sight appear,
A royal virgin clad in armour here!
Yet if distress a warrior's pity claim,
That pity give, and listen ere you blame.
  Where the calm Seine a richer verdure laves,
And circles Paris with its winding waves,
How bright my life's deceitful morning shone,
A nation's pride, and sister to the throne!
Yet to one brighter dream would fancy cling,   550
My spousal contract with the English King.
Alas! how ill our genuine good we know,
What seem'd a blessing, prov'd my heaviest woe.
While RICHARD's absence I with tears endured,
His roving gaze an artful maid allur'd;
New vows he form'd, nor thus content, to hide
His fickle heart, my virgin fame belied;

Oh! cruel blow! was't not enough to gain
My fond confiding love, and then disdain?
Why crush that flower so fragile and so fair, 560
To woman vital as the viewless air
That nourishes unfelt, but whose sweet breath,
Denied or tainted, is disease and death.
Yet worse remains: my brother, once so kind,
With him in bonds of policy combin'd,
In silence hears the tale, ah! wretched change!
And sees his sister weep, nor wreaks revenge.
Then blame not that I thus my sex disguise,
And seek myself the justice he denies;
Who else must live of lying tongues the sport, 570
Rude as those waves that wreck'd me at your port.
For this I sought thy camp, O Prince! and bring
Hate deep as thine to England's perjured King.
I fight, to force denial from his tongue,
Or bid his kinder sword complete the wrong:
Let me till then forget my injured name,
And in Zorayda hide Alasia's shame."

"Tis strange!" the Prince rejoin'd—" your knights declare
Their vow, their glory, to defend the fair!
Is innocence aspers'd, and shall not France, 580
Or generous England, yield her cause a lance?

Enough—I greet thee, daughter of the West!
And fear no treachery from a royal guest.
I meet thy frankness with as frank a heart,
Stay while thou wilt, and when thou wilt, depart.
Yet, for my sake, this robe of state assume,
And grace thy helmet with this sanguine plume,
And only to this faithful pair be known
What gentle bosom guards their monarch's throne."

But Aladin, while she her plaint preferr'd, 590
Lived in her looks, and hung on every word;
Wont, 'mid his harem's cool sequester'd bowers
With beauty's smile to cheat the idle hours,
Contending nymphs and rival charms compare,
And own how hard to chuse where all were fair;
To scorn, even while he felt, the petty wiles
That drest each eye in light, each cheek in smiles;
Complain of short-lived pangs he scarcely knew,
Speak as their slave, yet as their master woo—
He, nurst in climes where beauty, ripe too soon, 600
Flowers in the dawn, and fades before the noon,
Dreamt not of that high charm, that grace refined,
When beams through each fine form th'etherial mind;
That beauty, which in gentleness sublime
Awes yet allures, nor dreads the touch of time;

That urges man to more than human deeds,
For which the poet sings, the warrior bleeds;
And wins no favourite of an hour, but one
Still more endear'd when rosy youth is gone.

 Perchance not all these charms Alasia knew, 610
But all were her's to his enchanted view;
Her wrongs he felt, nor question'd whence it came,
That Philip, nay that Europe slights her fame;
If from her eye intemperate anger broke,
In that keen glance indignant virtue spoke;
True she was Christian, yet 'gainst Christians fought,
And spurn'd their worship whom as friends she sought;
But love such bars despised—did he require
His Persian nymphs to slight their God of fire;
Nay he had watch'd, to see the hinna shine 620
Through her long fingers, when some maid divine
Her flowery muntras told at Brahma's shrine.*
True she had barter'd for the helmet's pride
Her rank and virgin robes—but he might guide
Her steed in war, and combat by her side;
And (pleased to prove that chivalry was known
Not to the youth of western climes alone)

* The Hindoos as well as the Mahommedans are wont to use a string of beads to regulate the number of their prayers. The Hindu muntras or rosary is sometimes formed of the buds of flowers.

When at her feet he knelt, and sued the right
To wear her colours, and be called her knight,
Her scarf rewards the ardent proselyte. 630
Then to her tent the royal maid retires,
To seek that rest her weary frame requires;
While he, by hope and love sustain'd, again
Springs to the armies forming on the plain.

Oh, fatal night! oh, fatal gift of fire!
And thou, Alasia! scarce a gift less dire!
The Christians arm, and flush'd with hope and joy,
Crowd to the plain, and speak of triumph nigh:
Ah, wretched, if they knew their wretched doom,
But Heaven in mercy shrouds the ill to come. 640
   The Templars, prompt the conflict to renew,
O'er their black mail their snowy surcoats threw;
Awful, beneath their open helms appear'd
The dark stern visage, and the manly beard.*
Half black, half white, their banner fann'd the air,
And barded steeds their honour'd burthen bear.
Nor with less state sage Ermengard leads on,
In scarlet robed, the warriors of St. John:

* The Knights Templars wore beards: a circumstance which distinguished them from all the other military orders.

In life's gay morning from the world he fled
To tend the outcast leper's loathsome bed;   650
Nor less maintain'd his Saviour's cause in fight,
And the White Cross adorned no braver knight.*
His eye was keen, his features pale and spare,
And the rough casque had thinn'd his silver hair;
Yet strong must be his horse, and firm his seat,
Who dared that chief in battle-shock to meet.°

  Fill'd with like hope, with like desire of fame,
On their fleet steeds the flower of Asia came,
By Omar led, who now to strength restored,
Waves with redoubled hate his eager sword.   660
On either side they strive, they bleed, nor yield
One foot of ground, and equal seem'd the field,
Till Mosul's Prince, who through that desperate day
Seem'd more than mortal, where the fiercest fray
Raged round Rinaldo, on the hero flies,
And, warm with youth, to deadly fight defies:
Nor long they fought, for from the saddle tost,
Again the Templars mourn their leader lost.
The Christians yield—brave Ermengard in vain
Would save the living, and protect the slain;   670

---

* The mantle of the Knights of St. John, or Knights Hospitallers, was scarlet with a white cross on the shoulder. After their expulsion from the Holy Land they changed the colour of the mantle to black, in sign of mourning.

His knights in vain their rivalry forego,
They miss the arm of wounded Conrad now,
And he still foremost in the dangerous fight,
Oh, whither is he fled, the Emerald Knight?
And slighted Geoffrey, ever in the van,
And he, though less a warrior, Lusignan,
Whose holy standard was a resting place
Where rallying hope might turn, and brave disgrace?

 While o'er his mail the priestly surplice shone,
Hubert, the saintly Hubert, fights alone;   680
Alike prepared to act or to endure,
Nor death had terrors for a soul so pure;
Serene in good or ill, with equal eyes
He look'd on both, who look'd beyond the skies.
Where'er the Moslems most deform'd the field,
Where death stalk'd fiercest, there was Hubert's shield;
An arm less strong, a spirit less subdued,
Had dyed the thirsty sword more deep in blood;
But in that awful moment, truly brave,
He sought not praise, his triumph was to save. 690

 Meanwhile the King, confiding in his power,
Storms from his wooden fort th' "Accursed Tower;"
While in the second castle Alberic falls
With rage rekindled on the "Patriarch's" walls,

And heav'd with patient labour from the shore,
The third vast pile two sturdy galleys bore.
With Austria's Duke the gallant Flemings join,
Pisa and Genoa swell the frowning line;
(Who with the Adriatic Queen contest
Her ocean crown, and commerce of the west). 700
In twenty chosen barks, with naval state,
They seek that tower Moheddin sought so late;
The " Tower of Sacrifice," by Pagan doom,
Where bled to Jove the votive hecatomb;
Built on a rock, amid the waves it stands,
Protects the mole, the shelter'd port commands.ᴾ

First Alberic wakes the war—an arrowy shower
Drives its brave guardians from the Patriarch's tower;
He calls his warriors, lets the drawbridge down,
Springs to the wall, and rushes through the town. 710
The Moslems fly! he heaps the streets with slain,
Nor looks behind, nor chides his lingering train.
Rous'd by the clamour, Aralchaïs came;—
Though sprung from Karacous, his sinewy frame
Had more than manly bulk, but not a soul
Which, like his sire's, could half a realm control;
Boastful as brave, exulting in his force,
Greedy of spoil, and stranger to remorse.

"Turn, Christian, turn!" he said, "if aught thou seek,
Save vulgar foes, the timid and the weak,   720
Turn! for my sword the combat can compel;
Methinks those costly arms would suit me well."
  They met, and blows resound. The youth in height
And strength excell'd; in skill the generous knight.
So long they fought, and each so well withstood
His rival's rage, that neither yet subdued,
But wearied both, by mutual wish awhile
Suspend the conflict, and repose from toil.
'Twas where a temple rose to him who trod
The Syrian wastes, the herald of his God;   730
The sculptor's art his wond'rous story shew'd,
The desert rocks, and Jordan's sacred flood;
While sever'd heads, in grim and ghastly row
Record his death, and Herod's impious vow.[4]
So high the spot that thence their eyes command
The town beneath, the ocean and the land.
But what the sight that both confounds? and why
Does one with terror shout, and one with joy?
Three pyramids of flame, that rolling dun
Their murky vapours, hide the noonday sun;   740
Those clouds of smoke, those sanguine fires, too well
To Alberic's heart their fatal secret tell;

M 3

Benumb'd he stands, as by some wizard's charm,
Nor hears the Moslem call, nor sees him arm.
Weak as a lamb before his murderous foe,
He lifts no shield—his heart receives the blow.
Fierce Aralchaïs tore his mail away,
And left his corpse to prowling dogs a prey.

  Nor had his warriors, in his hour of need,
Thus left their valiant chief alone to bleed,   750
But Karacous, as in his glorious track
They strove to gain the walls, compell'd them back.
Soon o'er the crumbling battlement he hung,
And from his vase the fatal naptha flung;
O'er burning wood, o'er shrieking warriors plays
With suffocating stench, the quenchless blaze;
Nor acids here nor temper'd hides avail,
Nor cooling water, nor impervious mail;
All flame alike, men, weapons, engines, all
Catch the blue fire, and share the general fall.   760
The Count of Blois, the lord of fair Champagne,
And Joinville, by his King belov'd in vain,
Sink in th' inglorious heap, a loss more dear
Than all the engines years of toil could rear.

  Still Philip fought, and conquest crown'd his arms
With easy wreaths, when now a shriek alarms;

Turning, he sees the magic fires devour
The Christian boast, th' invulnerable tower;
He sees th' exulting Emir, who displays
His own intended fate, the flaming vase. 770
" To earth, to earth !" he cried, and happy they
Whose flying feet were swiftest to obey ;
Already to the sky the blaze aspires,
And the proud castle sinks in lurid fires.
Last of the band the young Antonio came,
His crested helmet caught the magic flame,—
He writhes in agony, his piercing cries
Drown even the Moslem shout, till soon he lies
A heap of dust : his spirit seeks the skies.

It chanced a spear that Montmorency cast 780
Flew through the flames and kindled as it past,
It fixed its point in Aboul Hagia's breast,
Vainly he tore it from his glowing vest,
He burns, to earth his failing limbs descend,
His scatter'd ashes with Antonio's blend.

Meanwhile the Austrian, in his floating tower,
Leads to the fierce assault his naval power ;
The fort was slightly mann'd, and ill prepared,
No arm of prowess animates the guard.

What though a random spear had pierced his side,^r
He mounts aloft, nor heeds the sanguine tide.
Where on the ramparts warlike engines stood
With flaming torch he fires the arid wood;
His followers scale the walls, and blazing brands
Shed fire at once from fifty valiant hands;
The Saracens retreat, the Christian host
O'er the hot embers mounts, and wins the post,
While raised in triumph on the fading fires,
'Mid wreaths of smoke the conquering Cross aspires.

But fell Demroosh, of all that race accurst   800
That met on Carmel, loathsomest and worst,
Unseen was near. With dire combustion fraught,
A small light bark the artful Pisans brought;
But not to man the coming hour is known,
Their foes destruction meant, it proves their own.
The watchful fiend on that ill-omen'd bark
Blows from the burning fort a floating spark.
Swift as light straw, or Autumn's wither'd leaves,
Her fatal freight the rapid ill receives:
She flames, nor flames alone, her rockets cast   810
On every side have lighted many a mast,
Warriors to steel inur'd, in conflict brave,
Shriek at the fire, and shudder at the wave.

In vain their eager hands unfurl the sails,
The canvas kindles as they catch the gales;
In vain they ply the oar, the burning wood
Drops from their grasp, and chafes the hissing flood.
Few were the barks their wretched crew that bore
Through flood and fire, to die by steel on shore.

   Nor ends the havoc here, on meteor wings   820
From the calm sea th' exploding fireship springs,
And like some vast volcano, sends on high
Its flaming entrails to pollute the sky.
The waters foam and swell, the thunder's roar
Shakes the still air, an earthquake rocks the shore:
Yet calm and solemn as the mountain's brow
In the clear moon, when tempests rage below,
Floats the proud castle, and that burning storm
But clothed in glory what it could not harm;
Till the dire fiend, who lights th' accursed dart,   830
Even in the penal flame that wraps his heart,
Strikes its broad base, the lambent volumes soar,—
The last, the proudest castle is no more.

   Stern on the hostile fort the Austrian stands,
And owns the malice of infernal hands.
Islam revives, his few brave friends maintain
Th' unequal fight, but mingle with the slain:

And one who marked him wounded, spent with toil,
Thought at light cost to win the princely spoil;
But in his groin the Austrian drove the wound,　840
Then spurn'd the falling wretch, and glancing round
A withering look, he plunged amid the main,
And rose, though cumber'd with his arms, again.
Though pour'd a crimson current from his side,
With strenuous arms he beat the foaming tide,
And reach'd the shore; but peace nor rest was there,
All was confusion, carnage, and despair.
To their strong camp the hunted Christians fly,
And thank the care that rais'd its walls so high;¹
While on their rear the Moslems press, to gain　850
That last defence, and make its shelter vain.
Before the open gate the Count of Bar,
A new Achilles, singly bears the war;
Like some vast elephant, whose native mail
His winged foes with puny rage assail,
He stood; the spears that bristled in his vest
He sent more deeply to their owner's breast,
And as the victims thickened round, he rose
Still more terrific on his gasping foes.
Screen'd by his mighty arm, the Christians haste　860
To their calm tents, and bless him as they past.

Alas! that strength which all the battle bore,
Which slew an hundred foes and sought for more,
That mail so finely wrought and knit so well,
Were weak as reeds before the powers of hell.
The conquering troops of Saladine to aid
Now Karacous the eager sally led,
While borne triumphant in the turquois vase
Of fire accurst a fatal remnant plays:
That fatal drop, with fury hurl'd from far,   870
Strikes on his lifted sword the Count of Bar;
He shakes it from his grasp, but shakes in vain,
It clings suspended by too strong a chain;
His arm already feels th' ascending flame,
And dreadful tortures spread through all his frame.
Enraged, to earth he cast his ponderous shield,
And snatch'd a spear, the last he e'er shall wield:
" Take that, misshapen wretch! and learn, if still
My better arm were faithful to my will,
Soon should thy soul regain its native hell,   880
And feel those torments thou canst give so well."
He spoke—his spear the Emir's shoulder tore,
And long that wound shall Karacous deplore.
Then with one shrill, one final shriek of pain,
He fell expiring on the mound of slain,

While spreading o'er the whole, that wondrous fire
Blends all his victims in one funeral pyre.ᵗ
 Yet even in death his weeping friends he saved,
And aw'd that foe his living arm had braved.
That mighty blaze, extending o'er the plain,   890
Drives from th' assaulted camp the impious train.
Secure at length the ponderous valves they close,
And weep their loss, and from their toils repose.

END OF BOOK IV.

CŒUR DE LION.

BOOK V.

THE ARRIVAL OF RICHARD IN PALESTINE.

ARGUMENT.

THE ARRIVAL OF RICHARD IN PALESTINE.

Conrad and Isabella—Entrance of Leopold—Marriage of Conrad—The Princess of Constantinople—Famine in the Christian camp—Arrival of Adel with succours to Saladine—Of the Duke of Suabia to the Crusaders—Richard's voyage, and battle with the Dromond—The illumination, the landing at Acre—Richard and Berengaria — Evanthe — Dissentions among the Chiefs—Richard surveys Acre by sea and land, and turns the course of a river—Distress in the city—The illness of Richard and perfidy of Philip—Albert and Ricardo—The Falcon—Pardo seeks the lost bird—Finds a secret way into Acre—Recovery of the Falcon—Preparations for assault.

CŒUR DE LION.

BOOK V.

THE ARRIVAL OF RICHARD IN PALESTINE.

Within the camp confusion reign'd, and shame,
Resentment, clamour, grief and mutual blame:
But man is blind; no warning, no remorse,
Arrests the wicked in his headlong course.
  The Austrian hastes where still in regal pride,
Sate reckless Isabelle by Conrad's side,
And cool'd his gashes with that herb renown'd,
That erst by Belus great Alcides found,*
What time the dying hydra gave the wound.

---

* The Colocasia.

Scarce patient of the Leech's short delay, 10
Propt on his sword, he urged his tottering way;
Yet smoothing as he came the rugged brow,
Which rage and agony convuls'd but now,
To Thoron's wife he made obeisance low :
" Health, royal lady—hands so fair as your's,
My friend attests, can work no common cures :
Ah, happy! while you heal the meaner part,
Could those bright eyes forbear to pierce the heart.
Hubert, that mitred Norman, dares to say,
That all the wreck of this disastrous day 20
Springs from your guilt, who left—oh deed abhorr'd!—
For this brave Prince your craven, woman-lord :*
And, but Augustus check'd his priestly pride,
The fools had come to force you from his side."

" To force!" cried Conrad, " can they then forget
The wounded lion is a lion yet?
The meddling knave were best his beads to tell—
Sooth! for a priest he wields the falchion well;
But mine, my friend, is weary of its rest,
And longs to find a scabbard in his breast. 30

* See the opening of the third book.

Have they forgot, in Syria's last alarm,
Whose was the single ship, the single arm?—
But I disdain to boast, I cannot teach
My worth in words, my actions are my speech.
To-morrow's dawn hails Isabelle my bride,
Nor dare they touch her raiment at my side.—
Forgive me, Princess, if my words be brief,
And I forget the lover in the Chief;
Augustus is my friend, nor durst he shew
An adverse semblance, were his heart my foe. 40
Once join'd with thee, I speak as Sion's King,
And drivelling Lusignan in vain may bring
That high-souled Prince, whose warlike worth I hate,
RICHARD may come, but he will come too late."

"Then mark me, Conrad!" Isabelle replied,
"No private rights beseem a regal bride;
Sovereigns and Peers must grace the splendid scene,
And all the nuptial state that fits a Queen."

That solemn mockery stains no stately pile,
Where storied tapestry hangs the vaulted aisle; 50
No dome time-hallowed, where the tinctured rays
Shine on the sculptured great of ancient days.

When Acre's siege began, the martial train
Had rear'd with simple skill the modest fane.
Yet those sleep there, whose souls now wrapt in bliss,
Had wept in blood to witness deed like this;
And on the walls in grand disorder shone
Turbans and scymitars, from Moslems won.
No deep ton'd music breath'd a solemn sound,
Nor gold nor rubies gemm'd the altar round;   60
Yet piety had breathed the humble prayer
O'er many a precious relic resting there,
With zeal as pure as where the tapers blaze,
And chaunting choirs th' eternal anthem raise.
Behind the shrine a veil of crimson hue
The sacred precinct veiled from vulgar view.

    Haughty yet mean, less studious to fulfil
His Maker's precepts than his Suzerain's will,
The Prelate of Beauvais, ministrant there,
Insults his God with vows he cannot hear.   70
Now came the Princess,—gold and purple blend
On her rich robes, and high-born dames attend;
Nor Gaul's degraded Majesty denied
To view the guilty rites, and give the bride.
Next moved the daring Prince; nor latent shame
Deprest his courage, nor his glance could tame;

Yet more than lover's rapture seem'd to speak
In his quick motion and his mantling cheek;
Something o'er which the wondering gazer ran,
Then shunn'd instinctive, and forebore to scan. 80
The Austrian next, whose summon'd smiles conceal'd
His lingering step, and smart of wounds half heal'd;
Behind, and blended with the Tyrian train,
His mail-clad warriors throng the narrow fane.

Already round the altar's glittering fence
Th' attentive Princes kneel,—the prayers commence;
When from behind the silken veil arise
Low sounds of smother'd sobs, and long-drawn sighs.
The curtain opens—well may Conrad start,
Well may the blood flow backward to his heart; 90
Well may he gaze upon that wasted frame,
And ask, thus changed, ah! can it be the same?
Gone was the wreath her braided locks had worn,
Her robes, once wrought with gold, defac'd and torn,
Her glassy eyes a wandering mind bespeak,
Yet beauty linger'd on her pallid cheek;
And something scarce defined, in speech or mien,
Of fair and noble, told what once had been:
As in the wither'd rose a faint perfume
Recalls the memory of its summer bloom. 100

Her low soft tones a pleasing grief inspir'd,
Yet sooth'd to pity, not to vengeance fir'd.
" Oh! Conrad, Cæsar, or if thou require
That name so dearly purchased,—Prince of Tyre!
Think not I come to mar thy bliss, nor fear
That hatred urges one no longer dear;
I will not vex thee long, will but resign
This ring, this precious ring that bound thee mine—
Take it, proud Isabelle, and may he prove
More true to thee, than to my slighted love.   110
Yet I was loved—and still beloved had been
Had Stamboul's wretched Princess reigned a Queen.
Nay, on my alter'd form your gaze forbear,
Nor what I was, nor am, is now my care:
I yet were lovely, had he thought me fair.
Nor think, though wild my sunken eye may seem,
That some dark deed is in its wandering beam :—
What though I felt not, when th' unpitying storm
Has raged at midnight o'er my houseless form;
Though I have flung me on the rocky brow,   120
And could not hear the cataract roar below,
The soul which once in duty's path has trod,
Not e'en when reason strays, forgets its God.

Still will I bear th' appointed load of pain,
One only vision—Ha! it comes again!
Avaunt, ye murderers! God of mercy, give
A longer span—let him repent and live—
Ah, me! unshrieved the guilty soul has fled,
And see! those phantoms thickening round the dead!
Those forms that are not of the sons of light—   130
Oh, save me, save me, from the maddening sight!"—

  She scream'd! her hands were clasp'd upon her head,
A burning blush her wither'd cheeks o'erspread,
And like a morning cloud, a broken spell,
She vanish'd—how or whither none could tell.

  With lips whose pride the struggling shriek forbore,
Though pale and trembling as the veil she wore,
Stood Isabelle; but her unbending lord
Own'd not his secret pangs in look or word;
Unchanged, unshrinking was his eagle eye,   140
As when it gazed on Raymond's agony.
With rapid glance he scann'd th' assembly round,
Beheld the cloud on every face, and frown'd.

  " Princes, I read resentment on your brow—
Say then, is Conrad's honour fall'n so low,
The sport of every maniac's breath—as frail
As the slight aspen in the summer's gale?

Can ye not trace the same infernal powers
Whose dreadful spells consumed our fire-proof towers?
I reck not, though an hundred phantoms fair   150
Should come like feverish dreams, and melt in air;
Nay I will thank them for this bridal ring,
It well beseems the daughter of a King;
I dread no ills its charmed round may breed—
Most reverend prelate, let the rites proceed."—

   Convinced or awed, no warrior took the word.
One hardy Tyrian stept before his lord,
But shrunk, for Conrad half unsheath'd the sword.
Fair Isabelle revived,—the rites were closed,
Nor Philip's voice forbade, nor heaven opposed.   160

   Already Ullah pours her baleful rains,
And drives the armies from the miry plains;
In Acre's domes her weary troops recline,
On Kaisan's height the bands of Saladine,
Alike unmenaced by the dearth and woe
That threat the Christians in the camp below.
Their fleets are wreck'd upon the stormy coast,
Their stores consumed, their famish'd coursers lost;
Want stalks abroad, and at her touch the skin
Cleaves to the bone, and furies rage within.   170

Gaunt, fleshless forms, their meagre friends appal,
And glide like spectres round the silent wall.
Here sullen apathy forgets to feel,
Here hunger revels on the loathsome meal;
Here avarice, whose insatiate greed has sold
His last sad pittance, dying, gnaws the gold.
Love bids Alecto's torch his lamp awake,
And dips his arrows in the Stygian lake,
While phrenzy never tamed, and horrid joy,
With dreadful laughter mock their agony; 180
With loud blasphemings load the fetid air,
And join, with Death, the banquet of despair.
Now swell the streams to torrents, from the plain
Wash the half-buried bodies of the slain,
And with corruption foul, rush headlong to the main.
Contagion comes, and through the wasted frame
Spreads,—as through Autumn woods the casual flame,
When town, and tower, and ripening grain, by turns
Feed the red fury, and a province burns.
The brave in arms, untaught to shrink at death, 190
Start from their friends, and shun each other's breath.
In vain the chiefs th' unbridled throng restrain,
And Hubert warns of angry Heaven in vain;

Shame flies with hope, they spurn the theme sublime,
And deeper plunge in misery and in crime;
When lo! a fleet!—as o'er the boundless blue
The banner'd Cross flung wide its sanguine hue,
That holy symbol seem'd again to bear
Mercy to man, and comfort to despair.
Oh, needless mockery; on th' unguarded strand   200
Proud Adel springs, and bids his Egypt land;
Tears down the bright delusion, and displays
His yellow standard to their sickening gaze.

With all the pomp of music, all the show
Of selfish triumph when it scoffs at woe,
Betwixt the Christians and the town he leads,
Uncheck'd, that host whose countless sum exceeds
The insect swarms that, far at distance seen,
Blot the broad sun, and chase the vernal green.
While from their walls they gaze, and blush to own
Their life, their safety in those walls alone;
While latent valour wakes, and aims the blow
The wither'd arm is powerless to bestow;
By turns his luxury mocks their need, by turns
His taunts assail the wretched troop he scorns.

Hope springs again, for hark, the trumpet's notes!
O'er the near hills th' Imperial Eagle floats.

'Tis Frederic's van! back, back, the portals fling,
And hail with rapturous shouts the conquering King!
Alas! Icomium's terror breathes no more,   220
O'ercome with toil, or fest'ring in their gore,
His myriads sleep, and those that yet remain,
Exhausted, pale, may wish them with the slain;
While their sad Duke, who mourns his mighty sire,
In filial sorrow sinks his martial fire;
Nor feels that, lurking in the cup of grief,
Disease has mark'd her prey, and mocks relief.
Through the dark camp they spread a double gloom,
And joined in misery, wail their common doom.

While thousands thus accuse his long delay,   230
" Why lingers RICHARD on the wat'ry way?"
The sun in sadness rose, in sadness set,
The waves are clear, th' horizon spotless yet;
Can RICHARD loiter when the clarions blow?
Or hear of want, nor hasten to bestow?—
Alike his spirit chafes; from day to day
By storms imprison'd in Limisso's bay;
At length escaped, in vain his sails expand,
Some demon drives them from the Syrian land.

Yet with two favourite barks, before the rest 240
The royal galley skims the ocean's breast,
And the clear waves play round each ruddy oar,
As if rejoicing in the freight they bore.
In the blue distance, faint and dim-descried,
Like rock or islet looming o'er the tide,
A shadowy form appear'd,—but soon it grew
Near and more near, and now distinct to view;
A mighty ship, with every mast defined,
And all her canvass spread before the wind.
Vast as those floating towns that bear afar 250
From pole to pole the storm of England's war;
Yet ship like this, on all the azure reign,
Nor Europe dreamt, nor Asia saw till then.
With awe the crew its mighty bulk behold,
And hostile pendants, bright as liquid gold:
But for the expected fight the Monarch burns,
And threats and promises inspire by turns;
His galleys arm; the mariners in haste,
On the sharp prow the frowning castle place;
The knights their helmets brace, their lances wield,
And from the gunwhale snatch th' emblazon'd shield.*

* The manner in which the shields of the knights were ranged round

the

Meanwhile with all the press of oar and sail,
And all the impulse of the strenuous gale,
Th' enormous "Dromond" comes, and strives to whelm
Her puny foes amid the watery realm.
They shun the fatal shock, yet rudely tost,
Now rise to heaven, and now in gulfs are lost;
While closing o'er her track the billows roar,
And chafe beneath th' unwonted load they bore.
But RICHARD's voice the faltering yeomen cheers,
" Gold for the valiant, death to him that fears !"
He bids his galleys turn and court the wind,
And pressing fast their heavier foe behind,
Before the breeze with forceful speed they glide,
And pierce with beaked prows her lofty side :
The grappling hooks are fixed ; the arrowy showers
Pour like a tempest from the wooden towers,
In vain—from plank or gunwhale they rebound,
And strew the ocean, guiltless of a wound;

the gunwhale of the galleys, when prepared for war, as well as the form of the wooden castle which it was usual to elevate at the prow when an action was about to commence, is shewn in that curious relic the Bayeux tapestry. In a MS. at the British Museum, of the time of Henry III., a vessel is represented having a castle at the stern as well as the *forecastle*, which has evidently bequeathed its name to that part of a modern ship, although the castle itself has shrunk nearly to a level with the main-deck.

While swarthy Egypt at her foes beneath 280
Aims the deliberate blow, and scatters death.
Nor thus content, with many a ready weight
Of stones and lead, prepares their general fate.
But England's King, whom no defence could bar,
Now to the adverse deck transfers the war;
For boldly standing on the castled prow,
He climbs its loftier side, and leaps below.
Him Leicester followed, fighting as he rose,
Richmond and Nevile, dealing blows for blows.
With envy fired, De Vere[a] and Sackville[b] spring 290
From either rival bark, to aid their King.
Fast flows the purple tide,—yet wherefore tell
How Albert fought, or stout Fitzharding[c] fell,
Or Pardo's strokes in quick succession came
With graceful ease, as war itself were game?—
Hid in the darksome caverns of the deep
Already twice their scanty numbers sleep;
Where late presumption vaunted, fear assails,
The clouded Crescent wanes, the Cross prevails.
The sable Acbar now, in whose command 300
That dread of ocean left th' Egyptian strand,
First in the fight while victory doubtful hung,
Now at the Monarch's feet his sabre flung.

"Thou, at whose touch the Faithful fall!" he said,
"Thou, who hast borrow'd Azrael's venom'd blade,
Rejoice; that arm which earth and Heaven defies,
Ne'er reaped by sea or shore so rich a prize.
Behold, contrived with what consummate art,
How vast, how strong, how finish'd every part.
From where the Nile its eastern tribute pours, 310
To Syria's strand we brought these warlike stores;
These arms, these liquid fires, this hoard of grain,
To Acre borne, had made your valour vain.[d]
Yet deem not, Infidel," and as he spoke
The slumbering furies kindled in his look,
"Deem not that these are thine,—my triumph mark,
Where yon green ocean oozes through the bark—
Learn how we combat on these wat'ry fields,
What thou shalt win, and how a Moslem yields!
Too blest to perish in destroying thee, 320
To ocean's caves I drag thee down with me."

"Die then thy chosen death," the Monarch cried,
"My weary weapon scorns to tame thy pride;
But vaunt no more:" and bounding o'er the rings
Of dead and dying, to his bark he springs;
Calls from their fancied spoil his warriors bold,
The grappling irons wrenches from their hold,

And safe and free his galleys ride again,
As their proud foe sinks darkly in the main.

   Now to their wishes shifts the prosperous gale, 330
They rest their oars, and loosen every sail;
Beneath the cloudless sunbeams glittering bright,
And sporting through a thousand rings of light,
Round the smooth keels the limpid waters play,
Till, as they purpled in the evening ray,
With rapture RICHARD hail'd the yellower line
That traced in mist the shore of Palestine.
Fill'd with one feeling, with one thought inspired,
At sight of that so long in vain desired,
One shout of holy joy the warriors gave,   340
A shout re-echoed by the dancing wave;
By angels echoed with a heavenly strain,
By fiends in mockery from their beds of pain:
With streaming eyes they view the distant strand,
And stretch their arms to meet the Promised Land.
   Nor less, from Acre's camp the Christians knew
The white specks glimmering on the boundless blue;
And gazing, linger on the darken'd shore,
Till fancy's self can fix their place no more.

But soon a mimic day illumes the dark,   350
And lamps light up in each advancing bark;
Round every mast are garlands wreathing bright,
And every galley's form is traced in light;
And Rams and Catapults, and engines dire,
Shine on the crowded decks, and vomit fire.
High to the clouds the living splendours glow,
The bright reflexion gilds the deep below.
O'er RICHARD's head, in lines of burnish'd gold
Flamed his rich crown, his royal standard roll'd;
And far above, a Cross serenely bright,   360
Beam'd, as from Heaven, its pure and silver light.

  It was an eastern night of loveliest calm,
Each wave was music, and each zephyr balm.
No mist the placid face of ocean knew,
No cloud obscured the æther's deepening blue;
And though no moonbeams played, a ruddier glow
In grandeur clothed majestic Carmel's brow,
And those devoted towers that shone so bright,
Like victims, lovelier in their funeral light.
No chilling blasts, no fatal dews were there,   370
To mar enjoyment of that tranquil air,
So lately heavy with the damps of death,
Now pure and fragrant as an infant's breath;

Or that blest eve, whose sacred dews arrest
With drops of healing power, the raging pest ;*
Disease and pain, and wounds and famine seem
From every bosom vanished like a dream ;
While as the fleet rows nearer to the shore
The billows blush beneath each glittering oar,
That dashes jets of living flame on high,   380
To shine and fade amid the lurid sky.
The rivers glitter in the spreading beam,
The brightening ocean seems a flood of flame;
From every brow has pass'd its hopeless gloom,
And answering fires the Christian camp illume.

  The morn that called the Moslem host to prayer
Still saw the happy Christians lingering there.
The blazon'd sails beneath the sunbeams glance
And gem, like floating clouds, the dark expanse.
Now drums and cymbals sound, the mellow flute 390
Blends its soft tones, nor is the clarion mute;
And timing to their oars, the myriads raise
The solemn chaunt or choral peal of praise.

  * The eve of St. John; the dews of which are believed, in the East, to stay the progress of the plague.

Borne on the waters now the music floats
Half lost in air, now swells its boldest notes,
Now higher strains the vocal brass inspire,
And angel voices seem to join the quire.
Bright as that reed, by Ganges, (sacred name!)
Whose scarlet blossom clothes her banks in flame,
The purple thistle on the Syrian wold,   400
Or fragrant asphodel that blooms in gold,
Now pennons wave; bend, eagle, cross, and shell,
The pomp of war or pride of lineage tell;
And long and loud the shouts of welcome grew,
Whene'er some well known banner flash'd to view;
Or fancy on the distant prow could trace
Some kindred shield, some long-expected face.
Near and more near, they reach the crowded coast,
Hope reads her triumph now, and doubt is lost;
The vessels ground, and many a friendly hand,   410
And rapturous greeting, hail them to the strand.[e]
First RICHARD springs to shore, and numbers spread
The costly tapestry for his courser's tread;
Favell, the noblest of the Cyprian spoil,
Gentle and graceful, and untired by toil,
In colour like the fields of ripening corn,
Crimson and gold his beauteous limbs adorn;

With high-arched neck the splendid cloth he trode,
Proud of his trappings, prouder of his load;
While envious of his state, in raven pride,   420
The Norman charger paces by his side.

  But wheresoe'er the Monarch's glances fall,
His grace, his bland demeanour gladdens all;—
Loud shout the Franks, the wondering Syrians prest
To gaze on him, the Hero of the West!
Admire his sable hauberk's woven mail,
His brazen axe that crushed where'er it fell,[f]
His silken mantle glorious to behold;
His saddle where the lions ramp'd in gold,
His lion shield, his helmet lion-crown'd,[*]   430
And the gold broom-flower on its glittering round.[g]
Behind, in long procession, moved the brave,
And notes of triumph swell, and banners wave;
The winds on high the English lions fling,
And dragon standard of th' Armoric King.

[*] On the first of King Richard's seals the shield bears two lions rampant. The second, which was engraved soon after his return from Palestine, is said to give the first example of the three lions passant gardant in pale. This was certainly his legitimate device. Henry II. had five lions in his shield, but he gave two of them, with his eldest daughter, to Henry, Duke of Saxony, who was afterwards called "Henry the Lion." The other three he kept for himself, and they have since been the acknowledged arms of England.

The Monarch kneels, with all his Princes round,
And kist with reverend awe the sacred ground;
While Hubert lifts to Heaven his tearful eyes,
And calls a thousand blessings from the skies.
Now Philip came; whate'er of jealous pain   440
Had rankled, and must rankle there again,
In neither heart such thought now found a place,
And mutual love prolong'd the strict embrace.
All, all was joy; for even Leopold
In simulated smiles his hate controll'd:
Conrad alone, unable to disguise,
Roll'd dark on Lusignan his baleful eyes.

Nor less delighted numbers press the strand
Where England's bridal Queen descends to land;
Admire her regal mien, Evanthe's grace,   450
The holy calm of pale Matilda's face,
Or sprightly Hermesind's aeriel bound,
As like a fawn she ran and gazed around.

Oh, talk of danger, talk of want no more!
From the tall ships in long succession pour
Men, armour, weapons, every warlike store;
Sicilia's matchless grain, Oporto's wine,[h]
The unpressed honours of the Cyprian vine,
The steer well fatted, and the salted chine.

All,—but their names the sated ear would tire, 460
All want could need, or luxury might desire.
The ships are drawn on shore, and now revealed,
Those portals fall that late the waves concealed;
The snorting steeds rush joyful to the land,
And neigh aloud for liberty regained.[i]
Rich stuffs are heap'd where'er the gazer turns,
And lances gleam, and polish'd armour burns,
And o'er their cups the jovial circles sing,
The power, the boundless wealth of England's King.

In RICHARD's tent was spread the gorgeous feast,
At RICHARD's board sate every noble guest;
Brave, courteous, generous, with untroubled mind,
To all around magnificently kind,
He dreams not that his gifts renew the smart
Of envy lurking in Augustus' heart;
While hovering nigh, Alkarmel sees with pain
The peaceful parting of the princely train;
Of those who ne'er shall part in peace again.

But whose that gay pavilion? Blazing bright,
Streams through the silk the many colour'd light,
Its ample space in Persian splendour drest,
And rich with all the perfumes of the east,

Vast as the tent for great Kerboga wove,^k
Each spicy gale seems redolent of love?
While all his vassals brave the dews, the wind,
Rests RICHARD here, in luxury's arms reclined?
No! his adventurous soul was bent to share
Whate'er his meanest serf might feel or dare:
But all that splendour to himself denied,
He freely lavish'd round his lovely bride.   490
" Enough," he thought, " she feels of toil and woe,
And small the comforts I can here bestow,
Yet, oh! while mine the power, from her be far
The fears, the horrors, and the wants of war."
 Her train dismiss'd, the Cyprian Princess there
Alone remains, her anxious thoughts to share.
Why, sweet Evanthe! does thy faded cheek
The secret touch of pining grief bespeak?
Ah! what avails that thine the winning smile,
The grace, the softness of thy native isle;   500
Thy golden locks, the languish of thine eyes,
But gain thee hearts that thou canst never prize!
Kind, gentle, modest, and sincere in vain,
Thy snowy bosom heaves alone with pain;
E'en from the hour that to thyself revealed
Thy fatal flame, with growing pain concealed,

Bereft of hope, for thine unspotted breast
Ne'er harbour'd guilty wish, or thought unblest.
Thy love, like lamps in Egypt's ancient tombs,
Nor chilling damps can quench, nor time consumes;
And should some fatal chance reveal the fire,
At once, like them, shall life and love expire.
Thy wither'd bloom the fruitless struggle tells
Of strong resolve with more than human spells;
Thine only joy to gaze on RICHARD's eye,
Yet thy sole hope, thy last resource to fly.
She rose, with pain the rising pang supprest,
And sought her couch:—oh! may she hope to rest.—

" Why," cried the King, with all a lover's fear,
" Why, Berengaria, wilt thou linger here?   520
That form, till now by trembling zephyrs woo'd,
Has braved the gales of ocean, keen and rude,
Must brave the journey o'er the sandy waste,
And worse than toil, the desert's sultry blast:
Yet, thy soft frame with equal toils opprest,
Thou scorn'st to sleep when hardiest warriors rest!
Short is their respite who with warriors live,
But take the little ease my care can give;
Nor let thy fading hue and heavy eyes
Betray the languor which thy tongue denies."   530

" And think'st thou, RICHARD, that my cheek is pale?
'Tis but these faithless lamps that tell the tale.
Why did I winds, and waves, and deserts dare,
But to partake thy counsels and thy care?
Oh, RICHARD! if my fragile frame must fail
At every toil, and shrink from every gale,
Why am I thine? oh! why did lavish fame
Teach me, unknown, to kindle at thy name,
And think how blest above her sex must be
The happy maid whom heaven should link with thee?
How throbb'd my heart in thee to find the Knight
I crown'd as victor of Pamplona's fight![1]
And oh! what joy my inmost spirit stirr'd,
To find myself by RICHARD's choice preferr'd!
Yet then I felt, amid my rapturous pride,
What Heaven demanded of a hero's bride;
Not with her foolish fears and puny frame
To check his course, and clog his rising fame;
Nor changing with each wild caprice of fate,
Too soon dejected, and too soon elate.   550
Arm'd 'gainst myself, I prob'd my heart with care,
Tried all its powers, to suffer or to dare;
And had I found no answering vigour move,
Dear as thou wert, I had resign'd thy love.—

Why all this pomp? why wilt thou feed mine eyes
With luxuries thou hast taught me to despise?
No more this gorgeous down is spread for me,
Lo! there the couch that I must share with thee.
What! could'st thou then his living rage deride,
And start'st thou, RICHARD, at the Lion's hide? 560
Nay! 'tis a beast in tuneful story known,
Generous his heart, and royal as thine own."

   Still on her face the Monarch fix'd his gaze,
Lost in an ecstacy of love and praise,
Again reminds her of the waning night,
And speaks of Council with the earliest light.
Exalted pair! unless your couch be blest,
What mortal eyes can hope untroubled rest!

   'Tis morn; and now th' assembled Chiefs debate,
How best their arms may seal the city's fate. 570
Three splendid thrones adorn'd the spacious ring,
One RICHARD fill'd, and one the Gallic King.
A third for him who in the Cydnus died,
Now Conrad claim'd, and Lusignan denied.*

   * In the hall where the principal personages who assisted in the siege of Acre met for council, three thrones were erected, for the Emperor of Germany

Meanwhile the Chiefs to royal RICHARD yield
The leader's staff, and bid him rule the field.
But Philip brook'd not this; the last night's feast,
The shouts, the triumph, rankled in his breast,
His spirit chafed to see the equal throne,   580
The fame, the riches, that outvied his own.

" Shall I to England stoop the pride of France,
And at a vassal's bidding couch the lance?
I whose rich blood from Rome's defender springs,
The first of Western thrones, the " King of Kings?"[m]
Be mine the sway, or I no more proceed,
I will not follow where I ought to lead.
And more—let RICHARD's avarice now resign
Half of that prize, by solemn treaty mine;
They may be rich who other's wealth withhold, 590
And generous that reward with other's gold;
And fools may still with hireling praise pursue
The hand so lavish of another's due;
But know thy Suzerain never can allow
The Cypriot crown in peace to bind thy brow;

Germany and the Kings of France and England. I cannot distinctly make out whether Lusignan had at this time a separate throne, but he and Conrad afterwards disputed that which had been intended for Frederic Barbarossa.

Nor she thy doting passion brings from far,
She called thy bride, the daughter of Navarre,
To reign as England's Queen, and boast perchance
You scorn'd for her the plighted maid of France."*—

" Nor think," cried Conrad, " that I tamely see
" A worthless rival here preferr'd to me.
Shall Lusignan display his white-veiled car,
And lead again his betters to the war?
Bid him that badge of sovereign power resign,
Once his indeed, but now as justly mine.
Mine, in the right of Isabelle my bride—
I blame thee, King, for thou abett'st his pride."

They ceased, and clamour rose : but RICHARD's look
Still'd every tongue to silence, ere he spoke.

" Strange welcome this! that on your comrade showers 610
The hatred due to Acre's stubborn towers !
Philip, our vows of Vezelay I own,
But not thy right to share the Cyprian throne;
Alone I won it, and I rule alone.
Yet mark—Theodoric's soul now wings its flight,
And leaves his wide domain his Suzerain's right;

---

* Alasia, sister of Philip, to whom Richard had formerly been betrothed.

One half of Flanders to my rule resign,[n]
And half of Cyprus, nay its best, is thine;
This justice wills—deny or grant the claim,
Our pledge was mutual, and our rights the same. 620
But chafe not that my troops are brave, that Heaven
To me a rich and pious land has given,
Whose loyal sons, to him how justly dear,
Press on their King the wealth thou envy'st here!—
If gold thou seek'st, lead on to yonder wall—
Let Acre yield—this strife delays her fall.

But for thy sister, for my bride, beware
The sacred theme, I warn thee to forbear.
I loved Alasia once, I loved too well,
Who dared for her against my sire rebel. 630
Thou heard'st when Heaven in awful thunder spoke,
When Heaven's red bolt the fatal contract broke;[*]
Thou know'st the cause, ah! bid me not reveal
What knightly honour would for ever seal.

" Conrad, I will not pause to question now,
If heaven or hell have register'd the vow
That sanctions thy wild hope—I boast no right
To pluck the beam that dims a brother's sight.

[*] Alluding to the thunderbolt which fell between the two armies, when Richard rebelled against his father, for the sake of this Princess his affianced bride, whom Henry detained from him.

Yet 'mid such clamour for an empty throne
If claims were wanting, I might bring my own.   640
From Fulk° I also spring—this biting blade
Perchance might make a substance of the shade,
And I, fit umpire, to the fable true,
Might gorge the prize, and leave the shell for you.
But Lusignan in me has placed his trust,
And I uphold him, for his claims are just;
Myself will be his rampart, and do thou
Who mocked a friendless wretch, respect him now."

 He spoke—th' assembled Princes own'd that hour
The force of justice from the lips of power.   650
Nor was it eloquence of words alone,
Each glance, each act, each modulated tone
Soft as the dews on sun-burnt Afric stole,
Sunk in the thirsty ear, and fertilized the soul.

 But Philip bent his brows—" Be warn'd," he cried,
" The hour may come when thou shalt rue thy pride.
I rush to war, but not to swell thy line,
Our fame, our fortune, can no more combine:
Go, waste your strength before you sullen towers,
To meet the Soldan's frowning front be ours;   660
Yet there are means, perchance to thee unknown,
By which the city may be all my own."

"By Heaven I thank thee! thou hast given to me
In wrath, what I had craved in courtesy,"
Return'd PLANTAGENET; his knights he calls,
Mounts his swift steed, and rides along the walls,
To mark were time or force had wrought decay,
Or careless guard might give th' assailants way;
Nor heeds the hostile darts that shower around,
Inglorious darts, that fall without a wound.   670

The monarch notes where ocean's hoarded tide
With copious draught the stagnant moat supplied,
A flowing river, devious o'er the plain,
That now approach'd the town, now shunn'd again,
But where th' Accursed ramparts rose in air,
Spread in a pool, and seem'd to vanish there.

"It cannot be," the King exulting cried,
"That space so small engulfs yon rapid tide!
Be secret, Albert; but when night shall hide
The daring purpose, then collect thy force,   680
And for this stream delve deep the hidden course,
So thirst shall rule in Acre, and prepare
The stings of death for those the sword shall spare."ᵖ

He spoke, and launching half his barks again,
Surveys the frowning bulwarks from the main.

Across the waves a mighty mole extends,
In form a crescent, and the port defends;
On all its length defensive ramparts rise,
And at its end the Tower of Sacrifice.
Thence to the Patriarch's tower, a mighty chain 690
Stretch'd its huge links, and dipp'd beneath the main.�q
This lowered with speed, admits the prompt supplies,
Then checks the pursuit, or secures the prize.
Here Austria late and baffled Pisa storm'd;
But holier zeal th' intrepid Monarch warm'd.
Careless of missiles showering from above,
His bark beneath the Patriarch's fort he drove,
Where to a granite pillar's ample round,
With massy rings its iron length was bound;
And seized his Norman axe,—that axe whose weight
Was then a wonder, and whose touch was fate.
He rais'd it high, and bending from the prow,
With all his giant force impels the blow;
He strikes, and strikes but once, the links divide,
And fall, harsh grating, through the gurgling tide:
Then to the port his gallant fleet he led,
And form'd with strictest care the close blockade.

Kahira,* "the Victorious," sends in vain
Her rice, her sesame, her golden grain,
The loaded vessels dread the guarded shore,   710
And plenty reigns in Acre's walls no more;
In vain her friends their anxious vigils keep,
The troops by land, the galleys on the deep,
Their Argus rests not, nor surprise can win
Its way without, nor sallies from within:
While Albert's train their nightly labour urge,
Till the long channel reached the ocean's verge.
Their task is ended,—with redoubled force
Flows the glad river in its new-made course,
And Acre's nymphs at morning's earliest beam,   720
Who sought with thirsty urns th' accustom'd stream,
Already weak with want, with watching pale,
In terror saw the copious river fail;
They call on Alla's name, their robes they tear,
And beat their breasts, and shriek in wild despair.

Yet could not Conrad's soul its hate resign,
Nor Gaul's proud King with warlike England join;
Their vassals sue, and frequent councils sate,
But fresh invective breeds increase of hate.

* The antient name of Cairo was Fostat, till Dgiouhar bestowed on it that of Kahira, or "the Victorious."

Oft Philip's rage his eager knights restrain'd,   730
And murmuring, in th' inglorious camp detain'd,
Forgetful why those sacred plains he trod,
False to his fame, and treacherous to his God:
Nor when he fought, could Montmorency's might,
Conrad, or Austria, or the Emerald knight,
Command the fate of war; the day's decline
Oft saw their forced retreat from Saladine,
Till RICHARD on the victors pouring down,
Redeem'd the half-won wreath, and made the field
    his own.

Three weeks have pass'd; on Acre's mouldering wall
Gaunt famine paces, and foredooms her fall.
Beneath enormous engines, day by day
Her ramparts crumble and her towers decay;
Yet on no lip an angry murmur hung,
Surrender breathed not from one dastard tongue.

Yet had her pride been quell'd, but fever reigns
In RICHARD's frame, and wastes his burning veins;
Weak as a babe his sinewy form reclined,
And wild chimæras vex his mighty mind,*

* The King's illness makes a principal feature in the romance. Vinsauf calls the malady with which he was afflicted *Arnoldia*. It occasioned the

loss

Till his good angel, with ætherial touch, 750
Compels the lingering demon from his couch;
His sunken eye reviving light illumes,
And his high soul the schemes of war resumes.
Augustus, jealous of his rival's arms,
Watch'd his returning strength with new alarms;
He vows to seize his prey, his heralds wait
On Asia's King, and treat of Acre's fate.
The Soldan, anxious to redeem the brave,
Yet scorn'd the haughty terms his avarice gave,
And Acre's warriors vow'd nor fire, nor sword, 760
Nor want should bow them to so stern a lord.*
Again Augustus sent: he craves to meet
The Arabian Ruler, and in person treat.
"No," cried the Soldan, "first must discord cease,
We hold that Monarchs can but meet in peace;
I could not here behold your Sovereign rest,
Nor spread the banquet for my princely guest.
'Twere strange, if, rising from the friendly board,
Our hands again should grasp the hostile sword."

loss of nails and hair; but I believe that the faculty have not yet been able to identify it.

* Historical; as is the subsequent speech of Saladine, which strongly marks the extent to which the Arabians carried their ideas of hospitality.

Meanwhile, unconscious of the snare below,   770
Impatient RICHARD plans a final blow;
To every post his battering train has drawn,
And fix'd the onset for the morrow's dawn.
That night, before his tent in pensive mood,
The purple concave restless Albert view'd,
And oft while thinking of his lonely bride,
To the mute stars his secret sorrows sigh'd.

" Remote from thee, how slow the moments move!
Increasing distance adds new force to love.
If but to Europe's neighbouring shores I roam,   780
Less keen the pang,—still something breathes of home;
But in these wilds not man alone is strange,
Beasts, birds, and plants, e'en hours and seasons change;
Each moment gives the sad reflection birth,
I see another heaven, another earth;
I cannot think that now thy dewy eyes
Watch yon bright planet through the purple skies;
No! when thou turn'st to court the placid moon,
On burning sands we dread the sultry noon;
And when thy landscape sparkles in the morn,   790
Here stars unknown the stranger heaven adorn.
I feel the lavish dews of night descend,
I see the skies unwonted radiance lend:

But vain their lustre, from thy presence driven
I long for Europe's less refulgent heaven,
And thy soft smile, more pleasing to my sight
Than all the splendours of a Syrian night."

Late sunk the warrior to his troubled rest,
And woke ere morning glimmer'd in the east.
He past to Pardo's tent;—prepared for fight,   800
His burnish'd armour caught the doubtful light;
A silver gauze was on the leopard shield,
Till fame should bid its blazon stand reveal'd.*
But all was silent, till Ricardo came
Pale from his vigils near his thoughtless dame.
"Up, Pardo! boaster, up! I little guest
That we must rouse thine eager soul from rest!"
No answer breath'd,—aloud they call'd again,
They search his tent, and wake his squires in vain.
"Ha!" laugh'd Ricardo; "does some damsel keep
His secret thoughts, and chase his vaunted sleep?"
"Say, rather," Albert cried, with terror thrill'd,
"Does some rash venture lure him to the field?
Oh! why so secret to his friend? and why
To share his danger or his fame deny?"

* It was no uncommon thing for young knights, who adopted the paternal shield, thus to screen the device till some glorious exploit should approve them fit heirs to their father's fame.

It chanced that Philip, more devoted far
To courtly pleasures than the toils of war,
Had brought to Palestine a countless race
Of hounds accomplished, trained to every chase,
And fearless falcons, that would even dare   820
Their own fierce monarch in his realms of air.
One morn the fleetest, best beloved of all,
His jesses broke and flew to Acre's wall,
And Philip, grieved to see his favourite roam,
A thousand marks proclaimed to him should lure him home.^r

With all a warrior's wrath young Pardo heard
Such princely ransom offer'd for a bird;
Yet,—for wild perils ever pleased him best,—
He scorn'd the gold, but vow'd to try the quest.

Clad in light arms, alone he took his way,   830
And scarcely waiting for the close of day,
Wrapt in his mantle, sought the town so near,
The oft repeated watch-word met his ear.
The truant bird upon a turret's height
There sate unshelter'd from the dews of night,
And while less dear its late-won freedom grew,
Regrets its dainty fare and gilded mew.

The Knight's soft whistle bids its slumber fly,
Instinctive it obeys, and flutters nigh;
Then fears the stranger voice, or, moved again 840
By powerful nature, loathes its silver chain,
Eludes his grasp, nor heeds the frequent calls
That check returning sleep, and chase it round the walls.

Long, long he follows, till at midnight hour
The falcon lighting on th' Accursed Tower,
Seemed like some demon on the fated wall
Malignant perch'd, portentous of its fall.

How oft, when wilder'd long in error's night,
Truth's daylight lustre flashes on our sight!
The darkness flies like mists when morning glows,
And Reason questions, whence that darkness rose?—
Thus Pardo, musing now where art had led
Th' obedient river from its ancient bed,
Felt, as at once the Heaven-sent impulse shone,
Through that deserted course to reach the town.
To think and act were one, he lingers not
To seek a comrade's aid; the bird forgot,
And with his pointed dagger arm'd alone,
He strikes the turf and time-cemented stone,
Fearful lest foes surprise him, or the sun, 860
With envious beam, reveal his work half done.

At length his toils a narrow opening win,
The trampled earth gives way and crumbles in;
Now by his hands he hung, and, rashly bold,
But breathed a prayer succinct, and loosed his hold.
Saved by the moisture lingering yet below,
Where erst the deepest stream was wont to flow,
Unharm'd he rose, without one guiding ray,
And groped along the side his dangerous way,
Save when his arms in rough collision call   870
Short gleams of splendour from the flinty wall.
Oh! should he wander in the dreadful gloom?
Should waves engulph him, should some pit entomb?
Or that mephitic damp, whose baleful breath
Haunts the deep cavern, lull him into death?—
But hail that stream of pure and fragrant air!
Hail to that ruddy beam! success is there.

Where late the river sparkled from its cave,
A pompous arch had spann'd the dashing wave,
Before its mouth the crackling faggots burn,   880
And Arabs watch;—oh! should the stream return!
Tall reeds that in the humid channel grew,
Concealed the listening warrior from their view,
While dimm'd with clay, his arms, his unsheath'd sword
Had now no lustre to betray their lord:

Though oft between him and the bickering flame
Gigantic, dark, the martial figures came.
He heard them speak of famine, thirst, and woe,
The tottering towers, the valour of the foe;
That, should their morning sally, nor the might 890
Of Adel aid them, they must yield at night.
Then when at sunrise other troops prepared
To change the watch, and rest the weary guard,
Unmark'd he sprang, and snatch'd with venturous hand,
Full from the piny pile a blazing brand;
And traced his backward course with steps so fleet,
An eagle's pinions seem'd to buoy his feet.

But Gaul's insidious King again had sent
His secret herald to the Soldan's tent,
What time to Saladine a soldier bore 900
An arrow, shot from Acre's nearest tower;
Its barbed point a fatal scroll revealed,
" Famine surrounds me; aid us, or we yield."—
" Alas! my Karacous, how great must be
The weight of woe that draws complaint from thee!"
Exclaim'd the anxious Soldan, as in haste
His rapid hand the needful mandate traced:

" A Gallic herald waits. Maintain the fight;
Or aid, or terms, I promise ere the night :"—
He wrote, and sought a messenger to bear,   910
Unseen, his bidding thro' the trackless air.
Far from the callow nestlings of her love,
Sate mournful in her cage a spotless dove.
The gentle bird her welcome duty knew,
And at his call with joyful instinct flew,
And raised her wing obedient, while his hand
Fix'd the small tablet by a silken band.
One moment on her smiling master's breast,
As in a loved sojourn, she paused to rest,
Rais'd to his face her mild and grateful eye,   920
Then spread her wings and vanish'd in the sky.*

   Meanwhile the earliest beam of orient day
Call'd round the English King his proud array.
So rich their mail, their arms so burnish'd bright,
Their helms, their lances, so profuse of light,
Their shields so precious from the limner's art,
They seem adorn'd to play some festal part;
But they, so late in beauty's halcyon hour
The grace, the glory, of her glittering bower;
Skill'd every courtly revel to prolong,   930
And every fleeting joy embalm in song;

When fame invites, regard nor toil nor scar,
Gentle in peace, but thunderbolts in war.

   Young Pardo now rush'd in, and from his hand
Cast the poor relics of his guiding brand:
" What, Pardo! thou, so active and so gay,
Why now so late? and thus besmear'd with clay?"

   " An hour has scarcely fled," the youth exclaim'd,
" Since that expiring brand in Acre flam'd;
I snatch'd it from the pyre, and yonder sun   940
Shall see it light the flames that blaze for Acre won."
He paus'd an instant, then in breathless haste,
All his long labours of the night retraced.

   " Oh! thou rash youth! yet in thy rashness dear,"
The Monarch cried, " what daring deed is here!
Must all our veteran cheeks be red with shame,
While Acre's trophies swell a stripling's fame?
Enough—when eve her glimmering light shall lend,
By Pardo led, to victory we descend."

   Scarce had he spoke, when in the air above   950
A hungry falcon chased a beauteous dove;
Who drawing courage in her last despair,
For man, once feared, forsakes the fields of air;

And, as on meaner perch she scorn'd to rest,
Instinctive refuge took in RICHARD's breast;*
While Pardo, as it blindly follow'd, caught
The wayward falcon, long so vainly sought.

 Upon the Monarch's silken scarf reposed,
Soon the faint bird her meek dark eyes unclosed,
While RICHARD mark'd, and loos'd the silken string
That bound the fateful billet to her wing.
Incensed he read, " Yes ! while we bleed, we toil,
To win these ramparts, Philip steals the spoil !
The fight he shuns, yet basely treats alone
For secret render of the falling town.
E'en now perchance he robs us of our right !—
Pardo, thine ambush must not wait for night ;
Tell Raymond France is false, but fortune ours ;
Then while again we storm those crumbling towers,
Lead thou his warriors through the secret track—970
'Tis Albert's charge to turn the sally back."

 Meanwhile the dove her lingering course pursued
To Acre, where ten thousand warriors stood,

---

* See the " *Gerusalemme Liberata,*" Canto xviii, 49, 50.

With upward glance, and watch'd with stifled breath,
The guiltless messenger of life or death.
Why comes she not as wont, with joyous spring
To yield her charge, and rest her wearied wing?
Too soon they guess'd, too soon in mute despair
Perceived her flagging plumes and drooping air.
No outward hurt her smooth white down display'd,
But, inly conscious of her trust betrayed,
Far from her mate she took her lonely stand,
Shunn'd all once loved, but most her master's hand;
To hear his call, to taste his bread denied,
Sate silent on her perch, and pined, and died.

END OF BOOK V.

CŒUR DE LION.

BOOK VI.

THE CAPTURE OF ACRE.

ARGUMENT.

THE CAPTURE OF ACRE.

Assault of Acre by Richard—Attack on the Accursed Tower—Death of Jerworth—of Rodney—Daring of Richard—Gallant action of a young Knight—Richard sets fire to the Tower—it falls—Entry of the Christians—Death of Aralchaïs—Of Karacous—Pardo leads his troop by a secret way into the city—Obtains possession of the citadel—Danger of Richard—He is succoured by Pardo—Almanzor—His combat with Richard—Success of Albert in repelling the sally from Acre—Complete conquest of the city—Despair of Saladine—of Philip—Quarrel of Richard and Leopold—Pardo and De Carreo rewarded—Release of Almanzor—Night-watch of Pardo—The story of Amina—Pardo conducts her from the town—Consigns her to an unknown warrior—Returns and is relieved by Albert—Lustration of the churches in Acre—Synod of the Genii on Mount Carmel—Their discontent—They are reproved by Moozallil—His threats against Richard—The call of Hassan—Maimoune and Saladine.

CŒUR DE LION.

BOOK VI.

THE CAPTURE OF ACRE.

Now wakes the contest—now those frames of wood,
That vast and high, in uncouth stillness stood,
Are all instinct with life;—Balistæ pour
The flaming Phalaric, or the stony shower;*
With ceaseless blow the heavy Ram is swung,
And blazing oils in dreadful tempest flung.
In vain the Moslems from the heights dispense
All that can wound the frame, or shock the sense;

* The name given to a species of burning dart, being a long stick of wood, tipped with combustibles, and hurled by the besieging engines.

The limbs of mangled comrades, sheets of flame,
And poison'd arrows, kindling as they came;   10
And wheels, those missiles most accurst and dire,
That wrap the struggling wretch in rings of fire.
In vain the clarions brayed, with awful clang
Boomed the deep gong, and batter'd armour rang,—
The Christians still press on ; the tortoise spreads
Its mighty buckler o'er their fearless heads ;
They heap the fosse, they mine the tower, they rear
Their ladders high, and mount undaunted there ;
Those frail supports give way, or from the wall,
Hurl'd headlong down, o'erwhelm them in their fall;
Yet still they climb anew, they storm the height,
And from their comrades' shoulders urge the fight.

Against th' " Accursed Tower" the Monarch set
His favourite engine, vaunted " Robynette,"
This Jerworth rules; by sixty winters bent,
His vigorous frame still proved his proud descent
From Caradoc, whose arm of steel might claim,
'Mid Arthur's Paladins no second fame,
The faithful partner of the truest dame,
The soul of war[a] —in youth had Jerworth's hand,
With England wrestled for his native land ;   30

And latest near the dying Hoel stood,
When the blue Ceriog blush'd with Cambrian blood;
Nor now less valiant, as the masses break,
With blows redoubled, and the ramparts shake,
Himself directs the Ram, and bending low,
Lends all his vigour to the mighty blow.
But Mestoc mark'd him, and the dart impell'd—
Too sure a course the fated weapon held;
And where the casque and plated mail combine,
Pierced through th' unguarded neck, and reach'd the
   spine.   40
Oft when sweet Spring with music loads the gale,
Shall Mona's Bards his silent harp bewail;
Oft, when solstitial storms unbridled roar,
And snow is drifting on her mountain shore,
Lament for one who wiled those nights away
With tales of climes beyond the setting day:—
For Jerworth sail'd with him whose patriot pride
Disdain'd a conqueror's yoke, across the tide
Where never yet had venturous pilot steer'd,
Nor Celtic speech, nor name of Christ was heard; 50
Where all to them was strange, and they to all—
Who won a kingdom, reared th' embattled wall,

Preach'd in Mexitli's fane th' Eternal Word,
And bow'd the strength of Astlan to his sword;*
With Madoc he return'd, but not again
Stemm'd with that daring Prince th' Atlantic main;
He staid, above his mother's grave to rear
The votive roses, nurst with many a tear;
Till England's Primate, in his vigorous age,
Relumed the Christian's zeal, the warrior's rage;
What time the priest, in sacred pilgrimage,
While countless miracles attest his truth,
Call'd to the Holy War the Cambrian youth.†

 Not unavenged he fell, his javelin leaves
King RICHARD's hand, and Mestoc's side receives

---

 * I need only refer the poetical reader to Mr. Southey's Madoc. The real or supposed expedition of that Prince is placed in the reign of Henry II., after the battle in which Prince Hoel fell, and which determined the fate of North Wales.

 † Baldwin, Archbishop of Canterbury, made a pilgrimage into Wales for the purpose of preaching the Crusade; and his journey is embellished by Giraldus Cambrensis with as many miracles and wonders as Amadis encountered in the Firm Island. The story of the young Elidorus, who lived some time with the Gnomes in their subterranean world, till he learned their language (which strongly resembled the Greek), is a very pleasing fiction. Baldwin is stated to have made many proselytes; and the ardour of crusading, which was new to Wales, began with nearly the same vehemence as in other regions; but it soon expired, and very few Welch were among the followers of Richard to the Third Crusade.

Beneath his lifted arm!—it spared the life,
But forced th' unwilling Emir from the strife.
Meanwhile the King, who mark'd his warriors fly
The fate of Jerworth, lifts his voice on high :
" And can ye tremble, Christians! ye who fight   70
For Him who framed yon firmament of light ;
Him whose least word could crush yon rebel towers,
Or arm embattled hosts of angel powers ?
But he to us ordains them, bids us dare
The might of hell, and earn salvation there.
Think of your sires, that o'er this race prevail'd,
Whom rescued Solyma triumphant hail'd ;
Whose names th' eternal scrolls of heaven record,
Then ' woe to him who wears a stainless sword.' "*

His rallying troops th' inspiring call obey,   80
Again the missiles fly, the engines play ;
He guides the dread Petraria,† high he heaves
A rocky mass ; the whistling air it cleaves,
It strikes the ramparts ; by its weight o'erthrown,
Twelve gasping Moslems sink beneath the stone.‡

---

* See the Oration of St. Bernard at Vezelai ; or Michaud, vol. ii., 124.

† Richard worked one of the Petrariæ for a considerable time.

‡ Vinsauf, who adds that the stone was picked up and sent to Saladine.

Again he loosed the engine, hurl'd below,
The batter'd fort receives the fatal blow,
Where Philip late had forced the breach; in haste
To prop the tower were wooden stancheons placed,
All seem'd secure, but now the facings fall,   90
And the crush'd stone betrays th' imperfect wall.
" A torch !" the Monarch cried, and Rodney's hand
Snatch'd with undaunted zeal the flaming brand;
The Moslems mark th' attempt, and from the height
Shower all their fury on the daring Knight;
Unharm'd he moves beneath his lifted shield,
And thrice rush'd on, but thrice compell'd to yield;
Again advanced, while England's archers drove
The wounded Syrians from the walls above;
'Twas then that Karacous infuriate spoke: 100
" Is death more fearful than the Christian yoke?
Women of Asia! forward to the wall,
What boots your dastard lives, if Acre fall?"
He spoke, nor pausing, with tremendous blow
Sends half the frowning battlement below;
Just as the Knight the fatal flame applies,
Crush'd by the weight a shapeless mass he lies,
Commends his parting soul to Heaven, and dies!

Grieved, yet unaw'd, the King review'd his bands,
No venturous Knight the dangerous task demands;
He smiled, and by his courage ruled alone,
" 'Tis well," he cried, " this glory is my own!"—
Then rose the general shout, his warriors spread
Their broad tough bucklers o'er their Sovereign's head.
Again the Syrian Chief dismiss'd the spear,
And aim'd too well, for RICHARD's fate was there;
But a young knight, intrepid, rush'd between,
And made his bleeding breast his Monarch's screen.
As his sad squires bore off their fainting load,
One hasty glance the grateful King bestow'd;   120
But paus'd not in his course, " On! on!" he cries,
He reached the tower, the bickering flames arise.

"Oh, water! water!" Long that fearful cry
Had Acre heard, nor found her springs reply;
All shrunk in dust, so well with RICHARD's care
The cloudless skies conspired, and glowing air,
Not her drain'd tanks, nor yet her treacherous stream
Could yield one drop to check that spreading flame;
The heavy ramparts nod, the fires devour
Their last support—down falls th' "Accursed Tower."

"On to the breach, ye flower of England, on!
The city falls, th' invincible is won."
"Not yet, blasphemers!" Karacous replies,
And by his hand the youthful Osbert dies;[b]—
Osbert, of Clinton's blood, whose knightly grace
And gentle worth adorned his noble race.
Rotrou of Perche next storms the yawning breach,
His rapid blows th' opposing Azim reach;
But soon a blazing hoop enwreathed them round,
In one infernal orb of torture bound,   140
They fight, they writhe, they struggle on the ground,
Till kindred fire their gallant limbs consume,
Foes in their lives, companions in the tomb.

    First on the height, uncheck'd by hosts of foes,
The Moslem dread, PLANTAGENET arose;
Next Bertrand sprung, the peril of the strife,
Wounds, clamour, death, to him were joy, were life;
His was an ardent heart, in youth deprest
By one sad blow, it sunk, but not to rest;
He loved to set his wealth upon the die,   150
He loved the banquets of intemperate joy,
The bleeding hurry of the battle plain,
Whate'er could rouse that heart to feel again.

The warriors follow fast, yet scarce behold
Mosques, cupolas, and minarets of gold,
And blossom'd groves, when lo! a wall of fire
Shuts out each marble dome, each glittering spire!
Vast piles of wood, for other labours placed,
And heaps of useless engines, fired in haste,
Oppose their progress; but the Monarch cast   160
One glance inspiring, " It must fade at last!
Even now it fades! beyond are fame or death,
The spoils of Acre, or the martyr's wreath."
Now ranged behind, a wall of steel appears,
So close the bucklers joined and glittering spears.
" 'Tis well!" again the ardent RICHARD cries,
" The truly brave would scorn too cheap a prize."

But was it lowering storm, or wizard spell,
That on the fight unnatural darkness fell!
No storm, for cloudless is th' aetherial blue,   170
Nor is it sober twilight's solemn hue,
Nor the chaste smile of Cynthia's summer night,
Her broad deep shadows, and her silver light.
Yet to their nests the screaming ravens fly,
And stars are glimmering in the mid-day sky!

Cold breathes the altered gale, a livid shade
Dims every brow, the glowing banners fade;
The moon invades the sun, whose golden ray,
Bright in solstitial pride, contests her sway.*

    Still at th' appointed hour the awful night   180
Spreads her black veil, the morn her saffron light;
Wrapt in the snowy tempest Winter comes,
And bounteous Spring in fragrant mildness blooms.
Nor pauses man, to question why or whence,
For the familiar wonder palls the sense.
He deems it awful, when the tempests wake
The mountain echoes, when the forests shake,
When lightning gilds the dark, and the gnarl'd oak,
That braved a thousand winters, feels the stroke.
Yet are those solemn changes most sublime,   190
That bursting seldom from the womb of Time,
Recall th' Almighty Architect, and hold
Their silent course, foreseen but not control'd;—
That, breaking Nature's common laws, sustain,
Her vast, immutable, eternal reign.

    The warring armies paus'd, and every eye,
In mute devotion, sought the darken'd sky.

---

* See Hoveden, folio 395. The eclipse lasted three hours.

" Ha! King of England, mark'st thou yonder sun?
As erst when Sion by our arms was won,*
That boasted emblem of thy Christian creed   200
Wanes to a crescent—do I rightly read?"

" Aye! for that Crescent shall expire as soon
As yon bright orb shakes off th' invading moon.
Come! thou that gavest those vaunting accents breath,
Come if thou darest! and prove it by thy death."

In murder'd Alberic's costly mail indued,
The giant son of Acre's ruler stood.
" Methink'st this spoil may teach your trembling host
That Aralchaïs breathes no idle boast."

He spoke; his hands the crooked sabre wield,   210
But dauntless RICHARD on his lion shield
Received, nor shrunk beneath the powerful stroke,
Nor flew the buckler, nor the weapon broke.
Wondering the Moslem gazed,—but RICHARD now,
That shield uplifting, with the sudden blow
Dash'd him to earth—upon his side he prest
His sinewy knee, and pierced his ample chest.

---

* At the time when Saladine approached the Holy City, after the battle of Tiberias, in which Lusignan was made prisoner, and at the moment when the deputies refused to surrender the town, a great eclipse of the sun " left all at once the heavens in darkness," which was interpreted as an evil omen to the Christians.

"Winton," he said, "strip thou this braggart foe,
And bear his spoils to Philip—bid him know
That I aveng'd his Marshal."—Then again   220
To the fierce charge he leads his eager train;
They break the adverse ranks, and hurrying on,
With blood and clamour fill the spacious town.
But louder than the angry din of war,
The voice of Karacous resounds afar:
"Hold, thou that slay'st the fairest of the fold,
Thou murdrous Lion, scourge of Islam; hold!
Hear, and let terror cloud thy brutal joy,
A childless father claims his valiant boy,
His Aralchaïs."—Stern the veteran stood,   230
His sabre reeking with a hero's blood;
The blood of Mowbray, o'er whose castle gate
The helmet hung in hospitable state;
Where still the warmest seat and choicest wine
Hail'd the tired pilgrim from the holy shrine;
Who to the Templars many a wide domain
Gave with a liberal hand, nor gave in vain;
Once had they saved him from the Soldan's chain,[d]
And sent to England,—happy if no more
His pious feet had trod the Syrian shore;   240

Yet to his worth a martyr's crown is given,
On earth he slumbers, to awake in Heaven.
  Now met the warriors; RICHARD casts below
A look of wonder on his pigmy foe,
With limbs curtail'd, unequal, and deform'd,
But the rude clay a soul of valour warm'd.
" Exult not, Monarch, in thy towering height,
Thy fair proportion, or thy boasted might;
The loftiest cedar feels the woodman's stroke,
And the red lightning strikes the proudest rock: 250
'Tis I have shed your Christian blood like rain,
And made one grave of all yon ample plain.
I bid thee now thy fancied spoil resign,
For while I breathe believe not Acre thine;
The city's fate is on our swords, on high
The vulture whets her beak, and knows that one shall
    die."
  Each held a spear, but, by one impulse sway'd,
Cast it to earth, and drew the deadlier blade.
The sword of Karacous, in Beder's field
And Bosra's, once had Ali's strength impell'd,   260
That giant strength whose single effort slew
The mail-clad warrior and the courser too.

But RICHARD's magic steel, six ages gone,
Was fram'd by Merlin for Pendragon's son.
The sage, lest meaner hand its edge should wield,
In wild romance the Monarch's death conceal'd;
How, nurs'd by fairies in their bowers of bloom,
Th' awakening hero should his reign resume.
But time reveal'd the truth—to England's King
Of Arthur's grave the bards of Gwyneth sing;   270
He sought fair Avalon's romantic isle,
Where Severn circles Glaston's time-worn pile,
And raised the stone beneath her altar's shade,
Where by Geneura's side the Monarch laid;
Time had not changed his form, august though pale,
Nor loos'd one rivet from his iron mail.
Kneeling, the King evoked the mighty dead,
Whose hand relaxing loos'd the gifted blade,
Then vow'd that sword, by favouring powers bestow'd,
Should fight the battles of his injur'd God.[c]   280
Now first he wields it, and with forceful sway
Rends half th' Egyptian's turban'd casque away.
But Karacous, with strength that more became
The arm of Ali than his stunted frame,
Strikes on the groin, and though the hauberk broke
Its force, the palsied limb confest the stroke;

Nor might the staggering King the blow repell
When on his arm the heavy sabre fell,
And but a chain the precious weapon bound,
Th' unrivall'd Caliburn had press'd the ground.   290
" Spirit of Arthur! dost thou see," he said,
" How ill this coward hand deserves thy blade!"
Stung with the thought he smites his gallant foe
Full on the chest, and blood succeeds the blow.
Now pours the storm of mutual wrath amain,
Nor e'er those gifted weapons fell in vain,—
For where no crimson current mark'd the stroke
Helmet and shield were pierced, and corselet broke.
But RICHARD's height, (though both alike were brave)
And length of arm superior vantage gave;   300
Till Karacous, who bled from many a wound,
Indignant flung his buckler to the ground;
Now with sinister hand the sabre held,
Now with the right, and now with both impell'd.
" Not, not alone!" he cried—but RICHARD's care
Check'd on his shield the effort of despair;
For where the dexter lion frown'd, the sword
Stuck in the golden mass; nor might its lord
Again withdraw, for RICHARD's angry thrust
Pierced through his side, and hurl'd him to the dust:

Yet fighting to the last, the vital breath
He yields unwilling, and contends with death.
" Proud conqueror, lay me by my gallant boy,
And thou, Mahommed, ope thy gates of joy."

  " Eternal source of good!" the victor cries,
As on the corse he fixed his thoughtful eyes,
" Is there no mercy? shall the trumpet wake
That gallant soul to haunt the penal lake?
Alas! his hope is built on sand; his trust,
Like Sodom's glittering fruit, shall fade in dust." 320

  A shout arous'd him! from the citadel,
On the glad breeze the notes of triumph swell;
From its high towers, in conquering pride unroll'd,
The red cross flames, the lion burns in gold;
For Pardo by the stream's deserted bed
With brave Thoulouse his bold Provençals led;
Through frighted streets with eager haste they flew,
Astonish'd all, dispers'd, o'erwhelm'd or slew.
In vain the citadel her portals barr'd,
They scaled the heights, o'erpower'd the feeble guard,
And made it theirs, while all that should defend,
Against the King their fruitless valour spend.

  But ah! while victory calls his careless host
From RICHARD's side, shall RICHARD's self be lost?

A band of foes, that strove to force their way
From the fall'n town, perceive the royal prey,—
They thank their Prophet, from their phalanx spring,
Enclose him round, and shout " the King! the King!"*
 " The King alone!" a voice familiar cried,
Young Pardo's blows the yielding train divide, 340
He springs exulting to his sovereign's side.
His troop succeeds, again the war they wage,
And, warm with fight, the yielding foe engage.
Amid the ranks, all red with Christian blood,
An Arab Prince, the bold Almanzor stood;
The dark egret, whose jewell'd sprays were seen
'Mid the rich foldings of his turban green,
Revealed his rank, while in that verdant hue
Respectful slaves the Caaba's pilgrim knew;
He struck the youth, and from his arm he drew 350
A crimson current, bright as ever dyed
The insect-laboured gem of Omar's tide.
With toil, with joy exhausted, with the pain,
Whose burning smart he never knew till then,
He faints—the Monarch caught him in his fall,
And, thus encumber'd, fights, and baffles all!

    * Historical.

He dreads no danger from th' unequal strife,
And trembles only for his favourite's life.
But soon that livid cheek was flush'd with shame,
From Pardo's eyes indignant lightning came,   360
He starts, in haste he binds the bleeding wound,
And wheels again his trenchant faulchion round;
While RICHARD through the shrinking numbers flies,
The great Almanzor singles and defies.
Seldom had either met an equal foe;
Careless at first they give the random blow,
Then, by experience taught, rejoice to feel
Their rival's worth, and summon all their skill.
They strike, they turn, they bend; the fell intent
Read in the eye,—they read it and prevent.   370
That scented scymitar of Syrian frame,^f
Swift, like the flash of Summer lightning came,
Tough, supple, keen; but RICHARD's shield defied,
Or RICHARD's cunning turn'd the stroke aside,
Or impotent its baffled fury fell
On the tough chainwork of his Norman mail.
Not so the Monarch's sword, though shunn'd with care,
Frequent its guiltless force was spent in air,
Nor Asia's hardest steel, in happy hour,
Temper'd with magic herbs and words of power,   380

Nor yet the Koran's holiest text, though brought
Even from his Prophet's gifted tomb, and wrought
By vestals on his silken vest, defends
The bleeding flesh where Caliburn descends;
And now, though stiff with gems and woven gold,
It pierced the Mecca turban's verdant fold,
Through the rich plaits the purple torrents flow,
Almanzor reels, he falls beneath the blow.

 Who next shall bleed? lo! only Pardo near,
Pours all his rapture in the Monarch's ear;   390
Now doubly joyous that his Sovereign's smile
Approves his prudence, and rewards his toil.

 Nor with a fate less prosperous Albert waits
Th' expected sally from the Patriarch's gates.
Happy that Syrian who survived to tell
To Asia's Monarch how his comrades fell!
While o'er the heaps of dead the victors pour,
Force back the closing gates, and win the tower.

 Nor less through Acre's streets, by Leicester led,
The English host her desert homes invade,   400
Till all, or slain, or captive, own their power,
Till Christian ensigns stream from every tower;
Those walls that England conquer'd first, alone
Her Lion-flag forgets to mark its own.

From what slight fault gigantic ills appear!
For, like that little cloud the Prophet's prayer
Called from the deep, that error shall expand,
Till its black shadow darkens all the land.

    Slight is the joy that shines in smiles alone,
In silent tears is warmer rapture shewn: 410
But there's a higher agony of bliss,
That knows nor tears nor smiles,—and such was this,
Such RICHARD felt;—so many conflicts past,
His prayer, his nightly dream fulfill'd at last.
And was She his, that city, dearly won
As Jove-prop'd Ilion, she whose every stone
Had cost a martyr's blood, whose impious pride
For three long years the Christian world defied?
Defiled the Cross, blasphemed each holiest name,
And gave her captive foes to lingering flame![g]   420
In one long upward look his thanks were given,
His silent gratitude communed with Heaven.

    Meanwhile with Saladine the heralds met,
And vain demands drew on a vain debate;
Till hark! that shriek from shuddering Islam sent!
He draws the silken curtains of his tent,—

One look reveals the whole; his sickening sight
Turns from that Cross on Acre's ramparts bright.
That slow disease, still watchful for the hour
When cankering cares the harass'd frame devour, 430
Holds its permitted reign, and round their lord
His servants tremble for a life adored.[h]

Nor envious Philip read with less affright
A rival's fame on every banner'd height;
His avarice by that prompt success betray'd,
His promised glories sunk in sudden shade.
But Austria's crafty Duke, whose thirst of gold,
His love, his hate, and even his fears controll'd,
Resolves to share the spoil;—he calls his powers,
Flies to the town, and mounts the conquer'd towers,
And (for no banner there in mastery shone)
His flag, presumptuous, marks them as his own.
His troops, whose scanty hire but ill was paid,*
For pillage ripe, his welcome call obey'd;
With Bertrand join'd, their bloody way they force,
And shrieks, and flames, and ruin mark their course.

* As in this Crusade each Chief was obliged to support his own troop, the leaders generally allotted a fixed stipend to each man.

But now the King, attentive to repair
The yawning breach his fury batter'd there,
Inspects th' Accursed Tower,—amazed, he knew
The golden Larks upon their field of blue. 450
" What means this insult? By those powers that crown
My conquering arms, I bid the pageant down!
Say whence, proud Duke, this daring madness springs,
To mate thy banner with the badge of Kings?[i]
Even on this tower, beneath that conscious sun
Which saw its ramparts by my valour won,
Canst thou believe I tamely will behold
Another's flag? the flag of Leopold?
Sooth! were thine own Imperial Suzerain near,
He well might dread to plant his eagle here. 460
Conrad alone, that Heaven and man defies,—
But words are idle,—there thy banner lies!"
Even as he spoke, beneath his sword it falls,
Th' offending ensign tumbles from the walls;
'Mid heaps of carnage in the moat it roll'd,
And dust and blood defiled the gaudy gold.
In wonder speechless stood its raging lord,
His threatening eyes flash fire, he grasps his sword.

" Hold! haughty Chief," again the Monarch spoke,
" Nor farther yet my righteous ire provoke, 470

I dread thee not;—yet pardon if my tongue,
By sudden anger moved, have done thee wrong.
What though sole victor o'er this stubborn town,
The glory is and shall be all my own;
I know the rights of three long years of toil,
And thou, and all, shall share her lawful spoil:
But I endure no plunder—late I knew
A lawless band, who bore thy cross of blue:—
Recall them, for should one red hand be stain'd
With needless blood, one sacred shrine profan'd, 480
By Heaven's bright throne, though Lydia's gold were there,
And India's gems, that wealth they should not share."

 Many there are to dare, but not uphold
The guilty deed, and such was Leopold.
Brave as the best, if valour lie alone
In shedding blood, or lavishing our own,
Opinion bound him in her stern control,
Nor he, like Conrad, ruled the shrinking soul.
If ever worth or rank might envy claim,
He envied RICHARD, long'd to blast his fame, 490
Yet dared not now his kindled ire resent;
Muttering and pale again he sought his tent.

"Enjoy thy triumph, Prince! and think my hate
Short as thy wrath, but thou shalt feel it yet;
This outraged flag, which long my fathers bore,
This outraged banner Austria bears no more.*
What though in flowers I deign my sting to hide,
'Tis but more surely to abase thy pride;
The shallow waters chafe, but where they sleep
Lurks danger most, for they are dark and deep." 500

But now the King, for all alike prepared,
Surveys the town, the towers, appoints the guard;
Gracious to all, a just attention paid,
Captive and friend, the dying and the dead.
Freed from th' incumbent load, a warlike bier
Now Rodney graced, and claim'd a passing tear;
Twined round his mangled limb, the Monarch's eyes
Its azure cincture mark, and thus he cries:

"Lo! first of those to whom that badge I gave,
The gallant Rodney bears it to his grave: 510

---

* Leopold changed his armorial bearings after the siege of Acre. His original shield was, six Larks Or, in a field Azure.—The story is that at one battle during the siege, he fought so bravely that his armour was entirely covered with blood, save his belt, which remained white. In commemoration of this circumstance, the Emperor assigned to him and his successors their new device, Gules, a fess Argent.

Thus may ye live to glory,—thus may all
In life adorn it, honour in their fall.
But say—who now the vacant prize shall grace,
Who best deserves to fill a hero's place?—
Thanks, my brave Peers, for this your silent voice,
Those speaking looks that single out my choice.
Pardo, if right thy generous heart I see,
Nor rank nor riches have such charms for thee;
This kindled envy once—young Knight, t'were wrong,
That heart like thine should strive with envy long; 520
With thee our fame in Acre's fall is shared,
Nor favour gives it, 'tis thy just reward.
Long since my love had given, and love alone
Deferr'd the guerdon, till thy worth had won."
From his own knee meanwhile with ready hand
He loosens, and presents the azure band.

But Pardo's swelling heart no words supplied,
Kneeling he kiss'd the badge, and flew to hide
The bursting stream of gratitude and pride.

"One debt remains," the generous Monarch said,
"A Knight whose shield a clouded moon displayed,
Whose legend mourn'd injustice—if severe
His hurt forbid not, lead the warrior here."
Borne on a litter came the wounded Knight,
And shunn'd with downcast looks his Sovereign's sight.

But vainly he a well known face conceal'd,
The Monarch paus'd, then rais'd the pictur'd shield :
"Say, my young friend, what clouds thy opening morn?
What wrongs oppress, what injury hast thou borne?
Why dost thou fight disguised? why leave behind 540
Thy train, nor give thy banner to the wind?
Why not to me thy secret sorrows bring,
And claim his ready justice from thy King?—
Thou answer'st not, De Carreo! must I then,
Where I had hoped to praise, reprove agen?
The forest laws my royal fathers framed,
By thy rash youth were outraged, and I blamed:
For this resigns't thou thy paternal state?
Was I unjust? or think'st thou I forget
The blood that from the Chiefs of Norway springs,
Thy sires ennobled ere my own were Kings?
Through whom my father's yoke proud Gwyneth bore,
Through whom I rule Ierne's emerald shore;
Thy noble parent, in whose guardian power
My mother rests, and Windsor's regal tower?
Or think'st thou I forget his loyal son
Who for my menaced life exposed his own?
Give me thy banner ;"—once again outspread,
The silver saltier parts the sanguine red.
He lopp'd the pennon's forked points,[i] and said—

" Disdain not from a grateful Sovereign's hand
A nobler banner, and enlarged command;
To thee the fame of Othoer's race I trust:
Now prove him false that called his King unjust."k

" Now most unjust," the blushing youth replied,
" My pride transgress'd, and thou reward'st my pride.
What wond'rous power thy princely soul displays,
With gifts to humble, with reproof to raise!
How I receive the lesson, Sire, my speech
Is poor to utter, but my life shall teach."   570

Faint he sunk back, the King's attentive mind
To his own Leech th' exhausted Knight consign'd.*
Then sought Almanzor's couch, whose desperate hand
Tore from his bleeding brow the healing band:
Unmoved by Ermengard, he mocks his prayers,
His pious skill, and unrelaxing cares,
And vows that never Infidel shall shed
His hateful ointments on a Hadji's head.

* The sons of Esculapius may be interested to learn that this was no less a personage than Richard de Higel, Bishop of London, and the first who is mentioned as bearing the title of King's Apothecary. In our degenerate days the functions of " soul-curer and body-curer" are not ordinarily thus united; but the clergy engrossed all the little learning of that semi-barbarous age, and the practice of pharmacy was not uncommon, even in the highest dignitaries.

" Brave Emir," spoke the King with generous heat,
" I love that spirit, proudest in defeat;
Yet for thy future fame consent to live,
And ask whate'er a Monarch's power can give." 580
   " What canst thou give, thou murderer of my fame,
Thou canst not give me back a warrior's name!
Yes! I will live, but live alone that thou
May'st lie my thrall, as I before thee now;
A living victim long thou should'st not be,
I scorn thy mercies, Christian dog, and thee.
Yet if thy words be not the idle breath
Of one whose secret malice seeks my death,
Send me to him I love, and Saladine
Shall teach to quell that arm which humbled mine."
   " So be it, Prince, as to thy grasp I yield
This glove, my pledge to meet thee in the field,
And on my casque thy proud egret will wear,
Nor wear dishonour'd; not thyself shall dare
To think it tarnish'd, when thou seest it there."

   'Tis night, and Pardo with a chosen power
Protects the gate that leads from David's tower.
The rising moon two female forms betray'd,
Who linger'd near, and seem'd to court the shade;

Seized by his warriors, one of matron years,   600
Drops her coarse veil, and through contending tears
Speaks of the robbers that had come by night,
And insults to her child that counsell'd flight.

  But accents gentle as the breeze that blows
In amorous fragrance o'er the expanding rose,
And sweet as murmurs of the streams that lave
The frail Mimosa imaged in their wave,
Reproving spoke:—" Dear guardian of my youth,
Stoop'st thou to falsehood who hast taught me truth!
Let guilt from fraud extort her poor defence,   610
But truth's the native guard of innocence.
Oh, Knight! nor fear nor insult we endure,
Still are the Haram's sacred bounds secure.
The city's fate unknown, I calmly led
Through folds of Syrian silk the golden thread,
When shrieks of woe, resounding from the street,
To the forbidden Golphor lured my feet.
Alas! my sire, whose smile at eve and morn,
Still told or promised of his safe return,
Low on a bier his senseless form was laid,   620
With honour borne, yet honour'd as the dead;
His bloody turban!—but I saw no more
Till my thick veil my weeping damsels tore,

And said Almanzor lived; but hence removed
To Kaisan's camp, nor nursed by those he loved.
Can ev'n the generous Saladine supply
A daughter's cares, or read the asking eye?
Then blame not that, emboldened by despair,
I bade my nurse two barracans prepare,*
Such as befit our meanest slaves alone,   630
So might we pass, I deem'd, unmark'd, unknown:
But ah! how helpless and how weak a flower
Is woman when she quits her guardian bower!
Oh, let me seek its sacred walls again,
To weep I left them, since I left in vain."

"No, not in vain! behold a loyal knight
Kneels at thy feet, and vows to aid thy flight;
I grant thy wish, for I believe thy tale,
Yet drop, one instant drop, that envious veil.
Perchance (and I methinks should bless the hour) 640
The fate of war may lead me to thy bower;
Warriors are rude when rushing from the field,
And I would know thy beauties but to shield."

* A large mantle or outer garment of dark brown cloth, which completely conceals the dress and rank of the wearer. These are worn by the women of the East when they go abroad. Those belonging to the lower classes are very coarse in their texture.

As shone the moon, then bursting from a cloud,
So dawn'd Amina from her sable shroud.
'Tis not the diamonds in her raven hair,
Or the strung jasmine wreath'd in contrast there,
The golden links that round her ancles hung,
The belt of perfume o'er her shoulder flung,*
Her jewell'd caftan, or her shawl of gold,　　　650
That the gay youth in mute enchantment hold;
But that fine form that match'd the palm in height,
Firm as the cedar, as the acacia light;
Those eyes, in which a chastened spirit dwells,
Mild as the dove's, yet bright as the gazelle's.
Perchance her cheek too warm a glow had won
From the keen ray of Yemen's fervid sun,
Yet o'er its charms the vivid blush that broke,
Outvied Damascus' rose, when thus she spoke:

"Not far are those who if this scene they guest,
Might deem their daggers' fittest sheath my breast;
Yet think not I a spotless fame despise,
If at thy suit I drop my dark disguise,
Nor worse than death abhor a stranger's eyes.

* This is a broad belt, formed of the choicest spices, and slung over one shoulder. The golden anklets are often massive to a very inconvenient degree.

Though now adorn'd with every Syrian art,
To lure a master's gaze, not touch his heart;
Such were not once my cares," she paus'd and sigh'd,
" Ere I was destined for Moheddin's bride:
The new restraint my liberal soul disdains,
For I was nurs'd on Yemen's happy plains,　　　670
Free as the soaring bird, the mountain gales,
Or streams that leap, rejoicing, to the vales.
My ardent spirit, from my dear kitarr
Delights to call the inspiring strains of war,
Or warriors' loves, but sickens when I suit
Voluptuous accents to the Persian lute.
I love to bend the bow, to urge the chase,
And on th' unsaddled courser win the race;
To dress my father's meal, and twine at eve
Those webs that only Arab maids can weave;[l]　680
Where towering date-trees shade the saffron mead,[m]
And tents are pitch'd, and peaceful camels feed;
But weep, now doom'd to waste the breezy morn
In joyless splendour, and in arts I scorn.
Perchance in Syria yet my soul retains
The Grecian fire that warm'd my mother's veins!
The ire that kindled when she told her doom;
Snatch'd by the ruthless Tartars from her home,

In a rude sack borne o'er the burning sand,
And sold, half-lifeless, to a stranger's hand.[n]   690
But steps approach:"—she ceased, and closely drew
The veil which Rezia o'er her features threw.

"Be swift," cried Pardo, "bring my stoutest steed,
Watch well the portal, I return with speed:
For thee, bright damsel, I transgress, nor pause
To risk my fame in beauty's sacred cause,
Nor fear a generous King the deed will chide:
To friendly hands I pledge me now thy guide;
But duty then requires to break the spell,
And my reluctant lips must breathe farewell."   700

Soon on the steed the grateful dames he placed;
Unbarred the gates and led them forth in haste.
By this the moon withdrew her guiding light,
The dark dense vapours blot th' etherial height,
From Carmel's brow the pealing thunders roar,
And the full clouds their angry torrents pour.

Unused to Nature's frown, Amina's breast
Heaves with the fears she check'd, but scarce supprest.
And Pardo, faltering in a doubtful track,
Thinks how his Sovereign's trust commands him back,
When sudden by th' electric flash was shewn
A warrior near, in armour, but alone.

"Whoe'er thou art, for by this fitful light
Ill may I read thy lofty crest aright,
Now by thy spurs, I bid thee aid the fair!
Now for the love of holy knighthood swear,
Ere Carmel's brow with orient crimson shine,
To lead these Arab maids to Saladine."

"In simple faith the precious charge to guide
Be mine," the youth in Eastern speech replied.   720
"Though I, uncall'd, assume the knightly crest,
Believe that honour fills an Arab's breast;
I will not sue to hear that maiden's tale,
Or see one eye beneath her half-raised veil."

"And wilt thou leave me," sigh'd the trembling fair,
"And leave me thus, beneath a stranger's care?"

"Alas! sweet maid, may ne'er thy tender heart
Be torn like mine,—unwilling I depart.
Thy charms this night have lured me to forget
A duty that was never irksome yet;   730
While back to Acre's joyless walls it leads,
My thoughts will linger where Amina treads."—

"Thus, then," she answered, "if we here must sever,
Thus, like this jasmine, and, alas! for ever,
At least forget not ere its bloom decline
The maid whose heart shall store each word of thine."

Then drooping her fair head, she parts in haste
The fragrant blossoms on her bosom placed;
And had a ray been there, th' enamour'd Knight
Had found a tear upon its starry white.   740

" No, till my death thy memory will be sweet,
If—but brave Arab *we* at least shall meet;
Ere this I should have ask'd with timely fear,
Thy name, and what thy secret purpose here."

" My name I tell not now, but thou may'st guess
My daring hope, that, careless in success,
Some ill-watch'd fort might yield our valour way,
And night reverse the glories of the day.—
I hoped in vain—farewell, till time shall shew
Thy faithful friend, at least thy generous foe;   750
My blue egret shall mark me in the field."—
" And me the milkwhite gauze that veils my shield,"
Rejoin'd young Pardo, as with hasty tread
And sinking heart he left the weeping maid.

Scarce on his midnight watch again he stood
When Albert came, and mark'd his musing mood.
" What! my best friend, my Pardo, art thou sad,
(Thou ever gay!) when all around are glad?

If budding honour thus thy spirit tame,
Heaven shield thee from thy growing weight of fame!
Come, I must rob thee of this gate's command,
Thy last night's toil, thy wound, this rest demand;
Go to thy couch—nay, why that louring brow,
Thou prompt'st the taunt I never thought till now:
I will not say 'tis deep, but there is one
Who loves thee as thou wert indeed his son;
How would he grieve to see thy spirit lost,
How mark that sigh! Come, I must have thy post.
Thine is an eye that knows the spells of sleep,
We love-lorn souls, thou say'st, but watch and weep;
If we must watch, it little matters where—
RICHARD and Love's commands alike I bear;
Yield to whiche'er shall please thy fancy best,
Thy friend's intreaty, or thy King's behest."

" To both," he cried, " and leave to thee the light,
Thy laughing brow has stolen from mine to night;
It may be that I feel a wound forgot,
That I am weary, though I knew it not."

But what bright image haunts his heated brain,
And frights that slumber, ne'er implored in vain? 780
" An infidel, another's destined bride,
I could not love, if love were mine," he cried.

" What witchery this? our ghostly legends tell,
That Demons oft in angel semblance dwell;
Yet, though I perish, ne'er can I believe
Her words unholy—that those looks deceive."
But hark! that distant strain,—the stormy night
Stills her rude blasts, and listens with delight.
In stoles whose rich embroidery sweeps the ground,
With censers breathing sacred odours round;   790
With tapers far their holy light revealing,
With solemn music on the darkness stealing;
With waving palms that fresher gales diffuse,
And cleanse each shrine with consecrated dews,
Sage Hubert speeds, amid his priestly train,
Chaunts the high mass, and lustrates every fane.
To Christian rites each blessed dome return'd,
To every Saint the votive incense burn'd,
And monarchs kneel, while zealous prelates raise
The notes of triumph, piety and praise.   800
How rarely thus, with flowers that never fade,
Religion's amaranth wreaths the CONQUEROR's blade!

   Those lofty strains o'er Pardo's restless mind
Breathed a pure calm, ennobled and refined:
Yet though to prayer his inmost soul was given,
Amina mingled with his thoughts of heaven;

Bright as she shone in Cynthia's silver beams,
The angel vision cheers his broken dreams.

   Far other orgies, other sounds than those,
From Carmel's dark divan of demons rose;   810
Abortive guile, and baffled hate were there,
Contention, fury, weakness and despair.—
Each blames his fellows, each himself extols,
Th' infernal throng Alkarmel scarce controuls.
" What madness, Genii, what blind rage is ours!
Our safety hangs not on yon conquer'd towers.
The wrecks of storm-tost barks that strew the main,
The steams of death that rise from Acre's plain,
Yon blighted fields, yon heaps of ashes tell
How duly each has labour'd, and how well.   820
Say next, what evils can our hate conspire,
By fraud, by force, by famine, plague or fire?
The Pest has fell'd whom swords assail'd in vain—
Speak, shall the deadly vapours rise again?
Their course to govern, their success to see,
Superb Moozallil, were a feast for thee."—

   " No! not for me, abhorr'd Alkarmel!—ask
Thyself or Ullah for so mean a task.

Her toad-like spirit would delight to sip
The last blue venom from each livid lip. 830
She smiles when by disease the peasant dies,
I joy alone in higher agonies;—
Guilts's labouring throes, the Hell of vain remorse,
And hate, and virtue writhing at its force.
Vile as the beasts they rode, th' imperial band
Might wait for thee, I lopp'd the master hand—
Not I Comnenus' craven soul controlled,
But the fierce Conrad, Bertrand, Leopold,
These are my slaves, and RICHARD's groans shall tell
My skill directs their deadly malice well. 840
The arrow from a foe would scarce offend,
Infernal hatred points it by a friend.
'Tis like that icy wind, whose odorous breath
Shall woo man's helpless race to drink their death;*
Or like those scented blades of Syrian steel,
Whose venom'd fragrance aids their power to kill.
Talk not of hope, from us for ever fled,
The truly brave fight on when hope is dead:
Let Adam's sons her baseless visions trust,
RICHARD must triumph, and ye know he must; 850

* The Sarzar, a cold and fragrant wind, which, according to the Mahommedans, shall blow upon the last day, and destroy all living creatures.

But let us keep him from the rich repast,
And drug the nectar he must drink at last."—

" And how?" cried Ullah, " not by idle words,
The sole resource Moozallil's wit affords!"—

" Peace, murmurer! do not these contentions tell
That discord is the deadliest curse of Hell?
Still in the Christian host the fiend shall reign,
Their efforts palsy,—make success their bane.
Let this suffice, nor farther seek to know,
Till Palestine in shrieks announce the blow."— 860

" But who shall match PLANTAGENET? for death,"
Mordash began, " arrests the Soldan's breath."

" Restore him—Asia from her terrors freed
Shall thank her Prophet for the specious deed;
Such task befits Maimoune's gentle mood—
She loves the guilt that wears the mask of good."

At this her form assumed a lovelier grace,
A smile just lighten'd on her pensive face;
On roseate clouds she flies, while deeper hate
And deadlier scorn on each swart visage sate. 870
As fades the moon, with wizard gloom o'erspread,
So darkness deepen'd, when the Peri fled;
Loud rose the voice of wrath, red lightnings glare
And all the furies fright the troubled air.

What spell arrests the storm? below, around,
More felt than heard, and yet it seem'd a sound.
At once they pause, their inward fears betray,
And curse that call they dare not disobey;
While low to earth the abject spirits bow,
And silence reigns where Etna raged but now. 880
Alone Moozallil stands erect,—his eye
Shoots angry flames, he mocks them as they fly.
" False to yourselves as to your God, away!
Lo Hassan calls, and Hassan's slaves obey!
Hence! lest th' Assassin Prince infuriate rise,
And dare arraign the children of the skies;
Lest on some icy peak he bid you pine,
Or deep in earth, in riven rocks confine.
Go! ye that fear a mortal; doubly curst!
Bound to those spells your folly taught him first. 890
Go! reckless now of your ætherial birth,
To Heaven rebellious, yet the slaves of earth.
For this ye lost the skies; ye would not bow
To man when sinless, yet ye serve him now!
Be Heaven or Hell my lot—delight, disgrace,
I make no compact with the hated race."

Meanwhile Maimoune sought th' Ascanian wave,
Whose limpid tides her fair pavilion lave.
Oft when at noon th' unrippled face is clear,
Through the blue glass the fairy halls appear,   900
White as those fanes that time and man defy,
Nor rue one stain from Grecia's lovely sky.
O'er half the lake the beauteous vision spreads,
Rich gilded domes, and marble colonnades;
While mortals, wandering on the shadowy shore,
Mourn for the buried palaces of yore.*
Here shells in mockery match the frailer flowers
That lend their beauty to our earthly bowers,
Soft banks of moss serenest sleep bestow,
And fragrant rills in soothing murmurs flow.   910
Nor lack'd there tenderer blossoms, such as give
Th' ambrosial scents by which the Peries live;
While all around, in rich profusion strown,
'Mid orient pearls the blushing coral shone;

* Nice, or Is Nik, the capital of Bithynia, is situated on the banks of the Lake Ascanius, now called Ac Sou (*Eau blanche*). The inhabitants pretend that, when the waters of the lake are low, majestic edifices and massy towers are seen beneath the waves, the remains of a submerged city, which they suppose formerly to have occupied the site, and to have been destroyed by an earthquake. It is possible that this fable may have originated from the reflexion of the buildings of Is Nik in the water, but similar stories are not uncommon in the East.

Th' amber's liquid light, and many a gem,
Rare as the boast of Stamboul's diadem.
Maimoune snatch'd a vase; in Paradise
Once had its radiance pleased celestial eyes,
And now, though sullied by her guilty touch,
Its light transcends the gems of earth as much   920
As Heaven's inferior angels would outshine
Those charms in Carmel's synod held divine.
Within that shrine of sunny topaz beams
A lucid wave from Eden's sainted streams,
With whose blest drops the Peri every day
Wash'd from her brow the stains of earth away.
And now, as she through night's calm æther flew,
Pleased with her task, and conscious that she drew
From that good office, from the vase she bore,
Charms, since her loss of Heaven unknown before;
Flowers from her waving tresses load the wind,
A wake of light and perfume spreads behind,
And from her lips such magic notes distil,
That Moslems deem them strains of Israfil.*

* Israfil is one of the four Archangels; the angel of music, who is to sound the trumpet on the day of resurrection, and whose ravishing strains will delight the true believers in Paradise.

Where faint and pale, scarce conscious of the sound
Of weeping friends and Imaums chaunting round,
The Soldan lay,—her radiant presence sent
Soft light and freshening odours through the tent;
And as above his wasted form she bent,
Scarce her mild eye severer sadness shews   940
Than pitying seraphs feel for human woes,
While from her hand Heaven's own sweet dewdrops
    came,
Smoothed his distorted brow, and cooled his frame.
Such magic drops, as Grecian poets tell,
From young Aurora's rosy fingers fell;
Nor more reviving those ambrosial showers
To Tempe's drooping shrubs and faded flowers;
Nor yet Mahommed's wounded, weary crew,
From Gilead's balm diviner virtue drew,
When at his prayers (for so the Suras feign)   950
The healing grove sprung up on Mecca's plain,*

---

* In one of Mahommed's battles many of his followers were grievously wounded: but, at the Prophet's prayer, the plant from which the balm of Gilead or Tolu is obtained, sprung up like a grove, and their gashes soon yielded to the force of the miraculous balsam. The Suras are the divisions or chapters of the Koran.

Than from those blessed drops, indeed divine,
Flow'd through the wasted frame of Saladine.
Nor warm with life, with health renew'd he seems,
Rose with the sun, and blest his golden beams.

END OF BOOK VI.

CŒUR DE LION.

BOOK VII.

THE MARCH TO ARSOUF.

ARGUMENT.

THE MARCH TO ARSOUF.

Departure of Philip and Conrad—Embassy to Tyre—Richard's march from Acre—The encampment at the fountain — Hermesind — Pardo—The Emerald Knight—Albert—The submission of Cesarea—The vale of Arsouf—The enchanted wood of Sharon—Terrors and delusions of the Christian Army—Of Richard—Flight of Moozallil—Appearance of the Moslem forces—Preparations for battle.

CŒUR DE LION.

BOOK VII.

THE MARCH TO ARSOUF.

Not vain Moozallil's threats: where'er it fell
His torch awaked the latent fires of Hell!
Till all who fought for Acre's towers erewhile,
Like ravening vultures now contest her spoil.
At length a seeming calm succeeds the storm,
And fiendish malice wears a fairer form.
With faltering voice, slow step, and visage pale,
The specious Philip gilds his artful tale,
How the long toils his pristine strength o'ercame,
And Asia's sun unnerved his northern frame.

" Brother of England! comrade of my youth!
With soul propitious hear the voice of truth.
The city's fall acquits my vow; the gales
With favouring breath invite me to Marseilles:
Weak as I am, I yet my course delay,
Nor heave one anchor, if thou bid'st me stay.
Oh! had I lived unwedded to a throne,
Drawn a free sword, and fought for fame alone,
Not life or Europe proffer aught so dear
As for the Cross to fight and perish here!   20
But since I more the Christian weal can aid
In France a monarch than in Asia dead,
I bow to Heaven, I seek th' inglorious West,
And leave the wrongs of Sion unredrest;
Doom'd, when thy triumph rescued realms proclaim,
To curb the jealous pang, and bless thy fame.
Yet,—for my pious zeal unwilling draws
One active weapon from the sacred cause,—
Ten thousand spears, the choicest of my train,
To aid your arms in Otho's care remain.   30
Then prove, my friend, though policy or pride
Have sever'd those in happier youth allied,
That, like the nectar in its bloomy cells,
Deep in our hearts one drop of sweetness dwells;

These chiefs have seen our discord, let them see
Thou hold'st my life as dear as thine to me."ᵃ

He spoke:—not oft to RICHARD's generous breast
Suspicion came, or came a welcome guest;
Yet when his rival, with such vain parade,
Asserts a friendship he so oft betray'd,   40
Distrust awakes, he sees the covert snare,
And feels for England's weal a sovereign's care.
"I too, Augustus, have been taught to feel
How ill these feeble bodies serve our zeal:
Thus ever, when an arm of flesh we trust,
We find th' important lesson, man is dust!
Our early love was like a golden chain,
Not lightly broke, nor broken, join'd again.
If rivalry could here our souls inflame,
Here, where our hope, our interest was the same,   50
Will fair occasion interdict the wrong?
Will distance make expiring friendship strong?
Then pardon, Philip, if I bid thee stay,
Again to pledge the vows of Vezelay,ᵇ—
Those vows, that even from a rival's hand
Demand the care of my unguarded land."

"And fear'st thou, RICHARD, I would forfeit troth?
Then fear no longer: I renew my oath;

So thou before these Princes yield again
A vassal's fealty for thy Norman reign."   60

But RICHARD, reading through the thin disguise
The wish to sink him in his comrade's eyes,
Paus'd not an instant; kneeling on the sand,
His sword he tenders to his Suzerain's hand.*

" For ducal Normandy, and Acquitaine,
Touraine and Poitou, half thine ample reign,
I render homage here; but England's throne,
Erin and Gwyneth, by my father won,
And Cyprus' conquer'd vales are mine, and mine alone."

The chiefs in wonder heard the King display   70
The various regions that confest his sway,
When Conrad rose, and with unbending look,
Disdaining art, in open scorn he spoke:

" Warriors farewell! I pray not for your weal,
I feign no friendship that I do not feel;
Nor courage fails me, nor my scrip is low,
Nor ape I sickness, 'tis my will to go.—

---

* It was the custom for the vassal, when rendering homage, to present his sword to his Suzerain, and kneeling on one knee, with his hands between the knees of his feudal lord, to repeat the vow of fealty for such and such lands, saving his allegiance to some other lord for other lands and honours, or excepting such possessions as were unconditionally his own.

For thee, O chief! I spread no artful gloze,
No love has bound us, and we may be foes,
Since thou permitt'st yon phantom king to wear   80
My lawful title, and my standard bear.
Nor think by words my purpose to restrain,
I lack not gold, and flattery I disdain;
Oh! may you mourn me, as th' Achaian host
In blood and fire once mourn'd Pelides lost."

They spoke and parted;—long with pain supprest,
Indignant virtue blazed in RICHARD's breast.
"Hence, hence, ye recreants! ye that vow'd to bleed
For Sion's love, yet leave her towers unfreed!
Hence, for if interest lures, or fear appals,   90
Ye are not worthy to behold her walls!c
The God of Truth a livelier faith demands,
And scorns the labour of reluctant hands."

Now with redoubled zeal he bends his care
The walls to strengthen, and the towers repair;
The ransom'd captives to their homes restor'd,
While those deserted by their cruel lord
Paid the dire forfeit of his broken word.d
Then to the Templars, bravest of the brave,
The conquer'd town, important trust! he gave;   100

And bids his knights (nor were they loth) prepare
For the long march, the toils and wounds of war,
To quit her glittering domes, her citron shades,
And the soft converse of her dark-eyed maids.

   But first from Acre to the Tyrian court
The Austrian Duke, and proud Beauvais resort;
Beauvais, who ere his limbs the hauberk wore,
The pastoral staff and golden mitre bore.
Them, charged with courteous speech, the Monarch sent,
So might, perchance, the angry chief repent,   110
And Philip, still in friendly Tyre confined
By adverse ocean, or his wavering mind.^e

   " He who restrain'd the west'ring sun," he said,
" And through the parted waves his chosen led,
Again may open yon ætherial realm,
With stones or fire an impious race to whelm;
Yet wills not that presumptuous man despise
The licens'd means his narrow skill supplies."

   Meanwhile the pilgrim host their course began;^f
First rode D'Avesnes, and either Lusignan,   120
The Templars, (all that Acre's safety spared),
And brave Toulouse, for every chance prepared.

Next with the centre royal ENGLAND came;
There round their King the glancing pennons flame;
There from its towery height the standard flow'd,
And princely dames on gentle palfreys rode.
Otho, behind, th' Ausonian force commands,
The Gallic chivalry, and Austrian bands;
With him, in robes of glittering scarlet, moved
The Champions of the Tomb, in combat proved. 130
Arm'd with their bows the yeomanry attend,
And, sheathed in stubborn mail, the flanks defend;[g]
While proudly riding o'er the purple tide,
The copious fleet each rising want supplied.[h]

The air was calm, and every hill around
Sent joyful echoes to the trumpet's sound;
The morn was bright, and every golden ray
Wanton'd 'mid tossing plumes and banners gay;
The winding Belus past, and Memnon's tomb,
And Kishon's stream, and Carmel's brow of bloom,
And Shafamora, that sequester'd lies
Beneath green ridges that successive rise
To princely Lebanon, whose peaks of snow
Shine o'er her dusky wilderness below;
'Mid many a fragrant herb they wander on
Through the delightful plains of Zabulon.

'Twas sultry noon,—'twas August,—yet the breeze
From the tall hills, the near though hidden seas,
Blew fresh and cool, while through the livelong day
A thousand beauties cheat the weary way; 150
Around profuse the purple thistle grew,*
That clothes whole regions in its gorgeous hue;
While Nature's hand, eternal wonder! weaves
A holy legend in its dappled leaves:
Like that bright flower which still (as bards have sung)
Laments the hero from whose blood it sprung;—
That, the sad record of a heathen's shame—
But this, of heavenly love and mercy's healing stream.†
The yellow cassia, with its rich perfume,
The cistus, lavish of its shortlived bloom, 160
Type of man's hopes, all lovely at their birth,
But falling with the slightest touch to earth;

* Dr. Clarke speaks in admiration of this beautiful and stately plant. Indeed I have scarcely changed the words in which he describes it on his journey from Acre to Nazareth. A variety of this thistle has its leaves dappled, as though some white liquid had been spilled upon it. The legend which ascribes this peculiarity to the milk of the Virgin, which accidentally fell upon the plant, seems to have borrowed somewhat of the fanciful character of Pagan mythology.

† Ajax, who contested with Ulysses the armour of Achilles, and who, when the prize was awarded to his rival, became mad and slew himself. From his blood sprung the hyacinth, which is said to have his name written on its petals.

A race as fair the next blythe morning weaves,
And woos th' expecting gatherer, and deceives.
There too that tree, whose rosy blossoms flame,
As blushing to record a traitor's name;
The name of him to self-destruction led[i]
In vain repentance for his Lord betrayed.
There loaded palms and ripening vines between
The tall opuntia rears its prickly screen, 170
And round each ample leaf its flowers unfold
Their rich festoons of crimson and of gold;[k]
And there that cane, whence sweeter juice distils
Than bees collect on Hybla's thymy hills.
Ill fated plant! for man's delight design'd,
But made by man the scourge of half his kind.
How blest had ne'er a Norman ruler's hand,
Pour'd the new nectar on Sicilia's strand!
Thrice blest, had ne'er Iberian sails unfurl'd,
With this dire gift to curse th' Atlantic world.[l] 180

All lovely yet appear'd that chosen land,[m]
Despite of war and Islam's iron hand.
With awe they tread where e'en th' unconscious sod
Was dear to memory, sacred to their God.
Yet oh! how much more fragrant and more fair,
When his celestial presence wander'd there!

When earth, delighted, round his infant head
Bade virgin flowers delicious odours shed;
When serpents died, and every herb of ill,
And native harvests redden'd every hill; 190
The thorny brakes with ruddy grapes were fill'd,
And the rough oaks a honied dew distill'd.*

At Cana now the pilgrims pause, where first
From the gross veil the present Godhead burst;
Where, while through every heart amazement rush'd,
" The conscious water saw its God and blush'd."
Next at Saphura, reverend in decay,
To Anna's shrine their duteous homage pay.ⁿ
Till one fair eve, while lavish dews descend,
And the clear stars attemper'd radiance lend, 200
Where the tall plane-trees join'd the acacia's shade,
And through the turf a crystal fountain play'd,
King RICHARD pitch'd his camp, and all around
Ten thousand tents conceal'd the dusty ground.
In haste the troops regale; with toil opprest
They laid the helmet by, and sunk to rest.

---

* Ipsa tibi blandos fundent cunabula flores.
  Occidet et serpens, et fallax herba veneni
  Occidet; * * * * *
  Molli paullatim flavescet campus arista,
  Incultisque rubens pendebit sentibus uva;
  Et duræ quercus sudabunt roscida mella.

But, lured by silver Cynthia's rising beam,
Round the green margin of the gurgling stream,
The knights and damsels court the evening breeze;
Of their rich burthen rob the bending trees, 210
On saffron turfs the rural banquet spread,
Or the cool tamarind's grateful acid shed
In the clear nectar from the fountain head.°
While RICHARD with his bride discours'd apart,
Each sought the lady dearest to his heart.
Flung on a mossy bank, young Raymond seems
To count the murmurs of the lucid streams,
But love was conscious of a sweeter spell,
Where on the waves Matilda's image fell;
Evanthe sought behind a leafy screen 220
A shadowy spot, where she might weep unseen;
Near the pale heliotrope, whose flower with pain
Turns to the sun, and loves, like her, in vain,ᵖ
Nor heeds that Lusignan's enchanted soul
Mark'd each bright tear that o'er her beauty stole.
In sooth each knight some soft attraction found,
Yet hid in fair excuse the chain that bound:
One loved the opening of a laurel glade,
One the broad sycamore's majestic shade;
But each, the spot where sate his favourite maid. 230

Gay Hermesind, amid the moonbeam's glare,
Drew all the youthful and the joyous there;
Soft flattery, breathing from the careless heart,
Or sighing slaves that dare not own their smart,
Bids on her blushing cheek new graces rise,
And calls fresh lustre from her laughing eyes.
With playful wit she points her conscious charms,
Fair, and capricious as those airy forms,
That where the moon shines clear, and brighter springs
Th' autumnal verdure, weave their mushroom rings,
And quit the lily's spacious bell, to tread
Their midnight mazes on th' enamell'd mead.

 Apart from all she mark'd the Knight Unknown,
Propp'd on his ample shield, his vizor down,
And as she spoke, with arch coquettish grace
Flung back the roseate gauze that veil'd her face.
" Why does the Knight of Solitude disdain
To mingle with Diana's vestal train?
Now by thy grassy plume and emerald shield,
By those coy lips in scornful silence seal'd,   250
Approach our ring; 'tis not the tell-tale noon,
And vestal's veils are lifted to the moon."

 " Nay, lady! point not thus, nor thus intreat—
I may not fill that envied, dangerous seat;

For oft, 'tis said, 'mid honour's deathless leaves,
If subtle love his fragrant roses weaves,
With hue less bright the glossy laurels shine,
Fade at his touch, and like the flowers decline.
While Salem's throne the bold Amalric claim'd,
While Baldwin ruled, this shadowy grove was famed;
At earliest summer, round this sacred spring,
His nobles wont to join Judea's King;*
They met, on fire for glory, prompt to ride
'Gainst Sanguin's force, or tame Noureddin's pride.
What fitter spot can hear the vows of one,
Whose heart now beats at honour's voice alone.
See, as I dipp'd my falchion in the stream,
The moonlight touch'd it with propitious beam;
I will not fear that e'en thy looks have shed
A softer power to enervate the blade;   270
Yet not too long I trust that witching eye,
I know my danger, and have strength to fly."

Piqued at his coldness, vowing that his heart
Should yet be hers if she had charms or art,

---

* This fountain, frequently mentioned in the history of the Crusades, is about a mile to the south-east of Saphura, between that town and Nazareth. It was a place of rendezvous for the armies belonging to the Kings of Jerusalem, particularly during the reigns of Amalric and Baldwin the Fourth. *Clarke's Travels.*

She ponder'd on his words, and vainly tried
To pierce the secret sense they seem'd to hide.
(The voice, through the barr'd vizor heard alone,
Nor yet familiar seem'd, nor quite unknown.)
With seeming triumph in her looks, the while
She blest Ricardo with her sweetest smile. 280
" Lo! he hath spoken—some few trials past
Shall find this Orson humanized at last."
Then glancing round: " How sweet these moonlight shades,
How blest the lot of Syria's happy maids!
No toils are theirs, no care but to enjoy
All art can give, beneath so pure a sky;
Where nature, prodigal of bounty, yields
All bards have fabled of Elysian fields."—

" Ah!" Pardo cried, " can Syria's daughters be
The source of envy to a maid like thee! 290
Will Hermesind confess her eyes require
The jetty cohol to enhance their fire?
Or would she brook to waste a morning's care,
The jasmine twining in her sable hair,
While stiff with gems her radiant vesture shone,
To please one cold or jealous eye alone?

No! for she emulates that orb divine
Whose sultry beams on all creation shine,
And brighter arms her eyes' destructive ray,
As more sad victims droop beneath their sway." 300

"Nay! scoffing is not safe! some luckless hour
E'en thy cold breast may melt in beauty's pow'r."—

Her words aroused a serpent at his heart,
Yet his gay brow refused to own the smart.
" Aye, nymph! but never will I bend to one
Who loves to break all hearts, but pities none;
That like the fen-fire shines but to beguile,
Death in her frown, and treachery in her smile;
Though thou hast brighter lips, and cheeks, and eyes,
Than grace the bowers of Moslem Paradise, 310
If such the heaven thou seek'st to gain, beware;
Mahommed paints his houris kind as fair."—

But Albert, silent on a bank reclined,
In fancy's glass compares each damsel's mind.
Some flowers there are so delicately bright,
Their leaves expand but to meridian light,
And drink, where most Hyperion's fervours stream,
With eagle gaze the fullness of his beam;
And such was Hermersind, whose beauty shone
In the broad sunshine of a court alone, 320

Where, while around imperial splendour plays,
Her eye might bask in, and reflect the blaze.
While pale Evanthe, gentle, anxious maid,
A pensive violet in its leafy shade,
Though from that sun her light of life she drew,
Dares not on him to lift her timid view;
Yet far unlike the cloister's pallid maids,
Or flowers that open as the daylight fades,
With charms half lost amid the doubtful light,
And incense wasted on th' unconscious night: 330
Her's was no useless bloom, no lavish'd balm,
She sought the lowly dell, the shadowy calm;
Yet smiling in the sun, serene in showers,
That crush'd or blasted, gayer, prouder flowers,
In weal or woe her sweetness would impart,
To please the joyous, cheer the drooping heart.
" But," thought he, as his mind the theme pursues,
And from the scene imbibes its eastern hues,
" What flower is she that in her lonely dell
Droops mournful now, my own sweet Rosabelle? 340
Ah! when, loved blossom, shalt thou cease to mourn?
When shall thy wandering nightingale return?"

 Now gentle sleep each sparkling eye deprest
And rich pavilions tempt to balmy rest:

For Europe's scanty tents were laid aside,
And Western warriors loved Arabian pride,
To see rich carpets on the turf unroll'd,
And every damask curtain loop'd with gold;
While flowery wreaths their midnight scents exhale,
And perfumed waters cool the sultry gale. 350
They loved whate'er of gorgeous and of gay
Might shed a grace o'er battle's stern array.

   Yet ere the East proclaimed the rising sun,
The tents were lifted and the march begun.
Beneath their feet profuse that lily springs
Whose golden bloom outvies the robe of kings,[q]
And the pale star, by pious pilgrims named
From that whose beams a Saviour's birth proclaim'd.[r]
But when at noon the heavy casque opprest,
In Nazareth's consecrated shades they rest; 360
Their golden beads with pious reverence tell,
And slake their ardour at the Virgin's well.
Still with the dawn Arabian maidens bring
Their thirsty vases to the sacred spring,
But all unconscious of its ancient fame,
They breathe no humble prayer to Mary's name;
No shrine records where once a Saviour trod,
And gladden'd earth confest the infant God.

Now through Esdrælon's smiling vale they crost,
Where Cesarea awes the rocky coast.   370
They halt—but none their conquering course oppose,
And at their call the friendly gates unclose.
An ample guard the Monarch leaves behind;
Then as through Arsouf's rocky vale they wind
He counsels caution.   Melting in the sky,
No more the vast horizon shuns the eye ;
Not this fair Zabulon's delightful plain,
Here ambush'd fraud might lurk, nor lurk in vain,
Where to the south, the angry seas enclose,
And to their left the heights of Napolose ;   380
While in the narrow space that wound between
Frowns many a broken rock and deep ravine.
Here torrents cut the path, here rampant grass,
And towering reeds betray the near morass.
Nor false the leader's fears—from every height
Soon flew the deadly shafts in frequent flight ;
From mighty blocks of weather-tinctured stone,
That seem'd in wrath by warring Titans thrown
On the crush'd forest, start the wary foes,
From each green tuft, each wall, each hollow, rose;
Each little hamlet seems a fortress now,
No spot is safe, no step without a blow.

Where each rude fragment is a post to gain,
Where not one stream is passed till choked with slain.
Strange to the ground, with practised foes they meet,
Prompt in advance and prompter in retreat;
Who see the Christians with their darts perplext,
Then quit this lair and wait them from the next;
While still the broken ground forbids to close,
Nor day brings safety, nor the night repose. 400
In vain is force before a viewless foe,
Or prudence, levell'd by a random blow;
No space is theirs to charge or to career,
Skill, valour, strength, alike are frustrate here.

At length a hoary wood the heights o'erspread;
With caution due the harass'd host survey'd,
And hope for safety in its friendly shade;
Yet deeply marvel that the Soldan's care,
Of late so wakeful, plants no ambush there!
The hasty trench is dug, the frequent stroke 410
Fells for the solid fence the knotty oak,
While the lopp'd branches, heap'd in many a pyre,
Prepare to guard the forest camp with fire.
One half the host their anxious vigils keep,
Stretched on their arms, the rest solicit sleep.

But soon their minds disastrous thoughts invade,
With withering hue they scan the wond'rous shade;
What though no mighty stems, luxuriant, wove
Their boughs umbrageous, patriarchs of the grove,
The trunks were white with age, with moss o'ergrown,
Deform'd, and struggling with th' incumbent stone.
Not like those woods where Nature's hand profuse
A thousand forms displays, a thousand hues,
Where all the children of the hill combine;
Nor like those stately sheets of towering pine
Whose graceful pyramids on Jura rise,
And blend her misty summits with the skies :—
One rounded dwarfish form, one sullen leaf,
Clothes the wide forest in perennial grief;
One leaf that, when the naked Winter mourns,   430
Fades not, nor brightens when the Spring returns.ᵗ
In vain their foes have fled the fatal wood,
No rest they found, by deadlier ills pursued.
Fiends, that to grieve the noble Tancred there,
Could erst the form of armed Clorinda bear,
Or wore Armida's smiles, but wore in vain,
Send the loud shriek, and clank the heavy chain.
Cold poisonous serpents hiss along the ground,
The vulture screams, the lion roars around,

And ever where the thickest branches play'd 440
His dreadful eyes are twinkling in the shade.
With naked swords the affrighted warriors hear,
Their snorting steeds are bathed in dews of fear;
In vain industrious hands provoke the fire,
The rebel flames in dust and blood expire.
With sad funereal sound the moaning breeze
Swells to a storm, and bends the stubborn trees;
The thunder roars, the forked flash appals,
And sanguine rain, that blisters where it falls;
To each scared wretch his ghastly comrade seems 450
Like those pale forms that haunt distemper'd dreams.
Loud scream'd the owl, the raven croaking flew,
E'en darkness wore a strange unnatural hue,
And her black void is fill'd with shapes of woe;
Terrific sights, that day shall never know.

Now valour falters,—they that proudly bore
The brunt of battle, are themselves no more;
Fearless alone, PLANTAGENET imparts
His own brave spirit to their sinking hearts;
Cheers, strengthens all—till now at random thrown
On a vast slab of dark and rugged stone,
Beyond that joyless scene his fancy soars,
Reviews the past, the future page explores;

When lo! a blaze of fiercer lightning came,
The wood is radiant with a lambent flame;
Shrill shrieks succeed,—Evanthe pale, aghast,
Bursts through the adverse boughs and rushes past;
Foaming with rage, a ravenous beast pursued,
And dreadful roarings echo through the wood;
From its broad shoulders streamed its shaggy hair, 470
And its red eyes with rage portentous glare.
No time to seek the spear or draw the blade,
Dauntless he rushed to screen the affrighted maid;
O'er his stout arm his velvet mantle wound,
And, undismayed, receives the dreadful bound;
Huge claws and gnashing teeth in vain assail,
Entangled, blunted by his woven mail;
Till, as more wide the furious jaws expand,
Down the fell throat he thrusts his mighty hand,
Tears with resistless force its heart away, 480
And far before him casts the lifeless prey."
Evanthe next he seeks,—with 'wildered look
Her slender arms entwined a rugged oak;
But, with the weight of gratitude opprest,
She comes, she falls on her deliverer's breast.
Loose are her tresses, bare her rounded arms,
Their faded hue gives interest to her charms,

Till, as new light inspires her opening eyes,
On her pale features burning blushes rise,
And, starting from his hold, she strives to hide   490
Her glowing face, and sinks at RICHARD's side.

"Oh! why again so generous? wherefore save
A wretch, whose only hope is now the grave?
Why, why for me so dear a life expose?
Too well, alas! this wretched bosom knows,
Too deeply feels the gratitude it owes."

Astonished at her words, perplexed, amazed,
Reproving, pitying half, the Monarch gazed,
While o'er his soul, but whence he knew not, came
The fascination of that mystic dream,   500
Which, when he slumber'd in th' expiring storm,
In added grace foreshewed the stranger form.
But soon his better thoughts the spell resist,
He answer'd calm, as though his ear had miss'd
The sense of words by strong emotion wrung,
Unknown, at least unbidden from her tongue.

"Nay, rate not thus," he spoke, "illustrious maid!
So slight a service,—in itself repaid.
Thou tremblest yet!—let Berengaria's care
Thy terrors soothe, thy harass'd frame repair.   510

Rise, Princess, nor disdain the aid I lend,
My arm shall guide thee to thy gentle friend.
"To her, beloved of RICHARD, shall I go,
And bid her, as she caused, enjoy my woe?
No, first, inhuman! shed my vital blood,
Or give me to the monsters of the wood.
Rent from a crown, myself, my sire a slave,
I bore resign'd,—I loved thee, and forgave;
I loved, I saw thee wed another bride,
And lived, alas! to wish I then had died.   520
Now self-betray'd—ah! whither shall I fly?
How meet thine own, or Berengaria's eye!
Oh! hide me in some cave, where none that knew
Her happier days, Evanthe's grief can view;
Some spot (if such there be) where never fame
With joyful tongue shall whisper RICHARD's name;
There shall cold vigils waste my youthful prime,
And tears efface th' involuntary crime:
Or rather, since those frowning looks disclose
Far less than pity for thy victim's woes,   530
Now let me quit this load of life, and find,
Chief of the iron-heart, this steel more kind."

"Hear not, ye Heavens!" cried RICHARD, as he sprung,
And from her hand the lifted dagger flung.
"Alas! unhappy maid! this awful night
Bereaves thy wandering mind of reason's light!
Is this Evanthe? she so meekly given
In calm devotion to her sire and Heaven?
Whose bosom seem'd so pure, that none might dare
To deem one thought forbidden harbour'd there! 540
Now in her words can guilty passion speak,
Glow in her eye, and redden on her cheek?
Where is the downcast look, the pensive air,
The Cross Evanthe ever wont to wear?
Hold fast, lost Princess! hold that sacred sign,
It cures all sorrows, let it solace thine."

"Ha! am I mock'd!" the beauteous semblance cries,
While each fair feature swells to giant size,
While blood-red arms the phantom limbs invest,
And the red helm displays a sanguine crest: .550
"Yet tremble, thou hast spurn'd Evanthe's charms,
But what shall save thee from infernal arms?"

"What but that higher Power that Christians trust,
A Saviour's blood, a God for ever just."

He hurls the fiend to earth; the bands unlace,
The falling helm betrays a female face,
Though not Evanthe's—but the blood forsook
The Monarch's cheek, and every fibre shook.—
He knew those charms in opening youth that stole
With such seducing witchery on his soul;   560
He dared for them with hostile France conspire,
For them in rebel arms assail'd his sire;
On holy Pandulph rais'd his impious spear,
Till Heaven in thunder check'd his mad career.[x]
From hence what length of wars, what weight of woes,
What long remorse,—but oh! what glory rose!
For hence in penance to th' Elect of Heaven,
With humble heart he sued to be forgiven,
And robed in sackcloth to their scourges bow'd.[*]
Hence, to atone the guilty deed, he vow'd   570
His banner on the Sacred Plains should shine,
His arm affront the conquering Saladine.

[*] Richard seems throughout his after life to have been actuated by a sincere repentance for his rebellion to his father. At his accession, he shewed no favour to those who had been his abettors, while he distinguished the faithful friends and counsellors of Henry. On one occasion he prostrated himself, clothed in sackcloth, to an assembly of priests and bishops, confessed his sins, submitted to their reproofs, and even to their scourges, and at last received their absolution.

Hence, where Calabria's mountain-hermit dwelt,
On each rude rock in pilgrim garb he knelt,
And wondering heard, what heaven-descended sights
On Judah's hills had blest his wakeful nights,
How from th' Apocalypse his gifted view
The past expounded and the future knew;
Where prescient Heaven, in mystic phrases seal'd
Its pardon of the Monarch's crime reveal'd;   580
And bade, when Syria saw his flag unfurl'd,
His name outshine the conquerors of the world.^y
Hence, when the vital spark should quit his breast,
Had RICHARD will'd, that though his heart might rest
In that dear city which he loved the best,
(Delighted when her Minster's fretted height,
Grew like a child beneath the parent's sight,)
His corse, where Everard's holy springs distil,
Placed at his father's feet, should ask forgiveness still.^z

Such painful thoughts officious memory rais'd,   590
As bending o'er the prostrate form, he gazed,
On charms unseen since he believed them pure,
And vow'd his love should with his life endure:
While feelings that had slept for years, again
Burst in full force upon his aching brain.

"Demon!" he cried, "how well thou know'st the art,
To torture though thou can'st not shake my heart.
'Tis but a semblance, yet Alasia's form
Arrests my vengeance and unnerves my arm.
Hence, in His name this blessed sign who bore,   600
Delude my sense, and vex these groves no more."

"Fond man! thou robb'st me of an instant's power,
I scent th' advancing dawn, and know my hour.
But mark this crest, this armour; mark them yet—
The face methink'st thou can'st not well forget;
Thy heart in vain the vision may despise,
The dread reality shall blast thine eyes."

As from her narrow cell Aurelia springs,
And spreads to summer suns her ample wings,
Thus from the bursting mail Moozallil rose,   610
The trembling wood its mighty master knows.
So vast his stature, that the proudest oaks
Reached not one ringlet of his raven locks.
On his dark brow a thousand furies sate,
Revenge, and pride, and ever-during hate;
He shuns th' approaching sun, but leaves the sod
All black and blasted, where his steps had trod.

What sacred spell is in the morning light,
That with the darkness melts the fears of night?
Fatigue and pain, and sounds and sights accurst 620
Are vanish'd, like the dreadful dreams they nurst;
Up springs each warrior, springs with joyous bound,
And calls with cheerful voice his comrades round;
At his own fears amazed, and the control
Of night and darkness on his alter'd soul.
Yet, though with that pervading radiance came
Health to the mind, and vigour to the frame,
Fresh care succeeds; those stores that prudence pil'd,
Are drench'd by rain, by birds obscene defiled.
In vain they seek, if haply there may twine 630
The juicy melon, or th' uncultur'd vine;
For every fruit in those dark brakes that grew,
Scared by its nauseous taste and livid hue.
Rank lurid herbs that wizard hands distil,
With potent juice to aid their powers of ill;
Some whose foul scents their innate guilt declare,
Or thorny fruits bid careless hands beware;
And some more dangerous far, of fragrant breath,
Whose taste is poison, or whose touch is death.

Beneath those shades (whose wondering echoes rung
With discord harsh) were holy matins sung,

When RICHARD bade to hasten on their way,
Nor lose one hour of vigour in delay.
" Ere night our swords shall all we need obtain,
Or force a passage to the friendly main."
Now Berengaria came, and on her arm
Evanthe, bright in every youthful charm.
Well had Moozallil mock'd her eye of blue,
Her lips, her cheeks, like roses wash'd in dew;
But could not mock that purity of soul,   650
Which breathed a holier beauty through the whole.
In every act, each modest glance exprest,
In every folding of her spotless vest.
Oh! if those powers accurst, that only live
In prompting man to ill, could ever give
Those charms one moment's sway in RICHARD's heart,
'Twas when in thought he scorn'd their baffled art.

 The march began, but wearisome and slow,—
Above the woods impede, the bogs below:
Blythe were the warriors, when the orb of day,   660
Thro' boughs less dense could send a brighter ray;
And when the tainted gale betray'd no more,
The damp unwholesome marsh it linger'd o'er.
But short their joy, the lessening umbrage shews
On Arsouf's heights arrayed the wary foes

Thick as the blades of grass in vernal hour,
Or locusts that those tender blades devour;
Gay as the fields when bright with summer dews,
Or beds of tulips, deck'd in rainbow hues.
(What time to cheat the Haram's weary hours, 670
Voluptuous lamps illume the gaudy flowers.)[aa]
" Ah !" thought the King, " how oft my eager sight
Has sought this foe, and long'd to close in fight !
But now with bands dishearten'd, spent, opprest—
Yet spare these murmurs, Heaven decrees the best.
Let our stout yeomen close in firmest rank
To form our van, and guard each lengthen'd flank,
While all the knights the white-veil'd car surround,
Nor trust their steeds amid the broken ground.
Albert, Ricardo, long beloved and tried, 680
To you with fifty warriors we confide,
In yonder wood, our sister and our bride.—
' St. George for England !' be the signal given,
Till then restrain your rage, and trust in heaven."

Oh, courage ! though thy bold, unshrinking hand
From flaming pyres could pluck the lighted brand,
An army's chief implores a higher power
To nerve his mind in battle's awful hour.

The cool quick sight that marks each peril nigh,
Nor madly braves, nor basely turns to fly ; 690
The soul that now its valour can repress,
Now seize the point when daring gives success.
All these were his, who with one piercing glance
Each present evil saw, each future chance;
How well their post the adverse army chose,
Where on one side th' Enchanted Forest rose,
On one fierce Arsouf's foaming torrent flows,
While pent in narrow broken ground, unknown,
Or known to fear, what perils wait his own;
Who marks each danger, marks it but to foil, 700
And, nobly conscious, glories in his toil.

And these are his whom Europe late beheld,
When vaunting Gaul, by British might compell'd,
Left her lost eagles on the fatal field !
Nor scorn, illustrious Chief! my humble praise—
Not yet the hour is come when bards shall raise
Thine far above an elder Arthur's fame;
When age shall teach, and infants lisp thy name.
I speak not of a bloody despot, hurl'd
From ill-got empire—or a rescued world— 710
But (dreadful only in his distant roar)
That present War deform'd not Albion's shore;

That still our altars and our throne endure,
Our fields are fruitful and our hearths secure;
That every peaceful home unaltered shews
Those nameless comforts England only knows.
All these, our grateful tears confess it true,
All these to thee, to thee and Heaven are due!

END OF BOOK VII.

CŒUR DE LION.

BOOK VIII.

THE BATTLE OF ARSOUF.

ARGUMENT.

THE BATTLE OF ARSOUF.

The Moslems begin the battle—Are driven back by D'Avesnes—Death of that hero—Exploits of Richard—He kills Omar and pursues the Saracens to the torrent of Arsouf—Adel and Saladine fall on the centre—Death of Anglure, of Ferrars, Percy, and the Duke of Suabia—Aladin, Zorayda, and Almahide defeat the van, and attack the standard—Death of D'Oyley and Perceval—Advance of the reserve—Piety of Saladine—His prowess—Death of De Coucy, and others.—Vision of St. George—Combat between Richard and Saladine—Meeting of Aladin and Pardo—Richard routs the Musulman army—Attack on the royal ladies in the forest—Captivity of Matilda—Danger and rescue of Hermesind—Noble conduct of Adel—The Emerald Knight—Hermesind and Ricardo.

CŒUR DE LION.

BOOK VIII.

THE BATTLE OF ARSOUF.

On Arsouf's hill the Moslem myriads shone,
Their yellow standards glittering in the sun.
'Mid shouts of " Allah !" and the martial call
Of shrill Nacaire, and Zel, and Atabal,*
The Soldan views his ranks,—a barded steed
On either side attendant Mamlukes lead ;

* The nacaire, or long Saracen trumpet, was much used in the times of the Crusades. It is figured in Mr. Hamilton Smith's Ancient Costume of England. The principal circumstances of the description in the poem are from the Arabic historians. The noise of drums and trumpets, and other martial instruments in the Musulman ranks, is frequently contrasted with the silence of the crusading armies.

There plumes and banners sink and rise again
Like foam on billows of the chafing main;
While, motionless as rocks that guard its flow,
And silent as th' untrodden mountain's brow, 10
The Christian army frowns in shade below.
The sable hauberks clothe the fields in night,
Save when some blazon'd pennon beams to sight,
Or glares the thirsty steel's portentous light.
The wolves, that hail the thunder-cloud of war,
Look from their dens; the vultures speed from far.

   Now showers of javelins hurtle through the sky,
Like wintry snows the plumy arrows fly;*
The Moslems bleed; their happier foes endure
The baffled storm, in stronger mail secure. 20
Their hearts with valour arm'd, their limbs with steel,
Unmoved as sculptured forms that cannot feel,
They stand,—till RICHARD mark'd the Moslems pour
From their exhausted sheaves a scantier shower:
The signal sounds,—at once the lances beam,
The banners wave, and, like a mountain stream,
Led by D'Avesnes, burst forth his eager knights,
Drive back the foe, and win the nearer heights.
But Mosul's lord, and Mosul's braver heir,
Arbelia's pride, and Sandjar's Prince were there, 30

Omar and Afdhal, like the morning star,
The Soldan's eldest hope, and new to war.
They meet the chief, who, all to fury given,
Shouts loud his war-cry, " 'Tis the will of Heaven!"*
Twice he rush'd on, and twice repulsed, again
Spurs his stout charger o'er the heaps of slain.
But Adel from a distant height survey'd
His brother's wavering bands, and hastes to aid.
The arrows bristled in each jewell'd fold
Of the rich turban round his helmet roll'd,   40
White waved his triple plume, but white no more,
Soon was its silver down bedew'd with gore,
And each bright fringe his chesnut courser wore.
Where'er he came gay shields in shivers flew,
Crests, arms, and mangled limbs the plain bestrew,
And steeds ran masterless,—deep groans were mixt
With clash of arms, and shouts that rose betwixt.
Pierced by his spear was sage Bertulpho slain,
Albrando next, both vassals of Louvain;
And Antwerp's lord; till, tired of meaner foes,   50
Furious he seeks with great D'Avesnes to close.

* This was, in former Crusades, the general cry of the soldiers of Christ, but is named as having been particularly used by James of Avesnes in this battle. All the circumstances of his attack and death are historical.

The Flemish lance on Adel's buckler broke,
But Adel's scymitar, with mightier stroke
Lopp'd one stout leg; nor present death can tame
The martyr's soul, such death as leads to fame;
His frighted steed pranced wildly o'er the plain,
Yet still he grasp'd the unrelaxing rein,
Collecting all his strength, to right to left
His sword descends, and helm and corslet cleft;
Though all the ground was redden'd as he past,   60
Though now each stroke was feebler than the last,
He yields not yet, till Adel comes again,
And hand and sword fall sever'd to the plain.
He sinks in blood, but with his dying breath
He calls on RICHARD to avenge his death.

"I come, brave Count!" th' impetuous Monarch cried,
And plunged his golden spurs in Favel's side:
Nor waits his troops;—determined squadrons nigh
Oppose his arm, they feel it and they fly.
Adel he seeks, but Adel distant far,   70
On Otho's bands now waged destructive war:
His Egypt bleeds the while; to one proud heart
Drove RICHARD's spear, then drawing back the dart,
He through his comrade thrust with mightier force,
And pinn'd him dying to his dying horse,

Whose spine received the point; the lance he leaves,
And to the brain his sword Benamar cleaves.
Now Reduan came:—where Thebes of old to war
Pour'd through an hundred gates the rattling car
His fathers dwelt; he bears no waving crest,   80
Nor brass nor steel his mighty limbs invest;
Once (when deserted by the ebbing Nile)
He found and slew the slumbering crocodile;
Sheathed in its spoils thenceforth he scorns the shield,
And either practised hand the sword can wield.
But Caliburn, 'gainst which no fence avails,
Shivers like glass the adamantine scales;
He falls, he stains the verdant skin with red,
His comrade flies, but shooting as he fled,
To Richard's ear th' unerring arrow sped.   90
Slight was the wound, such wound as but inspires
The hero's soul, and rouses all his fires.
He snatch'd an archer's bow,—the Egyptian steed
In vain was swift, more swift the winged reed;
Beneath his shoulder was the barb addrest,
The barb empurpled issued at his breast.
Now numbers perish'd, nor the muse may tell
Their names, or how by various deaths they fell,
Or bravely, or by wounds dishonest gored,
Yet few were found to wait th' Armoric sword.   100

Omar alone, to none whose valour yields,
Omar, the hero of an hundred fields,
Waves high the yellow badge of Ayoub's blood,
While his round shield in proud defiance shew'd
A Moslem trampling on the Holy Rood.
The King beheld; with fiercer fury stung,
He seized the axe that by his saddle hung;
The breaking helm was heard, the crashing bone,
And Omar from his seat a shapeless mass was thrown.

Nought now restrains PLANTAGENET,—his blows
In hideous ruin crush the shrinking foes;
While like some winged courser Favel flew,
To Arsouf's stream he drives the trembling crew;
Alike they fall beneath his axe, or brave
The foaming tide, and perish in the wave.
Now to the cliffs they rush, nor heed below
The rocks, the seas, so much they fear their foe.
Again in blood they dye that guilty shore,
Of old so deeply stain'd with virgin gore,
Till he, the saint that Albion's sons implore, 120
Freed from the dragon's jaws the royal maid,
And at her feet the slaughtered monster laid.*

---

* Andromeda is said to have been exposed to the monster on the rocks at Jaffa; and it was near Berytus that St. George conquered the dragon. The two stories have had their rise in the same allegory.

Unconquer'd RICHARD basks in victory's smile;
Defeat frowns darkly on his rear the while.
Before the flower of Asian warriors ride
The brother Sultans, more by love allied.
But though the practised eye on either face
Might read the kindred lines of Ayoub's race,
Well might it marvel at the tie which binds
In wondrous union such discordant minds.   130
One pale and spare, in sable robes arrayed,
No jewels deck'd, save on his Syrian blade;
No gaudy hues, save where the plumes that grace
His casque, attest his empire and his race;
But Adel, named the Thunderbolt of Fight,
In stature lofty, as supreme in might,
With diamonds flamed, and gloried to behold
His meanest followers clad in gems and gold.
Generous to friends, he could forgive his foes,
And yet his slaves would shun the path he chose; 140
With all an Arab's scorn of blood he slew,
And mercy was a fault he never knew.
While learned Imaums shared with Saladine
An hermit's meal, he quaff'd forbidden wine;
A nation's wealth his new seraglios hide,
While Saladine, with more of patriot pride,

Bade thousands toil Kahira's walls to frame,[b]
Or delve the well ennobled in his name.
Fate brought ambition, his reluctant guest,
Native she sprung in Adel's haughty breast; 150
Alas! when Azrael shall their love divide,
Young Afdhal's realms may rue his uncle's pride.

    Now first on earth was Norman Arnulph laid,[*]
A noble victim, worthy Adel's blade;
The Soldan's spear the Danish Silric found,
Pierced through the eye, the brain received the wound.
The brave Anglure, incensed, to vengeance flew,
But check'd the blow, the yellow crest he knew.
Nor less the Soldan mark'd the noble knight,
Of old his prisoner in Tabaria's fight, 160
And for his prowess tax'd at ransom high,
Ill might his scanty lands the mulct supply.
Him, at his earnest prayer, the Soldan freed,
Amid his friends to seek the glittering meed;
One year to Gaul's proud lords he sued in vain,
Nor longer could his bride the knight detain,
For honour call'd him to resume his chain.
Such virtue touch'd the Soldan's generous breast,
With gifts he graced him, and with freedom blest;

[*] Arnulph of St. Clair.

Now pleas'd that grateful thoughts his falchion staid
He dropp'd his own; "no! thou hast shared my bread,
" Seek other foes, if thou must fall," he said.
Alas! his doom was near, for Adel's hand,
Relentless Adel! stretch'd him on the sand;
But in Poitou, the eldest of his line,
For ever bears the name of Saladine.[c]

Earl Ferrars next at Adel aims the blow;
Pleased that its weight announced a worthy foe,
The King accepts the fight, and wheeling round,
E'en as he turns, his side receives a wound; 180
He rais'd his sabre, but the Earl with care
Eludes the steel, which spent its force in air;
Again the Norman struck, but struck in vain,
The shield's tough plates the fierce assault sustain;
The Earl's left shoulder feels th' avenging stroke,
Through arms, and flesh, and crashing bones it broke;
His powerful hand resign'd the ponderous shield,
His noble blood rain'd crimson on the field.
Yet still he grasp'd the sword—one effort more—
Again his eyes exult in Adel's gore; 190
He falls, yet blest that not in vain he dies,
Waits the stern stroke that sends him to the skies.

With grief and fear his shuddering troop was fill'd,
But rage in Percy's noble bosom thrill'd.
Furious, to meet th' Egyptian king he rode,
And couch'd his lance; but soon the brittle wood
Snapp'd in its rest, the Moslem aim'd his sword,
Full at the temper'd casque of Whitby's lord;
He leap'd aside, the steel with erring force
Miss'd the good Knight, but slew his generous horse.
Yet soon on foot recover'd, Alan stands,
And, rashly brave, th' unequal fight demands;
His blows more swift than autumn's clattering hail,
On Adel's buckler shower, and Syrian mail.
The Monarch, maddening that a single knight
So long detain'd him, summons all his might;
Beneath the helm a dreadful stroke he sped,
And from his shoulders parts the gasping head.

Alas! already had his princely line
Twice dewed with blood the sands of Palestine.   210
Again shall Percy's orphans mourn, again
With solemn dirges seek St. Hilda's fane.^d

Now, by the Soldan pierc'd, Vigano lies,*
Cleft to the brain, the noble Stourton dies;

---

* Vigano de Cherbourg.

When Suabia's hapless Duke, who, vainly brave,
With grief and sickness wasting to the grave,
Scorn'd on his couch to yield a sluggard's breath,
In glorious battle seeks a nobler death.
Attired once more in long neglected arms,
The feeble frame his ardent spirit warms; 220
As when by him Iconium's Prince was slain,[e]
His eyes flash fire, he seems himself again.
His reeking sword is drunk with Moslem blood,
But when against Damascus' lord he stood,
His transient vigour fail'd; in short career
Borne down, transfix'd by that unerring spear.
His Teuton knights to Arsouf's forest bore
Their lifeless leader, weltering in his gore,
And in the son, again the sire deplore.

 Nor sleeps the war, where Sion's sovereign stands,
The Red Cross champions, and Provençal bands;
There near young Aladin Seiffeddin fights,
Dark Mestoc there with Sandjar's Prince unites,
And one whose limbs in Christian armour drest,
Bore on the ruddy helm a sanguine crest;
A naked sword the ruby shield display'd,
And "Vengeance" glow'd around the threat'ning blade.

Alas! Alasia, does that martial gleam
Thy royal race, thy gentle sex beseem?
Far hence that sickly softness, skill'd to hide 240
Its selfishness in sentimental pride;
That not for others but itself afraid,
Weeps, faints, bewailing where it ought to aid.
But woman's courage needs no plates of steel,
Its gentler office not to wound, but heal;
To bear resign'd, to hide the starting tear,
To speak the hope her bosom cannot share;
O'er pain's cold brow a heavenly beam to shed,
And watch, unfearing, by contagion's bed;
These are its triumphs, which though Fame deny 250
An earthly crown, she writes in gold on high.

Yet thee I blame not, beauteous Almahide,
Noureddin's daughter, and Aleppo's pride:
But not in luxury train'd; that Prince forbore
In Haram bowers to waste the peasant's store,
Nor gems, nor purple his Sultana wore.
An Arab she, she taught her child to bear
The stubborn bow, and chase the dappled deer,
Where Pharphar cools Damascus' violet vale;
And breathes from neighbouring hills th' inspiring gale.[f]

But when her sire resign'd the flame of life
And from his ashes rose the bird of strife,
When Judah's Lord (than him less generous far
Who on a kingless state had scorn'd to war),
Assail'd his sorrowing realm, the royal maid
In martial weeds her lovely limbs array'd,
With dauntless breast opposed his bloody track,
And from Belinas turn'd Amalric back.
Then to the Soldan, who from Egypt flown,
Made Syria's princely bride by force his own,*   270
To him, who in her father's favour bred
Now spoil'd the royal house he once obeyed,
She knelt, and from his generous pity won
The vow to spare Noureddin's infant son;
But when (by long and fierce assault subdued)
For Mosul and its rebel Prince she sued,
Unwilling to forego a realm so fair,
So hardly won, he scorn'd the Virgin's prayer;
Yet after long with vain remorse would chide
Th' obdurate heart that woman's tears denied.   280
Thenceforth amid a peaceful realm she reign'd,
And war she never sought, but well sustain'd,[g]

* Ascalon, often called in the East the " Bride of Syria;" that name is also given to Damascus.

Till roused by RICHARD's fame new ardour warms
Her regal soul, again she shines in arms;
Nor RICHARD's self might scorn the martial pride,
And powerful spear of noble Almahide.

While Raymond hastes to check Seiffeddin's rage,
While Bertrand and Arbelia's Prince engage,
While Lusignan and fierce Zorayda fight,
While Geoffrey braves Moheddin's equal might,   290
Her javelin's force the wondering Templars know,
Or feel the vigour of her sounding bow;
By valour as by vows forbid to yield,[h]
With noble blood they dye the verdant field.
On every side she slays, her smoking steel
Provence and Flanders, Brabant, Syria feel;
Till all the van, in dire confusion tost,
Flies to the hills and mourns its bravest lost.

But Aladin pursues his glorious course
With all the lightning's swiftness, all its force;   300
Where frowns the central might of England's war,
His daring arm assails the sacred car.
Some sunk, the victims of his Syrian steel,
Some crush'd inglorious, by his courser's heel;
Behind their Prince the youth of Persia came,
Rapid as whirlwinds, terrible as flame;

With shouts they charge—but, resolute to die
Or guard their Standard, England's chivalry,
By Asia's brother Kings already prest,
To the new fight their dauntless fronts addrest.   310
There Multon, Tancarville, and Pembroke stood,
And Osmere, sprung of old Elphegius' blood;*
His golden sheaf there gallant Grosvenor rears,
There the white cross of Perceval appears;†
There Leicester first his father's banner spread;[1]
There shines De Karreo, who so nobly bled,
Adorn'd with recent honours; Dutton's lord,
Proud of great Odard's far-descended sword;
And Pelham's youthful pride—no braver name
Decks the long annals of his line of fame;   320
Not even that Knight to whom on Poitiers' field
Gaul's vanquish'd King his captive sword shall yield.[k]
But Osmere soon the Persian javelin slew,
And Pembroke's steed without a rider flew;
Reft of a limb, his squires afflicted bear
To calmer scenes the proud Fitz-Herbert's heir.

* Osmere was the son of Elphege de Toketon, now Tufton.

† The arms of Grosvenor are a wheat-sheaf: those of Perceval, three white crosses on a field Gules; motto, "*Sub cruce candida.*"

T'was then that D'Oyley,—he whom none excell'd
In mortal conflict or the listed field,
Who once unknown his Sovereign's spear engaged,¹—
With Aladin a doubtful combat waged; 330
Nor ever yet that ardent Prince had found
A knight more skill'd to give, or ward, the wound.
Now here, now there, on either batter'd mail
They strike infuriate, and by turns prevail;
Till fortune, to the Saracen inclined,
Instructs his powerful arm the pass to find,
Where the dark hauberk, forged with little art,
Admits his sabre to the Christian's heart.

But Perceval, long bound by grateful ties
To D'Oyley's house, enraged to vengeance flies.ᵐ 340
In vain,—his better arm the Persian cleaves,
And pale on earth the wounded Norman leaves;
And but his squire was near, on Arsouf's plain
The son of Ascelin had swell'd the slain.

And now the conquering Prince his rowels hides
In Safie's flank,—the affrighted crowd divides;
Alike he spurns the living and the slain,
And dares with impious touch the car prophane.

Bold Harcourt hastes to save; and Stanley's knight,
Talbot and Compton, dragons of the fight; 350
While Turneham and heroic Pelham spread
The groaning sand with heaps of Persian dead:
This soon the Prince observ'd,—his horn he wound
(His studded horn that gave a silver sound);
First at his call the youthful Osman rush'd,
O'er friends and foes impetuous Ghazi push'd;
Afdhal, Zorayda, Zenghi, Almahide,
Forego the spoil, and to his succour ride;
But (for what speed can match a father's fears?)
Seiffeddin first with foaming steed appears. 360
Now man to man and horse to horse opposed,
In one small space is all the war enclosed.
Here armour rings, and broken weapons fly,
Blood dyes the earth, and dust obscures the sky!
Now Hamo fell, the prey of Almahide;*
Khorassan's Prince by powerful Leicester died.
By Roland pierced, rose Alp's expiring yell,
By Afdhal's hand the conquering Roland fell.
The young Fitzaubert, who on Arsouf's plain
Nurs'd the fond hope of gilded spurs in vain, 370

* From Hamo is derived the family name of Amherst.

By Almahide to lasting slumber sent,
His faithful squire shall Leicester long lament.

 Loud rings the clash of arms;—the press of war
Nearer and nearer thickens round the car:
Its purpled wheels are choked with mounds of slain,
And its white veils receive a crimson stain.
The Christians yield! the Prince with powerful spear
Strikes from his seat the hardy charioteer;
While Solyman, of all the Mamluke train
Bravest and first, usurps the vacant rein.[a]   380
'Twas then, while Multon with impetuous force
On Mosul's hope impell'd his powerful horse,
That Grosvenor (from his hand the falchion thrown)
Springs on the wheels, and drags the Moslem down,
While his strong knee his struggling foe comprest,
His dagger's point th' unwilling soul dismist.
Orasmin, long his partner of the war,
Seeks from the field his dying friend to bear;
In vain,—his arms and gilded helm inspire
Fierce Bertrand's grasping soul with strong desire;
O'er his slain foe his mighty shield he spread,
And by his side he lays Orasmin dead.
Alike in Ayoub's yellow livery drest
The field Bedreddin and Miralis prest.

On Kaled next the bold De Karreo flies,
And, cleft by Harcourt's axe, Shirazin dies.
But Bertrand, like some massy tower, defied
Abdallah's strength and overweening pride;
Three half-armed Franks upon his lance had bled,
"Breathes there a fourth dares meet its force?" he said:
The Viscount, striking ere he deem'd him near,
Lopp'd with his trenchant blade the lifted spear;
Then as his arm his sabre's hilt explored,
Deep in his side he drove the fatal sword.

But now from Arsouf's forest moving on,
The knights of France and warriors of St. John,
With shrill-voiced clarions pierce the troubled air,
Fall on the Moslems, and reverse the war;
And, long victorious on the neighbouring height,
To seek fresh foes descends the Emerald Knight. 410
Graceful as Mars he reins his matchless steed,
A milk white jennet of Iberian breed.
Meantime th' Egyptian King the fight survey'd—
His arm in dust twice twenty knights had laid,
Whose dauntless fronts the snowy Cross display'd.
Now resting from the field, he sees advance
The fresh attack—he grasp'd his powerful lance,

And sought the Soldan—who from war retired,
As Moslem rites at glowing noon required,
First on his hands the cleansing water pour'd,   420
Then, bent to earth, the God of Heaven adored.
His beauteous dwarfs around the Monarch stand,
And chaunt harmonious, as their laws command,
That holiest Koran, traced by Omar's hand;
While all the rush of war, the mingled cry
Of rout or conquest, swept unheeded by.ᶜ
In admiration lost, th' Egyptian stood,
Nor on his brother's silence dared intrude
Till Saladine arose. Then, "Lo! he cried,
"Where from yon wood Gaul's red-cross warriors ride,
And with proud Austria's azure legions come,
Our ancient foes, the Champions of the Tomb."

"Charge, Adel! charge! we give them to the sword,
In Alla's name,—be Alla's name adored!"
And calm as when the quiet sod he prest,
The dauntless Soldan fix'd the lance in rest;
To check th' advancing squadrons, ere they gain
The level ground, and join the English train.
Half lost in herbage, where a torrent crost
The narrow path, he plants his little host;   440

Soon its blue waves run purple to the main,
And the rose-laurel wears a deeper stain.
First, pierc'd by Adel's hand, De Coucy fell,
Whose hapless tale Provençal bards shall tell;
For ere his soul its earthly prison broke,
With faltering accents to his squire he spoke:
" To Fayel's bride convey this bleeding heart,
Whose hapless passion scarce with life shall part;
Perchance, though to its living woes severe,
She then may grace it with a pitying tear;—   450
Fame, and her love, and Paradise, to gain,
I wear the Cross, nor let me wear in vain."—
Alas! the squire, while he his route explored,
Met in a wood the lady's jealous lord;
And, all unconscious, to his ear disclosed
Within the urn what precious heart reposed.
He hears, and credits half the tale: the rest
In frightful hues his jaundiced fancy drest;
His phrenzy deepens, nor believes the dame,
Loved by such knight, could scorn his faithful flame.
With savoury spice the wretched heart he drest,
And saw his bride enjoy the dreadful feast!
Then told the whole;—when she who prized his truth,
Even while her virtue shunn'd the hapless youth,

Would with no meaner food pollute his tomb,
And pining, met the voluntary doom.^p

Yet did not his fond heart forget to beat,
Nor Coucy's soul desert its earthly seat;
Till Ermengard, neglectful of the fight,
Of all his sins had shrieved the pious knight." 470

Meanwhile the battle bleeds. On Adel's spear
Died noble Clermont, and the brave Sancerre.
The Count of Dreux, beside his own arrays
His brother's troop, the vassals of Beauvais;
Vaunting he came—but when his eye beheld
The scene of death, by sudden terror quell'd,
He turn'd his steed; and through his squadrons spread
Their leader's fears, till all in tumult fled.
Not so St. Paul's brave Earl; beneath him slain,
Three noble steeds are stiffening on the plain, 480
Fearless he mounts a fourth; his dreadful brand
With hideous ruin sweeps the Mamluke band;
The Knights of Sion, fired with rage, imbue
Their scarlet mantles in a deeper hue.
Here Ermengard for deathless fame contends,
Here storms Fougères, and Mestoc there defends.

But, like some tiger springing from his lair,
In battle dreadful as devout in prayer,

The Soldan seems—on horse and foot alike,
His blows descend, and kill where'er they strike. 490
First of the noble fell Tillières, and then
Castillan's Baron, and the bold Turenne;
Gournay and Ponthieu;^q and a warrior drest
In sable arms, his helm without a crest;
A cedar, once the patriarch of the glade,
Crush'd by the bolts of Heaven, his shield display'd,
"How fall'n, and whence!" the mournful legend said.
Alas, he perish'd! Not a squire unlaced
His casque, or friend the words of peace addrest;
None knew that in that humble guise was quell'd 500
A chief that once Edessa's sceptre held,
Whose house should give (from Moslem conquerors won)
A race of sovereigns to Byzantium's throne.[r]

But when unhorsed the Lord of Newburg fell,
Lamenting thousands raised the piercing yell;
That heart which ne'er to asking want denied,
That hand which Europe's famish'd host supplied,
When, whelm'd with countless ills, on Acre's plain
They look'd to Tyre's relentless Prince in vain,[s]
Is cold! But angel harpings hail on high   510
The " faithful servant " to eternal joy.

Brave as that Lysoi, from whose triumph came
His lineal pride, and Montmorency's name;
Graceful in youth, the noble Joscelin flies
To proof of arms, and Saladine defies.
One in the flower of youth, when just began
The supple joints to knit and fix in man;
And one in vigorous age, ere slow decay
Unnerved those joints and stole his strength away.

Meanwhile where Hubert heap'd the field with dead,
"Turn, Sarum! turn!" a voice of thunder said;
"Turn, hateful recreant to thy vows profest!
How ill those stains beseem thy priestly vest.
Has earth or hell an union more abhorr'd?
Peace on thy lips, and carnage on thy sword!"
He turn'd,—his foe was red with Christian gore,
His shield the Prophet's moony ensign bore;
Th' unvizor'd helm Rodolpho's face betray'd,
A Templar once, but now a renegade.*
"Thou, traitor! say whom most his God shall prize,
The man whose sword defends him, or defies?"
The priest return'd; by righteous anger sway'd,
Deep in Rodolpho's throat he drove the blade;

* This incident of a Templar renegade is on record.

While the warm life-blood chokes his struggling breath,
His fate he curses, and blasphemes in death.

But near the Prelate's side Guiscardo stood,
And spoke aloud, by sudden fear subdued:
"St. George! thou guardian of our English host,
Now lend thy aid, or Christendom is lost."

Sage Hubert smiled: "Heaven loves not those that fear, 540
A firmer faith had made thy sight more clear.
O thou, the strength of England's line, dispense
A brighter beam to his benighted sense."

He pray'd, and Guiscard sees a stranger knight,
Steed, arms, and vesture, all of silver light;
But on his casque he bore a dragon crest,
A sanguine cross his diamond shield imprest;
His lance was gold, and as the lightning glides
Through hardest rocks, the Moslem mail divides;
Blood spouts around, yet not one drop might dare
To stain his radiant arms or glittering spear;
While each true martyr, ere he yield his breath,
Looks to that stranger's eye, and smiles in death.

Now shouts are heard! from Arsouf's crimson stream
With thundering speed triumphant RICHARD came.

He, not too far by present glory led
To scorn the havoc far behind him made;
Changed like a god the fortune of the war,
And the foil'd Moslems quit the half-won car.
Oh, Cœur de Lion! why withhold the name 560
With which applauding comrades stamp'd thy fame;
When armies fled before thy withering glance,
And victory waited on a single lance?
As earth, and rocks, and bristling wood betray
Where the spring torrent forced its furious way,
Though Alpine snows supply its rage no more,
And the hot sun have wasted all its store;
Of arms and steeds, the wounded and the slain,
A ghastly track grows dreadful o'er the plain.
Such then the terrors of his arm, that still 570
At Richard's name Arabian bosoms thrill!
The restive courser starts that sound to hear,
And infant cries are check'd by sudden fear."

Where yet by Arsouf's wood the Moslems fought,
Dismay and death his biting falchion brought.
What checks his conquering course?—a form, a face,
Whose youthful beauty oft he loved to trace,
Defaced with many a gaping wound, and known
By Montmorency's eaglet-crest alone.

"Ah! whence this cruel deed?"—The dying lord 580
Waves the red remnant of his broken sword,
And points to Saladine, who on the right
Still urged the fainting Lombards into flight.
The Monarch spurs to vengeance. "Turn!" he cried,
"By England's King is Saladine defied.
Ah! what avails this throng of martyrs slain?
While we, the authors of the war, remain?
Let angry strife suspend its mutual rage
While we for Sion and for fame engage—
Thy fabling Koran, and th' Eternal Page." 590

"I never brought a ruthless host from far
To seek thy crown, and rouse thy world to war;
Me not with curses ravaged Europe names,
Her harvests trampled, and her towns in flames!
The war is thine!—Yet come," the Soldan cried,
"Ne'er was it said that Saladine denied
To meet a foe that Islam's faith defied."

They wheel around, they rush in full career,
Each sits unmoved, and breaks his faithless spear.
The Soldan snatch'd a second from his slave, 600
To RICHARD's hand a second Pardo gave;
Again th' impetuous chiefs the course renew,
Again on earth the shining splinters flew;

Till either Sovereign, casting from his hand
The shiver'd truncheon, bares his glittering brand.
Now blows descend, above, below, around
The lightning flashes and the arms resound;
The Soldan's sword, at RICHARD's head addrest,
Cleft from his morion half its broomy crest;
While Caliburn through helm and turban glides, 610
And from the Soldan's arm the mail divides.
The Soldan strikes again,—his furious blow
Rings on the buckler of his mighty foe,—
It lops the golden boss; but RICHARD lent
A dreadful stroke, which, on his shoulder sent,
Forced him to earth, while, from his burthen freed,
Pranced through th' affrighted ranks the startled steed.
Now RICHARD springs to ground, to wage the war
On equal terms; but Mosul's generous heir,
Who mark'd his Sovereign's need, dismounts in haste,
And on his seat the wounded Soldan placed.
In vain would RICHARD now the fight prolong,
Around their Chief the faithful Mamlukes throng;
With England's King a desperate strife maintain,
And in the press was beauteous Favel slain.[x]
Just as the Monarch with an active bound,
Leaped to the seat, he felt the erring wound;

Deep in his side received the stroke of death,
Bent on his knees, and gasp'd his latest breath.

Oh! then what wrath in Richard's bosom rose, 630
A wrath that issued not in words but blows.
What wrath inflamed his Peers! on all the plain
With fiercer fires the combat wakes again.
On foot the Monarch fights,—the dastard crowd
Flies from his single arm; he shouts aloud,
" Bring forth my generous Lyard!"—at the sound
The Norman war-horse paws the echoing ground.
Black were his limbs as Pluto's murky reign,
And glittering bells adorn his glossy mane;
His furniture was gold;—with wings outspread, 640
A dreadful raven nodded o'er his head.
Long had he mourn'd to see the Cyprian steed
Usurp his master's love;—from bondage freed,
And prancing to his lord, he joys again
In his proud load, and spurns the purple plain.
He champs his golden bit, his eyes flash fire,
Beneath his hoofs the trampled crowds expire;
The living fly, they see their comrades bleed,
Nor deem that wond'rous horse of mortal breed.
While Caliburn now these, now those, bereft 650
Of life and limb, or to the saddle cleft.

Such fear ensues, that had not Adel's hand
Enforced the valour which his words command,
And been himself their shield, that fatal day
Had swept the boast of Ayoub's race away.

   But with surpassing rage the Leopard Knight
Pursues the Moslem who disturb'd the fight;
Seiffeddin's offspring, by his father's care
Already mounted, and engaged in war.
They met, and each the half sheath'd falchion drew,
And rais'd, and dropp'd; for each together knew,
One the veil'd shield, and one th' egret of blue.
" Nay," Pardo cried, " our force let others feel,
Nor hands once clasp'd in friendship urge the steel;
Farewell!"—" Yet pause," said Aladin, " and hear
If to thy heart Almanzor's child be dear:
Thou know'st that long (though wars might intervene)
Moheddin sought her for his haram's queen.
Prepared already was her ample dower,
And presents given, and fix'd th' auspicious hour, 670
When droop'd the nymph—in vain the Imaums pray'd,
Or bound with holy scrolls her burning head:
Pale as the unconscious tenant of the tomb,
Or blossom withering in the hot simoom,

Her spark of life seems twinkling to expire;
So Rezia weeping said—her wretched sire
Explores a cause in vain, but none can tell,
Unless thy conscious heart resolve the spell."

He paus'd ; but Pardo vainly sought reply,
Till feeling burst in one convulsive sigh. 680
" Ah ! what avails it—Oh ! could both forget,
Thus doom'd to meet no more, that e'er they met !
What now remains but to bewail thy doom,
And pine like thee, and perish on thy tomb !"

" Hope yet shall live!" cried Aladin : " attend—
Foe to thy faith, believe me yet thy friend :
Though sacred laws perchance, or jealous pride,
Have here to love his sweetest food denied,
Soft looks, and 'whispered thought of hearts allied :'
Yet he who swims the moat, and scales the wall, 690
Gains strength from bars like these, to leap them all.
He teaches language to the silent flowers;
And not a blossom decks Arabian bowers,
How scentless, small soe'er, or faint of dye,
But bears some sense to conscious beauty's eye.
Such will I twine—I know their legends well—
The passion-flower a Christian Knight shall tell;

And hope, and fear, and mutual love exprest,
Amina's fluttering heart may read the rest.
But see, while thus the precious hour I waste,   700
What demon sweeps our ranks!"—he waved in haste
His graceful hand, and spurr'd his foaming horse,
While death and terror mark his conquering course.

  But Pardo sits entranced:—the flying throng,
That RICHARD scatters, pass'd uncheck'd along,
Till Mahmoud spoke: "Is this a place of sleep?
" Christian! thy slumber shall be long and deep;
Deep as the grave."—But, waking from his trance
At the rude summons of the Arab lance,
Young Pardo spurs his steed; to earth he bore   710
The vanquished Saracen, to rise no more.
Urged by that inward grief that knows not balm,
And rage, which only Moslem blood can calm,
The Knight, whose courteous manners all admired,
Now seem'd some fiend, with wrath infernal fired.
Grave Ibrahim, whose beard of snowy white
Down to his girdle flow'd, a reverend sight,
Seized by that snowy beard, contends in vain,
His headless trunk falls bleeding on the plain.
Reft of an arm the Nubian Calaf died,   720
The deadly weapon pierced Melcazar's side:—

Melcazar, sweetest of the youths that sung
His own Bokhara's odorous shades among;
Her shepherds oft by fount or citron grove
Wept as he pictured hapless Mejnoun's love;
While nymphs, like Leila fair, the bowers would throng,
And with applauding roses crown the song;
Or shower'd sweet jasmine from their latticed screen,
Like fairy favours, dropp'd by hands unseen.

   Shahriar, who in Medina's house of gloom   730
Thrice saw his Prophet's self-suspended tomb,
And strove the sins of early life to clear
By fast and prayer, and penitence austere,
Despite of texts inwoven with his mail,
Falls, nor his Prophet nor his prayers avail.

   Thus (like Hyperion, when his orient ray
Gives gracious promise of a golden day)
While the young hero track'd his way with blood,
Aghast in wonder hoary veterans stood;
E'en Cœur de Lion check'd his foaming horse,   740
Amazed, exulting in his favourite's force.

   A Christian Knight,—but let the page of fame
Refuse its record to the dastard's name—

By Aladin's unsated sword pursued,
Sought fatal refuge in th' Enchanted Wood;
He sought and found—for through the waving leaves
White vests and glittering arms the Prince perceives;
Nor longer for the craven's blood he burn'd
But from the grove his docile charger turn'd;
An instant sees him at Zorayda's side. 750
" Bright moon of earth, my soul's best gem," he cried,
" Vain is our struggle here, our valour vain,
He who could yonder wolf of war restrain
Might bid the wither'd leaves be green again.
Yet if for vengeance pine my injur'd love,
The Monarch's Haram waits in yonder grove,
Slight seems the guard, not slight our triumph won
If in his consort's fate we rule his own."
 Strong in the willing aid of Almahide
They quit the field, and through the forest ride; 760
And soon they came where, fearless of a snare,
Far from the clash of arms, the shouts of war,
Each royal beauty through the waving shade
Seem'd nymph, or dryad of the shadowy glade;
Anxious, yet calm, their thoughts to heaven addrest,
With pious hopes they charm their fears to rest.

The reckless Hermesind, in smiles array'd,
Lists to Ricardo, who beside her laid,
Pours his delicious flattery on her ear,
Or turns with looks of livelier joy to hear 770
Her converse brilliant, sprightly, and refined,
But like the dew, that leaves no trace behind.

Unhappy youth, forbear the moonlight grove,
Break thy soft lute, and cease thy songs of love;
Nor hope, bewilder'd in her witching snare,
To touch that heart, if yet a heart be there.
Drown Love in War:—and hark! that war is near,
On his smooth shield rings Albert's warning spear;
And fifty warriors, starting at the sound,
In steely phalanx guard their treasure round. 780

His vizor down, his ashen spear in rest,
'Gainst Aladin the ready Albert prest;
But he, who saw th' expected prize so nigh,
Disdains the single fight, and past him by.
Not so Noureddin's child; with lance opposed
She meets her foe, and soon in combat closed;
Both hope an easy spoil, and grieve to feel
A warrior worthy of their practised steel.

Meanwhile the Persian Prince and Gallic maid
With baleful eyes the iron ring survey'd. 790

In vain with taunts they rouse each faithful knight,
Each curbs his rising wrath, and shuns the fight;
While sure destruction threatens him who dares
To rush, unhappy, on their hedge of spears.
But the young warrior, tempering force with skill,
Aims his light dart, to torture not to kill;
Helias' steed receives the smarting wound
In his left eye, and flinging to the ground
His startled lord, he spreads confusion round.
The line thus broke, prepared the Persian stood, 800
His vantage seized, and bathed his sword in blood.—
The Pisan Ugo welters in his gore,
Iberian Carlos sinks to rise no more;
Carlos, who loved the proud Castilian maid,
Whose heartless taunts his faithful vows repaid
His life unblest, yet happy in his death,
Since for her sake he yields his wretched breath.
Her lover's deeds Zorayda's soul inspire,
Her pride they kindle and her envy fire;
She spares not those of Gaul's paternal soil, 810
Nor those once dear in Albion's happy isle.
Where each devoted warrior seeks alone
His sovereign's safety, and neglects his own,
Rich were her spoils, her laurels cheaply won.

Of fifty, late the guardians of the shade,
Cold on the turf are thirty heroes laid;
While scarce the rest their ponderous arms sustain,
And with a sanguine deluge bathe the plain.
Count Mirlo piercing in her mad career,
(Her cousin once, when France or kin were dear.) 820
Now through the broken ring the fury flies,
And hope already grasps th' expected prize;
Evanthe, sickening, faints in mute despair,
With clasped hands Matilda sinks in prayer;
While Berengaria from a lifeless hand
Snatch'd the broad shield, and waved the shining brand.
" Death, not pollution for a hero's bride,
For RICHARD's Queen!" th' intrepid beauty cried.
" For RICHARD's Queen!" her ruthless foe replied;
" And who art thou that darest such rank assume? 830
False bird, this hand shall strip thy borrow'd plume."

But Albert sees, no more can Almahide
Detain the Knight, he seek his Sovereign's side;
What demon then might match Zorayda's rage,
Again compell'd a desperate strife to wage?
Robb'd of a prize that seemed already won,
Her glory tarnished, and her vengeance gone.

Nor less Aleppo's Princess blames the Knight,
She calls him craven, and demands the fight;
While anxious only from Zorayda's hand   840
To save his Queen, he slights her fierce demand.
And she, too generous with unequal force
To press a single warrior, turns her horse,
And crossing, as she fled, Matilda's way,
Bears through the forest her defenceless prey.

  Fair Hermesind's rich robes and courtly mien
To Mosul's erring Prince exprest a Queen;
Fawnlike she fled, she seeks the thicker wood,
While on his goaded horse the Prince pursued.
In vain Ricardo, desperate, crost his way,   850
To buy with life one instant of delay;
And seized with powerful grasp the rein of gold,
His wounded arm reluctant yields its hold;
Yet scarce he feels the smart, one pang possest
His faithful soul, and silenced all the rest.
It chanced a path the flying virgin took
Where dash'd o'er mossy stones a brawling brook;
So close the rocks arose, and twining boughs,
That scarce its dizzy verge a pass allows.
In need less desperate, ill the timid maid   860
Had dared that narrow dangerous way to tread;

At least had claim'd Ricardo's help, and shewn
A thousand pretty fears, half feign'd and half her own.
Yet fearless now she skims the slippery shore,
Nor sees the foam, nor hears the waters roar.

 Ricardo saw, and while the Persian steed
His tedious way with painful labour freed,
He, fleetest of the fleet, in wanton course
Who oft outmatch'd the stag, or generous horse,
Now in the tangled brake by love sustain'd, 870
Through nearer ways the angry torrent gain'd.
Where to the rock above a cedar clung
Impending o'er the path; aloft he sprung—
The crashing fibres yield, the falling shade
Divides the eager prince and flying maid.
In vain—his steed scarce pausing, dares the bound,
And lights uninjur'd on the slippery ground;
He gains each moment on her slackening flight,
He grasps her mantle; while the wretched knight,
Crush'd by the load, and struggling in the wave, 880
Hears her loud shrieks,—he hears and cannot save!

 Who in that deadliest peril rush'd between?
The Knight Unknown, the Knight of armour green!
He who by coy disdain and silent pride
Had touch'd a heart to pleading love denied.

In combat late with Egypt's King engaged
By Arsouf's stream, his dauntless valour waged
The lengthen'd contest, till when Asia's lord
With England stood, they sheath'd the mutual sword;
Nor since reviving war with fiercer hate
Her fires rekindled, had the warriors met.   890
Now warn'd by Salem's King, who love-inspired,
Mark'd where the Moslem Chiefs from fight retired,
With him he followed, and as Lusignan
To aid the Queen, to raise Evanthe ran,
For Hermesind he rush'd to fiercest fight,
For Hermesind,—who check'd her weary flight.
They fought, till Adel spurring through the shade,
" And think not thus to shun my sword," he said,
" Turn, Christian! turn; and thou young Prince, resign
The fight unjust, yon craven's spoils are mine."   900

   " Behold me here prepared," the Knight replied,
" For both or either; be ye both defied!
Yet better might thy taunts be aim'd at those
Who quit the field to war on female foes."

   " On female foes!" indignant Adel cries,
As round the wood he rolls his searching eyes;
" Now praised be Alla! praised the Prophet's name,
No true believer shares this deed of shame.

Thou, through thy visor'd casque so rarely seen,
Whate'er thou art, apostate, Nazarene, 910
And thou young Fatimite, far hence remove, ʸ
Too much ye trespass on my brother's love.
And know ye not that, when a city falls,
E'en the rude conqueror spares the haram walls ? ᶻ
Christian ! in combat we shall meet again —
Meanwhile accept for each fair victim slain,
Whate'er the price, her double worth in gold,
Or two, the fairest that my harams hold.
Hundreds they boast that well might pay the debt,
Whose veils to me were never lifted yet."— 920

" Moslem ! not thus a woman's worth we prize,"
With all a Christian's anger, Albert cries.
" Say, should thy walls some Cleopatra boast,
More fair than her for whom a world was lost,
Poor were that ransom for Matilda paid,
Our Monarch's sister, now dishonour'd, dead."

" Thy foul reproach, ungenerous Christian, spare,
Nor stain our glory with so base a fear,"
Cried Mosul's Prince ;—" by flattering demons led,
We sought in bonds to bind each royal maid, 930
That he who fills Damascus' walls with gloom,
Who makes our towns a waste, our lands a tomb,

Who loves the widow's and the orphan's cry,
Might find one grief to cloud his victory;
Nor farther had our sated rage pursued,
Nor stain'd one sword in unoffending blood;
Then fear not for your captive, none," he cried,
" Dares doubt the spotless faith of Almahide."

That dreadful name which oft had spread despair
Through marshall'd ranks, now silenced every fear.
" Enough," the monarch said, distrust and shame
Fly from her presence—I forbear to blame.
And you, brave Christians! let your valiant Lord
Forego his fears, and trust an Arab's word.
We fight as sovereigns, not as fiends, to gain
Or guard our faith, our glory, and our reign.
Revenge we love, yet boast our hearts have won
A generous spark from yon all-bounteous sun;
And by that only God, whose ruling will
Perchance for good designs this seeming ill,
By highest heaven, where saints and angels dwell,
By the dread bridge and endless flames of hell,
To England's King an Arab's faith I plight
To bring the Princess with the orient light."   950

He spoke, and from the scene of contest leads,
Abash'd and sad young Aladin proceeds;

While Gaul's proud maid her rival lingering view'd,
And curs'd the sword that fail'd to shed her blood.
Oh! if our will such baleful power could give,
No mortal eye might meet that glance and live.

  But Hermesind, whose vanity was still
Her beacon-light, that led to good or ill;
Graceful before her brave preserver knelt,
Pour'd all her thanks, and more than all she felt. 960
Oh! who could hear unmoved, of mortal mould,
Such gratitude, so eloquently told
In tones so sweet, from lips of hue so bright,
Such glowing cheeks, and eyes of liquid light!
Yet if slight waving of the warrior's crest,
Or silken scarf, some rebel thoughts confest,
His words were calm and few.—" T'was knighthood's
    care,
Her boast, her oath, to guard and aid the fair,
T'was duty and no more."—" Yet hear," she said,
" Nor deem that guile inspires a simple maid,   970
Or curious folly, if I fain would know,
To whom my life, or more than life, I owe?
Whate'er the cause that makes thee court disguise,
My lips shall guard the trust my heart will prize,

Safe as the wealth to caves of ocean given,
Nor breathed, save in my orisons to heaven;
Those orisons which call its saints to save,
For deathless fame, the generous and the brave."

 In swifter beat the heaving scarf appear'd,
The murmur of preluding speech was heard;   980
When, as by some mistrustful thought inspired,
He bowed a mute refusal, and retired.

 Baffled again, her angry feelings rise,
And lightnings flash indignant from her eyes,
They glance upon Ricardo's pallid face,
And all again is gentleness and grace.
Devoted more, but less by fortune blest,
Still the fall'n tree his wounded limbs opprest.
Who knew like her each fascinating art,
In dreams of heaven to lap the willing heart!   990
Her eyes shone bright in tears, her tender hand
Was gentlest, first, to fix each needful band;
Nor her warm thanks with less of nature came,
Though often check'd, as if by virgin shame;
Or fear to raise,—since love to hope is prone—
Hopes that her calmer reason might disown.

 Drest by such hands could wounds forbear to close,
Could heart so happy vainly court repose?

As on his couch a lingering moon he lay,
Bright rainbow visions wiled its lapse away. 1000
His was a courteous soul, whose livelier powers
Could gild the stream of pleasure's social hours;
But 'twas a radiance cold and rarely given,
Like gleams of sunshine on December's heaven.
Sweet were his songs, and framed with tuneful art
To soothe or soften, not to raise the heart;
While love, which fires the proud to arduous deeds,
In his mild breast its native sadness feeds.
Yet ne'er had pleasure spread such halcyon calm,
Ne'er seem'd his hours so redolent of balm, 1010
As now, though oft to thrilling pangs a prey—
(Unheeded pangs)—for still with every day
She came, like some angelic guest, to bring
To his exhausted thoughts another spring.
Short was her stay, by modesty restrain'd,
Yet like soft fragrance on his soul remain'd
Some look, some motion, as she left the tent,
Some word or tone, as o'er his couch she bent.
He longs for strength, for her to fight, to die;
He trembles lest his dream of bliss should fly. 1020

END OF BOOK VIII.

NOTES.

NOTES

TO

CŒUR DE LION.

BOOK I.

Note (a), page 8, line 42.

Alkarmel, fellest of Messiah's foes.

MOUNT CARMEL is memorable in Sacred History as the spot on which Elijah confounded the priests of Baal, and also as the scene of his retirement. The cavern which the Prophet inhabited is still shewn. This mountain seems to have been indeed one of those " high places " selected for religious ceremonies in all ages, and to have witnessed them in all their variety. After the fire of Heaven had thus once destroyed idolatry, we have the authority of Suetonius, that a pagan divinity of the same name with the mountain was worshipped there. He had an altar, and sacrifices, but no temple or statue. Him the Romans transformed into the Carmelian Jove, to whom Vespasian offered a sacrifice, when he came into Syria to subdue the rebel Jews. The Convent of the Virgin next occupied the height; it was in its turn profaned by Mahommedan superstition, but was afterwards restored, and gave rise to the military order of " Our Lady of Mount Carmel," instituted by Henry the Fourth of France. I believe this convent is still in existence. Carmel has shared the fate of the rest of Syria, where neglect and oppression have made a desert of regions that nature formed a garden. Its summit is craggy, but even there a few wild vines and olive trees attest the fertility for which it was once so famous, and whence it derived its name, Carmel signifying in Hebrew, " the vine of God." The mountain forms one of the most remarkable headlands on the coast of the Mediterranean.

Note (b), page 9, line 77.

Joy! for this night the Queen Sybilla dies.

Sybilla was daughter to Amalric King of Jerusalem, by his first wife Agnes de Courtenay, only child to Joceline de Courtenay, third and last Count of Edessa. She was first married to William Longsword, son of William the Third, Marquis of Montferrat, and elder brother of Conrad of Montferrat. By him she had issue Baldwin the Fifth. Her first husband dying, Sibylla married Guy de Lusignan, whom she is said to have chosen for his personal beauty. At her father's death, her brother, Baldwin the Fourth, succeeded to the throne of Jerusalem: but he was a leper, and his talents, though considerable, were not equal to supply the inexperience of youth and the defects of nature. He soon fell a victim to his malady, and the unhappy realm of Jerusalem, already involved in dangers from which only the greatest prudence and courage could extricate it, devolved on the infant son of Sybilla and Montferrat. Raymond Count of Tripoli was chosen as his guardian and regent of the kingdom: but he insisted, as he was next male heir to the throne, that the custody of the young king should be shared by Joceline Count of Edessa. The character of Raymond might have been deemed above suspicion, but the event shewed that his fears were prudent, for in less than six months the little Baldwin died, and his mother succeeded him as Queen, not without suspicion of having contributed to his death.

Note (c), page 11, line 109.
The Cyprian sceptre base Comnenus sways.

At the period when the poem commences, Cyprus was in the possession of the usurper Isaac Comnenus, the descendant of that Alexius who filled the throne of Constantinople during the first Crusade, and whose hollow friendship, perhaps, cost more lives to the noble leaders whom he had invited from Europe, than his enmity could have done. It is impossible to read the history of those times, without wondering at the duplicity of the Greeks and the forbearance of the Latins. The feeling that the Greeks were Christians, and that their vow was to combat the enemies of Christianity seems to have had extraordinary force upon bands of warriors strong enough to have crushed the faithless empire, and who when in Europe were not remarkable for their moderation. In the middle ages (notwithstanding the glorious exception of two Emperors of the Comnenian line) the name of Greek appears indeed to have been synonymous with every possible aggravation of meanness, treachery, cowardice, and cruelty. Vinsauf, in a furious tirade against the Greeks, observes, that the vices of their ancestors remained to them, but that their virtues had all passed into Italy. The perfidy of Sinon, the craft of Ulysses, and the atrocity of Atreus, were still theirs by inheritance.

Note (d), page 12, line 148.

Have we not crush'd Imperial Conrad's host?

These lines allude to the disastrous event of the second Crusade. The Emperor Conrad the Third of Germany and Louis the seventh of France pursued different roads through Asia Minor; and the valour of the Seljouk Turks of Iconium was not more fatal to the followers of Conrad, than the perfidy of the Greek guides, who injured their health by supplying them with unwholesome provisions, and either led them into deserts, where myriads perished from famine, or betrayed them to their enemies. The Emperor, at last, with less than one tenth of his original numbers, succeeded in joining the army of Louis, which had also met with many disasters, but was in greater force, and had been amused by the Greeks with tales of the feigned successes of Conrad. The battle of Laodicea followed, in which the Turks suffered a defeat so signal, that the Greeks acknowledged the moderation of the Crusaders in not having levelled Constantinople with the ground. But many miseries again awaited them on their road to Antioch, and the second Crusade terminated in the fruitless attempt on Damascus. The town was already in the extremity of despair, when the Syriac Christians became jealous that their western allies should enjoy the spoils which their valour was about to win, and by treacherously prevailing on them to change their point of attack, rendered the whole expedition abortive.

Note (e), page 12, line 153.

We fill'd with leprosy the courts of kings!

The successes of Saladine had been assisted by an earthquake, which overthrew the fortifications of several cities that would otherwise have opposed him. These lines allude also to the comets and meteoric phenomena so often noticed in the history of the Crusades, to the frequent famine and drought from which the Christians suffered, and to the leprosy of Baldwin the Fourth.

Note (f), page 13, line 170.

Who trifles with his friendship, sports with fate.

The conduct of Frederic Barbarossa, in resenting the duplicity of the Greeks was more spirited than that of his precursors had been. In one instance he shewed his resentment by causing the standard of the western Empire to float from the walls of Constantinople, and Isaac Angelus found it thenceforward prudent to treat with somewhat better faith, a monarch that he found had the will as well as the power to punish him. The Sultans of Iconium followed the double policy of the Greeks, by feigning a friendship for the army whose approach they dreaded, and then profiting by its fancied security. But Frederic, though attacked in the mountains, and at disadvantage, when the two divisions of his army were at a distance from each other, gave the Turks a signal defeat. The Emperor and his son, Frederic Duke of Suabia, both distinguished themselves highly in this engagement.

Note (g), page 19, line 293.

"To rule the Eagle!" cried the Prince of Tyre.

The house of Montferrat was descended from the Dukes of Saxony, and was at this period one of the most powerful in Italy. William the Third, surnamed the *Old*, had married a sister of the Emperor Conrad. He had four sons: Boniface, who received the crown of Thessaly as the reward of his achievements at the taking of Constantinople in 1203; William *Longsword*, the second son, has been already named as the first husband of Sybilla. Reynier, the third, died in the Holy Land about three years before the loss of Jerusalem. The fourth son, who after his imperial uncle bore the name of Conrad, was the most distinguished; and the graces of his person were no less remarkable than his valour. After the surrender of the Holy City, he arrived at Tyre in the very moment when the inhabitants were about to deliver up the town to Saladine. His presence inspired fresh courage, he forced the Soldan to raise the siege, and thus preserved the only city which the Christians still retained in Palestine. His assumption of the government and title of Prince of Tyre was a natural sequel to these events, but it is to be regretted that his subsequent violence destroyed the esteem which he had acquired by his talents.

Note (h), page 20, line 304.

Or when her warlike peers no more obeyed.

Scarcely had Baldwin the Fifth expired, when his mother became desirous to reign in his stead, and disdained neither stratagem nor false promises to satisfy her ambition and that of Lusignan. While the Count of Tripoli assembled the Barons of the empire at Napolose, the daughter of Amalric, acting by the advice of Heraclius, Patriarch of Jerusalem, and Eudon, Grand Master of the Templars, announced her intention of separating herself from her husband, and choosing a warrior who was able to defend the kingdom: on condition that the Barons would acknowledge as king, him whom she should elect. The Barons, who expected that her choice would fall upon Raymond, readily consented. The gates of Jerusalem were closed, and Sybilla repaired to the church of the Holy Sepulchre, attended by her nobles, and crowned with a garland. Mass was sung before the sacred tomb. Heraclius vowed fidelity to her in the name of the clergy and the people, pronounced aloud her divorce from Lusignan, and commanded her in the name of Heaven to bestow her hand and the sceptre on the man whom she believed to be most worthy. Sybilla next prostrated herself, to implore the guidance of Providence in her choice; then rising, she raised the chaplet from her head, and placed it on with solemnity on the brows of Lusignan, declaring that " man could not separate those whom Heaven had united." The nobles felt that they were duped: and if a few, imposed upon by the splendour of the scene, applauded the conjugal fidelity and affection of Sybilla, the majority foresaw the evils which so imprudent a choice was likely to bring upon Jerusalem; and the friends of Raymond, in particular, felt indignant at the elevation of one, who while he filled the high office of Regent during part of the reign of Baldwin the Fourth, had proved how unequal he was to the government of a kingdom, already involved in difficulty and danger.—Hoveden, Michaud, Mills, &c.

Note (i), page 21, line 342.

Like some strong tower, stood Austrian Leopold.

Leopold Duke of Austria. Shakespeare has introduced him in his play of King John, but he died four or five years before the accession of that monarch.

Note (k), page 23, line 376.

Your robes polluting with a Herald's blood.

The Prince of the Assassins, stimulated, as is supposed, by the wish to be freed from a tribute which he paid to the Grand Master of the Templars, sent offers of alliance to Baldwin the Fourth, and a proposal to embrace Christianity with all his followers. To these advantageous terms Baldwin had agreed, but the Grand Master was loth to give up his tribute, and as the Envoy left the King's tent, two of the Templars (some say Eudon himself) fell upon him, and dispatched him with their daggers.

Note (l), page 23, line 392.

The bonds of life, this pains my sires in heaven.

In this part of my story I have followed the judgment of Messrs. Michaud, and Marin, who endeavour to repair the injustice which appears to have been done to the character of Raymond by the greater number of historians. His discontent at the election of Lusignan to the throne of Jerusalem, led him to form a party in favour of Thoron, but Thoron declined the proffered honour, and Raymond retired to his county of Tripoli. Lusignan, instead of conciliating him, determined to besiege his town of Tiberias, or Tabaria; Raymond prepared to defend it, and in his anger implored the assistance of Saladine. At this time dreadful portents were seen in heaven and earth, and the Knights Templars and Hospitallers were nearly all cut off by a Musulman army, which had advanced into Galilee, on its way, it was said, to the assistance of Raymond. The terror of this defeat appeased the discords of the Christians, and Lusignan and Raymond were reconciled. The forces of the kingdom assembled in the plain of Saphoury, to the number of fifty thousand, when intelligence was received that Saladine had taken and burned the town of Tiberias, and now besieged in its citadel the wife and three sons of Raymond, who intreated his instant succour. The Barons assembled in the tent of Lusignan, when Raymond demanded to be heard: " I am about to offer," he said, " a counsel that will surprise all; but I give it with more confidence as it is contrary to my interest." In a word, he declared that he could not prefer the defence of his own family and possessions to the safety of the Christians of the East; the army now assembled at Saphoury was their only hope, and that to lead it into a dry and barren desert would be its destruction. He swore before God and men that he would voluntarily abandon the county of Tripoli, and all his possessions to save the town of Jesus Christ. Their only interest was to destroy Saladine, and to preserve defenders to Jerusalem; and that all the evils which might fall upon him would become a source of good, since he endured them for the cause of his Saviour, and the welfare of his people. The more generous this advice appeared, the less was it believed sincere. The Grand Master of the Templars blinded by his hatred to Raymond, interrupted him many times with allusions to his treaty with Saladine, and said that *the hair of the wolf might be seen under the sheep's skin.* When Raymond invoked the name of Christ, Eudon replied that *Mahommed* would sound better from a traitor. Raymond scorned to recriminate, but offered to submit to death if events were not as he had predicted. Marin compares the blindness of the Christians to that of the Trojans concerning the prophecies of Cassandra. They persisted in accusing Raymond of treason. Yet the force of his reasoning prevailed, and it was determined to remain at Saphoury. But during the night the Grand Master of the Templars came to Lusignan, and filled him with the blackest suspicions of the treachery of Raymond. The weak Prince gave orders for the army to advance: for the first time he was obeyed, and it was for the ruin of the Christians. This army was indeed the only hope of Palestine, for even this was equipped from sources not her own. England had already begun to supply the necessities of other nations; it was supported by the treasures which Henry the Second had sent to Jerusalem; and to associate that monarch in the glory of the expedition, the arms of England were emblazoned on the banners of the Christian forces. All was lost at Tiberias: the wood of the True Cross was taken, the army was annihilated, and Lusignan a captive. If the heroic valour of Raymond on this dreadful day, if the fulfilment of his words, be not evidence of his truth, it might be inferred from the wildness and incongruity of his calumniators. Raymond found refuge at Tyre, and on his return to defend Tripoli, was attacked by a mortal illness, caused by grief at the downfal of the Christians, and the shame of having been suspected of treason by those for whom he had sacrificed every thing. His ardent character changed to a deep melancholy, which ended in madness. The time of his death is variously stated. I shall say nothing of the idle stories, that he and Saladine had drank human blood as a pledge of friendship, that he fought masked against the Templars, that he had embraced Islamism, that he was smothered in his bed by his people, who wished to force him to surrender, or that he was stabbed by the envoys of Saladine. Mr. Mills, I perceive, is among those who doubt the fidelity of Raymond, but in my opinion the very violence of his character places it above suspicion.

Note (m), page 25, line 427.

But lauded Hubert's martial pilgrimage.

Hubert, Bishop of Salisbury, and afterwards Primate of England, deserves to be singled out even from a crowd of heroes; he was one of the bravest warriors of the third crusade, and not more distinguished for his martial prowess than his Christian virtues. This prelate and the amiable Hugh, Bishop of Lincoln, form a striking contrast with the haughty Philip, Bishop of Beauvais, and the libertine Geoffrey, Archbishop of York (son of Rosamond), who became the helmet much better than the mitre.

Note (n), page 26, line 449.

Till contrite hearts appeas'd the offended Lord.

As the crusades were supposed to be undertaken under the immediate sanction of Heaven, those who embarked in them expected some evident interposition of divine favour in their behalf. They disdained the common precautions of war, and murmured when they felt those evils to which their own imprudence had exposed them. In those cases, the clergy and leaders who shared the enthusiasm of their followers, or who were at least interested to support it, found their best resource in the assertion, that the crimes of the Crusaders (which were in truth sufficiently glaring) had forfeited the favour of the Almighty, and that it was in vain to hope for success, until a general reformation of manners and morals, accompanied with sincere penitence and humiliation, should first have washed away the stain. The appeal was seldom vain, reformation followed, and the enthusiasm which accompanied it frequently prepared the way to the anticipated success; and though the good resolutions which had been formed, quickly vanished in the delirium of victory, the licentiousness which ensued only gave fresh force to the next admonition. Antioch witnessed two or three of these alternations of feeling. While that city was besieged by the Christians, a severe famine led to the most horrible crimes: but the exhortations of the pious Adhemar were at length answered by a return to the strictest rules of moral discipline. Immediately afterwards Godfrey recovered from a violent illness, and a victory was obtained over the forces which were hastening to the assistance of Baghasian. It would have been heresy to doubt that these happy events were marks of the restored favour of Heaven. Again, when the Christians, having conquered Antioch, were in their turn besieged by Kerboga, and reduced to extremity by a famine still more dreadful than the former, the " pious fraud" of the Sacred Lance was the harbinger at once of the restoration of order, and the signal victory which annihilated the army of that prince. Mr. Mills has drawn a very pleasing picture of the good conduct of the Christian army before Nice. " The camp presented the rare and edifying spectacle of a chaste and sober soldiery; and although not free from the common disposition of exalting past ages at the expense of the present, the confession was drawn from the severest censors, that there was far more virtue among the crusading warriors, than among the hosts of Israel in old time. The simplicity and purity of the early church were revived. So affectionate was the union between the brotherhood, that all things were held in common. The generals not only commanded and fought, but watched, and did the most humble duties of the camp: so that the officer and the soldier were scarcely to be distinguished. Artificial discipline was needless, when virtue pervaded every part of manners."—*History of the Crusades*, vol. 1, ch. iv.

Note (o), page 29, line 513.

My mother gave me, an unwilling bride.

Mr. Mills has justly observed, that in the middle ages, whenever a divorce was desired, a pretext was easily found. Yet if ever nonage could be admitted as a plea, it must be allowed that Isabelle was entitled to claim it, as she was but eight years old when her mother bestowed her on the Count of Thoron.

Note, page 30, line 543.

Four reverend priests the BOOK OF LIFE sustain.

This Standard is described by Vinsauf and most of the writers on the third crusade. Mailly observes, from Le Gendre that the custom of placing the banner on the top of a tree, itself raised on a scaffold, and drawn on a car by six oxen with velvet housings, adorned with the arms of the leader, was prevalent in the twelfth century, and that it came from Italy. The Crusaders probably owed the idea to the Pisans and Genoese, who sustained a considerable share in the siege of Acre. Vinsauf evidently speaks of it as a novelty. The fashion appears to have lasted only about one hundred and twenty years, being found cumbrous and inconvenient. It must have been almost impossible for a defeated army to save its standard.

Note, page 30, line 544.

Near it rode Lusignan, whose vest displayed.

For the arrangement of this battle see *Marin; Histoire de Saladin*, vol. ii. p. 184.

Note, page 32, line 570.

Who in Tabaria's field its guards subdued.

Tekieddin Omar was the nephew of Saladine, and one of the bravest of his generals. He was the bitter enemy of the

Christians, who had but too many reasons to deplore his valour. At the fatal battle of Tiberias he took Lusignan prisoner, and also the True Cross, which Rufinus, the Bishop of Acre, according to custom, carried that day in battle. The Bishop was armed with a cuirass, contrary to the usage of all the other Prelates, who before him had carried that Holy Wood unarmed, yet had never received a wound, whereas he, notwithstanding his armour, was shot quite through the heart with an arrow. Omar, in presenting the cross to Saladine, observed, " it should seem, from the lamentations of the Franks, that this wood is not the least important fruit of our victory." After Saladine's entry into Jerusalem, the splendid gold Cross which the Christians had erected on the summit of the mosque built by the Caliph Omar, and which occupied the site of the Temple of Solomon, was cast down and dragged through the streets in the mud, to the Tower of David, amid the lamentations of the Christians."—*Maimbourg, Marin, &c.*

Note, page 34, line 628.

Five dauntless Mamlukes, in his palace bred.

With this slender guard, five of his principal Mamlukes (for the number is specified) Saladine passed many times through the enemy, and endeavoured to rally his flying troops. Speaking of the Mamlukes, Marin observes, " we must not confound those whom we have hitherto called Mamlukes, with those that afterwards reigned in Egypt. This name properly signifies a domestic slave, and was given to those who were particularly attached to the service of the Prince or his Emirs. In the commencement the Mamlukes were the children of the concubines of the Sultan, but afterwards the latter purchased slaves, of which they formed their *halca* or guard; and they often passed from the vilest employments to the command of armies. Saladine was the first who formed them into a body of soldiers, subjected them to severe discipline, and employed them on the most important occasions. It should be remarked that these Mamlukes wore a sort of yellow livery, yellow being a colour which distinguished all his household and which was affected by those who wished to appear attached to it. His successors in Egypt bought many of these slaves, who became at last the principal force of the state. They defended it at first with courage, but concluded by invading it themselves. We must not forget to say, for the history of manners, that these Mamelukes *wore the arms* of the Sultan, but that, to distinguish individuals, bars of crimson, roses, birds, griffins, and other figures were added to them upon the shield."—*Histoire de Saladin,* tom. i.

Note (p), page 36, line 674.

In sable folds (the hue of Islam,) bound.

Under the Abassides, black became the standard of the Caliphs, and has ever since continued the distinctive colour of Islam, or Mahommedan orthodoxy, in opposition to the green banner of the Fatimite Caliphs, and the white one of the Suffees " the Inspired."' It has always been the custom for the principal Arabian or Moorish families to distinguish themselves and their followers by appropriate colours; of which many amusing exemplifications may be found in the History of the Quarrels of the Abencerrages and the Zegries, in the " Civil Wars of Granada." Yellow was the peculiar badge of the house of Ayoub, the father of Saladine; and the Soldan, no less proud to display his orthodoxy than his personal power, always took care to blend the *black and yellow* in his standards. Omar, as the nephew of Saladine, bore a yellow plume, and a yellow banner. In his wars with the Christians, the Koran was always carried in state in the army of Saladine; a proof that he, no less than the Crusaders, considered himself engaged in a religious contest.

Note (q), page 37, line 684.

Observes the battle, and on Mestoc calls.

Some writers mention five governors of Acre; others only two. It appears certain that Karacous and Mestoc were the highest in authority. Aboul Hagia, and the other two whose names are mentioned, were probably no more than lieutenants.

Note (r), page 39, line 707.

Unheeding Erard pass'd his brother by.

Erard, Count of Brienne, and Andrea his brother. This trait is mentioned by most of the writers on the Third Crusade as a striking instance of the effect of momentary fear on a mind naturally brave. Perhaps Erard did not even see his brother.

Note (s), page 42, line 769.

Who own'd a kinsman in the noble Kurd.

Ismail commanded the Saracen reserve in this battle. Saladine belonged to a tribe of Kurds.

Note (t), page 43, line 806.

But Lusignan his rival's danger saw.

Perhaps there is no moment of Lusignan's life in which he appears to so much advantage, as in this rescue of his most virulent enemy. Vinesauf, who omits no opportunity of expressing his dislike to Conrad, says " he was unworthy of his humanity." It does not appear to have inspired him with gratitude. Lusignan would perhaps have been the victim of his generosity, but for the prompt assistance of his brother Geoffrey.

Note (u), page 44, line 808.

He call'd for aid, th' illustrious Glanville came.

Ranulph de Glanville is named among the Norman Knights, and it is therefore probable that he was a Norman by birth as well as by descent. In his youth he was a distinguished warrior; he led the armies of Henry the Second more than once, and took the King of Scotland prisoner at Northallerton. He was afterwards Justiciary of England, and is reported to have been the author of the law-book which bears his name; the earliest which gives any coherent account of English laws, and perhaps the first treatise on jurisprudence which appeared after the dissolution of the Roman empire; but Mr. Reeves (Hist. of English Law, vol. i. p. 121) seems to think it unlikely that in those days a great political character should have been also an author. He suggests the possibility that the work might bear his name, from having been composed under his patronage and superintendance. When Henry the Second died, Glanville, to avoid engaging in his old age under a new master, took the cross, and sailed to Palestine, where he seems to have arrived soon after the commencement of the siege of Acre, about two years previous to the battle in which he fell.

Note (w), page 44, line 826.

Lulo, and Karacous, and Mestoc's might.

Lulo was the commander of the marine of Egypt, but he fought on land in this battle.

Note, page 45, line 830.

The heaven descended Oriflamme unfold.

The Oriflamme, or sacred banner of France, was reported to have descended from heaven, in honour either of Clovis or Charlemagne. It was, according to Mailly, a square banner of flame-coloured taffeta, without figures or embroidery, but with three deep indentures at the bottom; and suspended to a gilded lance. Hence was derived its compound name, the word *flamme* relating to the colour of the silk, and being also a name commonly given to banners of that form. Other writers have said that it was embossed with the golden lilies of France; but they have possibly confounded it with the royal standard, of which notice will be taken in a subsequent note. Mr. Southey, in his Joan of Arc, states that the Oriflamme was originally used only in wars against the infidels, and that in after years it became a signal that no quarter was to be given; he adds that when Philip (as reported by some historians) erected the Oriflamme at Crecy, Edward in return raised up his burning Dragon as the English signal for massacre.—The Oriflamme was in fact only the standard of the abbey of St. Denis, and borne in its wars by the Counts of Vexin, as *Avoués* or secular champions of the abbey, till Philip the First united the Vexin to the Crown, when this banner being in high reputation, he gave it place before even his own standard; the taste of the age enveloped its history in fable, and it was believed to ensure victory. The fallacy was at length proved, and the Kings of France found it expedient to forget it, or to feign that it had been reclaimed by Heaven under Charles the Seventh.

Philip Augustus, previous to his embarkation for the Crusade, received the Oriflamme, and the *bourdon*, or pilgrim's staff, with great solemnity in the church of St. Denis.

Note (x), page 48, line 908.

And the glad seas feel lighten'd of their weight.

In ages when the ocean has become the readiest means of communication between distant regions, it is hardly possible for us to conceive adequately the terrors of such an expedition as the voyage from France or England to Jerusalem in the twelfth century, and it is probable, that nothing short of the almost incredible waste of human life which had been occasioned by the land journies of the pilgrims, would have prompted the hazardous enterprize. In the time of Magnus the third of Norway, Skopte Augmundson, allied to the Royal Family, had warm discussions with the king about the succession of an estate, and not obtaining his demands, left the court. In 1100 he equipped five vessels for the East, and took with him his three sons: but they all died before they reached Palestine. He was however the first Scandinavian who had passed the straits. The ardour of crusading was kindled. Sigurd, one of the sons of Magnus, embarked from Norway with sixty vessels; was well received on his way by Henry the first of England; took the fort of Cintra in Lusitania from the Saracens, beat them next at Lisbon and Alcazar; twice fought their piratical fleet, passed the straits, and in the Isle Formentera attacked the cave of some infidel pirates. It was overhung by a rock, which the Norwegians mounted, and crushed them with stones; then lighted wood before its mouth, and almost stifled the brigands, who made a desperate sally, but in vain; they were all destroyed. Sigurd gained a great booty, and received the solemn thanks of Yvica and Formentera for their deliverance. He was afterwards kindly received by Roger the Second of Sicily, and in 1110 landed at Ascalon, whence he made the pilgrimage to Jerusalem, and assisted at the siege of Sidon. The voyage had occupied more than two years, and this expediton, which has been strangely neglected by historians, was considered as one of the most remarkable of those which occurred during the Crusades. But it was only the nations of the Baltic and Adriatic who possessed any share of maritime spirit or power. In the days of Charlemagne, France had something like a navy, but it declined under his feeble successors, and was annihilated after the usurpation of Hugues Capet. England was not better provided. The Saxons had lost all the naval pride of their ancestors, and the Normen, or Normans, whose Danish forefathers had been the scourge of Britain, after their conquest of England, bounded their voyages to the passage of the channel. Genoa, Pisa, Venice, and the Saracens of Barcelona, engrossed the whole commerce of Europe, and Philip Augustus and RICHARD were alike compelled to hire from the Genoese the vessels which conveyed them to Palestine. Nor were these vessels the floating castles of modern England. Closely resembling the Liburnian galleys of the Romans, they trusted more to oars than sails. The compass was not then in use, and every nautical art imperfect and ill understood. The relation which Hoveden and others have given of the voyage of RICHARD, proves how completely the pilots stuck to the shore, and how much they feared the element which they pretended to govern. Even in the thirteenth century it was rare for a British ship to be seen in the Mediterranean.—*Catteau Calleville, Révolutions de la Norvège.— Mailly, &c.*

BOOK II.

Note (a), page 54, line 30.

And Berengaria, his affianced bride.

Vinesauf speaks of the vessel which contained the Queens as being light and fragile.

Note (b), page 58, line 116.

Though stripes and slavery be the stranger's doom.

All those frightful tales of cruelty to the unhappy wanderer, which now appear almost as dreams of imagination, seem to have been realized in Russia during the middle ages. That country was then sunk in the abyss of slavery and ignorance—knowledge was forbidden, and even the recent introduction of an imperfect Christianity had not ameliorated the condition of the people. The unfortunate pilgrim who was shipwrecked, or led by any accident to that inhospitable shore, became a slave, and the attempt to return to his own country was punished with death.—*Mailly*, &c.

Note (c), page 59, line 141.
Methinks Byzantium's exiled Lords retain.

Cyprus was at this period under the dominion of Isaac Comnenus, nephew to Manuel Comnenus, the last of that house who filled the throne of Constantinople. In the disorders which followed on the usurpation of the imperial dignity by the infamous Andronicus, Isaac fled to Cyprus, and forging letters from the new emperor, and obtaining the assistance of the fleet, sent by William King of Sicily to the Crusades, he was acknowledged as governor of that island. But he soon threw off his feigned allegiance, and usurped the imperial title.

Note (d), page 59, line 148.
Was still a haven to the tempest tost.

" Henry so far abolished the barbarous and absurd practice of confiscating ships which had been wrecked on the coast, that he ordained, that if one man or animal were alive in the ship, that the vessel and goods should be restored to its owners."—*Hume, Henry II.*

Fuller commends RICHARD for confirming and extending these laws. The rules which he enacted for the maintenance of order on board his fleet, though strongly marked with the character of the times, seem to have been dictated by good policy. RICHARD has also had the credit of a set of regulations compiled in France under St. Louis, and chiefly borrowed from the " Consolato del Mare," or earliest maritime code of the middle ages, which was promulgated at Barcelona in the beginning of the thirteenth century, and being acceded to by Philip Augustus and the Count of Provence, became binding in the Mediterranean. Mr. Hallam says, that these regulations were called the "Laws of Oleron," from an idle story that they were enacted by RICHARD I., while his fleet lay at anchor in that island on its voyage to the Holy Land. But it is unlikely that another nation should give an English Sovereign the credit of any improvement which it might itself have disputed, and I think it probable that the "Laws of Oleron" originated with RICHARD, though they may have been first collected and consolidated under St. Louis. The time of RICHARD was then too recent, for a forgery to have derived any advantage from the supposed antiquity.

Note (e), page 61, line 186.

They lanced their veins, and drank the mingled gore.

Vinesauf, after having observed that Cyprus, which had formerly been a source of wealth of Palestine, now became its enemy, adds, in speaking of Isaac, "Saladino dicebatur familiaris, et mutuum singuli hausisse cruorem, in signum et testimonium initæ invicem confæderationis, tanquam ex commixtione sanguinis exterius revera fierent consanguinei." The story is probably fabulous, but this superstitious and revolting rite of friendship does not yet seem to be totally obsolete among the Greeks.

Note (f), page 62, line 200.

As guests we enter'd, but as captives staid.
This account is principally taken from Vinesauf.

Note (g), page 63, line 234.

Or life or freedom may be theirs no more.

It appears to have been a custom with Isaac to rob and imprison strangers, but the rank and power of the guests whom he was now incensing should have told him that humanity was prudence.

Note (h), page 68, line 341.

A boat puts off—'tis Pembroke comes at last.

The name of the clerk was Hugo del Mare; the anecdote is from Vinesauf.

Note (i), page 69, line 349.

Reft of his ears, will scarce offend again.

It is a great proof of the respect in which RICHARD held the laws of honour and of nations, that notwithstanding his impetuous character, and the distressed state of his vessels, he should have waited so long for the return of his ambassadors, whom Isaac had the temerity to dismiss with insult. The incident of the Seneschal is from the metrical romance of "Cœur de Lion," in which the Emperor orders his *nose* to be cut off, and the reader is gravely informed that his face was spoiled in consequence. The story accords sufficiently with the historical character of the Usurper, and is likewise countenanced by a passage in Hoveden, which has been already noticed by Mr. Ellis.

Note, page 70, line 376.

'Tis Turnham's well known banner shines on high.

Sir Stephen Turnham, the King's Marshal and Treasurer.

Note, page 70, line 377.

One Bosco seized, for knighthood scorn'd not then.

William de Bosco, a Norman. See Vinesauf.

Note, page 71, line 399.

The gallant Robert, heir of Grosvenor's line.

Sir Robert le Grosvenor distinguished himself at Messina and at Cyprus, as well as in the subsequent events of the Crusades.

Note (m), page 75, line 490.

To bid the senseless blossoms whisper love.

The women of Cyprus are said to be skilful in the language of flowers, and to be remarkable for their attachment to them as an ornament, in preference to any other; notwithstanding that the island abounds in mineral wealth, and that the Paphian diamonds are exported to many nations of the Levant, who value them more highly.

Note (n), page 80, line 603.

The Persian tyrant's doom, to starve on gold.

The Persian monarch Khosroes, having an idea of causing his son Mardasan to be crowned as his successor, his eldest born Siroes, jealous of this preference, followed the example which Khosroes had set him in rebelling against his own father, and shut him up in a place called the Tower of Darkness, which he had built as the repository of his treasures. Gold and precious stones were heaped around him, and when he asked for food, he was bidden to feast on that wealth of which he had been so insatiable: and thus grief and hunger terminated the existence of a prince, whose reign had been among the most glorious in the Persian annals.

BOOK III.

Note (a), page 87, line 92.

From Tancred forced her freedom and her dower.

The author must here beg pardon of all who may be interested in the fame of William the Second of Sicily, for having, to suit her story, bestowed upon that monarch a less amiable character than history assigns to him; in short, for having arrayed him rather in his grandfather's colours than his own; though the appellations of the Bad and the Good are neither of them perfectly consistent with historical truth. At the death of William, Sicily became a scene of confusion. Constantia, daughter of Roger, the father of William, and married by the ambitious policy of Frederic Barbarossa to his second son Henry, afterwards emperor, was the legitimate heiress. But Tancred, the bastard offspring of William, with the aid of a strong party in the island, which could ill brook the idea of a foreign master, or a female reign, usurped the sovereignty, and threw Matilda the widow of William into prison. RICHARD arrived shortly after at Messina, when Tancred found it prudent to set her at liberty, and to compromise the claims which RICHARD made upon him for her dower, and for the wealth which William had bequeathed to Henry the Second of England, by the payment of twenty thousand ounces of gold as a compensation for the dower, twenty thousand ounces for the legacies, and by agreeing to equip ten gallies and six palanders or horse transports, for the use of the Crusaders.—*Hoveden, Mills, &c.*

Note (b), page 87, line 100.

To England's Primate gave the Cyprian crown.

Matthew Paris gives a particular account of the ceremonies of King RICHARD's Coronation in England; and as the forms of this august festival have lately been so much an object of public interest, I perhaps cannot do better than transcribe Dr. Milner's translation of, and remarks upon the passage, from his letter in " Carter's Specimens of Ancient Sculpture and Painting." " As we have in Matthew Paris, an account of the dress in which Henry the Second was buried, so have we of that in which RICHARD the First was crowned. Having described the ornaments, and mode of procession of the assistants, the monk of St. Alban's goes on : ' They then stripped him of all his clothes except his breeches and his shirt, which was unsewed between the shoulders, for the convenience of anointing; being thin-shod with sandals worked with gold; the Archbishop Baldwin anointed him King, upon the head, between the shoulders, and upon the right arm, with prayers appointed for this purpose. Having then laid a blessed linen cloth upon his head, he placed the bonnet thereon. Having then clad him with the royal robes, together with the tunic and dalmatic, the Archbishop gave him the sword to subdue the enemies of the Church, which being done, two Counts put on his spurs, and having then received his mantle, he was conjured by the Archbishop, on the part of God, not to accept of the royalty unless he intended to keep his oath. Then taking the crown from the altar, he delivered it to the Archbishop, who placed it on the King's head; he at the same time received the sceptre into his right hand, and the royal wand into his left. In this account I shall only notice the following particulars, namely, that the royal robes consisted partly of ecclesiastical ornaments, namely, the tunic and dalmatic, which are the principal dresses of deacons and subdeacons; secondly, that the spurs, which are the emblems of knighthood, were fixed on, not by the Archbishop, but by secular Barons; and lastly, that the King first took his crown into his own hands, and so delivered it to the Archbishop, to signify that he did not hold his temporal power of the Church. This circumstance was of the utmost importance, at a time when the Church had recently forbidden Bishops and Abbots to receive investiture from temporal princes, by the pastoral staff and ring, lest it should be inferred that temporal authority was held of the Crown.'"

Dr. Milner dismisses the subject with the mention of a few of RICHARD's exploits, and speaks of his valour and magnanimity with admiration as warm as they elicited from Mr. Gibbon.

Note (c), page 89, line 136.

What knights in tilting or Castilles excel.

A tournament usually lasted several days, and the exhibition of each day was different. As the tilt and the mêlée answered to the single combat and the battle, so did the Castilles to the assault of a castle. The attack was generally made with violence, and was often attended with bloodshed. In 1546 the Court of France passed the winter at La Roche Guion, and amused itself with the construction of Castilles, which were bombarded with snow balls. The weapon may appear harmless enough, yet these Castilles cost the life of the Duke D'Enghien. See M. de St. Palaye sur l'Ancienne Chevalerie.—Some idea of this martial sport may perhaps be formed from the attack on the Castle of Beauty, at Camacho's wedding, described in Don Quixote.

Note (d), page 89, line 144.

The martial pomp, the blaze of gems and gold.

The same pride which in the Greek empire reserved the purple for members of the imperial family, extended itself to the west, where scarlet was appropriated to knighthood. To this circumstance many allusions are made in Don Quixote, particularly when a scarlet mantle is thrown over him, on his arrival at the Duke's castle. Our forefathers were also much attached to costly furs, with which they bound or lined the mantle, as may be still seen in the state robes of our nobility. The favourite furs were the royal ermine, the miniver, the sable, the *gris*, and the vair, or grey squirrel. The knights sometimes wore surcoats of vair or other furs, whence they have been introduced in many families as the field of their armorial bearings.—*St. Palaye, &c.*

Note (e), page 90, line 148.

The swan, the pheasant, all that swim or soar.

The swan was one of those royal birds which were reserved for the state banquets of our chivalrous progenitors. Modern England is apt to think its flesh somewhat coarse and tough, and I believe that Norwich is the only town which retains so much of knightly manners as to have this bird regularly bred and fattened for its civic feasts, where its presence is indispensable.

Note (f), page 90, line 160.

Press'd from the golden grapes of Cyprian vines.

The Cyprus wines have long been celebrated. I have already mentioned the Commanderia, which is esteemed the best. It is principally made near Paphos, is sweet and syruppy, and may be kept open without spoiling.

Note (g), page 90, line 161.

Clairette in fuming beakers, and the juice.

Metheglin, mead, or hydromel, though much fallen from the high repute in which it was held by our Saxon ancestors (who could devise no greater delight for the souls of departed heroes, than to quaff this sparkling liquor from the skulls of their enemies), is still too well known to need explanation. Pigment, hypocras, and clairette seem to have been mixtures of wine with honey and spices. The hypocras was the most esteemed. The Clairette is said to have been sometimes served warm: perhaps, if we allow the substitution of honey for the modern luxury of sugar, which the Crusades had then but partially rendered known, the familiar names of mulled wine and negus may give a tolerable idea of these favourite beverages. Vinesauf speaks in high terms of the general magnificence of RICHARD's bridal feast. Nothing was to be seen but vessels of gold and silver, enriched with precious stones.

Note (h), page 91, line 174.

And each fantastic interlude between.

It was the custom at these state feasts to remain many hours at table, and the intervals between the several courses were beguiled by various "interludes," or theatrical representations, which took place on the very table round which the guests were seated. The personages which figured in these interludes were generally allegorical, and contrived to flatter the principal guests. The machinery was probably very inferior to that now used in pantomime, and the astonishment of the historian has undoubtedly not taken from its effect, yet it often raises an idea of more ingenuity than we are apt to expect from so rude an age. A more particular account of one of these interludes will be given in the note to the Vow of the Peacock. In the History of the Civil Wars of Granada the strange devices which the knights exhibit on their entry to the tournament held by Abenamar, and the wonderful transformations which occur, are so much in the style of these interludes, as to leave little doubt that the latter must have been of oriental origin.—*St. Palaye, &c.*

Note (i), page 94, line 233.

Chose for her home the court of high Navarre.

The courts and castles were excellent schools of courtesy, of politeness, and virtue, not only for the pages and squires, but also for young ladies or damsels. They were early instructed in those accomplishments which accorded with the manners of the age; were taught to receive with politeness the knights who arrived at the castle; to disarm them, to give them fresh clothes, serve them at table, and even attend to their wounds. But perhaps it would be difficult to convey a better idea of these feudal customs than is to be found in many of the speeches of that mirror of chivalry, the valiant knight of La Mancha. It was usual for the inferior knights to send their daughters for education to the castles of their feudal lord; but any lady of distinguished rank, beauty, and merit was solicited even by those whose lands lay at a distance, to accord to their children the advantages which they would derive from her instruction and example.—*St. Palaye, Ellis, &c.*

Note (k), page 95, line 255.

That touch'd with tuneful skill the mandoline.

The mandoline is a sort of guitar with only one string, and the skill of the musician is shewn in causing it to produce every variety of tone. The mandoline was a very favourite instrument with the antient Spaniards, and particularly employed in serenading.

Note (l), page 99, line 362.

Of stones and fire assail her haughty towers.

RICHARD caused many warlike engines to be made during his stay in Cyprus. To the largest of these the romance gives the name of Robynette.

Note (m), page 101, line 398.

In loftier numbers breathed Tyrtæan fire.

Bertrand de Born was one of the most extraordinary characters of his day, and Millot, (Hist. Littéraire des Troubadours), remarks on the manner in which he has been passed over, both by literary and political historians. He was Viscount of Hautefort, in Perigueux, and began his career by depriving his brother of his share of inheritance. The unhappy Constantine obtained the support of the Count of Perigord, and Talleyrand Lord of Montagnac (ancestor to that Talleyrand, who held so distinguished a place in the cabinet of Napoleon), while RICHARD of England, then only Count of Poitou, and the Viscount of Limoges, suspended their own quarrels to embrace the cause of the injured. On the other side, Bertrand was supported by the Viscounts of Ventadour, Segur, Gordou, Gévaudan, Tartas, and Turenne The Counts of Foix, Angoulême, and Armagnac; the Lords of Puiguillen, Clarensac, Gragnel and St. Astier, great Barons, of Perigord, and, to crown the whole, the Prince Henry, elder brother of RICHARD, was to take the command.

Many of these names are as uncouth as if they had been borrowed from the Tartars, and have little interest to an English ear, but their number shews the manner in which the fiery Bertrand always contrived to engage in his own quarrels all the princes who were within the reach of his friendship or his reproaches. As violent in love as in war, his impetuous passions exhaled themselves on every occasion in songs, which have more of the strength than the sweetness of poetry. By these he animated his soldiers, he encouraged his allies, he irritated his enemies, he sustained his own hopes; and, when the flame of war was extinguished, by these he had power to rekindle it. It would be useless to follow Bertrand through the story of his life, or rather of his wars, but some farther particulars will be given in another part of the poem. Suffice it to say, that RICHARD, by negotiation, contrived to avoid an engagement with his brother, and that Bertrand, after many alternations of friendship and hatred, finished by becoming the implacable enemy of the Lion-hearted King.

Note (n), page 102, line 412.

Since by his valour in Messina's fray.

During the residence of the English and French Monarchs at Messina, many affrays took place between the former and the natives; in one of these the English being victorious, RICHARD's standard was planted on the walls of the Town, in a spot which Philip considered as a part of his own quarters—Philip highly resented this insult, (the more that he was fond of displaying his feudal suzerainty) and insisted that the standard should be taken down; RICHARD obeyed and peace was restored. Vinesauf, however, says, that RICHARD would not remove his own standard but consented that the banner of the French King should be hoisted by its side.

Note (o), page 103, line 444.
Placed on a golden dish of rare device.

Of all the "noble birds," the peacock and the pheasant enjoyed the highest rank. They appeared only at the most splendid feasts, they were dressed with the richest spices, decorated with gold, and jewels, and borne to the table by the most distinguished ladies. To carve the peacock or the pheasant, was also one of the proud privileges of the bravest cavalier, and he to whom it was offered, was obliged in courtesy to protest his own unworthiness, and not to accept the office but upon "great persuasion." The vow of the peacock is perhaps one of the most romantic features of chivalry. The lady bore the honoured bird, which was always adorned with its gayest plumage, to every knight in succession, beginning with him who was first in valour and rank, and each knight was expected to signalize his courage and his love by some vow, made "before the peacock and the ladies." When this ceremony was completed, the peacock was borne back to the table, and placed before the chosen knight, who drawing his sword, began to carve it with great ceremony; and it was expected that he should so divide it, as to give a morsel to each guest, however great might be the number. To illustrate this subject, and that of the interludes already mentioned, I will abridge a part of the account given by M. de St. Palaye of the feast held at Lille, in 1453, at the court of Philip the Good, Duke of Burgundy, on account of the crusade against the Turks, who had just reconquered Constantinople: "At last the festal day arrived. If the magnificence of the Prince was admired in the number and abundance of the courses, it shone still more in the spectacles then known by the name of "*Entremets.*" Divers decorations, machines, figures of men and uncommon animals, trees, mountains, rivers, even a sea covered with ships, appeared in the hall. All these objects, intermixed with men, and birds and other living animals, were in motion in the hall or on the table, and represented a sort of allegorical ballet. It is difficult to suppose what must have been the size of this apartment, which contained a table so spacious, besides the multitude of guests and spectators. All at once a giant appeared, armed like a Saracen of Grenada. He conducted an elephant, who bore a castle, in which was a distressed dame clothed in black like a nun. In vain she requested the giant to stop: he led her forward to the table of the Duke, and there the captive lady, who was intended to represent Religion, recited a long complaint of the evils which she suffered from the Saracens, and the tardiness of those who ought to deliver her. Toison D'Or, King at Arms of the Order of the Fleece, then advanced, preceded by a long file of pursuivants, with a living pheasant on his finger, adorned with a collar of gold and gems, and presented to the Duke two damsels, of which one was Violante, his illegitimate daughter, and the other Isabeau of Neufchatel, daughter to the Lord of Montague; each lady being accompanied by a Knight of the Golden Fleece. Then the King at Arms offered the bird to the Duke, in the name of the ladies, who recommended themselves to the protection of their Sovereign, " to the end that the antient customs might be observed, according to which at feasts and other noble assemblies, a peacock or other noble bird was presented to the princes and lords, that they might make vows in behalf of the dames and damsels who besought their assistance." The Duke replied, " I vow first, to God my Creator, and to the most glorious Virgin, and after them to the pheasant and the ladies," to carry the war among the infidels, &c. &c. The signal was followed by all his court: each knight vowed to distinguish his courage against the Turks by some singular exploit; and imposed upon himself some arbitrary penance. Some would not sleep on a bed, others would not eat off a table-cloth, some would abstain from meat or wine on certain days, some would not wear a particular piece of armour, or would wear it day and night; some clothed themselves in sackcloth; in fact, the admirable ridicule of Cervantes was but the echo of these vows, which we that live in soberer days are apt to believe only the inventions of romance writers. The vows finished with a new spectacle. A lady clothed in white, like a novice, and bearing her name of *Grâce Dieu* in golden letters on her shoulder, led in twelve damsels, who represented the Virtues, which were to accompany the Crusaders. Each bore her name also embroidered in gold, and recited a few verses. These twelve ladies were the knightly virtues of Faith, Charity, Justice, Reason, Prudence, Temperance, Fortitude, Truth, Generosity, Diligence, Hope, and Valour. *Et toutes enfin commencèrent à danser en guise de mommeries, et à faire bonne chère pour remplir et rachever plus joyeusement la fête.*" One of the most singular of these fantastic scenes is the Vow of the Heron, which forms the subject of an ancient poem, printed also by St. Palaye. The Count D'Artois being banished from France, took refuge in London. One day his falcon caught a heron. The Count was at first indignant at so vile a capture, but afterwards gave orders to his " officiers de la bouche" to pluck and dress it. At night, when Edward the Third was at supper with his nobles, his Queen and her damsels, he entered, attended by minstrels and two noble ladies, bearing the heron between two silver plates, and advancing with great state to Edward, presented to him this most cowardly of birds (which is said even to fear its own shadow), as the reward of his indifference for a crown which he allowed to remain in the hands of his rival. Stung with this taunt, the enraged King swore that the year should not pass before Philip should see him in France, bearing fire and sword, to avenge this affront, were the French army ten times greater than his own. The Count D'Artois then went round to the nobles, and all hastened to bind themselves by some wild condition. The gallant Sir Walter Manny, whose ancestor accompanied RICHARD to the third crusade, engaged to take a certain town defended by Godemar du Fay. The Earl of Salisbury declared, in honour of the lady of his heart (the daughter of the Count D'Erby), that he would not uncover his right eye during the war. It is impossible to read the vow made by Queen Philippa without shuddering, for she called heaven to witness that she would destroy herself and her unborn infant, if the period of its birth should arrive before her husband had taken her across the seas, in acquittal of her oath. Edward was filled with horror at her words, and forbade the vows to be continued. The heron was cut up and eaten.

Froissart mentions, that at the battle of Poitiers there were many young knights who had one eye covered with cloth, and that they had sworn to their ladies not to restore it to its use till they had signalized their prowess in France. But most of these conceits were the refinements of a later age of chivalry than that in which the poem is placed.

Note (p), page 105, line 481.

Next sate D'Arselles, and high St. Valery's heir.

Louis D'Arselles and Bernard de St. Valery, two noble Normans, who are mentioned in the annals of that country among the " Preux Chevaliers" of the third crusade.

Notes (q) and (r), page 105, line 482.

And stout St. John, and Arnulph of St. Clair.

Roger de St. John, descended from the family of Ports, Lords of Basing, in Southampton, from the time of the Conquest, and maternally from William de St. John, of St. John, near Rouen, who came to England with William the Conqueror, as grand-master of the artillery, and supervisor of the waggons and carriages; whence the horses' hemes, or collar, was borne as his cognizance. One of his descendants was second wife of Bernard de St. Valery, Lord of

Ambroseden, in Oxfordshire, and who took his name from the castle and town of St. Valery, in France, whence the Conqueror sailed to England. This Bernard was, I believe, the grandfather of the Bernard already mentioned.

(r) Another Norman, who appears, in the history of that country, as one of its bravest crusaders.

Note (s), page 105, line 483.

Harvey, whose axe was never rais'd in vain.

The Harveys, anciently Fitz-Harveys, descended from Robert Fitz-Harvey, younger son of Harvey Duke of Orleans, who came over to England with William. Harvey de Yuon, in the reign of Henry the Second, died on his way to the Holy Land. His son, Henry de Harvey, accompanied RICHARD. Of this family come the Earls of Bristol.

Note (t), page 105, line 484.

And Nevile, skilful on the troubled main.

Henry de Nevile, descended from Gilbert de Nevile, who was admiral to William the Conqueror. Henry died without issue, but his sister, Isabel, was the maternal ancestor of the Earls of Abergavenny, who thence bear the name of Nevile, and the motto *Ne vile velis.*

Note (u), page 105, line 485.

Spencer, whose name was to his office due.

Hugh, fourth son of Thurstan le Despencer, steward to Henry the First. The office had been hereditary from the days of William the Conqueror, and gave its name to the family. The *de* was afterwards omitted by some branches, hence Spencer.

Note (x), page 105, line 486.

And Ferrars' valiant Earl, and Fortescue.

Henry, Earl of Ferrars, in Normandy, was rewarded by

the Conqueror with the lands of Etingdon, in Warwickshire, which had belonged to the family of Sewell from the time of Edward the Confessor. Sewell, however, still held the manor under Count Ferrars, whom he acknowledged as his feudal lord; and one of his descendants married the heiress of the Norman Earls, and thus regained his ancient honours. A similar fortune attended the representatives of many of the dispossessed Saxons.

Note (y), page 105, line 489.

Grosvenor, whose house held kindred with the Dane.

The ancestors of this family came from Denmark with Rollo, and settled in Normandy, where they took their name from the office of master of the royal buck-hounds. Gilbert le Grosvenor, who accompanied William to England, was nephew to Hugh Lupus, Count of Avranches, and first Earl of Chester, himself nephew to the Conqueror. The ample posssssions of this family in Cheshire and the adjacent parts of Wales are well known.

Note (z), page 106, line 501.

The brave De Vaux, in arms a mighty name.

Ranulph, or Robert de Vallibus, corrupted into De Vaux, one of the ancestors of the family of Dacre: that Barony having originally belonged to the family of De Vaux, of whom three brothers settled in England after the Conquest.

Note (aa), page 106, line 502.

And Roland, who from stout Belasius came.

Belasius (now Belasyse, Earls Fauconberg) was a Norman knight, who accompanied the Conqueror to England. I have ventured to substitute the family name of Roland for that of Robert, which belonged to his descendant under RICHARD the First.

Note (bb), page 107, line 522.

With Dædalean art for beauty's fairest flower.

Patric, Earl of Salisbury, being the King's lieutenant in Acquitaine, was slain by Guy de Lusignan (afterwards King of Jerusalem), on his return from a pilgrimage to St. James, in Galicia, leaving Ela his sole daughter and heir, of whom, says Dugdale, it is reported, that being so great an inheritrix, one William Talbot, an Englishman and an eminent soldier, took on him the habit of a pilgrim, and went into Normandy, where wandering up and down for two months, he at length found her out. He then disguised himself as a harper, and being practised in mirth and jesting, became well accepted at the court where she resided. Here becoming acquainted with her, he after a while took her to England, where he presented her to King RICHARD, who received her courteously, and bestowed her in marriage on William Long Espee, one of his father's sons by the Fair Rosamond, at the same time surrendering to William the Earldoms of Rosmar and Salisbury as her inheritance. Ela was descended from Walter de Eurus, Earl of Rosmar, who came to England with the Conqueror, and whose surname still lives in the noble house of Devereux.

Note (cc), page 107, line 426.

And Curzon's pride, the youthful Giraline.
Properly Robert or Richard, but Giraline is a family name.

Note (dd), page 108, line 533.

And Harley, sprung from that victorious Thane.
The family of Harley is so ancient, that that of Harlai, one of the most eminent in France, is believed to be descended from it. One of this house, in 1013, commanded an army under King Ethelred, and defeated Swane, King of

Denmark, near Pershore, thus saving the town. Sir William de Harley was distinguished under Godfrey of Bouillon, and was one of the first Knights of the Holy Sepulchre. He was buried in the Abbey of Pershore, where his tomb still remains, and was the only one which escaped in the time of Henry the Eighth.

Note (ee), page 108, line 537.
The noble Harcourt next, in whom combine.
The house of Harcourt is descended from Bernard, of the blood royal of Saxony, who being born in Denmark, was surnamed the Dane. He was chief counsellor to Rollo, and second in command in his descent on Normandy in 876. He was afterwards minister to William Longsword, Rollo's son and successor, and guardian to his child during his minority. He married a lady of the royal family of Burgundy; from his eldest son descended the ancient Earls of Leicester, while the offspring of the second took the name of Harcourt, and were renowned both in England and France. The Sir Robert Harcourt mentioned in the poem was the son of Ivo, and inherited his father's English possessions, leaving those in Normandy as the portion of his brothers; but it was properly his descendant William, the same that took so distinguished a part in the siege of Damietta in 1218, that acquired the surname of the Englishman. The Harcourts seem to have been particularly stricken with the mania of crusading, and there is scarcely a single expedition to the Holy Land of any importance, in which they were not conspicuous.

Note (ff), page 108, line 542.
The conquer'd spoils, and fame of Erin's war.
William Marshall, Earl of Pembroke, Strigulph Strongbow, Earl of Clare, and Robert Fitz-Harding, Lord of Berkeley

castle, were the three warriors most distinguished in the conquest of Ireland under Henry the Second. The Fitz-Hardings were descended from the Kings of Denmark, and came to England with the Conqueror. In 1168 Robert Fitz-Harding entertained, at Bristol, Dermot Mac Murrough, King of Leinster, with a company of sixty followers, when he came to England to solicit aid from Henry: which event brought on the war with Ireland.

Note (gg), page 108, line 546.

The silver stags upon an azure bend.

Lydulph, of Audleigh in Staffordshire, eldest son of Adam de Audley, bore his father's arms, Gules, a fret Or, and was progenitor of the Lords Audley. Adam, the second son, bore the same arms, with a label of three points Azure in chief, for difference. It was his son, William de Audley, who becoming possessed of the manor of Stanley in Staffordshire (so called from its rough and stony soil), took the surname of Stanley. The arms of this branch (now Earls of Derby) are, on a bend Azure, three stags heads Argent.

Note (hh), page 110, line 579.

His name renown'd on earth, his " Hope in Heaven."

The name of Percy comes from a town in Lower Normandy, near to Villedieu, and not, as some have supposed, from the accident of *piercing* a King of Scotland's *eye*, at the siege of Alnwick Castle: for though that accident is said to have befallen Malcolm the Third (who was contemporary with William Rufus), the officer that slew him was named Hammond, and had no connexion with the Percy family, who did not possess lands in Northumberland till the time of Edward the Second. Its progenitor was Mainfred, a Danish chieftain, who made irruptions on France prior to the expedition of Rollo. Two of his descendants, William and Serlo, assisted

William of Normandy in his conquest of England. William was much beloved by the Monarch, and obtained large grants of land in Hampshire and Lincolnshire. He was also in habits of close friendship with Hugh Lupus, who bestowed on him the lordship of Whitby, where he restored or rather founded the abbey of St. Hilda. His brother Serlo became the first Prior, and his nephew William, who was at Serlo's death chosen Abbot, was of such high renown for sanctity, as to be afterwards canonized. This first Lord William de Percy was surnamed Alsgernons (aux Moustaches); he went with Duke Robert and other Normans to Palestine in 1096, and died at Mount Joy, so named by the pilgrims who usually had the first view of the holy city from that eminence. Here his followers interred his body, but brought over his heart, according to the practice of those ages, to be deposited in Whitby Abbey. His wife was Emma de Port, for the Conqueror having bestowed on him Semar, near Scarborough, and other lands, " he wedded her that was very heir to them, in discharging of his conscience." Emma outlived her husband, and was herself a benefactor to Whitby.

Their son, Alan, called the great Alan, was also so beneficent to the Abbey, as to acquire the title of its second founder; but his warlike achievements are wrapped in oblivion. He had seven sons, and the eldest of these had four children, but they died early, and he and his brothers passed away and left no heir. Maud, the eldest daughter, had married William de Plesset, Earl of Warwick: but he also died childless in Palestine, and the only hope of succession remained with the youngest daughter Agnes. She married Josceline de Lovain, son of Geoffrey Barbatus, Duke of Nether Lorrain, Count of Brabant and Lovain, and brother to Adelicia, second wife of Henry the First of England. He took the name of Percy, but was permitted to retain his hereditary device, *Or, a lion rampant, azure,* which with a change of colour only, is still the arms of Brabant and Hainault. Josceline was of one of the noblest families in Europe, being descended from Charlemagne, and from the illustrious Duke Regnier, who was taken prisoner by Rollo the Dane.

Henry de Percy was the true representative of this illustrious line at the time of RICHARD's Crusade; but to avoid confusion, from the endless repetition of the same familiar name, I have changed it to one frequent in the family annals. In 1234 his younger brother Richard had contrived to get possession both of lands and honours, and it was not till after a solemn trial before Henry the Third, that his nephew William (son of Henry de Percy) obtained justice.

The motto alluded to in the text is, " Espérance en Dieu."

Note (ii), page 110, line 593.

His look appall'd, and death was in his blow.

The elder Percevals seem to have been remarkable at once for talent and cruelty. They are sprung from Robert, younger son of Eudes, sovereign Duke of Brittany; but were thence transplanted into Normandy, and at the time of the Conqueror possessed the castle of Yvery, with great estates and power, and the hereditary office of chief butler. Some of the family came to England with William; but Roger de Yvery, faithfully adhering to Robert, his eldest son, against William Rufus, was by the latter dispossessed of many of his lands, and particularly the castle of Yvery in Oxfordshire, which was bestowed on Guy de St. Valery, and was thenceforward called St. Valeria.

In the meantime the main stem of the family reigned at the castle of Yvery in Normandy, which was built by Albreda, wife of Ralph, Earl of Yvery and Baieux, who had more of the lioness than the dove in her composition, for when the castle was finished, she ordered the architect's head to be struck off, that he might not build another like it; and afterwards, attempting to retain possession of it against her own husband, was killed by him in the attempt. Their son Ascelin (sometimes called Gouel de Perceval) inherited all his mother's ferocity, and acquired the surname of Lupus from his violent character. He was a great warrior, and commanded the Norman forces at Mantes, where William the Conqueror received his death-wound. But one of the most remarkable features of Ascelin's life, was his war with the Earl of Bretevil, on account of a woman which his (Ascelin's) youngest brother had ravished. He defeated the Earl, took him prisoner, and confined him three months in the castle of Breherval, where he was treated with the utmost severity, and exposed at the upper windows of the fortress to the frost in the depth of winter, covered only by his shirt, which was previously dipped in water, and in this situation was he compelled to remain till it froze to his back. Nor could he escape *ex ore Lupi*, from the jaws of the wolf, till he agreed to give three thousand dreux pounds for his ransom: and, what must have been more galling than all the rest, to yield his only daughter in marriage to Ascelin. Nevertheless the war revived, till in three years the Earl was nearly ruined, but he found means to interest Philip King of France and Robert Duke of Normandy in his cause, and also the clergy, who were incensed against Asceline for the little reverence he had shewn them. In Lent, 1095, the Earl, with the forces which all these allies could raise, assisted by Robert de Belesme, a very expert officer, and an inveterate enemy to Ascelin, and by the engines which had lately been used at the siege of Jerusalem (they having been invented about that time by a famous engineer in the first crusade), attacked Asceline, in Breherval; but he defended it two months against them all, and at last made a treaty, by which he remained in possession of all his honours, only allowing the Earl of Bretevil to retain quietly his castle of Yvery, the suzerainty of which Duke Robert had bestowed on him, and which was one cause of quarrel. Ascelin not liking to pay to the Earl the homage he had formerly paid to the Duke.

The second son of Ascelin, William, surnamed *Lupellus*, or *the little wolf*, rebelled against Henry the First. After an unsuccessful battle, he was taken prisoner by a peasant, but bribed him with his arms to let him escape. The peasant shaved him in the manner of an Esquire, and carrying a staff in his hand he reached the Seine, where he was forced to give his shoes to the boatman for his passage, and so go barefoot home.

William took part with Matilda against Stephen. After his death the surname of Lupellus seems to have become general among his descendants.—Richard his fifth son continued the line, and being nearly related to Earl Strigulph whose mother was like his, a daughter of the Earl of Mellent, he accompanied him in his Irish expedition—and was with RICHARD in the Holy Land.

I ought to apologize for the length of this note, but the history of this family seemed to me to present so good a view of the darker manners of the times, of the discourteous Barons against whom knight errantry was really useful, that I felt unwilling to curtail it.—Ascelin must certainly have been one of the greatest as well as one of the worst men of his time.

Note (kk), page 115, line 688.

And wondering wisdom warbled from his tongue.

Pierre Vidal was one of those strange contrasts, so often met with in the history of the middle ages. The character of his muse was different, or he might perhaps bear a comparison with Alfieri, for while good sense and sound feeling reigned in his poetry, his life was marked by an eccentricity little short of madness. St. Palaye calls him the Don Quixote of Troubadours. The professed admirer of every beautiful woman, he believed himself equally the object of regard, and often boasted of imaginary favours. Having once indulged his vanity at the expense of a Provençal lady, her husband punished him by slitting his tongue. Hugues, the Lord of Baux, took compassion on him, and had him cured. He remained attached to the family, and soon became enamoured of Adelaide wife to Barral de Baux, the head of the house. His whimsical passion was a source of great amusement to this lady and her husband; and the latter, far from being jealous of his extravagancies, gave him arms and habits like his own, and allowed him the freest access to his wife. Adelaide on her part pretended to return his love: but being soon disgusted with the presumption which her affected smiles inspired, she forced her husband to dismiss the unhappy minstrel, who while exhaling his sorrow in verses which are yet remarkable for their sweetness, sought consolation in war, and went with Cœur de Lion to Palestine.

The bravadoes in which he announced his prowess were not less extravagant than the complaints in which he breathed his love. "My enemies," said he, "tremble at my name, and the earth shakes beneath my steps. All that oppose me I cut to pieces."

It may well be believed that such a character was a source of great amusement to the young Knights who accompanied our Lion-hearted Monarch, and they alternately amused themselves with feeding and exposing his follies. During the King's residence in Cyprus, they contrived to marry him to a lady, who appears to have been distantly related to some one of the families which had sate on the throne of Constantinople. They persuaded him that she was niece to the Emperor, and was to have the diadem transferred to her. No more was needful to heighten Vidal's eccentricity to madness. He usurped the Imperial state and title, gave that of Empress to his wife, had a throne carried before him, and expended all his earnings in support of his Utopian dignity. Nay, so incurable was this fancy, that five and twenty years after, he succeeded in collecting a little troop as mad as himself, and made a crusade to Constantinople, in the hope of recovering his empire.

But perhaps the most ridiculous proof of his wildness, was that elicited by his passion for Louve de Penautier, a lady of Carcassonne. As her name signified a female wolf, he thought himself bound not only to assume in her honour the name of *Loup*, but to wear the *wolf*-skin also, and in this disguise to be hunted by his own dogs, whom he would not permit to be called off till he was at the point of death. The lady's compassion prompted her to dress his wounds, but she laughed with her husband at his folly.

This folly, however, scarcely ever touches his writings, and the moment that the muse possessed his fancy, she seems to have inspired him with a discrimination and prudence, which it would have been well if he could have carried into the affairs of life. His tale of the Jongleur not only gives admirable lessons to the young Troubadour for his conduct in the world, but some hints by which his patrons might be benefited. He also composed a treatise on the government of the tongue, an invective against Philip Augustus for not redeeming the Holy Sepulchre; another against the King of Spain, for buying peace from the Moors instead of subduing them. He complains of the conduct of the priesthood, and the encouragement given to heresy by their bad lives. And, finally, he launches into invective against the Emperor Henry the Sixth, for detaining RICHARD in prison, against the faith of nations and the privileges of Crusaders. In short, his themes were various, and generally handled with power.

Note (ll), page 119, line 792.

This zeal in age is fed with Christian blood.

One of the first exploits of Saladine was the overthrow of the Egyptian or Fatimite Caliph, who had his residence in Cairo, and was of course the determined enemy of the orthodox caliph, or Caliph of Bagdad. Saladine was through life remarkable for his strict adherence to the doctrines and observances of Islam; and though the Crusaders often forced his noble mind to respect individuals, his hatred of their religion seems to have been not less virulent than theirs for Mohammedanism.

Note (mm), page 120, line 804.

And Mosul's lord was vassal of his hand.

Yemen, or Arabia Felix, was conquered for Saladine by his brother Touranschah, a man whose bloody and violent disposition formed a strong contrast to that of the Soldan. Saladine was long engaged in war with the Sultans of Mosul, whom after a violent contest he subdued.

Note (nn), page 120, line 806.

My fatal reign, my sorrow, and my shame.

There is little temptation to enlarge on the melancholy picture presented by the last years of the kingdom of Jerusalem. Amalric was a brave soldier, and might have made his power respectable, but his avarice and inconsistency ruined his cause. The blind passion with which he sought to obtain the wealthy dominion of Egypt led him into long and useless wars, while at the same time he had the inconceivable folly to sell some of his strongest fortresses to the Saracens and the next moment to break the peace formed with them, if the slightest prospect of advantage was held out from another quarter. His son Baldwin the fourth was only thirteen when Amalric died, and was afflicted with leprosy. Raymond of Tripoli became Regent during his minority, but his reign from the first hour of its commencement was disturbed by the dissensions of his nobles. As Baldwin grew up to manhood he took the reins of government into his own hands and signalized his brief authority by the complete defeat of Saladine near Ascalon. But his spirit and activity gave way beneath a fresh attack of disease; an unworthy jealousy of the power and commanding character of Raymond led him to prefer Lusignan as Regent, and he soon after died, leaving the crown to Baldwin the Fifth, the infant son of Sybilla, and William of Montferrat. The events immediately subsequent have already been noticed in the First Book.

Note (oo), page 121, line 832.

And at my feet down dropp'd Chatillon's head.

The humanity of Saladine, and the cruelty of RICHARD CŒUR DE LION, are phrases which must be familiar to many of my readers.—It is not my wish unduly to exalt the character of my hero, neither would I rob the Conqueror of Jerusalem of one well earned laurel. His conduct to the vanquished in the City deserves the highest praise, and is an instance of that generosity of which the history of the East offers so many striking examples, and which does not in those climes appear incompatible with acts of the greatest cruelty in the same individual. Rinaldo of Chatillon was the object of peculiar resentment to Saladine. Raised by the preference of Constantia, widow of Raymond of Poitiers, to the throne of Antioch, he was for many years the captive of Noureddin. When he regained his freedom, Bohemond, the son of Raymond, was old enough to govern his dominions, and Constantia was no more. Rinaldo married the widow of Humfrey of Thoron (father to the Thoron who appears in the poem) and thus became Lord of the impregnable fortresses of Carac, and Krak or Montroyal. From this latter place he ravaged the frontiers of Arabia, and when peace was concluded with Saladine, still continued his incursions. Saladine remonstrated to the King of Jerusalem, but Baldwin the Fourth had not power to punish or restrain his vassal. Rinaldo who had often plundered the caravans of Mecca and Medina, now conceived the bold project of penetrating even to those cities, and of pillaging the Caaba and the

Tomb of the Prophet. Assisted by a band of Templars, he surprised the Egyptian merchants, who were conveying along the Red Sea, the treasures of India, and entered triumphant into countries which had never yet beheld the Christians. He reached the valley of Rabid, about ten leagues from Medina, where he was attacked by a Syrian army and defeated. Rinaldo and a few others escaped as by miracle to Krak. Part of the prisoners were executed as criminals, and we have the authority of the Arabian historians, Schahabeddin, Tabari, and Aboul-Feda, for stating that the rest were immolated at the same time with the victims sacrificed at the ceremony of the Grand Beiram. This horrible execution did not satisfy the vengeance of Saladine, and he invaded Syria, incessantly repeating the vow to kill Chatillon with his own hand. It was not, however, till the battle of Tiberias, that this daring warrior fell into the hands of the Soldan, when the circumstances of his death are faithfully given in the poem. The day after the battle witnessed a scene which was still less in accordance with the humanity ascribed to Saladine. He caused such of the Knights of the Temple and of St. John, as were among the prisoners, to be led before him, and declaring, that he " would deliver the earth from those two abominable races," he permitted the emirs and doctors of the law, who surrounded him, to kill each a knight. Loaded with chains and incapable of resistance, these devoted warriors disputed with each other the honour of first receiving the crown of martyrdom, and many who had never belonged to the military orders, cried aloud, that they were Templars or Hospitallers, and gloried in partaking their fate. Saladine, seated on his throne, beheld and applauded the execution.

Note (pp), page 121, line 836.

Compell'd at length to own the Soldan's reign.

After the battle of Tiberias, in which Lusignan was taken

prisoner, Jerusalem, under the orders of the veteran Baléan D'Ibelin, made a more resolute defence than could have been expected from its destitute condition; but was at last forced to surrender. The Latin historians remarked that the Crusaders had entered the Holy City on a Friday, at the very hour when their Saviour submitted to death to atone the crimes of man. The Saracens re-took the town also on a Friday, the Mahommedan day of religious observance, and, according to their belief, on the anniversary of the day when their prophet arose from Jerusalem on his miraculous journey to Heaven: but an eclipse of the sun, which took place at the moment the conditions of surrender were adjusting in the tent of Saladine, was regarded as an evil omen.

Note (qq), page 123, line 866.

" And the twelfth moon," he said, " shall find him free."

Saladine was touched by the grief of Sybilla, and promised that as soon as his power was established, he would restore her husband to liberty. He also felt for those who had lost their friends at Tiberias, and liberated such of their sons or husbands as were among his prisoners. Many of the Christians had abandoned all their wealth, to bear out on their shoulders their infirm friends or parents. Saladine rewarded their disinterestedness by liberal gifts, and permitted the Hospitallers to remain in Jerusalem to nurse the sick.

Note (rr), page 125, line 908.

And Acre fall, and Palestine be free.

See Rastell's Chronicle. - Origin of the Garter. " Some do affirme that this order beganne firste by KING RICHARD CŒUR DE LYON, at the siege of the citie of Acre, where in his great necessytie there were but twentie-five knightes that firmlye and surelye abode by him, whene he caused them all to weare thongs of blue leythere aboute their legges, and afterwards they were called knights." Sir

Egerton Brydges, in his notice of the family of St. John, in Collins's Peerage, says, " This Roger de St. John was with RICHARD THE FIRST at Acre, when that Monarch thought of this device. He tied a leathern thong, or garter, around the left leg of a certain number of his knights, to excite them to greater courage. This some think was the first occasion of the institution of the Order of the Garter." It suited me better to place the investiture at Cyprus than at Acre.

BOOK IV.

Note (a), page 134, line 22.

For want and thirst have keener stings than war.

Vinesauf speaks of the Bedouins or Bedeuvini, " horrible, darker than smoke, bearing the bow and quiver and the small round shield."

Note (b), page 134, line 34.

And Rome's degenerate eagles learn'd to dread.

Some of the most splendid monarchs of Persia belonged to the Seljoukian dynasty, which expired in the year 1194. The kindred Sultan of Roum, whose capital was first at Nice, and afterwards at Iconium, rent many of its fairest provinces from the Greek empire, and maintained itself till 1308. It is from this branch of the Seljouc Turks that the Ottomans now upon the throne of Constantinople are descended. The Seljouc dynasties of Caramania, of Aleppo, and Damascus, were of shorter date. The last was that of Damascus, which city was given up to Noureddin by Ayoub, the father of Saladine, who was then Vizir to the last Seljouc prince, Modgireddin Abc. Ayoub had been under great obligations to Noureddin, and his brother,

Shiracoush, was then in his service. The Sultan rewarded them both with liberality, and Ayoub received the government of the yielded town as the meed of his treachery. These two emirs were also endowed with the peculiar privilege of sitting in the presence of Noureddin, without waiting for permission.

Note (c), page 136, line 64.

The placid Soldan fill'd his simple throne.

Luxury has been the common reproach of the east: yet it may be remarked, that its greatest conquerors, at least in modern days, have been distinguished by the simplicity and even austerity of their manners. Such were Noureddin and Saladine, Ghenghis Khan, and his descendant Tamerlane.

Note (d), page 136, line 71.

And Aladin, whom youth's warm hopes inspire.

From the many names which belong to these young princes, I have endeavoured to select those most capable of being moulded into English verse. The history of the Arabs (Universal History) relates, page 514, that Saladine, having alighted from his horse to take a more ceremonious leave of Kaisar Shah, son of Kilidge Arselan, Sultan of Iconium, and who had married a daughter of Malek Adel, Kaisar Shah in return held the stirrup and assisted the Soldan to remount, while Aladin arranged his clothes, on which a bystander observed, "O, son of Ayoub, you need not now care what death you die; a prince of the house of Seljouc has helped you on horseback, and a descendant of the Atabek Zenghi has adjusted your garments." Seiffeddin, the father of Aladin, had been engaged in long and ruinous wars with the Sultan, and his friendship was never cordial.

Note (e), page 138, line 108.

The labouring steers drag on the ponderous towers.

These towers were similar in nature to those employed by Godfrey at the siege of Jerusalem, and even in an age when we hear familiarly of the destructive powers of our modern artillery, there is something imposing in the account of such gigantic engines; these were higher than the walls of the city, and each was capable of containing five hundred men. They consisted of three stories: in the first story were the battering rams; in the second, the Balistæ and Catapults, which threw darts and stones to the distance of one hundred and twenty-five feet. The stones were from three hundred to four hundred pounds weight; they crushed the roofs of houses, overturned the machines of the enemy, and shook the walls; the third and last story contained one hundred warriors, who were armed with axes, maces, &c., and protected by a roof from the stones and fire which were hurled from the engines of the besieged. It was also provided with a *pont levis*, or flying bridge, which could be let down upon the walls. These moving castles were raised upon wheels, and covered with leather hardened in vinegar, to render them impenetrable to common flame, and to the ordinary Greek fire. After the earth had been levelled, and a part of the fosse filled up, they were rolled forward by means of levers. *See Mailly, Marin, &c.*

Note (f), page 138, line 121.

To shivering want his own rich mantle gave.

The banners of France were three, the royal or personal standard of the King, the "Chape de St. Martin," and the oriflamme. The royal standard was a square banner, or gonfalon, of a blue colour, and powdered with lilies of gold. This was usually entrusted to some vassal of valour and consequence, who was called the gonfalonier, a name in later years confined to him who bears the standard of the Holy See. At the battle of Bouvines, the standard of Philip Augustus was borne by Gallon de Montigny, who, when the King was unhorsed, gave notice of his danger by lowering it several times. The "*Chape de St. Martin,*" according to Le Gendre, was a banner of taffeta, on which the Saint was depicted, and which had acquired extraordinary virtues, from having been allowed to remain some time upon his tomb. Other writers assert that it was the mantle of the Saint, and some have pretended that it was worn by the Kings of France in battle. Others suppose it to have been the banner belonging to the Abbey of St. Martin of Tours, and others again contend that it was not a banner, but a coffer or portable pavilion, containing the relics of many saints, and among others those of St. Martin, which the Kings of France held in the highest veneration. Whichever of these opinions may rest on the best authority, the presence of the Chape de St. Martin was supposed to ensure victory, and its place in battle was immediately after the royal standard. The oriflamme has been already considered, but the dignity of bearing it was sought by the most renowned knights, and contested with almost as much eagerness as the principal command, at least if we may judge from the instance of Arnoul d'Andrenhem, who under Charles the Fifth resigned his office of Maréchal of France, that he might exercise that of *Porte Oriflamme.* The bearer, however, had no authority, except over the troop at the head of which he carried his banner; but that troop consisted of all which chivalry could boast, of most noble and most valiant:—added to which, the oriflamme was always in the van, either in march or in battle, consequently in the post of danger and honour; and when it was present, even the banner of the King became of small account, and was called only the royal pennon.

Nothing can more decidedly mark the respect in which the oriflamme was held, than the oath administered to the bearer. " You swear and promise, on the precious body of Christ Jesus, here present, and on the bodies of Monseigneur St. Denis and his companions, here also, that you will loyally, in your own person, guard and govern the oriflamme of our Lord the King, also present, to the honour and profit of himself and his kingdom, and that you will not abandon it, neither for the fear of death nor for any other cause, but that you will in all things do your duty as beseems a good and loyal knight towards your Sovereign and liege Lord."— *See Mailly*, vol. i.

Note (g), page 142, line 205.

While Philip's hand his keen francisque displayed.

The francia or francisque, a kind of battle-axe, from which the Franks are supposed to have derived their name, as the Saxons did from the se-ax, a similar weapon which they used in battle. Some modern authors assert that the axe and bipennis were solely used by the Danes. Perhaps a weapon of this sort was originally employed by all the barbarous tribes of northern Europe, but relinquished in the progress of civilization; and the Danes being the last of the northern invaders, might also be the last to abandon it.— *Smith's Antient Costume of England.*

Note (h), page 144, line 257.

He moves not, speaks not, lives to pain alone.

The general suffrage of mankind seems to have established Saladine as the greatest man of the age in which he lived; yet in the power of supporting any reverse of fortune, he shewed himself much inferior to his antagonist, Richard Cœur de Lion. Some historians have said that the English Monarch was never so great as in his dungeon of

Trivallis; but the Sultan of Damascus, whether from mental weakness, or constitutional infirmity, seems to have been sunk into a deplorable state of despondency by every defeat. The picture in the poem goes not beyond that which is drawn by his annalists, and after the loss of Acre, we have the testimony of the learned Abdollatiph to that morbid state of mind, which would not admit even the presence of his sons. This great physician, after having acquired by travel a knowledge of the learning and antiquities of India and Damascus, was then on his road to Egypt, and felt it a point of duty to pay his respects to the Sultan *en route:* but the unhappy Monarch was in a state which precluded his admission. M. Michaud's observations on the general character of Mahomedan courage are not inapplicable to this subject. " The reader may have remarked, in perusing this history, that the religion of Mahommed, all warlike as it is, does not inspire in its disciples that obstinate bravery, that perseverance under misfortune, that unbounded devotion, of which the history of the Crusades offers so many examples. The religion of the Musulmans requires the stimulus of victory to preserve its strength and violence. Trained in the blind doctrine of fatalism, they are accustomed to regard success or defeat as the decree of heaven. Victorious, they are full of courage and ardour; but when vanquished they allow themselves to be cast down, and feel no shame in yielding to an enemy, whom they regard as the instrument of destiny. Their courage is rarely excited by the desire of acquiring renown, and even in the moments of their military ardour, it is rather the fear of punishment than the thirst of glory that detains them in the field. The power to brave their foes must be derived from a chief whom they dread, and despotism appears necessary to their valour."—Vol. ii. p. 213.

Note (i), page 145, line 266.

Oh! had I Ali's strength, or Kaled's sword.

The valour of Kaled and Ali is conspicuous in the wars of the Prophet. The strength of Ali, who wrenched off one of the gates of Bosra, and used it for a shield, appears beyond belief, and the exploits by which Kaled acquired the surname of "Seif-Allah," or the "Sword of God," are not less wonderful. Ali was vindictive and ambitious, and his struggles for the Caliphate led to that great schism, which has separated Persia from the standard of Mahomedan orthodoxy. Kaled seems to have been without ambition, ferocious, amd delighting in battle for its own sake. The enthusiastic character and marvellous achievements of the companions and successors of the Prophet, gives to Mr. Gibbon's account of the origin of Mahomedanism all the interest of romance.

Note, (k), page 147, line 322.

His Genii workmen brought to Giamschid.

The Gem of Giamschid, frequently alluded to by Oriental writers, is by many supposed to be a carbuncle, and this idea is adopted by the author of Vathek; but, according to D'Herbelot, the Gem of Giamschid was a large cup or vase, made of a single turquois, which was found by the Genii his subjects, when digging the foundations of Istakar. This vase has long been lost. Giamschid was the son of Caiomurs, the first of the Preadamite Sultans, who reigned over the Genii before the creation of man. He is said to have been the inventor of wine, which, from its intoxicating qualities, he named "the charming poison."

Note, (l), page 149, line 350.

And vanish'd in a pyramid of light.

The idea of this incident is taken from a passage in the *Histoire de Saladine*, which says that many fruitless attempts had been made by the besieged to set fire to the wooden castles of the besiegers, or to overturn them with stones. Saladine promised great rewards for their destruction; at last a young man of Damascus flattered himself that he would burn them by means of an inflammable matter of which he possessed the secret, and which was different from the common Greek fire. In reality, after having mixed various drugs with naptha or petroleum, in brazen vases, these vases were hurled against the castles, and consumed them in an instant. Michaud says that they were reduced to ashes, as though they had been struck by the lightnings of Heaven. In the *Pièces Justificatives*, at the end of his second volume, is an extract from the MS. Life of Saladine by Renaudot, which bears upon the subject. " It is certain," says M. Renaudot, " that the artificial fire, called Greek fire, *feu de mer*, or liquid fire, whose composition is found in the Greek and Latin historians, was very different from that which the Eastern nations began to use at this period, and of which the effect was the more surprising, as its cause was entirely unknown; for, while the common Greek fire was prepared with wax, pitch, sulphur, and other combustible matters, the principal ingredient of this was naptha or petroleum, of which there are natural springs in the neighbourhood of Bagdad, similar to those remarked by the ancients near Ecbatana, on the confines of Media, and in other parts of Persia. It appears probable that the Orientals first made use of it at this siege (Acre), and that the Christians, from its resemblance, called it also Greek fire, and believed it to be the same which was known throughout the Levant. The Greeks and Mahomedans afterwards continued to employ their respective fires, without communicating the secret to other nations. The Greeks distinguishing the naptha fire of the east by the name of *Median fire*; and the Latins confounding both under that of Greek fire; in the same manner as the

Orientals afterwards gave the appellation of naptha to the gunpowder by which it was superseded." M. Mailly enters into a digression on the subject of the Greek fire. Its effects are doubtless exaggerated; and, though I have availed myself in the Poem of such exaggerations, there are not perhaps many who will now seriously believe on the authority of some old historians, that it consumed the very stones, or that, while the tendency of all other flame is to aspire, this had at least an equal inclination to burn downwards. M. Mailly, whose work was published in 1780, states that some of his contemporaries had pretended to a re-discovery of its composition. It was not ten years before that a person named Dupré, had died in the receipt of a pension paid him by the French Government on condition of burying his secret in oblivion. Mailly had himself known a physician, who had made the same discovery, or at least one similar, but to whose labours the ministry gave no encouragement, "a humanity," he adds, "as honourable to philosophy, as to our country; the only one perhaps, where persons in place may be found, sufficiently the friends of mankind, to forbear multiplying the sources of their destruction; and to remember, that if unhappily wars are sometimes necessary, infernal secrets should be left to infernal armies, and that we already possess too much, in the use of gunpowder!!" The English Government would certainly have drawn upon itself the anathemas of M. Mailly, and have afforded a fine field for the display of his national vanity by its patronage of the Congreve rockets, had they then existed.

Note (m), page 149, line 361,

Oh! who but courts th' emprize, the glory rare?

The conveyance of Greek or Median fire to the city was, throughout the siege of Acre, a service of great importance and danger. It was generally effected by means of swimmers or divers. Vinesauf mentions one who was carrying it in an otter's skin, but being caught by some fishermen, was brought to the camp.

Note (n), page 153, line 443.

But call'd in after years " the English stone."

In some of the histories of the Crusades there is mention of a rock on the sea-shore very near Acre, which received the name of *La Pierre des Anglois :* but I do not known on what account.

Note (o), page 162, line 656.

Who dared that chief in battle-shock to meet.

Ermengard D'Aps was grand master of the Knights Hospitallers before the taking of Jerusalem, and enjoyed that dignity for more than five years. The Grand Masters of the Templars were less fortunate, for at least four or five were successively slain in the same period.

Note (p), page 164, line 706.

Protects the mole, the shelter'd port commands.

The form of Acre is triangular. It is defended by the sea on the north, western, and southern sides, and on the northeast or land side is guarded by walls and strong towers. At the northern extremity, or apex of the triangle is the Tour du Diable (Satan's Fort). In the middle of the line, and at a projecting angle, is the Tour Maudite (Accursed Tower), the scene of the most violent assaults. At the south-eastern extremity, very near to the sea, is the Tower of David, or Tour du Patriarche; beyond this the wall extends a short distance into the sea, and is terminated by a small fort to which I find no distinguishing name. The sea encroaching on the southern side, or base of the triangle, forms a sort of bay defended by a mole, which springing from the shore near the southwestern corner, stretches half across, and is bounded by a strong tower, built on an insulated rock. This rock was formerly the site of a temple of Jupiter, and the place where the priests retired to inspect the entrails of the victims. From the number of flies which were hence attracted to the rock arose its name of *Tour des Mouches*. I have endeavoured to retain the pleasanter part of the idea, and have called it the Tower of Sacrifice. I may perhaps here be permitted to make a short observation on the names of Acre and Ptolemais, respecting which much has been written. The former name, or at least such modification of it as arises from the different pronunciation in various languages, seems to have been both the ancient and modern appellation of the city, and it has been questioned whence it acquired that of Ptolemaïs. Some writers have suggested that this last name, though employed by the Greeks of the Lower Empire, and the Latin authors, may never have become general among the natives of the country. Vinesauf, I think, gives a satisfactory explanation. The old town of Acre, as appears from the remains of its walls, did not occupy more than the lower half of the triangle, and Vinesauf says that to the north or on the side nearest to the hill of Turon, was that part of the city called Ptolemaïs, having been more recently built.

Note (p), page 165, line 734.

Record his death, and Herod's impious vow.

To the left of the mosque, on the north of the city of Acré, are the ruins of a building still known by the name of King RICHARD's Palace. Dr. Clarke calls its architecture *gothic*, and from the representations which I have seen, the arches are decidedly pointed. Two lofty arches and part of the superstructure remain; the cornice is ornamented with enormous stone busts, of very distorted countenances, whence the building has derived its name; these being supposed to represent the heads of the Saracens whom the Lion-hearted Monarch killed, or ate, according to the romance. Dr. Clarke thinks it more probable that it has been a church of St. John the Baptist, and erected during the time when the Christians were in possession of Acre, whether before or after its capture by Saladine. It is possible that from this very structure the city assumed its title of St. Jean D'Acre.

Note (r), page 168, line 790.

What though a random spear had pierced his side.

This wound is historical, as are also most of the subsequent incidents, and particularly the manner of Leopold's retreat.

Note (s), page 170, line 849.

And thank the care that rais'd its walls so high.

The Christian camp at Acre, by means of successive additions and entrenchments had become (like the town of Santa Fé, built by Ferdinand and Isabella under the walls of Grenada), almost the rival of the city it besieged. It contained streets and churches: not indeed such as would have been erected in a situation where they were likely to be permanent, but such as a residence of three years must have supplied with all the necessaries, and even some of the luxuries of that half-civilized age. These were incessantly filled with warriors from almost every nation of Christendom. The Arabian writers say that so many languages were spoken in the crusading army, that they could not find interpreters for the captives; and in another place, that the camp was so well fortified, that not even a bird could get in.

Note (u), page 172, line 887.

Blends all his victims in one funeral pyre.

See Michaud, vol. ii. p. 392, where he speaks of a Christian knight who singly defended one of the gates of the camp against a crowd of Saracens. The Arabian authors compare him to a demon, animated by all the fires of hell. An enormous cuirass covered him entirely; arrows, stones, and lances were showered in vain upon him; destroying all that approached, he seemed himself invulnerable, till at last he fell a victim to the Greek fire—" *Dévoré par les flammes, il périt, semblable à ces machines énormes des Chrétiens que les assiégés avaient brûlées sous les murailles de la ville.*" Marin distinguishes this hero as the Count of Bar, to whom his valour had procured the title of the French Achilles.

BOOK V.

Note, page 177, line 32.

Whose was the single ship, the single arm?

Conrad of Montferrat first visited Palestine at the time of the second crusade, when his father with his four sons accompanied his uncle, the Emperor Conrad the Third, on that unfortunate expedition. He afterwards distinguished himself in Italy in the contests between the Emperors and the Holy See; conquered some of the Islands of the Adriatic, which he sold to Venice, and then passing a second time to Constantinople, he assisted Isaac Angelus to establish himself on the imperial throne, having killed in battle the leader of the rebels. The sister of this monarch was at first a bait for his ambition, but finding that his marriage gained him nothing but the title of Cæsar, and the right of wearing purple slippers, he left the unhappy Theodora, and sailed to Palestine in quest of more substantial laurels. He arrived at Tyre in a single ship, on the very day when it was engaged to surrender to Saladine if not relieved. The Sultan threatened to place the old Marquis of Montferrat, who had been some time his prisoner, in front of his army, and to expose him to the arrows of the besieged if the town did not surrender; but Conrad was either too well convinced of the humanity of Saladine to fear his threat, or was insensible to the appeal, and replied that if the Soldan were barbarous enough to cause the death of one who had surrendered on his parole, he should glory in being the son of a martyr. Tyre remained his own; he assumed the title of its Prince, and enlarged its territory. Vinesauf says, that he had also another wife in Germany, high born and beautiful; I think her name was Emilia; but many of the heroes of the crusades would not have been sorry to claim at least one of the indulgences of the Mahommedan law.

Note, page 178, line 69.

The Prelate of Beauvais, ministrant there.

The nuptial ceremony was performed by the Bishop of Beauvais, most of the other prelates protesting against it. Baldwin, the old Archbishop of Canterbury, died a few days after, of grief, it is said, at this disgraceful scene.

Note, page 184, line 195.

And deeper plunge in misery and in crime.

Vinesauf gives a distressing picture of this famine, and devotes no less than twelve sections to bitter invective against Conrad, who withheld from the army the provisions with which he had agreed to supply it. Perchance he had them not.

Notes (a) and (b), page 188, line 290.

With envy fired, De Vere and Sackville spring.

Alberic, or Aubrey de Vere, second Earl of Oxford, and married to Adelicia, daughter of Roger Bigot Earl of Norfolk. De Vere was so great a favourite with John, as to be reckoned among his evil counsellors.

(b) Sackville or Salkavilla, now Dukes of Dorset. Herbrand de Salkavilla came to England with the Conqueror. Nigell de Salkavilla was excommunicated by Thomas à Becket, for detaining a manor belonging to the Archbishop, at the same time that he inflicted a similar punishment on Robert Brock, who had cut off the tail of a horse which was carrying provisions to his palace. This was only four days previous to his murder. Sir Jordan de Salkeville, nephew to Nigell, married Clementia, daughter of Alberic de Vere, Earl of Oxford.

Note (c), page 188, line 293.
How Albert fought, or stout Fitzharding fell.

Fitzharding, was the ancient name of the House of Berkeley; which descended from the Kings of Denmark. In 1168, Fitzharding entertained at Bristol, Dermot Mac Murrough, King of Leinster, with a company of sixty, when he came to England to solicit aid from Henry the Second: which event brought on the conquest of Ireland. Maurice, his eldest son, married Alice, daughter of Roger de Berkeley, and was one of the rebellious barons in the reign of John.

Note (d), page 189, line 313.
To Acre borne, had made your valour vain.

The Dromond was bound from Damietta to Acre. Both the European and Oriental writers vaunt its magnitude, and the importance of the stores which it contained. It was said to hold corn sufficient to supply the city of Acre for two years, besides great quantities of Turkish bows, of urns with Greek fire, and, among other ammunition, of venomous serpents, which were destined to sting or bite the Christians to death. To modern ears, this seems an extraordinary weapon of offence, as the serpents might be perverse and bite the wrong party; it is possible that these were some warlike engines, bearing the form or name of serpents, though the other idea is not unworthy of the fancy, which supposed RICHARD to have brought to Acre no less than thirteen ship loads of bee-hives, the denizens of which did good service against the besieged. See the Romance:

> Kyng RICHARD into Acre's cyté
> Leet keste the hyves gret plenté.
> It was hoot in the someres tyde,
> The bees bursten out on every syde,
> That wer anoyed, and ful off grame;
> They dede the Sarezynes ful gret schame,
> For they hem stungge in the vysage,
> That alle they gunne for to rage;
> And hydde hem in a deep selèr,
> That none of hem durste com neer;
> And sayde Kyng RICHARD was ful fel,
> When hys flyes byten so wel!

A similar incident occurs in the history of the Caliph Vathek, where Carathis introduces small pots of venomous serpents into her apartments, to destroy her unsuspecting visitors. The Oriental writers agreed, that if the Dromond had arrived in safety, the Christians would never have been able to take Acre. The Romance has the same idea:

> " For, hadde the drowmound i-passyd the see,
> And comen to Acres fro Kyng RICHARD;
> An hondryd wyntyr afftyrward,
> For alle Crystene-men under sunne,
> Hadde nevyr Acres ben i-wunne!"

Note (e), page 193, line 411.

And rapturous greeting, hail them to the strand.

I cannot give a better idea of RICHARD's magnificence, or of the joy of the Crusaders on his arrival, than by quoting two passages from Vinesauf, the former of which describes his entrance into the harbour of Messina, the second his appearance in the bay of Acre. After observing on the necessity of splendour in princes, *qualem te video, talem te esse spero*, and the disappointment of the Messinese, who on going out to meet Philip at his arrival, found him in a single ship, like a fugitive, and hastening to hide himself in his castle, as though he feared the sight of men; the chronicler continues: " Porro Rex Angliæ ille magnanimus, ex quo fama prædicante divulgabatur adventare, catervatim ruunt populi, illum cernere cupientes; et in littus se ingerentes certatim occupant sedes illum ascendentem visuri. Et ecce eminus prospiciunt mare galeis opertum innumeris, et vox à longe intonabat in aures eorum tubarum reboantium, et lituum clarius et acutius resonantium, interea propius accedentibus fuit videre galeas seriatim remigantes, variis undique ornatas et refertas armaturis, ventilantibus ad aurum innumeris penuncellis, et signis, ordine decoro, in hastilium summitatibus; rostris galearum varietatibus picturarum distinctis, appensorum in singulis proris, scintillantibus radiis scutorum, videres ex multitudine adventantium remigantium mare fervescere, tubarum intonationibus, quas trumpas vulgo dicunt, audientium aures tinnire, et ex vario tumultuantium acessu delectationem excitari. Cum ecce rex magnificus juxta navigantium galearum catervatim obsequio stipatus, cæteris eminentiori et ornatiori præstans in prora, tanquam ignota visurus, sive ab ignotis videndis fertur in littus obsitum densarum turbarum agminibus, et omnibus tanquam se ultro videndum exponens, eleganter ornatus in littus ascendit, ubi nautas, quos eo præmiserat, cum cœteris addictis obsequiis suis reperit, eum gratanter excipientes, et dextrarios, et equos suos nobiles, sibi pridem commissos ad vecturam exhibentes. Confluunt hinc inde cum suis indigenæ prosequentes ipsum usque ad hospitium suum. Super cujus tanta gloria vulgus attonitum conferebat ad invicem, hic quidem dignus Imperio, hic merito constitutus super gentes, et super regna, cujus fama olim audita multa junior est ipsa veritate quam videmus."

It was on the day of St. Barnabas, or of the summer solstice, that RICHARD appeared before Acre. The whole army advanced to meet him, and the earth shook with the exulting shouts of the Christians, while the Turks, who heard their trumpets and acclamations, were deprest and terrified. " Duo Reges à portu sese mutuo deducentes gratanter officiosis alter utrum venerabantur obsequiis. Deinde Rex RICHARDUS in tentoria sibi preparata se recipiens de gerendis negotiis disponebant. Multa quidem meditabatur solicitudine qua instantia, quo artificio, quibus Machinis civitas expeditiori comprehenderetur compendio. De cujus adventu nec calamus absolute poterit populi describere lætitiam, nec cujusquam lingua retexere, noctis etiam serenitas aere solito puriore eidem æstimabatur arridere; sed et hinc trumpæ perstrepunt, illinc intonant tubæ, hinc acutius modulantes concinunt tibicines, illinc tympana concrepitant, sive gravioribus harmoniis susurrant Heroinæ: et tanquam ex variarum vocum dissonantiis mulcens auditem captatur Symphonia; nec enim inveneritur de facili qui more suo cessaret à laudibus et gaudio: aut enim cordis testantes lætitiam resonant populares cantiones, aut antiquorum præclara gesta, priora exempla recitabantur in incitamenta modernorum. Hi cantantibus vina propinant in vasis pretiosis, alii quibus libet indifferenter accipientibus pusillis cum majoribus summo cum tripudio noctis transigebant instantiam. Accessit in augmentum lætitiæ, quod Cyprum insulam tam commodam, tam necessariam, Rex RICHARDUS nostræ subjugasset ditioni, quæ tam oportune tantæ serviret exercitui. Nihilominus in testimonium exortæ laetitiæ in cordibus omnium, et ad removendas noctis tenebras, ubique cerea scintillabant lampades, luminaria flammantia, et multiplicato fulgore nox diei videretur usurpasse claritatem; ita ut totam vallem Turci reputarent igne succensam."

Note (f), page 194, line 427.

His brazen axe, that crushed where'er it fell,

The tremendous axe of RICHARD, with which he was wont to " crush the bones" of misbelieving Saracens, is said to have had twenty pounds of steel in its head. Mr. Smith, in his Ancient Costume of England, mentions the axe of Baldwin *Bras de Fer*, Earl of Flanders, which is preserved in the Belfort Tower at Ghent, and gives a figure of it, bearing a strong resemblance to the description of that weapon. It weighs eighteen pounds, and is only a single axe.

Of RICHARD's axe the romance says:

" King RICHARD, I understond
Or he went out of Englond,
Let him make an ax for the nones,
To breke therwith the Sarasyns bones.
The head was wrought right well;
Therin was twenty pounde of stele;"

Note (g), page 194, line 431.

And the gold broom-flower on its glittering round.

In the portrait of RICHARD on the first of his seals, the upper circle of his helmet is surrounded by an ornament which is supposed to be the flower of the *Planta Genista*, or broom, whence the house of Anjou took the surname of Plantagenet. This device originated either with Geoffrey Earl of Anjou (the grandfather of our RICHARD the First), who is said to have worn a sprig of broom in his hat when on a pilgrimage to the Holy Land, or with his father Fulk of Anjou, the fourth King of Jerusalem, who on his way thither used a branch of broom or furze as a scourge. Henry the Second of England, son of the above named Geoffrey, was the first of our Kings who bore the name of Plantagenet. He is reported to have placed a sprig of broom in his helmet, on taking the vow of the crusade.

Note (h), page 195, line 457.

Sicilia's matchless grain, Oporto's wine.

A part of RICHARD's army, in its way to Messina, assisted Sancho, the first King of Portugal, in the conquest of Sylvia from the Moors; in the same manner that the soldiers of Conrad the Third, and Louis the Seventh, had in the former crusade enabled Alphonso, first King of that country, to take Lisbon, which the Portuguese feign to have been founded by Ulysses. There can therefore be little doubt that Portugal, as well as Sicily and Cyprus, contributed to the victualling of the English fleet.

Note (i), page 196, line 465.

And neigh aloud for liberty regained.

The palanders or horse transports were drawn on the beach, and the horses introduced by a sort of shelving platform, which was afterwards turned up to close the opening. This door was then well secured, and was entirely under water while the vessels were at sea. When it was desired to land the horses, the palanders were again drawn up on shore till the gate was exposed; the fastenings were removed, and the horses descended to the shore without inconvenience or injury.—*See Mailly, &c.*

Note (k), page 197, line 483.

Vast as the tent for great Kerboga wove.

Of the immense booty which fell into the hands of the first Crusaders, at the battle of Antioch, nothing was so highly prized, or excited so much admiration, as the superb tent of Kerboga, King of Mosul, one of their principal antagonists. It was adorned with gold and silver in every part, was of such vast extent as easily to contain two thousand men, was divided into streets, and defended by towers, like a fortified town. This tent, the only one perhaps of the kind which had been seen since the time of Constantine, who caused a similar one to be constructed, became the property of Bohemond, who sent it to Bari in Italy.—*Mailly, &c.*—The crusading Princes appear to have quickly caught a taste for this oriental luxury, and their small and clumsy tents were soon improved upon an Eastern model; though they never attempted to vie with this pompous specimen of Asiatic luxury, which will remind the reader of the tent given by the fairy Paribanon to her lover Achmed, in the Arabian Tales. Another splendid tent is named by the historians of the first crusade; it was sent by an Armenian Prince, Nichosias, as a present to Godfrey, but fell into an ambuscade prepared by Pancrates, who sent it to Bohemond, as a gift from himself. Godfrey reclaimed it, and it became the subject of much altercation between the two leaders, till Bohemond was at last compelled to yield.

Note (l), page 199, line 542.

I crown'd as victor of Pamplona's fight.

RICHARD is said to have been struck with the beauty of Berengaria, Princess of Navarre, while he was only Count of Poitou. I do not know where to turn to my authority, but I have some recollection of his being present at a tournament given either by her father or brother.

Note (m), page 201, line 585.

The first of Western thrones, the " King of Kings."

Mailly says, in speaking of the letter of Hugues le Grand to Alexius, " that such was the opinion which those ages entertained of the power of a King of France, that the title of *Roi des Rois* was not only often claimed for him by his subjects, but bestowed by writers of other nations; such as Matthew Paris, who gives it to him *par excellence.*" In like manner the daughters of the French King are said to have disdained the name of Princesses, and to have pretended that the title of Queen was due to their birth alone.

Note (n), page 203, line 617.

One half of Flanders to my rule resign.

Among other things to which the two Monarchs had bound themselves, when they met at Vezelay to make arrangements for their journey, was an exact division of conquest during the Crusade. Philip therefore claimed one-half of Cyprus from RICHARD: but that monarch insisted that though they were bound to share whatever they should acquire together, Philip had no right over that which was won without his aid; nevertheless he was willing to divide the island with him, if Philip would in like manner give him half the county of Flanders, which had just reverted to its Suzerain by the death of Theodoric, who expired at Acre on the very day of RICHARD's arrival. To this Philip would not agree, and the quarrel was never perfectly accommodated.

Note (o), page 204, line 641.

From Fulk I also spring—this biting blade.

Fulk, fourth King of Jerusalem, was by his first marriage father to Geoffrey Earl of Anjou, so that RICHARD stood in exactly the same relation to Fulk with Baldwin the Fifth, they being both his great-grand-children; and if it were to be considered that a female was unworthy to fill the throne of Jerusalem (as had been asserted at the accession of Sybilla), he became the legitimate heir.

Note (p), page 205, line 683.

The stings of death for those the sword shall spare.

RICHARD, almost immediately on his arrival before Acre, addressed himself to the consideration of the means likely to compel its surrender; and one of his most efficacious manœuvres was the turning the course of a river which supplied the city with water. This circumstance has possibly been the occasion of some difficulty into which geographers have fallen respecting the river Belus. This river formerly so celebrated for its silicious sands, and the accidental discovery of glass, is joined near its mouth by another river, which being figured in some charts as a separate stream, doubts arose as to which really deserved the name of Belus. More recent surveys having proved their junction, it is probable that the lesser stream was that which formerly supplied Acre with water, and which RICHARD diverted from its course. M. Michaud observes that Acre is perhaps the only city of which we possess an original plan, taken so early as the thirteenth century.

Note (q), page 206, line 691.

Stretch'd its huge links, and dipp'd beneath the main.

See the description of Acre in the note on the Fourth Book. This chain is mentioned in history, but the manner in which RICHARD destroyed it is from the Romance.

> " How the folk off the hethene lawe,
> A gret cheyne hadden i-drawe,
> Ovyr the havene of Acres fers,
> And was festnyd to two pelèrs,
> That noo schyp ne scholde in-wynne,
> Ne they nought out that wer withynne."
> * * * * * * * * * * *
> " And Kynge RYCHARD, that was so good,
> With hys axe in foreschyp stood;
> And whenne he com the cheyne too,
> With hys axe he smot it in two,
> That all the barouns, verrayment,
> Sayde it was a noble dent."

Note (r), page 212, line 825.

A thousand marks proclaimed to him should lure him home.

I avail myself of this incident to notice a characteristic difference between the third Crusade and those which preceded it. Louis the Seventh of France, and the Emperor Conrad, followed the track of Peter the Hermit and Godfrey of Bouillon. They had to contend with all the fatigues of a long and difficult journey, with all the miseries of famine, and all the dangers arising from open hostility and secret treachery; in Hungary, Bulgaria, and the Greek provinces bordering on Constantinople. These evils redoubled, when, passing into Asia Minor, they became entangled in mountain passes, and exposed to the incessant attacks of the Turks, under the dominion of the Seljouc Sultans of Iconium. Scarcely a third of their numerous armies reached Palestine, and those who did not perish in the journey, or whose sufferings did not cause them to turn back before they attained the Holy Land, arrived there in a deplorable state of exhaustion and poverty. Destitute of provisions, of money, frequently of arms and clothing, warriors of high birth, and ample European possessions, were often reduced to subsist on the charity of wealthier or more provident leaders; and all were in need of assistance. Frederic Barbarossa, whose lamentable expedition forms a part of the third Crusade, still pursued the beaten track; and even the courage and ability which had been displayed in a long life of war, could not save himself and his army from the fate of their precursors.

Philip Augustus and RICHARD of England, however, took warning from the sad example, and emulating the adventurous spirit displayed by the Norwegian Sigurd, and other warriors of the Baltic, they dared to entrust themselves and their armies to the ocean, and hired for the voyage the galleys of Genoa and Piso; for Venice, though then the first of maritime powers, took little part in the crusades, till her own interests were attacked in the contest for Constantinople. Some dangers were encountered in the course of the voyage, part of which may be reckoned among the ordinary casualties of the sea, but of which the greater proportion should be ascribed to the imperfection of the galleys, and to the ignorance of pilots. Still the French and English crusaders encountered neither toil nor privation, and the nobles transported into the East the comforts and many of the luxuries of their feudal castles. The passion for the chase, which then began to rage in France, and had even shewed symptoms of its future dominion in England, prompted many to carry with them their hounds and their falcons. The hunting equipages of several were even scandalously magnificent, and the Syrian nobles thought that their new allies seemed better prepared to wage war with the wild birds and beasts of their country, than with the Saracens. The numbers of dogs and falcons belonging to some individuals is almost beyond belief; and Philip Augustus was determined not to be outdone by his vassals. The bird whose loss is mentioned in the poem, was the subject of a serious embassy to Saladine, the conditions of its restoration were debated with all the solemnity of a treaty, and a sum of money was offered, which would have been sufficient for the ransom of many christian knights. A fact which gave just offence to those whose relations or friends were prisoners to the Soldan.

The private interests of Philip Augustus, and the lukewarmness or disagreement of other princes, prevented the third crusade from being equally glorious in its result with that of Godfrey, but it was distinguished by more of discipline and conduct, and was free from those disasters, those deplorable scenes of human vice and suffering, which cause the mind to revolt from the history of almost every other expedition to the Holy Land. In the preceding crusades, the examples are distressingly numerous, and, in those which followed, the names of Constantinople and Damietta are sufficient to prove that the leaders of the Latin armies, brave and pious as they were, had not yet learned to be generals. When I say that

I ascribe the less disastrous issue of the third crusade to the influence of RICHARD CŒUR DE LION, I shall perhaps raise a smile, and be thought unduly partial to my hero, but the consideration of this subject will be more in its place when I have occasion to speak of the march to Arsouf, and the battle of Jaffa.

Note (s), page 216, line 921.
Then spread her wings and vanished in the sky.

During the siege of Acre the Christians often received intelligence of the intentions of the besieged by means of arrows with labels attached, which were shot into the camp by some friend within the town, and who was supposed to have perished before the surrender of the place, as he never made himself known. Saladine kept up his communication with the city by means of divers, and of carrier pigeons. These winged messengers had long been in use in the east, and were particularly employed under his predecessor Noureddin.

BOOK VI.

Note (a), page 224, line 29.
The soul of war—in youth had Jerworth's hand.

Both the houses of Cadogan and Hampden trace their lineage back to the renowned Caradoc *Friech bras* or *Brise bras*, one of the most famous of Arthur's peers, and no less renowned for his fidelity in love, than his valour in war. The poem alludes to the Fabliau of "The Mantle made amiss," in which Sir Caradoc's lady wins the magic garb, which would fit no damsel whose heart had ever been touched with inconstancy. Jerworth was a family name of the house of Hampden or Trevor.

Note (b), page 230, line 134.

And by his hand the youthful Osbert dies.

Osbert, descended from Geoffrey de Clinton, Lord Chamberlain and Treasurer to Henry the First. His descendants are now Dukes of Newcastle.

Note, page 234, line 218.

" Winton," he said, " strip thou this braggart foe."

Roger de Quincey, Earl of Winchester. There were but two Earls of Winchester of this family.

Note (d), page 234, line 238.

Once had they saved from him the Soldan's chain.

The great benefactor to the English Templars, was Roger de Mowbray, who accompanied Louis the Seventh to the Holy Land in 1148. He granted to the order various manors in Leicestershire. The knights, as an honourable return, gave him the privilege of pardoning any Templar who was doing penance. But they did him the more valuable service of ransoming him from the Saracens, after the battle of Tiberias; for one journey to Palestine did not satisfy this pious chieftain. In the days of Edward the Third, the Hospitallers, as possessors of the lands of the Templars, conferred the privilege of pardoning offending knights upon John Lord Mowbray, the lineal heir of Roger.

Note (e), page 236, line 280.

Should fight the battles of his injur'd God.

It was in reality Henry the Second, and not RICHARD, who explored the tomb of King Arthur, in Glastonbury Abbey; the songs of the Cambrian Bards having revealed to him that monarch's place of sepulchre. The bodies of himself, and his Queen Geneura, were found in two stone coffins by the side of the high altar, and were little changed by time. RICHARD afterwards bestowed Caliburn on Tancred King of Sicily, but it is to be regretted that he did not retain so interesting a relic. Warton's poem of " Arthur's Grave," is probably familiar to my readers.

Note (f), page 240, line 371.

That scented scimitar of Syrian frame.

The pliability of the damask sabres is more remarkable than the keenness of their edge. They appear upon close examination to be striated, or composed of filaments of steel and iron, in a manner similar to the alloys of steel and silver obtained in the experiments of Messrs. Stodart and Faraday. The best damask sabres are not only richly mounted, but are said to be strongly impregnated with a perfume, which they never lose.

Note (g), page 242, line 420.

And gave her captive foes to lingering flame!

Fanaticism was not confined to the Christian army, for the Saracens of Acre exasperated their besiegers by offering every possible outrage to the symbol of their creed. They raised crosses on the ramparts, beat them with rods, covered them with mud and dust, and broke them into a thousand pieces in sight of the Crusaders, who vowed anew to revenge their outraged faith. In the excess of religious animosity, the Moslems often massacred their unarmed captives; and on more than one occasion, they were seen to burn their Christian prisoners on the field of battle.—*Michaud.*

Note (h), page 243, line 432.

His servants tremble for a life adored.

See note (h), pages 408-409.

Note (i), page 244, line 454.

To mate thy banner with the badge of kings.

This seems to have been the true reason of the quarrel between RICHARD and Leopold, that the latter, being only a Duke, ordered his banner to be placed on the ramparts, which the high spirited Monarch considered as an affront to his regal dignity, and flung it into the ditch without any ceremony.

Note (i), page 248, line 560.

He lopp'd the pennon's forked points, and said.

Knights were divided into two classes, Knights Bannerets and Knights Bachelors: no man being properly a Knight Banneret, who could not bring into the field a certain number of lances, from fifty to twenty-five, this last was the lowest number; he had also a right to a war cry, which other knights had not. He was distinguished by the square banner, carried by a squire at the point of his lance, whereas the Knight Bachelor had only the cornet or forked pendant. When a Banneret was created, the general cut off the ends of his pendant to render it square, but this honour conferred no command except over his own dependants. Olivier de la Marche makes a distinction between the Bachelor created Banneret on account of his estate or merit, and the hereditary Banneret, who took a public opportunity of requesting the Sovereign to unfold his family banner, which he had before borne wound round his lance: the first was called *rélever bannière*, the second *entrer en bannière*. Sir John Chandos was still a Bachelor when he led part of the Black Prince's army into Spain, and first raised his banner at the battle of Navarette, where it was *unfolded, not cut.—See Hallam's Middle Ages.*

Note (k), page 249, line 564.

Now prove him false that called his King unjust,

The authority for this little episode is in Vinesauf, who records that one of his knights voluntarily received the blow which was aimed at RICHARD, and also the circumstance of the Monarch's reconciliation after the battle, with one who had previously offended him, but whom he forgave on account of his valour.—He also makes frequent mention of Baldwin de Carrio (now Carew) who must have been either the son or nephew of William, Castellan of Windsor, whose fidelity was so conspicuous during the absence of RICHARD.—This William was hereditary governor of Windsor Castle, that office having been confirmed to his father by the Empress Maude, and from it his family took the surname of Windsor, which is still retained by their descendants the Earls of Plymouth. That of Carrio, perpetuated in the Carews of Cornwall and Devon, was derived from a fief which William inherited in right of his mother.—This family is by some antiquaries derived from the Dukes of Tuscany, who are said to have passed from Florence to Normandy, but its descent appears pretty well established from Othoer, a powerful lord under King Alfred, and of Norwegian ancestry. Gerald, great grandson of Othoer, was sent by Henry the Second against Owen Rhys, Prince of Gwyneth or North Wales, whom he reduced to submission, and was made Castellan of Pembroke, under Montgomery Earl of Pembroke. Having also slain Owen, son of Cadugan ap Blethyn, chief Lord of Cardiganshire, he was made president of the county of Pembroke, chamberlain to the King, and married the Princess Nesta, daughter of the vanquished Prince of Gwyneth. His second son, Maurice, was the principal person by whose aid Ireland was conquered, and distinguished in most of the principal actions there. From him descended the Fitzgeralds, Dukes of Leinster, Fitzmaurices, Earls of Kerry, and the Fitzgeralds,

Earls of Desmond (now extinct); of the same stock were the Geralds, Earls of Macclesfield (now also extinct); the Lords Gerald of Bromley, the Geralds of Bryn, in Lancashire, and many other noble families of the same name. The ancient armorial bearings were Gules, a saltier argent.

Note (l), page 254, line 680.

Those webs that only Arab maids can weave.

A sort of coarse cloth, the manufacture of which is peculiar to the women of Arabia.

Note (m), page 254, line 681.

Where towering date-trees shade the saffron mead.

Saffron was one of the principal exports of the East in the middle ages, and the Crusaders were delighted when on arriving there they beheld whole fields of the favourite plant.

Note (n), page 255, line 690.

And sold, half-lifeless, to a stranger's hand.

The "Letters from Tripoli" contain many distressing relations of the manner in which Georgian and Circassian girls are kidnapped by the Tartars, and hurried across the desert in sacks slung on the back of a camel. Many die on the journey, or never recover their fatigues, though they are afterwards fattened with the greatest care, and instructed in such accomplishments as are considered most marketable. Of these stories the most interesting is that of Lilla Halluma, who after many sufferings was sold to Hadgi Abderahman, afterward ambassador in England; and by her beauty and gentleness not only induced her master to marry her, but to grant her many indulgences not often accorded to the Moorish females, and among others, that of receiving intelligence from her native country, and relieving the wants of her family, who had fallen into distress. Many of the poorer Georgians educate their daughters expressly for the

Turkish market, and themselves dispose of them to the Tartars.

BOOK VII.

Note (a), page 273, line 36.
Thou hold'st my life as dear as thine to me.

The speech of Philip Augustus is very nearly that which history ascribes to him; there appears little doubt that his sickness was affected, and that his religious ardour having never been great, his reasons for returning to Europe were purely political. These were the death of Theodoric Earl of Flanders, in consequence of which the Earldom reverted to his Suzerain, but which he was in danger of losing, if not at hand to take care of his interests; and the convenient opportunity which the absence of CŒUR DE LION afforded him for attacking his ill-defended states, and gratifying the jealousy with which he regarded the superior wealth and martial fame of his rival. The friendship of Philip Augustus had been fatal to RICHARD while only Count of Poitou, for it led him into rebellion against his father, and his hatred in after life was his perpetual bane. The Crusade produced a faint and false accord; each had bound himself by the most solemn oaths to a participation of peril, of glory, and of conquest; to defend as his own the possessions of his comrade, both at home and abroad; and the Church had rivetted these vows by the most deadly imprecations on all that should violate "the Peace of God." Yet were all these vows made but to be broken; real friendship needs no such covenants, and it has been ever obvious that the most solemn engagements are as wax before the flames of ambition. RICHARD and Philip were seldom together for three days without a quarrel; and though, as at Messina, the influence of the Holy Cause terminated these discords by a renewal of their vows, yet, as Michaud observes, there could be but little faith in a friendship which it was necessary to obtest so often. As soon as RICHARD arrived at Acre, the contest about Cyprus rekindled the sparks of jealousy, and the two Kings never once joined their forces against the foe; the most that could be obtained was that, one should attack the army of Saladine while the other assaulted the city; but on more than one occasion, as has been already noticed, Philip would have retired with disgrace before the Soldan, if RICHARD, forgetting his animosity, had not withdrawn his troops from the town and redeemed the victory. His martial superiority was thus rendered but more manifest. It was the duty of each leader to support his troops: and the monthly allowance which RICHARD granted to each man, was one-third more than that bestowed by Philip. It was natural that all who lived upon " debateable land" (and when we remember how many of the fairest provinces in France belonged to RICHARD, these could not be few), should be eager to profess themselves the followers of the most munificent master: Philip therefore accused RICHARD of seducing his soldiers from their allegiance. In a word, he had less irritability than the English Monarch, but as he also wanted his frankness, he seems never to have forgotten their former discontents, even at the moment when he again pledged an inviolable friendship; and when envy was in secret rankling in his heart, new grounds for quarrel could never be long absent.

Note (b), page 273, line 54.

Again to pledge the vows of Vezelay.

Vezelay is a small town in Burgundy, not far from Auxerre, and was the place where Philip and RICHARD met to make final arrangements for the crusade. The vows taken at Vezelay were nearly the same as those by which the Crusaders, at the council of Clermont, bound themselves to abstain from all private or Christian warfare, and by which all the Princes and Nobles became reciprocal guardians of each others dominions during the crusade; such as might remain at home, or might return before the rest, pledging themselves to respect the rights of the absentees. Philip and RICHARD made a farther agreement, that neither should abandon the crusade without the consent of the other; it was hence that RICHARD, when that consent was asked, required as a condition that Philip should again bind himself not to commit any outrage on his undefended states, of which his eagerness to return made him justly suspicious; and that Philip, in reply, demanded the renewal of RICHARD's homage for the extensive fiefs which he held of the French crown; so extensive, indeed, that when it is remembered that neither Burgundy, nor Lorraine, nor Flanders, then belonged to the Kings of France, it may well be asked, on what pretensions they founded their right to the title of " King of Kings," and first of the Monarchs of Europe.

Note (c), page 275, line 91.

Ye are not worthy to behold her walls!

This memorable expression has been ascribed to RICHARD by the historians of the times, though they differ in their account of the occasion which called it forth. Some say, that during his residence at Jaffa, he penetrated, on one of his romantic hunting excursions, to a hill whence he had a distant view of the towers of Jerusalem. He was then preparing to return to Europe, and the Holy City seemed to upbraid him with his want of power to relieve her, and with his meditated desertion of her cause. He wept, and veiling his head in his mantle, exclaimed, " that those who could not deliver, were unworthy to behold her." Other writers address this expression, as I have done, in reproach to some of his companions, who deserted their vows for the deliverance of the sepulchre.

Note (d), page 275, line 98.

Paid the dire forfeit of his broken word.

This is the least graceful feature of King Richard's life, and that which I have felt most difficulty in managing. To have passed it over entirely, would scarcely have been allowable, but after much consideration, I determined to touch it as slightly as possible. I could not hope to imitate Mr. Southey's extraordinary power of identifying myself and my feelings with those of the age or country of which I treated, neither could I expect or wish, in the nineteenth century, to obtain the sympathy of my readers in an attempted extenuation of massacre. Yet it would surely have been as unjust to Richard, as it was inconsistent with a story of which he was the hero, to hold forth to the detestation of posterity, an act not only excused, but applauded by the fanaticism of his contemporaries. The facts were briefly these: when Acre was surrendered, about 4,000 captives remained in the hands of the two Sovereigns, Richard and Philip. A treaty had been entered into with Saladine for the payment of a large sum of gold, the surrender of the wood of the True Cross, &c. &c. on condition of which they were to receive their liberty: but if he failed to fulfil the treaty before a certain day, their lives were forfeit. The day expired, the conditions were unfulfilled; a good deal of fruitless negociation followed, which only led to mutual exasperation; and, after waiting three weeks, Richard, who was preparing to commence his march, gave orders for the massacre. The numbers who are reported to have fallen vary from 1,500 to 4,000 or 6,000: I am inclined to think the lowest number the most correct. Many of the more wealthy had been already ransomed, or were reserved for ransom; and Philip, who had in the meantime departed to Tyre, took *his* share of the captives with him. Richard often sent for them, but he who was about to leave Palestine seemed rather inclined to obtain money for their freedom, than to strike terror by their murder; and if at last he gave them up to his rival, it does not appear that he did so previous to the massacre. Aboulpharagins says, " that the time being expired, Saladine sent to the Franks, ' Dismiss all the Arabs who are in your bonds, and I will give you the third part of the gold, and hostages for the other two; or otherwise, ye shall give me hostages for the third part which ye have received.' But the Franks said, ' Our word alone is sufficient to you, and our honour: why should we give hostages?' Then the heart of Saladine was hardened, neither would he consent, and the Franks being enraged, bound all the Arabs with cords, and leading them forth from the city on to the hill, having clothed them in vile garments, they ran upon them with drawn swords, and slew them in sight of the Moslem camp." The author of the Life of St. Louis relates the event in a manner which lays the first guilt of massacre on Saladine, and implicates Philip in the retaliation inflicted by the Christians. " Cinque mille hommes qu'il y avoit de garnison demeurèrent prisonniers, à condition d'être relachés en faisant rendre la vraie croix, et les esclaves Chrétiens: sinon qu'ils demeuroient à la discrétion des vainqueurs. Mais *Saladin, ayant fait mourir un grand nombre des prisonniers qu'il avoit de son côté*, bien loin de tenir la capitulation, ces 5,000 hommes eurent tous la tête tranchée, *un moitié au nom de Philippe, et l'autre au nom de* RICHARD. Ce fut *Eudes, Duc de Bourgogne, qui ménagea cet honneur à la France avec tant d'exactitude*." The Romance of CŒUR DE LION, which by its naïveté renders amusing those scenes of horror which would otherwise disgust, increases the number of the captives to 60,000, commands their destruction by the voice of an angel, and dwells with peculiar pleasure on the edifying effusion of Pagan blood. At the same time it is not sparing in its abuse of Philip, whom it accuses of avarice in liking better to receive ransom for his prisoners, than to follow the good example of putting them to death. I ought not to omit, that Saladine was certainly not slow in making reprisals on the Christian captives in his hands; and Mr. Sharon Turner, in his admirable sketch of the Third Crusade, relates an interesting anecdote of a young warrior whom the Soldan kept for two days with him in his tent, conversing with him, and endeavouring to convert him, or to find some reason which might excuse to his own bigotry the disposition which he felt to exempt him from the fate of his companions. At last he gave orders for his death, an instance of cold blooded cruelty, of which Mr. Turner seems to think, that RICHARD, ferocious as he has been deemed, would have been incapable.

Note (e), page 276, line 112.

By adverse ocean, or his wavering mind.

There were at least three embassies sent to Conrad at Tyre; of these the Bishop of Salisbury, Otho of Burgundy, and Roger de Quincy, Earl of Winchester, formed part; but as the several negociations are not important to the story, I have mentioned but one, and engaged in it those personages that best suited my subject. The Bishop of Beauvais was certainly with Conrad at the period when he was engaged in treaty with Saladine. He was one of the most distinguished for valour among the martial prelates of the age, but he did not, like Hubert of Salisbury, and the venerable Baldwin, Archbishop of Canterbury, combine the clerical virtues with the prowess of a warrior. During the captivity of RICHARD, the Bishop proved himself one of his most malignant enemies.

Note (f), page 276, line 119.

Meanwhile the pilgrim host their course began.

The historians of the time are followed in this arrangement

of the troops. Whatever was most precious moved in the centre, surrounded by the knights of England and Normandy; while the auxiliary cavalry, if I may so call the smaller troops belonging to other nations, formed the front and rear, and the infantry protected the flanks. The Templars and Hospitallers frequently exchanged places, but one was always in advance of the army, while the other formed the rear-guard. They were engaged in constant skirmishes with the infidels, especially after leaving Cesarea, and many acts of signal valour are recorded. The disposition and conduct of the troops in this long and difficult march, though not one of the most splendid achievements of our lion-hearted King, is among those which have gained him the greatest credit in modern times, and proves that in his military arrangements, he was not deficient in that prudence which has so often been denied to him. He is allowed to have been the first who in the age of chivalry consented to make use of infantry as a body, and who knew how to place it to advantage.

Note (g), page 277, line 132.

And, sheathed in stubborn mail, the flanks defend.

The Saracens complained in this march that their javelins and arrows made no impression on the Christian yeomanry, whom they described as men of steel, and said that a javelin which would have pierced one of their men to the back-bone, dropped powerless from the European coats of mail. Some of them are said to have had not less than ten arrows bristling in their breast-plate and habergeon, yet to have marched on unwounded.

Note (h), page 277, line 134.

The copious fleet each rising want supplied.

The fleet manned by the Pisans and Genose followed the line of coast along which the armies marched, so as to be ready to supply them with arms and provisions on any emergency.

Note (i), page 279, line 167.

The name of him to self-destruction led.

The Judas-tree, which is common in all parts of Syria, owes its name to a belief that it was on this tree that Judas Iscariot hanged himself. Its blossom is abundant, and of a bright rose colour; but it perhaps rather deserves the name of a large shrub than of a tree.

Note (k), page 279, line 172.

Their rich festoons of crimson and of gold.

The cactus opuntia, or Indian fig, of which hedges are made in many parts of Syria, where their proliferous stems form hedges of fourteen or fifteen feet high, and eight or nine feet thick. This extraordinary plant, which I have already had occasion to notice in a note on a former work (the Veils,) forms an almost impenetrable barrier to the passage of an army, and appears capable of becoming even a greater annoyance than the kantuffa of Abyssinia. Its prickly leaves wound the horses, and, if torn, their acrid juice is still more distressing in its effects. It is not easily cut down, and it will not burn. It does not however appear to have been so common in Palestine in the twelfth century, as to cause any inconvenience to the Crusaders. Mrs. Tully, in her admirable Letters from Tripoli, admires the beauty of its red and yellow blossoms, which she describes as hanging like festoons on the edge of its gigantic leaves.

Note (l), page 279, line 180.

With this dire gift to curse th' Atlantic world.

The history of the sugar-cane is curious. Indigenous in Egypt, and cultivated with success in Syria, in Cyprus and

Rhodes, this important plant was first made known to Europe by the Crusades. The soldiers of Raymond of Tholouse in 1098 discovered it in the neighbourhood of Tripoli, and when the march to Jerusalem was determined, they were with difficulty torn from the novel luxury. The mode of extracting the sugar was simple, but appears to have been efficacious. The inhabitants, when the canes were ripe, pounded them in a mortar, and then permitted the juice to coagulate in a cake " whiter than salt or snow." The "*Canna Mellis*," as it was called, (the Crusaders seeming to consider its juice as another species of honey) was soon transplanted into Sicily, where it appears to have flourished, and to have given rise to the extravagant passion for sweetmeats which existed in Italy in the fourteenth century, and of which traces may yet be found in the Carnival. Egypt was the principal source whence this consumption was supplied. From Sicily the culture of the sugar-cane passed to Grenada, thence to Madeira, and from Madeira to Brazil, whence it spread over the New World.

Note (m), page 279, line 181.
All lovely yet appear'd that chosen land.

The present appearance of Palestine corresponds so little with the glowing description of " a land flowing with milk and honey," or with the bunch of grapes which attested its fertility to the Children of Israel, that most of the writers on the Crusades have thought it necessary to enter into some details respecting its past and present state. A long and narrow tract of sandy coast, bounded by rocks and deserts, and but imperfectly and partially watered by mountain torrents, which, while they spread lavish fertility in their immediate neighbourhood, leave the rest a waste, conveys no adequate idea of the Land of Promise; the chosen Land, which was selected by Divine Will as the residence of his favourite people; the scene of his miraculous interpositions in their behalf, and finally the incarnation of his Son, and the redemption of mankind. The religion of Mahommed, like the locusts which visit most of the regions in which it predominates, seems to spread devastation in its course. The comparison may be fanciful, but it is true, that while Christianity is on every side ameliorating the face of nature, in the same proportion that it improves the social condition of mankind, draining the bog, levelling the mountain, overcoming the rigour of the frozen north, or the drought of tropical climes, Mahommedanism, the religion of war, of oppression and cruelty, has been long at strife with the bounty of nature in some of the fairest portions of the globe. Even the provident labours of their ancient cultivators are neglected and despised. The canals of Egypt are suffered to go to decay, nor can the diminution of that belt of verdure which still clothes the bounteous Nile, warn the careless and oppressed inhabitants to oppose in time the encroachments of the desert upon that Granary of the Ancient World. In Palestine, the descriptions of the Crusaders seem to present a middle point between its former beauty and its present state of neglect. It had suffered much and often, from war and pillage; and the martial spirit of feudal discipline in a kingdom struggling for existence was nearly as unfavourable to the husbandman, as the rapacious inroads of the Turks; yet there had been intervals in which it had revived, and its beauty, though blighted, was not destroyed.

I cannot resist the temptation of subjoining to this note the comment of a literary friend. " The fertility of that country depends upon moisture and shade; humidity is encouraged by trees. It has never been observed that the fatal and *predestined* blow was given to Palestine by Titus. To frame those immense works with which he assailed the capital, he cut down gardens, groves, and forests, for many leagues around. Deprived of shade, the ground has ever since remained scorched and barren, for no attempts were or could be made to replant, &c. This, in a word, is the reason of the barren state of the country."

Note (n), page 280, line 198.

To Anna's shrine their duteous homage pay.

Dr. Clarke speaks of the church of St. Anne at Saphura, as a stately *Gothic* edifice. The pointed arch is not uncommon in eastern ruins of the time of the Crusades; among these may be noticed the palace of Saladine at Cairo built under his directions, or those of his vizir Karacous.

Note (o), page 281, line 213.

In the clear nectar from the fountain head.

The fresh pods of the tamarind steeped in water, form a cooling and delicious beverage, of which the acid is peculiarly agreeable beneath the fervour of an eastern sky.

Note (p), page 281, line 223.

Turns to the sun, and loves, like her, in vain.

The heliotrope, so much admired for its fragrance, was the sun-flower of the ancients, and the flower into which Clytie was supposed to be transformed. It is said always to turn its blossoms to the sun, and to follow him through the skies: but this "fond idolatry" is so much more conspicious in the common American sun-flower, which has in addition the advantage to resemble the object of its adoration, that it has sometimes caused confusion; and a celebrated Italian artist, in painting the story of Clytie has introduced the sun-flower instead of the heliotrope.

Ovid describes the flower with sufficient exactness:

> Perque novem luces expers undæque cibique,
> Rore mero, lachrymisque suis jejunia pavit:
> Nec se movit humo. Tantùm spectabat euntis
> Ora Dei: vultusque suos flectebat ad illum.
> Membra ferunt hæsisse solo: partemque coloris

> Luridus exsangues pallor convertit in herbas.
> Est in parte rubor: violæque simillimus ora
> Flos tegit. Illa suum, quamvis radice tenetur
> Vertitur ad Solem; mutataque servat amorem.
>
> *Metam. lib.* 4.

Note (q), page 287, line 356.

Whose golden bloom outvies the robe of kings,

Sir James Smith supposes the amaryllis lutea, a very beautiful flower, which is as common in some parts of Palestine as the buttercup in our English meadows, to have been the plant alluded to by our Saviour when he says: " Consider the lilies of the field, they toil not, neither do they spin, yet verily I say unto you that Solomon in all his glory was not arrayed like one of these."

Note (r), page 287, line 358.

From that whose beams a Saviour's birth proclaim'd.
Ornithogallum, or Star of Bethlehem.

Note (s), page 288, line 378.

Here ambush'd fraud might lurk, nor lurk in vain,

The country between Cesarea and Jaffa is one of the most difficult and dangerous which an army can have to struggle with. On the left is that prolongation of the chain of Lebanon, known by the general name of Mount Sharon, though in parts it borrows that of Napolose, of Sichem, and other places in the vicinity. A straggling forest, composed entirely of cerrial oak, extends over the sides of the hills, and sometimes approaches very near to the sea; the intermediate space is broken by rocks and torrents, whose stony beds are scarcely less difficult to cross in the summer, than their furious waves in winter. A French traveller (M. Paultre) compares this tract to that extraordinary region in the neighbourhood of Fontainebleau, which any of my readers who have had a taste of its cross-roads cannot fail to remember. Large blocks of calcareous stone, grey without, from the effect of weather, but white at their more recent fractures, protrude on every side through the soil, and force the stunted trees to assume a thousand ungraceful forms. Indeed they appear rather the remains of a nobler forest, crushed by these gigantic masses, than to have sprung up around them. The forest of Sharon, of Arsouf, of Napolose, of Ascalon, or of Jaffa, for it bears all these names, is about six and thirty miles long, and from seven to nine broad. Many recent writers on the subject have exerted themselves to prove that this is the spot whence the leaders of the first crusade derived materials for the construction of their warlike engines; and which Tasso has embellished with so much of romantic fancy. Their arguments appear to be well supported; the situation of the wood of Sharon answers with tolerable precision to that of the Enchanted Forest, which was formerly supposed to have had no existence but in the imagination of the poet; and the idea derives new force from its being the only place within any probable distance from Jerusalem which could have afforded timber for the purposes of the siege. The more the Poem of Tasso is compared with the history of the time, and the geographical localities of Palestine, the more does his scrupulous accuracy become manifest: an accuracy the more surprising when it is remembered how much less of foreign countries or of ancient history was generally known, than in our more enlightened days, and that perhaps few of his readers would have detected or condemned any departure from historical truth.

Note (t), page 290, line 431.

Fades not, nor brightens when the Spring returns.

It has already been observed, that this forest is entirely composed of cerrial oak; *Quercus Cerris*. The trees growing in a shallow soil, near the sea, and scarcely ever receiving a due portion of moisture, do not attain any great size. Their appearance announces extreme age, yet their height does not exceed twenty-five or thirty feet, while eight or nine inches is the diameter of their stems. Their growth is seldom upright, and their summits affect an orbicular form, like that of trees which have been pollarded. The wood is very hard, the stems are knotty, yet the bark is smoother than that of our English oak: the leaves more shining and less deeply indented; the acorns large, and with a cup unusually wide. M. Paultre observes, that the scales which cover the cup are not rounded, as in our European acorns, but pointed and bent back in a sort of volute, which has acquired for this tree the name of *Quercus Crinita*. He compares the general appearance of the forest of Arsouf to the straggling woods on the gravel hills of Lower Burgundy.—*See Michaud, Pièces Justificatives.*

Other writers describe the *Quercus Cerris* or Turkey oak, and the *Quercus Crinita*, hairy cupped oak, or Burgundy oak, as distinct species; but the Oriental oaks in particular do not seem to be accurately known.

Note (u), page 292, line 481.

And far before him casts the lifeless prey.
" Before whose fury and unmatched force
The awless Lion could not wage the fight,
Nor keep his princely heart from RICHARD's hand."
King John.

The writers of the middle ages, not contented that RICHARD's surname of CŒUR DE LION, should be supposed to have arisen from his bold and warlike character, have fabled that he derived it in a more *literal* sense, from tearing out the heart of a Lion, with which he was engaged in single combat. The romance of CŒUR DE LION says, that RICHARD on his return from a private pilgrimage to the Holy Land, was taken prisoner by the King of Almayne.

The King's son challenges RICHARD, and is slain by him. The King's daughter Margery falls in love with the gallant captive; this her father discovers, and consults with his counsaylleres how to get rid of his enemy.—Ser Eldryd says:

"Ye weten wel, it is no lawe
A Kyng to hange and to drawe.
Ye schal do, be my resoun:
Hastely take your lyoun,
And with-holdes hym hys meete;
Three dayes that he nought eete;
And RYCHARD into chaumbyr ye doo,
And lete the lyoun wende hym too:
In this manere he schal be slawe.
Than dost thou nought ayeyns the lawe.
The lyoun schal hym ther sloo;
Then art thou wroken off thy foo.

The Princess warns Richard of his danger, and advises him to fly with her.

RYCHARD sayde: "I understande
That wer agayn the lawe of lande,
Away to wende withouten leve:
The Kyng ne woll I nought so greve.
Off the lyoun ne geve I nought;
Hym to sle now have I thought:
Be pryme, on the thrydde day,
I geve the hys herte to pray."
Kevercheves he askyd of sylk,
Fourty, whyte as ony mylk:—

These kerchiefs he winds round his arm, and awaits the Lion.

With that com the jaylere,
And other twoo with hym in fere,
And the lyon hem among.
Hys pawes was bothe scharp and long.
RYCHARD cryed: "Help, Jesu!"
The lyon made a gret venu,

And wolde have him al to-rent;
Kyng RYCHARD thenne besyde he glent.
Upon the brest the lyoun he spurnyd,
That al aboute the lyoun turnyd.
The lyoun was hungry and megre,
And bit his tayl for to be egre:
Faste aboute, on the wowes,
Abrod he spredde alle hys powes,
And roynyd lowde, and gapyd wyde.
Kyng RYCHARD bethought hym that tyde,
What it was best, and to hym sterte,
In at hys throte hys arme he gerte;
Rent out the herte with hys hand,
Lungges, and lyvere, and al that he fand.
The lyoun fel ded to the grounde:
Rychard hadde neyther wemme ne wounde.
He knelyd doun in that place
And thankyd God off hys grace,
That hym kepte fro schame and harme.
He took the herte, al so warme,
And brought it into the halle,
Before the Kyng and hys men alle.

The King is at dinner with his Peers.—RICHARD presses the blood out of the heart; dips it in the salt and eats it without bread.—The King exclaims

"I-wis, as I undyrstande can,
This is a devyl and no man,
That has my stronge lyoun slawe,
The herte out of hys body drawe,
And has it eeten with good wylle!
He may be callyd, be ryght skylle,
Kyng i-crystenyd off most renoun,
Stronge RICHARD *CŒUR DE LYOUN!*"

I can well believe that RICHARD would not have made more difficulty either in killing or eating a lion, than Antar, his rival enemy to the king of beasts.

Note (x), page 296, line 564.

Till Heaven in thunder check'd his mad career.

Alasia, or Alice, or as some have called her Adelaïs, Princess of France, and sister to Philip Augustus, was unhappily betrothed in infancy to RICHARD, afterwards King of England, and was sent to the court of Henry the Second, to be educated for her future husband. When the Princess grew up, RICHARD demanded his bride, but Henry would not yield her. RICHARD rebelled against his father, and joined with Philip Augustus, who espoused his quarrel; the armies met at Gisors, and were on the point of coming to an engagement, notwithstanding the remonstrances of Pandulphus, the Pope's legate, the same to whom King John afterwards surrendered his crown. The impetuous RICHARD was not to be persuaded out of a quarrel, in which he felt that justice was certainly on his side, though his rebellion was a crime, and in the heat of his passion, he lifted his spear as if to strike the Legate. In the meantime a thunderstorm arose, and *the thunderbolt fell between the two armies.* This extraordinary circumstance, which may be naturally accounted for by the attractive influence of the polished arms and armour on the electric matter, was regarded as the manifest interposition of offended heaven. A peace was soon concluded; Henry consented to create RICHARD Duke of Normandy, to acknowledge his right to the succession, which he had wished to alter in behalf of his favourite John, and to give up Alasia at a fixed time. The latter clause he never fulfilled. He also renewed his vow of the Crusade, while Philip Augustus, RICHARD, and most of the Barons, took or resumed the Cross.

On RICHARD's accession, Philip expected that he should immediately marry the Princess; but his attachment appeared to be cooled. Philip resented this slight upon his sister, and the unfortunate lady, after having been the cause of many private altercations, was on the point of seeing herself again made the subject of open war. RICHARD is however said to have given Philip a satisfactory reason for his change of purpose, in the discovery that his father had detained Alasia from him, on account of a criminal passion which he himself entertained for the young Princess. He gave proofs of her having even borne a son to Henry, and Philip was fain to close the quarrel; and to thank the knightly honour of RICHARD, which prevented him from making the scandal public. Alasia was afterwards mentioned in the dispute at Messina, but she is never named as a cause of feud in the after-wars of the Kings, though they were undertaken by Philip, on pretext of recovering her dower of Gisors and the Vexin, which RICHARD would not yield.

Note (y), page 297, line 582.

His name outshine the conquerors of the world.

This extraordinary man was the Abbé Joachim, who after his return from Jerusalem retired to the mountains of Calabria, where he passed for a Prophet. In austerity of manners and life, he affected to emulate St. John the Baptist. His pilgrimage to the Holy Land had been blest with visions, and Christ himself had taught him to understand the Apocalypse, and to read there, as in a faithful history, all that was to pass on earth. The account of him may be found in Hoveden. He at last incurred the censures of the Church, but at the time of RICHARD's voyage he was in the full odour of sanctity, and the Monarch's superstition was piqued to see the fancied saint. He did not however go to Calabria, but sent for Joachim to Messina, where he was questioned as to the result of the Crusade. Joachim said that Saladine was one of the seven heads of the Dragon in the Apocalypse, and predicted that Jerusalem should be delivered seven years after the conquest of the Soldan. "Why then," said RICHARD, "should we go so soon?" "Your arrival," replied the Hermit, "is very necessary: God will give you the victory over his enemies, and make your name celebrated above the Princes of the Earth." This reply, which was more flattering to the vanity of RICHARD than to the impatience of the Crusaders, give especial umbrage to Philip, and possibly it was less his superiority to the superstition of his age, than his jealousy of the glory announced to his rival, which made him affect to despise the prophet and his predictions.

Note (z), page 297, line 589.
Placed at his father's feet, should ask forgiveness still.
RICHARD the First bequeathed his heart to his favourite city of Rouen, and it was buried in the Cathedral (begun by his father and continued under his reign), at the right side of the altar. On the other side was the body of Henry le Jeune, his elder brother, who died before Henry the Second. RICHARD, however, still penitent for his youthful rebellion, gave strict orders that his body should be buried at the feet of his father, in the Monastery of Fontevraud, or the Fountain of St. Everard, founded by Henry II. It is there that the statue exists from which the portraits of RICHARD have been taken. At Rouen, the stone with the inscription to his memory has been removed, I believe when the present altar was erected, but the Lion-heart still rests beneath.

Note (aa), page 301, line 671.
Voluptuous lamps illume the gaudy flowers.
Aboulfeda. The position of the armies is also historical.

BOOK VIII.

Note (a), page 308, line 18.
Like wintry snows the plumy arrows fly.
Froissart compares the flight of the English arrows, headed by the white goose feather, to a shower of snow.

Note (b), page 314, line 147.

Bade thousands toil Kahira's walls to frame.

Amrou, a general of the Caliph Omar, won Egypt from the Emperor Heraclius, and in the place where he encamped (near to Babylon, which still existed) he built a new town, called *Mars Fostat*, the City of Tents, in which the governor of the province afterwards resided, till Egypt was conquered by Djouhar, in the name of Moez, the Fatimite Caliph who reigned in Africa. Djouhar awaited in his camp the arrival of his master. He caused it to be surrounded with a strong wall, which was soon filled with palaces and mosques, and grew into a town, which he called Kahira, or Al Kahira, the Victorious (corrupted by the Christians into Cairo), and Mars Fostat thenceforward went by the name of Old Kahira. Saladine, after his establishment in Egypt, determined to build a wall, which should enclose both the new and old town. This labour was continued during his life principally under the eye of Karacous, who was governor of Kahira, till summoned to the defence of Acre: but the successors of the Soldan neglected to complete it. Saladine also raised a superb mosque over the tomb of the Imam Shafei, founder of one of the principal orthodox sects of Islam, and added to it an hospital for the poor, and a college for theology, history, poetry, medicine, and arithmetic; at the same time he constructed the Castle of Kahira, or the Castle of the Mountain, the only place of defence which now exists in Egypt. It was celebrated for its extent and magnificence, and the ruins which still remain are interesting. The arches are pointed. Joseph's Well is another monument of the reign of Saladine, and was called after him, for the Soldan was proud of his name of Yusuf, or Joseph, which he inherited from his grandfather, and he loved to trace his descent from the Patriarch himself.—*See l'Histoire de Saladine, &c.*

Note (c), page 315, line 176.

For ever bears the name of Saladine.

This Knight has been called the Regulus of France, and it is related that the Soldan's gifts were so munificent, as to enable him to build on his return the Château de Jour in Burgundy; on its roof are two little armed figures, which are said to be those of Saladine and Anglure. The same story is also told of the castle of Anglure in Lorraine, but I leave it to the French genealogists to determine their rival-claims.

Note (d) page 316, line 212.

With solemn dirges seek St. Hilda's fane.

The first of these was Lord William de Percy, surnamed Alsgernons, who died at Mountjoy; the second was William de Plesset, Earl of Warwick, who married Maud, sister of Agnes de Percy, and who died without issue in Palestine, in 1184.

Note (e), page 317, line 221.

As when by him Iconium's Prince was slain.

Melkinus, the same whom the history of the Arabs calls Kaisar Schah, son of Kilidge Arselan, and nephew to Saladine by marriage. After various skirmishes, and one successful battle against the treacherous Sultan of Iconium, Frederic Barbarossa stormed and took his capital. Melkinus was slain in one of the combats, I believe by the hand of the young Frederic, whose valour was often conspicuous.

Note (f), page 318, line 260.

And breathes from neighbouring hills th' inspiring gale.

Damascus has been often admired for the beauty of its situation and gardens. A river, which falls roaring from the mountains, rolls over a gold-coloured sand, and spreads coolness and fertility in the valley of Abennessage, or the "Vale of Violets." It had so long been celebrated for its delightful situation, that Mahommed, who affected great temperance, refused to enter it, declaring " that there was but one Paradise destined to man, and that he was determined not to take his in this world!"

Note (g), page 319, line 282.

And war she never sought, but well sustain'd.

Saleh, the son and rightful heir of Noureddin, was but six years old when his father died, and fled for protection from Saladine to his uncle the Sultan of Mosul. Saladine was successful in every campaign, and Saleh, who feared to be given up to the victor, endeavoured to make peace with him. After the treaty was signed, and Saladine was in consequence preparing to withdraw his army from the siege of Aleppo, a young Princess arrived in the camp, escorted by a great number of slaves. She endeavoured to throw herself at the feet of the Soldan, but he who recognised the daughter of Noureddin, raised her, and inquired what she wished. She asked the safety of her brother, and the restitution of the fortress of Ezaz, which Saladine had recently won by a sharp siege. He granted her request with courtesy, and added many valuable presents. Some time after this, when Saleh and his protector the King of Mosul were both dead, Saladine continued the war; and Mazoud, son of the latter, being besieged in his capital, had recourse to the same means which had before moved the pity and blunted the sword of the conqueror. He sent the daughter of Noureddin, accompanied by his own mother and many noble ladies, to implore again the clemency of Saladine, and the restoration of the towns of Mesopotamia. This step was considered as a mark of the greatest submission, and from the humanity and generosity of the Sultan, its success was confidently anticipated. But Mazoud deceived himself. Saladine had found him too troublesome an enemy to let slip his prey in the very moment of success. He received the Sultanas with kindness, and with all the honours due to their rank; but intreaties and tears were vain; he was inflexible for the first time. On this subject M. Marin observes, "that to the political spirit of the present times it would appear surprising that a hero should yield his conquests at the tears of a few women, for they asked no less than the kingdom of Mesopotamia. Nevertheless, the manners of a nation which we are accustomed to call barbarous, caused the firmness of the Soldan to be regarded as an act of the greatest harshnesss. Many Doctors of the Law, although his subjects, dared publicly to reproach him in their writings, and it is remarkable that he himself repented of what he considered an act of inhumanity." I have less authority for the martial character of the daughter of Noureddin. At the death of Baldwin the Third this noble Arab had replied to those who counselled him to invade Judea, " that it was inhuman to molest the grief of a people that deplored its master, and that he should believe his own glory tarnished, by the attack of those who were not in a condition of defence;" but when Noureddin himself died, Amalric did not think it necessary to imitate his generosity. His invasion of Syria, however, had not the success which he had anticipated. At Paneas or Belinas (Cesarea of Philippa), he was stopped by a woman. The widow of the Atabeg who had been its governor, defended the place with such spirit, that he was glad to hide his retreat by permitting it to be purchased. I have ventured to give this exploit to Almahide. Saladine married either the daughter or the widow of Noureddin, but it is uncertain which.

Note (h), page 320, line 293.

By valour as by vows forbid to yield.

The Knights Templars wore the red cross on the shoulder, like the other knights, but none on the back, "lest the sign of the cross should ever be seen to fly." They were however forbidden by their vows, ever to turn their backs on the enemy, as were also the Knights Hospitallers, and the Teutonic Order.

Note (i), page 321, line 315.

There Leicester first his father's banner spread.

It was in this battle that Robert Fitz Parnel first unfolded the banner of his house, which on his father's death became his by inheritance.

Note, page 321, line 318.

Proud of great Odard's far-descended sword.

Odard, the eldest of five brethren, who came to England with Hugh Lupus, nephew to the Conqueror, is the Patriarch of the Duttons, Lords Sherbourne. In 1665 Odard's sword was in possession of the ladye Elinour, Viscountess Kilmorey, sole heiress of Thomas Dutton; having past from hand to hand like Agamemnon's sceptre.

Note (k), page 321, line 322.

And Pelham's youthful pride—no braver name.

The family of Pelham, now Earls of Chichester, was distinguished in England before the Conquest. John de Pelham, afterwards knighted, was one of those who claimed the honour of taking King John of France prisoner, at the battle of Poitiers, the King having surrendered his sword to him and Sir Roger La Warr. For this achievement the crampet, or chape of the sword, was adjudged to Sir Roger La Warr, and the buckle of the King's belt to Sir John de Pelham, who quartered it in his arms. It is also the occasional crest of the Earls of Chichester.

Note (l), page 322, line 329.

Who once unknown his Sovereign's spear engaged.

See the Romance of CŒUR DE LION. Sir Thomas Multon, and Sir Fulk D'Oyley, are, next to RICHARD himself, the heroes of this poem, but I do not find their names in the history of the times.

Note (m), page 322, line 340.

To D'Oyley's house, enraged to vengeance flies.

It has already been stated, that the House of Perceval, or Yvery, can trace its genealogy beyond the Conquest. Two of the family came to England with William, one of whom, Roger, was brother in arms with Robert D'Oyley, a noble Norman, and the friends bound themselves by mutual oaths to share each other's fortunes. The conqueror rewarded the services of D'Oyley with the only daughter and heir of Wigod de Wallingford, a potent Saxon lord, and in virtue of the agreement, Roger de Yvery obtained of his friend one of the honours, thenceforward called the Barony of Yvery in Oxfordshire. Roger had besides large possessions, and was Chief Butler of England, while some of his family held the same office in Normandy. In 1074, in conjunction with Robert D'Oyley, he founded the Church of St. George, in the Castle of Oxford, and in 1077, he also founded a Benedictine Monastery to the Virgin, near the Castle of Yvery, not far from Evreux in Normandy.

Richard Lovel, or Perceval, attended RICHARD to the Holy Land, and held a principal command in his army; but, being disabled by the loss of his leg, returned to England.

Note (n), page 324, line 380.

Bravest and first, usurps the vacant rein.

Many were the Emirs that perished at the battle of Arsouf, but none were more regretted than a Captain of the Soldan's Mamlukes, whose heroic bravery is celebrated by the Arabic historians. Not one of the Saracen warriors was more prompt to meet the hostile sword; he was always the first to succour his friends, and was himself never in need of their assistance. After his fall, the Moslems ran to raise him: " but he was already among the inhabitants of Heaven."—*Michaud.*

Note (o), page 326, line 426.

Of rout or conquest, swept unheeded by.

It ought to be had in continual remembrance, that the spirit of fanaticism was not confined to the crusaders; and that the name of " The Holy War" was mutually employed by Musulmans and Christians. While the Gospel was carried in state before the leader of the Christians, the Koran, a Koran written under the auspices, if not by the hand of the Caliph Omar, was borne with equal ceremony in the ranks of Saladine, who would pause upon the field of battle to perform his stated prayers, or hear a chapter of the sacred volume.

Note (p), page 328, line 466.

And pining, met the voluntary doom.

The brave Hangest de Coucy was wounded to death at the battle of Arsouf. In a song which has been preserved he bade adieu to France, saying that he sought the Holy Land in quest of three things most dear to a Knight: *Le Paradis, la gloire, et l'amour de sa mie.* The rest of his story is in the chronicles of the times. It bears a strong resemblance to that of the unfortunate Troubadour, William de Cabestaing, as well as to one of the *Novelle* of Boccaccio.

Note (q), page 329, line 493.

Gournay and Ponthieu; and a warrior drest.

All these warriors, as well as those named hereafter, are mentioned among the noble French or Normans, most of whom perished in the Crusade. The flight of the Count of Dreux, brother to the Bishop of Beauvais, is in Vinesauf, as well as the valour of the Count of St. Paul, who had many horses killed under him.

Note (r), page 329, line 503.

A race of sovereigns to Byzantium's throne.

Josceline de Courtenay, third Count of Edessa, was deprived of that principality by the Soldan, and his fate, subsequent to the taking of Jerusalem, is unknown. He left no male issue. The family of Courtenay, in the beginning of the thirteenth century, gave three Emperors to Constantinople; but this House, after having been raised to unexampled honours in Asia, fell, at least in France, into a decline as rapid as its elevation had been wonderful. The passion for crusading seems to have touched almost every branch of this noble family, and many were the martyrs whom it gave to the holy cause. Reginald de Courtenay, a very powerful peer, was in Palestine with Louis the Seventh, and was among those who vindicated the character of Eleanor of Guyenne, when charged by her husband with nuptial infidelity. He afterwards came to England with Henry the Second, and promoted his marriage with the divorced Queen. The prophetic motto of Courtenay seems to mourn for ever its departed grandeur, *Ubi lapsus. Quid feci?*

Note (s), page 329, line 509.

They look'd to Tyre's relentless Prince in vain.

Robert, Lord of Neuburg, is, as Vinesauf has observed, immortalized by his liberalities. During the famine at Acre, the generosity of many of the wealthier Knights saved the lives of thousands. Among these Robert de Neuburg was distinguished. The others are Walkelin Earl of Ferrars, Robert Trusebot, Henry, Count of Champagne, Josceline de Montoirs, the Count of Clermont and Hubert Bishop of Salisbury. Conrad of Montferrat bears the odium of having at least increased this famine by withholding the provisions which it was in his power to furnish from Tyre; and Vinesauf devotes no less than twelve sections to a description of its horrors, concluding each with execrations against the obnoxious Marquis, towards whom, indeed, he never omits any opportunity of shewing his detestation. But while he gives so much space to the especial abuse of Conrad, he seems to have hated Leopold so completely as to wish to rob him even of the immortality of infamy, and notwithstanding his many gallant actions in the Crusade, he never once names, even in a catalogue, that arch-enemy of his own heroic sovereign. He does indeed say that it was an addition to the grief of the English, that RICHARD was captive in *Osterricia*, rather than in Germany; but even there he never hints that the Duke had been in Palestine.

Note, page 330, line 513.
His lineal pride, and Montmorency's name.

The Montmorencies derive their name from an incident in the time of Charles Martel. A Moor having given a challenge to single combat, Martel selected Lysoi to meet him. After a day's hard fighting in lists, Lysoi was victorious, and cried out, *Mon maure est occis,* or *mon maure occis*, now corrupted into Montmorenci. Of the French cavaliers who fell at Acre or in the Crusade, none was more regretted than the young Joscelin de Montmorenci; Madame Cottin has made him a principal character in her Mathilde.

Note (t), page 331, line 538.
Now lend thy aid, or Christendom is lost.

" Now, O, St. George! if thou dost desert us, Christendom must perish."—The vision of St. George is also historical. M. Michaud thinks it was the green knight that was mistaken for him; but supernatural assistance was seldom wanting in the battles of the crusades. M. Mailly seems to have little doubt that the band of martyrs who came to assist their living brethren at Antioch in the first of their expeditions were actually seen on that occasion, that is, that they were a troop drest up by the priests to excite the enthusiasm of the rest.

Note (u), page 332, line 573.

And infant cries are check'd by sudden fear.

RICHARD continued to be the terror of the East, and was celebrated by the Saracens and Turks in their proverbs, long after the Crusades. If a child cried, the nurse frightened it into silence with the threat that RICHARD was coming; and if a horse started, the rider exclaimed, " what! dost thou see King RICHARD?" In like manner Saladine became the hero of the West, and the Saracen's Head is not yet obliterated from our sign-boards.

Note (x), page 334, line 625.

And in the press was beauteous Favel slain.

The Saracens, who saw their sovereign unhorsed, interrupted the combat. The death of Favel has had the honour to be frequently mentioned by the poets who have spoken of RICHARD; and among others by Drayton. Vinesauf says that his velocity was incomparable. The romance states that Favel and Lyard were both among the spoils of Cyprus: but as Normandy was celebrated for its horses, its capital having given its name to the *roan* steeds still so common in that province, I have ventured to make Lyard a Norman. It was the coal-black charger of RICHARD which the Saracens declared to be a devil. The raven upon Lyard's head is from the romance.

Note (y), page 347, line 911.

And thou young Fatimite, far hence remove.

Aladin, being a Persian, was probably a Shiite, or Fatimite; that is, a Mahommedan of the sect of Ali. The orthodox Musulmans hold these sectaries in still greater detestation than either Christians or Idolaters, and believe them to be farther from paradise. As one of the earliest exploits of Saladine was the suppression of the Egyptian or Fatimite Caliphs, and as the Soldan prided himself on his orthodoxy, none of the house of Ayoub were likely to look with complacency on the worshippers of Ali.

Note (z), page 347, line 914.

E'en the rude conqueror spares the haram walls?

The Mohammedan nations, barbarians as they are, have at least one refinement unknown to Greece or Rome. The haram of the monarch is sacred, and all who can find refuge therein. The respect paid to the sanctity of the haram is well illustrated in "Anastasius," in the war between the Beys of Cairo.

Note, page 348, line 948.

By the dread bridge and endless flames of hell.

The bridge of Al Sirat, which lies over the midst of hell, and which the souls, both of the just and unjust, will be obliged to pass. This bridge is finer than a hair, and sharper than the edge of a sword, and is besides beset with thorns and brambles. Nevertheless the good will pass over it with the rapidity of lightning, whereas the wicked will soon miss their footing, and fall headlong into hell. The orthodox Mahommedans maintain that the torments of hell are of eternal duration.—*Sale's Koran.*—*Preliminary Discourse.*

END OF VOL. I.

LONDON:
PRINTED BY COX AND BAYLIS, GREAT QUEEN STREET,
LINCOLN'S-INN-FIELDS.

CŒUR DE LION.

VOL. II.

OR

THE THIRD CRUSADE.

A POEM,

IN SIXTEEN BOOKS.

By ELEANOR ANNE PORDEN,
AUTHOR OF
"THE VEILS," "THE ARCTIC EXPEDITIONS,"
AND OTHER POEMS.

RICHARD that robb'd the Lion of his Heart,
And fought the Holy Wars in Palestine.—*Shakspeare*.

IN TWO VOLUMES.

VOL. II.

LONDON:
PRINTED FOR G. AND W. B. WHITTAKER,
AVE-MARIA-LANE.

1822.

LONDON:
PRINTED BY COX AND BAYLIS, GREAT QUEEN STREET,
LINCOLN'S-INN-FIELDS.

CŒUR DE LION.

BOOK IX.

THE EMBASSY OF ADEL

ARGUMENT.

THE EMBASSY OF ADEL.

Behaviour of Richard on his victory—His confidence in Adel—Advance of the procession—Adel restores Matilda, and proposes terms of peace—Meeting of the Council—Lusignan resigns the crown of Jerusalem to Richard—The self-devotion of Matilda, and expostulation of Raymond—Hubert advises an appeal to the Pope—The march to Ascalon—Discovery of Helim among its ruins—He relates its destruction by order of Saladine—Determination of Richard to rebuild the city—Story and death of Helim—Richard surveys Jerusalem from a distance, and captures the caravan of Mecca—Aladin and Pardo.

CŒUR DE LION.

BOOK IX.

THE EMBASSY OF ADEL.

But Richard ceas'd not from the work of death,
Sheath'd not his sword, nor gave his charger breath,
Till not one turban'd warrior stood to rear
The useless sabre or presumptuous spear.
Then on the turf his painful helm he threw,
In Arsouf's torrent cleansed his sanguine hue,
And, with uplifted hands and ardent gaze,
To Heaven he gives the glory and the praise.
Sad thoughts succeed; the blood that stains his wreath;
The grief, that conquest must be bought with death!

For Percy's blighted youth he now deplored,
D'Oyley the brave, and Ferrars' veteran lord;
But most, where pale the great D'Avesnes was laid,
His manly sorrows mourn'd th' illustrious dead.
He bids whate'er of funeral pomp may give
Fame to the past, or solace those that live,
In Arsouf's walls the honour'd corse await—
(Arsouf, where ruled his valiant sires so late).*

New grief succeeds; Matilda's loss he hears!
Now wrath inspires, and now fraternal fears.— 20
Now would he follow through the night, and claim,
By force and threat'ning arms, the ravish'd dame.
Now reason rules; his calmer feelings rest
On Adel's pledge, and Raymond's rage represt.
" Nay, seek not useless death, my friend; distrust
Provokes deceit, and makes the falsehood just.
Arabs have faith, and Adel's worth is known
In deeds not prais'd by Moslem lips alone.
But if the dawn a broken compact shew,
Thou shalt not find a brother's vengeance slow."— 30

* Valour, and the passion for crusading, were hereditary in the family of D'Avesnes; and Gerard, the ancestor of James, was appointed to the government of Arsouf, on its reduction by Godfrey of Bouillon. The funeral of James D'Avesnes was celebrated by RICHARD with peculiar honour, on the day succeeding the battle of Arsouf.

Meanwhile the Christians, resting from their toil,
Spread through the desert camp, and share its spoil.
Night closes round, but frequent watchfires gleam
On Arsouf's tented slope and mountain stream;
And ruddy torches glanced along the plain,
Where hasty tombs received the nobler slain,
Where friendship waked, the last sad rites to pay,
Or the rude plunderer stripp'd his lifeless prey;
And flash'd, while frighted wolves at distance bay'd,
On dusky hills and Sharon's magic shade. 40

The morning dawn'd, but ere its earliest light
Had Raymond climb'd to Arsouf's giddiest height,
While yet the mist forbade an eagle's ken
To rest on plain, or stream, or shadowy glen.
Around, the clouds engage in fearful clash,
And forked light'nings glance, and thunders crash.
Terrific thunder, heard by those alone
Who list the giant on his mountain throne!
Then sunk the storm, and many a verdant brow
Shone, like blest islands on a lake of snow; 50
Broad rose the rayless sun, and widely spread
The skies with gold, the billowy mist with red.—
But lo! those mists have melted in his beam,
Or lingering only near each mountain stream,

In fleecy wreaths, like clouds of summer skies,
Hang o'er the winding waters whence they rise.
   Far off, emerging from a woody glen,
Now seen, now veil'd by hills or groves agen,
A moving line appears, and flashing light
Glows, as from helms or spears, on Raymond's sight.
Now borne upon the breeze a gentle sound,
Like strains of elfin harpers, breathes around;
A crag obstructs his gaze, but on his ear
The welcome music swells, till full and clear
The royal drum proclaims a Monarch near.
Now from the hill to view distinct advance
Warriors with glittering helm, and shield and lance;
Standards whose black and tawny volumes roll'd
O'er turbans, rich with purple, green, and gold;
Eunuchs, whose robes of spotless muslin flew,   70
In wayward contrast to their Nubian hue;
And Mamlukes, leading by the gilded rein
Arabian steeds, that scarcely touch the plain;
And fair-form'd slaves, whose veils of dazzling white,
Imperial presents screen'd from vulgar sight.
Next Adel rode, conspicuous o'er the rest
By the white waving of his triple crest.

Behind, two chosen youths of Georgian race
Led on a camel, train'd to gentlest pace,
The roseate folds of whose rich palanquin   80
From curious eyes some royal beauty screen.

  No more th' enraptured Raymond paus'd to view,
On wings of love from Arsouf's cliff he flew,
And breathless reach'd the distant camp, as staid
At RICHARD's tent the gorgeous cavalcade;
As on its knees the well-taught camel bends,
And glad Matilda from her seat descends.
The courteous Adel guides her trembling frame,
And to her brother yields the royal dame;
While his fair Queen, her peer in youthful charms, 90
Folds her loved sister in rejoicing arms.
To Adel then a thousand thanks were pour'd,
And ready menials spread the festive board.
In each bright eye confiding pleasure sate,
And concord smooth'd the wrinkled front of hate.
But when his Mamlukes spread to RICHARD's view
The Soldan's gifts, the sister-Queens withdrew;
And Raymond too retired, to ease a breast,
With rapture now, as erst with grief opprest.

Rich vests of honour, gems that knew no price, 100
And bowls enchased with many a rare device;
Hot Saba's spicy wealth, and Yemen's gums,
Whose fragrant fume from silver censers comes:
Conserves, till now to Western taste unknown,
And fruits, the produce of a warmer zone;[b]
Sabres, whose blades delicious odours breathe,
And amulets, that warn of guile or death.
All these display'd, the slaves stood meekly round,
With folded arms and eyes that sought the ground,
When Adel spoke: "I do not wait to hear   110
Repeated thanks that sicken on my ear,
But I, myself no common herald, bring
The proffer'd friendship of no common King.

"Thus then of Ayoub's blood, of Joseph's line,
Shield of the Faith, speaks mighty Saladine—
His days may Alla guard, his power increase,
Till earth be changed for Heaven's eternal peace!

"When baffled hunters quit the idle chace,
When distanced runners feign to yield the race,
Fear prompts, or shame; and some might deem that fear
Brings me for peace a vanquish'd suppliant here:

Yet think what hosts shall arm at my command
From Cashmere's vales, from Nubia's sultry sand;
From Egypt, where within his giant tomb
The Patriarch sleeps from whom my fathers come;*
To mighty Kaf, on whose untrodden brow
The Bird of Ages dwells in endless snow,
Where Sultans ruled ere Adam's race began,
Where Angels bow'd, and Eblis scoff'd at man.[c]
All these, and more, beneath my favour shine, 130
And blend in prayer their Caliph's name with mine!
Then say if fear can dwell with Saladine?
To one less great could Joseph's heir descend,
Or seek one less than RICHARD as a friend?

"Perchance as numerous tribes thy rule obey,
And realms as various bless thy Western sway,
That other seasons, other stars adorn,
And fade in night when ours salute the morn:
Yet what of wealth shall mightiest conqueror save,
But the cold sheet that winds him in the grave?[d] 140

* Joseph, who according to Mahommedan tradition was buried in one of the Pyramids. The delight which Saladine had in asserting his descent from his patriarchal namesake has been before alluded to.

While one poor peasant from his hamlet driven,
Has power to blast him on the bridge of Heaven.*
A few short years, perforce our strife must cease,
Our sons may fight, but we shall sleep in peace.

" Behold me then, for either chance prepared,
For peace or war, as now thy lips award;
Say why, innumerous as the crested waves,
Your annual fleet the wondering Ocean braves?
What rancour fires to quit your tranquil reign?
What shun ye there, what here attempt to gain?" 150

" Twice fifty snows are gone since Godfrey bore,"
Thus RICHARD spoke, " the Cross on Syria's shore,
And asks your Monarch now, why all most dear,
Friends, kindred, home, we leave to perish here?—
The land from hence to Jordan's sacred tide,
The precious Cross where meek Messiah died,
His tomb, and where Jehovah's temple stood—
These have we vow'd to purchase with our blood."

" And these," said Adel, " while these climes retain
Their faith, their Prophet, must thou never gain. 160

* The bridge of Al Sirat, which has been already mentioned; where the curses of those whom we have injured in this life will become gusts of wind, to shake our footing on its perilous edge.

That senseless wood ye prize—it once was ours;
But, if by Genii curst, or Angel powers,
Rapt from our view, 'tis ours to yield no more,
Might we that scandal to our creed restore.
Nor can we to rebellious hands resign
The sacred City (and it ne'er was thine),
Salem, nor last nor meanest of the seven
That Islam honours by command of Heaven;
For there the faithful Genii meet, and there
Rose the great Prophet through ambrosial air,   170
What time, yet clothed in mortal flesh, he trod
The sevenfold heavens, and view'd the living God.
But if thou wilt, this contest yet shall cease,
And Strife's crude apple yield the seeds of peace.

" As late thy sister to the Soldan's breast
Recall'd a form in halcyon youth imprest,
When Eleanora with her former lord*
In Antioch dwelt, by Turk and Frank adored,
He wept to think how he with deadly strife
Pursued her son—that late he sought thy life;   180
But I with less paternal eyes beheld
Matilda's charms, and rued my pledge to yield.

* See Note on Book III. respecting the supposed acquaintance between Eleanor of Guyenne and the young Saladine, at Antioch.

"Hear then, great King! and if your martial vow
And jealous faith such bridal rites allow,
Beneath our blended sway shall Syria bow;
In all that splendour shall Matilda live
That Egypt's wealth to Judah's throne can give.
Free as in Christian lands, her gates of gold
To all she lists shall unreproved unfold;
While in my realms, unquestioned as in thine, 190
Shall Christians pass to every sacred shrine;
My slaves obedient shall protect their faith,
And aid them dying, and entomb in death.

"Then ponder well, a hostile realm to gain,
By arms to win it, and by arms maintain,
Or bid at once the strife of ages cease,
And all the ends of war acquire by peace."

"Vast is the stake, nor lightly to decide
Becomes my youth;" the English King replied.
"True, I have kingdoms, fruitful realms and fair, 200
That now, perchance, demand a Sovereign's care:
Unmatch'd in arts and arms, a fertile isle,
Whose vales are green in Summer's temperate smile;
Where nor hot winds nor fierce tornadoes blow,
Nor Winter brings unmitigated snow;

While half those regions Philip calls his own,
In corn and vines are clothed for me alone:
Yet may I not desert a promise given,
Or quit for earthly cares the Cause of Heaven.
Salem has yet a King,—a King my friend,   210
Can I crush rights I pledg'd me to defend?
Or should nor Heaven nor Lusignan withstand,
Without her sanction plight Matilda's hand?—
I call my council,—thou meanwhile may'st bear
My courteous greetings to the Soldan's ear;
Whate'er of friendship war like ours can know,
Christian and Infidel, or foe and foe.—
Say, should we close our contest or renew,
If e'er again my native land I view,
Not his own bards in warmer phrase than mine   220
Shall sing the power, the worth of Saladine."

  Soon to his Peers convoked, the Monarch shew'd
The proffer'd terms of peace, and then pursued:
" Thus speaks the Soldan—and I yield the choice
Of truce or conflict to the general voice.
Think, if such terms our faith with Heaven fulfil?
To leave the Turk on Sion's Holy Hill;
To yield a Christian Princess, and to prize
As friends and kindred those our God denies?

Ye ministers of Heaven! its will explain;   230
Thou, Lusignan! thy menaced rights maintain;
Be every claim in equal balance tried,
Weigh well, oh Princes! weigh them, and decide."
   He spoke, and wondrous, not a breath was heard,
Nor whispered murmur, nor dissentient word.
It seem'd as some Lethean spell had crept
Round each fierce heart—that even discord slept:
Till, like the last faint sigh when tempests cease,
One sound they uttered, and that sound was " Peace!"
The Asian prelates, Acre, Nazareth, Tyre,   240
And peers of France, that France and home desire,
Wearied of war, and conscious that the shame
Or praise alike will cling to RICHARD's name,
Each in his turn the offered rites allows,
And brings meet instance of resembling vows.
How oft Amalric leagued in strict accord
With great Noureddin, and Iconium's Lord;
Nor fear'd in Egypt Chaver's cause to join,
Even in his youth, the foe of Saladine.ᶠ
" Ha!" Raymond thought, " no martial voice, not one!
Discord and valour both with Conrad gone!
But Lusignan arises,—heavenly power!
Thy priests are faithless in this fatal hour,

Make then the claims of pride and interest strong—
Matilda's fate is trembling on his tongue."

  Yes, Lusignan arose, and ne'er before
So sweet a grace his calm, fair visage wore.
From his bright hair Judea's crown he took,
And view'd awhile with mild and pensive look.
" Beloved in life, and honour'd in the grave,   260
To me this wreath Amalric's daughter gave;
Pledge of her truth, affection's sweet reward,
I hail'd the glittering weight, and vow'd to guard.
Yet few like me, the sport of fate, have found
What thorns are hidden in its golden round;
That this wide earth contains no wretched thing
Despised, insulted, like a throneless King!
Not by ambition, but by duty driven,
I prized what seem'd the sacred gift of Heaven;
Nor grief, nor chains, nor Conrad's threats unjust, 270
Could make my faithful soul desert its trust;—
But now if heaven resume it, I resign—
Heroic RICHARD, be its glories thine!
Guard if thou wilt, or where thou wilt bestow,
No jealous pangs this grateful heart shall know;—
May he who wears, his realm in triumph free,
Like me be faithful, but more blest than me.

Some tranquil small domain, alone I crave;
A place of rest, an uncontested grave."—

" Enough, my friend—till Heaven's decree be known, 280
In trust I take the delegated crown;
Not for myself—my own paternal land
Is amply vast to fill one sceptred hand.
Yet must not thou, who saw'st the mightiest bend
Beneath thy rule, from kingly rank descend.
My recent prize, beyond description fair,
Deserves a Monarch's undivided care;
One half the Templars hold, the rest be thine
Its wealth, its regal honours I resign."g—

" Too generous King!" glad Lusignan replies, 290
" Not the wide earth could yield so dear a prize.
Hail, Cyprus! fairest isle beneath the sun,
So freely yielded, as so nobly won."—

The Monarch smiled, when Raymond, struggling long,
For looks less troubled and less faltering tongue,
Abruptly spoke :—" Is all our virtue gone?
" Plead I for heaven's, for glory's rights alone?—
Is war so irksome now, that in the field,
The hour of conquest, ye those conquests yield!

Acre, that three long years your arms withstood, 300
Acre, whose stones are red with kindred blood;
Acre upbraids ye with each sacred stain,
Arsouf implores ye by her glorious plain.
All they adjure—but thee with holiest power,
By the warm pride of victory's purple hour,
Oh! Cœur de Lion! theirs, thy fame to save,
And shield from grief the spirits of the brave.
Soul of D'Avesnes! alas! I deem'd thee blest,
That in the grave thy senseless ashes rest,
But thou shalt grieve in heaven—the injured slain 310
Shall nightly shriek round each polluted plain;
Till Islam's frighted slaves the region shun,
And yield again the realm their valour won.
Oh! if in vain a Saviour's tomb implore,
Does Honour, does Ambition fire no more?
And Richard—late I saw thy manly brow
Pale with fraternal fears,—and canst thou now
For ever yield her—yield her spotless soul
To barbarous hands, to Infidel control—
Force to a spouse abhorr'd her struggling will?"—320

"And can'st thou, Raymond, judge thy friend so ill?
Now, by this Cross, I would not yield a rood
Of all these regions, purchased with our blood;

Or give Matilda to a yoke abhorr'd,
To reign wide Asia's uncontested Lord.
Call forth Sicilia's Queen." In steady tone
He made the terms of proffer'd treaty known.
" Think not," he added then in soften'd voice,
" I give the name without the power of choice.
Think not, though all a Monarch's cares I feel, 330
My power more precious than my sister's weal.
Adel is generous, has a princely soul,
But his fierce passions never felt control;
Splendour would wait thee on Judea's throne,
But thine is not a heart for pomp alone.
This hour assembled Princes wait thy voice,
And peace or war may hang upon thy choice:
But should they all with armed hosts demand,
I would not yield him thy reluctant hand;
Circled by those of alien faith alone, 340
Frightful to view,—speech, manners all unknown;
Perchance without a friend thy heart to share,
Matilda! think, could'st thou be happy there?"—

 While thus he spoke, a bright but quivering streak
Oft flush'd and faded on Matilda's cheek;
At length it died, yet still her eye was bright,
Bright with a loftier and diviner light;

Her air serene contrasting with the glow
Of troubled passions all around her shew,
With the deep terrors Raymond's looks express,   350
She bow'd her head, and meekly answer'd—" Yes!"

All eyes had centred on her beauteous face,
The slightest signs of labouring thought to trace:
While RICHARD, on whom her's were fix'd alone,
To hide conflicting passions, screen'd his own;
Yet now he shares in Raymond's shuddering start,
And a deep sob betray'd his tortured heart.

" Matilda! Princess!" eager Raymond cried,
" Oh! pardon feelings which I cannot hide,
Nor let—but can I speak and be forgiven,—   360
Ambition lure thee in the guise of heaven.
To be the bond of peace, to free again
That Tomb which myriads bled to win, in vain;
Proud is the destiny—so proud, so high,
How gladly could I grasp such prize and die!
But years of misery wait thee; 'tis not now
Thy heart shall pay the penance of thy vow:
Wounds are but spurs in battle's glorious day,
'Tis the slow cure that wears the soul away.
To one—ah, pause!—a lawless Moslem, chain'd,   370
Thy faith contemn'd, thy liberty restrain'd,

That sickness of the soul, the exile's curse,
Which thine own virtues shall conspire to nurse—
Like the cold silent drop that wears the stone,
Shall waste thy cheek, till all its bloom be gone;
And as the wretch, becalmed on Indian seas,
Decks the loath'd billows with imagin'd trees,
Shall pining fancy paint thy natal shore,—
E'en Etna's fires may charm, when fear'd no more.
Think, though thy brother, as his rank commands,
Supprest his grief, and named these hateful bands,
Still anxious for thy weal he bids thee chuse—
His heart will bless thee, should thy lips refuse."

 A painful blush her burning visage dyed,
And with a voice supprest the Queen replied:
" He could not glory in his sister's shame;
His love might pardon, but his reason blame.
Oh! Raymond, more than thou or he I know
Each certain sacrifice, each threaten'd woe:
What 'tis to part with all that sweetens life,   390
Yet lack whate'er endears the name of wife.
Yet why such thoughts, when Solyma shall be
Freed to each Christian step, and freed by me!
Can I at such exalted lot repine,
When pilgrims, crowding to each honour'd shrine,

With every bead a grateful tear shall shed,
And call a blessing on Matilda's head?—
When, should my heart confess a moment's gloom,
My lifted eye shall view a Saviour's Tomb;
And hope spring upward to that happier shore,   400
Where all I love shall meet—to part no more.
Then rouse thee, RICHARD, hast thou cause for shame?
Oh! no, thy sister will not taint thy fame.
Look on thy own Matilda, look, for here
'Tis I should falter, and 'tis thou should'st cheer."

" Alas!" he answered, " all the pride I feel
In thy pure faith, thy self-devoted zeal,
Makes but thy loss more dear; yet shall not He
Who feeds the desert bird have charge of thee?
Strong in thy loneliness, perchance design'd   410
A torch of truth to that benighted kind;
But thy mild eye implores me, and I will—
Down, rebel heart! ye struggling thoughts be still.

" Princes! who know what strife was wont to stain
Our loud debates, and make our prowess vain;
If now with me ye deem some mightier power
Attunes our souls in this auspicious hour,
Be peace our choice; but let us still retain
All by our swords redeem'd from Moslem reign;

Nor knit the bonds of concord, till we know 420
If Tyre's proud Chieftain rest a friend or foe.
Fierce though he be, in one communion join'd,
No separate truce our selfish hands should bind."—

" Yet hear me, King, one moment I implore,
By this, the ensign of my pastoral power!"
'Twas Hubert spoke. " I had not paused so long,
" But hoped the sanction of some elder tongue.
RICHARD, not yours the choice of war or peace,
Nor can yourselves your own free vows release :
Alone to one on earth such power is given, 430
The one, unerring delegate of Heaven;
It may be He this compact shall allow,
His praise confirm Matilda's generous vow :
Yet, by your wealth, your blood, so nobly shed,
Risk not his censure on your regal head ;
Still let the choice be his, his sacred word,
Which rous'd to war, direct or sheathe the sword ;
We need not fear our conquests to maintain,
Till your swift envoy seek these shores again."

" Such mild reproofs, oh! Prelate, ever bring
The keenest shame," rejoin'd the generous King;
" I blush to think that my rebellious thought
Could dream of treaty, his consent unsought.

To Celestine shall Leicester now repair,
Our mandate thou to Asia's sovereign bear:
Say Heaven's vicegerent only can release
Our plighted faith, and sheathe our swords in peace;
Till his decree be known, we still must keep
Our hostile state, nor let the conflict sleep."

The Synod parts, and with a friendly wind   450
Soon Leicester leaves the Syrian shore behind.
And now the changing gales to RICHARD bear
His mother's tablets, fraught with weighty care.
" How Ely govern'd with too proud a hand,
Till discontent was rife throughout the land;
And John, to rebel courses ever prone,
Declared his brother dead, and claim'd the throne."
" Alas! dear England! while I speak, perchance
These broils are foster'd by perfidious France.
(Forgive me, comrade of my youth, that now   460
My heart has bodings which distrust thy vow;)
Yet hence vain fears—to Heaven my sword was given,
And my lone kingdom is the charge of Heaven."

Arsouf meanwhile, despoil'd of all her pride,
Daroun and Ramla fling their portals wide;

While Jaffa, which the Soldan threats in vain,
Exulting turns to Christian rule again.
From Tyre to Gaza, Palestine implores
The conqueror's mercy, and receives his powers.
The Moslems, scarce in menaced Sion sure, 470
With stronger walls her native strength secure;
And RICHARD leads his gallant comrades on,
To win Damascus' rival—Ascalon.

Each eager eye explored the naked plain,
And scann'd th' horizon's ample bound in vain.
No marble domes the vacant scene adorn,
No gilded turrets glitter in the morn;
From no strong fort the tawny standard flies;
Nor walls, nor towers, nor minarets arise.

" Oft have I heard," the wondering Pardo cried,
" That imps malign in Asian wilds reside;
In arid sands bid seeming lakes delude,
And shade with gorgeous piles the mimic flood:
But now, methinks, some envious demon shrouds
The actual city in aerial clouds."—

" Nay," Albert spoke, " observe upon our right
Those low-built dwellings, glittering in the light,
Like Moslem tombs; they speak the city nigh,
'Tis but yon grove that veils it from the eye."

Swift to the spot the eager troops advance,   490
Then, fill'd with awe, exchange th' inquiring glance.
" Where is the proud, the mighty city gone?
Were these white stones imperial Ascalon?"

Far as the keen-eyed lynx can measure round
The splendid fragments cover all the ground;
The column's broken shaft, the painted dome,
Soft carpets, glowing from the Persian loom,
Mirrors and cloth of gold, defiled and scorn'd,
That tell how rich the halls they once adorn'd.
But all was silent, save the breeze that sigh'd   500
O'er those fair ruins, late an empire's pride.

Has earth, beneath the weight of marble prest,
Heaved the proud structure from her jealous breast?
Or man, unfaithful to his father's trust,
The work of ages levell'd with the dust?
Oh! not when Carthage met her dreadful doom,
In rival vengeance seal'd by conquering Rome,
When nor rude axe nor hungry flame forbore,
And night and silence fled th' affrighted shore:
Not then her sons o'er fairer domes bewail'd,   510
In ruin scatter'd or in fire exhaled.

Now changed the scene: with painful steps they trod
Where treacherous ashes hide the burning sod;

And ever, as some smouldering heap they broke,
Oozed from its black recess the heated smoke.
The vulture haunts the desert house of prayer,
The ruin'd palace is th' hyena's lair;
And wondering thousands unreproved explore
Sequester'd beauty's desolated bower—
Her pomp, her pride, her busy crowds are gone, 520
And Syria's spouse is fall'n like Babylon.

One tower alone, a massy structure, stood,
Reared on the confines of the land and flood;
Though scathed with flame, with angry blows assail'd,
Dark frown'd its antique walls, and steel and fire had
    fail'd.*

Wondering the warriors view th' unshaken stone,—
When from its vaults resounds a sullen moan!
Keen was their search, and soon in piteous plight
They drag a wasted wretch to upper light.

On his dark brow, though stain'd with dust, were seen
Some tatter'd shreds of Mecca's holy green;
His beard was silver'd with the snows of age,
Yet glared his eyes with unextinguish'd rage;
While, as from some sepulchral cavern, came
A voice ill-suited to so worn a frame,

---

* This tower is said to be still in existence.

With quivering lips, but unabated pride,
To RICHARD's words the spectre form replied:
"But that the tale may grieve thee, Infidel!
Not all thy tortures should one sound compel.
Go gaze on Shiraz, on Damascus gaze,   540
Or where through Cassius' vale Orontes strays;
Bid Saba all her spicy wealth exhale,
Cull all the sweets of Cashmere's palmy vale;
Then may'st thou guess how fair thy treasure gone,
And half the pride of ruin'd Ascalon!
But far her splendour and her wealth above
Her zealous offspring prized their Prophet's love.—
That never here should Infidel command,
Or Egypt's wealth be borne to Christian hand,*
They vow'd—they heard of Acre's fall—again 550
The screaming vultures told of Arsouf's plain;
Dark o'er the splendid domes a cloud was hung,
And night and day with direful portents rung.
The fated city knew her hour was come,
And the sad Soldan, shuddering spoke her doom.
Yet t'was not when the powerful throng'd the gate,
When camels sunk beneath their costly freight;

* Ascalon was the principal port of communication between Syria and Egypt.

When music wail'd, or houri forms were seen
Half to undraw the silken palanquin,
To see once more the only home they knew, 560
And left but once, yet left for ever too;
Nor when the new, the gorgeous palace fell,
That desolation rais'd her fearful yell.
The great have wealth to win another home,
And spread a Paradise where'er they roam;
But when the poor, that saw their dwellings fall,
In every little hut bewail'd their all,—
When houseless infants round their fathers clung,
When on their arms their wives imploring hung,—
E'en by their very weight to stay the blow, 570
And check an arm already weak with woe;
'Twas then the Soldan wept, and in despair,
Called on his Mufties to relent and spare—
Th' averted head, that sought the mantle's fold,
The frequent sob, their dreadful sentence told;
' Oh! I had rather that these walls had stood,
Like Acre, purpled with her offspring's blood;
But Islam's weal demands'—he spoke, and then
Snatch'd the red torch, and led his weeping train.
Himself he fired whate'er was precious, rare, 580
The tombs of ancient saints, the mosques of prayer;

Till the high feeling caught from man to man,
Each with his home the work of fate began;
O'er its slow wreck his sullen vigil kept,
The eye was tearless, 'twas the heart that wept.
Each fatal hour some princely pile consumed,
Night after night terrific fires illumed;
Till the dark heavens their silent sorrows shed
O'er the wide havoc which their winds had spread.h

"Mourn, then, thou miscreant! thou the cause of all!
On thee may Islam's gather'd curses fall!
Think of this jewel lost, the weight of care,
The toils, the battles thou hast yet to dare,
With those who thus to death and flames consign
All they most love, ere they will yield it thine."

"Think thou what fervor Christian hearts must fill
Who strive with such, nor doubt of conquest still!
Short is your triumph:" thus the King replies,
"This phœnix from her funeral flames shall rise.
Exult! my friends! proud city! live once more. 600
Thy sons destroy'd thee, but thy foes restore.—
Go! tell thy Lord, in vain his soul exceeds
All record shews of great and daring deeds;
Undazzled we his radiant course can trace,
And hope to match—perchance outstrip his race."

" Even as thou wilt, but here my sorrows close ;
This spot that first beheld shall end my woes—
Once blest with all that mortal might desire,
A happy husband, an exulting sire,
I prized Morayma's worth all wealth above,   610
Nor gave a rival to her faithful love.
The plague broke forth—with every wretched day
My comrades died, my household pined away ;
My children sicken'd—less than mother's care
Had turn'd appall'd from features late so fair;
But fearless, speechless, o'er their couch of death
That angel watch'd, nor shunn'd their tainted breath;
Till as her fingers, moisten'd in the wave,
To their blue lips a moment's freshness gave,
She sunk, Affection's martyr, at my side,   620
Raised to my face her pitying eyes, and died !
What followed ask not—stupor seized my frame,
I saw not, heard not, till when reason came
I stood on yonder tower ; the Eunuchs gave
My heart's lost treasure to a wat'ry grave ;
Pale, but yet lovely, for not death might dare
To change the mansion of a soul so fair.
Still with her last, her fondest look, she gazed,
And as she fell her snowy arms were rais'd—

Was it a dream—they pointed to my boy, 630
The latest, dearest pledge of vanish'd joy!
I snatch'd him from the slaves, I watch'd the wave
Till even its ripples died, then sought the cave
Where late you found me stretch'd, and, spent and wild,
Gazed like a nurse that tends her sleeping child.
I could not pray, I had no hope,—I sate
As one whose senseless sorrow mock'd at fate.
Methought he moved, and with the sudden start
The blood thrill'd backward from my stiffening heart.
For hours I felt his languid temples beat, 640
And gently chafed the slow-returning heat;
Till tears, to ease my bursting bosom, came,
Warm'd his cold limbs, relax'd his rigid frame.—
Why need I say how my young Ali grew
Whate'er my hopes had feign'd, my wishes knew,
And pleasure's emptied chalice brimm'd anew!
Nor careless of the power that saved his days,
On Mecca's sands I knelt in prayer and praise.
Heard'st thou not, Heaven!—but gaze not thus on me,
Christian! my woes shall be no jest for thee!" 650

" Where is this boy?"

" Where! that should I demand—
" On Arsouf's plain he perish'd by thy hand!

Where sleeps he now? perchance that cruel breast—
'Tis said thy hatred loves the impious feast."¹

"Nay, 'tis thy frenzied malice forged the tale—
Old man, I know how little words avail,
Yet oft I mourn the blood my hand has shed;
What would'st thou now? can I relieve or aid?"

"No! nought from thee—not aught from Christian hand;
Not e'en to hide these aged limbs with sand,   670
Will Helim ask—not sorrow's last request
To share his Ali's grave—that barbarous breast.
Recoiling Nature points a fitter tomb;
Yet glory not, while gazing on my doom;
Here in the grave shall all my griefs repose,
But thy rash triumph finds no quiet close.
For me the gates of Paradise unfold,
For me Al Cawthar chafes its sands of gold.*
For me th' eternal groves of Eden flower,
For me Morayma decks her pearly bower.   680
Hark! for the warbling gates invite me in—
But thou, aye drain thy painted cup of sin;
Drain to the dregs, for poison harbours there,
Then sleep—the trump shall wake thee to despair."

* One of the fountains of the Mahommedan Paradise.

At once his limbs a youthful vigour found,
And breaking from th' astonish'd guards around,
Onward he springs, with Herculean power
Clasps the rough stones, and climbs the lofty tower.
" That prayer at least th' Eternal heard," he said,
" The axes broke, the hungry flames were staid, 690
Now fall, and whelm yon interdicted train;"—
Then wildly gazing on the foaming main,
" I come, Morayma, to thy tranquil grave."—
He spoke, and plunged and perish'd in the wave.

Now through the desert town the Monarch hies,
Marks the wide moat, or bids the ramparts rise.
" Here form the massy citadel, and here
Shrin'd in its breast Messiah's temple rear;[k]
A princely bower, a spacious arsenal there;
And where those orange groves bloom fresh and fair,
Let the calm convent from their bosom rise,
And holy hymns, and penitential sighs,
Float with their native incense to the skies."

Vast was the labour,—but the means were vast;
An army wrought, and proudest Princes cast
Their crested helms and blazon'd vests aside,
To mix in works a Monarch deign'd to guide:

While, proud to labour on a foreign soil,
The meaner crowd resum'd their wonted toil;
And many an Arab youth, or Nubian slave, 710
Wrought for his hire, yet curs'd the hand that gave.
The portly Mede, the supple Greek were near,
And frigid Georgia's blue-eyed mountaineer;
The Israelite, scarce suffer'd in the land
Where rul'd his father's by divine command,
And rich Armenia's active sons unfold
Their gem-wrought hangings and their stuffs of gold.
They blend with gothic masses, rude, grotesque,
The varying charms of playful arabesque,
The forms of classic Greece, severely chaste, 720
Or the light polish of Ionian taste.

Yet not to Ascalon the mighty mind
Of England's Monarch all its force confin'd:
Oft with slight train he scour'd the hostile land,
Strong forts subdued, and routed many a band;
His rank in vain a crestless casque conceal'd,
The puissant arm the "Lion Heart" reveal'd.
Once, when the King and two tried warriors more
The white Bernoose of Arab wanderers wore,

They reach'd a lofty hill, whence glancing down 730
With raptur'd eyes they view'd the Sacred Town.
Bright in the glowing autumn's sunset beam
Thy vale, Gehenna, and the winding stream
Of torrent Kedron, while a ruddier glow
Tinged the Green Mount, and Sion's adverse brow.
Beneath, half cloth'd in light, half lost in gloom,
That fane whose walls enclose a Saviour's tomb;
And that proud mosque, whose gilded turrets shine
Where erst Jehovah fix'd his chosen shrine;
There beams the crescent, there in triumph glow 740
The yellow banners of Messiah's foe.
It was a sight to fire a warrior's brain:
With armed hosts he crowds the vacant plain;
Godfrey, Rinaldo, Bœmond, Tancred, rise,
From huge machines the stony tempest flies,
And martial clamours thicken on his ear,
Triumphant notes, himself may hope to hear!
With outstretch'd arms he views the beauteous town,
" Shalt thou," he cries, " shalt thou be yet my own?"
And tears, yet such as valour's cheeks may grace,
Unbidden, wondering, dew'd his manly face.

Fast wanes the day; they spur their camp to gain,
Till in a glen they mark'd a Moslem train.

Bold in disguise, the hostile ranks they scan,—
'Twas sultry Mecca's annual caravan:
Bound from thát shrine where countless pilgrims hold
The double rites of Islam and of gold.*
The Zemzem's sacred wave, and odorous spice†
From India brought, and silks of rare device,
Brooms with the Caaba's precious cobwebs graced,‡
And Korans that the holiest hands had traced;
A thousand treasures dear to Moslem eyes,
Oman's rich pearls, and gems that all can prize,
The loaded camels to Damascus bear,
Safe in the guard of Mosul's dauntless heir.

But RICHARD with a leader's rapid sight
View'd as he past th' encampment of the night;
Then home he hastens, and selects with care
A knightly band, the bold emprize to dare.

While yet their course the doubtful twilight veil'd,
Each in a Bedouin's ample cloak conceal'd,

---

* The Koran expressly permits the Pilgrims to trade; and it may be doubted whether the yearly caravan be not more indebted for its numbers to avarice than to piety.

† The Holy Well of Zemzem is within the enclosure of the Caaba, in a separate building, and it is customary to send presents of its waters.

‡ See the History of Vathek.

Urged his fleet Destrier; morning mists were still
Drawn like a curtain round each swelling hill,
When the glad Monarch from a lofty brow
Points to the pilgrims in the glen below.
Some stretched beneath their steeds repose supine,*
Some on huge bales of costly stuffs recline;
Some, where light tents exclude the dews of night,
Or the dim watchfire fades in purer light;
While some, more wakeful, roused the lingering
    guard,   780
The camels loaded, and the steeds prepared.

  Now all was life, and 'mid the busy train
The camels knelt, and burthen'd, rose again.
The prancing steeds the breath of morning feel,
The fearless pilgrims snatch their simple meal;
When hark! the tambour every breast alarms!
The coward flies, the warriors spring to arms:
Yet half in scorn survey the scanty band
Of Bedouin wanderers, refuse of the land;

---

* The genuine mode of Arabian bivouac is to sleep under the horse's legs, the animal remaining standing. The fabled Centaur seems to be almost realized in the intimate union of man and horse, which takes place among the tribes of the desert.

Hardy and brave, yet all unskill'd to cope 790
With Mosul's veterans, and her princely hope.
But soon their pride was quell'd, when doom'd to feel
The weight of England's mace, and England's steel.
From rank to rank a panic terror spread,
And from the little troop the thousands fled.

 Join'd by the few that fought, with lance in rest,
To RICHARD's front Seiffeddin's offspring prest.
" Shekh, of what tribe and whosoe'er thou art,
Not this methinks a true believer's part—
When foreign wolves, rude, merciless, and bold,
Molest our faithful flocks, for lust of gold
The shepherd should not rob his neighbour's fold."

 No answer RICHARD deign'd, but cast aside
The downy cloth that veil'd his helmet's pride.
The Prince look'd round—are all his warriors gone!
Gone at that dreaded glance?—he stands alone!
Yet unabash'd, resolved his fate to brave,
Nor stain a life that flight might fail to save.
When RICHARD: " Thou whom e'en thy foes admire,
For happier fields restrain thy martial fire; 810
Go to thy Sultan, to thy warlike Sire,
And say that England's King rejoiced to see
How truly fame had spoke in praising thee.

Say more, we bid them not too idly trust,
For Ascalon is rising from her dust;
Ourselves have seen where Sion's towers ascend—
When next we see, we warn them to defend."

With graceful mien th' intrepid Prince obeys,
Pleased and yet blushing at a Christian's praise.
T'was strange, the syren that his fancy sway'd,   820
In darkest hues the once-loved King pourtray'd,
He vow'd revenge—yet whensoe'er they met,
He gazed admiring, and forgot to hate.
O'er fraud so much prevail'd his generous mind,
Nor strife could jaundice, nor affection blind.

Now whispering Pardo near, he gaily smiled,
" Hast thou no greetings for Almanzor's child?"—
" What should I send? why speak of smouldering fires,
Of memory lingering on, when Hope expires?"—
" Send love and joy," his laughing friend replies:
" If thou hast seen where Sion's ramparts rise,
Thou know'st by Silöe's brook her Golden Gate;*
If there some moonless night thou dare to wait
Till the mid-watch be set, I know a spell
May ope the Haram's jealous doors—farewell.—

* The golden gate of Jerusalem opened into the valley of Kedron, not far from Silöe.

Better to rush on death than thus to pine,
And if betray'd, my life is risqued with thine."
    But RICHARD's eye o'er countless spoils has run,
And marvell'd at the wealth his valour won.
Nor were his numerous vassals less elate,   840
When camels throng'd the city's spacious gate;*
And e'en the miser wearied to behold
Silks, carpets, camphor, frankincense and gold.
Largely he gave to each confederate band,
And friends and aliens blest his bounteous hand,
In terms that sicken'd Otho's envious ear,
And Gaul's proud Barons burn'd with shame to hear.
But as the sun through cloudless æther glides,
Regardless of the meaner orbs he hides,
In plenitude of splendour beaming round   850
His light of life to earth's remotest bound;
Thus through his radiant course the Monarch goes,
Blest in each blessing that his hand bestows.

    * Seven thousand camels with all their merchandize were the spoil of this adventure. I do not know the precise number of RICHARD's troop, but it was inconsiderable.

END OF BOOK IX.

CŒUR DE LION.

BOOK X.

THE QUARREL OF RICHARD AND LEOPOLD.

ARGUMENT.

THE QUARREL OF RICHARD AND LEOPOLD.

Return of the Ambassadors from Tyre—Departure of Philip and obduracy of Conrad—His assassination—Grief and death of Theodora, Princess of Constantinople—Marriage of Isabelle and Henry of Champagne—Obsequies of Conrad and the Princess—Conspiracy of Otho and Leopold against Richard—Their quarrel on the walls of Ascalon—Departure of the French and Austrians—Richard hunts in the forest, and falls asleep by a fountain—Meeting of Pardo and Amina—Amina's story—Escape of Lyard—Pardo pursues him and is bewildered—He returns to Ascalon—Absence of Richard, and consternation of the army—Loyal behaviour of Albert—Generosity and knighthood of Saladine — Disappearance of Evanthe—Malignity of Bertrand, and noble confidence of Berengaria.

CŒUR DE LION.

BOOK X.

THE QUARREL OF RICHARD AND LEOPOLD.

So swift, while myriads lent their willing aid,
The city rose, so wide her circuit spread,
That Islam ponder'd on her tales of old,
When Solyman the sons of fire control'd,
And piled stupendous many a fabric fair,
Colossal works! man's envy and despair.

  'Twas night—with unaccustom'd toil opprest,
Now Peers and Princes seek the couch of rest;
When hark! a thousand clamorous tongues require
The wearied king—the lords return from Tyre.

Impatient throngs explore each clouded look,
That told of evil ere a word was spoke.
And soon with tears was many a cheek bedew'd,
For sad the tale—a tale of guilt and blood.

   From Acre's plain the noble envoys crost
Scandalion's ridge, and gain'd the Tyrian coast.
By Asia's fervid suns unnerved no more,
Now Philip linger'd on Phœnicia's shore;
While Saladine, with policy refined,
In princely gifts display'd his courteous mind.   20
With these, to heal the Monarch's languid frame,
Abdollatiph, the pride of Asia, came,[a]
With all the lore of Ind or Persia fraught,
That Avicene, or sage Averrhöes taught;[b]
That Grecian erst, or wise Chaldæan told,
And all Damascus' royal schools unfold.
Unwearied yet he hastens to explore,
What lingering knowledge lives on Nilus' shore;
That shore where first she lit her mystic fire,
So soon to flourish, and so soon expire.   30
And now, though grief for Arsouf's ravish'd fight
Secludes the Soldan from his servant's sight,
His bounty graced the sage—he bids him shew
His wonted wisdom, and restore his foe.

But vain was all his healing skill to find
The King's disease, the canker of the mind;
As vain the zealous Prelate's earnest prayer,
Or envious Austria's, fill'd with timely fear,
Lest hated RICHARD rule without a Peer.

"Canst thou," the Duke began, "so deeply taste
Of glory's cup, yet quit the rich repast?
Or see those laurels by thy vassal won,
Which, near his lord, he durst not call his own?"

"Degenerate offspring of a sainted sire,"
The priest exclaim'd, with all a zealot's fire,
"How far unlike to him whose active youth
Bled in the cause of Sion and of truth;*
Whose honour'd age a pontiff's wants supplied,
And gave that home his rebel states denied.
Thou, but that bounteous Heaven delay'd thy reign,
Hadst join'd the kings of England and Almayne.
How may'st thou now, oh, sceptred recreant! bear
That outraged palm, that Cross abandon'd wear?
Or yield at Dionysius' honour'd shrine,
With festal hymns, his Oriflamme divine?†

---

* Alluding to the Crusade of Louis VII.

† The pilgrims to the Holy Land were furnished with staff and scrip. On their return they usually carried, in addition, a branch of palm.

Philip

Thy injur'd God beholds; he speaks his claim
In that gaunt malady which wastes thy frame.
His curse shall linger on thy tainted life,
Treason, and conflict, and domestic strife."

   They plead, they threat,—but prayers and threats are vain,   60
He climbs his ship, and launches on the main;
To Paris' walls the Soldan's gifts he bore,
A nation's wonder on that distant shore.

   Far other Conrad's mien,—austere and high,
He checked reproof, and made a proud reply:
" Prelate, forbear thy threats, and thou, my friend,
These vain entreaties,—Conrad cannot bend.
I once defied your church, and know that man
May live and prosper though he bear its ban.*
Me nor false hopes nor bigot zeal inspire,   70
My quest dominion, glory my desire.
Would RICHARD win my love, its price is known,
I treat with none that brings not Sion's crown:
Though well is all his former scorn repaid,
When that proud tyrant seeks Montferrat's aid.

Philip Augustus, at his arrival in France, replaced the Oriflamme with solemn pomp in the church of St. Denis, and hung the palm branch over the altar.

  * Alluding to the schism in the church which has been already mentioned. Conrad was the nephew of Barbarossa

Yet Leopold, even for thy triple claim
Of kindred blood, of danger, and of fame,
Thus far I yield:—On my behalf to treat,
Now Sidon's Prince and Asia's Soldan meet;
Wait then th' event,—should Ayoub's son decline 80
The peace, then RICHARD's foes again are mine.
But mark! no more in common fight to blend—
Foe of his foe, but never RICHARD's friend."

Impatiently they waited many a day,
Till Conrad kindled at the long delay,
His greatness outraged in his herald's stay;
He scorned to veil his thoughts, and at a feast,
Whose princely splendour dazzled either guest,
" Let Saladine beware," he sternly said,
" Dire be my warfare if he scorn my aid!"   90

The Prelate, anxious still th' accord to bind,
And fix the changing current of his mind,
Cried, as he pledged him in Ionian wine,
" As I your guest, be you to-morrow mine."

Day past, and bright the evening banquet shone,
And Conrad graced the feast, but not alone;
Rinaldo swell'd his train; and, ere he spoke,*
The envoys knew th' expected concord broke.

* Rinaldo, Prince of Sidon.

Their blighted hopes alike the Tyrians feel,
And all in silence sped their tasteless meal; 100
When Conrad rising, from his purple vest
Drew forth a scroll, and thus the Peers addrest:

"The Soldan, yielding to our terms of peace,
Is well content to bid the contest cease;
Unransom'd he restores our captive sire,*
He owns us sovereign potentates of Tyre:—
Envoys of England, learn your errand vain,
And tell your Lord, that when we meet again
The ground he holds his falchion must maintain."

The Austrian stood aghast, in mute amaze,— 110
"All-seeing power!" cried Philip of Beauvais,
"Was ever yet so foul an union sped?
Heaven linked with Hell, the living with the dead!"

"Peace, Prelate, peace! and practise what you teach:—
Go! to your own neglected Normans preach;
But learn I govern here; and Tyrian lords
Are wont to guard their honour with their swords.
What, thine is sharp! but let its hilt be still,
This froward humour suits thy mitre ill;

---

* The captivity of the Marquis of Montferrat, father to Conrad, has been named in a former note. He continued for some years in the hands of Saladine.

Though well I deem, of Asia's Pagan throng 120
Thy steel has more converted than thy tongue.
Nor on my head the holy thunders cast,
My breast is adamant, it scorns the blast;
And policy forbids to hurl them forth
Save on the fools whose terrors raise their worth.
Yet more,—that RICHARD, whom your zealots sing
The Church's prop, the model for a King,
He too is leagued with Saladine!—'tis said
He yields his sister's charms to Adel's bed.
Nay why that unbelieving scorn? Behold 130
The wondrous legend, character'd in gold!
May I not now the proud example own?
Or are his faults in RICHARD prais'd alone?"

"Not so, blaspheming wretch! Alike on all
Who stain our faith, th' impartial censures fall;
The more I lately prized his worth, the more
I blame his fall—I wonder and deplore.
But thou, that Heaven's great delegate defied,
Thou worse than faithless to a blameless bride,
Link'd with another's wife, in bonds that shame 140
Revolted Europe, and the Christian name!
No wonder can another crime impart;
The interdict I spare is in thy heart.

Heaven suffers long, but will not always bear;
Its vengeance may be near thee—Prince, beware!"
   The Prelate ceased; but where was Conrad gone?
Threat'ning he left the crowded hall alone,
But back he came not. Hark! that piercing shriek,
Which drives the blood from every fading cheek!
Each seized a torch, and rushing forth in fear,   150
Ran to a grove that rose in darkness near.
They start, they scream, 'twas Conrad's bleeding form,
So lately rich with life, with fury warm,
Thus murder'd, unconfessing, unforgiven,
And meditating outrages on Heaven.
Beside him sate a female, ghastly, fair,
As though to shame the torches' ruddy glare,
Struggling through stormy clouds, the moonlight threw
On her pale form a cold unearthly hue.
How sunk her rayless eye! her cheek how spare!
Yet beauty, rapture, love, had once been there;
And passion's April changes lent their glow
To features fix'd in deadliest anguish now.
Forgetful of herself, of all around,
Her soul seem'd lost in Conrad's gory wound.
" Too well avenged," in smother'd tones she cried,
And tore her robes to stop the welling tide.

Scarce was their midnight deed of horror sped,
When at her phrenzied shriek th' assassins fled.
With desperate impulse to his side she flew, 170
At once her pitying glance he caught and knew;
O'er his stern brow a strong convulsion past,
The pang she gave his keenest and his last.

The Leach approach'd; with accents of command
And frantic look she check'd th' officious hand;
"Hold! hold! not Isabelle should now divide
My Conrad from his first, his lawful bride.
She has not rights so holy, so divine,
Hers was his living couch, his grave be mine.
Methinks (yet ah! these sunken eyes are dim, 180
And all around unreal shadows swim,)
Yet if some bold Crusaders hear me now,
That heard in Sophia's fane our bridal vow,
Defend, I charge ye, by your fathers' fame,
To that last home sad Theodora's claim.
Oh! from that hour when fame too truly shew'd
His broken faith, and o'er the angry flood
I came, rash pilgrim, fated to behold,—
But hush! and be the guilty rites untold,—
I fled, I lived,—but ask not where or how; 190
Somewhat of cold, of drenching damps I know,

Of mountain caves, of chambers of the dead,
Of hinds that from my moonlight spectre fled,
Of happy chance, behind a leafy screen
That shew'd my Conrad's form, my own unseen:
One hope sustain'd me—Oh, mysterious Heaven,
Why is it cross'd? why died he unforgiven?
I lived to tread the earth that Conrad trod,
To reconcile the offending wretch to God;
I lived—I saw him fall a murderer's prey, 200
I saw his spirit pass unblest away.—
Earth is a desert now, and oh, despair!
Heaven too were joyless, for he is not there!

" But see that drop—those noble limbs are chill!
But round his heart warm life may linger still;
Mine too are cold—the fever of my brain
Has suck'd the blood from every wasted vein.
Yet could I to his bleeding frame resign
The last faint heat that feebly beats in mine,
'Twere worth whole lives for meaner purpose given,
The stake eternity, the purchase Heaven."

She stretched her limbs upon his lifeless breast,
To his cold cheek her paler lips she prest,
And clung with such a fond, devoted grace,
She seem'd to slumber in the dear embrace.

At length they raised her, but her languid head
Hung powerless back, and either soul had fled.

How fares the Queen?—the heart that shed no tear
For her lost sister, mourns not o'er their bier.
Yet for herself she feels, her power is gone, 220
Her dreams of glory fled—she stands alone.
Where may she fly, to what protector turn?
The good must hate her, and the proud would spurn.
Thoron once loved her, and if she descend
To kneel for pardon—no! she could not bend.
In sooth the dame, of rarest beauty vain,
Had mark'd its power on Henry of Champagne;
She knew him young, ambitious, fond of rule,
Yet one a meaner mind than hers might school,
And more, his blood to England's King allied, 230
Might win respect for claims he late denied.—
She called her maidens, deign'd such weeds to wear
As made each beauteous feature seem more fair;
Left Tyre and all its weeping train behind,
Coil'd like a serpent round her lover's mind;
And ere the day when funeral anthems gave
Her lord and victim to their silent grave,
Again was Acre stain'd with guilty joy,
At rites that outraged every holy tye.[c]

" Oh!" cried the Prelate, " dim the day arose, 240
And sad and silent linger'd to its close,
When through the Tyrian streets the funeral train
With solemn pomp moved on to Mary's fane.
The night array'd in sorrow's dismal hue,
Round each red torch her gloomy circle drew,
And faintly shew'd, on one dark bier disclosed,
Where, pale in death, th' illustrious pair reposed.
No sound was heard, nor sob, nor labouring sigh,
Though the big tear stood round in every eye,
Till with the dirge the solemn chorus rose, 250
The single utterance of a nation's woes.
For Conrad, though on Heaven's behests he trod
Reckless, and chose ambition for his god,
To regal cares his powerful mind addrest,
And made his city great, his people blest.
The priests in stoles of unpolluted white,
The mournful household clad in robes of night;
Warriors whose hearts a warrior's loss deplored,
Youth, manhood, age, all sorrowing for their lord,
Exiles to whom his power a home had given, 260
And monks and virgins dedicate to heaven:
All wan and ghastly as th' unconscious dead,
Breath'd a low prayer with every tear they shed.

But most that aged priest, whose just alarms
For menaced Sion rous'd her sons to arms;
To Europe's Kings his Tyrian crozier bore,
And preached the new Crusade from shore to shore.
He from his cell, where sinking to the tomb,
He writes in tears his chronicle of gloom,
Look'd on the world once more; with feeble breath
The aged patriarch rais'd the chaunt of death.
Yet oh! if ever prayer from heart sincere
Avail to speed the parted soul, or e'er
Might earthly mould angelic soul enshrine,
Or human sorrow touch the ear Divine,
William of Tyre, thy tears for Conrad shed,
Thy hymns, not idly o'er the marble said,
Shall aid the latest wish, the latest sigh
Of her he wrong'd to win his peace on high."[d]

Such was the tale that spread through all the host
Dismay and gloom, but RICHARD sorrow'd most;
And from the hall in mournful silence stole,
To vent alone the sadness of his soul.
The Princes linger'd there, and still aghast
In every varying light review'd the past;

Till Otho, who with Hautefort's Baron bold,
And Raymond talk'd apart, and Leopold,
Exclaim'd, " Methinks the weightier sense we lose
Of Conrad's death, in Theodora's woes.
No stripling's arm could stretch him on the sand, 290
Whose then the guiding will—the acting hand?"

" Whose!" Bertrand spoke, by hatred self-deceiv'd,
To utter words *that* hatred scarce believ'd;
" Whose, but the man that profits in his fall,
He, now the proudest, mightiest of us all;
Who talk'd of peace (a peace he means to break),
Yet brook'd not Conrad separate terms should seek;
'Tis plain—his nephew weds the widow'd dame,
To rise on Lusignan's abandon'd claim."

" Prais'd be St. Ursula!" cried Leopold, 300
" A stranger's tongue my secret thought has told.
Princes! for Conrad's blood, so basely shed,
His kinsman claims revenge on RICHARD's head.
Yet who would dare a frowning front to shew,
Who breathe suspicion on so proud a foe?"

" Who?" Raymond answer'd in indignant tone,
" All that believe the tale! not England's throne,
But RICHARD's virtue makes our swords his own.

Vengeance on him, if he that blood have spilt,
Vengeance on both the partners of his guilt! 310
On Philip of Beauvais, on Leopold—
Nay, let its sheath thine angry weapon hold;
But if by RICHARD's will the Prince were slain,
The murderous hand was in his envoy's train."

" Nay! who," said Otho, " heeds th' ignoble hand,
If his the profit, his the will that plann'd.
Be silent, flatterer! for the glorious sun
Oft shews a blot, and RICHARD may have one."

" Methinks I ill have earn'd a flatterer's name,
Who singly dared the peace he urged to blame; 320
Nay, deem'd me wrong'd, because he ne'er descried,
And outraged feelings I had sought to hide.
Yet, prais'd be heaven! his merit shines too high
To dread the mists that dim our nether sky.
Pause, ere you dare so base a thought impart,
Or meet the scorn of every honest heart."

Speaking he turn'd—fierce Bertrand through the gloom,
Gazed on his stately step and tossing plume:
" Go thou, for nought thy trusting soul could move,
So fix'd in RICHARD's—or his sister's love; 330

Thy generous zeal has something wildly great,
I honour thee for loving him I hate."

"Will then that hatred," Otho urged, "combine,
In quest of just revenge, thy force with mine?"

"Aye, where ye list—slight cause unsheathes my
 brand,
But hate like this might nerve a dead man's hand."

The wily Austrian murmur'd: "Count, beware!
Let Raymond's anger teach a timely fear;
He shines too high for force to reach his throne,
Our vengeance lies in secret means alone." 340

But Bertrand starts,—his eyes that flash with fire,
And wrinkled brow, bespeak ungovern'd ire.
"By secret means! could I to such descend,
He had not lived to trust thee as a friend.
I hate him, and to feed that hate have given
More than my earthly bliss, my hopes of Heaven.
Those black suspicions, crafty Leopold,
That first I dared to breathe, I dare uphold.
'Twere joy to find them stablish'd, but beware!
For should your meanness meditate a snare, 350
A timely warning in his ear to speak,
Where the best vengeance Bertrand's hate could seek?"

He too is gone; with eyes upon the ground
Stood either chief, then cautious glanced around;
Then rais'd, then dropp'd, as each had fear'd to trace
Indignant virtue in his fellow's face;
Till half assured the wary Austrian bends,
Half breathes in smother'd accents, "Are we friends?"
"Yea, to the death!" stout Otho's answer came
From lips that moved not, and a rigid frame.   360
"What then the means?" the fraudful Duke exprest;
"All means are sacred, and the safest best;
But to my tent for further speech remove,
Lest Bertrand's honour watch, or Raymond's love."

Short was the rest the active Monarch knew,
And the cool dawning's first empurpled hue
Amid his rising works beheld him stand,
To aid his noble labourers and command.
"Yet why, my Lord of Austria," RICHARD said,
"Do now your knights withhold their wonted aid?
Such high-born chiefs have mingled in the task,
'Twere scarce too much your princely hand to ask."
"No, proud PLANTAGENET, I am not skill'd
The block to fashion, or the trowel wield.*

*Leopold answered, that he was not born either mason or carpenter.

Such arts may suit thy kestrel kind, for fame
Hath been familiar with thy mother's name—
Thou should'st not bid expecting heirs inquire
If England's Sovereign had a regal sire;
My high-bred eagle soars a nobler flight,
Nay, scorns to slay a foe except in fight." 380

Oh! who can speak the Monarch's wrath—his hand
Unconscious grasp'd, half drew, then sheath'd the brand.
" Now by yon orb that rising gilds the sphere,
A coward only would insult me here!
Thou know'st the holy vows that bind me fast;
In Europe breath'd, those words had been thy last.
Yes is it here, beneath Duke Robert's hand,
Where fell the leader of the Parthian band,
Whose trophies yet the dauntless deed proclaim;
Thou darest to trample on my parents' fame! 390
But give thy slander words, injurious Lord!
What secret blood has tarnish'd RICHARD's sword?"

Now had he fail'd, but Otho's piercing eye
Forced from his livid lips the firm reply.
" And think'st thou, tyrant, did no bonds confine
My lips from challenge, I would wait for thine?
That Conrad's blood had cried to Heaven so long,
Had less than Heaven compell'd to bear the wrong?

But here I brave not one beyond the laws,
Nor trust to doubtful steel a kinsman's cause; 400
For Rome I sail, and even thou may'st dread
The only bolts that strike a regal head."

"Proud Duke, thy aid is free—or sail or stay;
Thou need'st not storm, I shall not bar thy way.
Thy falsehoods to repel, to shew thy guile
I will not stoop, they but deserve a smile.
And, Lords, ye know that for the general weal,
Not for my own, I urged your willing zeal,
To raise these towers; yet if by conscience moved
To shun a treaty ye so late approved, 410
On to Jerusalem, but vow with me
Never to leave her till you leave her free,
While our tough lances boast one barb of steel,
Or our best steeds can yield a single meal."c

His truncheon high exulting Bertrand shook,
"Spake I not sooth, these hateful bonds are broke!
Oh, how I love the very name of war,
And like a vulture snuff the scent afar!
Yet think not, King, that Leopold alone
With Conrad's murder stains the English throne, 420
For all who know what shameless rites combine
Champagne and Isabelle, the rest divine."

"Nor think," said Otho, " we will bleed and toil,
That thou may'st wear the glory and the spoil;
I sail with Leopold, and with me bear
The force Augustus trusted to my care.
Thou too wert best to quit this purple field,
To guard thine honour, and thy realms to shield."

" Sail then!" cried RICHARD—" may the favouring gales
Be ever prompt to swell your recreant sails, 430
That your own lips may first your flight reveal—
Oh! never truly touch'd with holy zeal,
To yield a prey that almost courts your hand!
Sail then—but here I fix my proudest stand;
My glory living or my death betray'd,
Shall stamp your infamy, and mock your aid.
And oh! for England—solemnly 'twas given
To noble Eleanor, to guardian Heaven,
To Heaven's vicegerent here; and Celestine
Will brook no hand should strike one fort of mine;
While still she boasts her ships, her hearts of oak,
Let those be strong that meditate the stroke:
Her steel to death such sheep-clad wolves shall doom,
The Pontiff's curses to the death to come."

They sail'd, but still the lofty works went on,
And rose in finish'd beauty, Ascalon;
While all the faithful host with one accord
Confirm their vows, and rally round their Lord.
Yet small the space their narrowing camp conceal'd,
And thin their columns on the darken'd field;   450
No longer theirs the overwhelming weight,
To rush on Sion, and command her fate.
Their leader, watchful precious blood to spare,
Now bids them frame those vast machines of war,
The Catapult, the Ram with brazen head,
The giant slings that blazing arrows shed,
The light fascines in hollow moats to fall,
The rolling towers that match the hostile wall;
With all those " Torments" Roman art employed,
And all that Milan's massive works destroy'd.*   460
Yet, for the mind its generous force may spend,
And skilful archers oft their bows unbend,
Not seldom was the tilt; the new built halls
Were gay with sumptuous feasts and courtly balls,

* The siege of Milan was one of the most arduous enterprizes of Frederick Barbarossa, who employed against that obstinate city all the artillery of antient and chivalrous times.

And oft in Sharon's woods the tardy morn
Rous'd at the chiding of the hunter's horn;
And oft, a polish'd boar-spear in her hand,
Behind some copse would Berengaria stand,
Robed like the Virgin-Huntress of the wood,
To watch the beast and shed his sable blood. 470
Or on her palfrey, whose resplendent white
Display'd his jewell'd seat and housings bright,
With hooded falcon on her wrist she came,
To wound in air the many-tinctured game.

One morn more loud th' inspiring bugles blew,
To higher pitch the keen-eyed falcons flew,
The full voic'd hounds the guiding leash disdain,
The snorting steeds impatient tug the rein.
Fired at the sight, "Do thou, my gentle bride,
War with the plumy race, while on we ride 480
For nobler game," the royal hunter cried.

Already had his eager chace subdued
Th' inferior tenants of the mazy wood,
And to the camp his train in triumph bear
The cunning fox, swift deer, and timid hare;
When high in cloudless noon the orb of day
Pierc'd the thick branches with a sultry ray;

And RICHARD sought, to shun the burning heat,
In thicker shades a cool and calm retreat.
Albert and Pardo by their sovereign rode   490
In converse on the chase, when near them stood
A mighty boar, the monarch of the wood.
Him nor their weapons nor their shouts dismay—
He views, he circles, and affronts his prey.
Furious, immense, the dreadful beast appears,
With horrent bristles and erected ears;
With hideous roar th' affrighted grove he fills,
And o'er his gnashing tusks the foam distills;
But RICHARD, watchful to prevent his foe,
Aim'd at his mighty chest th' unerring blow;   500
Deep sunk the spear, but high the monster stood,
Seized with his paws, and tugg'd and snapp'd the wood.
Maddening with pain and rage now twice he tried
To wound the King, who leaped his steed aside,
Then sternly waits him as he springs again,
And drives his biting falchion to the brain.
The knights his tusks and mighty bulk admire,
And eyes, yet red with half extinguish'd fire.

Delighted now they view th' inviting scene;
Close girt with jealous shades a fairy green,   510

A shadowy lawn, which tender hearts might chuse
For amorous speech, or bards that court the Muse;
For ne'er by confluent streams, or lake, or grot,
Did fabled Naiad hallow lovelier spot.
A fountain, bursting from the earth, became
A lucid pool, and fed a murmuring stream;
Its emerald verge a thousand blossoms dyed,
And azure lilies gem'd the crystal tide.
A sycamore, the patriarch of the glade,
O'er the clear spring his ample foliage spread; 520
Behind, amid the olive's darker green,
Gleam'd the blue fig, the ruddy grape was seen.

 Soon o'er the Monarch's eyes soft torpor creeps,
And by the waters lull'd young Albert sleeps;
But lovelorn Pardo mark'd the moon on high,
A thread of silver in the midday sky.
" Fair planet, never lover watch'd in vain
Thy swelling orb, as I thy lingering wane!
Swift through thy sphere of viewless crystal roll,
Auspicious Cynthia! to thy western goal, 530
And veil the stars in darkness, when I wait
The midnight hour by Sion's Golden Gate."
Then in bright wreath his nimble fingers wove
The jasmine, sacred to Amina's love.

"Sweet flower," he sigh'd, "thy freshness shall not fade
Ere these glad eyes behold the blushing maid;"
And as more thick a lover's day-dreams throng,
His buoyant fancy prompts the minstrel song.

" Oh sing not of love with his bended bow,
And the silver fillet that binds his brow, 540
   And his fluttering plumes behind;
For the love that wounds is a smiling pest,
The love that has wings is a treacherous guest,
   And worthless the love that is blind.

" No! love is a frank and a brave cavalier,
His saddle is jasper, of gold is his spear,
   And his armour the diamond bright:
Mirth dips his gay mantle in rainbow dyes,
His cheeks are the bud of the rose, and his eyes
   Are the stars on a moonless night. 550

" Sweet Modesty comes, as his blooming bride,
The bride-maiden, Mercy, attends at her side,
   And Loyalty rides as his squire;
The roses spring up at his palfrey's tread,
And the woodbine blossoms around his head,
   To the songs of the feathery quire."—

He ceased—do sportive fairies haunt the glade?—
Or does he clasp his own Arabian maid?
Trembling and breathless, both with haste and fear,
Drawn by the sound, yet dreading danger near, 560
She came,—then screaming in her wild delight,
Darts like a sunbeam to th' enraptured knight.
Now melts in tears of extasy, and now
An angry father sees in every bough;
Scarce can she trust her dream of bliss, or tell
The chance that guided to that leafy dell.

Oh! from that hour, that wretched, rapturous night
Of Acre's capture, and her hasty flight,
Her thoughts still linger'd on one sacred spot,
And him once seen, but never more forgot; 570
Her only solace, when Almanzor blest
The cares, the silver voice that lull'd to rest,
Or Philomel in sympathetic strain
To Eve's pale star deplored a love as vain.
With grief her sire beheld his drooping flower,
And bade Moheddin speed the nuptial hour.
Each drop that o'er her faded beauty stole
But fix'd the fatal purpose of his soul,
" No more," he cried, " this childish coldness shew,
Nor feign disgust for one thou cans't not know; 580

Soon shall his fondness dry these tears, and move
E'en thy young heart to feel the power of love."

Alas! too well the power Amina knew
That robb'd her cheek of youth's celestial hue,
And made those lips that mock'd the aloe's bloom,
Or breath'd the blushing Amra's mild perfume
Pale as the lily, "ah!" she thought, "how vain
The tardy blessing, should we meet again!
My heart would but a deeper grief deplore
When these changed features should be loved no more.
But hark!"—'twas mellow evening's stillest hour
When the soft Vina sounded near her bower,
(That bower which eastward from the Town of God
Look'd out where Kedron's winter torrent flow'd,
Where silver Silöe bubbles into light,
And dusky olives clothe the farther height;)
And soon a plaintive song attention moved,
For sweet the strain, though not the voice beloved:—

" The Bulbul sings in the distant bower,
 Far, far from his Rose's anxious ear; 600
But the Zephyr may waft to the drooping flower
 The sigh of the heart that she holds most dear.

" And hid in this garland of mystic bloom,
   She may feel the breath of that sacred sigh;
In the scentless amaranth's rich perfume,
   In the pale acacia's deepening dye.

" Let it fan the blush on her faded cheek,
   Till it glow as though her lover were near;
For even this silent wreath may speak
   The wish of his soul to a faithful ear." 610

A wakeful eunuch heard the closing strain,
And sought the venturous youth, but sought in vain;
While the sweet maid, no longer languid, pale,
Snatch'd the blest wreath that told so sweet a tale.
   But Aladin to Asia's lord declares
Fierce RICHARD's menace; Solyma prepares
For instant siege, and deep in Sharon's shade
Almanzor's care secludes the timorous maid,
Where murmuring streams, and birds, and fragrant
      flowers,
Erst join'd with youth to chase her careless hours.—
But ah! that loved retreat is wrapp'd in gloom,
The birds have lost their voice, the flowers their bloom;

And she whose lips responsive music breathed,
Or in gay knots their fleeting glories wreathed,
Sits pale beneath her favourite tree, and flings
Her hands, scarce conscious, o'er the gilded strings
Of her soft lute; now wakes a plaintive strain,
Now drops it from her hand, and weeps again.
The past is like a vision of delight,
For ever lost, the future veil'd in night. 630

But Saladine, who held Moheddin dear,
With myrtle wreaths would bind the brows of war;
To Lidda's camp he now the maid invites,
And speeds with courtly pomp the bridal rites.

In mirth and pomp Almanzor's household vied,
And all were joyful, save the wretched bride.
Passive, amid her maiden slaves she stands,
While the red hinna stains her snowy hands,
While with rich gems they deck her ankles fair,
And braid with orient pearl her glossy hair; 640
Then in a gay and gilded palanquin,
Whose gaudy splendour mocks the grief within,
They place their victim, and the march begin.
But as, to wile the sultry noon, they staid
Their weary steeds in Sharon's deepest shade,

While all around her careless guardians slept,
From her soft couch the timid virgin crept;
The roughest path, the wildest brake she chose,
Anxious alone, when death should end her woes,
To perish faithful—or perchance to move   650
Some wandering knight to guide her to her love.

  Such was her story,—but till poet's art
Can paint the joy that shone in either heart;
Her silver tone, the inexpressive grace
That lit her dark blue eyes, and glowing face;
Ill may he teach what made that hour so dear,
Or that slight tale so sweet to Pardo's ear.
  But never on affection's stream, in sooth,
Long smiles the sun, or is its channel smooth.*
The sable Lyard, RICHARD's favourite steed,   660
With one bold effort from his bridle freed,
Bounds through the glade, while Pardo strives in vain
To rush before and catch the broken rein:
Still as he came the wayward horse was gone,
Yet such slight space as lured the warrior on;
Nor marked he, till again he soothed its pride,
How far it led him from Amina's side.

* "The course of true love never did run smooth."

Bewilder'd now, and by his haste betray'd,
He wanders farther from the anxious maid.
" Thou sable beast," th' impatient lover cried, 670
" Scarce are thy pranks by Moslem fears belied,
Which swear some demon fills thy dusky hide!
Yet poor the sport, all vicious as thou art,
To wring with grief a true and tender heart."

 The daylight sunk—in vain he look'd on high,
And curs'd, what late he wish'd, the moonless sky;
Bewilder'd, wearied, till the morning shone
On the new walls of distant Ascalon.
Revived by hope, he spurs his steed, but there
All was confusion, terror and despair;   680
Pale every cheek; one single thought opprest
And still'd the warring crowd of every breast;
And soon he hears a dreadful tale, that drove
Even from a lover's heart the dream of love;
In one sad tone, one mournful phrase they spoke,
" Their Monarch captive to the Soldan's yoke."
Th' assembled Peers in dismal conclave sate,
How best to bear, and how reverse his fate;
Their minds benumb'd, partake the general gloom,
A thousand plans propose, reject, resume;   690

Even heroes scarce were men; when needed most,
Courage, and hope, and sense itself seem'd lost.—
But hark! a shout—they see a knightly train,
As captives long deplored, or wept as slain;
The matted locks, the pale and wrinkled brow
Spoke suffering past, but all was rapture now;
And happy Albert from the grateful ring
Bounds in his transport, and demands the King.

" Hast thou not heard,"the mournful Raymond said,
" How in his slumber to the foe betray'd—" 700

" Nay! my loved friend, no Moslem chains confine
The L<small>ION</small> H<small>EART</small>, the captive lot was mine!
With sylvan sport and noontide heat opprest,
A gurgling fountain lull'd the King to rest;
I slumber'd near, when from a happy dream
I started, waken'd by a woman's scream,
And saw a maid, who wept with anguish wild
As stern Almanzor claim'd his truant child.
Large was the hostile band, too large for strife,
The pressing danger threaten'd R<small>ICHARD</small>'s life, 710
(For well I knew, by honour unreprest,
What deadly hatred fired the Arab's breast;)
And boldly rushing 'mid the armed ring,
' Preserve my life!' I cried, ' preserve the King!'

Nor fail'd the fraud,—though all in battle field
Had known his broomy crest and lion shield,
The peaceful garb deceived; the valleys rung
With shouts of rapture as we pac'd along,
And oft my secret fancy wander'd here
To paint your fears, and joy that vanquish'd fear. 720
Yon woods may still the wandering King detain,
But England's glory wears no Moslem chain."

" Alas!" said Raymond, " 'twere a happier doom ;
Some beast may tear him now, or gulf entomb."—

" Peace, Raven! croak not yet," young Pardo cried
" Hope is a fairer and a safer guide.
'Tis madness thus th' inflicted grief to swell ;—
But speak, dear Albert, how thy fetters fell?"

" Nor were the tale of pleasing interest void
In happier hour," the gentle youth replied. 730
" They led me to the Soldan : nor his eye
Flash'd with the meteors of intemperate joy,
Nor glared with rage, when, as the truth I shew'd,
His baffled satraps clamour'd for my blood.
' That King must ill a Sovereign's duty know
Who harms the loyal, though he serve a foe,'
He answer'd mild ; ' such zeal in half my train
Had made thy Monarch's bold invasion vain,

Yet not too lightly must such knight be freed—
Twice fifty thousand bysants be the meed.'   740

"With grief I heard, beyond a subject's power,
My ransom rated at a princely dower.
When now the Soldan smiling led me forth,
' Nor mourn,' he said, ' this tribute to thy worth;
The Christian warriors, when they hear thy plight,
Shall vie with gifts to ransom such a Knight:
And trust me, though a different faith be mine,
I hold the name of chivalry divine;
Too well, in sooth, its foes are taught to prize
What makes frail man so glorious and so wise.   750
Fain would my soul th' ennobling precepts hear,
And fain my limbs the sacred tokens wear.'

"Amazed I ponder'd—could the holy flame
Descend to warm a misbelieving frame?

"' Believe,' he cried, ' with no impure desires
To join your Order Saladine aspires,
Nor were its glory tarnish'd, should a part[h]
Of its pure doctrines reach an Arab's heart.'

"So modest! thought I—could I still forbear?
I waived the vigil, waived the rites of prayer: 760
But in the bath his hardy limbs I laved,[i]
Symbol of man by vows baptismal saved;

Then at my will a simple couch he prest
In sleep, the emblem of our mortal rest,
And rose regenerate—o'er him next I threw
The linen robe of truth's unspotted hue,
That asks as pure a frame; the scarlet vest
That claims devotion from the constant breast,
Danger and death for knighthood's sake to brave,
And loath dishonour far beyond the grave. 770
Then passing, by his rank imperial sway'd,
Th' accustom'd blow, the friendly accolade,
I bade him guard a soul from falsehood clear,
And more than wealth or power the truth revere;
With liberal heart enjoy what heaven should send,
Observe the holy rites the church ordain'd,
And still be prompt, by selfish views unsway'd,
His life or limbs to risk in beauty's aid;
For ill that wretch the name of Knight may bear
Whose callous heart is closed to woman's prayer. 780

" ' No more I muse,' th' attentive Soldan cries,
' For from such source can less than heroes rise?
And let me prove I bear no heedless mind—
Go! seek the gold from all of Christian kind:
But if two summers past thou suest in vain,
My power unwilling claims its thrall again.'

" I knelt my thanks:—yet ere I journey hence,
I here my suit at knighthood's feet commence;
Largesse! Largesse!—from thee so wise and bold,
I ask a portion of the Soldan's gold!   790

" ' Who trusts in Saladine shall never find
That trust betray'd,' the new-made Knight rejoin'd;
' I like thy suit—deem half thy ransom told,
And ten brave warriors that my dungeons hold,
There lingering since Tabaria's fatal fight,
By thee restored to liberty and light.'

" He spoke, and leading past the ample gate,
In solemn council where his Emirs sate,
From all around, to loose my captive chain,
He craved their bounty, nor he craved in vain.   800
Seiffeddin and his son with prompt accord,
And Egypt's King, and Sindjar's valiant Lord;
Young Afdhal, worthy shoot of Ayoub's race,
And bold Zeineddin, fair Arbelia's grace,
Vied in their gifts; alone Almanzor frown'd—
When thus the Chief for sanguine arms renown'd:*
' Warrior, this gem is thine, but know that He
Thy fraud preserved had found no grace from me;

* Zorayda.

Say that the Soldan's camp is rich with one,
Whose wrongs, whose hatred seek his life alone; 810
Nor care I, though the haughty boast display
The Western lineage that my lips betray.'

"Wondering I heard, for strange it seem'd to find
Such rooted hatred in a stripling's mind;
Whose form and beardless cheek seem'd fitter far
For lady's service than the toils of war.

"Now all had given, but of the mighty debt
Twelve thousand bysants were uncounted yet;
When from his stores the Soldan these demands,
And gives the treasure to my wondering hands. 820
'Receive this pledge of just esteem,' he cried,
May still the laws you teach your actions guide;
And still your garners every blessing hold,
As you, when I reclaim, shall pay the Soldan's gold.'

"Thrice happy gold! too long in bonds opprest,
The Monarch's gift what captive pilgrims blest!
I claim'd my steed, and hasten'd to depart,
With lighten'd hands, but with a lighter heart;
My fate, my safety, eager to declare
To those, I knew, who held that safety dear, 830
Nor thought, alas! what hopeless grief was here."

"Not so! till we have trodden every glade,
In yon ill-omen'd forest," Pardo said.
"We might have known, from Arsouf's dreadful eve,
What demons there the spells of horror weave.
Yet bless me, Prelate! and with heaven my guide,
Through all its glens undaunted will I ride;
Bring back my living Liege, or find my rest
On the cold sod his princely limbs have prest."

Her sorrows shrouded in her ample veil,   840
The anxious Queen had heard the warrior's tale;
But yesterday, to treacherous ease betray'd,
By the cool breezes and the fragrant shade,
She linger'd, while her maidens sporting round,
Spread the light banquet on the mossy ground.
Her gay guitar th' Iberian virgin strung,
And to her sprightly songs the forest rung;—
There Lusignan beneath the conscious shade
Told his soft story to the captive maid:
"How blest were he, would Cyprus Princess deign
To share her just, hereditary reign."
Her glowing cheeks, moist eyes, and heaving breast
Emotions strong as love awakes, confest;
Th' enamour'd King in breathless rapture gazed,
But soon she crush'd the hopes her silence rais'd:

" Ah no!" she sigh'd, " the fates have fix'd my doom,
A lonely heart, a convent's pious gloom."—

 She spoke, and wandering sought the thickest shade,
Till sober twilight sadden'd every glade.
" Alas!" she thought, " while yet a reckless child, 860
How oft have I at Cypriot maidens smil'd,
When gathering flowers, that, bathed in mystic dew,
Should kindle love, or bind their lovers true.
Officious memory marks their bloom too well,
But honour, duty, bid me shun the spell;
Yet there are plants which, cull'd in twilight hour,
O'er love unblest assert a holy power."—

 Alas! how weak against Maimoune's guile
All the soft magic of her amorous isle!
Not her's imagination's love-sick dream, 870
Which fancy wakes and fancied balm can tame.
Yet might she bless the idle search that now
Had spared her wounded breast a heavier blow,
And led her distant from the scene of woe;
When on the breezes borne, the billows roll'd,
The Moslem shouts their fancied capture told.

 As maids, that dancing in the blossom'd mead,
Hear the deep thunder pealing o'er their head,—

As mariners, when winds with sullen moan
Portend the storm, that find their rudder gone,— 880
So fared the Christian host; even bearded men,
That oft had fronted death, were children then.
In tears the mild Matilda melts away,
And lost in stupor Berengaria lay;
Not soon her flowing sorrows gave relief,
Or her firm spirit rose to strive with grief.

The hope that long on Albert's words reposed,
Died in her bosom, ere his story closed;
In silence now she turn'd her to depart,
New cause of anguish smothering at her heart, 890
When Bertrand loud in scoffing accents spoke
(For RICHARD's loss his gloomy rapture woke:)

" Ye, who beguil'd the hours in yonder shade,
May tell perchance where pale Evanthe stray'd,
And what soft scenes conceal the pensive maid;
Or they who mark'd how oft her faded cheeks
Glow like the morn, when royal England speaks,
May bid our hearts from idle fears be freed,
And guess the riddle she alone can read?"

Impetuous anger blazed in Raymond's eye, 900
And Lusignan prepared the warm reply;

But Berengaria's glance reproachful stole
To the dark depths of Bertrand's sullen soul.
" And were it thus," the Queen indignant cried,
" What fiend is he that tells it to his bride!
Alas! sweet maid, too much my wretched lot
Usurp'd my soul; her absence was forgot.
It wakens hope—with joy her loss I learn
May she with RICHARD stray, with him return;
For know, base slanderer, wheresoe'er they ride, 910
Heaven is their guard, and honour is their guide."

With hasty steps the noble dame withdrew,
And baffled Bertrand shrunk abash'd from view.

END OF BOOK X.

CŒUR DE LION.

BOOK XI.

THE PRINCE OF THE ASSASSINS.

ARGUMENT.

THE PRINCE OF THE ASSASSINS.

Pardo determines to explore the wood, and takes leave of Albert—The forest fountain—The deserted mansion—His journey through the desert—The snowy mountains—The cavern in the rock—Appearance and story of Hassan—His early friendship and quarrel with Nizam—His mysterious power—The temptation of Pardo—The paradise of Hassan—Pardo and Maimoune.

CŒUR DE LION.

BOOK XI.

THE PRINCE OF THE ASSASSINS.

Pardo meanwhile, in lighter mail array'd,
Prepares on foot to tempt the dangerous shade.
But first he calls his gallant friend apart,
And thus relieves his agonizing heart:

" I would not, Albert, that our comrades fear
I too am lost; ye know not how or where,
But do not ask my venturous quest to share.
I brought the sorrow, let me brave the pain;—
Nay start not, conscience shall not speak in vain.

Fool that I was! absorb'd in selfish joy; 10
For Lyard heard, and warn'd of danger nigh.
 But thou wilt laugh, my friend, and while I speak
Shame well may redden on my burning cheek,
That I, who scorn'd the wanton archer's power,
Lost my proud freedom in one luckless hour;
That many a night, for fair Amina's sake,
My heavy eyes have learn'd like thine to wake;
Well mayst thou taunt me, none so well as thou—
But check those smiles, I cannot bear them now;
In happier hours, should happier hours befall, 20
Pour forth thy gibes, and I will bless them all.
 " Farewell! if now my eager search be vain,
And I am lost, in heaven we meet again;
But should my King, my more than sire return,
To hear my wandering doom, perchance to mourn,
Say, if his erring favourite still be dear,
'Twas my last hope that pious hands might rear
A simple pillar by yon forest side,
To mark for RICHARD's love that Pardo died.—
Oh! had I bled to guard his precious days, 30
Or shared thy danger, Albert! and thy praise!
 " Still with one anxious wish my heart is fraught—
My steed—yet 'twas not of my steed I thought;

I know that thou the faithful beast wilt take,
And prize my noble roan for Pardo's sake.
But she, Almanzor's child—Oh! while I vow
My days to RICHARD, peril waits her now!
I dare not think—but if impell'd by fear
She seek this camp, and one no longer here,
On thee, my generous Albert, I depend;   40
Receive, protect her,—be indeed my friend.
Once more farewell—nay give one smile to bless
My venturous way, bright omen of success."—

   And is he gone? He sprung upon his quest,
As though his haste might give his feelings rest,
And thought, with all her torturing train, depart,
Like the pale phantoms at the dreamer's start.
But though the sun in morning splendour glow'd,
To him dark horror wraps the hateful wood;
Ah, that those hills, those conscious shades would tell
At least the fate of him he lov'd so well.
His anxious eye in vain he glanc'd around,
Or on his horn the well-known summons wound;
'Tis but the fawn that from his presence flies,
'Tis but the echo to his call replies.

At length (for oft through devious paths he stray'd)
With weary steps he reach'd the fatal glade;
As sweet a fragrance fills the balmy air,
As cool the fountain seems, the fruits as fair;
And the soft spirit of departed joys   60
Breathes from each flower, and swims before his eyes.
What froze his glance?—a scarf distain'd with gore!
A scarf! just Heaven! that late Evanthe wore.
" Oh! then were Bertrand's base suspicions true!
And what dread tale is in that sanguine hue?
Yet ever be the hateful lie abhorr'd,
Think, Pardo, think more nobly of thy Lord;
And emulate his Consort's trust, to prove
Thy heart, like hers, deserves a hero's love.
And for that stain, behold where all around   70
The slaughter'd boar has died th' enamell'd ground;
I will not fear—no not till proof be found.
Be hope my guide, and lo! those flowers betray
The tread of steeds—sweet seraph, lead the way!"—
    Scarcely he stays to lave his burning brow,
Or pluck the purple clusters from the bough;
And fresh as at the earliest hour of morn
Onward he hastes, and winds his mellow horn.

But daylight fades,—he ill may brook delay,
Yet fears again in tangled wilds to stray; 80
Nor dares he slumber on the mossy green,
Lest wolves assail, or scorpions wound unseen.
" I love," he thought, " a soldier's death to brave,
But would not wish a lion's paunch my grave,
Or court an aspic's bite—perchance 'twere best
To make yon sycamore my eagle's nest,
Though snake perchance, or vulture harbour there,
Fearless I trust our common parent's care."

Up the broad trunk with agile grace he wound,
To the tough boughs his ample mantle bound, 90
And slept;—unnoticed sung the bird of night,
Nor e'en Amina charms his dreaming sight.

What odours from a thousand glowing flowers,
Fair as the bloom of Irem's fabled bowers![a]
What strains from birds all glorious to behold,
With wings of purple, emerald and gold,
All strange to Europe's niggard summers, borne
Round the young sleeper, speak th' awakening morn.
Again the wood his hasty meal supplied,
Again his steps the frequent footprints guide; 100
Here stately trees obstruct the cheerful day,
Here time-bow'd veterans bar the weary way;

Here rocks arise or narrow lawns are spread,
Here tangled brushwood closes all the shade.
And now he reached a stream; through narrow space
The sunbeams break upon its crystal face;
Th' acacia with its tufts of golden hair,[b]
And taller trees, and flowers more fresh and fair
Hang o'er its waves, to view their image there;
Save where the lotos, as in wanton pride,   110
Spreads her broad leaves, and veils the lucid tide.

   Scarce mark'd the wanderer that the forest grew
Thin and more thin, and now retired from view;
For still, to screen him from the noontide beam,
A belt of verdure clothed the winding stream.
Till now a moss-grown arch contracts the wave,
In darkness chafing through the echoing cave;
And by a wall where clustering ivy twined,
Still veiled in wood, the devious path declined.
It reach'd a narrow gate; the iron pin   120
Yields to the warrior's hand,—he ventures in.
It was a garden, such as Arabs love,
Half art, half nature, wilderness and grove.
Myrtle and orange here, and cassia grows,
The dusky olive, and the glowing rose;[c]

Here the lost stream, in mazy channels led,
Cools the hot breeze, and visits every shade;
The thick-wove foliage of the laurel bower,
And the pale star of sad Amina's flower.
But all was lonely, not a living sound—　　　130
And now he ventures on forbidden ground;
The Haram walls, as infant, maid, or wife,
Where Moslem beauty wastes her captive life.
'Twas not the thought that death might wait him there,
That with a strange oppression loads the air;
That stole its freshness from each fount that falls
In diamond showers within the glittering halls,
Where eastern luxury all her pride displays,
In many a lamp of gold and sculptured vase,
Or made the gay kitarr and amorous lute,　　　140
E'en to a lover's active fancy, mute.
The bath, whose waves a costly scent diffuse,
And shine o'er marble of a thousand hues;
Where roseate curtains shed voluptuous light,
And silken seats the weary limbs invite;
Charm'd not the warrior's free-born sense, nor stole
One softer feeling through his kindling soul.
" No!" he exclaim'd, " a purer stream I quaff'd,
This Circe's cup has poison in the draught;

The bird within its gilded cage may sing, 150
That never knew through azure fields to spring;
And beauty may be idly happy here
Nor dream that heaven had will'd a higher sphere;
That she has sweeter duties, nobler powers,
Or soul more lasting than those birds and flowers.
And yet I love an Arab maid!—but why?
Because her spirit sparkles in her eye,
And inborn greatness lifts her far above
These idle triflings that her sisters love."

Swift through the gloomy passages he ran, 160
That join the Haram to the halls of man.[d]
But could a despot's lone abode impart
A sense more grateful to a Christian's heart,
Without one spell the hateful truth to hide,
They spoke of rapine, cruelty and pride.
The cells where many a wretched, hopeless slave
Toils, bleeds, and sinks unpitied to the grave;
The long divan in Persian silks array'd,
The curtain'd galleries round the chamber spread,
Or those beneath, where day shall never come, 170
Where martial spoils are shrouded in the gloom,
Or murder hides the victim and the tomb;[e]

Shuddering he saw; but all was lonely there,
And forth he rush'd to breathe a freer air.
He reached the court, where still in Arab state,
Chain'd by the foot, two harness'd coursers wait.*
One dark as stormy clouds or wintry night,
One as the lily's spotless blossom, white.

" Wide is the plain, and hot the noontide ray,
No branches now will check a horseman's way; 180
Fortune, I take thy proffer'd gift—Oh! speed
My anxious wandering, as thou send'st the steed;—
For thee, thou raven beast, my cause is slight
To love thy dusky hue,—I choose the white."

But little use he found of spur or rein,
For like an arrow glancing o'er the plain,
As with his freedom pleas'd, th' unfetter'd steed
Holds on his course with more than mortal speed.
Soon has he left each cultured scene behind,
He skims the sand, he snuffs the desert wind; 190
Bounds where th' enduring camel moves with pain,
And the red waves are like the stormy main.
The warrior faints beneath the noontide heat,
'Gainst the hot casque his painful temples beat,

* It is a piece of Arab state to have one or more horses, ready saddled and bridled, chained by the foot in the court-yard of the house.

Yet o'er the waste, with unabating force,
The wondrous courser holds his arrowy course.

  At last, 'twas at the sunset hour, he staid
Where fruitful palms a desert fountain shade;
And cooler gales its belt of herbage fann'd,
A verdant island in that sea of sand.   200
With joy the wanderer quits his wilful guide,
Culls the ripe dates, and drinks the cooling tide,
And slept—till with the morn beside him stood
The wond'rous horse, and seem'd to court his load.

  " Methinks, if once from this waste region freed,
The sluggish ass shall be my battle steed;
I well deserve to lunar wilds to soar,
If, black or white, I trust in palfrey more!
Who knows the treason should the traitor fly,—
But sands surround me, I must mount or die."   210

  Thus still the Knight o'er desert realms was borne,
While swelling Cynthia fill'd her silver horn;
Nor man he saw, nor aught of living kind,
Save the vast ostrich, running with the wind;
Or the swift pelican, that flies to bring
Her nestlings water from the distant spring,
While still the courser stopp'd, as evening fell,
Where clustering palm trees shade the lonely well,

And welcome sleep the wanderer's strength renew'd,
The spring his beverage, and the date his food. 220
At length more wild the barren region grows,
Near the hot desert snow-crown'd mountains rose;
The dews fell thick, the evening gale blew chill,
As rush'd the steed up many a rugged hill.
Each glen seem'd ruder, keener every blast,
And each steep ridge was loftier than the last.
And now he reach'd a height—one well might deem
The moon shed coldness in her piercing beam,
On naked peaks and brows for ever white,
And azure glaciers, glittering in the light. 230
But still by many a torrent's dangerous edge,
By many a precipice, whose slippery ledge
The mule might fear, with unabated speed,
And surer footing bounds th' unwearied steed.

From a broad arch of undissolving snow
A rushing torrent sought the dell below;
Undazzled by the foam, or glittering light
Of pendant ice that fringed that vault of white,
The steed plunged in, where not a straggling beam
Shew'd the dark cradle of the roaring stream. 240
Onward he holds, nor heeds the dashing spray,
Nor fails his footing on that dangerous way;

The dread abyss might seem the path of hell,
Till opening on a rock-encircled dell,
Whose smooth steep sides shake off the feathery snow,
And shut the moonbeams from the depth below;
Save where one fallen peak with ruin strew'd
The rocky bottom, fragments vast and rude;
And, through the chasm, one silver ray was flung,
Where on the adverse wall a bugle hung.   250

Its ample round the youth with music fills,
And wakes the echoes of a thousand hills;
When lo ! the flinty barrier rolls away,
And unseen doors a lamp-lit cave display.
" Almighty Power ! what now thy will?" he cried,
But be thou yet my guardian and my guide."

He quits his steed, which started off agen,
Draws his bright sword, and plunges in the den.
Again the valves have closed, the walls repeat
Nought save the echoes of his rapid feet;   260
Shew nought but rocks with tawny moss o'ergrown,
Or where the snow-damps filter through the stone;
The half-froze drop that caught the flickering light,
White clustering spar, and pendant stalactite.

" Oft have I heard, in Arab story told,
How scaly dragons guard the cavern'd gold,

And fain would court such bold emprize: but fear
Aladdin's glittering garden shines not here;
And though I rubb'd yon rusty cressets bright,
They would not bring one giant friend to light; 270
Else should his lips a monarch's story tell—
Alas! my own is doubtful! who can dwell
In scenes like these, whose savage gloom would fright
The holiest sage, the sternest Eremite?
My living dungeon, and perchance my grave!
But lo! where yon white veil divides the cave."—

T'was but a bound,—he long'd to know his doom,
He drew it back, and stood within a room,
Shewn by a single lamp, half glare, half gloom.
Its lustre fell upon a plain divan, 280
Where sate in robes of white an aged man.
Nor joy nor fear his changeless cheek exprest,
To daunt or welcome his astonish'd guest,
While pointing to the coarse repast that spread
Th' untap'stried floor, in tranquil tone he said:

" Hail, Christian! thou art late—advance and eat,
Hunger like thine should make the banquet sweet;—
Nay! pause not—warriors are not nicely fed,
Nor need voluptuous, and 'tis wholesome bread."

"Nay, father! who art thou, by seeming spell
That wait'st me here, and know'st that need so well?"
"Hassan, the Mountain Prince!"
"Ah! then too late,"
The youth exclaim'd, " I know my dreadful fate,
For thou hast murder's deadliest arts, to strike
The distant victim and the near, alike;
Once mark'd by thee, the tyger knows his prey,
Or wasted wretches pine their lives away.
One only boon, Assassin Chief! accord,
Thy poisons spare, and kill me with the sword."

No feeling o'er his furrow'd visage past, 300
And cold and rayless was the glance he cast.
"Trust me, young Knight! thou hast no cause of fear,
For murder wherefore should I bring thee here?
It had been easier far to bid thee fall
While lingering in Almanzor's lonely hall,
Or by the forest fountain—foolish boy!
My wish is now to save thee, not destroy."

"Then in the name of heaven I eat," he said,
"For He who walked the printless waves, and fed
Thousands with less than this; whose power divine
Lives in the sacred wafer (mystic sign!)

Shall sanctify the meal."—Yet oft he gazed
On that old man, and still the more amazed.

The winters of that desert realm had shed
Their whitest snows upon his aged head;
The rose his pallid cheek might once have known,
The modulation of his youthful tone,
The lustre of his changeless eye were flown.
Fix'd as th' uncoffin'd dead, or those that, lost
In Alpine regions, feel the grasp of frost;   320
Yet not the kindly calm of pious sage,
Nor wrinkles those of meek and reverend age:
Though anger sate not on his brow, nor trace
Of evil passions darken'd on his face,
It was an apathy that told of sin,
And seem'd to speak the silent heart within
Cold as the glaciers, that but melt to shew
The dark abyss or flinty rock below;
Nor spoke it false; who knew his youth might know.

Health shed her beam on Hassan's vernal hours,
And pleasure woo'd him to her tempting bowers;
Glanced in each mountain damsel's laughing eye,
As like the fleet gazelle she bounded by,
And breathed voluptuous in each scented gale
That swept the flowers of Casbin's fairest vale.

So cool the fountains, and the banks so green,
Such tranquil beauty clothed the smiling scene,
The parted soul might wish its Eden there,
Or Peries for their odorous feast repair:
Behind, Elburza's rugged chain arose,   340
High o'er the clouds, a wilderness of snows.
But smiling beauty won not Hassan's love,
The stream soft murmuring, nor the shadowy grove,
Nor yet to see those glittering peaks arise,
Fair as fond fancy pictures distant joys;
Oft would he break the charm that distance shed,
And plant on horrid heights his venturous tread;
Nature he loved, but in her wildest form,—
The raging sea, the earthquake, and the storm.
He fled from Shiraz' palace-groves, afar   350
'Mid the lone halls of column'd Istakar,
To tread her ruin'd terraces, and gaze
On the cold moon, or Naptha's fitful blaze;
And think upon those wretches that below
Move in one whirl of burning, endless woe.

 As yet young Hassan's heart was free from crime;
But trust him not, the tempter knows his time—
The sting of pain, or sorrow's wasting rage
May cloud with frowns the wrinkled brow of age:

But trust not him who, yet in sunny youth, 369
Wants the frank smile, the open glow of truth;
Whose cold perverted fancy never roves
To dream of faithful friends and happy loves,
But rashly wanders in ambition's maze,
That winds, and knots, and darkens as he strays.
Not that ambition which for glory stakes
Peace, health, and life, and gilds the wreck it makes;
But that which, mindful of the present hour,
Stops not for crime, and grasps alone at power.

Yet Hassan had a friend, and one whose mind 370
No bonds, save virtue's, ever yet confin'd;
His thought through nature's various realms would range,
Explore her wonders, ponder every change,
And own in all that Being, whose control
Created, keeps, and renovates the whole;
Bids the same laws the small and great confine,
Bids for one end discordant means combine;
One power renew what other powers destroy,
And clothes the whole in beauty and in joy.

Oh! how could darkness love the cheerful light,
Or Nizam's smiles with Hassan's gloom unite?

Perchance, that though of different race, they drew
Milk from one breast, or through the morning dew
Chaced the fierce panther, or the rapid deer,
Each, save his equal friend, without a peer.
Perchance, that both insatiate in the draught,
They from one fount the streams of science quaff'd.[f]
Nizam would snatch the blossom from the shoot,
And in its embryo trace the future fruit;
His friend would poison from the leaves distill, 390
And try on puny beasts its power to kill;
Honey from each the mind of Nizam stole,
From each its venom flow'd to Hassan's soul.

The Persian Sultan heard of Nizam's worth;
From Casbin's peaceful shades he call'd him forth,
O'er all his realms his sole vicegerent made,
Loved as himself, and like himself obey'd.
But the young sage, though pomp and power were new,
To seek his friend from courtly scenes withdrew.
He found him on a rock, intent to throw 400
His baits upon the stream that foam'd below,
And while his panting victims round him lie,
To wanton in their dying agony.
" Up, Hassan—throw these childish sports aside,
Seek nobler game, an empire's cares divide;

Our bounteous Prophet," thus the youth began,
" Showers on thy friend the smiles of Arselan.
Come then to Shiraz—trust thy Nizam's care—
My wealth, my power, my Sovereign's favour share."

   His moody friend scarce rais'd his sullen eyes,   410
And thus with proud and curling lip replies :
" What should I share ?—think'st thou the gaudy gold
That decks thy caftan and thy turban's fold
Has charms for me ?—that Hassan would resign
His own free mountains for a fame like thine ?
My simple robes exclude the heat as well,
Thy pomp but makes them heavier.—Canst thou tell
For thee if richer fruits adorn the tree,
Or shines the sun with brighter light—for thee ?"

   " Dear Hassan, is it thus ? Hast thou forgot 420
Our youth, our vow to share one common lot ?*
Art thou content ! has thine aspiring mind
All its ambitious views at once resigned ?"—

   " No, fool ! Ambition still is Hassan's joy,
I scorn thy proffer, for I look more high ;

---

  * The two friends had vowed that whichever should first obtain wealth or honours should immediately share them with the other : a vow often paralleled by the knightly " brothers in arms."

He that is foremost when the race begins,
May cheat the betting crowd, but seldom wins.
'Tis thou that never yet her fire hast nurs'd—
The second in the realm, and not the first!
Thou lovest to hear the throngs that trumpet forth
Thy mercy, justice, piety, and worth,
(A thousand gifts that none discover'd here,
But heap them all upon their new Vizier;)
Nor think'st those talents, now so lustrous grown,
Would blaze with tenfold light beneath a crown.
Thy master to thy grateful heart is dear;
Be kind, and send him to a happier sphere.
Thou start'st—then, Nizam, we are friends no more:
Thou would'st not dare to look where I will soar.
Without one bright tomaun, one robe of state, 440
I'll fix my power beyond the reach of fate;
High as the Simurgh's nest shall be my home,
Where thou or Arselan can never come;
I'll stand erect upon a lofty wall,
When he shall totter—thou perchance may'st fall."

Vex'd at the drops that gather'd in his eyes,
With hands uprais'd sad Nizam thus replies:
" Eternal God! is then the vision o'er?
Can Hassan speak it, we are friends no more!

Ah, then farewell, clear streams and shadowy groves,
And each dear witness of our early loves;
Like the sad flowers that waste their virgin bloom,
The lamp that glimmers in the silent tomb,
Ye speak of broken ties, of pleasure past,
Bright as the rainbow, and to fade as fast."

 Years roll'd away, and Nizam still approved
His wondrous worth, by king and people loved,
Bokhara's farthest bounds their rule obey,
And flowery Cashmere courts so mild a sway.
But to the west, amid Elburza's snows,   460
A mountain chief to strange dominion rose.
He had not wealth the sordid soul to move,
Nor those free manners that the generous love,
Nor could his dwelling youth or age invite,
The strongest fortress of a desert height.
Yet he had followers, eager to fulfil
What they believed their God's dictated will;
Nay, some declared that wondrous man had given
To them a foretaste of his promised heaven;
And he who dared to doubt what they should tell,
Or on his mind a strange conviction fell,
Or murder struck him in his inmost cell.^z

Slaves trembled for their lives, and kings were prone
By his alliance to secure their own.[h]

Yes! Hassan knew to work upon the soul,
Till e'en instinctive conscience lost control.
He knew each power that cuts the thread of life,
What taint will enter with the venom'd knife;
What unobserv'd will present death procure,
What saps the hardy frame, unmark'd, but sure. 480
The toad, the basilisk of dangerous glance,
The snake, whose noise betrays his swift advance,
The shining fly with wings of emerald light,
The dog that maddens with its phrenzied bite;
Each weed that curses Afric's sands, or grows
By fens contagious, or on desert brows;
The sullen yew, the fatal manchineal,
Or those blue flowers that sense and feeling steal;*
And all those mineral poisons, deadlier still,
That earth secretes, were subject to his will. 490
Nor these alone—at midnight he would dwell
On those dark books that things forbidden tell,—
The spells of numbers, and in baneful hour,
How holiest names may have unholy power.

* Certain alpine regions are said to produce a small and beautiful blue flower, whose exhalations deprive the gatherer of sense. It is even reported that its effects have been fatal when conveyed in a letter.

By Kaf, in the Domdaniel's caves accurst,
At Istakar, beside the fires they nurst,
He talk'd with those 'twere impious but to name;
At night on highest hills unhallow'd flame
Blazed for his orgies, and the cloudless moon
Withdrew her beam, though in her fullest noon. 500
 But Arselan was gather'd to his sires,
And his brave son, whom frequent conquest fires,
From Omar's gulf to Oxus' frozen wave
Convenes his force to crush the rebel slave.
In vain—that Prince whom half the east obey'd,
Was powerless here; his army fear'd and fled.[i]
His star grew dim, nor ever brighten'd more,
For Nizam, bulwark of his giant power,
Fell from his favour in that fatal hour.
Too late recall'd, while yet he rued the smart 510
Of courtly wrong, a dagger reach'd his heart.
Lamented Sage! was this thy mournful end?
Did Hassan thus requite his early friend?
 Sanjar, the Sultan, with a bolder train,
Assaults Alhamout's rock-built fort in vain.
Amid his guards, and in his tent of pride,
The Ataghan was planted by his side:

" Did not the Mountain Prince thy worth revere,
Thy heart were softer than this marble here."ᵏ

 Such was the Chief that sought the Christian yoke;
That Eudon and that Conrad dared provoke,
And Saladine disdain'd, till Hassan sent
Three midnight murderers to his inmost tent.
Startled he woke, and darkling baffled all,
Till the rous'd menials hasten'd at his call.
One wretch his arm had slain, a second fled,
And headlong leap'd the lofty balustrade;
The last with poison'd weapon pierce'd his side,
And gloried that in Hassan's cause he died.ˡ

 Such man was he, if he indeed were man,   530
Whose wondrous life surpass'd our mortal span,
Till he like Egypt's cavern'd dead became,
Nor time had power upon his wither'd frame.
He sate in silence, and with serpent gaze
Watch'd the young Knight, whose cheek no dread
  betrays.
" Chief, I have proved my trust; requite it now.
Why am I here?"—In accents calm and slow
Grave Hassan spoke: " that all thy race may be
Won through thy teaching to my faith and me."

"Nay, Hassan! I am better skill'd to bleed 540
In Heaven's pure cause, than reason on its creed;
And if its mysteries pass the mind of man,
Ill may I read what prelates cannot scan.
Prepare thy tortures,—Prince, I dare to die!
But never shall my recreant tongue deny
My vows baptismal, or this sacred sign
Given but to Christians, knighthood's badge divine."
"If but to Christians, how to Saladine?"
The Chief rejoin'd; "but be thou mute and hear :^m
Like thee the One pure Being I revere; 550
And He whose humble steps Judea trod,
Inspired of Heaven, though misbelieved a God.
Nay, start not—is this truth unheard before?
Do half your Christian sects confess him more?—
But not to Him alone my faith is given,
For Islam's Prophet is the priest of Heaven.
But nor Mahommed's creed, nor Christ's can win
Eternal joy, without that light within,
That faith—yea Christian thou account'st them blest,
Who quit the world, upon some mountain crest 560
To tame their rebel flesh by fasts severe,
Vigil, and prayer, and penitence austere."

" Aye, Mountain Chief, the anchorite we prize,
Yet holiest they," the ardent youth replies,
" Who pure as hermits in their rock-hewn cell,
Have yet a sword to strike the infidel."
"Forbear, rash Christian—curb thy venturous thought,
Nor give me vantage farther than I sought,
For such am I—for many a lonely year,
Such were my hours of abstinence and prayer ; 570
Till the cold moonbeams blanch'd my naked head,
And from my brow the trace of passion fled ;
Then dawn'd upon my soul a heavenly light,
By glimpses first, then purely, calmly bright.
Thou deem'st me curst, that human victims bleed
At my behest ; and doubly curst indeed
Where I, if human passion bade their death :
But Heaven's own oracles inspire my breath.
I know the holy transport,—calm and still
My humbled soul receives th' Eternal Will ; 580
Its chosen Avenger—yet my eyes grow dim,
And nature shudders, till I think of Him
Whose realm was ravaged by th' offended Lord,
When human mercy check'd his conquering sword ;
What praise was His, that with unmoisten'd eyes
Led forth his Son, the destin'd sacrifice ;

How Judith's hand th' Assyrian's life-blood shed,
How last, for man a Holier Victim bled."—

"Pervert not thus," burst forth th' indignant youth,
"To ends accurst th' eternal Word of Truth.— 590
Vengeance is his! or when to mortal given,
Has stamp'd in blood the characters of Heaven.
Its Will confined not to one narrow breast,
The sun has paus'd to view, the world confest.
But for a Holier Name—this den of death
Would sink in ruin, if I gave it breath.
Think of His life, thou fiend! and think of thine!
If thou hast power, miscall it not divine."

"Misjudging youth! nor at thy warmth I muse,
Nor chafe to hear—I pity and excuse 600
The zeal I soon shall prize; and give indeed,
To win thy faith, what should have been its meed.
My power, like that to zealous Peter given,
To those I love unfolds the gates of heaven;
Living they enter, living to return,
But ever, thirsting for that blest sojourn,
They work my bidding, nor can pain annoy,
Nor death appal—a death that leads to joy.
Say! if my spirits waft thee hence aloof,
Wilt thou believe? wilt thou abide the proof?" 610

"Chief! I am in thy power," the Knight replied,
"And well I guess that, were the proof denied,
Unarm'd as now thou seem'st, thy lightest words
Could fill these cups with death, this cave with swords.
Yet, wizard! practis'd as thou art, beware;
Clear be thy fountains and thine houris fair,
And green thy shades—they have not to deceive
One half-convinced in wishing to believe,
But one who trusts in Heaven's sustaining power
To pierce the spells of thy Circean bower." 620

"Nay! think not of deceit, or death, or fear,
But share my cup, and know my love sincere."
Th' Ismailian spoke, "and more, if doubt oppress,
"Or weariness intrude, (though well I guess
Thy stay will seem too short, that bower too dear),
One wish sincerely breath'd will waft thee here.
I know thee, Pardo! though not here display'd
Thy leopard shield; I know the hand that laid
Thee, helpless babe, where monarchs past, nor guest
That royal currents mingled in thy breast;— 630
Nay, let not eager hope thy cheek inflame,
The hour, rash youth, that tells thy princely name,
Shall be an hour of torture and of shame.

To prove my friendship, hear one wonder more,—
Thy Monarch lives, but on a western shore."

He spoke, and deep the grateful liquor quaff'd,
The knight in silence took, and pledged the draught,
And sank, with deep and sudden trance opprest,[n]
Ere he could ask one blessing on his rest.

Sure there are hours when gentle spirits keep   640
Their hallow'd vigils o'er our reckless sleep;
And e'en though dreams be hush'd, the conscious mind
Awakes to pleasure, nameless, undefined.
Yet now less pure the subtle spell that stole
A soft voluptuous thrill through Pardo's soul;
Or that sweet voice, whose mellow cadence seems
To echo those that charm'd his rapturous dreams.

" The dews of morning gem the flower,
The morning gales refresh the bower,
And grateful birds to Heaven prolong   650
The incense of their matin song;
Yet still their watch the Peries keep,
To bless one earthly pilgrim's sleep.

"Awake thee, youth! the moments fly,
Too short will be thy dream of joy;
Earth claims thee back to woe again,
Till Azrael burst thy mortal chain.
Then wake, thy store of rapture reap,
Nor waste one hour of Heaven in sleep."

The knight in thought had vanquish'd all the joys
Voluptuous Moslems hope in Paradise,
But lo! his sylphlike guard his breast alarms
With no exuberance of obtruded charms;
Her braided hair, her starry circlet bright,
Her zone, her vesture of embodied light,
That changed through every hue—Oh! could a form
That aw'd assembled demons, fail to warm
Such youth as his? through his delighted soul,
With every glance insidious passion stole,
So calm, so pure, that nor his virtuous pride,   670
Nor e'en Amina's image, rose to chide;
Such love it seem'd as pious vestals feel
For Saint or Angel watching o'er their weal.
The pensive languor of Maimoune's eye,
The breathing perfume of her gentle sigh,

Charm'd more than smiles by earthly beauty given,
They look'd, they whisper'd of her native heaven.

  She led him forth, while still the duteous grove
Bow'd o'er her head in reverence and in love.*
She shakes ætherial odours from her hair,   680
Disdains the envious turf, and glides in air.

  " And is this Heaven? was ever, since the birth
Of Sin and Death, such Paradise on earth?
Can all be true that bards reveal'd of yore,
Armida's garden, and Acrasia's bower?
Or of those starry halls where Peries wonn,
Throned in the splendours of the evening sun?
Shadukiam's golden towers, for ever bright,
And Amberabad, sublime in purple light?"†

  A thousand fountains glitter'd in the beams,   690
A thousand flowers were imaged in the streams;
And trees unknown extended wide and high
Their long arcades, a leafy panoply.

---

  * Alluding to the Mimosa, " that courteous tree," which bends its graceful branches as a sort of welcome to the traveller who seeks its shade.

  † Shadukiam and Amberabad, two cities of the Peries in Ginnistan, or fairy land. The brilliant colours of the setting sun are the reflection of their splendour.

Th' unfading amaranth, with its gorgeous hue,
The lotos, robed in empyrean blue,
The rose, whose hundred leaves of beauty spread,
Th' agave, rearing high its stately head;
Less fair by Pharphar's banks the flowers appear,
Or Yemen's glens, or valleys of Cashmere,
Not brighter green the groves of Shiraz clad,   700
Less pure Choaspes' fount, or vaunted Rocnabad.

  It were a joy to list the waters flow,
Or watch them rippling o'er the stones below;
While fearless of the hook the fishes glide,
Like living gems, and wanton in the tide;
And birds like those (as Moslem tales presume)*
In which just spirits wait their day of doom,
Wave their green plumage o'er each lucid rill,
Soft music murmuring from the rosy bill.
And for the fragrance, 'twas that sense refined,   710
That breathes a sweet delirium through the mind;
That says a kindred spirit lingers nigh,
And wakes the memory of forgotten joy.

---

* There is much difference among Mahommedans as to the state of the soul between its separation from the body and its final judgment; but there is a popular belief that the spirits of the just inhabit the gardens of Paradise in the shape of green birds.

And oh! Maimoune's converse—ye who prove
How trifles charm us from the lips we love,
May guess what grace her look, her dulcet tone
Lent to her speech, and made each theme her own;
How doubly sweet to him, who left but now
Elburza's cliffs, and Hassan's awful brow.

 Nor lack'd there aught that fabling Suras tell 720
Of that blest garden where Believers dwell;
The crystal dew that falls in odorous showers,
Cool streams of milk and wine, and pearly bowers;
And here were palaces, that shine and seem
As they had caught the morning's violet beam,
While seats of flowers unfading, undeprest,
Surround the glittering halls and tempt to rest;
And banquets, such as kings in vain desire,
Come with the wish, and at a wish retire.

 " How fair," the youth exclaim'd, " how glorious
  this! 730
Yet why for us alone such lavish bliss?"

 " Is yet thy sight so dim?" Maimoune said,
And on his brow her rosy fingers laid;
" See where on mossy banks my sisters lie,
And lap the Faithful in eternal joy."

He look'd again, and radiant forms were seen
In each cool grot, each shadowy walk of green,
Beneath each trumpet-flower's gigantic bell,
On each sweet tuft of golden asphodel;
Their sylphic weight the docile peacocks bear,   740
They wanton in the waves, they glide in air,
With the light clouds they wheel in mazy dance,
And rapture beams in each ætherial glance.

Night comes not here; those dark and silent hours,
When the warm sun no gladdening influence showers,
Are gay with lamps, whose silver radiance falls
In tenfold splendour from the crystal walls;
The founts that breathing coolness through the glade
Beneath his beams in rainbow beauty play'd;
Blush as he sets, with innate lustre bright   750
Send through the gloom their thousand jets of light.
New glory gilds th' acacia's polish'd stems,
Its flowers are spangled with the dancing gems;
And as she sits beneath its feathery shade,
A halo dances round Maimoune's head.
E'en thus, beneath Magellan's southern skies,
The ocean brightens as the daylight dies;
And half alarm'd the mariners admire
Their oars, their vessel, bathed in liquid fire.

Here pleasure leads her joyous train along,   760
In one gay round of frolic, feast and song;
Fatigue and pain the happy region fly,
And slumber sits not on th' unwearied eye.
The youth, forgetful how he braved the spell,
Whose soft oblivion proved its power too well,
Nor doubting if those bowers of bliss had given
All pious Christians hope and dream of heaven,
If sad reflection once asserts her power,
Looks in Maimoune's eye, and thinks no more.

END OF BOOK XI.

CŒUR DE LION.

BOOK XII.

THE PILGRIMAGE OF BERENGARIA.

ARGUMENT.

THE PILGRIMAGE OF BERENGARIA.

Return and story of Evanthe—Her wandering in the forest—The cemetery—Mysterious appearance of Leopold—His prisoner—Humanity of Aladin—Raymond accuses Bertrand of treachery—Story of Bertrand—Embassy of Aladin, and truce with the Soldan—Confession of the Assassin, and departure of Bertrand—The vision of Berengaria—She sails with Albert for Europe—Her shipwreck—Albert proceeds to England—Queen Eleanor—Narrative of events in Europe—Rebellion of John and perfidy of Philip Augustus—Albert arrives at his castle, and finds it deserted—Discovery of Edric—He relates the surprise of the castle and seizure of Rosabelle by a band of unknown warriors—Death of Edric, and departure of Albert for Germany.

CŒUR DE LION.

BOOK XII.

THE PILGRIMAGE OF BERENGARIA.

Three days are past—in vain is every glade
Explored for Richard and the captive maid;
To all the saints are solemn vows addrest,
Each soul is bow'd; in many a haughty breast
Wakes slumbering conscience; crimes forgotten long
Speak from their graves, and force th' accusing tongue.
Dire penance follows, vigil, fast, and prayer,
A thousand pious frauds to cheat despair;
So may offended Heaven avert the stroke,
And spare the judgment which those crimes provoke.

At length Evanthe came, but weak and pale,
As flitting spectres in the twilight vale.
She sought the council-hall, and fearful roll'd
Her hollow eye, " Where, where is Leopold?"

" Ha!" thought her lover, "did he share her heart?
" Know'st thou not, Princess, since we saw him part,
The moon has wax'd and wan'd? But dost thou bring
No words of hope, no tidings of the King?"

" The King!" she cried—" Oh Heaven! what
   dreadful light
Breaks on the doubtful visions of the night!   20
But, save for ill, could Austria linger here?—
Nay do not smile, I am not crazed by fear,
Last night I saw the traitor—must I call
The LION HEART his victim or his thrall?"

Chill horror reign'd, while each revolves too late
His mutter'd threats and ill-dissembled hate.
Yet how contrived? such treason might demand
A bolder genius and a firmer hand.

The Queen approach'd, but soon Evanthe's tears,
Chase her young smiles and waken darker fears; 30
Silent she clasps her friend, her sorrows flow
In mournful prescience of th' unutter'd woe.

But she who seem'd as though her breaking heart
Had ceas'd to beat, arises with a start:
" I must not linger, or my strength will fail,
Ere I can utter half the dreadful tale.

"That night," (but here a blush her cheek o'erspread)
" When from your side in yonder grove I stray'd,
Heedless I wander'd, seeking many a flower
In childhood cherish'd on my natal shore,   40
Till darkness gather'd round—I sought again
My distant friends;—I ran, I call'd in vain;
And fear, that rous'd my cries, at length subdued,
Fear of the savage beasts that haunt the wood.
Now midnight came, but then I reach'd a dell,
Where a cool fount in pleasing murmurs fell;
I drank the clear fresh wave, and almost blest
The chance that gave so sweet a place of rest.
Day dawn'd at last, the turf was stain'd with gore,
Nor was the victim far, a mighty boar;   50
The King perchance to this green spot had chased
The lordly prey, abandon'd in his haste.
Yet slowly I the track of steeds pursued,
My steps were feeble, and the way was rude,
And daylight faded ere I left the wood.

Blue misty hills the northern prospect crown'd,
But where the ocean form'd a nearer bound
White buildings rose; with all the little force
I yet could summon, I renew'd my course.
Alas! too soon I found my hope betray'd; 60
O'er turban'd domes the mournful cypress spread,
A place of grief, a City of the Dead;
Vast as Larneca, where in endless line,
On Cyprus' shore the marble fabrics shine.
My heart grew sick—was this my destined home,
E'en while I breathed, a tenant of the tomb?
Living to waste beside the wasting dead,
No eye to mourn me, and no prayer to aid.
Yet Fancy slept with all her idle gear
Of goules and goblins, childhood's favourite fear; 70
Nor was my heart unnerv'd by conscious sin,
I call'd on Mary's name, and ventur'd in.
Soft gleaming from a new-built tomb, a light
Shone, like a friend amid the dismal night.
The senseless clay was sepulchred beneath,
But o'er the bier, in all the pomp of death,
The snow-white pall was spread; soft odours came
From virgin flowers, and lamps of silver frame
From Saba's oils dispens'd a fragrant flame.

For here with every Jama's sacred morn,   80
To weep their friend the Moslem maids return;
Renew the lamp, the votive wreath bestow,
And feed with tears their unavailing woe.[b]

" Alas! like them, my tale prolongs the grief,
Its lingering cannot change, I will be brief.—

" I know not if to lengthened toil a prey,
Or that those odours stole my sense away,
Entranced I sunk :—I saw, but all might seem
Illusive shades, and past as in a dream.

" Before the gate my hand forgot to close,   90
O'ergrown with moss, a humbler fabric rose;
Two men approach'd :—the first in seeming dread
Started and paus'd, but took me for the dead.
How had I pray'd, while yet the prayer seem'd vain,
To hear the sound of human voice again!
Christian or Moslem seem'd not then my care,
So my last sighs were breath'd in human ear;
But with the sight of armed men, a chill
Crept o'er my heart, and terror held me still.
Their hands unbarr'd the antique tomb, and led   100
A fetter'd captive from its awful shade;
No ray reveal'd his face,— though dimly seen,
His form was noble and august his mien.

But as his jailor parting turn'd, I knew
The crest, the mail, the Cross of Austrian blue:
I do not fable, as my soul would hold
Its hope of heaven, that man was Leopold!—
With haste that seem'd beyond my wasted frame
I rose, pursued, implored him by his name:
They heard me, Princes! yet they did not heed, 110
Or, deaf to pity's claims, increas'd their speed;
Nor had I reach'd them, but the prisoner broke
His chain, and levell'd with a vengeful stroke
His other foe; but soon a lawless throng
Pour'd from the ship, and forced their prey along.

" The last was springing through th' empurpled wave,
' Oh, aid a dying wanderer! aid and save!'
I cried:—he answer'd with a mournful sign,
' Hush thee, poor maid, or instant death is thine!'
The galley sail'd, I sunk upon the sand; 120
A glittering baldric lured my feeble hand,—
Say, has my fancy coin'd one horror more,
Or is this belt the belt that RICHARD wore?"c

Alas! the Queen's convulsive start has shewn
How well to her each fatal gem was known;

While pale as hers each hardy cheek became,
And only Bertrand's brow was flush'd with shame.
" Was then that captive Richard?" Albert cried;
" Such were not then my thoughts," the maid replied.
" I could not dream such guilt—but deem'd him come
To seek some Moslem, prison'd in the tomb.
Yet never, sure, had Richard heard the cry
Of feeble wretch, and left her there to die!"

" Alas!" said Lusignan, " thus faint and worn,
What guardian saint has sped thy safe return?

" Strength fled with hope—this belt depress'd my mind
With fearful bodings, dark but undefined.
Hours past unheeded—for the sun was high
Ere I again unclosed a conscious eye,
Propt in a stranger's arms:—but alien tongue, 140
Nor turban'd brow could wake my terrors long—
T'was Aladin, who with the tenderest cares
Revived my wasted strength, and sooth'd my fears.
He gave me nectar from the wounded palm,*
That bleeds by day in wine, by night in balm;

---

* The liquor which flows from the palm by night is a mild and pleasant beverage, while that which is obtained by day is of an intoxicating nature: the heat probably causing it to ferment as it distills.

Before him placed me on his Arab steed,—
' Bound to yon northern hills, the Soldan's need
Ill brooks delay,' he cried, ' yet would he fain
That need should wait, ere woman sued in vain.'
Each dingle of the tangled wood he knew,   150
And, heedless of the weight, his courser flew;
He bore me to the gate of Ascalon,
Staid not my thanks, but like a dart was gone."

" Heroic youth!" cried Philip of Beauvais,
" Alas! that Moslem should extort my praise."

" Alas!" said Raymond, " that a prelate's mind
Should harbour thought so earthly, so confined!
But mark that scowling Baron—while I speak,
Mark each quick change on Bertrand's felon cheek!
And lurks not treachery there?—in him who first 160
With Conrad's blood the godlike Prince aspers'd?
Nor deem'd it shame secluded speech to hold
With Philip's bosom snake, and Leopold!
Chain'd though he be (and may an evil end
Befall the traitors!) RICHARD has a friend."[d]

He spoke, and Bertrand rose;—his eye of fire
Flash'd for a moment with ungovern'd ire,—
But soon a starting tear supprest the glow,
And deepest sadness gather'd on his brow.

" Raymond ! proud Raymond ! I thy taunts forgive :
Yet none but thou should make such speech, and live.
I hate the Monarch, nor my hate disguise,
And he who fears not him, the world defies.
In youth, on whom could fairer fortunes shine?
What hopes so gay, what heart so light as mine?
Dear to Prince Henry, to his sister dear—
Yes! royal Helen smil'd on Bertrand's prayer.
How firm my friendship, and how fond my love,
To distant years my ardent lays shall prove.
I hate not RICHARD for our early strife,—   180
A passing storm-cloud in the morn of life;
Nor that I bow'd beneath his matchless sword—[e]
He, generous then, my life and lands restored;
But deepest vengeance, deadliest hate attends
On smiling enemies, and faithless friends.
Young Henry died,—my grief, that mock'd control,
Drew love and pity from his father's soul;[f]
That fatal blow was dealt by heaven alone—
The death-wound of my peace was RICHARD's own!
'Twas he who fix'd on Helen's charms mine eyes, 190
And, pleased to see my fond emotions rise,
Bade me so high my daring wishes raise,
And taught my willing lyre to sound her praise;

Yet while with treacherous hopes my flame he fann'd,
The Saxon Duke was graced with Helen's hand! ᵍ
What would I give, brave youth, to feel agen
The boiling agony that tore me then!
With brow erect I met the shaft of fate,
And made all Europe subject to my hate.
Witness the ceaseless wars, the floods of gore,   200
From Ebro's stream to Brabant's eastern shore;
The strife with Philip, oft with pain subdued
By Pope or Legate, and as oft renew'd. ʰ
The blood of thousands scarcely quench'd mine ire,
Oh! that their curses could relume the fire!

" Fame had no charms, and vengeance died at last,
A deadlier calm succeeded to the blast;
My frozen heart nor love nor hate could warm,
Grief had no sting, and pleasure lost its charm.
The youthful wonder'd that my cheek was wan,   210
And shunn'd the silent, melancholy man;
Nor could the aged rest on me their cares,
My woes could never sympathize with theirs.
I fled wherever tumult held her reign,
For there alone I seem'd to breathe again;
And but where battle's fiercest fury glow'd,
My torpid blood with healthful vigour flow'd.

" Twelve tedious years my grief have soften'd now,
And toil and pain have blanch'd a youthful brow,
Yet from my heart one pang can never move— 220
The conscious memory of its outraged love!
E'en when my lips a smile fallacious wear,
One mournful feeling broods for ever there,—
A silent, secret pang that none can share.
That love in heaven could make my hours unblest,
That hate for RICHARD vex a martyr's rest!
Then, Chiefs, suspect not Bertrand's soul of guile,
He dares to frown, but treachery wears a smile."

" Yet," cried the Emerald Knight, who ne'er till then
In council spoke, and never spoke agen, 230
Why vents a Knight his rage in idle words?
Warriors should trust their quarrels to their swords!"

" I would, but RICHARD ever shunn'd the strife,
He said, his sister bade him spare my life;
His sister!"—here a scornful laugh he tried,
But the feign'd mirth in sobs convulsive died.

" Indeed," ('twas Raymond spoke) " I did thee wrong,
My zeal transgress'd,—forgive th' intemperate tongue;
May heaven like mine thy cause of wrath remove,
And bind again the broken links of love. 240

Hate should not live in souls where honour grows,
For demons triumph when the good are foes."

Another week, a week of anxious care,
Brought to their council Mosul's generous heir.
In peace he came, and those that wont to shun
His arm in war, his mild demeanor won.
" From Joseph's royal seed, from Asia's King,
Her Shield and Sword; health, greeting, love I bring:
Such love as heroes mingle with their war,
And pity, such as noble foes may bear.   250
His soul is panting to renew the strife,
Where sword with sword contends, and life with life;
But like a viper darkling to destroy,
Becomes not him;—the eagle perch'd on high,
Respects the helpless dove that roosts below;
The hungry lion spares the slumbering foe.
And from yon regions where the prince of day
Bursts through the hills, to where his parting ray
Gilds with ætherial hues the dancing brine,
His scouts have scour'd the plains of Palestine.   260
Whate'er his lot, the dungeon or the tomb,
Our hands are guiltless of your Monarch's doom.

Yet more—the godlike Soldan scorns to press,
Ev'n on his foes, in weakness and distress;
Till him you mourn, returning like a star,
Dispel your darkness and restore the war,
Or till the moons bring round the various year,
Rest! Christians, rest! unharm'd and harmless here.
Bid yon ripe fields their nodding gold resign,
Press the fat olive, ease the burthen'd vine;   270
But when the days of proffer'd truce expire,
As warriors wait him, or as friends retire."

 But Raymond now, who mark'd that every eye
To his was lifted, gave the prompt reply:
" Bear back our greetings—bid the Soldan own
Our souls are worthy, since we take his boon;
Peace, for our Monarch's sake, we stablish here,
Till RICHARD come, or till the closing year."

 The Prince but staid to share with cheerful soul
The pledge of truce, the feast, the brimming bowl,
Then, vaulting on his faithful steed, once more
To Syria's lord the pledge of concord bore.

 Yet still with spicy sweets the goblets flow,
And chace the clouds from each relaxing brow;
When 'mid the Chiefs, with mien uncouth and rude,
A dark brown man in garb monastic stood.

"Whence and what art thou?" fiery Bertrand cried;
"What thou wilt blush to hear," the monk replied.
"Slave to the Mountain Prince, and Conrad's foe—
He will'd the murder, and I gave the blow;   290
I and Alkamor, who already lies
Blest in our master's promis'd Paradise.
Thou deem'st a Christian King the poniard sped,
But he who smiles when heaven enjoins to shed
The blood of Misbelievers, bids ye know
He hated Conrad, and he laid him low."[i]

"Unhappy wretch!" ('twas Hubert's holy voice)
"Deluded, canst thou murder and rejoice?
Nor conscience checks thee, nor the timely fear,
That death and tortures wait th' Assassin here." 300
"Death!" he exclaim'd, "oh, ne'er for idle breath
Did coward sue, as Hassan's slaves for death.
Who once has tasted heaven, finds earth a void;
Yet sheathe your swords; not thus to be destroyed,
To me his hands the happy poison gave—
Your tortures cannot reach, your malice save."

O'er his pale brow the painful flushes came,
And strong convulsions shook his sinewy frame;
Yet with each pang his phrenzied raptures rise,—
"Now rend my flesh, insulting Giaours," he cries,
My soul is blest—it soars to Paradise."

And backward as he fell, his clenching hand
And angry brow defied the awestruck band.ᵏ

But fix'd as though th' infectious venom spread
Through his cold veins, and pallid as the dead,
Fierce Bertrand stood,—and when at length he broke
His silent trance, he felt not that he spoke.
" How little deem'd I, in my years of youth,
When all my thoughts were love, my accents truth,
That one black drop could poison all my mind!— 320
Must I, who held that passion was not blind,
Nor hate unjust—e'en while my slanderous tongue
Spoke what my heart denied—confess the wrong?
Perfidious RICHARD!—oh, the time has been,
Who injured thee had found my falchion keen;
When I, methinks, had wonder'd less to see
The sun all darkness, than a spot in thee.
Had'st thou been faithful, I could bend me yet—
But to be humble, where I vow'd to hate;
To thee, yet tarnish'd with so deep a stain—   330
Oh! could that blot be cleans'd! could'st thou again
Seem to my soul what I believed thee first,
That, that were rapture, though my heart might burst!"

That very eve, array'd in palmer's weed,
With staff and palm-branch, shell, and scrip and bead,

Alone he left the camp : and none might tell,
If foes enthrall'd him, if he lived or fell;
His squires in vain the Baron's fate explore,
And Perigueux receives her lord no more.

'Twas at the midnight hour when all was still, 340
Save the soft zephyr and the murmuring rill,
The convent chaunts that glided on the air,
Or the low murmur of secluded prayer;
That RICHARD's bride the Virgin's name adored,
And called a blessing on her absent lord.
Small was the chapel, but no vulgar hand
Had framed the holy fabric, simply grand.
Light rose the cluster'd shafts, till far aloof
They branched and knotted on the gilded roof;
Or broke in pointed arches, where between, 350
The foliaged tracery form'd an open screen.
There never prying eye or noon-day glare
Burst on the tranquil sanctity of prayer,
But through the windows' rich and complex frame,
Solemn and soft, the various radiance came;
On the rich pavement deeper hues were thrown,
And sculptured Saints in holier grandeur shone.

But most the Virgin's form—oh! surely wrought
By hands inspired, the marble breathed and thought!
Her look so radiant with maternal grace,   360
Such opening glory in the infant's face!
She stood behind a gem'd and gilded shrine,
That made her simple beauty more divine;
While mimic stars and skies of purple hue,
O'er the bright vision purer lustre threw.
One lamp alone diffused a steady light
On Berengaria's robes of spotless white;
For though, while dubious of her consort's fate,
She quench'd each taper that in festal state
Had deck'd the shrine, and meekly laid aside   370
Her splendid robes and ornaments of pride,
She shunn'd the mourning vest Matilda wore,
And aught might whisper, RICHARD lived no more!
She forced her cheek the hue of hope to wear,
Nor flow'd her tears, save at her secret prayer.

In meek devotion bow'd her pious soul,
Her eyes were raised to heaven; her sorrows stole,
Silent, unconscious——But what light divine
Beams from the sculptured form, the gorgeous shrine?
The gilded glory grew to lambent flame,   380
O'er the cold cheek a living lustre came;

'Mid gales from opening Eden breathed around
One heavenly light, one pure seraphic sound:
Yet sweeter far than angel harpings, broke
Th' entrancing accents, when the Virgin spoke.

" Rise, Berengaria, Heaven approves thy prayer,
Thy dauntless RICHARD claims celestial care;
Let prudence now thy daring purpose veil,
But Europe waits thee,—spread the willing sail;
Nor tremble thou when whirlwinds chafe the tide, 390
The power that bids thee go, shall guard and guide."

She ceas'd,—th' aerial music sunk away,
The form grew cold, the glory ceas'd to play;
But one pure beam, thence never more to part,
Of faith, of comfort, fill'd the mourner's heart.

Now to her sight the brave Toulouse she bade,
Albert, Matilda, and the captive maid.
With joy they heard the words of hope, and prest
To share her toils, and heaven-directed quest;
But smiling she her mild reproof addrest, 400
" When thus supernal wisdom points the way,
It fits not us to question, but obey.
While to your prudence only I confide
My venturous errand, be it yours to hide.

Alone I mount the bark,—or if indeed,
Whom angels guard a mortal champion need,
Let RICHARD's choice be mine; a noble knight,
Beloved by all, alike in bower or fight,
Whose open truth with strictest honour blends,
Whose frankness charms, whose freedom ne'er offends.
Say, gallant Albert! know'st thou whom I seek?
Or has thy modest worth a sight too weak?
A monarch traced the portrait, when he gave
The charge, erewhile, to guard me o'er the wave."

" Nay, generous lady, whose th' ungrateful ear,
That would not glow at praise thus doubly dear?
To RICHARD, who the knightly badge bestow'd,
And RICHARD's Queen, my faithful sword is vow'd;
But thus preferr'd, while hopes I dared not speak
Strove in my heart, and burn'd upon my cheek, 420
What words may now my secret transports tell!"—

" Aye," said the Queen, " I read thy riddle well,
Thou long'st to cheer thy widow'd Rosabelle,—
But sigh not now—I hear the matin lark!
His next blithe strain shall call us to our bark.
'Tis meet that we to RICHARD's mother shew
The dire occasion of our public woe.

To fix what means may loose the Monarch's chain,
What war must force, or embassy may gain,
Albert, the care be thine—thy mission known, 430
Shall blind suspicious eyes, and hide my own.
My sex and rank a pilgrim's weeds shall veil,
Nor blazon'd arms betray the royal sail."*

 Mild breath'd the southern breeze, the vessel flew,
Now Ascalon, now Jaffa sinks from view;
Dark Arsouf's wooded heights, and Napolose,
And Cesarea fade; then Carmel rose,
And conscious Acre;—still in sanguine hue
St. George's Cross from every rampart flew.
Alas! how different was th' extatic hour 440
When first she hail'd that long-expected shore!
When countless galleys gem'd the ocean round,
And lights were glimmering on the blue profound;
When streamers waved, when every joyful tongue
In holy transport rais'd the sacred song;
And rapture woke, till every heart became,
Like earth and ocean, bathed in floods of flame.
How many, then so full of hope and joy,
Live but in fame, yet fame that cannot die!

 * It was a custom of the middle ages to blazon the arms of illustrious persons on the sails of the galley, or, more properly, to make the whole sail a large coat of arms.

And he the loftiest—but she might not dare 450
To feed such thoughts, they bordered on despair.

 Scandalion now, and Blanco's jutting coast,
And the dim peaks of Lebanon are lost;
Desponding Tyre, and Sidon, great no more,
Or honour'd only for her fame of yore;
And that capricious stream, now pure and clear,
That erst, when spring revived the flowery year,
Ran purple, mindful of Adonis' wound,
With annual rites bewail'd, with annual garlands crown'd.*

 Berytus now, and Tripoli they past, 460
And now, rejoicing in the changing blast,
For Cyparissa's favourite isle they steer;—
First Famagousta's marble domes appear,
And known Limisso; next Colosso rose,
Soft shadowy Paphos, and th' Olympian snows;

---

* The river Adonis falls into the sea between Sidon and Berytus.

  "Thammuz came next behind,
Whose annual wound in Lebanon allured
The Syrian damsels to lament his fate,
With amorous ditties all a summer's day,—
While smooth Adonis from his native rock
Ran purple to the sea, supposed with blood
Of Thammuz yearly wounded."

    Paradise Lost.

Till leaving far those conquer'd shores, again
The vessel bounded o'er th' Ionian main;
From Rhodes, where soon, 'mid famine, fire, and death,
Thy Knights, St. John, shall earn th' unfading wreath,
To white-cliff'd Crete, Jove's once selected shore; 470
Corinth and Argos, mighty now no more.

But soon dark clouds the azure heaven o'ercast,
From southern regions came the angry blast;
In vain the pilot seeks Sicilia's coast,
For with the hidden stars his hopes are lost.[l]
He drives by Cephalonia's fruitful isle,
Zanté, where cloudless suns for ever smile,[m]
And old Corcyra; now Ragusa's towers
Are near, and now Ancona's rival shores.
Now through the falling torrents dimly seen, 480
Shone like a star the Adriatic Queen.
In vain with strenuous oar and shifting sail
They seek the harbour, for the furious gale
Drives on the bark, while, oh! portentous sight,
Burns on the helm dire Helen's fatal light![n]
The shore, so long desired, is now too nigh,
Where countless shoals in fatal ambush lie!

Alone, unmoved, serene amid despair,
With folded arms, and lost in silent prayer,

On the tall prow the seeming pilgrim stood,   490
And gazed unfearing on the boiling flood.
The billow broke, the crashing beams give way,
The lordly castle is the ocean's prey!
She sinks beneath the wave—then Albert sprung,
Her name, her secret trembles on his tongue!
But crowds withheld the youth, "Behold," they cried,
" Heaven chose its victim! mark the sinking tide,
Mark on the helm th' auspicious fires divide!
Let yon feign'd saint his secret guilt atone
(Pure as he seem'd), nor all be risk'd for one."   500

   He heard them not, nor had the loyal knight
Been thus restrained, but now the flashing light
Beams o'er the calmer deep, and bids him mark
How on that wreck, as on a gallant bark,
She stems the sea; and every surge that tost
Their heaving galley, wafts her to the coast.
And now she quits her hold, she springs to land,
Treads firm in hope, and waves them from the strand.
Nor vainly waves,—before the changing gale,
Down the deep gulf the merry seamen sail;   510
Messina's dangerous straits are past, more near
Sardinia's ile and Atlas' snows appear;

Steep Calpé's brow and Lusitania's shore
Retire,—they hail their native cliffs once more.

   Soon Albert spurr'd his steed, nor paus'd to view
How different from the prosperous realm he knew,
The peaceful happy home, was England now!
Where fear and sorrow darken'd every brow!
He hastes where Windsor, from her height of pride,
Awes woods and vales, and Thames' meandering tide;
Nor lingers, saddening o'er the alter'd scene,
When ruin mark'd where recent war had been,
Till now—he bends before the Regent Queen.

   Years, more than oft the temperate peasants know,
Had traced deep furrows on her polish'd brow;
To silver hue had changed her raven hair,
And thinn'd her cheek,—but still its rose was there;
Not yet one sparkle from her eye was fled,
Unbent her form, and firm her stately tread.

   Once that keen eye and flushing brow confest 530
Passions too strong to fit a female breast:—
But wrongs arous'd them,—she had heard her name
In Antioch blacken'd with unworthy shame;
Divorced, despised, had fled the Gallic strand,
With vows of vengeance on her native land;

Again a Queen, in captive gloom had borne,
Her faithless Henry's private, public scorn.
Her rage broke forth, she sought in desperate hour
Her lovely foe's involved and wondrous bower;
'Twas said the venom'd bowl and murderous brand,
In dreadful choice she tender'd to her hand:
But this was slander, Rosamond the while,
Atoned her guilt in Woodstock's convent pile;
Now o'er her dust the sculptured marble rose,
And daily masses sought her soul's repose.°

But Eleanor the pilgrim Knight embraced,
Then, while her heart its swelling grief represt,
Ask'd of her favourite son,—that son whose reign
Freed her from bonds, and gave to power again.ᴾ
" Fear not to speak—his fatal loss we know—   550
Ill news fly fast, 'tis good that travels slow."*

" Lady, he lives! and heavenly lips betray,
Or soon his foes shall yield their royal prey."
Then to her ear alone the Knight confest
The wondrous vision, and his Sovereign's quest;
Till she, who never bent in adverse hour,
Pour'd from her aged eyes a joyful shower;

* Philip Augustus was immediately informed of RICHARD's captivity by a messenger from the Emperor. From France the news passed into England.

And oft and oft, with growing interest, sought
To hear the deeds her CŒUR DE LION wrought.
" Speak of that battle, Albert! speak again— 560
'Tis my sole solace now—Oh! that Mortaigne
Had been like him we mourn, or never been.
Look out, on all this once delightful scene,
Look through the land, its curses breathe in vain
On him, alike unfit to serve or reign:
False to his King, and, worse, Augustus' tool;
A traitor to the state he seeks to rule!
Leagued with its foes—but he may find too late
Their specious friendship deadlier than their hate."

 Sad was the tale.—Though faithful, Longchamp's hand
Had proved too feeble for a realm's command;—
With power inebriate, he opprest the land,
Affected more than courtly state, defied
His mitred colleague, and inflamed his pride:
Till Durham, conscious of his wealth and power,
Call'd his new Primate from the Norman shore.[q]
He, son of Clifford's fair and erring child,
Led for his reverend robes a life too wild;
Loved more the midnight bowl and wanton lyre,
Than Ebor's matchless fane and solemn quire. 580

And royal RICHARD, ere he left the west,
Gave with a brother's kiss a King's behest;
(The same to John with oaths confirm'd before),
For three full years to shun the English shore.ʳ
But John was early false, and Geoffrey now
Deem'd that his priestly rank absolved the vow.
With Pembroke join'd, the princely pair demand
The delegated seals from Longchamp's hand;
While Eleanor, by frequent insults moved,
Too rashly sanction'd what her lords approved.ˢ   590
But the torn kingdom, drown'd in blood and tears,
Soon proved the justice of her Monarch's fears.

How little, when with lavish hand he shed
Princedoms and honours on his brother's head,
Had RICHARD seen from whence the storm should lour,
Or thought his gifts but gave rebellion power!
In scorn of Arthur's infant rights, Mortaigne
Now spoke of heirship to his brother's reign.
Homage at Philip's feet he hastes to pay;*
Philip, who false to heaven and Vezelay,   600
Now claims the Norman rule;—with virtuous pride,
Her hoary Seneschal the King defied;

* It is said that he even did homage to Philip for the crown of England.

Enraged he prest to arms,—but vainly prest,
For honour, banish'd from the Sovereign's breast,
Lived in his nobles,—" they had truly sworn
To guard his rights, till RICHARD should return."t

Sick at the light that makes his glory pale,
(For RICHARD's triumphs breath'd on every gale,)ᵘ
He heard of Conrad's fall—his slanderous tongue
With darker scandal swells the Austrian's wrong; 610
And swears the Monarch, now by practice grown
Expert in murder, next intends his own.*

Indignant England smiled, but soon deplored,
Captive or slain, her dear heroic Lord;
As when o'er Egypt heavenly vengeance moved,
Seem'd each sad heart to mourn its best beloved.
Revered, yet not for regal pomp alone,
His martial fame and far-descended crown,
But for that hand, whose gifts prevent distress,
That soul, which revell'd in its power to bless; 620
Whose first command absolved the prisoner's chain,
Lest one lorn wretch should hear and curse his reign.ˣ

* When Philip summoned Rouen to surrender, the seneschal of Normandy replied that the doors were open, if he chose to enter: but Philip was too wary to risk his safety upon such doubtful ground. He burned his magazines and retired.

He loved the dance, the feast, the minstrel song
Himself could raise so well, the glittering throng
Of princely jousts :—oh ! could his realm forbear
To worship one to whom its sports were dear !

   Guilt drops her mask,—the rebel, bolder grown,
Now fables RICHARD's death, and mounts the throne.
Through Gloucester's fruitful vale, (her ample dower)
Avisa spreads revolt*—from Thikehill's tower,   630
From Durham's hill, from Derby's massy keep,
To where th' Atlantic laves St. Michael's steep,
The battle raged ; but soon from Neustria's coast
Th' intrepid Queen leads on her little host ;
With York, who, faithful to his Monarch, now
Laments his rash revenge and slighted vow.
Against the rebel force her powers combine,
The martial Durham, Cestria's Palatine,
Leicester, in Syrian fields with glory crown'd,
Bardolf and Stuteville; Strigulph, long renown'd 640
In Erin's wars, and for his matchless bow,[y]
All sheathed in arms, with loyal ardour glow.
Windsor they save, they guard the menaced shores,[z]
And draw their lines round Thikehill's reverend towers.

  * Avisa, the second wife of John, was the daughter and heiress of the Earl of Gloucester, and promoted the cause of her husband throughout her extensive domain.

The Norman confines Philip threats in vain,
The Queen upholds her Son's invaded reign.

"Yet," she resumed, "not yet is Thikehill ours,
Nor Nottingham, nor steep St. Michael's towers;
Ill may the cause one faithful Baron spare,
This weighty mission must be Albert's care.   650
Before th' Imperial synod boldly stand,
And from the Austrian Duke the King demand;
When to his Peers his treason you proclaim,
If not to justice, he must yield to shame.—
Seek then with happiest speed thine own domain,
And from thy vassals chuse the fitting train;
But think, a nation's curse will brand delay,
Not e'en thy lovely bride must win thy stay."

Six times the dawn beheld him on his course,
Six welcome nights reposed his weary horse;   660
But with the seventh, at sunset's purple hour,
Peer'd o'er the dusky woods his well-known tower.

"See, see, my squire, the light that glimmers there,
In that lone cell thy Lady chose for prayer!
To Syria's holy war her fancy roams—
Yes! heaven has heard thy wish, thy Albert comes.

Swift, swift, and she shall soothe thy pride, and feed
And bless thee for my weal, my faithful steed;
Swift! thou hast yet some weary leagues to pass,
And deep and dangerous is the green morass."   670
    Not idle was the fear,—while yet he spoke,
The ground beneath their floundering palfreys broke.
With much of time and labour freed at last,
Their way was dangerous and the daylight past;
The dancing wildfire gleams on every side,
Bewildering only whom it seems to guide;
Oft in deep bogs the faithless path is lost,
Oft by tall reeds and tangling brushwood crost;
And ere again they reach'd the open wold,
The night was black, the midnight bell had toll'd. 680
Slow rose the clouded moon, long shadows fall,
And dark and massive frown'd the castle-wall.
"The bridge is down!" cried Albert; "why so late?
No bolts secured, no warder at the gate?
The light is vanish'd from my Lady's tower,
Sweet dove! thou sleep'st in an unguarded bower;
This horn must chase thy dreams." Alas! how well
That deep full strain was known to Rosabelle!
How oft, when seated in her father's hall,
Her blush betray'd she knew the distant call!   690

How oft would she from dreams of pleasure wake,
When echo bore it o'er the moonlight lake!
Why wakes not now? has she forgot the strain!
And all his vassals?—hark! he breathes again.
Yet no reply—the silence chills his breast,
With naked weapon o'er the bridge he prest;
He reach'd the hall—the embers still were red,
There still the fragments of the feast were spread,
But all was lonely; to his lady's bower
He flew; his cries re-echoed through the tower! 700
In vain—her snowy veil is on the chair,
Her favourite dove securely roosted there;
And where her maidens wrought th' embroidered vest,
Still in th' unfinish'd work their needles rest;
And in that cell, where every morn and even
She poured her fervent orisons to heaven,
Her opened missal on the cushion spread,
Her cross and rosary by its side were laid;
And from the wreath which bound her auburn hair,
A vagrant rose still bloom'd unwither'd there; 710
There was the book she laid aside for prayer,
The plaintive lay some troubadour had wove,
A mournful legend of forsaken love.

Still her mild spirit seem'd to breathe around,
And fancy, starting at the slightest sound,
Hears in the wailing breeze her silver tone,
Or light approaching step,—but fancy hears alone.
Oh! height of grief! but Bernard ventures near,
Half roused to mirth and half deprest by fear:
" Sure some magician rules these lonely halls! 720
The steeds yet feed securely in their stalls,
But not a wight is nigh—yet come, for you,
My master, have I spread the feast anew;
The crackling blaze shall cheer the wakeful hour,
At morn, perchance, the spell may lose its power.—
But why that vacant gaze? and from thy hand
Why drops, unconsciously, the blazing brand?
No signs of war, nor blood nor arms are here,
Nor wert thou wont the wizard's art to fear—
Trust me, my lord, to cheat her lonely hours, 730
Thy lady seeks Fitz Ranulph's Cestrian towers;
Her lovely cousins there with her prolong
The lively dance, the feast, the choral song."

" Peace!" Albert cried, "oh! think not to deceive
" With hopes you cannot, while you speak, believe;
If mirth like theirs could cheer her widow'd heart,
Would Edric, would my warlike train depart?

What spirit dropp'd the veil, the rosebud there,
Or through this lattice shed the treacherous glare?
Curse on the bog, the dark and tangled shade—
With that lost hour my earthly bliss is fled!
Yet bring my steed,—if Ronald struck the blow,
Yet Ronald ever was a generous foe,—
Nor here one trace of war; this murky night
Again may wilder, we must wait for light.
In such an hour to lose thee, Rosabelle,—
Ah! no—the morning will not break the spell."

 A cheerful blaze was in the lonely hall,
That shew'd the banners on each trophied wall; 750
The rounded arch, through which the night wind sigh'd,
And shook the mouldering wrecks of martial pride;
The mighty chesnut beams, that, in disdain
Of time and mining worms, the roof sustain;
Where shapes grotesque barbaric sculpture traced,
Or the fine forms of classic Rome debased.
The oaken board—whose merry guests were gone,—
The chair of state and bench of massy stone;
On all by turns the flickering radiance play'd,
Here broad in light, there sunk in sable shade. 760
With vizor down, that Bernard might not trace
His varying thoughts reflected on his face,

The warrior sate remote, and watch'd his squire
Drain the red bowl or slumber by the fire;
One might have deem'd that grief had conquer'd rest,
But the long toil his weary frame opprest,
And nature claim'd her hour,—as long he mused
On his dear loss, still more and more confused,
His aching head perplex'd the painful theme,
And wild conjecture glides into a dream.   770

Through the long windows now the morning light
Streams various on the hall—up starts the knight:
" Wake! Bernard, trim the fading fire once more,—
But lo! what mean these blood drops on the floor?
Perchance these dancing rays confuse my sight,
No! it is blood, nor was it here at night!"
Full in their view and vivid was the stain,
No man was near them, and conjecture vain.
Why should a friend have fled? and if a foe,
What from his slumbering prey withheld the blow?
And whence the blood? what hand could give the wound?
They rise and search, above, below, around;
Each winding corridor, each trophied room,
The turrets' airy height, the dungeon's gloom.

The bridge their haste at night forgot to raise,
Is lifted now, and sanguine stains betrays;
Hence, if for good or ill, the walls contain
The mystic guest, whom yet they seek in vain.

His blood flow'd freely in the dauntless chief, 790
Hope waked again, and wonder master'd grief;
But every noise the trembling squire appalls,
Rejoiced when Albert sent him from the walls.

" Go to Lord Ronald's border tower, and well
Observe his bearing, and conjure him tell,
If aught he know of Lady Rosabelle?
Mark, at my greeting if his cheek be pale,
Or his frank nature kindle at the tale,
Then speed thou here; some mystery hovers round,
Nor will I hence until its clue be found." 800

Forth rides the gladden'd Squire—the knight alone,
His grief and wonder wore a softer tone,
And pausing as he paced the echoing hall,
Or gazed on trophied arms that graced the wall,
His memory waked again the hopes and fears,
The woes, the pleasures of his early years.
Oft on that seat reclined the aged pair,
Who train'd the friendless orphan as their heir.

One stormy night, when all was drear and dark,
Sunk on Northumbria's rocks a founder'd bark;   810
One plank alone through tossing surges bore
An helpless female and her child to shore.
Vain were the Baron's cares, his lady's vain,
For scarce her languid eyes unclosed again;
She gazed upon her sobbing child, she sigh'd,
Drew from her hand an emerald ring,—and died!

 Above his years appear'd the orphan's pain,
But kindness won his rosy smiles again;
Nurs'd by the childless pair, who saw with joy
His grateful heart, and blest his laughing eye.   820
Oft, breathless, had he listen'd when they told
Of ancient worthies, courteous, wise, and bold;
That shield, which now the rust of ages wore,
Great Arthur's Peer, white-handed Ivain bore,
And that, whose orb the spotless steed reveal'd,
The Conqueror braved on Hastings' fatal field.
The Baron gloried in his grandsire's might,
Who bled for freedom and his country's right,
Then, 'mid the wreck of all her native band,
By arms maintain'd his honours and his land;   830
While Albert's heart his alien race denied,
And felt in each bold chief a filial pride.

Here, too, as years increas'd, his fancy wove
The fairy day-dreams of awakening love.—
Oh! how was every happy vision crost!
His reverend guardians gone, his lady lost!
Call'd by his Sovereign in his bridal hour,
To bear the Holy Cross on Syria's shore;
Yea, on the day that should have crown'd his bliss,
Yet e'en a lover's fears had spared him this.— 840
He sought her chamber, and with throbbing breast
Kiss'd her white veil, her silent dove carest;
He rais'd her book, oh! sacred song has power
To calm the wildest, soothe the saddest hour!
And well this tale might charm, whose lofty tone
Now rais'd the hero's soul, now bade him moan
O'er kindred griefs—but as the interest grows,
He hears behind the chamber door unclose;
He starts, he lifts the falchion at his side,—
From the rais'd latch a hand appears to glide; 850
Forward he springs, he speaks, but nought is there;—
In vain he rushes down the winding stair:
He hears a closing door, and following fast,
He reach'd a room, whose narrow windows cast
A doubtful light, and columns, thick and plain,
The low-brow'd arches of the roof sustain.

The walls are darken'd with his moving shade,
The floor re-echoes to his iron tread;
But there he stands alone—nor foe was nigh,
Nor way appear'd through which such foe might fly!

 Wearied and sad, he yet his search renew'd,
Till Bernard spoke, re-entering from the wood.
" Courteous was Ronald's mien, nor blanch'd his cheek
With conscious treachery, as he bade me speak :
' I greet Lord Albert on his safe return,—
His Sovereign's fate, his lady's loss I mourn.
When Europe sees Messiah's foes subdued,
Our hands again may wake our Border feud;
But doubt not me, my fury never falls
On helpless women and unguarded walls :   870
True to the peace for Sion's holy cause,
And true to honour's yet severer laws,
Had I but known this treachery, aim'd too well,
My sword, my life, had guarded Rosabelle.'
As home I sped, not careless of my quest,
My cautious speech each labouring hind addrest;
But war has spared thy halls—nor has Mortaigne,
With lawless plunderers ravaged thy domain;
And yesternight, as for her honour'd lord,
Thy lady's will had spread the bounteous board." 880

Alas! the hope that buoyed is fading now,
And blank despondence sits on Albert's brow.
The evening shadows long and darker fall,
The rusty armour rattles on the wall;
Chill breathes the wind—forth fares th'officious squire,
To seek fresh fuel for the fading fire.
What means that shriek? lo! gasping, pale, aghast,
Comes Bernard back, and speaks with pain at last,
" I saw him! there the hooded spectre past—"
" Peace! Peace! thou dream'st—But soft! what form
    is there?"—   890
Up springs the knight, and down the winding stair,
Regardless that the figure seem'd to tread
A different path, to that dark chamber sped.
Screen'd by a pillar's shade, with aching brain
And breath suppress'd, he watch'd, nor watch'd in vain:
With shrouded torch, that scarce his features shew'd,
And tatter'd garments, black with clotted blood,
Silent and slow, as though his tottering frame
Scarce bore his weight, the hideous phantom came.
It bent to earth, and from the hollow floor   900
Strove, feebly strove, to raise a secret door;
But from his lair the watchful Albert springs,
Prone on the ground th' astonish'd wretch he flings:

" Speak or thou diest,"—

" Yes! rather will I die,
Than shew thee where my master's treasures lie."

" Edric!—just Heaven!—then all may yet be well,
'Tis Albert speaks—but where is Rosabelle?"

"My master! thou art safe!—then prais'd be Heaven!
Yet was it but for this my life was given?
To tell thee this—but fear may worse foresee,   910
She lives, I trust, and yet may live for thee."

Soon Bernard drest the couch and spread the board,
When Edric spoke, to transient strength restored.
" Alas! 'tis vain—my wound can never heal,
Yet let me, while I may, its source reveal.
But yestermorn so fair, so blythe of cheer,
Here was my lady, all thy vassals here;
Long had she loved to muse and weep alone,
But then warm hope inspired her cheerful tone:
' Long hast thou seen, good Seneschal!' she said, 920
' How ill my cares this niggard myrtle paid;
Behold it now, how gay since yesternight,
In fragrant blossoms drest of bridal white!
Say, Edric! wilt thou mock my lively cheer,
Or trust my omen that my lord is near?

Nay, smile not—if a dream, 'twill fade too fast—
But let this day in martial games be past;
Too long my sadness has your mirth represt,
But now I bid you spread the joyful feast.'

" Ill-omen'd feast! perchance less strongly barr'd
Our gates were left, less watchful was our guard.
The sun was set, the goblet circled round,
All lesser noise our jovial chorus drown'd;
When lo! an armed band, unmark'd before,
From the full board three struggling yeomen bore.
'Twas dusk—helm, sword, and shield were laid aside,
But with such arms as haste and chance supplied
We rose—across the bridge and through the wood,
The stranger villains fled, and we pursued;
Unconscious of the lurking ambuscade,   940
To death or slavery were our band betray'd.
Confused, unarmed, the flower of all our train
With thee in Syria, our defence was vain;
To each unguarded heart the falchion sped—
Yon bog engulph'd the dying and the dead.

" And now a troop, who shamed the spurs they wore,
Thy weeping lady from the castle bore,
And all her train!—Oh! had I then been free,—
Yet what were one?—I bent the suppliant knee,

I proffer'd half thy wealth.—With scornful smile, 950
Their Chief replied, ' For many a weary mile,
O'er land and flood, from distant realms we came
For this fair prize, and shall I yield the dame?
Forego the hope!—yet be thy treasures shewn;
Her freedom heed not, but secure thine own:
So thou, if here thy wandering lord return,
May'st tell thy tale, and teach him how to mourn.'—
" Never"—I said. " Die then, rash fool!" he cried,
And pierc'd, unknightly, my unguarded side.
Senseless I fell:—when thought return'd, I found 960
The villains fled, and all in silence round.
Feebly I totter'd here, a knight and squire
Were all I saw, safe slumbering by the fire.
Oh! had I guest it thee, my gallant Chief,
What joy had given my bleeding heart relief!"

" And know'st thou not from whence the traitor came,
His rank, his arms, to give my vengeance aim?"

" His speech was Austrian, and his antique shield,
A Griffin dreadful on a crimson field."

Soon Edric's spirit wing'd its peaceful flight, 970
And weeping England claim'd her lingering knight.
" Too long have private woes delay'd," he cried,
" Alas! those fatal words, ' not e'en thy bride.'

Yet said he not an Austrian? Heavenly Power!
Thy ways are wondrous! teach us to adore.
For there at least shall Schorndorf's noble heir
My sorrows lighten and my dangers share.
Friend of my youth, oh! should'st thou, Theodore,
At once my Sovereign and my bride restore!"—

He left his desert halls and lone domain;   980
Two reverend Abbots form'd his peaceful train,
And favouring breezes bore him o'er the main.

END OF BOOK XII.

CŒUR DE LION.

BOOK XIII.

THE CASTLE OF TRIVALLIS.

ARGUMENT.

THE CASTLE OF TRIVALLIS.

Berengaria assumes the garb of a minstrel—Meets with Count Maynard of Gortz, and accompanies him to his castle—Entertains the lady with her minstrelsy—Gathers information from the domestics of an unknown prisoner at Trivallis—The lady warns her of danger from the Count, and assists her to escape—The castle of Trivallis—The song, and recognition of Richard—The meeting with Longchamp.—Journey of Albert through the Black Forest, and appearance of the mysterious flame—His arrival at Schorndorf—Behaviour of Ulric and Theodore—Discourse of the vassals at table—The captive lady—The shield—The ring—Theodore and Albert—The prophecy—Departure of Albert—The rural bower, and appearance of Rosabelle—Arrangements for her escape—Albert loses himself in the forest, and follows the mysterious fire to the sepulchral cavern—The treachery of Ulric—The death of Theodore—Fulfilment of the prophecy—The Queen and Longchamp arrive at Schorndorf.

CŒUR DE LION.

BOOK XIII.

THE CASTLE OF TRIVALLIS.

Meanwhile the Queen, in safety borne to land,
Knelt, meekly thankful, on the desert strand.
Nor town nor tower were near;—she sought repose,
Where on the beach a fisher's hut arose:
There, lone in age, a hospitable pair
The wanderer welcomed to their homely fare.
 A minstrel youth, his lowly state above,
Who saw his lady's charms, and dared to love,
Erewhile, as from his jealous lord he fled,
To this lone shore malicious fortune led.

To ocean's winds he pour'd his plaintive song,
Or sigh'd that river's shadowy banks along,
Which, bursting from Goritia's heights, retains
Its mountain cold in Aquileian plains.*
One sultry noon he sought the frigid wave,
Too rashly dared, and found a wat'ry grave.
Now for her dripping weeds the gentle Queen
His harp assumes, and vesture, white and green;†
With liberal hand a due reward bestow'd,
And took at early dawn, her lonely road. 20
Oft as she stray'd, while passing fancies fire,
She wakes soft music from the trembling lyre.—

'Twas autumn: yet, by fervid noon opprest,
Now on a shelter'd bank she paus'd to rest;
A knight who homeward leads with gentle pace
His train, victorious in the morning chace,
Glanced on the bard,—who, heaven-directed, strung
The ready harp, and thus spontaneous sung:

* The Frigidus, or cold river, a small but memorable stream in the territory of Gortz, near Aquileia; now called the Vipao.

† White and green were the appropriate colours of the wandering minstrel.

"Turn, knight! a weary minstrel sings;
The dews relax his trembling strings,   30
   And hunger chills his tongue;
Yet blest shall be the hand that brings,
   A cup to cheer the Child of Song.

" From fair Provence, my native land,
I've roam'd to many a foreign strand,
   Nor found my wanderings long;
While still my strains repaid the hand,
   Which cheer'd the vagrant Child of Song.

" Thou goest—then take the minstrel's curse,—
Be bold, be great, but never verse   40
   Thy memory shall prolong;
Forgot, ere lifted from thy hearse,
   For thou hast scorn'd a Child of Song."

" A winning strain!" the haughty Maynard cried,
Thy saucy boldness I were best to chide:
Yet come with me, I reck not of thy curse,
But my sick dame may love thy southern verse;
And (or thy art will poorly pay thy pain)
For lady's ear thou tunest a softer strain."

Dark was Count Maynard, and his scowling look[a]
Had yet less promise than his accents spoke.
The towers of Gortz, upon the forest side,
Less shew'd his liberal spirit than his pride.
'There all was grand, and numerous vassals found
His ample board with daily plenty crown'd;
But 'mid the guests still lurk'd distrust and fear,
Nor habit chaced restraint, nor wine could cheer.

His dame was one whose early fancy wove,
And young experience broke, her dreams of love;
She found her lord still first in tilt or fight,   60
Still drest in smiles for high-born beauty's sight,
But the smooth brow, the courtier grace, that shone
In other mansions, never cheer'd his own.
Though still due honours to her rank he gave,
And gilt his victim's cage—a splendid slave—
Her heart was chill'd, her hour of rapture o'er,
Her roses wither'd, ah! to bloom no more.
Her disappointed spirit oft was shewn
In look of discontent, or peevish tone;
And her harsh chiding, 'mid her virgin train,   70
Oft sprung the tear her kindness dried again.
And now, though anxious for his promis'd heir,
Count Maynard's pride could ape affection's care;

His tardy smile was answered by a tear,
And wrung the heart it beam'd too late to cheer.
As for a friend, she languish'd for the grave,
And wish'd to perish in the life she gave.

 A gorgeous couch her faded beauty bore,
As Berengaria near the chamber door
Leant on her harp;—a blush was on her cheek,   80
And her soft eyes her pitying soul bespeak.

 " Advance, young bard !" began the pensive dame,
" I love the heart that beats alone for fame;
Yet thou, who livest 'mid visions of thine own,
Of bliss and virtue to the world unknown,
Has thine ideal realm one charmed strain,
To wake departed hope, or lull the stings of pain?"

 " Oft, lady, boasts the muse such magic power,
But such, perchance, is scarce your minstrel's dower;
Yet where her spirit in Provençal vales,   90
Plays in each stream, and breathes in all her gales,
My youthful ear her noble minstrels heard,
And caught a strain from each sublimer bard.
Vidal, who roams in fancy's wildest maze,
Soft Marie's tales,[b] Alphonso's princely lays;[c]
His Sister, who beloved by Phœbus' quire,
Wakes in Provence her Arragonian lyre;
Bertrand de Born, whose youthful songs were fire;

Arnaud, whose strains the female heart allure,[d]
And England's pride, her Royal Troubadour.   100
Erewhile, in famed Avignon's shadowy grove
When the gay Monarch held his " Courts of Love,"
Oft have I heard, while raptured crowds were mute,
Sweet Philomel, Love's Advocate, dispute
On points of tender faith, with all the train
Of gaudy Finches, fickle, light, and vain.
For fancy wanton'd thus in frolic guise,
When Princes sought, and Queens adjudged the
    prize."[e]

" And who art thou, whose vaunting phrases tell,"
Observ'd the Count, " of greatness known so well?"

" Blondel my name ; and, but I prize the lyre
Above the glory gallant deeds acquire,
My birth might well to knightly rank aspire."
Thus spoke the Queen, by love impell'd to wear
The name of one in youth to RICHARD dear.

" And well such title fits a form so fair,"
The dame replied, " those eyes, that golden hair.
Now tune thy harp,—I fain would learn to live
In that bright clime poetic fancies give ;
But sing not love, for love is wild and mad,   120
Wrings the lorn heart, and makes the happy sad;

It dreams of joy that mortals never gain,
And faith, that lives but in the Minstrel's brain;
Sing not of love—I could not bear the strain."

"Nay, Lady, would'st thou break my sweetest
 string?—
Yet can your bard in phrase romantic sing
Those bolder notes that swell the northern lyre,
And knightly youth to deathless deeds inspire.[f]
Of awful magic, erst to Merlin known,
Or lighter pranks by moonlight fairies shewn, 130
Of glorious war, of wounds with sword and lance,
Great Arthur's peers, the Paladins of France."—

"Strange songs for lady's ear! Thy wayward muse,"
The dame rejoin'd, "some gentler theme may chuse.
Let warriors court the laurel glory weaves,
I shudder at the blood that stains its leaves."

"Would then some biting satire please thy mind,
That paints the crimes and follies of mankind?
Such Pierre[g] has framed—"

"Nay, nay, thy themes are strange,
Capricious bard, hast thou no fitter change?" 140

"Nay, by my knighthood, the caprice is thine,"
The Count burst in, "or hear him or decline.

Sing what thou wilt, keen satire, arms, or love,
Or blend them all, and all shall then approve."

    Blondel obey'd—a pleasing air he rung,
As Huon's wild and wondrous quest he sung.
The merry squire, but most that beauteous fay,
Whose tiny limbs celestial grace display;
His lily crown, his never-fading youth,
His dance-inspiring horn, the test of truth;   150
His bowl, whose ever-brimming sweets allure
The guiltless touch, but shrink from lips impure:
Of Huon's love, of Rezia's charms and woes,
Their mutual crime, and how the tempest rose,
Till in a desert isle they found repose;
And by their matchless truth at length restored
The fond Titania to her elfin Lord.*

    At first the dame with taste fastidious heard,
Scann'd every thought, and carp'd at every word;
Then sigh'd if fabled woes recall'd her own,   160
Then thought and felt in Huon's fate alone;
Till on her cheek the long-lost colour rose,
And her rous'd spirit mourn'd to hear the close.

---

  * Alluding to Wieland's Oberon, founded on the old Romance of Huon de Bordeaux, and translated by Mr. Sotheby into English verse.

"Take this," she cried, and loos'd her golden chain:
" Take this, young bard, 'twill better pay thy strain,"
The Count began. With grateful glance he took
And kist the chain, but turn'd with careless look
From the full purse : " I am no venal bard,
Your praise, your favour, are my best reward."

" Ha! 'tis not now, as when in years of old, 170
Castalia's fountain quench'd the thirst of gold,
Too long, too well, our northern bards have known
To scorn the muse that pays with smiles alone ;"
Thought the stern Count, and dark suspicion spoke
In his black brow, and keen inquiring look ;
Till as the seeming youth in haste withdrew,
All her soft sex was in her glowing hue.

In fear, yet forced her terrors to restrain,
Silent she sate amid the menial train;
Resolved to quit the fort with rising morn, 180
Nor thought how oft she pass'd th' untasted horn ;
Till now she ask'd what princely halls were near,
Whose bounteous lords the wandering minstrel cheer.

" Few," said an aged page, " since Leopold
Grasp'd this fair duchy in his iron hold,
Their wealth betray, or dare their gates unfold;

And since his minions, from a foreign shore,
That unknown captive to Trivallis bore."—

"Nay wherefore pause? oh! why should fear inspire?
Lurks fraud in youth, or treachery in the lyre? 190
Oh speak! the Muse on tales of sorrow feeds,
Reveal the path that to Trivallis leads."

"Deep in a mountain wild, sublimely grand,
And black with age, the triple turrets stand:
'Tis whisper'd those forbidden chambers hold
Unnumber'd victims, and uncounted gold;
This much is sure, whoe'er the Prince offends,
In speech or action, foes, suspected friends,
Those walls receive. They enter—ask no more!
For never yet did that relentless door 200
Disgorge its prey, th' irremeable bourne,
Whence, like the gates of hell, is no return.
Nay, there are tales (and bold we deem the wight
Who views that castle but by noonday light)
Of dreadful screams, and sounds of mortal pain,
And sheeted forms that drag the clanking chain;
And one who there, amid the moonlight stood,
Deem'd that each guilty turret blush'd with blood.
These halls erewhile a transient shelter gave
To one departing for that living grave: 210

To speak was death, none knew his name or face,
Yet sure such care betray'd a princely race;
And once, from yonder loophole dimly seen,
I gazed at distance on his martial mien:
I longed to give him arms, and bid him stand,
Or fall as fits a warrior, sword in hand;
And mourn'd to think that famine's slow decay,
And grief and chains, should wear those limbs away—
But thou art pale, poor youth—thy wish forbear,
The bard, believe me, wins no favour there." 220

While yet he bends to hear, a damsel came
And call'd him forth, to cheer her pensive dame.
But pensive, languid she appear'd no more,
A healthful glow her lingering beauty wore.
"Fair youth," she spoke, "or, by that blush betray'd,
If right I guess thy secret, lovely maid!
My Lord has said,—'he is not what he seems,'
And chains are near when thus Count Maynard deems.
Nay, do not speak, nor to my ear confide
What wedded duty should not hear and hide; 230
But I am grateful for the only joy
That years have brought, and would repay it, boy.
Go to thy couch, but ere the dawning day
My damsel guides thee by a secret way,

Beyond our walls; if then a thought I claim,
Breathe one brief prayer for Gortz' unhappy dame;
Thy youth has many a rainbow dream to come,
But mine are past, I sigh but for the tomb."

"Nay, gentle lady, rouse thee from despair,
Not less than thou I know the weight of care; 240
Perchance had all for which thy nature sighs,
Perchance have lost what most thy heart would prize.
But for the grave! oh! if thy fearless soul,
Recoiling, start not from the dismal goal,
Think that its rest is but for those who tread
This darksome vale unfaltering, undismayed.
'Tis that beyond, for which we bravely bear
The ills of life—oh! fix thy wishes there.
It cannot chase thy woes, but they will seem
Like passing clouds that melt beneath the beam; 250
While every flower that decks the glistening spray,
Each bird whose carol hails the orient day,
Shall lift thy grateful thought to Him on high,
Who in that radiance gives them life and joy."

"I would—I will—oh! could'st thou safely stay—
Thou heed'st not gold, but, can I aid thy way?"

"Lady, these paths are rude; my weary feet
Bleed at th' unwonted toil."

"My steed is fleet,

And shall be thine—farewell, be heaven thy guide;
But mark me, where thou see'st the way divide, 260
Turn to the right,—'tis to our Austrian pride,
Vienna! but beware the left hand path,
It leads to dread Trivallis, chains and death.
Farewell, and pray that I may sleep in peace."—

"Dame, I will pray that soon thy griefs may cease;
But, rous'd to hope, new joys and softer fears,
And proud of all a mother's pleasing cares,
Till thou, like Huon and his bride, shall find
Heaven yet is gracious, when it seems unkind."

Freed from the castle ere the dawn of day, 270
The minstrel Queen pursued her anxious way;
Scarce on the right hand path one glance bestow'd,
But took, impetuous, the forbidden road.
Scarce could she still the beatings of her breast,
Or pause herself, or give her palfrey rest,
When the hot sun in cloudless skies was bright,
Or glimmering stars diffused a doubtful light.
She trod the burning crags, whose ruins spread
The dizzy ledge, and beetled o'er her head;
Plunged in rude dells, unconscious of the beam, 280
Or to its cradle traced the brawling stream;

Nor sought the goatherd's shed,—her scrip supplied
The scanty meal, she drank the limpid tide.
Till when at last those awful walls appear'd,
Which cowards fled, and e'en the valiant fear'd,
They seem'd like forms in waking visions wrought,
When hope obsequious paints the secret thought.

 Fell'd was the nearer wood—beyond, it rose
To screen the fort, but not to hide its foes:
High on a hill, the triple towers were seen,   290
On three huge crags, with horrid depths between;[h]
A triple fosse the vast enclosure bound,
And massy walls the triple vallum crown'd.
The stones were black with age, the struggling day
Scarce through the loopholes sent a scanty ray.
From those dark halls no sounds of welcome breathe,
No hamlet shelters in its shade beneath;
One awful beam th' autumnal evening threw,
That tinged the western front with sanguine hue;
While from behind, the moon arising bright,   300
Clothed the pale landscape in contrasted light.

 She left her steed beneath the beechen shade,
" And art thou there, my best beloved !" she said,

" Upbraiding all that to thy help should fly,
Nor think'st what fond, what anxious heart is nigh."

  Eve's last soft flushes fade, and all is still,
While veil'd in gloom, she climbs the arduous hill.
Rude was the path, nor oft by pilgrim worn,
O'ergrown with briars, long, wildering and forlorn:
Scarce might the horseman trace that dangerous way,
Through brakes, impervious to the summer day,
Now wrapt in night; while onward as she hies,
Scared at her step the birds of carnage rise.
At last, yet shrouded in the castle's shade,
Cautious she crost its spacious esplanade;
Marked each strong wall with towers begirt around,
The massy keep what lofty turrets crown'd;
The boy who never dreamt of war might know
Those awful ramparts would but mock the foe;
While not one light the abode of man confest,   320
Or gave the weary pilgrim hope of rest.
Those grated loopholes o'er the gate—ah there
Perchance her RICHARD wastes with secret care!
Whose gifts were kingdoms, now by famine dies—
His only prospect those relentless skies,
His only visitants the bats, that prowl
Round the grim tower, or nightly hooting owl!

Mournful she stood; but soon the breeze that sighs
Through her lone harp, bids other thoughts arise:
"Yet, yet," she said, "some dear familiar strain 330
May reach his cell, and bolts and bars be vain;
While, should some jealous warder mark the lay,
'Tis but a minstrel sings to cheer his way.
Ah, me! that air to early love so dear,
Even in the tomb might rouse my RICHARD's ear;
Oh! could I pour his deep clear tones along,
And steal his accents as I steal his song.ⁱ

  "Frown, frown, Clorinda—I would prize
    Thy smile o'er all that arms might gain;
  O'er wealth and fame; yet mock my sighs, 340
  My faded cheek, my tears despise,
    Nor I my fate arraign;
  While every rival's grief I see,
  And know that all are scorn'd like me."

 She ceased, for from on high a fuller tone,
Though faint in distance, blended with her own;
That voice, those words could come from one alone.

"Oh smile not, if thou e'er bestow
 On others, grace I think sincere;
Such smiles are like the beams that glow   350
On the dark torrent's bridge of snow,
 And wreck the wretch they cheer.
Thine icy heart I well can bear,
But not the love that others share."

Bright hour of rapture! who may dare to tell
In her fond breast what blended feelings swell!
With parted lips, closed eyes, and hands comprest,
To still th' impetuous beatings of her breast,
Listening she stood; while conscious memory strays,
To that blest hour when first she heard the lays. 360
Extatic dream—at length her faltering tongue
Its grief exprest in emblematic song:

"The widow'd dove can never rest,
The felon kite has robb'd her nest;
With wing untired she seeks her mate,
To share or change his dreadful fate."

Again she paused, and listening, from on high
Caught from the friendly gale the faint reply.

"But kites a higher power obey,
Th' Imperial Eagle claims the prey,—^k 370
Hence! to his spacious eyrie go,
The Eagle is a nobler foe."

She strikes the harp—" Farewell! farewell!"
Her thrilling notes of transport swell:
" The monarch bird may build his nest
On oak, or tower, or mountain crest,—
But love can match his daring flight,
Can fell the tree, or scale the height."

" Ho! who art thou," a surly warder calls,
" That darest to sing beneath Trivallis' walls?" 380
" A wandering bard, good friend, who fain would win,
These awful gates to let the weary in."
" Nay, hence—nor dare to touch thy harp again,
And thank thy saints 'twas I that heard the strain;
Tired as thou art, fly swiftly o'er the heath,
And shun these walls as thou would'st shun thy
        death."
But was that pilgrim weary? oh! less fleet
The mountain chamois plies its fearless feet:

" Farewell! my ears are blest though not my eyes,
Thy chains shall fall," she warbles as she flies ; 390
" Thou gentle guardian of my steps, my will,
Take my soul's blessing and direct me still.
At Haguenau soon the empire's magnates meet,
Oh! touch the Eagle's heart—oh! guide my wandering feet."

For many a day through Austria's wide domains,
By woods of tapering pine, or mountain plains,
By hills the venturous goat alone had track'd,
By placid lake or rushing cataract,
She wander'd on ; and still at evening fall,
The woodman's hut, the convent or the hall 400
Had given her rest, till now at day's decline
Near Eglisau she reach'd the rapid Rhine ;
Where from the lake its azure current pours,
And antique forests crown the lofty shores.
Along the verge the lingering sunbeam show'd
Before her far a rough and shadowy road.

She glanced around, but saw no cottage nigh.
A cross was on the crag ; her shuddering eye,
Turn'd, awe-struck, from the monument of blood,
But stray'd not far, for, bosom'd in the wood, 410
Rear'd o'er a spring, a humble chapel stood.

No glittering shrine, with paltry gems disgraced,
Or gaudy hues, deform'd its simple taste;
The fount within its marble basin play'd,
And, gushing downward in a full cascade,
Curl'd o'er its pebbly channel, calm and bright,
Then leap'd tumultuous from the woodland height;
Huge stones disturb its course, and thickets hide
Its humble confluence with the mightier tide.
Above the spring, in spotless stone pourtray'd,   420
Near her grave husband stood the Mother-Maid,
While He whose voice inspired his Lord foreshew'd,
Pour'd on his head divine the sacred flood;
The opening heaven reveal'd the Dove divine,
Beneath, this legend graced the modest shrine:

" Whoe'er thou art, lone pilgrim, pause and pray,
For one like thee, who trod this woodland way;
But in the fane his holy zeal had plann'd,
Fell by a midnight villain's impious hand.
This stream, now deeply purpled with his blood, 430
Ere thou can'st see, shall roll a stainless flood;
And HE Immortal, who in mercy gave
A holier power of cleansing to the wave,
Bids prayers for his salvation breath'd alone,
In heaven's bright book be treasur'd for thine own."

" Nor shalt thou lack them, whosoe'er thou art!"
Cried the fair wanderer, " 'twere an ingrate's part,
To rest me by thy fount, nor ask thy weal;
Hear me for him—yet oh! with warmer zeal,
Hear me, Great Source whence all our blessings
  spring!   440
For my loved lord, for England's captive king."—

" Her captive king!" a voice behind began.—
Starting she saw a venerable man,
In convent cowl; she fear'd her trust betray'd—
" May I not pray," in faltering tones she said,
" Albeit in realms where ne'er his virtues shone,
For him whose gentle sway has blest my own?"

" Nay, fear not me, poor youth! but thou hast said
The *captive* monarch—I had mourn'd him dead."

" Dead! reverend father—can'st thou think the foe,
Who work'd his death would hide so bold a blow?
Christian or Moslem were too proud to tell,
By them the first of English heroes fell."—

" Oh! I had hoped thou had'st some cause of trust—
Nay, I will buy thy frankness if I must.
A faithful subject never will betray
His Monarch's friend—this cowl of humble gray

Hides the proud Longchamp—thou hast heard my fall,
My flight, my dangers—I deserv'd them all.
My soul, too high by power unwonted wrought, 460
Forgot the meek humility it taught;
Durham forgot it too, but that is past—
His rage is sated—and forgiven—at last—
Yet 'mid my countless crimes my faithful zeal
Was ever, only, for my Monarch's weal;
Tell me he lives, that I to him may fly,
May ask for pardon at his feet, and die."

She rais'd her minstrel cap—her locks of gold
O'er her green cloak in bright luxuriance roll'd;
" Talk not of death, but live to set him free, 470
And know his first, most anxious friend in me."

Of all her joys, of all her griefs she spoke,
And on their speech the early morning broke.
" Now let us forth : to Haguenau's towers I go,
Where meets th' Imperial Court."

      " But dost thou know,"
The Prelate said, " in whom thou wouldst confide !
Imperial Henry, with his father's pride,
Though green in years, combines the Austrian's guile :
Think, should he know thee, should some daring wile

Send thee to share that lot thou seek'st to change; 480
Where not a tongue could tell, or hand avenge.
Or go, with thine acknowledg'd rank thy shield,
Or safer, in some envoy's train conceal'd:—
We, thus disguis'd, through every Gallic ward,
May reach thy Norman Peers, and chuse thy guard;
Then as to Henry's court we boldly come,
Rouse to our aid the thundering wrath of Rome."

  The Queen consents, and with her reverend guide
Track'd, many a weary mile, the winding tide.

  Albert, meanwhile, to shun suspicious eyes, 490
Leaves far the Flemish coast, and courts disguise:
France he avoids, and quits his priestly train,
By routes distinct th' Imperial States to gain,
And meet at Schorndorf's friendly fort again.
Fears for his bride, affection for his King,
Lent him the swiftness of the falcon's wing.
While near the Rhine he now his course pursued,
Through those vast forests of primeval wood;
Hercynian shades, that, like an awful cloud,
Whole regions darken with their sable shroud; 500
Where from their rocky springs the rivers run
Their long dark course, and never see the sun;

Where vales in vain their ample bosoms spread,
And lordly mountains lift th' aspiring head,
Nor know the dazzling realm their peaks invade.

 The noontide twilight fades, and long and loud,
Ferocious beasts yell dreadful through the wood;
Scarce Albert's heart was firm, and Bernard's breast
Is chill'd with fears, increasing, ill supprest:
When full before their way a globe of light,   510
Of crimson flame majestically bright,
Sends forth its magic glare! Some hidden cause
Their hastening steeds with strong attraction draws:
Nor would the Knight resist, he feels the glow,
The mystic ardour souls superior know,
Twinborn of hope and dread, and wildly sweet,
That bids them rush uncertain ills to meet;
And long, albeit with natural terrors pale,
From airy shapes to draw their midnight veil.

 " Oh, turn, my master," cried the trembling squire,
" Infernal spirits light that sanguine fire!
Thou know'st me brave,—I never shrunk with fear,
From aught that man could threat, or thou could'st dare;
But I was warn'd by her who gave me breath
To shun this forest more than pain or death.

These wilds, where bears and fiercer ruffians prowl,
And stronger, nameless horrors thrill the soul;
Where Druid orgies mock the Name Divine,
And human victims heap Irmensul's shrine:
Where guilt and fear the avenging kindred shun,   530
And wizards meet for rites that blot the sun;
Lure hapless wanderers to the fatal wood,
Or roam as wolves, to feast on human blood.¹
She told of murder'd forms that ride the gale,
Weep in the rain, and in the tempest wail;
Of shrieks and howlings—Ha! dost thou not see,
Where tortured spirits writhe on every tree?
Oh! 'tis in scenes like these, in such an hour,
That sleepless demons know their baleful power!
Turn, turn, while yet our steeds may fly the spell, 540
No eye can see thy shame, no tongue can tell."—

" And think'st thou, Bernard, Honour has no power
In noble breasts, though at the midnight hour?
That I could wear these spurs a monarch gave,
And know me base, yet mingle with the brave?
Trust me, if hellish sprites have influence here,
'Tis not on those who dare, but those who fear.
My head by Heaven's anointed servant blest,
The sacred symbol glittering on my breast,

I mock them all, and would not turn me now,   550
But for my faith to that ill-omen'd vow.
My mission done, if yon red beam invite
(And I will court it,) fear to whisper flight."
He spoke—his steed obey'd the rein once more,
The flame was gone, the spell had lost its power.

   The night was starless and the hour was late,
When Albert blew the horn at Schorndorf's gate:
In vain the warrior told so great a name,
And urged a knight's, a stranger's, pilgrim's claim;
Or hints at mission from the Holy Land:—   560
No gate was loosen'd from its iron band.
At length he spoke, " If Theodore be near,
" Tell him that Albert, that his friend is here;
Not thus your youthful Chief would bid me wait,
Or bar so long th' inhospitable gate."

   His words at length a surly yeoman bore,
And from the revel came young Theodore.
Flush'd was his cheek, his eye shone wildly bright,
But he with rapture hail'd the wandering Knight:
While compliments and fair excuse he showers,   570
Of dangerous times, and late, unwonted hours,
Through many a hall he leads the wondering guest,
To where the Baron urged the midnight feast.

With courtesy that pride well knows to wear,
He seats his friend, and calls for choicer fare.
Vast was the hall, and bright the taper's glow,
And large the knightly troop that sate below;
But in each swelling lip and fiery eye
Shew'd more of pride than ruth or courtesy:
Loud was their converse, unrestrain'd and bold, 580
Of love, of arms, in coarser phrase they told;
And Albert fears their next reply may claim
The burning blush of anger, or of shame.

Grave was Lord Ulric,—yet no frown represt,
Nor angry word rebuked the boisterous jest;
While as the goblet circled 'mid the crowd,
The eye grew brighter, and the laugh more loud.
Even Albert's brow a gayer aspect wore,
At the blythe wit of ardent Theodore;
When thus a youth his fellow squire addrest: 590
" Hugo, to-night, as from the hunt I prest,
I pass'd our lovely prisoner's woodland bower,—
Beneath the porch she stood, its fairest flower;
Lonely and sad, her tears in silence stole,—
Fool that I was! her sorrow pierced my soul.
Think'st thou that if to distant lands I rode,
And my bright Maude contending nobles woo'd,

She thus would lock my image in her breast,
Nor deem the *present* lover was the best?"

" Soon wilt thou prove her, when on Syria's coast,
With our young lord we brave the Paynim host."—

" But will he sail?—no more he longs to rove;
He knows his sire suspects his rival-love.
The more the Baron's haste, the more his fear
To leave her in his power, defenceless here;
And, what will both their ghost-rid fancies fright,
The mystic Beacon re-appear'd to night!"—

"Hush! these are themes we may not speak so near;
Our lives may answer, should the Baron hear."

As Albert listening turns, his glances fall   610
Where, brown with age, a trophy graced the wall:
The mail was canker'd, but the massy shield
Bore a fierce griffin on a crimson field;
And of conflicting thoughts a torturing train
Rush'd, like a whirlwind, through his dizzy brain.
He rais'd his hand his alter'd brow to hide,
When, while in vain a careless tone he tried,
Lord Ulric spoke : " If to admire," said he,
" Be wrong, your pardon for discourtesy,
But ne'er beheld I emerald ring so bright,—   620
Perchance some token of triumphant fight?"

The Knight presents it:—" If by fortune mine,
Baron, thou likest it, and 'twere freely thine,
But 'twas a Mother's gift,—the only trace
She left in death to find my name or race."

The Chief return'd the ring, nor more inquir'd,
Broke up the revel, and in haste retir'd.
A thousand fears torment his guilty mind,
Nor was his guest to calmer thought inclin'd.
Why on his ring should Schorndorf's Baron dwell?
And could th' imprison'd dame be Rosabelle!
The Shield, the Beacon, seem to form a train,
All link'd to him by some mysterious chain!
He longs for morn, that Theodore may hear
Each strange event, each wild conjecture clear.

Grey Bernard now, attendant on the Knight,
Told dreadful stories of the forest light.
Beloved by all the vassals of his land
Was Schorndorf's former lord, brave Hildebrand.
Some twenty winters past, he sought alone 640
The morning chace, sithence his fate unknown;
But from that eve, with bright and sanguine beam,
Deep in the wood a light was seen to gleam:
All gazed in wonder, but the vulgar said,
That where it shone a murder'd corse was laid!

Perchance their lord's!—that flame a warning gave,
To guide th' Avenger to the Victim's grave:—
To reach the spot his bravest warriors swore,—
The wood they enter'd, but return'd no more.
A wife he had,—a dear, an only son, 650
But soon by prowling ruffians both were gone;
And from the hour Imperial Frederic's hand
To Ulric's claim resign'd his brother's land,
The light had vanish'd; and his vassals fear
To name the theme; they know their lord severe:—
He said that Memory could not bear to dwell
On the sad fate of those he loved so well.

The Squire scarce gone, young Theodore appears;
With oft-reverted glance, like one that fears,
Slow step, and finger on his lip imprest— 660
While, springing from his couch, his joyful guest
Meets his loved friend, and strains him to his breast.

The youth began, while strong emotions trace
Their quick succession on his changing face.
" Albert, for life reciprocally given,
Our faith was plighted in the sight of heaven;
By vows on Sylvia's conquer'd ramparts made,[m]
I come at once to claim and promise aid.

" My Sire, in youth, by lust of glory fired,
The future fortunes of his life enquir'd; 670
The forest trembled, and these words divine,
In flames were murmur'd from Irmensul's shrine:
' THOU SHALT BE SCHORNDORF'S LORD, BUT MARK,'
 it said,
' THE HOUR THAT SEES THEE CHILDLESS, SEES THEE
 DEAD!'
A numerous race he own'd; but all are past,
Like summer blossoms,—I remain the last;
And hence, more careful of the double life,
He long withheld my eager soul from strife:
Now, strange reverse! for Sion's holy land
He bids me sail; and, Albert, I withstand! 680

" I could not stoop to fear a stepdame's reign,
And heard with joy his will to wed again;
I hoped that female smiles again might shower,
Serener beams on Schorndorf's gloomy tower.
He brought his bride; she seem'd of foreign race,
But grief and hate were pictur'd in her face;
What human heart could see her tears unmoved?
Mine paid its tribute,—I beheld and loved.
I promis'd help, but my returning sire
Check'd my unfinish'd speech, and storm'd in ire. 690

Deep in the wood, sequester'd from my aid,
Oh! can I sail and leave the wretched maid?
Nought but his death his purpose can withstand,
I am his son—that thought restrains my hand;
But thine is free!"—

     With horror Albert hears
The knell of friendship sounding in his ears;
" Accursed wretch! no farther taint the air
With words so impious, that I blush to hear;
My heart enshrined thee once,—but Theodore,
Spare thy lost friend, and let us meet no more." 700

 Upsprung the youth, with sad but eager look
He seized the Knight's reluctant hand, and spoke:
" Nay, Albert, cast me not in scorn away—
Think of our mutual deeds in battle fray;
How we one board, one couch, one danger shared,
How oft this hand hath been thy guide, thy guard;
Or how thy words, when resting from our toil,
Fell, still I hope, on no ungrateful soil.
Yet scarcely wean'd from dark Irmensul's shrine,
We bow, but coldly, at the Name Divine; 710
And deeds that startle in your happier clime,
'Mid these rude shades were scarcely deem'd a crime.
Inur'd from earliest youth to blood and war,
To push the spear, or whirl the scythed car,

Scarce stronger bonds unite the sire and child
Than bind the tenants of yon sable wild;
And why should mine be dear? His stern control
Check'd each kind feeling of my opening soul;
In his harsh sway my mother droop'd and died,—
His pride, not love, my infant wants supplied; 720
My hawk was kinder; I was forced to roam,
And seek from beasts the love denied at home.
Thou can'st not tell how hearts, long doom'd to find
All they should prize, repulsive and unkind,
Cling to a friend—how dear thou wert to mine!
I listen'd, and my soul seem'd wrapt in thine.
Behold thy sway, the thought that stain'd my heart,
Once blamed by thee, for ever shall depart;
I vow to guard his life—but this fair flower,
And thou, dear youth! thou too art in his power. 730
Despise, distrust, detest me if thou wilt,
Yet 'twas for thee I plunged so deep in guilt;
And, but my father knows our fates entwined,
I had not lived to thwart his jealous mind.
But late I left his side—with smother'd breath
He said he fear'd thee, bade me work thy death.
'Father,' I said, 'if thou my friend destroy,
The hour that Albert falls, thy son shall die.'—

' Then perish first, rash fool !' he madly said,
But o'er his brow a livid paleness spread :   740
' The Prophecy !' he cried, and dropp'd his blade.
Not less the guilt that made him Schorndorf's heir :—
Depart at dawn, and oh! my friend, beware !"

He rose, and slowly to the portal crept,
Then turn'd, and fell on Albert's neck, and wept.
" We meet again, perchance—but jealous eyes
Will watch, thy safety then will need disguise;
Thou can'st not feel what weight is at my heart—
Could'st thou forgive me, Albert—ere we part?"

" Alas !" he answer'd, " plunged so deep in ill,—
Hast thou, poor youth, such kindly feeling still?
Farewell,—thy pardon must be sought from heaven,
By my full heart thou wert too soon forgiven."

His parting paid, at dawn the generous Knight
Rides from the fort, now hateful to his sight :
Yet round the walls, though danger hover near,
He still must linger, till his train appear ;—
Meanwhile he purpos'd 'mid the forest shade
To seek the guiding light and captive maid.
He traced a devious path, now smooth and plain, 760
Now sunk in wood, and now reveal'd again ;

Yet deeper in the endless groves it wound,
And darker, denser, closed the forest round.
Gigantic elms, vast sheets of sable pine,
With beech, and birch, and knotted oak combine;
And blasted trees, whose branches scorch'd and bare,
To fancy's eye terrific semblance wear.
The raven croaks above the warrior's head,
And wolves howl dreadful in the dismal shade;
And bears, scarce shrinking from the doubtful day,
Stalk through the brakes, and seem to mark their prey.
When lo! enshrined amid the darkest wood,
A fairy bower in sweet seclusion stood!
The groves retiring, left a lovely vale
Bare to the south, but screen'd each ruder gale;
And flowers of sweetest scent diffused around,
With living gems enamell'd all the ground.
The gentian here in heaven's own azure glows,
The lily pale, and Austria's golden rose;
On this fair scene the moonbeams longest play, 780
The sun enamour'd darts his earliest ray;
And when the woods a sober livery wear,
His latest radiance loves to linger there.
Low was the bower, through woodbines dimly seen,
Sweet eglantine, and ivy's clustered green;

But jealous care secures th' enchanted ground,
Deep trenches guard, and iron spikes surround.

By hope and fear, and love's impatience torn,
The Knight yet dreads to wind his bugle horn;
When, murmuring from a cell, unseen though near,
Soft female accents strike his joyful ear;
Oh, love alone those whisper'd words might hear:

" Ela, my keeper grants my suit—once more
To see my friend, the generous Theodore;
Yet little does he deem, by him restored,
That my fond bosom trusts to meet its lord.
How can this Baron think my faith to move!
Ere Albert sought me I repuls'd his love—
But hark! that horn!" With hurried hand she drew
The branches back, and blest her warrior's view. 800
Who then might paint their eloquence of joy,
In speech, in silence, or th' expressive eye;
Yet vainly Albert scann'd the guarded ground,
His starting steed refused the dreadful bound.

" Oh, tempt it not, sweet Lord!" she cried, " to-night
My love and prudence shall contrive our flight;
At midnight, by his snowy plumage known,
Comes Theodore, in silence and alone.

Wear thou the silvery plume, thy sure defence,
Prevent th' appointed hour, and bear me hence: 810
The bridge once down, the portal once unbarr'd,
Weak is my keeper's arm, and slight the guard.
But hark to yonder bugle's warning notes,
See where on high the bloody banner floats!
My tyrant comes; oh, shun his jealous eye!
The hateful Ulric—do not speak, but fly."

  He turn'd, and plunging in the thickest shade,
" Ride thou before, my trusty squire," he said,
" And to that hamlet where the passes met
Bring the white signal ere the daylight set." 820
The knight, meanwhile, whose joyous fancies rove,
Lost in delightul dreams of bliss and love
That break and knit a thousand times the chain,
Drops on his palfrey's neck the careless rein;
Nor mark'd his devious wanderings, till at last
An oak's rough branches brush'd him as he past.
The sun already sinking in the west,
Of time mispent the sickening thought imprest;
At every step he marks the fading light,
And fate, malicious, seems to urge the night; 830
While if his steed some fancied track pursued,
His hopes deceitful, sunk in denser wood.

Chill darkness reigns, when lo! with brighter beam,
Large and more near, shines forth the mystic flame.
Fain would he now repulse the potent spell,
And turn his struggling steed to Rosabelle;
But vain the curb, each moment gives it force,
He yields at last, and spurs his foaming horse.
He follows long, till full before the Knight,
Deep in a cavern fix'd the wondrous light! 840
Sure awful nature in her wildest hour
Framed this stupendous monument of power!
Less vast, less splendid, Staffa's vaunted cave,
Whose broken pillars chafe the northern wave.
White as the spacious vault they bore aloof,
Light, slender columns rear the fretted roof;
'Mid the rich spars the mimic flowers appear,
And ghastly faces grin grotesquely there:
In arches here the rich concretions bend,
And bases there to meet their shafts ascend, 850
Thick twined with wreaths of rainbow crystal round,
As if some fay the mimic garlands bound.

 Not long the Beacon stood,—its wondrous light
Again leads on, unfolding to his sight
New caves, new arches, regular and grand,
That mock the pigmy toils of mortal hand:

At length, condensing all its scatter'd fires,
The sanguine globe shoots upward and expires.
Th' affrighted steed stops short, and hark! the sound
Of roaring streams beneath the hollow ground.   860
The Knight dismounts, but every beam is fled,
And deepest darkness gathers round his head:
When glimmering torches through the woods appear,
And clattering hoofs announce pursuers near.
The brightening lights approach, and now they shone
On a tall aisle with ivy half o'ergrown:
Scarce had he reach'd its shade, when sword in hand
Perfidious Bernard leads the treacherous band;
With blazing torch he rushes to the cave,
"This way he past, nor all his saints can save,   870
Yet wield your weapons well, my lord is brave!"
He spoke—they gallop'd o'er the cavern floor,
Sunk in the hidden gulph, and rose no more.

Scarcely the Knight his grateful soul had rais'd
To guardian Heaven, when lo! the Beacon blazed;
And stood majestic on a mouldering pile,
Embosom'd deep within the vaulted aisle,
Where the dark cypress in funereal gloom,
Wept o'er the mound that should have been a tomb.

But all uncover'd, on the stone was laid 880
The wasted form, in splendid arms array'd,
And yet untouch'd by time, his burnish'd brand
Grasp'd in the skeleton's unyielding hand.
His crimson shield the griffin's wings display'd,
The sable griffin nodded o'er his head.
Brave Albert touch'd the sword, the rigid clasp
Was loosen'd, and he fits it to his grasp;
Admiring, as its ponderous length he sway'd,
The jewell'd hilt, the red and fiery blade.

But now a second, larger band appears, 890
And heavier steeds, and louder shouts he hears!
He turns, he trusts to see the flame expire,
But broader, brighter glares the magic fire;
Shoots back its beams from every sparry height,
And wraps the warrior in one sheet of light:
While as again the fiery sword he raised,
The wondrous blade with living lustre blazed.
They hurry on, impetuous as the wind,
Ulric alone, fierce Ulric lags behind—
But when they saw the dread, mysterious light, 900
The well-known armour of the lifeless Knight,
The funeral mound, as if by sudden spell
The steeds were stopp'd, the lifted lances fell.

THE CASTLE OF TRIVALLIS.

The hoary Seneschal, at Albert's feet
(Stung by remorse) drops powerless from his seat:
" It is fulfill'd!—my murder'd master's brand
Gleams in his injur'd son's vindictive hand!
Albert of Schorndorf—here I saw him bleed—
Arise, avenge him—'twas his brother's deed!"

" 'Tis false!" cried Ulric; " seize the stranger Knight!
What! do ye doubt? then arms shall prove my right!"
But guilt unnerv'd his arm, and Albert sway'd,
Strong in his truth, th' hereditary blade.
The Baron fell,—when now his comrades bore
The lifeless corse of ardent Theodore:
The silvery plume the youth to death betray'd,
The father's treason reach'd his offspring's head.
Sadly they laid him by his parent's side,
Who own'd just Heaven's avenging hand, and died.

And now the flame dilating, broad and bright, 920
Moves in a pyramid of sanguine light:
Wrapp'd in one blaze, in one sad heap were piled
The murder'd lord, the brother, and his child;
All night it glow'd, a self-sustaining fire,
Till with the dawn th' unearthly flames expire.
Soon in a temple's consecrated gloom
The pious Albert shrined his father's tomb;

And where to Heaven appeal'd the righteous blood,
The cloister rose, the nightly anthem flow'd.

'Twere long to tell what Albert now was told, 930
His father's fate, and Ulric's crimes of old;
How with her infant son his mother fled,
To all unknown, the Baron deem'd them dead;
Or how that prophecy, concealed from all
Save Theodore, and that grey Seneschal,
"When Schorndorf's heir shall wield his father's sword,
Then shalt thou perish, childless, undeplored."
How waked suspicion, and how Bernard sold
His honour and his master's life for gold.

'Twas night—the lute's soft sound, the trumpet's clang 940
Was heard, the dance had ceas'd, the beakers rang;
With love and joy the antique chambers ring,
And merry minstrels touch'd their blythest string,
While the full vaults their richest nectar pour'd
To Albert's bride, and Schorndorf's new-found lord.
The warder came, "beneath the castle door
Two weary strangers rest and aid implore;
A hoary pilgrim one, sedate and sage,
One bears a harp, and seems of tender age."

"Fling wide the gates, and spread the choicest cheer,
Our deadliest foe to-night were welcome here,"
Blythe Albert spoke, and then with gesture bland,
"Hail! pilgrims, hail, from Syria's holy strand!
Speak, if perchance your happier speed may bring
Tidings of England's host, or England's King?"

"Oh, joy unhoped!" the younger stranger cried,
Stout Longchamp flung his broad-brimm'd hat aside,
While Berengaria, o'er her neck of snow,
Gave her rich locks of burnish'd gold to flow.
Th' astonish'd vassals knelt—with courteous grace,
Their Queen uprais'd them in a warm embrace;
Each of the other's fate in haste inquir'd,
Nor fail'd the theme, nor mutual wonder tired,
Till o'er the zenith night's black coursers flew,
And each glad guest to late repose withdrew.

END OF BOOK XIII.

CŒUR DE LION.

BOOK XIV.

THE IMPERIAL SYNOD.

ARGUMENT.

THE IMPERIAL SYNOD.

The departure from Schorndorf—Meeting with the Archbishop of Cologne and Count Maynard, who are escorting King RICHARD to Haguenau—Interview between Albert and his Monarch—The Envoys of Austria resign their captive into the hands of the Emperor—Visit of Berengaria and Longchamp to RICHARD in his prison—The assembling of the Diet—The Ambassadors of England demand the King, and threaten the Emperor with war.—The reply of Henry—The charges against RICHARD—His vindication—The ransom proposed—Magnanimity of the German nobles—Transactions in Palestine—Behaviour of Hermesind at a tournament—Arrival of a band of female Pilgrims; and meeting of the Princess Helen with Matilda—Continuation of the Pilgrimage, and illness of Helen—She is sheltered in the cell of an Anchorite—Her confession; and discovery of the Hermit—Death of Helen, and of the Hermit.

CŒUR DE LION.

BOOK XIV.

THE IMPERIAL SYNOD.

Long years had past since morning rose so bright
On Schorndorf's towers, or waken'd hearts so light;
The nightmare-weight of Ulric's rule was gone,
And like a sunbeam Albert's virtues shone:
But shone not long, to claim their Lord again
The reverend Abbots came, and knightly train.
One hour of busy grief, one sad farewell,
Were all that love might yield to Rosabelle;
The Queen impatient sees, and hastes to part—
Such scene was torture to her suffering heart.

Rode proudly forth the princely cavalcade,
And plunged undaunted in th' Hercynian shade;
While all around their hope's green livery wore,
Exulting in the gloom they fear'd before.
Thrice had the evening sooth'd them to repose,
Thrice on their early way the morning rose;
When on a heath with not one dwelling nigh,
Hut, convent, castle, church, to fix the eye,
Where each low hill the same dull curve defined
And many a chance-worn path perplex'd the mind, 20
The sound of distant drums, and light that play'd
On burnish'd arms, a knightly band betray'd.
Soon by his gorgeous gonfalon was known
The proud arch-priest, Rinaldo of Cologne :*
He guards some prisoner — hopes fantastic spring
In each glad bosom—'tis indeed the King !
 " Whence and what are ye, Knights?" the Prelate cried.—
" From England's Regent Queen," the youth replied;
" Before his Peers we hasten to demand
Redress and justice from th' Imperial hand; 30

---

* Rinaldo, Archbishop of Cologne, who played a distinguished part in the contests between Frederic Barbarossa and the Holy See.

And pray your gracious pleasure to accord
A moment's parley with our captive Lord."
  " My leave is yours," Rinaldo then replied.
" Would Henry brook such leave?" Count Maynard
    cried.
  " Thy master is not mine," Rinaldo said;
" Nor am I here to load a captive's head
With fresh dishonour,—but, to justice true,
Alike I guard him from his friends, and you.—
Escape thou murmurs't—nay, dismiss thy pain,
These Knights have honour, and th' attempt were
    vain,   40
My single sword might quell such scanty train."
  Some paces back th' obedient guards withdrew,
And to his Lord impatient Albert flew:
Who o'er his neck his arms in rapture flings;—
Yet not such joy as from despondence springs.
For not when first on Acre's walls he stood,
Not when on Arsouf's field his mace rain'd blood,
Nor when on him th' anointing oil was shed,
Such glory brighten'd round the Monarch's head;
As, when in chains a felon scarce should wear,   50
The rock his couch, and coarse his scanty fare,

He paced his dungeon; when his sickening eye
Saw but the gloomy woods, the wint'ry sky,
Unchanged save by the varying light, the blast
That shook their tops, or clouds that hurried past.
A bride despairing—a defenceless host,
Perchance his fame aspers'd, his kingdom lost,
He felt and bore; with more than poet's fire,
Frequent he swept the long familiar lyre;
Throng'd his scant cell with heroes famed of yore, 60
And cheer'd the gloom with gleams of fairy lore.

Thus, wafted onward by Etesian gales,
Up the broad Nile the rapid Canja sails,
Steady yet swift, the adverse current braves,
And with unerring keel divides the waves;
While he whose hopes are all on fortune cast,
Like that same bark, bereft of sails and mast,
Floats sidelong down the stream, without a guide,
The prey of rocks, the puppet of the tide.

" My faithful friend! amid her dreams of bliss, 70
And prompt release, Hope scarcely whisper'd this!
How fares my realm, my Mother?—how my host?
Is Sion rescu'd yet, or Acre lost?"

"Thy Knights," the warrior said, "have sheathed
    their eager swords,
Safe in the truce a generous foe accords;
But Philip's vows were like his sickness, vain,
And—oh, my Liege, I grieve to give thee pain!
Thy brother seeks thy crown; a hand less strong
Than thy sage Mother's, might not hold it long."

"And let him seize it—'tis my lightest fear,   80
An hour wins back his conquests of a year.*
I loved him—hence his power to prove unkind,—
Why will he shew a brother's love was blind?
My mother toils and treason has defied,
Nor bends with age thou say'st—but my sweet bride?"

Speaking he turn'd, for she, unmark'd though near,
Who drank each word with love's attentive ear,
Strikes her light harp, and guides the longing eyes
Whose anxious fondness pierced her slight disguise.

But Albert gazed upon his Monarch's brow,   90
"How will it glad each loyal heart to know
That thou art found, and thus unchanged by woe!"

"Aye! else I ill deserve to wear a crown,—
He earns not Fortune's smiles who dreads her frown;

---

* Alluding to the speech of RICHARD, that he would recover in a day all that John could conquer in a year.

Insult and torture I might well defy,
My only fear was unavenged to die
Where none should hear my fate; but now I fare
To meet my trial—nay, that glance forbear:
If nought of Roman soul be their's beside,
These German Cæsars have a Roman pride;   100
'Tis much their jealous hatred does not grudge
A court of Princes and Imperial judge!
But let their petty rage exhaust its skill,
My dauntless soul shall prove me England still."

   The hour drew on,—the squires of Leopold
Resign'd the prisoner and receiv'd their gold;
And Frederic's wily son, who half in fear,
And half in transport, found his victim near,
(Unlike his Sire, whose greatness veil'd his guilt,
And dried with glory's beams the blood he spilt,)   110
Through all his circles bade the summons fly,
And urged the moment that he felt too nigh.
   And now to Haguenau Peers and Primates throng,
One thought each heart possess'd, one theme each
    tongue;
But temper some, some policy controll'd,
One sides with RICHARD, one with Leopold,
One Henry's threats seduced, or Philip's gold;

One hated England's power, or RICHARD's fame,
Nor came prepared to try, but to condemn.
Yet some more nobly thought;—thy prince, Louvain!
Who mourn'd by Henry's craft a brother slain;
Maguntium's Primate, and the Saxon pride,
Her Lion-Duke, to RICHARD more allied
By kindred virtues, than his English bride;
He of whose race imperial Otho springs,
And happy Britain waits her future kings.*

The eve of trial came;—the wintry night
Hid spires and turrets from the prisoner's sight;
Th' Hercynian mountains, and the silver line
Of hovering mist, that traced the nearer Rhine: 130
Yet horses tramp, and trumpets bray'd around,
And hammers ring and clamorous shouts resound.
Now torches gleam—in vain he strives to throw
From his high grate the anxious glance below,
Though sure one faithful eye is watching there;
He paced his cell, half breath'd the broken prayer,
Or listen'd as the jealous bolts were drawn.
With feverish eagerness he longed for dawn,

---

* The present House of Brunswick descends from the Emperor Otho, son of Henry the Lion of Saxony and the Princess of England.

Or eyed th' untasted meal, which ne'er in vain
Had woo'd before, or shook his heavy chain :   140
Till, by the rush of warring thoughts opprest,
He flung him on his couch and strove for rest.
Sudden the hinges grate,—surprised he rose,—
Two strangers entered, and the portals close.
Dim burn'd the lamp, but darkness could not hide
The one loved form, who flings her harp aside,
Springs to his heart, and faints in rapture there;
Her bonnet falls, and loose her golden hair
O'er his dark robe in waving lustre flows,
While as again her glistening eyes unclose,   150
She reads in his what grateful wonder glows.

Their broken speech tumultuous joy controll'd,
Till calm'd at last, the Royal Captive told,
How, in his sleep secured with many a chain,
His foes had seized and borne him o'er the main;
Yet had his hand their treason half repaid,
Prone at his feet Burgundia's Duke he laid,
And the black soul in lingering tortures fled.[b]
Next Berengaria, while her dewy eye
Shot many a conscious beam of present joy,   160
Told her past griefs : how all bewail'd her lord,
As captive first, and then as dead deplor'd.

The Soldan's proffer'd truce, the heavenly light
That shone to cheer; her shipwreck, and her flight.
The guidance given by Gortz' unconscious dame,
Of Albert's weal, of Longchamp's grief and shame.

But now a sigh arous'd the Monarch's ear:
" Who then art thou that sitt'st in darkness there?"

" One who has err'd, nor, till by thee forgiven,
Dares sue for pardon of offended heaven."   170

" My faithful Longchamp! can'st thou think that I,
Who sin so oft, forgiveness would deny?
Say, was I wont to play so stern a part?
Or dost thou deem that sorrow steels the heart!"

With warmth the King his gladden'd friend embraced,
On either cheek his kiss of peace he prest.
" If I could grieve o'er memory of the past,
This meeting, Longchamp, how unlike our last!
I then the Sovereign of two prosperous lands,
Girt with such fleets, with such unrivall'd bands;   180
And thou the friend, the delegate of one
Who own'd no prouder prince beneath the sun!
Now all that rests,—so fast our fortunes move,—
Courage to me, to thee thy Monarch's love.

Nay, check that sigh—regrets and shame are vain,
Resume thy Seals, and be thyself again;[c]
Aside that penance garb must now be laid,
And Ely's Prelate speak in Albert's aid.
Yet sorrow strengthens—should I else have known
Thy constancy, dear Longchamp! or mine own? 190
And one yet dearer! how her fragile form
Bow'd like the reed, but broke not with the storm;
And well redeem'd the boast of tender pride,
In softness bold, indeed a hero's bride!
Oh! Berengaria, think'st thou not our bliss,
When fortune smiles, shall be more rich for this?
But thou hast yet a task; I know thy zeal
With smiles can leave me, if to seek my weal.
At dawn my trial comes;—but why so pale?
What can I dread at which thy heart should quail?
They dare not bring me to the block or stake,
For angel-guards o'er Heaven's vicegerents wake.
Suspense and durance, there I read my doom,—
My freedom, dearest! must be won from Rome.
Wait not this solemn farce, this mockery,—go,
Ere Maynard's glance the truant minstrel know;
And hark! I hear the outer door unfold,—
Here is thy bonnet,—hide those locks of gold.

Wait not to speak, thine accents will betray
A heart too full,—my dearest love, away;— 210
Remember, Longchamp, be thyself again!—
Minstrel farewell! I thank thee for thy strain."

The Diet met, and purple glory shone
Round the vain man who fill'd th' Imperial throne;
And seldom King might boast a nobler band,
Primates and princes, Magnates of the land,
In wonder gazing on their captive there,
His form majestic, and commanding air.[d]

The envoys entered, and with dauntless look
The tyrant's seat confronting, Albert spoke. 220
" From England's Regent Queen, and each that bears
A loyal soul, her Prelates and her Peers,
We ask—no sign of hostile will foreshewn,
Why thus thou hold'st our Monarch from his throne?
And more: from thee, O Cæsar! we demand
Justice on one, a vassal of thy land,
The Duke of Austria,—who, against the troth
Of men and nations, and his solemn oath
Of Christian concord, dared by fraud enchain
Our slumbering Sovereign, and in bonds detain." 230

"One not" (as Albert ceased the Priest began)
" Sacred alone as monarch or as man,
But by that Cross which holy Pandulph gave,
To God devoted; and his God shall save."

" And I am charged," again the warrior cried,
" If his just freedom shall be still denied,
From England, Normandy, Guyenne to bring
Defiance, battle, till thou yield our King."

" Defiance, not from England's strength alone,
But every Prince who fills a Christian throne.   240
From all, by Clermont's solemn compact bound,
In Holy War to tread the sacred ground,
Or guard their absent comrades' lands from scathe,
As they reposed upon their comrades' faith;
And more, for every day his Tomb is stain'd
By Moslem rites, by brutal scorn profaned,
For every martyr's blood, for every harm
The faith endures, deprived of RICHARD's arm,
An angry Deity now speaks in me,
And claims in wrath the mighty debt from thee." 250

The Prelate spoke, and Henry's cheek of pride,
Pale as he listen'd, glow'd when he replied:
"Strangers! I chafe not, though your speech be bold;
Your Sovereign there, and there my Peers behold:

All that as vassals own Imperial sway,
The mighty whom these ample states obey.
Unheard I judge not, but from Austria's yoke
I claim'd her captive, and these lords convoke:
Be they the umpires;—but if I shall prove
Your King not only worthless of your love,   260
But all unfit on any rights to call
To be his shelter, who has outraged all;
And black with crimes, by Heaven and man abhorr'd,
That barbarous states had scrupled to record;
Then, for this care of Europe's general weal,
Your thanks, not censure, shall requite my zeal:
Meanwhile, if to this court no cause appear
To thwart our gracious wish, remain and hear."
"Monarch," said Albert, "I my seat demand,
As Schorndorf's Lord, and heir of Hildebrand.   270
As such to thee" (he knelt and loos'd his sword)
"I tender homage as my Suzerain lord;
Saving the faith to England's Monarch ow'd,
For lands and honours by his love bestow'd."

 Nor Henry dared the proffer'd homage scorn,
He loos'd the collar which himself had worn,
And while he fix'd it on his vassal's breast,
With well dissembled joy the youth carest.

To Ely's Prelate gave an honour'd place,
Then spoke with measur'd speech and plausive grace.

" Princes and Peers, and Thou, illustrious Thrall!
Fain would I win th' impartial ears of all;
Fain every good and loyal heart incline
To feel how painful is this task to mine;
For Kings with livelier sorrow must expose
A Monarch's guilt, or mourn a Monarch's woes.
Sadly we sympathize, when such are brought,
Even like the least, to answer deeds they wrought
In wanton power; but sadder were the time,
Should regal mantles prove a shield for crime.   290

" RICHARD PLANTAGENET, OF ENGLAND KING,
Branch of a stock from which myself I spring,
Think not a jealous rival seeks thy wrong,
That hate misleads, or guile inspires my tongue;
Thy Lion-heart I loved, thy daring deeds,
For every pang my kindred bosom bleeds;
And while on thee my heaviest charges fall,
'Tis my first wish thou may'st repel them all.

First then I charge thee, King! that in despite
Of my Constantia's claims, and well-known right,"

Despite those rights of blood which all respect,
And Kings who rule by them should least neglect,
Thou did'st compel th' unwilling realm to crown
The base-born Tancred on Sicilia's throne,
Perchance not William's child, at least no lawful son.

"And next I charge thee, while affecting zeal
For the lost Sepulchre, the Christian weal,
That thou, to swell thy greedy power, hast bent
On Christian kings thy mighty armament;
My kinsman Isaac hurl'd from Cyprus' throne, 310
Made his rich spoils thy minions' or thine own;
And, as a thousand tales of scandal prove,
His daughter's youth abus'd with lawless love.

"And next, that on the day thy single powers,
The rest defrauding, seized on Acre's towers,
Even from the rampart where his valour placed,
Thine envious hand my vassal's banner cast;
Him with a blow, and it with filth disgraced.
Oh! must I speak the hateful truth aloud,
And own that Austria's flag to such dishonour bow'd!"

'Twas here the Duke upon his captive roll'd
Such glance as serpents on the prey they hold:
But sunk abash'd beneath the mute reply,
The calm, majestic scorn of RICHARD's eye.

"And more," th' Imperial youth resum'd his tale,
"I charge thee King, that still beneath the veil
Of zeal and reverence for our Holy Cross,
Thy stubborn pride has wrought it shame and loss.
Still with new broils the Christian Princes vex'd,
Their efforts baffled, and their plans perplex'd; 330
Till one could brook a vassal's scorn no more,
And Gaul's brave Sovereign fled th' unconquer'd shore.
'Tis Thou must answer now for every day
That injur'd Sion weeps a Moslem sway;
For loss of all that Philip had subdued,
Had saved of Christian, shed of impious blood.

"Next, as his Suzerain, I of thee require
The price of blood for Conrad, Prince of Tyre;
Whose murder by thy coward hate was plann'd,
In midnight darkness slain, and by an unknown hand.

"Next, that the same base treason aims the knife
Of lurking villains at Augustus' life;
And he, till now unwont to dream of fear,
In every stranger dreads th' assassin near.

"But specious words might gloze these charges past,
A seventh remains, the weightiest and the last:
That while (despite that pride, which day by day
Made half the host but gazers on the fray,)

Still the full current of success roll'd on,
T'was thine to stay its course at Ascalon. 350
In servile tasks were noble hands employed,
Vainly to raise those works the foe destroyed;
While thy smooth speeches almost could incline
The Chiefs to impious peace with Saladine.
With him! the Infidel! in all his state,
Still Sultan of the East, and Lord of Salem's fate!

"Say, Princes! say, is this the Hero's sword,
That weeping Sion has in dust deplor'd,
The "CŒUR DE LION," who alone could cope
With Asia's King! the Christian's second hope! 360
Shall we not strip this Lion's hide, and shew
The subtle fox, the coward sheep below?
And what, though treason brought him to our throne,
Shall we not make the cause of man our own?
Or must we fix this monster in his reign,
And give this demon back to power again?ᶠ
But I transgress: he yet may all deny,
Or with prompt wit some fair excuse supply;
Yet, though I know his sweet and plausive tongue,
I cannot, dare not, hope to find me wrong." 370

He ceased, and RICHARD hasten'd to reply,—
Calm was his mien, but lightning in his eye.
His not the pining captive's faded hue,
From smother'd rage a livelier crimson grew;
His ample beard and hair's neglected length,
Seemed but an earnest of superior strength.
With graceful air, yet as in high disdain,
Oft as he spoke he waved his cumbrous chain.

" And who shall claim my answer? who shall bring
A King to trial? who condemn a King? 380
There is one only court which Kings should fear,
A Court Divine—and Thou shalt meet me there;
But by th' anointing oil, the solemn hour
That gave my sceptre, I deny thy power!
Oft have I err'd,—and who that looks within,
On memory's glass shall find no stain of sin?—
Yet if I e'er misus'd my rule, or them
He made my children, let my God condemn:
To Him I here appeal, to Him I trust;
I know him Good, nor dread to know him Just. 390
Yet, while your haughty summons I deny,
For my own honour, Henry! I reply.

" Me no kind purpose to Messina drove;
In hate I enter'd, though I left in love.

A widow'd sister's freedom to restore,
Her massy throne to claim, and regal dower,
That ample board, whose golden round might hold
Th' Armoric Peers or Paladins of old,^g
With all the wealth that William's last command
Gave to my sire, I sought th' unfriendly land.   400
'Tis true that soon was every doubt dispell'd,
And Tancred's faith my hostile purpose quell'd;
Yet if such concord breed distrust in thee,
Why breeds it less to Philip than to me?
Is't that he urged him to destroy me there?—
But the firm youth refus'd, and warn'd me of the snare.*

" And next at Cyprus, wearied, tempest-tost,
What was my welcome on that Christian coast?
Chains to my soldiers, treachery to my Bride,
Myself forbad to land, and aid denied!   410
What were he Anna's spouse, or Manuel's son,—
I had not spared him, had he been thine own!

" But for his daughter,—let a Knight beware
How with incautious speech he wound the fair!
Nor, save with chaste devotion, breathe a name,
Pure as the snow in Cynthia's virgin flame;

* Tancred shewed to RICHARD a letter, in which Philip Augustus urged him to join in a conspiracy to put him and the English to the sword.

Let Berengaria's matron praises tell
The virtues she has known and loved so well.

"And for that rapturous hour, that glorious strife,
More worth than thousand years of meaner life, 420
When Acre yielded, when my single powers
(Yes, they were single!) storm'd her haughty towers;
When England's unassisted might prevail'd,
Where France—where Europe and the East had fail'd!
Was I to brook, upon the very day,
The very rampart where I forced my way,
A meaner flag,—a flag that did not share
The glorious toil,—in rival triumph there?
Thou art no warrior, yet perchance are here
Some that may hold a warrior's feelings dear. 430
How would thy sire, at princely Milan's fall,
Have brook'd an English banner on the wall?
I tore it down—but if it wrought such hate,
Why not acknowledg'd then, or shewn so late
Must Conrad's death the poor pretext supply?
But 'tis enough,—unless my life belie
That foulest charge, I stoop not to deny."*

* RICHARD declared that unless his whole life had proved him incapable of such an action, it was useless to assert his innocence.

He paus'd, for Albert rose : " Forgive," he said,
" Th' intrusive speech, but while I still delay'd
On Syria's shore, a wretch before us stood,   440
Whose fiendish soul rejoiced in Conrad's blood;
Sent by th' Assassin Prince he dealt the blow,
And with his death confirm'd the tale of woe."

" Praise to that Power, our guardian and our guide!
Praise to the God of Truth!" King RICHARD cried.
" Must I speak more, or melts each charge away,
Like mountain mists beneath the morning ray?
I have not wrought in shade—a crystal screen
Is rear'd the Monarch and his realm between,
That not one foible veils from vulgar eyes,   450
But while it parts, displays and magnifies.
Through such is Philip seen, and thousands know
'Twas Flanders lured him from his holy vow;
And thousands heard him, when he pledg'd again
Those oaths of friendship, pledged so oft in vain.
Yet wherefore broke—the wondrous tale display—
Not that my absence left my realm his prey;
He talks of darts which I from Syria's shore
Could hurl, perchance, or dark Trivallis' tower;
Of treacherous swords—but oh! if such my power,

I were a fool to aim no shaft at thee,
And live enthrall'd, when such might set me free.

" One charge remains—the peace with Saladine,—
Was it approved by all, or wholly mine?
Forced on the Chiefs for interests of my own;
Or broke by me when left to fight alone?
If any doubt my zeal, its truth shall breathe
From earth, from heaven, and from the gulfs beneath;
Thanks to that God for whom I all endure,
The curse of dying Moslems makes it sure. 470
Whose was the flag that waved on Acre's height?
Whose the red hand that won proud Arsouf's fight?
Or whose the name that routed Islam fears,
That Europe boasts, and Asia speaks with tears?
I scorn to vaunt, but oh! when England's fame,
Now dawning bright, shall cast its zenith flame;
When even your cowering Eagles shall attest
The Lion's friendship guards their tottering nest;
Then shall she bid her sons observe on high,
Where shine my deeds in scrolls that cannot die. 480

" Now let these Princes, if indeed to them
Such power be given, acquit me or condemn.
Or if in thy belief I rightly deem
The purple paler than the golden gleam,

That Cæsar's sceptre were itself a jest,
Did no embroidery deck the Tyrian vest,
What is my ransom? how must I unclose
These dainty chains, so fit for noble foes?
Yet mark me, Henry! I thy claim deny,
To the last denier, and would sooner die   490
By daily torture in the darkest lair
Of dark Trivallis, (if a worse be there,)
But I am vow'd to Heaven—my idle sword
That heaven rebukes, and England claims her Lord."

He ceased; but through the hall loud murmurs rise,
And tears are glistening in unwonted eyes;[h]
In dread his ransom and his thrall to lose,
Preventive of their speech, the Emperor rose.
  "Hail! CŒUR DE LION!—I with joy receive
Thy proud denial, and I will believe.   500
Such be thy ransom as beseems thy fame,
As fits with thee to yield, and me to claim;
Ten thousand pounds, each thousand ten times told,
Of Cologne weight, and of the purest gold."[i]
  The Emperor paus'd, the Synod stood aghast:
" What King, they thought, " might pay a sum so
    vast!"

But Richard's soul no mean surprise could move,
He knew his England's wealth, his people's love.

"It shall be thine, ere yonder sun that now
On southern regions sheds his summer glow   510
Turn from the goat; yet haply I might fear
Some treachery still, for treason brought me here."

But ere he ceased the young Louvain arose,
Still inly sorrowing o'er his private woes:
"Nay, by that ghost which nightly round my bed
Demands just vengeance on his murderer's head;
May he through whom the deed of death was done,
Ne'er for his guilt in penal fires atone;
May this right hand, that never fail'd me yet,
In my next field its wonted skill forget;   520
May thy just fury tear it from my side,
If I behold thee wrong'd!" the warrior cried.

"May Heaven in righteous judgment deal with me,
On its Great Day, as I am true to thee,
Thou injured Prince! Heaven's cause is now thine own.
I swear!" exclaim'd Rinaldo of Cologne.

And rising, all the Magnates of the land
Vow'd on their croziers, or their arm'd right hand,
To make their Emperor guard the faith he swore,
Or yield allegiance to his crown no more.[k]   530

On their free vows the dauntless King reposed,
And Henry parted, and the Council closed.

Meanwhile in Palestine the months roll'd on,
And Spring dawn'd bright on finish'd Ascalon.
Already Albert comes: proclaims with joy,
His Sovereign found, and bids them hope him nigh.
Now either host the genial year inspires
With martial zeal, with rival ardour fires;
Yet who might think, to see the blended train,
They once were foes, and shall be foes again ?   540
Arabs with Christians break a harmless lance,
To Arab lutes the merry Christians dance;[1]
While mutual presents mutual kindness bound,
This gives a hawk, and that returns a hound.
Led by the Arabs, now the Knights invade
The boar or panther in his native shade;
By Christians taught, the Arabs course the hare,
Or mark the falcon wage the fight in air;
And when the Christians seek the fierce Castille,
Or their light bands in mimic skirmish wheel,   550
The generous Saladine in wonder sees,
"Who may contend with foes whose sports are these?"[m]

And now, disburthen'd of her heaviest cares,
In each gay scene the calm Matilda shares;
Evanthe's bloom revives, and joy inspires
Gay Hermesind's dark eye with keener fires;
Elate when call'd the evening dance to lead,
Or at the tilt bestow the victor's meed.
Once for that envied meed the Knight unknown
Knelt at her feet, yet still his vizor down;   560
O'er his green helm the laurel wreath she threw,
Then as she held the token forth to view,
" May this poor glove," she said with winning grace,
" Beneath that trophy find an honour'd place,
Proof that thy heart, as courteous as 'tis brave,
Scorns not her thanks whom thou hast deign'd to save."

"Nay, loveliest work of Nature's master-hand!
My only badge must be this laurel band;
I serve a jealous goddess, nor must wear
The pledge of mortal maid, however fair;   570
Would'st thou be grateful, wait awhile," he said,
" Then weave my shroud for Honour's bridal bed."

His voice had sunk, and something stirr'd her mind,
Remembrance vague, and terror undefined;
But on her cheek indignant blushes burn'd,—
To pale Ricardo's trembling gaze she turn'd;

"Wilt thou redeem me from unwonted scorn?
Shall this poor token on thy casque be worn?
The Knights of old, or false our tales declare,
Served honour best when best they serv'd the fair;—
I, for my sex's fame, this glove require
At the next tilt to waken all thy fire;
So may'st thou tear yon scornful wreath away,
And claim the prize, the thanks misplaced to-day."

He kiss'd the precious gift, and would have spoke,
When on the sports a strange appearance broke;
All clad in pilgrim garb a female band,
The palm and ozier cross in either hand.

"From distant shores," they cry, "to every shrine
We track the weary plains of Palestine;   590
Weep in each spot to pious memory sweet,
Kiss each green turf that bore Messiah's feet;
Then let your bounty prove your faith as true,
And feed the hungry lips that pray for you."

But one of pallid front and lofty mien
Sought private audience of Sicilia's Queen;
Her veil thrown back, she stood in silence there:
"Whence art thou, gentle friend, and what thy prayer?"

"Are we then both so changed?" the stranger cries;
But at the well-known voice Matilda flies,   600

"My sister!" and her tears impetuous throng,
To dew the warm embrace that held them long.
　But Helen, as she fix'd her anxious gaze,
Spoke with a smile,—a smile of other days;
　"What years, what changes, ah! what griefs have past,
My own Matilda! since we parted last!
I, wont to seek a King's paternal hall,
And lead in spirit as in rank the ball;
To shine at jousts the gayest of the gay,
Or listen Bertrand's plaintive virelay; 610
(Bewitching dreams, why will ye haunt me yet?
When 'tis my wish, my duty to forget;)
Thou in thy cell, thy heart no sorrow knew,
Thine eye no tear, save what devotion drew;
While to thy buoyant hope the world unknown,
Seemed like that Heaven whence thy young thoughts had flown.
Methink this staff and tippet should be thine;
Thy front's ambrosial wreath should circle mine!"
　"Yet I had sorrow too," Matilda cried;
"That I have borne, I praise a heavenly guide." 620
　"Yes! but thou could'st not madden, day by day,
To think thy folly flung thy peace away;

That thou had'st all which seem'd to make thee blest,
Yet not one gleam of sunshine in thy breast:
Yes! thou art changed! but not like me, for thou
Wert ever calm, and art as lovely now;—
But I—is this my bloom, my open brow?
These dim sunk eyes, oh! grief and death are there—
Nay, do not weep to think my rest is near;
I did not come, Matilda, to increase   630
Thy woes or mine; I came to pray for peace.
Is Bertrand here?"

        " Oh no! ere Autumn's rain,
He took a pilgrim's garb, nor comes again."

  "'Tis well! we should not meet—but thou may'st say
His hatred wrongs my brother—bid him pray
Heaven's mercy on that sin, and curse alone
The only heart unjust to him—my own."

  " Nay, Helen! Sister! wherefore feed thy grief?
The God that bids us ask can give relief."

" My crime was dark, nor is my penance light,   640
But it is nearly past—we part to-night."

"To-night! dear Helen?"

        " Yes! our pious band
Takes but such rest as nature's wants demand.

Of late I bade my princely lord farewell,
Then sought my brother in his gloomy cell;
Frank, generous, gay, as in his youth's first hour,
Unbent by sorrow, as unspoil'd by power.
This parting is my last, and if again
We meet on earth, it shall not be in pain;
I pray for peace,—and if in vain I call,   650
I yet shall find it, where 'tis found by all.
Thou weep'st again! yet thine are griefs that break
But for a moment the clear placid lake;
While mine are flaws, that scarcely speck the glass,
Yet spread and lengthen till they burst its mass.
Once more farewell!"—and her white arms are thrown
Around Matilda's neck; she kiss'd her and is gone.

  The gentle pilgrims still their course pursue,
At holy Bethlehem yield observance due,
Forbidden Salem's distant towers adore,   660
And trace the winding Jordan's shadowy shore.
Diverging now, o'er wide Esdrælon's plain,
Jesreel and Nazareth's sacred walls they gain;
Till as by Thabor's lonely base they tread,
Tiberias' ample lake before them spread,

Whose fruitful shores perpetual harvests rear,
And bid the vine blush purple through the year.
Its waves they pass, and on its eastern coast
See mountain peaks in stormy chaos tost
To Jebel's height, whose rounded summits show 670
The velvet softness of eternal snow.
Here, in those wilds where long a Saviour trod,
And angel-legions serv'd th' acknowledg'd God;
Or he who shew'd the coming light, and gave
A holy virtue to the simple wave;
Or those the Saints of later times, that fraught
With ardent zeal, his great example caught,
Here from their kind to rocks and ravens fled,
And life sustained with what the desert bred :
They kneel at every Cross; yet shuddering hear
Of stripes and fasts, and penance most austere;
Nor covet, while they praise, a glory bought so dear.

Now pine-crown'd cliffs meet darkling overhead,
Huge stones their path; beneath, a torrent's bed;
And Helen's feet, unus'd to ways so rude,
Miss the smooth rock, or stain the stones with blood.
She faints—she grasps a crag—one moment more,
And she may sink amid the deafening roar.

Worn like herself, yet form'd of stouter mould,
The sister band her sinking frame uphold.   690
No roof is nigh—far distant is the height,
Crown'd by the convent they must reach to-night;
But where a Cross surmounts yon beetling brow,
That shades the cataract, yawns a cave below;
There may she rest, a sister at her side,
Till Anna's Monks send back a surer guide.

  Low was the arch, but inward as they wound,
Say, do the rocks send forth that solemn sound,
The Virgin's vesper hymn? The pious train
Repectful paus'd, then rais'd th' accordant strain. 700
The dusky cedars on each chalky brow,
The rocks, the caves, the flood that foam'd below,
Join the full voice,—from hill to hill it flies,
And glen to glen, and stream to stream replies.

  Still o'er the heights the closing echoes ran,
When from the cave appear'd a reverend man;
As towards the train his pious hands were spread,
One golden sunbeam touch'd his hoary head.
" The peace of heaven, th' eternal peace that knows
Nor change, nor sorrow, on your duteous brows!
Yet whence inspired to trace a path so rude?
For, save the mule that brings my weekly food,

The goat, or eagle on yon craggy height,
For months no living thing hath blest my sight."

"As pilgrims we thy solitude invade,
A fainting sister craves thy pious aid."

Onward he led where Mary's image stood,
And a rude altar bore a Cross as rude:

He from the rock had scoop'd the forms divine,
And a rough lamp that burn'd before the shrine. 720
A skull and hour-glass spoke of time and death,
A scourge of penance; o'er the wither'd heath,
That form'd his couch, a faded scarf he spread,
Which had been gorgeous once; "Approach!" he said,
And on its folds their senseless load they laid.

"Our vows, O Hermit! and the coming eve,
Forbid delay; but in thy charge we leave
Our helpless friend. Thou laugh'st at pomp and power,
But she was once a kingdom's fairest flower,
And nurs'd in purple; aid her in her need, 730
For Mary's sake, and to yon convent lead
Her steps recovered; so our prayers shall rise,
And win thee wealth in worlds beyond the skies."

With ivory crucifix, whose classic taste
Mock'd the rude sculpture o'er the altar placed,

He kneels, and on th' unconscious pilgrim throws
The torrent's gelid wave—her eyes unclose.

"And have I pray'd for death, yet fear to die!"
Inly she groan'd,—" Oh! were some Father nigh
To hear my parting shrift, to hear and save!" 740
She started up, and glancing round the cave,
"Oh blessed Hermit! if thou art indeed,
By heaven commission'd at my utmost need,
Attend! and may a Gracious God bestow
One hour of strength!" She bared her livid brow.
"Not she who nurs'd my youth would know me now,
But I, when English Henry's name was fear'd,
Was deem'd his favourite child, and then appear'd
As fed on roses, wild with health and bliss—
The weight of secret guilt hath made me this!" 750

The Hermit starts, and as he draws more near
His open cowl, replies in tone severe:
"Yes, Helen! for upon thy soul shall rest
The crimes, th' eternal doom of those who loved thee
    best."

"Have then these deserts breath'd it? Human ear
Yet never heard!—Thou man of faith austere,
To thee a dying penitent I sue:
Be just, yet in thy justice gentle too."

" Daughter proceed ! If endless pangs are thine,
The lips that doom thee never shall be mine."   760
" 'Tis not thy pity I would seek to move,
Or mock thy saintly ears with tales of love.
All Europe knew my Sire—too fond of rule,
A kingdom's idol, but Ambition's fool !
Through me fresh schemes of worldly power he plann'd,
Pleas'd when the Saxon Henry sought my hand.
Warriors, who named him Lion of the war,
Bespoke him brave, and maidens called him fair :
The voice of fame his presence soon approved,
His worth I honour'd, and believ'd I loved ;   770
And, save my tender years forbade the band,
I then had given an unreluctant hand. —
But there was one, I know not if his lay,
His form or valour stole my heart away,
Or that my generous brothers held him dear ;
For I was blest but when De Born was near.
Profuse, or proud, or rash—let others call
These things his faults, I loved him for them all.
Thou art impatient, and I will be brief :—
Yet, Hermit, 'tis that I have wrong'd this Chief, 780
'Tis that my fancied falsehood warp'd his brain,
I thus have pined for years—oh ! is my sorrow vain ?"—

" But *seeming* false !" th' indignant Hermit cried,
" True to De Born, and yet the Saxon's bride!
Trifle not, daughter! think how small the sum
Of earthly years, to those of pain to come!"

" I do not trifle—turn thou not away
In scorn—I heard with torture, day by day,
Of Bertrand's falsehood—how Amanda's charms,
(Turenne's fair daughter) lured him from my arms.
I wrote, and no reply—and while my brain
With torture reel'd, my father urg'd again
The Saxon's suit—indignant phrenzy came
To dry my tears! 'He shall not blast my fame
Though he have wreck'd my peace; nor boast I died,
Or pined his victim,' stung with rage I cried,—
And the next eve beheld me Henry's bride.

" Thou groan'st! O, Father! but alas! I seem'd
In stupor lost, and ah! that yet I dream'd!
Mirth wanton'd round, yet nought of joy I knew, 800
Nor aught of pain, till, laughing, from Poitou
Gay RICHARD came, and as his hand display'd
The fatal scroll, ' A boon! a boon!' he said;
' Forgive a loiterer,' and he kiss'd my brow;
' Though to thy lovesick heart time linger now,
As erst to mine when from Alasia barr'd;
I found the means to cheat her wily guard,

And basking in her sight so long denied,

Forgot thy tears my selfish stay might chide.'

  " Seek pardon at the Cross!' I cried, and tore 810

The letter from his grasp and ran it o'er.⁰

  ' I cannot hide the grief I feel

That thou should'st doubt my truth, my zeal;

  But may my soul in torment pine,

When absent if I seem to live;

If aught another love could give,

  Delight me like one word of thine.

' May the fell eagle from on high

My falcon on my wrist destroy;

  Oh! may my casque obstruct my sight,   820

My steed nor spur obey nor thong;

Short be my reins, my stirrups long,

  And I the first to fly in fight.

' A captive, coop'd with those I hate,

The scorn of man, the sport of fate,

  May evil luck my dice pursue;

The wind refuse to swell my sail,

My purse be void, my harvests fail,

  If e'en in thought I prove untrue.

' May I behold thee courted long,   830
And want the sense to venge the wrong;
   May porters beat me, may I find
No hour to wreak revenge, if they
Who swear that I thy trust betray,
   Are not more false than dice, or wind.'

" Oh God! each word that spoke of joy and youth,
Of martial glee, and fond confiding truth,
Proclaim'd me perjur'd, pierced my guilty soul!
But why dilate? too soon I knew the whole.
My fancied foe now reign'd in Perigord,   840
De Born but stayed to give her to her Lord,
And grace, as friendship bade, the bridal feast,
Which Talleyrand display'd for every guest.*
My brother's pitying heart was still the same,
His patience sooth'd me, and forbore to blame;
' And oh!' I pleaded, ' by our early years,
' By my lost peace, by all these fruitless tears,
Since I and Bertrand ne'er must meet again,
Let him believe me false, unfeeling, vain;

---

* The daughter of Turenne married Talleyrand, Count of Perigord. I cannot help being interested in the early annals of houses, which have since so largely influenced the fortunes of the world.

Think that my worldly soul to Mammon sold, 850
Loved his frank homage less than rank or gold;
Let him despise me, for he less will rue,
Than thus to find me lost, yet feel me true.
And ah! kind RICHARD (for I know De Born),
Should he by frenzied act, or word of scorn,
Insult thy name, or mine, in pity spare,—
Think how thy sister wrong'd him, and forbear;
It were a torture yet to dread that those
I cherish most, should ever meet as foes.' "

"All gracious Heaven! th' astonished father cried,
Was that the cause which tamed the Lion's pride?
A lamb to Bertrand, fierce to all beside!
Who knew him best believed it struggling shame,
That he had urged thy vows, and conscience made him
 tame!"

"Hermit, they knew him not, and I was wrong!
My fancied wisdom did not cheat me long.
I heard how Bertrand's hate our house pursued,
Till 'gainst my father's throne his first-born stood,
And RICHARD, when he sought his promis'd bride
And rightful dukedom, both so long denied, 870
From his unnatural rage to Philip's aid
Was forced to fly, by him at last betray'd.

I knew too late, while writhing with the smart,
From my kind Lord to hide my bleeding heart,
To let no sigh my inward grief betray,
And check the tear he still would kiss away;
Still in his sight with feign'd delight I smil'd,
Alone, my thoughts would madden o'er my child.
I might seem blest, yet pining day by day,
As flowers decline beneath too warm a ray;   880
For poisons may be viewless as the beam,
Nor give a colour to the tainted stream.
Oh! had his harshness but excused my woe,
Or given one scalding tear pretence to flow;
Of all my pangs his kindness gave the worst,
I was ungrateful, and I felt accurst!

  "The stormiest ocean must have rest at last.
Years fled—my bitterness of grief was past;
His worth awaked esteem,—my child grew dear,
And how did RICHARD's glory soothe my ear!   890
Till he was captive, and I heard, oh shame!
That Bertrand stamp'd him with a murderer's name!

  "Thou groan'st again,—but ah! that night of dread!
I seem'd to die!—a vengeful angel led
Me, trembling, through the realms of penal flame;
Thousands I saw of yet unsullied fame,

Who writhe for secret guilt, though glory write
Their names on brass;—but most he fix'd my sight
On one, a ghastly trunk distain'd with gore,
And in his hand his sever'd head he bore.' 900

"'Lo! who was Bertrand once! frank, loyal, true;
But he with hatred dared the good pursue:
Against his Sovereign and his friend conspire,
And bade a son in arms affront his sire.
He was the tempting fiend, th' Achitophel
Who led this second Absalom to hell;
That those whom heaven had join'd he dared to sever,
He bears his guilty head disjoin'd for ever.'

" I shrunk away,—but wheresoe'er I turn'd,
Before me still the dreadful spectre burn'd; 910
Towards me it seem'd the livid head to hold,
The blue lips moved, the flaming eyeballs roll'd!

"' I led my Prince to crime—for that I groan,
And heaven is just—but not to me alone;—
Whose soul the burthen of *my* sins shall bear?
For whom does hell a hotter flame prepare?'

" I see his fiendish laugh—I hear again
Those dreadful accents, branded on my brain!—
I woke, for nature could endure no more,
And fled for peace to Sion's sacred shore. 920

Oh! Father! is there mercy yet in heaven?
Can I save him, or be myself forgiven?"
  But he replies not—on his hands outspread,
Veil'd in his cowl, is bow'd his holy head;
They fell—" And does he sleep!" the Pilgrim cried,
And drew with angry grasp his hood aside—
She shrieks, for ah! too well she knew the face,
Through guilt, and time, and sorrow's deepest trace;
And Bertrand too revived—upon the sand
He knelt with kindling look, he seiz'd her hand. 930
  " Friend of the wretched! first to Thee I raise,
And Thou shalt read, th' unutterable praise.
Oh! I had deem'd the hour that told me this
Had been my death,—but 'tis o'erwhelming bliss!
I'd rather know myself a wretch, than hold
My friend ungrateful, or my mistress cold;—
Helen! sweet Helen! oh! to breathe again
That name, nor think thy brightness has a stain!—
Load not thy soul with sins another wrought,
For heaven were hell, by thy perdition bought. 940
Can sorrow seek relief in crime alone?
My misery was thy work, my guilt my own.
And did'st thou think Amanda could subdue
This heart?—yet ah! I deem'd thee treacherous too.

Thy judgment err'd, our mutual pangs attest
The path of truth must ever be the best;
The only path which safe through toil and fear,
Leads to the goal, and ends not in a snare.—
But thou art faint again! my zeal transgress'd,
Nor saw thy wasted frame had need of rest: 950
Go to that couch! in years of hope and love,
Know'st thou by whom that faded scarf was wove?
The heath is soft, and oh! may every flower
With holiest balm thy wither'd strength restore,
And angels soothe thee. When the tempests lour,
Such couch is mine,—but now some mountain crest;
There will I pray for blessings on thy rest,
Till morning break, and we together raise,
With hope renew'd, the strain of prayer and praise."

" Stay! Bertrand, stay! 'tis but one little hour—
I ne'er shall see the flush of morning more;
Thy gentle words have calm'd my burning brain,
My strength is ebbing,—'twas the strength of pain.
Wilt thou not pray with me, that I may die
By thee forgiven, and hoping peace on high?"

" Forgive thee, Helen! Pray with thee!" he cried,
And placed her kneeling by the altar's side;

" May the pure Virgin never plead for me,
If my worst madness wish'd a pang to thee."

" Oh, ever kind!" she breath'd—the altar stays
Her clasp'd and bloodless hands, her earnest gaze
Fix'd on the Cross, her cheek as coldly fair,
Her look unchanging as the image there.
But Bertrand stood, aloft his arms were spread,
His penance-faded cheek had lost its red;
But when his heart to fame and love beat high,
Ne'er had such splendours lighten'd from his eye.

" Thou, holiest Virgin! Thou, the Sire of Heaven!
Thou, in whose death man trusts to be forgiven;
And Thou, the Comforter, who now hast pour'd 980
Thy balsam here, be each and all ador'd!—
Behold this kneeling victim, ye who hear
The secret sigh, and see the lonely tear!
Such tears, 'tis said, shall quench the scarlet stain,
And shall they plead before your throne in vain?
While in your Name, that Name for ever blest,
I here absolve her sin, Great Power! attest
The solemn pledge, and heal the wounded breast.
Oh! I am dark with guilt; yet if the noon,
The dawn, the vesper hour, the midnight moon 990

Have heard my groans, have seen me kneeling here,
Oh! let my sorrows never reach your ear;
For me no Saint have sued, no Saviour bled,
Ere my least fault be charged on Helen's head.
How oft have I at highest altars stood,
To curse my King, to ask his sacred blood!
Thou heard'st me not, O God! for that be Thou
For ever prais'd: but hear me, hear me now!
Now, when I call thine angel host to shed
Their richest unction on his holy head!—   1000
He prosper'd in the curse a villain breath'd,
Now be his brows with brighter glory wreath'd;
Each tale, by malice forged to blight his fame,
Oh! let it cling but to my guilty name!
Be mine accurs'd, forgot, while day by day,
His wins from every sun a brighter ray!

   " Father of mercy! read the grateful zeal
That mocks our words, our chasten'd bosoms heal!
Make every wish, each inmost thought thine own!
Lo! we have kiss'd the rod—Thy will be done!"—

   Awhile he bow'd his head in silent prayer—
He rose, his Helen still was kneeling there;
Her glance was upward, on her cheek there shone
The calm of holiest joy,—but life was gone.

"This task should not be mine, but it shall prove
A sacred sadness, less of grief than love."
On her cold breast the crucifix he laid,
And wreath'd with virgin flowers her lifeless head;
Chaunts o'er her bier the solemn prayers of death,
With voice unfaltering gives the requiem breath;
Then laid her in the grave he meant his own,
And, as he flung him on the senseless stone:
"I had not thought in distant lands to hear
Of thy last breath, nor shed a single tear!
Is my heart cold before its hour?" he cried,
"Or have my sins the fount of sorrow dried?"—
 He thought of other days, while long his bane,
For a last struggle pride revived again.
"My name dies with me—not a kinsman, none
Shall claim my heritage when I am gone.   1030
My brother!—oh! how vain, how dark, appears
All the long discord of our early years;
Would I could now what then I sought resign,
That life (my life) and all the land were thine!
Hautefort! thy towers have lost their feudal state,
No banner'd throngs are pouring from thy gate;
Thy trophied arms shall be the vulture's nest,
And ravens scream where kings were proud to rest;

Nay, should some passing wanderer ask who sway'd
In those proud halls, majestic though decay'd,   1040
My peasants, vassals of some chief abhorr'd,
May pause, forgetful of their ancient Lord.
Yet there were time to seek for love and fame,
To build another race, a fairer name:
But no!"—and on his lips there beam'd again,
A smile that had no bitterness, no pain;
"My hours are number'd,—nay, I must not meet
My injur'd friend, and cast me at his feet;
Hope, love, and hatred, all that stirr'd me here,
Sleep in this grave!—Oh, slept I with them there!—
Sweet Saint! for never unblest spirit shed
A smile so heavenly on the lips it fled;
Sweet, sainted Helen! from thy world of bliss,
Look on the wretch still doom'd to crawl in this;
And pray that soon our sever'd fates may join,
My griefs sleep here, my soul ascend to thine."—

One eve, the faithful mule that brought his food
Return'd, unlighten'd of its weekly load;
And Anna's wondering monks, who sought the cave,
Found him, still strech'd upon his Helen's grave,
Lifeless and cold as she that slept beneath.
They laid him by her side; their chaunt of death

Peal'd o'er the closing stone;—a cross arose,
That still to many a holy Pilgrim shews
Where Helen's soul its load of anguish cast,
Where Bertrand's fiery spirit rests at last.

END OF BOOK XIV.

CŒUR DE LION.

BOOK XV.

THE RETURN OF RICHARD.

ARGUMENT.

THE RETURN OF RICHARD.

The attempted treachery of the Emperor, and noble firmness of the German Princes—Return of Richard to England; his transactions there, and departure—Behaviour of Pardo in the Paradise of Hassan; he resists the tears of Maimoune, and demands his promised freedom from the Assassin—Maimoune saves him from his vengeance, and becomes herself its victim—Appearance of Hassan to Pardo in the Desert—His threats—He summons Maimoune and Amina—The death of Hassan—Wanderings and danger of Pardo and Amina—Interposition and gratitude of Maimoune—They reach the encampment of Aladin, who relates the successes of the Soldan and distress of Jaffa—Arrival at the Forest Fountain—The Trophy—Pardo resumes his arms and reaches Jaffa on the evening of a solemn fast—He finds the town pledged to surrender on the following noon, if not relieved—The moment arrives—The sails of Richard are seen in the distance—The Christians rush to battle; are overwhelmed by numbers—The mistake of Richard, and intrepidity of Pardo—Richard lands, and obtains the victory—Death of Mirzalis, and danger of Saladine.

CŒUR DE LION.

BOOK XV.

THE RETURN OF RICHARD.

Thou, Loyal Spirit! in the noble mind
Who dwell'st with all of generous and refined,
Thou, whom a happy realm exults to feel,
Source of her public fame, her private weal;
And boasts she gave,—oh, be it long her pride!—
Thy home, when banish'd from the world beside:
Ne'er was thy call with readier love obey'd,
Ne'er at thy shrine were purer offerings paid,
Than when his weeping myriads vied to bring
Their several portion, and release their King.

The poor his mite, untax'd the Abbot yields[a]
His gold, the lord the produce of his fields:
Yet time roll'd on; and all on Syria's shores,
Or war-vex'd England, count the weary hours;
For two there were, whose secret treachery strove
To render vain a generous nation's love;
Philip of France, and he whose impious sword
At once assail'd his brother and his Lord.

'Twas now at Spires,—for RICHARD, as in sport,
Was doom'd to follow that capricious court,—   20
Th' Imperial Synod met; from England there,
Her envoys half th' expected ransom bear;
The rest with willing zeal shall London bring,
When her proud gates again enfold their King.

The Monarch hails his hour of freedom nigh,
And every noble breast is touch'd with joy;
When Henry, rising, with a gloomy look,
Whose fiendish malice wither'd ere he spoke,
Two scrolls unfurl'd: the first display'd to view
The Gallic lilies on their lake of blue;   30
The next—oh! whose the rebel hand might dare
To fix proud England's regal lions there?

" From France and England,—for his nobles now.
To valiant John that kingly name allow,—

Friendship and love these welcome scrolls convey,
With liberal proffers ;—wealth for every day
We guard our captive ; so may discord cease,[b]
And Europe prosper in the shade of peace.
Methinks some short delay, devoid of blame,
Our vows may pardon, and their friendship claim."

 In silence RICHARD heard the words of guile,
His hope sunk low, but scorn enforced the smile ;
" Perjur'd and base !" th' indignant Envoys cry,
" Restore his ransom, or his chains destroy."
When rising with one will, th' Imperial Lords
Touch'd their rich croziers or their glittering swords :
" Have we not sworn ?"[c] a voice of thunder says,
And Henry shrunk from virtue's angry gaze ;
" Nay ! think not I could let dishonour sway,
Delay is all I seek,—a short delay."   50

 " Delay, and reign no more !" The echoes round
Seemed pleased to double the portentous sound ;
When lo, new terrors !—Longchamp entering there,
Deigns no obeisance to th' Imperial chair ;
But briefly greets the Primate of Cologne :
" Now Brother, make this sacred mandate known !"
All stood aghast,—but most was Henry pale,
He knew the golden keys, the Pontiff's seal.

Solemn and slow Rinaldo then began
The dread Anathema, the Holy Ban 60
That breaks allegiance, arms the subject's hand
Against his Lord, and spreads o'er all the land
Funereal gloom; when closed is every fane,
Nor may confession ease the heart of pain.
No sacrament is given, nor prayers are said,
Nor nuptial rites, nor requiem for the dead,
Nor vows baptismal; " and this Curse shall hold
On Cæsar's head, and Austrian Leopold,
Till, moved by fear or conscience, they restore
The English RICHARD to his subject shore; 70
And This on Him who seeks his Brother's life,
And faithless France, till they forego the strife,
Waged in contempt of Clermont's holy laws,
On one, the Champion of his Saviour's cause.
He who for Her nor blood nor wealth has spared,
The Church adopts her son, the Church shall guard."

 Oft had his Sire the Pontiff's power defied,
When his ambitious Lords upheld his pride:
But Henry stood alone, his crimes arise
In ghastly phalanx to his shuddering eyes; 80
He feels the curse :—he seems already chased
From his high throne, and hunted o'er the waste;

His voice was hoarse, his brow convulsed with dread,
While, torn by avarice and by hate, he said,

" Strike off his bonds, and be the Monarch free!—
Most noble King, Count Maynard wends with thee
To bring the ransom back; yet ere thou go,
Embrace in friendship one whom time may shew
True to thy cause, though late he seem'd thy foe."^d

But firm Rinaldo knock'd the chains away,   90
And clasp'd the grateful King; " no weak delay,
" 'Twere folly here another hour to waste,
A steed awaits thee—Oh! be wise, and haste."

And never when at Easter's festal time
He rode to Mass, or in the summer's prime
Chased the fleet stag, such train could Henry's pride
Command, as rode in love by RICHARD's side!
'Twas Christmas, yet December's darkest sky
Has beauty to th' enfranchis'd captive's eye;
Her cheerless snows outshine the blooming spring, 100
Her blasts are sweeter than the zephyr's wing;
They breathe of liberty: but sweeter yet
The Monarch's joy, when at Maguntium met,
Unstaid by age, by distance or alarms,
His bride and mother clasp'd him in their arms;

From England one, and one from favouring Rome,
Arrived to guide their cherish'd Pilgrim home.

Next at Cologne, in her unrivall'd pile,
While music breath'd through every spacious aisle,
Rinaldo's self the solemn Mass has said, 110
And shared with pious hands the sacred bread;
While the loud Anthem swell'd in choral peal,
" Prais'd be the living God, for now I feel
From Herod's hand His Angel saved me; power,
And love, and praise be His for evermore."*—

The Lion Duke, who in his inmost heart
Still mourn'd his Helen, hasten'd to depart,
And wept on RICHARD's breast; but young Louvain
Leads on where Antwerp bounds his rich domain,
And the broad Scheldt runs foaming to the main. 120
No idle speed,—while yet his flying sail
Gleams in the distance, pursuit loads the gale;
Another hour, nor had his regal home
Received the King, nor England known his doom.
But skill'd in all that fits a seaman's care,
The open rock to shun, or shallow snare,

---

* Nunc scio vere quia misit Dominus angelum suum, et eripuit me de manu Herodis, et de expectatione plebis Judæorum." *Hoveden, fol.* 413.—Rinaldo accompanied RICHARD to Antwerp, where, according to Hoveden, the *Rhine* falls into the Sea.

Now Trenchemer joys to steer his long-lost lord,[f]
And Sandwich hails him; thence, by all ador'd,
While myriads weep for rapture, and around
Velvet, and gold, and tapestry hide the ground, 130
He hastes to London; 'twas no purchas'd state,
No heartless homage of the rich and great,
That rais'd the arch of triumph, chas'd the night
With one undying blaze of festal light,
Beneath the palfrey's feet rich carpets spread,
Or from above upon the Monarch's head
Shower'd wreaths, that suit his deathless glory more
Than all the flowers which flaunting summer bore.
His nobles were not there,—in camp or siege*
They fought the combats of their distant liege; 140
It was his people's love—and myriads throng
With shouts of welcome as he rides along.
The meanest bondsman had his hour of pride,
Who o'er the crowd his tossing plume descried,
Thrice blest was he, permitted to behold
His gracious smile, or touch his mantle's fold;

* The historians are particular in remarking, that the rapturous and splendid manner in which RICHARD was hailed at London, was the spontaneous ebullition of popular loyalty. His nobles were all engaged in subduing the rebels, and durst not desert their post, even to welcome their King.

Now "Cœur de Lion" sounds, now "Palestine,"
And not a minstrel wins one cup of wine,
That cannot sing brave Richard's deeds of might,
In Acre's fall, or Arsouf's glorious fight. 150

Admiring, envying, dark-brow'd Maynard cried,
" Had Cæsar known thy London's wealth and pride,
O King! or how her people held thee dear,
Not twice thy ransom would have brought thee here!"g
Yet those whose fame disloyal deeds had stain'd,
In terror heard the Lion's strength unchain'd;
St. Michael's Castellan, whose power defied
A two years siege, but heard him free and died.*
Soon his strong arm redeem'd his Norman reign,
And made each rebel hold his own again. 160
As through his shires in martial pomp he past,
They yielded,—Nottingham resists the last:
Prince David, brother to the Scottish crown,
Nor martial Durham, might reduce the town.
Hark! to their clarions now the valleys ring,
With shouts and clamorous joy they hail the King;
But blind with pride, the traitors madly deem
Those raptures feign'd, and nurse their fatal dream,

* This obstinate rebel is said to have expired with terror, immediately on receiving the news that Richard was again in England.

Till RICHARD's might is felt[h]—beneath his power
The ramparts yield, and justice claims her hour. 170

But Asia calls the muse;—she may not dwell
On RICHARD's thousand acts of fame, nor tell
How once alone in Sherwood's groves he rode,
And met her merry outlaws of the wood.
He fought and quell'd their chief, whose bearing told
A mind as courteous as his heart was bold;
Nor scorn'd the King to share his sylvan cheer,
The river's swans, the forest's fattest deer,
And praise the guardians of the rustic scene,
An hundred bowmen, gay in Lincoln green.— 180
Nor may she sing of him whose jovial soul
And martial spirit lurk'd beneath the cowl;
Her who for love her kinsman's halls forsook,
The arrow guided, and the javelin shook;
Fair as the huntress goddess famed of yore,
Or Venus, when Diana's robes she wore;—
Nor when the outlaw knew his royal guest,
How his brave soul its loyal faith profest:
Oppression, ruling in the Monarch's stead,
Proscribed his name, and drove him to the shade;

Yet had he bravely held the royal wood,
And John's stout rebels fled from Robin Hood.[i]

  Nor how the King, whose wrath his speech disarms,
His manly frankness, and Clorinda's charms,
Gave his free pardon and his lands agen,
And pardon eke to all his merry men;
So they would bind their scatter'd sheaves anew,
And choose them bows of Sherwood's toughest yew,
To wage with beasts inglorious war no more,
But slay the Moslem hosts on Syria's shore.   200

  Nor may she pause on Winton's gorgeous scene,
Where Berengaria and the Mother-Queen,
And Geoffrey, by his brother pardon'd now,
(His loyal aid redeem'd his broken vow;)
Rouen's sage Primate, Erin's, and the might,
Of haughty Durham, unexcell'd in fight;
Ely, and Lincoln, with all virtues fraught,
Himself a model for the faith he taught;
Bold Strigulf-Strongbow, Leicester, Hereford,
And Cestria's Palatine, and Richmond's Lord,   210
All throng the ample choir, a splendid train!
While Priests and Vestals raise the solemn strain;
And RICHARD, great in honours and renown,
With more than former pomp resumes the crown:

And they at Henry's death who loved to tell,
" How the sun set, and yet no darkness fell,
But a new day rose brighter than the last,"k
Exult to see that former dawn surpast.

" And now for Palestine!" the Monarch cries,
While sheath'd in arms his subjects round him rise;
Nor did he doubt to bid his yeomen bear
The dreadful Crossbow; though in Christian war
The Patriarchs of the Church its use forbade,
He might not deem that sage injunction made
For those who, struggling in the cause of heaven,
Used the best means to human wisdom given.[l]
Now from his Mother's kiss, his Bride's embrace,
The tears, the blessings of a loyal race,
The hero bursts away, he mounts once more
The ruddy galley, and forsakes the shore.   230

But lull'd meanwhile in Hassan's fairy bowers,
How sped the youthful Knight's voluptuous hours?
Time glides unfelt, while joy succeeds to joy,
Nor care steals in, nor rapture stays to cloy.
Yet, 'mid unceasing pleasures, Pardo's mind
Seeks for a something that it cannot find;

Longs for that dark and solitary hour,
When calm reflexion reasserts her power.
'Mid roseate bowers, or citron's fragrant shade,
Demands the barren heath, the forest glade;   240
Or that fresh breeze, so purely, keenly cold,
That breathes refreshing o'er the mountain wold.
Oft conscience to his startled soul would bring
A dying mistress, an offended King;
A thousand glorious visions of renown,
Of conquer'd Turks, and Sion's rescued town;
And oft he rose, resolved to use the power
Which bursts the charm, and frees him from the bower:
But ere his trembling lips can breathe the call,
He sees Maimoune, and forgets them all.   250

   Yet once his guardian Saint so strongly stirr'd
The springs of thought, she sung, and sung unheard;
While round the themes accusing conscience woke,
His fancy play'd, scarce weeting that he spoke.

   " What mockery of enchanted wiles is this?
No Paradise, although a bower of bliss.
The blest can ne'er so deep an interest know,
Yet ask in vain the fate of those below.
Perchance dark Hassan not to me has given,
Because I spurn'd him, such delight in heaven,   260

As those who perish in his wars may share
In bowers less green, with houris half as fair."

Surpris'd, alarm'd, his beauteous guard appears
More fair, more dangerous through her gushing tears.
" Ah me! tis sooth that mortals change as soon
As sands or waters, or th' inconstant moon;
Unblest the sprite who loves a child of clay,
Yet has not passions that like his decay:—
Speak! do these gardens pall upon thine eye,
Or is't Maimoune that thou seek'st to fly?" 270

" Thee, thee alone! for ne'er my soul resign'd
Its trust in Him who died to save mankind;
And but for thee, these grots, this fairy bower
Had scarcely held me one reluctant hour.
I blush that thus I staid when duty prest!
I weep to think thou can'st be aught unblest!
Yet here can aught of angel nature dwell,
A murderer's slave, the minister of Hell?
In bliss, alas! we cannot meet again,
I cannot hope that we shall meet in pain. 280
Now then we part—yet could the scalding tears,
Prayer, vigil, toil, the agony of years,
Or even my heart's best blood, thy doom repeal,
Not Egypt's hermits, in their holy zeal,
Devised such penance as these limbs should feel.

Nay, weep not thus, for I must break the spell
Which strengthens by delay—Farewell! Farewell!"
  " Oh, pause! rash youth—one moment—I entreat,
And sue immortal, at a mortal's feet.
Unblest indeed, since first thy race began;   290
When, call'd to bow before the earliest man,
I linger'd in the fount of life to lave,
And draw new beauties from its wondrous wave.
Vainly I hoped his chosen bride to prove,
And teach his new-born heart to beat with love.
Too late I came—th' appointed hour was o'er,
And fell with those that fell to rise no more;
On whom, from all their native birthright driven,
Almighty vengeance shuts the gates of heaven.^m
Too just thy fear we cannot meet again,   300
Thy doom is bliss, and mine, eternal pain!
Yet spurn me not—my hands are free from blood;
Guilty myself, I yet can love the good.
Stern Hassan bade me mould thee to his faith,
And give thee back his slave, or back to death;
I spared, I held thee here,—I could not know
A heart like thine, and work its endless woe.
Then force me not to weep thy youth betray'd,
To see thy pangs, yet want the power to aid;

Nor amulet can save, nor magic rite, 310
Nor all the Genii, for they fear his might.
Oh! spare thyself—and though thy soul may hate
The lost Maimoune, rush not on thy fate."

" That Power, mild Spirit, which has steel'd my heart,
Which stirs within me, and exclaims " Depart!"
Shall it not guard me? 'Tis that meek despair,
That sigh, that pleading look which most I fear.
Too soft, too gentle, thou should'st rather rave,
And call me false, and drag to Hassan's cave;
But I were worthless should I now remain 320
And know thee—what I will not speak again.
And yet shall man, all guilty though he be,
Find hope of grace, and is there none for thee!—
Hassan, I call! Assassin, now redeem
Thy fatal word, and burst this witching dream."

" What hast thou done!" she shriek'd—the thunder peal'd,
Grots, gardens, groves, and bloomy mountains reel'd;
They vanish like a cloud,—a lurid light
Reveals the lone Elburza's desert height,
And Hassan's awful cave;—his leaden eye 330
Beams for a moment with infernal joy.

" Return'd and not convinc'd! if pleasure fail
To bend thy spirit, torture shall prevail:
If thy nice taste Elburza's Eden tire,
Hence, and enjoy her penal caves of fire."
But Pardo heard no more, some force unknown
Snatch'd from th' assassin's grasp, and whirl'd him on,
Till in the midst of Syria's burning sands
He dropp'd, half senseless, from Maimoune's hands.

" Alas! unhappy youth, my power is o'er,   340
Here reigns Demroosh, and I can aid no more;
Saved for an instant, to celestial care
I leave thee now, and Heaven receive thy prayer!"

One moment all was heat and dazzling light,
The next benumbing cold and deepest night;
The morn return'd, and all was changed again,
While fever throbb'd in every burning vein:
Nor guide, nor food, nor cooling spring were there,—
Resign'd to death he knelt in earnest prayer.

" Father of Mercy! may an erring child   350
Draw thy pure eyes to this abandon'd wild?
How did thy liberal hand its blessings pour!
How have I wasted days that come no more!
Alas! enraptured to contend with Hell,
To my own strength I trusted, and I fell!

Yet let my dying lips thy favour move
For him who gave an orphan child his love;
For her whose trusting faith, whose gentle charms
Were still remember'd in Maimoune's arms.
Ah, for that outcast might I yet implore!   360
But to thy will I bow me, and adore."

  Still knelt the warrior, when before him stood
Hassan, the calm, remorseless man of blood.
"Lo, I am here! and dost thou loath my view?
Thou may'st, for I shall claim the vengeance due:
Thou thought'st to shun me, but the linnet, tyed
In silken bondage, has a flight as wide.
Know, I have lived beyond the life of man,
Yet cannot all my power prolong the span,
Unless by deep and frequent draughts renewed,   370
From human veins I drink the living blood.
Choose then, my victim or my slave,—obey
My darkest, worst behests,—enlarge my sway,—
Work midnight murder, drug the deadly bowl,
Know me a fiend, yet yield me up thy soul;
Or by that Power thou fondly call'st divine,
Thine instant life shall be the food of mine."

  "Too idly have I work'd His will, in death
To hope the glory of a martyr's wreath,

Yet gladly will I glut thy brutal thirst, 380
And lingering perish in a rite accurst,"
The youth replied, " if Him whom I adore
Be less than God, or vain the Cross he bore."

He spoke, and kneeling, made the sacred sign,
And strong in faith adjured the Name Divine.

" Ha! mock'd again,—but thou art yet my prey,
For thou shalt weep thy heart's best blood away."

The famish'd locusts strew'd the burning sands,
Their wither'd limbs he piled with active hands;
With magic perfumes rous'd a livid flame, 390
And breath'd 'mid words of power Maimoune's name.

A cool refreshing breeze, a plaintive air
Of wonted sweetness, told the Peri near;
But ah! how changed,—the glance on Pardo thrown,
Which mourn'd his pangs, forgetful of her own,
Was all which spoke Maimoune;—Hassan's spell
From the wild waste had forced her to his cell.
He call'd her perjur'd, bade her then restore
The rescu'd youth, and cross his will no more,
Or meet the vengeance of infernal power. 400
Maimoune smiled, a smile almost divine,
" Heaven's curse I bear, and shall I shrink from thine?

Not all the tortures of thine impious art
Wound like th' undying fire which wraps my heart."

 Wild with delight, his horrid Afrits came
And tore her lovely limbs with thongs of flame;
She shrunk not, strove not, breathed no plaintive cries,
To save those charms for which she lost the skies.
To Carmel then her bleeding form he bore,
Mock'd by those fiends her beauty aw'd before.   410
Then deep in Kaf's eternal ice he rent
A dreadful chasm, and there his victim pent;
And she, perchance, for ages yet to come,
To ruthless winds had wail'd her dreadful doom;
But now the sorcerer, with malicious art,
Would wring with keener pangs her gentle heart:
In thunder told, she knew his hateful will,
And cannot shun, though loathing to fulfil.

 A tear her own worst pangs had fail'd to move,
Fell as she gazed upon her earthly love;   420
And with reluctant, lingering hand disclos'd
Where, wrapt in sleep, Amina's form reposed.
Weak as she seems, with all a mother's care,
Her gentle arms her senseless rival bear.

 Calm was th' Assassin, but a dreadful joy,
A laughing fiend sate mocking in his eye.

"Christian! whose charms thy dastard life ensure,
Hast thou a spell thy minion to secure?
Thou seest what pains rebellious genii wait;
Can mortal virgin hope a milder fate? 430
Behold these gems, that treachery's touch proclaim,
These talismans, that bear her Prophet's name;
Behold, I break them thus! and thou shalt call
On all thy saints for aid, and curse them all;
Shalt see her glut my rankling malice first,
Then waste beside her, waste with want and thirst!"

"So lately taught thine impious boasts are vain,
Inhuman monster! darest thou threat again?
Blest Champion of my native England, thou
That saved thy menaced Sabra, aid me now! 440
Aid in a virgin's cause!" With vigorous hand
The warrior hurl'd the Sorcerer on the sand;
Sternly he grasp'd his throat, nor gave him time
To call his fiends, or breathe one magic rhyme,
Till the dark spirit fled; the wizard frame
Vanish'd in noisome fume, and he became
Like those white bones that, bleaching on the waste,
Shew where the erring caravan has past.

"Great is the Christian's faith!" Maimoune said,
And veil'd in mist the thirsty desert fled; 450

While Pardo rais'd his soul in praise and prayer,
Then with a kiss arous'd the sleeping fair.
She clapp'd her hands; " and am I then," she cried,
" In these dear deserts, and with thee my guide?
Or am I dead, and does thy blessed ghost
Rejoin me here?—for I have mourn'd thee lost."

" Nay, thou fair dreamer! we must leave behind
These cumbrous limbs, ere we can ride the wind;
True, I have dwelt with spirits, been to fame
And duty dead, but wear this mortal frame.　　460
Alas! these wastes, that seem so fair to thee,
These thirsty sands, that know nor spring nor tree,
Will make us ghosts too soon;—but God is great!
Come when it will, we share one common fate."

" Fear not," she answer'd, " I these sands have crost
When food and water, nay our track was lost,
And yet the spring my faithful camel found;
I know the desert signs:"—she gazed around,
Till hope forsook her eye; on either hand
The smooth horizon touch'd the shoreless sand;　470
No scatter'd palms of food or shelter tell,
No patch of verdure marks the distant well;

Nor rocky rift was there, nor deep ravine,
To hide the hoarded rain, or nurse the niggard green;
Nor snake nor lizard, offspring of the day,
Nor the long line that marks the beetle's way;
Nought save that spider, God's peculiar care,
Sole living thing, that seems to live on air.^o
'Twere joy to hear the shakal now, or meet
The dreadful traces of the lion's feet!   480
All, all is silent, save their quicken'd breath,
(The silence and the solitude of death,)
Save when around their limbs the hot winds play,
As if they marvell'd what obstructs their way.
Yet on they roam'd, while still, to stifle fear,
To cheat the pangs of thirst, or chase despair,
Would Pardo tell of Christians brave and proud,
Whose hearts like his to Moslem beauty bow'd;
How Becket's sire in Arab durance lay,
His master's daughter broke his chains away,   490
Forsook her faith, her sire, and natal tongue,
And from their loves the sainted martyr sprung:
Or, how the brother of the English Queen,
Loved by the sister of Mirammolin,
When died his sire, and rebels seized the throne,
Beheld the generous Moor restore his crown;^p

And she recounted how Almanzor's pride,
With stern Seiffeddin, Saladine defied;
And thus anew her hateful nuptials crost,
While wrapp'd in grief she wept her lover lost. 500
And how, as late by glowing noon opprest,
With lute and voice she sooth'd her sire to rest,
Deep stupor came, and all appear'd a void,
Till in the waste she waked by Pardo's side.
She knew not, by Maimoune's spells beguil'd,
How her fond father wail'd his dying child;
Drank her last breath, and in his bosom warms
The senseless semblance of her faded charms.

But thirst consumes them soon, and speech is pain,
Scarce may their tottering limbs their weight sustain,
While growing torture racks the fever'd brain.
A purple haze bespeaks the dread Simoom,—
It comes, it wraps them in its scorching gloom;
Speechless they sink,—they raise the mutual eye,
Hopeless of aid, yet scarce resign'd to die;
While life, now felt but in the sense of pain,
Ebbs from each burning limb and bursting vein.^q

Meanwhile Maimoune in her coral cave
Starts at her image pictur'd on the wave;

"Ah, me! yet I to Heaven and Hassan bow! 520
Those fatal charms—what were they to me now?
One mortal proves how vain each boast I made;
I could not fix him, and I cannot aid!
Thou, sole memorial of my happier days,
Companion of my fall, beloved vase!
I will not waste thy last unsullied wave,
My bleeding brow or burning wounds to lave;
Yet when my limbs th' unpitying Afrits smote,
My heart approved me, and I felt it not.
Oh! if one deed of good, unstain'd with ill, 530
Can yet my breast with aught of sweetness fill,
With fiends accurst must I for ever rove,
And work the guilt I loathe on those I love?
Thrice happy mortals! to th' Eternal ear
Your veriest wretch may lift his hands in prayer,
And know the God that grants not, yet will hear;
But I—I feel the outcast's keenest pain,
Who wish the power of good, and wish in vain.—
Yet oh, celestial drop! that still dost shine,
As ever conscious of thy source divine; 540
Since not my guilty touch, my fruitless tears,
Nor all th' offences of uncounted years

Have spent thy virtue—aid them in their need,
And let these tortur'd limbs for ever bleed."

   She snatch'd the sun-bright vase, and hover'd nigh,
Where in each other's arms the lovers lie.
Now short and heavy came their panting breath,
Their lips are yellow with the crust of death ;
But bending from her cloud, her hands of snow
Cool their stiff limbs, and bathe each burning brow.

   Painful and slow, as when distemper'd dreams
Have crush'd the mind, returning reason gleams ;
Through their parched veins the languid pulses play,
And death unwilling yields so fair a prey ;
Till now they wake to life, their eyes unclose,
With strength renew'd and lighten'd hearts they rose.
While, as she flings the precious drops around,
Wond'rous to tell, where'er they touch the ground,
The thirsty sands a sudden verdure find,
And fruits expand, beneath whose golden rind   560
In clear cool streams refreshing juices flow,
That speak the sacred waters whence they grow.

   For ages bent to earth, Maimoune's eyes
Sought in spontaneous thankfulness the skies.
" Omnipotent ! from one who dare not raise
Her hands in Prayer, accept the voice of Praise!"

She starts! for in her breast a power divine
Allays its pangs, and cries " to Saladine!"
" Oh, joy unhoped! am I permitted still?
I fly, too blest to work thy gracious will."— 570
    Meanwhile from Pardo's hands Amina quaff'd
The juicy melon's sweet and copious draught,
When lo! the pelican—she flies to bring
Her young ones water from the distant spring:
" Behold, my friend!" the Arab virgin cried,
" On! let us hasten—Alla sends our guide."
    Soon has she vanish'd from their anxious view,
But nerved by hope they follow where she flew;—
Vast ridges, heaving like the stormy main,
Oppose their painful progress, but in vain; 580
In vain the flying columns round them rise,
That precious fruit a wond'rous strength supplies.
At length Amina faints: but full in sight,
Rise the near palms, her lover bears her weight;
With day's last beam he reach'd the shady well,
And staggering, at an Arab's feet he fell.
    He woke—'twas Aladin that o'er him bent,
And Mosul's maids that watch Amina's tent,
And Mosul's warriors that, encamp'd around,
Slept by their faithful coursers on the ground. 590

"Oh!" cried young Pardo, while his cheeks attest
Shame, hope, and fear, contending in his breast,
"Tell me if lives my King? what fates befal
Our Christian heroes?—tell me, tell me all."

"Believe me, warrior, that I share thy joy,
Thy Monarch lives, and Jaffa hopes him nigh;—
And then forgive me, if I cannot join
Thy grief, that danger threats the Christian line."

Brief were his words,—the term of truce drew near,
The Soldan bade the Christian host prepare 600
As foes to wait him, or as friends depart;
But the brave Chiefs replied with joyful heart,
"Bear, Heralds, to your lord these words again,
King RICHARD lives, King RICHARD ploughs the main."
He call'd his satraps round, and spoke of war;
But those whose kingdoms lay dispers'd afar
Languish'd for home, and, as with one consent,
Refused their aid, and left the royal tent.
First in revolt the proud Seiffeddin stood,
And Sindgiarshah, and Zenghi's youthful blood; 610
With frequent scrolls in haughty phrase exprest,
They vex'd the Soldan's scanty hours of rest.

He smiled, disdainful of each rebel foe,
Of taunt and threats, and calmly wrote below,
" To what protector would my subjects flee ?
What seeks the Prince who scorns a friend like me ?"

 Truth had its force ; to duty all return'd,
The proffer'd grace alone Seiffeddin spurn'd :
The Soldan wrote, and from an angry heart,
" Base and ungrateful, haste thee to depart ! 620
Ne'er did I stoop thy friendship to intreat,
But thou hast lick'd the sod beneath my feet !
His realm, his life, to me Seiffeddin owes,
I saved him from his subjects and his foes ;
And what the succour, what the thanks I gain ?
The groans of those that curse his iron reign ;
His own ingratitude, his sloth, distrust,
And murmurs, rising like the desert dust.
Go ! revel on in rapine and in strife,
Fear for thy days, and yet provoke the knife, 630
Seek some new rock, beneath whose shade to live,
Again offended, I no more forgive."

 " My sire, alas !" the young narrator cries,
" Yet never knew the Soldan's worth to prize ;
With jealous doubt his lofty soul was moved,
And him distrusted whom it should have loved.

I then was distant, but with all his force,
Inflamed, yet troubled, as he held his course,
I met him, nor could filial fear restrain;
I urged the Soldan's love, his gentle reign, 640
His power of vengeance,—but I urged in vain.

"'Go, willing victim!' was my sire's reply,
'Caught by the serpent's fascinating eye,
Rush on thy doom;—but I no more will bend,—
Go! in his wars thy youthful vigour spend,
Till thou shalt rue the shouts that spread thy name,
When the quick bowstring checks too proud a fame.'

"But could I stoop to feel so mean a fear,
Or think the generous Soldan insincere,
When for my truth my parent he forgave, 650
And in a warm embrace uprais'd his slave?
'Twas then the war resumed;—the Christians ran
To meet our arms, and each was more than man;
But numbers girt them round; each hour their host
Deplored a hero or a bulwark lost.
Now Cesarea falls, the wolves again
Expect their feast on Acre's funeral plain;
O'er the young Ascalon a sable cloud
Hangs, and her bridal vest shall be her shroud.

In vain their guardians seem in love with death, 660
In vain their valour mates thy Monarch's wreath,
For Jaffa's walls are dust;—nine days her tears
May plead with Heaven, but if no aid appears,
Pledged to surrender, all our strife is o'er,
And Christians rule in Palestine no more;
Her warriors must the Soldan's chains endure,—
Behold the troops that make his conquest sure!"

"Ah!" groan'd th' afflicted youth, "my force how slight,
Yet, if my death might save some worthier knight,—
Dear Aladin! on thee my hopes depend, 670
Am I indeed thy captive, or thy friend?"

Around the Arab's tent the palm trees grew;
He culls the dates that seem of richest hue,
And shares them with the Knight, and hastes to bring,
Pour'd in the melon's rind, the bubbling spring;—
"Now by the desert bread, and desert wine,
Which here we pledge, whate'er thou wilt is thine;
Were it the pearls of Indus to bestow,
Or fetch thee ice from Kaf's untrodden brow."

"Then, if my wish be not beyond thy power, 680
To Jaffa lead me, ere her fatal hour."

"An easy boon, for there my duty lies,
And with the dawn we part," the Prince replies.

 Seven nights have past, another noon is fled,
They quit the desert for the forest shade.
The young Amina rules a fiery steed,
And ever loves the foremost band to lead;
Exults in liberty regain'd at last,
Nor shrinks from scorching sun or evening blast.
But as the lovers reach a fragrant dell,   690
Why do their cheeks of fond remembrance tell?
And whence that marble obelisk, which rose
Where from its source the conscious fountain flows;
While as in memory of one rapturous hour,
The jasmine wreathes it with its starry flower?
Above, the arms that Pardo wont to wield,
The helm, the hauberk, and the leopard shield;—
He starts, and blushes with a ruddier shame,
At the brief record of his early fame.

 " Christian or Arab, who shall wander here,   700
To youthful virtue give one generous tear.
Heaven, that his glory might be all his own,
Reveal'd his rank, but kept his race unknown;

And they on Arsouf's plain or Acre's tower,
Who wept his blows or gloried in his power,
Confess'd him born to grace the spurs he wore.
To Cœur de Lion dear, his worth he proved,
Who perish'd, seeking for the King he loved;
And that bright Angel, in celestial flame,
That consecrates each bold Crusader's fame, 710
Amid his martyrs blazons Pardo's name."

" Oh! were it true! oh! had a glorious death,
Had toil, had suffering earn'd the envied wreath!
But wake my soul! regret and shame are vain,
Bright glory hear! I will be thine again."

Thus while he speaks the arms his limbs invest,
He shakes the lance and nods the waving crest;
But in his scarf he wraps the leopard shield,—
" There shalt thou slumber, till to fame reveal'd!
Oh! could I from the world and memory hide 720
My tainted honour, as I veil thy pride!"

But never yet, in all his past career,
Seem'd he so form'd to kindle love and fear;
For Asia's sun had tinged too fair a face,
And time had lent his form a manlier grace;
While round his lips the smile that ever play'd,
Temper'd the fire his piercing glance betray'd.

Amina fondly gazed, then whisper'd near,
While pride and rapture struggled with a tear:

"In the wild waste, thou chosen of my heart, 730
By power supernal join'd, no more we part!
Yet pardon, Christian, if I sometimes feel
My friends, my country, weep thy biting steel;
And when with Kings thou wakest the purple war,
Think there is one Amina bids thee spare."

"Christian, farewell!" the Persian warrior cried,
Thy truant steps will need no farther guide;
And let us hold these hours of concord sweet,—
How shall we feel, brave youth! when next we meet?"

"As friends!" was Pardo's quick reply, "for those
Whom honour rules, in heart are never foes;
They not in malice bid the arrow fly,
And fight for fame,—to conquer, not destroy."

The evening glow was fading into night,
When Jaffa's ramparts met their anxious sight.
The shatter'd towers, the ruins strew'd around,
The turf defaced and worn, the new rais'd mound
Spoke of the strife, while, from the ramparts roll'd,
Its fatal end the yellow standards told;

And on the farther height (a chosen post),   750
Like a crouch'd lion, camp'd the Moslem host.
Yet where, supreme in height, the massy keep
Commands the town and awes the chafing deep,
Still from the church the glittering cross arose,
Still unsubdued St. George's banner flows;
And the red streamers bid them haste to reach
Where a low postern open'd on the beach.
The Christians here their jealous nightwatch hold,
But soon at Pardo's voice the gates unfold;
And Albert clasps him, while a transient joy   760
Glows in his care-worn face and sunken eye.

"Where hast thou linger'd, till we thought thee dead?
Or why return'd, my friend! when hope is fled
And infamy is shunn'd but in the grave?"—

" Why? but to share it, if I cannot save;—
To share their fate for whom I should have died:—
Ask me no farther now, " the youth replied,
" But let me to Matilda's royal care,
And gracious counsel, yield this Arab fair."

" As our best hope, and now alas! our last,   770
This day the Chiefs proclaim'd a solemn fast,
To move offended Heaven—and all our host
(That all how few!) save we that guard this post,

Meet in yon fane; the English Princess shares
The general grief, and mingles tears and prayers
To change the adverse winds;—the morrow's sun
Must bring our gallant King, or all is gone.

 The warrior to the throng'd cathedral drew
Amina, wondering at a sight so new.
Sad was the pomp, for sable clothed around   780
The ancient walls, and sable hid the ground.
Dark, save before the shrine, where tapers beam,
And waving censers shed a ghastly gleam
On many a martial form that knelt below,
Arm'd as for fight, but worn with toil and woe.
White as the novice robes and veil she wore,
The silver Cross herself Matilda bore.
In mourning vests, and shrunk amid the crowd,
Her graceful form with grief and sickness bow'd,
Evanthe, late by every eye ador'd,   790
Seems hastening to the Sire her tears deplor'd.
Before the altar, in the solemn pride
Of highest mass, where gold and crimson vied
With Tyrian purple, saintly Hubert stands,
Swells the loud psalm and lifts his earnest hands:*

* See Psalm lxxix.

" Lord ! in thy Sion now the Heathen reign,
Her dwellings raze, her holiest Temple stain ;
The blood of saints is pour'd her walls around,
Like autumn rain that soaks the thirsty ground ;
And none remain to hide with pious care   800
Their limbs from ravenous beasts and fowls of air.
They taunt our griefs,—they hold our name in scorn,
But shall thy wasting wrath for ever burn ?
Look on our woes, and for thy glory's sake,
Forget our sins : Omnipotent ! awake !
' Where is their God ?' the proud blasphemers say ;
Oh, stretch thine arm and give thy lightnings way ;
Avenge thy servants' blood, thy power proclaim,
Chastise the lands that call not on thy name.
Oh ! hear the captive's secret sighs, and save   810
The victim, destined to th' untimely grave !
Repay their horrid blasphemies, and shew
'Tis thine Almighty vengeance deals the blow.
So we, that are thy people and thy flock,
Shall ever clasp thy Truth's eternal rock ;
To Thee our hymns of peace and gladness raise,
And sing from age to age Jehovah's praise."

So pray'd they, deeming in that wretched hour
The Psalmist's words had yet the holiest power.
Humbled in soul, low sunk each haughty brow,   820
And eyes were wet that never wept till now.
At length in silence, for each swelling heart
Forbade to speak, the mournful train depart.
Screen'd by a pillar, as his comrades past,
Young Pardo watch'd their forms, and follow'd last.
For many a friend his eye has sought in vain!
Long might he seek,—they slumber with the slain!

Where now Matilda dried the silent tear,
By pious hope sustain'd, and earnest prayer,
His knee has prest the ground—she rais'd the Knight
And kindly greets th' expected Proselyte.

"Weak are the words of man if Heaven deny
The grace that saves," was then her meek reply.
"Hundreds could strike the rock, but only one
Drew forth the stream—yet be my work begun.
Nor, damsel, let thy fears suggest that those
Around thee now are aliens, strangers, foes,—
No! think that each her dearest blood would spend
To hail thee as a sister and a friend:
A sister, link'd by those diviner ties,   840
Whose mystic force regenerate bids us rise,

From the pure wave, combined in bonds of love,
One family on earth, joint heirs above.—
And Pardo, to my brother's heart so dear,
This darksome hour thy glad return shall cheer,
A pledge of heavenly grace—oh! may thy Lord,
Like thee lamented, be like thee restor'd."

The morning dawns, but RICHARD comes not yet;—
Can Heaven its own, its once-loved land forget?
The fated noon draws on, and numbers strain   850
Their fruitless glances o'er th' unspotted main.
Ranged in the square the troops already stand,
The keys are seen in Henry's trembling hand,
(Champagne's young Earl, from Acre call'd to bear
His Uncle's truncheon, and direct the war.)
Now groupes of weeping females round them close,
And loud upbraidings mingle with their woes.
" Save us!" they cry, " your wives and daughters save,
From death, or shame more dreadful than the grave."
But they so fierce in battle want reply,   860
Nor speak, nor move, save when th' impatient eye
Turns from the Ocean to accuse the sky.
Already shines aloft th' ætherial fire,
Inch after inch the lessening shades retire;

The proudest towers that flank th' embattled keep
Now scarce withhold one sunbeam from the deep.

"Stay!" Pardo cried, "we have an instant yet!"
And climb'd in haste the loftiest minaret;
While thousands watch'd his lessen'd form on high,
And hope turn'd sickening from his drooping eye. 870
At length it beam'd—"A sail! a fleet!" he cried,
"See the red flag floats proudly o'er the tide."

As when some billow on the troubled deep
Swells with a sullen, silent, solemn sweep,
At once the dusky mountain breaks, it pours
Its sparkling floods of foam, and spreads, and roars.
Thus changed the awful stillness of despair
To murmur'd sounds of joy, and busy care.
Like statue warm'd with life, Champagne's brave lord
Flings down the keys, and grasps his shining sword!
Where Saladine leads on his countless force,
In peaceful pomp, the Herald stops his course,
And tells of RICHARD nigh.—Great Ayoub's son
Mourns for an instant o'er his conquest gone;
Then yields to fate, displays a leader's care,
And bids his trumpets sound the note of war.

Rous'd by th' inspiring call the Arabs throng;
Flush'd with new hope, the Christians pour along.

See him, the Emerald Knight, who long had prest
A feverish couch, again in armour drest! 890
And who is she, that like a radiant fay
Glides towards the gate, and checks him on his way.

 " Pause! though thy heart of adamant deny
To lift thy vizor to a human eye,—
Though deaf to beauty's prayer, to beauty's sigh,
Hear for thyself! Indeed thou must not go,
With wounds half heal'd, to brave so fierce a foe!
Come, let me steal this heavy lance away—
Too rash, too eager, ride not forth to day."

 " And can'st thou, lovely tempter! truly deem 900
That I am cold and senseless as I seem?
Yet ill the Knight would merit beauty's smile,
Whom even her tear from duty could beguile;
It should be beauty's pride, in honour's track
To urge her hero, not to lure him back:—
How for thy grace I languish, how thy spell
For ever wraps me round, no words can tell!"

 " Aye! nor no ear believe," the maid replied,
" With my first suit, so slight a suit, denied."

 " Nay, by St. James! fair nymph, 'tis not to hide
Some face more foul than wizard ever knew—
I boast two eyes, and both of hazel hue;

Nay, ladies, when a boy, would call me fair,
And wreathe their fingers in my clustering hair.
But, for some youthful sin to me 'twas given
To love a maid who changed like April's heaven;
Now full of promise as its sunniest morn,
Now saddening into tears, now dark with scorn;
Hence my rash vow, no more to woman's gaze,
In weal or woe this iron front to raise, 920
Till in that hour, when at the altar shewn,
By holiest rites I claim her as my own.—
Oh, Hermesind! perchance too high I rate,
Duped by fond Hope, thy interest in my fate;
Perchance—yet may I trust that rising flush—
Oh! say not pride or anger prompts the blush,
Nor draw that jealous mantle o'er thy cheek,—
Thy looks must answer, if thou wilt not speak."

Yes! through her heart a crowd of feelings past,
The voice, the seeming scorn explain'd at last; 930
'Twas for her sake he still had shunn'd her eyes
To please unknown, to win her in disguise!—
She trembled, and her eye a tear betray'd,
Joy, shame, remorse, and hope, alternate sway'd.
She sigh'd,—the hand he kneeling sought to clasp
Drop'd unreluctant in his eager grasp;

She strove to speak—when lo ! Ricardo near,
Meets her rais'd eye, the image of despair :
From her bright cheek the crimson ebb'd again,
And trembling Coquetry resum'd her reign.   940

" Indeed ! Sir Knight, thy hopes have blossom'd soon ;
Unsown at morn, and flourishing at noon !
Hast thou some talisman to charm unseen,
Or think'st thou I can love that casque of green ?
At thy first sigh forgive a long neglect ?—
Rate thyself lower, Knight ! and learn respect."

" Unfeeling woman ! trifling to the last,
Aye ! to the end,"—he mutter'd as he past.
She seiz'd his arm ;—he push'd her hand away,
Remounts his steed, and gallops to the fray.   950
Too late repentant, self-abased she stood,
But with forced smiles resumes her sportive mood.

" Ha ! is it thou, Ricardo ? Did'st thou hear
That wayward Knight ? 'tis pleasant thou wert near ;
Of all our damsels me he treats with scorn ;
My glove, forsooth, must not by him be worn,
'Twould taint his honour !—Then the chilling gale
Shifts to the south, and sighs and tears prevail ;
And I may fill poor Honour's place, and then
To his new bride he'll lift his helm agen.   960

Whate'er his charms, as high I'd rate my own,
Nor wed, like Psyche, e'en a God unknown;
But hear'st thou not, my friend,—when I am nigh,
What means that drooping crest and vacant eye?"

" Yes, Hermesind, I heard! nor can thy smile
Again to bliss this breaking heart beguile.
How I have loved thee—with a zeal how strong
Thou know'st too well, and hast abused too long;
I could not fancy, spite of warning fame,
Less than an angel in an angel's frame. 970
To love thee now—or live and love thee not,
Exceeds my power, I bow me to my lot;
Yet sometimes—if in other years thou cast
A pensive glance on days and feelings past,
If then my memory wake one thought of pain,
I shall not live, or love, or die in vain."

Thus as he spoke he closed his helm, to hide
The bitter tears that flow'd in spite of pride.
She clasp'd her hands,—and is he also gone,
And left her to repent and weep alone? 980
Oh Hermesind! not all thy beauty's power
Gave thee one joy were worth this wretched hour.

The battle raged; the worn and wasted bands
Strive with the chosen of a thousand lands.

Where in the conquer'd town a temple rose,
Its ample nave conceal'd a host of foes;
There Hubert's holy zeal the fight began,
Geoffrey, Champagne, and gentle Lusignan;
While in stern order on the Moslem side
Frown'd Aladin, Zorayda, Almahide. 990
Now from the column's shade their arrows fly,
Now for close fight their daggers gleam on high;
Tombs, pillars, shrines, their barbarous hands o'erturn,
They hurl the craggy stone, the sculptured urn;
The broken saints to earth their votaries bore,
And holiest altars float in mingled gore.

Nor on the plain where dauntless Raymond stood,
And Albert's plume is red with Moslem blood,
Less raged th' unequal war; each Christian's mind,
Fearless of death, devoted and resigned. 1000
Yet may they scarce sustain th' o'erwhelming weight,
Another hour, and RICHARD comes too late!

What power detains him?—Pardo climbs again
A turret's height, and scans th' unruffled main:
" Oh God! those ships, that on so proudly bore,
Now turn their towering prows and shun the shore!
Alas! those yellow flags on every post
Deceive the King, and Palestine is lost!

Does Heaven indeed forsake us?"—But he caught,
Even as he breath'd despair, th' inspiring thought:
" One hope remains, one only hope," he cried,
And from that height plunged headlong in the tide!—
Vast was the fall, but mercy deign'd to save,—
Unharm'd he rose, and buffets with the wave;
Redoubled hopes his waning strength supply,—
It fails—but lo! the regal bark is nigh,
First in the morn, but now in flight the last;
O'er its steep side his weary arms he cast:

" Turn, Monarch, turn! thy faithful comrades save!"

He spoke, and sunk exhausted in the wave.' 1020
An hundred arms in instant succour vied,
And snatch'd the fainting hero from the tide,
As Richard to his Leach the Knight consign'd,
Again the willing vessels court the wind;
(While Princes rush to ply the rapid oar),
Crowd all their canvas, and approach the shore.

There slaughter still was rife—by Christians slain
Though twice their number load the crimson plain,
Fresh foes press on:—but where one Christian died
No comrade rush'd to fill the dreadful void. 1030

But two were there, prepared for desperate strife,
By native valour and disgust of life.
Like some commission'd scourge, the Knight unknown,
'Mid lanes of falling foes spurs proudly on;
By wounds, by fever drain'd, again he bleeds,
But feels it not, nor gash nor scar he heeds,
Urged by a sting he cannot leave behind,
The wounded heart, the fever of the mind.
Like him Ricardo—long his tortured soul
Its martial ardour bow'd to Love's control;   1040
Fired by despair a ruthless sword he sway'd,
And hecatombs might curse th' Iberian maid.

   Lorenzo, proud the Gonfalon to bear,
(Given by the Pontiff to the hero's care,)
Waves high its sacred folds, where brightly shone
The Golden Keys beneath the triple Crown;
And many a Chief, whom Arab hosts oppress,
Feels in its sight an omen of success.
Elate with hope young Mirzalis came on,
Whose yellow plumes proclaim'd the Soldan's son;
While one firm hand the gorgeous Standard clasp'd,
Hid in his left the Ataghan he grasp'd:
Lorenzo's heart receives the sudden wound,
He yields his precious charge, and bites the ground.

But Ezzeline, of Este's race, whose steed,
Train'd to the fight, reveal'd Bayardo's breed;
(While, by no chanfron hid, his forehead bore
The milkwhite star that Frontaletto wore)*
Flies to revenge his friend.   With mighty force
The wond'rous steed assaults the Arab's horse;   1060
His better hand engaged, without a shield,
Still scorns the Prince his maiden spoils to yield:
Again his dagger gleams,— the courser's eye
Receives its fatal point, he rears on high,
Breaks through the ranks, impatient of the pain,
Then falls and bears his rider to the plain.
Ricardo rush'd between, "Almighty Power!"
Inly he pray'd, "befriend my closing hour."
Swift fall his strokes, the wintry rains less fast;
Till sorely prest, the Syrian Prince at last   1070
Amid the Mamluke troop the Standard cast;
Then drew his sabre, and by seeming flight
Seeks from its rescue to delude the Knight.
But on he springs, amid the Arab band,
Where now the banner graced Zeineddin's hand;

---

* Bayardo and Frontaletto, the horses of Rinaldo and Ruggiero in the Orlando Furioso. Bayardo was trained to assault the enemy's steed, while his master engaged the rider.

He seized the staff, his sword with sudden sway
Falls on the Prince, and lops his arm away—
Just then his side Moheddin's javelin found,
The wood breaks short, the steel is in the wound;
In triumph once its glittering folds he waved,   1080
Then fell, envelop'd in the flag he saved.

But, watchful of th' event, the Knight Unknown,
With vengeful blade pursued the Soldan's son;
His snow-white Jennet, fleeter than the wind,
Cut short his artful flight, he seized behind
His victim's casque, and with a mortal wound
Divides the throat, then hurls him to the ground.
But soon mild pity calms the Spaniard's ire,
" Fair, valiant youth! I would not be thy Sire."—

" Then meet his father's friend!" Moheddin cried,
" And be thou here for Saladine defied!"
Grief gave the weapon force, the frequent stroke
Through his green helm or high-wrought corselet broke;
A thousand colours dance before his sight,
And all but courage fails the generous Knight.
By mutual wounds their noble coursers slain,
They rise and wage the combat on the plain.
Th' Iberian's limbs no more their burthen bear,
But on his knee he yet maintains the war;

Victorious to the end, he waves around 1100
His sword—Moheddin feels the mortal wound,
Where the stout greaves and polish'd cuirass join:
They fall beside the son of Saladine.

But hark! that panic shriek, that rapturous shout!
See from yon temple pours the Moslem rout!
Whose is the prowess whence the foe retires?
Whose, by the terror which his sight inspires?
Whose, by the godlike port and broomy crest?
Whose, by the Lion shield and silken vest?
Triumphant RICHARD! not the baleful breath 1110
Of the hot pest thus strikes dismay and death!
Where Saladine, sequester'd from the crowd,
To meaner hands the cheap success allow'd;
He hears the shriek, and hastening to enjoy
The fancied glory, sees his army fly!
" And who the Knight on yonder hill?" he cried:
" The King! the King!" an hundred tongues replied;
" The King on foot! then be this steed of mine
Led for his use."—cried generous Saladine.^u

Forth Adel sprang to stop the flying crowd, 1120
" Base slaves! so late of easy laurels proud,
In danger humble as in council loud!

Turn ! if ye love your Soldan's fame," he cries,
Turn if ye love the bowers of Paradise.
And thou, oh Mestoc ! in our palace bred,
Nurs'd with our sons, and with our dainties fed,
Turn for thy faith — that dreadful Giaour defy,
The sun should blush when Mestoc seeks to fly !"

But Mestoc said, " go ! bid that mound of slain
Arise and fight, and be destroyed again !   1130
It is a demon, dreadful in his wrath !
Shall autumn's scatter'd leaves obstruct his path ?"

" My arms ! my arms !" was now the Soldan's cry,
" When fades his glory, Saladine must die."

And now, perchance by some ignoble hand,
The best of Asia's Kings had prest the sand ;
But He the Christian's God, whose mercies shower
Even on the impious that blaspheme his power,
Watch'd o'er his sacred days ; the heavenly will
Maimoune feels, and hastens to fulfil :   1140
Yet she, who when to ruthless fiends a slave,
Still mix'd with balm the envenom'd cup she gave,
In mercy summon'd to a sterner part,
Now weeps each pang she gives a father's heart.
As the brave Soldan, o'er the death-strewn field
Towards England's King his starting steed compell'd,

He sees—oh Alla! 'tis his favourite child,
Senseless and pale, with blood and dust defiled!
His Mirzalis, on whom he sought to place
The crown that Afdhal's elder brows should grace!
He staggers from his steed, his tearless eyes
Fix on the dead, his grief upbraids the skies;
He casts his regal turban to the ground,
Or wipes with fruitless care the stiffen'd wound.
He shrieks, he raves, he clasps th' unconscious clay,
And reason wavers; but the pitying Fay
In soothing Lethe steeps the shaft of pain,
His eyes grow dim, he sinks upon the slain.

 Thick crowds are hurrying past—nor foe nor friend
Paus'd on the ground one casual glance to bend;
His horse alone (which erst Seiffeddin's heir
Had train'd his dangers and his toils to share,
Till he at Arsouf, in the hour of need,
Gave for the Soldan's use the favourite steed,)
Stands o'er his fallen lord; his wistful eye
Turn'd to the throng that pass'd regardless by;
Not now exulting in his yellow crest,
Or burnish'd poitral, but with head deprest;

Till Aladin the golden plumage spied:
" Poor Safie! wherefore art thou here?" he cried.
" Oh Adel! Afdhal! stay and let them live—
Unless their blood these dearer lives could give."—

 All flew to Saladine, and Adel view'd
His senseless form, " There is no wound, no blood."
He loos'd his belt—he felt the living heat
Warm in his limbs, his languid temples beat;
" O, Saladine, my brother and my lord!—
Prophet of Islam! be his life restored!"—
But Afdhal o'er his clay-cold brother kneels,
While down his cheeks the tear unbidden steals. 1180
" Thou did'st not love me, Mirzalis!" he said,
" But I will weep thy death."—He rais'd his head:
" Poor youth! may Paradise be closed to me,
If e'er I grudged my father's love for thee."

 The tide of war rolls near ;—in silent haste
On their good steeds each senseless load they placed;
Their camp is fill'd with foes, and like the wind,
His flying squadrons leave their chief behind.
What roof a shelter to his griefs will give?
Shall he whom myriads ask'd for leave to live, 1090

Even like their Lord whose blood his armies shed,
Find not a spot to rest his weary head?
Not so, sad Monarch! Ramla shall bestow
Her ready shelter, and arrest the foe.
While there he weeps, the royal drum shall sound,
And call again the scatter'd legions round.

END OF BOOK XV.

CŒUR DE LION.

BOOK XVI.

THE HOLY SEPULCHRE.

ARGUMENT.

THE HOLY SEPULCHRE.

Visit of Hermesind to the field of battle—Death of the Emerald Knight and Ricardo—Distress of the Saracens in Ramla, and their vows of vengeance—RICHARD, while reviewing a part of his troops on the plain of Jaffa, perceives the approach of a Moslem Army, and at the same time is informed that Almanzor has attacked the town—He leaves the infantry to sustain the assault of Adel, and hastens with his Knights to relieve the City—He declines the challenge of Zorayda, and overcomes Almanzor—Combat of Pardo and Zorayda—The recognition of Pardo, and death of Zorayda—Meeting of Aladin and Pardo—RICHARD obtains the first victory of Jaffa, and returns to the plain—He kills Mestoc and Schaunah, and disables Adel—The challenge of RICHARD; and second victory of Jaffa—The meeting of Amina and Almanzor after the battle—Bigotry and death of Almanzor—The treaty of Peace—The Princes of both armies assemble in the church of the Holy Sepulchre and swear to observe its conditions—Behaviour of Saladine and RICHARD—The celestial vision—Conclusion of the Poem.

CŒUR DE LION.

BOOK XVI.

THE HOLY SEPULCHRE.

Meanwhile in Jaffa's walls what transports glow!
What festal pomp succeeds the pomp of woe!
The Christians' hopeless tears to rapture changed,
Their King recover'd, and their shame avenged:
While he, rejoicing in their zeal, looks on
To Sion freed, and laurels yet unwon.

    The stars are high in heaven, the moon is bright;—
What lonely wanderer seeks the field of fight?
'Tis Hermesind! her locks all wildly spread,
No mantle wraps her form, no veil her head.   10

Her's not the soul to shake with idle fear,
Yet might a warrior shrink to wander here;
When the pale light in ghastlier horror shew'd
Distorted faces, pale, or dark with blood;
When through their tatter'd scarfs the night-wind sighs,
When the cold beam reflected from their eyes
Gives an unnatural life; and, feasting nigh,
Hark! to th' hyena's laugh, the shakal's cry;
Or the low groan, the gasp, the rattling breath,
Where still some suffering spirit strives with death. 20
And now the rush of wings—her footsteps near,
From their dire feast the heavy vultures scare!
What horrors spread below?—ah! look not there.
Her brow is fix'd in anguish, but her eye
Gazed on the dead as if on vacancy;
There were but two on all that sanguine plain
Whose sight could wring her guilty soul with pain.

   All day she watch'd—they came not, and the cry
Of hope, despair, delight, and victory
Fell cold upon her sense. Could conquest cheer 30
Her self-accusing soul, if blood be there?

   The slippery field beguiles her hurried tread,
She wades in gore, she stumbles o'er the dead.

One wretch, convulsed in nature's latest gasp,
Seized her loose robe—she frees her from his clasp,
But stops not on his livid brow to gaze,
Though well that face was known in happier days.

   She reached a spot with thicker carnage spread;
There headless trunks and limbs dismember'd laid,
Coursers, that perish'd where their masters died,   40
Turbans and sabres, helms of knightly pride,
Shields where the bloody Cross dishonour'd shone,
And crescents, glittering in the kindred moon.
On all she looks, but pauses not, her mind
Fix'd upon those she seeks, yet dreads to find;
Pale but unshrinking—lo! where yonder beam,
From that bright helm awakes an emerald gleam!
She shrieks—her grasp her burning brow comprest,
But goading conscience urged severer haste:
She sinks beside the Knight; her hurried hands   50
The vizor raise, and loose the helmet's bands;
With patient toil she chafes his lifeless head,—
Oh! is that cheek with mortal paleness spread,
One that once mantled in her smile, and took
Its form, its colour from her changing look?
Is that closed eye the one that proudly shone,
Speaking each thought, nor droop'd but at her frown?

Those curls—the casque's incessant weight had worn
Their auburn beauty, but in youth's gay morn
How had she loved (so pride confesses now) 60
Their sunny radiance and luxuriant flow!
She looks, till other years revive again,
A flood of tears relieves her burning brain:
And see! upon his breast, like marble cold,
Warm as they fall, his languid eyes unfold,
Then closed, as if some hateful sight to hide,
" Hence! let me die in peace," he faintly sigh'd,
And give at least my parting thoughts to heaven." 70

" No never, never, till by thee forgiven;
Though here I perish, kneeling at thy side,"
With broken voice the sobbing maid replied.
" Yet—yet thou liv'st—and if the skill be mine,
Which once—nay, wherefore that impatient sign?
If e'er thou loved'st me, do not scorn my aid;—
Thou can'st not wish thy blood upon my head."

" Oh thou fair Syren! can'st thou yet deceive?
Thou dost but speak, and I again believe!
Yet here thy aid were vain—I know of old
The smart of wounds, but now my heart is cold.
Yet there is one—and he may linger still, 80
On yonder mound—there, there renew thy skill,—

His blood is heavier on thy soul than mine;
Again those eyes in borrow'd light must shine!—
What! can it be so hard once more to feign?
Oh Hermesind! if it be now a pain,
Be it thy penance—soothe his parting hour;
Or should thy cares his fleeting life restore,
Confess thy faults, and if he love thee still,
Then be thou his, and study all his will.
Heaven treat thy wrongs to me, as thou art true 90
To what I charge thee now—Oh, God!—adieu."—

  Yet still she holds his head,—she lingers there,
Pale as himself, a statue of despair.
Again his eyes unclos'd—no word he spoke,
But oh! the pointing hand, th' upbraiding look.
" And must I leave thee, ere thine hour be past?"
She hears a sigh, and feels that sigh his last,—
Then 'mid the bitter tears that gush'd so fast
She sees not where her reckless footsteps tread;
Weak, trembling, pale, she staggers o'er the dead.
A voice breathes low—the cold, the sense of pain,
Had waked Ricardo from his trance again;
Her whisper'd name arrests her startled ear,
" Oh, once again!—yet can I wish her here?"—

He sees her at his side—In life's last throe,
Can then the soul such heavenly rapture know?
O'er him she bends, her eyes in sorrow swim;
Those precious tears! and are they shed for him?
O'er his pale brow a sudden crimson past,
" Sweet Hermesind, I thought this hour my last, 110
But oh! thou com'st to cheer me and forgive,—
How can I perish, if thou bid'st me live?"

" Live then! this hour shall Heaven attest my vow,
I dare not trust my changing fancies now;
Live! and by holiest ties I pledge me thine;
If not—yon convent is thy grave and mine;
There will I o'er my wretched victims moan,
Bewail their death, and fit me for my own."

She look'd, the transient glow had left his cheek,
He gazes still, and strives in vain to speak, 120
But to his lips her yielded hand he prest,—
A smile proclaim'd his parting spirit blest.

In Ramla's walls the Soldan's scatter'd powers
Meanwhile convene, and throng her narrow towers.
The first false daybreak, faintly seen afar,
Called to the Mosque the leaders of the war;

There camphorous torches half dispel the gloom,
And all Sabæa fills the spacious dome;
While he whom Asia's thousand thrones obey'd,
Wrapp'd in the tarnish'd robes of grief, and laid
On a high bier, with funeral white o'erspread,
Weeps o'er his slaughter'd child. The Imaums there
Awake the Koran's holiest rites of prayer;
They laud th' Eternal God, an endless theme,
Creator, Ruler, Merciful, Supreme.
Blest had they said no more, nor while they own
Th' Almighty Sire of Heaven, denied the Son,
Nor for the promised Paraclete adored
Th' Impostor's name, th' Apostle of the sword!

  Now stung with rage, as less by grief subdued, 140
Full in the midst gigantic Adel stood,
Completely arm'd, while high his triple plume
Like some pale meteor shone amid the gloom.

  ". Enough! for Mirzalis our tears are shed;
To death and silence let us yield the dead,
And wake to vengeance. Gracious Saladine,
Shall yon bright sun upon our shame decline?
So many leaves of golden glory past,
Shall our stain'd annals write in tears at last,

'Behold, one Christian landed, and we fled,   150
While unavenged the seed of Joseph bled!'
Forbid it shame, forbid it Him on high,
Who holds th' eternal scroll of destiny;
And hark! those clamours—they announce a band
Now fresh from Egypt's unexhausted land,
Untaught to tremble—wilt thou waste their zeal,
Nor prove this fiend accessible to steel?
Oh! as his impious deeds shall surely shine
In Sejjin, record of the wrath divine;[a]
As never he in Eden's streams shall lave,   160
Nor quaff by Alla's throne of Tasnim's wave;
I call to war, and in the Prophet's name
I breathe the curse that dooms defeat and shame."
He paus'd, and raising high his clenched hand,
Cast towards the Christian camp th' opprobrious sand,
" The curse of Beder, where the Koreish fled;
Confusion, Death, upon his impious head."[b]

Slow rose the aged Soldan, whelm'd with fate,
" See here how little Azrael spares the great!
The dark and narrow home, the simple shroud   170
Are all that wait the wealthy and the proud;
And let us reap the lesson, taught to know,
Perchance his next dread summons calls our foe.

But this frail arm no more the lance may wield—
My brother, lead my squadrons to the field."

  Almanzor frown'd : " Upon th' accursed tower
I fought, I bent before that dreadful Giaour ;
Behold this scar ! my turban, ne'er before
Profaned with dust, was crimson with my gore ;
Behold this belt ! the pledge of mortal fray,—   180
When next we meet the wolf shall find his prey."

  " A stronger claim is mine," Zorayda cries,
" The wrongs which feed a hate that never dies."

  " And mine," cried Afdhal, " Christian blood shall rain,
And orphans' tears embalm my brother slain."

  But Mestoc, blushing for his recent flight,
Fell prostrate : " Adel, lead us to the fight !
Oh ! Saladine, forgive thy guilty slave !
Wealth, honours, power, to me thy bounty gave ;
Rais'd from the dust to stand beside thy throne,   190
What but his life can Mestoc call his own !
That life I here devote ; in Alla's eye,
And Islam's cause, I vow to kill or die."

  Fired by new succours, while they thus prepare
By one dire blow to end the lingering war,

King Richard views his troops, alarm'd to find
That scarce a tenth of those he left behind
The sword had spared, and on the open shore
Arrays the little band his vessels bore;
His kingdom's troubled state allowed no more. 200
Five hundred yeomen; half could bend the yew,
Half bore the cross-bow, and the quarrel drew;
And ten brave knights—yet each himself an host,
In later years had been a nation's boast.

While there in sport they practise on the plain,
Nor deem the routed foe could form again,
They mark a thickening cloud, and hear the sound
Of distant drums, and steeds that shake the ground.
Soon Richard's skilful eye their numbers knew;
Seven thousand strong, and his brave troops how few!
An instant's pause decides—with cheerful air
He bids them form th' impenetrable square:
The kneeling front a hedge of pikes present,
Next o'er their heads the ready archers bent;
Erect behind, the tallest yeomen stand,
The dreadful cross-bow charged in every hand.

" Comrades, be firm !" he cries; " a warrior knows
His own desert, nor ever counts his foes;

Danger is fame! not always shall belong
Wreaths to the swift, nor victory to the strong;
Heaven holds the balance, and at will supplies
Wit to the foolish, or confounds the wise.
Be fix'd, be motionless; sustain their shock,
Nor wounds must tempt, nor keener taunts provoke:
The first that stirs shall die, since he who draws,
In private battle, risques the general cause.
Expect my word,—no useless javelin cast,
Nor on the foe one guiltless arrow waste;
Till from your pikes recoils the startled steed,
And death may fly on every slender reed." 230

He spoke; the weak grew strong, the coward bold,
A general shout their cheerful ardour told:
They knew their Monarch, and his single might
Was more than thousands in the hour of fight.
But as the dusty cloud approaches near,
And the loud music swells distinct and clear,
An Envoy speaks, by RICHARD heard alone,
"While here you ride, Almanzor storms the town!"
" Peace! on your life," the prudent King replied:
" Soldiers be firm! for further aid I ride, 240
But will not linger:"—to his side he calls
The knightly ten, and gallops to the walls.

Already on the south the combat raged,
And brave Champagne superior force engaged.
Where, through the batter'd walls they forced before
Their bloody way, again the Arabs pour;
Almanzor heads their fierce assault, nor heeds
What dangers threat, or how the battle bleeds.
Half heaped with stones, the moat is choaked with slain,
The crumbling towers a second siege sustain;   250
When RICHARD, entering by th' unguarded north,
Spurs through the town, and leads the Christians forth.
Their sally daunts the foe, their shouts confound,
And turbans fall, and blood is streaming round;
While, dreadful as the desert winds that sear
The reddening harvest, and defraud the year,
He smites the faltering crowd; his coal-black steed
O'er dead and dying bounds with reckless speed,
Champs his rich curb, and shakes his glossy mane,
Rejoiced to bear his royal load again.   260

   Still unrelenting in his fierce advance,
Young Hamsa perish'd on his rested lance;
He drew it back, and though at random cast,
Through stern Mozaffer's lifted arm it past,
And pierced Khorazin. Zulemah beheld
His father's fall,—and, firm in grief, impell'd

The heavy spear; aside the Monarch sprung,
And in his courser's woven mail it hung.
He rear'd his mace,—that mace whose iron weight,
Studded with horrid spikes, was instant fate; 270
Struck with new fear, the youth retires in vain,
A shapeless mass he tumbles to the plain.
Again the mace was rear'd,—Abdallah nigh,
Benumb'd with terror, lost the power to fly:
His angel saved him—for the Monarch's eye
Fix'd on stout Richmond, who dismounted stood
Against a host, and dyed the field with blood.
He seized a Persian charger's golden rein,
And hurl'd the startled rider to the plain;
Mounts the brave Earl, then rushes on the band 280
That fell like grass before his mighty hand.

Soon, as with undistinguish'd carnage tired,
His noble soul a worthier foe requir'd,
Zorayda saw;—in vain her lover tried
To check her course, and generous Almahide;
Impell'd by fate, or by a woman's pride
To veil her fears, " No ! no ! to me belong
The risk, the fame, and justice makes me strong.
Oh thou !" she cried, " in virtue's specious name,
Who stabb'st the trusting friend, the virgin's fame,

RICHARD OF ENGLAND, now for fight prepare,
A victim calls, and vengeance guides the spear,"—
 " There breathes not one whom RICHARD ought
   to fear :"
Firmly he answer'd ; when before him stood

The blood-red knight of Arsouf's magic wood.
For once the ruddy glow his cheek forsook,
And in his grasp th' Armoric falchion shook ;
" No, not with thee ! for thee my heart has bled,
Lost as thou art, thy blood I cannot shed."

 Zorayda's laugh hysteric burst to hide 300
How conscience strove with hatred and with pride :
" Ha ! this is well ! 'twere poor to see thee bleed,
To see thee tremble is revenge indeed ;
The Lion's hide reveals the Hart below,
And CŒUR DE LION fears—a female foe !"
 " Hence, hence from honour's field !" the King
  replied,
" Hence ! in the harem's secret chambers hide ;
False to thy God, apostate to thy sex,
Go, where thy sight no Christian eye may vex.
What though thou know'st that, true to knighthood's
  vow, 310
I will not write thy guilt upon thy brow,

Dread, lest again th' offended skies should flame,
And Heaven's red bolt bear witness of thy shame."

 She strove for speech, but Aladin detains
Her gentle steed, her rash design arraigns :
" Not for my sake, but for thine own, retire;
His skill, his strength, a manly arm require.
Cold as thou art, to me this fight belongs—
The slave at least may feel his lady's wrongs."

 His generous zeal the Monarch's pity draws; 320
" Brave youth! thy worth deserves a better cause."
Rejoiced, he saw Almanzor's headlong speed
Before the Prince impel his snorting steed.

 " Turn, braggart! less than woman, turn! for now
My jewel blushes on thy recreant brow.
Turn, 'tis a fight which thou art sworn to bide."

 " And one I would not shun," the King replied.

 Now here, now there the well taught chargers wheel;
The helmets ring and gleams the azure steel;
But RICHARD, as in martial pastime cool, 330
Prevents th' intended stroke, and fights by rule :
While, urged by wounded pride, his fiercer foe,
Intent to give, forgets to ward the blow,
And bleeds at many a wound. Not oft avail
His deadly thrusts to pierce the Norman mail;

While Caliburn, where'er its edge descends,
Divides the buckler and the corselet rends;
Yet, with each wound Almanzor's fury grows,
And swift and swifter fall his deafening blows.
Long hung the doubtful fight, till RICHARD's mind,
Oft wandering to the band he left behind,
Impels th' impatient steel; the Arab's vest
Receives the blow, it pierced his mighty chest.
Inly he bleeds; his waning strength he feels;
Before his eyes the fading landscape reels;
Yet either hand the dreadful sabre bore,
Despair and torture prompt one effort more,
Where o'er the Monarch's pliant hauberk roll'd,
On his rich scarf the lion grins in gold:
But RICHARD leap'd aside—the mighty thrust   350
Baulk'd of its aim, Almanzor bites the dust.

 Brave Pardo mark'd his fall; in thought he hears
Amina's shrieks, and sees her flowing tears;
While the fierce King the sorrowing Arabs chaced,
Their dying leader on his steed he placed,
And bore to Jaffa's walls; but dares not stay
To kiss the flood of filial grief away:
Once more he gives his eager roan the rein,
And breathing war, he gallops to the plain.

He meets Zorayda, lost in troubled thought,   360
Not now, as late among the first she fought;
But mused apart—" If with no braver Knight
Engaged to meet, thou shun'st promiscuous fight,
Here let our swords our mutual prowess prove,
And try the combat for our ladies' love."

" Behold my mistress here!" she fiercely said,
And rais'd her shield : it bore the Gorgon's head.
" Would it could turn thy hated race to stone :
Revenge and hate are all the loves I own.
But words are vain; What stripling he, who dares
To brave that arm which CŒUR DE LION fears?
Thy mien is noble; but that ample shield—
Has treason stain'd its badge, or why conceal'd?"

" And would'st thou, warrior! of my birth inquire?
The Church my mother, and this sword my sire;
I knew no parent's care; this shield alone—
But no! I would not it should make me known,
Till the first Prince might wish me for his own.
And for the rest—these spurs a Monarch gave,
A proof he loved me, and believed me brave.   380
For thee, thy speech and arms betray that those
With whom thou combat'st, should have been thy foes;

But I inquire not, lest thy lips declare
A name some noble race might blush to hear.
  " Presumptuous boy!" she said, " methinks thy tongue
Should be less bold, unless thy lance be strong."
  They wheel'd around, and met in short career,
Backward he bent beneath her powerful spear;
But his light lance has broken on her shield—
Taunting she flung the fragments on the field.   390
" 'Tis well, stout champion!—next thy sword should shew
If aught but words be thine to wound a foe."
  " Nay, courteous Knight! behold its azure sheen,
I would not that my wit were half so keen."
They closed in fight, Zorayda fought with all
A warrior's strength, and more than warrior's gall.
For woman, when she bursts the bounds assign'd
By Heaven and nature, no restraints can bind;
As some fair garden, should its fence decay,
Becomes to wolves and ravenous birds a prey,   400
Fruits fade and flowers, while weeds accurst and vile,
With rampant vigour choke the fruitful soil.
Thus droop the Virtues, thus, without control,
All the fell Furies riot in her soul.

But Pardo, proud of his excelling skill,
Proud of a steed that seem'd to guess his will,
Wheels here and there; each lawful vantage took,
And now eludes, and now prevents the stroke;
Nor fought by knighthood's strictest laws alone,
But gave to combat graces all his own. 410
Alas! his soul is buoyant with delight;
Nor sees where laughing demons watch the fight,
Nor deems he soon shall curse that fatal hour,
And, lost in grief, bewail his falchion's power.

Zorayda maddening to be thus withstood,
And madder yet to see her flowing blood,
With hasty impulse waves her weapon round,
And his unguarded knee receives the wound.
Slight was the hurt; but, at th' unknightly blow
His anger rose; he rushes on the foe. 420
While her fierce charge his lifted buckler bore,
Beneath the heart his weapon drinks her gore,
And from her steed she sinks, to rise no more.
But on inclement Thule's wondrous coast,
When high to Heaven the steamy jets are tost,
Not swifter, when the hidden fires subside,
Within its basin sinks the calm clear tide,
Than Pardo's burst of sudden fury died.

He kneels beside her: "Warrior! 'tis the hour
When earthly things should fix the soul no more, 430
And Mercy, pointing to her native Heaven,
Bids us forgive, that we may be forgiven.
Perchance thy soul in secret holds her faith;
Still pious rites may soothe the pangs of death,
And Holy Church receive thy parting breath."

 She heeds not, but in either trembling hand,
With shorten'd hold she grasps her shining brand;
In haste he rais'd his shield,—with feeble sway
The treacherous blow but rent its veil away,
And a broad burst of brighter light reveal'd   440
The spotted Pard upon its azure field.
He points his sword; "'Twere madness now to spare."
But with a thrilling shriek, she cries "Forbear!"
And senseless sunk,—it seem'd her latest gasp;
His pitying hands her tight-drawn helm unclasp,
While, from their net of gems and gold unbound,
Her long black tresses flow'd upon the ground.
He props her on his knee, amazed to trace
The softer moulding of a female face,
Whence hate's unnatural scowl had parted now,   450
Though death and horror bathe her livid brow.

Breathes she no more?—ah yes! her labouring breast
By starts the throe of inward pain confest,
The crimson flush'd and flitted on her cheek,
There is some grief she would, but cannot speak;
Death claims her soul, and yet it will not part
Till that dread secret ease her bursting heart—
" Relentless Heaven! it waits but for a time
That sterner justice may o'ertake the crime.
Thus should my tainted blood indeed be spilt,— 460
Thus by my Child—the offspring of my guilt."—

" What words are these?" he cried, " Oh! speak
   again!
Or let me think them phrenzied dreams of pain.
Great God! on either side is madness now—
Speak, if thou can'st—who am I? who art thou?"

" Let me embrace thee first, and on thee cast
A mother's gaze—my earliest and my last.
Nay! look not thus—what though thy hands be red,
'Tis by my guilt that now my blood is shed,—
I scoff'd—I would have braved it to the end; 470
But vengeance rules, and even I must bend.
No more of my dishonour'd race inquire,
Suffice, an English Monarch was thy sire.

My parents bade him train me up in truth,
He should have guarded, he abused my youth;
That crime be his—'twas mine my guilt to hide,
Bound as I was, his son's contracted bride.
I listen'd vows that injur'd son preferr'd;
I knew them impious, yet I heard, I heard,—
And when his breaking heart, my falsehood known,
Forbore reproach, intent to veil alone
My shame, and save my honour by his own,
My hate pursued him—but the die is cast;
Once warn'd—th' avenging bolt has fall'n at last."

" Fall'n, fall'n indeed,"—a well known tongue replied.
'Twas CŒUR DE LION, weeping by her side.
" Oh lost Alasia!—nay, one instant hear,
For thine eternal weal, a voice once dear.
I come not one reproving glance to cast,
Oh! think not on this life, for that is past,— 490
What are our passions in the silent home?
What all this little world to that to come?"—

" Forbear, forbear!" she sternly cried, again
Her spirit rising over death and pain;
" There are but two whose eye my soul would shun,
Whose sight could vex in death—and thou art one.

I want no counsel, and could not unveil
To some dull priest my circumstantial tale,
That he may give, at lost Alasia's name,
With wink and shrug a royal house to shame,   500
And boast how all upon this changing scene
Meet sin and judgment—I, by birth a Queen!^c
And if I cannot, like some Sovereigns, kneel ^d
To pale-faced monks for stripes I scorn to feel,
Still less I deem that prayers in dying hour,
Or priestly pardons, have salvation's power.
Curse on such arts—and curse on those who live
In watching pangs for which they feign to grieve:
Hence!—she now mistress where I once was dear,
May chide those drops so idly lavish'd here—   510
If I have lived unworthy of my sire,
Worthy of both my lovers I expire,
The interdicted King—the parricide,—
Oh! start not thus, my child, my child," she cried.
" That fatal word—it was not meant for thee,—
Thy hands are guilty, but thy soul is free.
Oh! I am faint—th' avenging skies that gave
Years undesired, deny the hour I crave;
But justice, when it bids my ghost endure
Its doom of torment, shall proclaim thee pure,— 520

Abandon'd, sought so long, and known too late,—
It was not thou that seal'd Alasia's fate."

Around his neck she hung, to hide the strife,
The last convulsion of contending life;
Nor sigh nor groan her parting tortures tell,
Till in his arms a senseless load she fell.
" Oh dreadful end!" the shuddering Monarch cried,
" Unhallow'd hour!" the weeping son replied.

But prest no more by RICHARD's arm of might
The Moslems rally and renew the fight. 530
" Rest here, poor youth, and ease thy bursting heart,
Mine is a warrior's and a Monarch's part."
He said, his vizor o'er his face he drew,
And on the foe with double fury flew.

But Pardo, deaf to all that once had charms,
The shrill voiced trumpet, and the clang of arms,
Regardless now of who might win or die,
Lost in that grief that knows nor tear nor sigh,
Gazed on the form that still his arms enfold,
Pale as herself, as motionless, as cold. 540
Till speaking loud in grief and wonder near,
A well known voice arous'd his startled ear.

" And have I sought thee o'er the plain," it cried,
" To find thee thus, the dark Destroyer's bride?—

Pardo—I will not linger now, to know
Why thou usurp'st my privilege of woe,
But, by thy Knighthood, who has struck the blow?"

"One, who to save her should have welcom'd death,
Her child has pierc'd the mould that gave him breath."

"Her Child!" cried Aladin, with mantling brow—
Zorayda's Child!—but that is nothing now:
Where lurks the monster, that my hands may tear
And give him piecemeal to the fowls of air?"

"Oh! but for one sad duty to fulfil,
And one sweet flower that clings around me still,
How gladly would I rush upon thy sword,
And lose at once a being—now abhorr'd:
Prince—in a parent's precious gore embrued,
Ne'er shall this steel be wet with other blood:
A mournful relic to my latest hour— 560
Spare then, or strike me, I am in thy power."

The Prince a moment paus'd—a deathlike dew
Suffused his frame, and hoarse his accents grew.—

"No! no! I strike not him who shared my bread,
For one—but let our thoughts respect the dead!
If thou art guilty, live! thy curse is life—
If error struck, I have no cause of strife.

Fulfil the mournful rites, I could not bear
To view those eyes, and find no meaning there.
Zorayda! while the bitter shower I shed,   570
I'll think thee pure, and but bewail thee dead,
I'll rush to fields so often shared with thee—
Perchance some quiver holds a dart for me."

Meanwhile the fight is won; their leaders slain,
The routed Moslems hurry from the plain—
" Now, Raymond! Albert! now your forces join,
Press on their rear, pursue, destroy, confine!"
The Monarch cries, and leaves the finish'd fray,
With double wreaths to crown one glorious day;
Where his brave archers on the distant plain,   580
Unconscious of the fight, a tenfold force sustain.

Three times the foe had charged his heroes there;
Three times had broken on th' unshrinking square;
Their steeds recoiling from that hedge of spears,
Whose every point a waving pendant bears.
Three times the baffled chiefs had ridden round
The equal sides, nor point of vantage found:
In vain their taunts or steely javelins fell,
Scorn smiled at those, and these their shields repel.

Again they come, the charge stern Adel leads,
And swarthy Mestoc, fam'd for daring deeds:
Full on the pikes they urge their generous steeds;

Drum, cymbal, trumpet, join their martial sound,
And dust in volumes veils the squadron round.
But still from every pike the pendants stream,
Still shines through mist the iron's deadly gleam;
The coursers start, obey nor spur nor rein,
But break their ranks and riot o'er the plain.
" Be fate upon thy point," fierce Adel cried,
And flung his dart,—it pierced Llewellyn's side; 600
Next, calm in silence, powerful Mestoc threw
His heavier spear, that youthful Harold slew.
" Now, Charge!" he shouted, " Charge! the day is
  ours;"—
But Sherwood's archers pour their iron showers
With aim so true, that where their comrades died,
A mound of slaughter'd Ethiops fills the void.
 As daring Mestoc aims another wound,
His head, his arm fall sever'd to the ground;
'Twas Cœur de Lion's blow—so swift he came,
His deeds alone the matchless King proclaim. 610
The faithful steed, affrighted, bathed in gore,
Through shuddering ranks their headless leader bore.
While fear and wonder fill the shrinking host,
Grief swell'd in Schaunah's brother bosom most;

Dark as a cloud when big with autumn rain,
And towering o'er the height of vulgar men;
On foot he fought, while from the burthen freed
Of his huge bulk, reposed his weary steed.
A groupe of spears his slaves attentive bear,
He chose the weightiest, one that few could rear, 620
And backward bending, as he aim'd its course,
That all his body's weight might aid its force,
Hurl'd at the King—it pierced each stubborn fold
Of his tough shield, his surcoat wrought with gold,
Pierced his stout hauberk, but his vest beneath,
Stiff with embroidery, check'd th' approaching death.
He cast the frustrate weapon on the sand,
And snatch'd a crossbow from a yeoman's hand;
The well aim'd quarrel flies with hissing sound,
And Schaunah's eye receives the torturing wound. 630
Bleeding and blind, and giddy with the pain,
He drops his shield, and staggers o'er the plain,
When through his casque a second arrow flies,
And pierced the brain—he bites the ground and dies.

Incensed to see his loved Egyptians bleed,
The royal Adel spurs his chesnut steed!
He foams with rage, and bids his Prophet hear
His vows of vengeance, lost in empty air.

For soon the powerful quarrel check'd his pride;
His better arm hangs useless by his side; 640
And where the jewell'd rein his fingers grasp,
A second fixed it in their nerveless clasp;
A third—though hung with glittering fringes round
His charger's neck received th' unerring wound:
Mad with the smart he gallops from the plain,
Nor can his powerless lord his flight restrain.

 Strange was the conflict—gazing on the King
Like some fell tiger, crouching ere he spring,
The Christians wait, while one brave chief defies
A mighty army, and that army flies— 650
Yet, as when rocks the hunted stag oppose,
If bold through fear he turns, and fronts his foes,
Then baying dogs and archers gird him round,
But stand at distance, lest his antlers wound.
So forms the host aloof; and darts are thrown,
And stones and arrows shower'd on him alone:
But like that stag when insect swarms assail,
From helm and shield he shakes the dreadful hail.
He couch'd a lance, and while his broomy crest
Flamed in the splendours of the purpling west, 660
While from his arms ten thousand glories shine,
Singly he rides along their crowded line;

" Hear, Asia, hear! 'tis ENGLAND claims the fight,
'Tis ENGLAND's lance defies your proudest knight!
Sons of the East! who boast yon glorious flame
Inspires your valour, shall his parting beam
Bear to our Western Isles the tale of shame?
Breathes there not one for Islam's sake to meet
His Prophet's foe, and veil his Faith's defeat."

   Ye generous Sons of Ayoub, had you heard,   670
What grief were yours! for not a warrior stirr'd—*
Awhile the Monarch paus'd—then backward drew;
" Now pour your darts," th' obedient arrows flew,
While from the arbalist, with deadlier weight,
The iron bolts shower fast, and scatter fate.
If Christian priests pronounced those weapons curst,
Well might the Moslem crowd who felt them first,
By secret fears already urged to flight,
Deem them some engine of infernal might,
On Acre's plain and Arsouf's taught to know   680
The wondrous force of England's antient bow;
A deadlier curse was here—they break, they fly—
The bolt pursues them, and in flight they die.

   * It is here that Gibbon exclaims, " am I writing the History of Orlando, or of Amadis?"

"St. George for England—Charge!" exclaim'd the King,
And from the ground his eager warriors spring.
Their bows are cast to earth, their falchions gleam;
But soon in blood was quench'd the azure beam.
In vain contending with his adverse fate,
The Soldan sounds retreat,—but sounds too late,
'Twas headlong flight; while, pouring from the town,
Each Christian joins to hunt the Moslems down;
Once, since the dawn, with signal victory graced,
Their pious zeal a second harvest blest.
There was the martial prelate, Raymond's sword,
Champagne and Nevile, Winton's gallant Lord;
Grenville and Mortimer, and Lusignan,
Mauléon, Multon, ever in the van,
And stout De Mauny, whose descendant's name
Calais and Poictiers give to lasting fame.*
But ever first the matchless RICHARD flew; 700
Now for some chosen foe the quarrel drew;
Now bade some wretch his flying javelin feel,
Or plied untired the unrelenting steel.

* The readers of Froissart will not require to be reminded of the achievements of Sir Walter Manny.

Night darken'd on the chace, the moon arose,
Yet still the Christians press their routed foes.
The trembling slave that sought the veil of night,
Curs'd the clear beam that guides the arrow's flight.
Shame woke revenge, nor slept th' unsated blade
While that soft light one turban'd head betray'd.

'Twas midnight ere the pious King could raise 710
In Jaffa's fane the rapturous voice of praise!
On trophied biers Llewellyn, Harold lay,
The easy price of that triumphant day.^c
The grateful host, while loud their anthems peal'd,
Own'd Heav'n not more their falchion than their shield.

Who but has known the blended thrill of joy,
And pride, and grief, that waits on victory?
When patriot rapture half repels the tear
For those, oh! never, never, held so dear;
And the lorn heart reproves the rising glow, 720
For what to it is fame or conquest now?
Though its freed country be a name once more,
Or rescued realms a thousand blessings pour.
But what the pure, th' unsated rapture then,
If the bright laurel shew no sanguine stain?

And generous Pity, not Affliction gives
The sacred dew that consecrates its leaves.
  Yet ev'n in Jaffa's walls two hearts o'erflow
With more than pity for a conquer'd foe.
With many a fruitless tear young Pardo gave   730
His wretched parent to the silent grave;
And tapers burn'd, and ceaseless mass was said—
If aught our pious cares avail the dead.
Beneath his trophied pillar, vainly rear'd
By Sharon's fount, a simple pile appear'd,
Where filial love, still jealous of her fame,
Alone inscribes Zorayda's mystic name.
  Meanwhile, her heart with equal anguish wrung,
Above her father's couch Amina hung.
With herbs of power she cool'd his burning head,
And as her hands each healing bandage laid,
Sobb'd to believe his wounds beyond her aid.
Oft to his couch with noiseless step she crept,
And indrawn breath, to mark if yet he slept;
Trembling to break a rest so calm and deep,
Yet fearful death might wear the mask of sleep.
Then watch'd retired, that every breeze which came
From the calm deep, might cool his fever'd frame.

If evil fate in evil glances lie,
Drops less than balm from that mild dovelike eye?

   At length Almanzor moved,—he waked, he smiled;
Delightful moment! for he knows his child.
Rapt from his sight, Maimoune's spells had shed
Grief through his soul, and he had mourn'd her dead;
But now he marks her renovated charms,
And blest, and strain'd her in his feeble arms;
While, as she fondly watch'd his brightening eye,
And terror strove with gratitude and joy,
She tells her hopes;—he, struggling with his pain,
Smiles, for he feels, but will not speak them vain.

   Yet oft, his frame as keener tortures stung,
Deep, deadly curses falter'd from his tongue
On all of Christian faith—Amina nigh,
Averts her waning cheek and tearful eye.

   " Light of my age, what means this changing cheer?
Sure thou wilt curse with hatred as sincere?
Though not by insult stamp'd so deep," he cries,
" The impious race by which thy father dies?
Thou art their captive too—but see! again—
My daughter!—has some Afrit warp'd thy brain?"

With trembling voice, clasp'd hands, and downcast
   eyes,
" My mother was a Christian !" she replies.
  " Aye, till by nuptial rites my fondness gave
To me and Mecca's faith my best loved slave.
Oft have I marked thee bend at Issa's name,
More lowly than a Hadgee's child became ;
Yet did our holier Prophet's rites engage,
Thine eye still sought his heaven-dictated page ;
But had I thought—far sooner had thy death—
Amina, speak ; thou art not of their faith ?"   780
  " No !" was her quick reply, but something stirr'd
On her flush'd cheek, and half denied the word.
True to her sex, she fear'd her father's frown,
More than to rush where naked falchions shone.
Her captive mother, hopeless to be freed,
For rank and power embraced the Prophet's creed ;
Then learn'd her brother, at his fortune's cost,
Had else redeem'd the gem he valued most.
With fruitless tears her hidden Cross she prest,
To Mary still her secret vows addrest ;   790
And when Almanzor's love her grief beguil'd,
And opening beauties charm'd her in her child,

She whisper'd truth in many a cautious speech,
And bade her love the faith she dared not teach.
Now by Matilda led, that daughter's sight
Hail'd the mild dawnings of Redemption's light;
But had the heavenly beam unclouded shone,
Had the pure wave baptized her for its own,
Undaunted she through roaring flames had trod,
Nor e'er with faltering lips denied her God.   800

    She shook before the glance that probed her soul,
The voice more dreadful than the thunder's roll.
" No more! 'tis guilt alone that dreads to speak,
Thy heart is falser than thy changing cheek;
Nay, 'tis my pure and pious blood disdains
To aid deceit, and swell th' Apostate's veins;
But may this curse,"—with fix'd, dilated eye,
Kneeling she sunk in breathless agony;—
His voice relax'd:—" thou wert a duteous child,
I spare thee, but,"—again his look grew wild, 810
On those whose arts thy childish ear beguil'd
I call the Prophet's vengeance—may the beam,
The ocean breeze, the date, the mountain stream
To them be death; their portion want and shame,
Their head in whirlwinds wrapt, their heart in flame;

May grief and pain their manly strength consume,
And the curs'd Goules defraud them of their tomb."—

Rage burst the half-closed wound; her trembling hand
Would stanch its flow and join the broken band;—
He flung her from him, and the dressings tore,   820
" I did not curse, but thou art mine no more;—
Thy touch is poison, and if thou could'st give
A thousand lives, I would not wish to live."

Across his face his mangled vest he threw,
As if to hide her from his loathing view;
While in that state when thought is crush'd by grief,
And tears flow on, yet do not yield relief,
Even where she fell she lay—and hours had past,
Ere terror rous'd her into life at last,
And thought return'd, but with a deadly chill;   830
She sought Almanzor's couch:—there all was still;
Wan as the dead, she rais'd the silken fold,—
His dreadful glance was fix'd, his lips were cold.

Now change the strain—let holy joy inspire,
And angel warblings join the rapturous lyre;
The silver moon has linger'd on her wane,
And fill'd her orb of vestal fire again;

Nor earth nor ocean, wood nor mountain height,
Has roused its echoes at the din of fight.
In tower and town the rival hosts repose,   840
In triumph these, in conscious weakness those.
Maimoune's heaven-commission'd spells incline
To meeker thoughts the generous Saladine;
The Great Eternal bids contention cease,
And hatred sleeps, and every heart is peace,
Now Sion's courts and Sion's fanes are free,
At every altar bends the duteous knee;
And the loud cymbal calls the pilgrim host
To joust or banquet at the Soldan's cost.

    On Sion's hill, beneath the awful dome   850
That rose majestic o'er Messiah's tomb,
Europe and Asia met,—but foes no more,
For Christian knees have prest the hallow'd floor.
The mystic bread adorns the glittering shrine,
The emerald chalice holds the sacred wine.

    Beneath the altar's tap'stried steps appear'd
Two humbler piles, in equal splendour rear'd;—
On one, the pride of Syria's vaunted loom,
The crescent gems a velvet field of gloom,
With ivory clasp'd the sable Koran laid,   860
And Moslem rites by Moslem priests were paid;

On yellow down the beauteous dwarfs incline,
And chaunt that fabling page they deem divine.

In spotless white the firstlings of the fold
Had drest the rival altar, starr'd with gold.
Clad in the hue of heaven, as best beseem'd
That sacred Book which tells of man redeem'd,
The Holy Volume spread; and round it stand
Prelates, the pride of every Christian land:
These Hubert leads to pay their holy vow,   870
Long England's glory, and her Primate now.
While They, the valiant Champions of the Tomb,
So long expell'd, their solemn charge resume:
Their hoary master, Ermengard, appears,
With pious transport fill'd, yet bath'd in tears,
For ah! how few the dear-bought triumph share
Of those who once had vow'd him fealty there.

Before the sable altar Adel stood,
With all of Joseph's and of Ayoub's blood,
Arbelia's youthful prince, and Mosul's pride,   880
And she, the Arab Pallas, Almahide.
Beyond were waving plumes and turbans seen,
Of royal tincture, crimson, white, and green;
Rich vests, that Syria knows alone to weave,
And daggers glittering like the stars of eve,

And high-born chiefs from many a distant shore,
Of feature various as the robes they wore.

   Nor less diverse appears the princely train
That Europe sends to crowd the ample fane:
From Etna's fires, or Cimbria's louring sky,   890
They mix with Asia's ardent chivalry.
But courteous smiles, or holy reverence now
The frown attemper'd on each haughty brow,
Nor though bright swords and corselets glitter'd there,
Was more of war than festal pomp might bear.
O'er burnish'd mail or woven hauberk roll'd,
Surcoat and scarf in many a blazon'd fold;
The buckler's massy orb was cast aside,
And doff'd th' oppressive helm and plumy pride.

   And (well such scene might Moslem eyes alarm)
There royal beauty hangs on valour's arm.
With holy rapture fill'd, by Raymond's side
Moves meek Matilda, now his plighted bride;
Smiling through tears her proselyte succeeds,
Sad Pardo's hand the beauteous orphan leads.
But who is she, that mid the lovely train,
Comes with the young and arrogant Champagne?
Courteous yet noble, smiling and serene,—
No! 'tis not Salem's self-elected Queen,

In feign'd disease she hides her pride and shame, 910
That beauteous form is Pembroke's noble dame.

But there were two who yet distinguish'd stood,
And could not blend, though with a sceptred crowd:
Whom Heaven itself with innate glory crown'd,
Sought by each eye, and linger'd on when found.
Great Ayoub's son, in Majesty severe,
Unbent though aged, grave but not austere;
Yet even now was regal pomp forgot,
And gold and purple robes, he needs them not;
Nor though within a Christian fane he stands, 920
To yield a kingdom to a victor's hands,
Around his form less awful grandeur shone,
Than when he mounted on its conquer'd throne.

Far different RICHARD—o'er his polish'd brow
His curling locks still shed their sunny glow;
And in his eye that playful archness strove,
Which charm'd of old his subject Courts of Love.
His robes were costly,—nor the gazer deem'd
That aught less rich had such a form beseem'd,
Yet none might pause to look on clasp or gem, 930
He does not gain, but splendour gives to them;

And many a timid eye which fear'd to know
A hateful gorgon in its country's foe,
Admiring gazed; nor scorn nor hate are found
In that calm look which meekly sought the ground:
For to a Christian heart, how worthless here
Must earthly fame and regal pomp appear!
Here was Ambition's grave, for here was given
Th' eternal blow to him that troubled heaven;
And here celestial mercy deign'd to bear   940
That doom of sin which e'en the proud must share;
Here stoop'd to death, that death itself might die,
And life immortal call his saints to joy.

    While thus he mused, the solemn chaunt began,
" Glory to God, good-will and peace to man."
Robed, veil'd in white, with spotless garlands crown'd,
An hundred virgins rais'd the choral sound.
Some courts or palaces forsook, and some
Left for this pilgrimage their convent dome;
And hence return'd, as different duties call,   950
To social circles, or the cloister's wall.
But two for heaven designed, though unprofess'd,
Drew the deep sigh from many a pitying breast.

Wrapt in her veil, with faltering steps and slow,
Her once clear voice now broken, harsh, and low;
That form, still graceful, wakens soft regret,
The mournful mien betrays Evanthe yet.
Quick was her sister's step, and trembling, pale,
With hurried hand she lifts the novice veil;
Ran with a troubled eye the circle o'er,   960
Then sigh'd, and dropp'd it to be rais'd no more.
Hid were her raven locks, her smile was gone,
The full bright eye was Hermesind's alone.

Now perfumes burn before the conquering King,
And fair-hair'd slaves the costly presents bring,
Whatever Asia boasts of spice or gem,
And Sion's long contested diadem.
Again exulting on a hero's head,
The conscious gold a ruddier glory shed;
And Lusignan, who quits contention's roar   970
For calmer scenes and Cyprus' smiling shore,
In unrepining wonder sees the crown
Sit light on other brows, that scorch'd his own.

And there were treasures misers would not store,
Yet then esteem'd above the richest ore;

All earth retains of holy men, who first
Bade Truth's mild radiance on its darkness burst;
Their touch could then sublimer fervour shed,
And sickness shrunk, and howling madness fled;
And though, perchance, a less believing age   980
Reject the relic while it guards the page,
Still might they fix the meek and pious eye
On death, and hope, and immortality!
And they who lived, and toil'd, and died to save,
Speak truth, and faith, and comfort from the grave.

   Hush'd is each sound, e'en murmuring whispers
      cease,
The mutual Heralds read the terms of peace;
And now on either side advancing there,
At either shrine th' assembled Princes swear,
These on the Gospel, on the Koran those,   990
To sheathe their swords and be no longer foes.
But They, whose will the rival hosts obey'd,
Who waked the conflict, and the conflict stayed,
Alone adjured not heaven—with one consent,
While on the kingly pair each eye was bent,

" Be peace between us!" they exclaim, and stand
Full in the midst, and pledge the friendly hand.
O Majesty! thy simple word had then
A force beyond the oaths of meaner men.

But hark! that shriek, that groan! such sounds might
    rise   1000
From baffled demons in their agonies!
And hark again! what heavenly strains succeed!
More sweet than amorous lute or pastoral reed.
What perfumes breathe! what amber glories swim!
What sudden splendour makes the daylight dim!
A lambent flame, whose heaven-descending blaze
The altar circles with ætherial rays,
Plays round thh Priests, and lights with fire divine,
The sevenfold lamps that stand before the shrine.
Amazed the Soldan saw—but, self-deceived,   1010
He doubts the wonder—saw, yet disbelieved;
Thrice he commands, and thrice his impious crew
Suppress'd the flames, and thrice they blazed anew;
Trembling he owns the wonder, while the strain
Of Christian transport fills the spacious fane:

But he, still erring in his bigot faith,
Reads in that fire the oracle of death.

 And now a cloud descends; but lovelier far
Than those which follow day's declining car,
Or those which in the balmy nights of June,   1020
With silver fleeces gird the full-orb'd moon;
It rests upon the shrine, and seems to rise
Brighter and brighter, till it touch'd the skies.
Now thunder roars around, and lightning plays,
Harmonious thunders, and a temper'd blaze!
Now it unfolds—to mortal view is given
A glorious vision of the joys of heaven.
Veil'd in the wondrous, vast abyss of light,
The Triple Godhead shuns created sight;
But seraphs kneel around, and angel choirs   1030
Strike, robed in light, their everlasting lyres;
And they that erst for Sion bled, adore,
In bliss eternal, Him whose Cross they bore.
Beneath, the Arch of Peace and Promise spread,
The type of safety, born in doubt and dread;
And lo! within its ample circle beam'd
The sacred sign that marks its pledge redeem'd.

Lost to man's touch, though to his reverence given,
Bright cherubs bear the Holy Cross to Heaven!
Now golden radiance gilds the sacred wood, 1040
While every precious stain that once was blood
Glows like that gem which needs no borrow'd light,
But scorns the earth, and shines amid the night.
Far brighter than that starry Cross, on high,
Sublimely circling through the southern sky;
Which oft with joy on trackless floods descried,
The Pilot's that, as this the Christian's guide,
Shews him his path through trackless floods to find,
And calms with faith and hope the doubting mind.

But at its foot, dejected, weeping there, 1050
What that thin form, so faded, yet so fair?
Which dares not look tow'rds that resplendent throne,
Or ask that mercy, meant for man alone?
Ah! sweet Maimoune! angel tears were moved
For their lost sister, erring, yet beloved;
Well then might they, from Hassan's deadly snares
Saved by her suffering, aid her with their prayers;
Nor were they vain—from out the central flame
A voice divine,—a voice of mercy came;
A voice unheard on earth since angels trod 1060
This nether ball, and man communed with God.

So sweetly awful, so sublimely mild:
" Come to my bosom! come, thou erring child!
Come! and let joy exalt the bliss of Heaven,—
The lost is found, the Penitent forgiven."

Upward she flies, and brightening as she flew,
O'er her light harp her glowing fingers threw;
Again she pours th' unwearied hymn of praise,
Again partakes the beatific blaze.
When now that voice the warlike host addrest,　1070
And fill'd with transport every faithful breast:
"Soldiers of CHRIST! by CHRIST with conquest crown'd,
Think, while your hearts with grateful rapture bound,
Mine is no Temple framed with human hands,
Beyond the stars my chosen Sion stands.
Soldiers of CHRIST, depart! your goal is won,
Well have ye wrought:—THE WILL OF HEAVEN IS DONE.

Louder, yet sweeter swells the chaunt divine,
And brighter yet th' immortal glories shine;
Till clouds of perfume closed the vision round,　1080
And faint in distance sunk the rapturous sound.

Bowed with one heart before the Almighty Lord,
Christian and Saracen alike adored.
On many a doubting mind conviction stole,
And Truth illumin'd many a darken'd soul.

All own'd the PRESENT GOD; but chiefly they
Whose worth and valour bought that glorious day;
And never aught of earthly hope fulfill'd,
With bliss so pure the heaving bosom thrill'd;
Sweet as unfading, Time could not impair,   1090
Nor pain nor death,—it glows for ever there.
To holiest joy was CŒUR DE LION moved;
His task was ended, and his GOD approved.

END OF THE POEM.

NOTES.

NOTES
TO
CŒUR DE LION.

BOOK IX.

Note (b), page 8, line 105.

And fruits, the produce of a warmer zone.

MANY of these articles sound trifling in a modern ear; but fruits, sherbets and ices, were frequent presents of Saladine to the Christian chiefs.

Note (c), page 9, line 129.

Where Angels bow'd, and Eblis scoff'd at man.

Kaf is believed in the East to be not only the residence of the Simurg, but the spot where the Angels were commanded to worship Adam, which Eblis refused. He said that the Angels whom God had created out of fire, could not worship a creature of clay: for Adam had been formed of the dust of the earth.

Note (d), page 9, line 140.

But the cold sheet that winds him in the grave?

This celebrated remark of Saladine has been related in various ways. It is generally believed that a few hours before his death he caused his winding-sheet to be paraded through the streets of Damascus, with the proclamation, " Behold all that shall remain to Saladine, the Conqueror of the East!"

Note (e), page 11, line 164.

Might we that scandal to our creed restore.

This was the excuse alleged to King RICHARD. It was supposed that the true Cross had been burned either by accident or in the first fury of conquest, and that the Mahommedans were unwilling to confess it. I have abridged these negociations as much as I conveniently could. Jerusalem was esteemed as sacred by the Mahommedans as by the Christians, it having been at first chosen by the Prophet as the Kiblah, or place to which the Faithful were to address their devotions: it was also the scene of the Mérage, or his night journey to the seventh Heaven.

Note (f), page 14, line 249.

Even in his youth the foe of Saladine.

The revolutions of Egypt, at the time to which these lines allude, were too various to be more than glanced at. Chaver, or Schaour, Vizier to the Fatimite Caliph, was chased from Cairo by his rival Dargham. He applied to Noureddin, who sent Shiracoush with an army to assert his cause, and compelled the luxurious and reluctant Saladine (then only twenty-five years of age) to accompany his uncle. Dargham besought the aid of Amalric, but it did not arrive in time, and he was defeated and killed. Chaver, however, soon found that his friends were about to become his masters, and shutting the gates of Cairo against Shiracoush, formed a fresh alliance with Amalric, who had been summoned to Egypt for his destruction. The mismanagement of the King of Jerusalem made the campaign disadvantageous to the Christians; and the chimerical idea of conquering Egypt, which he retained ever after, was the source of continual misfortunes, and tended to bring on the ultimate ruin of his realm.

Note (g), page 16, line 289.

Its wealth, its regal honours I resign.

One half of Cyprus had been previously sold to the Templars, and in making this exchange of regal honours with Lusignan, RICHARD was perhaps more governed by sound policy than would at first appear. He bartered for an empty title only a conquest which it might have been troublesome to maintain; and had he ever gained possession of Jerusalem, he would no longer have been bound in honour to uphold the claims of a monarch, whose restoration to a throne which he was unequal to fill, must probably have been followed by a second loss of his kingdom.

Note (h), page 29, line 589.

O'er the wide havoc which their winds had spread.

The destruction of Ascalon was extremely painful to Saladine; and he passed a sleepless night in great agitation before he could give the necessary orders. When he came in sight of the city he shuddered, and after a melancholy silence exclaimed, " my children are very dear to me, but I would rather lose them than touch a stone of this city; yet if the welfare of religion, and of my people, exact this sacrifice, I will make it without regret." The Imams and Cadis insisted on the ruin of Ascalon. " The orders of Heaven must then be obeyed," said Saladine, and commanded the citizens to quit their houses. The scene grew more and more distressing, but the Soldan relieved their sorrows as far as was in his power. The walls had been battered for many days with little success, and it was probable that Richard would not long delay his advance. The Soldan therefore set the example of destruction, and fires were lighted in every quarter. The tower which has been mentioned was soon the only building which remained standing in Ascalon.

Note (i), page 32, line 664.

'Tis said thy hatred loves the impious feast.

The Mahommedans seem to have had an idea that RICHARD did not scruple to eat the bodies of his enemies, and the Romance delights in making him a complete cannibal. He recovers from his illness by eating Saracen flesh, which is served up to him as pork, and afterwards feasts the ambassadors of Saladine with the heads of their own friends, expressing great astonishment at their lack of appetite. Such enormities do not appear historically to have ever tainted the character of the third Crusade; and the belief probably arose from a confused remembrance of the dreadful famine at Antioch during the first expedition to the Holy Land; when the Crusaders are said to have even disinterred the bodies of their enemies that they might feed upon them. Previously to the surrender of Antioch, Bohemond, who sought to deliver the camp from the spies by which it was infested, caused twelve Saracen captives to be slain and roasted before a large fire, proclaiming that he had discovered this resource against want, and would treat in like manner all his enemies that should fall into his hands. After Richard's arrival in Palestine, there was never any want of provisions to prompt such unnatural acts.

Note (k), page 33, line 698.

Shrined in its breast Messiah's temple rear.

The church was usually adjacent to or in the citadelle for the greater security; and as the citadelle was fixed on the most commanding height, it hence derived the advantage possessed by so many of the continental cathedrals, of being visible from a great distance.

BOOK X.

Note, page 43, line 6.

Colossal works! man's envy and despair.

As the superstition of Europe ascribes to the industry of the devil every extravagance of nature, or stupendous relic of forgotten antiquity, the traditions of the East suppose the mighty works of elder days, the ruins of Ctesiphon and Persepolis, &c. &c. to have been raised by genii, the offspring of fire, who laboured at the command of the Preadamite Sultans.

Note (a), page 44, line 22.

Abdollatiph, the pride of Asia, came.

The humanity of Saladine was aided by policy in the courtesy which he displayed towards a departing enemy. To the perishing luxuries of fruits and ices, and the ordinary gifts of Arabian horses and splendid robes, the Soldan added a supply of the precious Balm of Gilead, the panacea of the East, and sent with the presents a celebrated physician, to inquire into the malady of the French King.

" Abdollatiph was born at Bagdad, and travelled, like the ancient philosophers of Greece, over many parts of Asia. He was about twenty-eight when he began his travels, and went first to Mosul and then to Damascus, but did not stay long at either. The first was engaged in the chemistry of the day, in which he was already skilled; at the second he vanquished some opponents in philology.

" He now bent his steps towards Egypt, and to this journey the consent and patronage of Saladine were necessary; but when the Arabian physician arrived at the camp near Acre to solicit it, he found the Saracens bewailing a recent defeat; a defeat so honourable to the skill and valour of our English RICHARD, that nothing less than the late matchless defence of this fortress, by a handful of British seamen and mariners, could have eclipsed its glory; hence the lofty spirit of the Soldan was plunged into a morbid melancholy, which excluded the traveller from his presence; but the favours he received, evinced the munificence of Saladine, and he persisted in his design of exploring Egypt. One strong inducement, which influenced him on this occasion was the instruction which he hoped to derive from the society of the celebrated Maimonides, the disciple of Averrhöes; and by Alcadi al Fadel, who had in vain intreated his return to Damascus, he was furnished with such recommendations as insured him the most flattering reception.

" From this intercourse with the great and learned he withdrew, however, to present himself before the Sultan; who having concluded a truce with the Franks, then resided in the Holy City.

" He was received with marked respect by Saladine, who granted to Abdollatiph a pension of thirty dinars per month, as a testimony of his personal esteem and his love of science. After the death of the Sultan this sum was raised by his sons to one hundred dinars, till their unnatural uncle drove them from the throne of Egypt and Syria, and Abdollatiph was forced to return to Damascus.

" He afterwards travelled over many parts of Asia, Aleppo, Greece, Syria, Armenia, and Asia Minor, and died at Bagdad, whither he had gone to revisit his native abode previous to a pilgrimage to Mecca."—See White's History of Abdollatiph. Monthly Review for 1802.

Note (b), page 44, line 24.

That Avicene or sage Averrhöes taught.

Avicene, or Avicenna, a celebrated philosopher of Bokhara, in Khorassan, died in 1036, in the 58th year of his age. Modern critics are inclined to allow him the praise of a good botanist, but his talents do not appear to have equalled his reputation, and the intemperance of his life disgraced his character as a physician.

Averrhöes, the cotemporary of Abdollatiph and of Saladine, was born at Cordova, the principal city of the Moors in Spain. He studied theology, mathematics, and the Aristotelian philosophy, at Seville, and the fame of his talents caused the Caliph Jacob Almanzor to appoint him supreme magistrate and priest of Morocco and Mauritania. This rapid advance excited the jealousy of his rivals, who soon brought about his disgrace by the charge of heresy. His pupil Maimonides left Cordova that he might not be compelled to join the outcry against him. Averrhöes afterwards confessing himself a penitent, was restored to his honours. He died in 1206. Averrhöes appears to have deserved his fame by his temperance, his learning, and his clemency as a judge. He was a warm admirer of Aristotle, and of the medical treatise of Avicenna. He was a great commentator on the writings of others, composed many works on medicine, and is the first who records the observation that the same person could have the small-pox but once.

Note (c), page 45, line 49.
And gave that home his rebel states denied.

In the contest for the papal supremacy, the legitimate Pontiff Alexander the Third fled into France from the successful VICTOR, and the fury of Frederic Barbarossa by whom he was supported. Henry the Second of England, and Louis the Seventh of France, vied at first in the honours which they paid to him, but on the quarrel between Henry and Thomas à Becket, the magnanimity of Alexander refused to yield the interests of the Church to the claims of private gratitude, and the King of England became thenceforward one of his persecutors. Alexander, on the other hand, did not forget, that though deprived of his temporal power, he was still armed with the thunders of the Church.

Note (c), page 53, line 239.

At rites that outraged every holy tye.

Henry of Champagne had been left at Acre on RICHARD's advance to Arsouf. These nuptials had still less of decency than those with Conrad, and it seemed as if Isabelle were afraid lest they should be prevented by the general execration of the Crusaders.

Note (d), page 55, line 279.

Of her he wrong'd to win his peace on high.

William Archbishop of Tyre was one of those who brought the fatal news of the loss of Jerusalem to Europe, and excited her warriors to arm for its recovery. He assisted at the council of Mayence, which was summoned by Frederic Barbarossa; and his pathetic description of the state of Palestine drew tears from Henry the Second and Philip Augustus, at the meeting which he induced them to hold at Gisors. There is some doubt whether this venerable historian were living at the time of RICHARD's crusade, or whether the see of Tyre were then occupied by a second prelate of the same name.

Note, page 60, line 388.

Where fell the leader of the Parthian band.

The combat of Robert Duke of Normandy with the "Parthian," at the battle of Ascalon, in the days of Godfrey, is depicted on the Bayeux tapestry. This Parthian was the standard-bearer of the Sultan of Egypt. "Le prince, frappé de la broderie d'argent et de la pomme d'or qui brilloit au dessous de la pointe de la lance, où étoit attaché le grand étendard des ennemis, l'arracha avec la vie à celui qui le portoit, en l'abattant aux pieds du Sultan." It was estimated at twenty marks of silver, and hung up before the Holy Sepulchre, as was also the sword of the Sultan Al Aphdal, which he lost in his flight, and which was purchased of the soldier who found it for seventy besants.—*Mailly.*

Note (e), page 61, line 414.

Or our best steeds can yield a single meal.
Historical.

Note (g), page 74, line 714.

" Preserve my life!" I cried, " preserve the King!"
The generous devotion of William de Pratellis, who on this occasion saved the life of his defenceless King, is well known. I have taken a poet's license to substitute another hero.

Note (h), page 76, line 757.

To join your Order Saladine aspires.
See the well known Fabliau of " The Order of Knighthood." The story that Saladine was knighted by one of his prisoners, or by Humphrey of Thoron, at a tournament, and that he also procured that honour for his two eldest sons, is congenial with the belief that he died a Christian, or that he ordered his funeral alms to be equally divided between Mahomedans and Christians. Such fables at least prove the esteem of his enemies.

Note (i), page 76, line 761.

But in the bath his hardy limbs I laved.
The succeeding lines describe the ceremonies of investiture with all their mystic meaning, and the charge usually delivered to the new made knights.

BOOK XI.

Note (a), page 91, line 94.

Fair as the bloom of Irem's fabled bowers!

Irem was, according to Oriental tradition, the name of a magnificent city and garden, formed by Shedad the son of Ad (first king of the ancient tribe of Ad) in the deserts of Aden. The idolatrous prince intended to imitate the celestial paradise, and to arrogate divine honours, and when the work was finished he set out with a numerous attendance to view it: but having arrived within a day's journey of the place, the whole company was destroyed by a terrible noise from heaven. The city and garden of Irem are believed still to exist as a monument of divine vengeance, but to be generally invisible to mortals. One Abdallah Ebn Colabah pretended to have accidentally reached this wonderful place while seeking for a stray camel.—See Sale's Koran. Preliminary discourse and notes.— Mr. Southey has made a fine use of the whole story of the presumption and punishment of the idolatrous tribe of Ad, in his Thalaba.

Note (b), page 92, line 107.

Th' acacia with its tufts of golden hair.

The acacia vera, or mimosa; not the robinia pseud-acacia which so frequently usurps its name in European gardens. The flower of the genuine acacia resembles a small tuft of yellow silk or hair, and its foliage is much more light and feathery than that of its false namesake.

Note (c), page 92, line 125.

The dusky olive, and the glowing rose.

The Asiatics, notwithstanding the delight with which they dwell on the very name of a garden, seem not to carry their

Note (o), page 103, line 444.
Placed on a golden dish of rare device.

Of all the "noble birds," the peacock and the pheasant enjoyed the highest rank. They appeared only at the most splendid feasts, they were dressed with the richest spices, decorated with gold, and jewels, and borne to the table by the most distinguished ladies. To carve the peacock or the pheasant, was also one of the proud privileges of the bravest cavalier, and he to whom it was offered, was obliged in courtesy to protest his own unworthiness, and not to accept the office but upon "great persuasion." The vow of the peacock is perhaps one of the most romantic features of chivalry. The lady bore the honoured bird, which was always adorned with its gayest plumage, to every knight in succession, beginning with him who was first in valour and rank, and each knight was expected to signalize his courage and his love by some vow, made "before the peacock and the ladies." When this ceremony was completed, the peacock was borne back to the table, and placed before the chosen knight, who drawing his sword, began to carve it with great ceremony; and it was expected that he should so divide it, as to give a morsel to each guest, however great might be the number. To illustrate this subject, and that of the interludes already mentioned, I will abridge a part of the account given by M. de St. Palaye of the feast held at Lille, in 1453, at the court of Philip the Good, Duke of Burgundy, on account of the crusade against the Turks, who had just reconquered Constantinople: " At last the festal day arrived. If the magnificence of the Prince was admired in the number and abundance of the courses, it shone still more in the spectacles then known by the name of "*Entremets.*" Divers decorations, machines, figures of men and uncommon animals, trees, mountains, rivers, even a sea covered with ships, appeared in the hall. All these objects, intermixed with men, and birds and other living animals, were in motion in the hall or on the table, and represented a sort of allegorical ballet. It is difficult to suppose what must have been the size of this apartment, which contained a table so spacious, besides the multitude of guests and spectators. All at once a giant appeared, armed like a Saracen of Grenada. He conducted an elephant, who bore a castle, in which was a distressed dame clothed in black like a nun. In vain she requested the giant to stop: he led her forward to the table of the Duke, and there the captive lady, who was intended to represent Religion, recited a long complaint of the evils which she suffered from the Saracens, and the tardiness of those who ought to deliver her. Toison D'Or, King at Arms of the Order of the Fleece, then advanced, preceded by a long file of pursuivants, with a living pheasant on his finger, adorned with a collar of gold and gems, and presented to the Duke two damsels, of which one was Violante, his illegitimate daughter, and the other Isabeau of Neufchatel, daughter to the Lord of Montague; each lady being accompanied by a Knight of the Golden Fleece. Then the King at Arms offered the bird to the Duke, in the name of the ladies, who recommended themselves to the protection of their Sovereign, "to the end that the antient customs might be observed, according to which at feasts and other noble assemblies, a peacock or other noble bird was presented to the princes and lords, that they might make vows in behalf of the dames and damsels who besought their assistance." The Duke replied, "I vow first, to God my Creator, and to the most glorious Virgin, and after them to the pheasant and the ladies," to carry the war among the infidels, &c. &c. The signal was followed by all his court: each knight vowed to distinguish his courage against the Turks by some singular exploit; and imposed upon himself some arbitrary penance. Some would not sleep on a bed, others would not eat off a table-cloth, some would abstain from meat or wine on certain days, some would not wear a particular piece of armour, or would wear it day and night; some clothed themselves in sackcloth; in fact, the admirable ridicule of Cervantes was but the echo of these vows, which we that live in soberer days are apt to believe only the inventions of romance writers. The vows finished with a new spectacle. A lady clothed in white, like a novice, and bearing her name of *Grâce Dieu* in golden letters on her shoulder, led in twelve damsels, who represented the Virtues, which were to accompany the Crusaders. Each bore her name also embroidered in gold, and recited a few verses. These twelve ladies were the knightly virtues of Faith, Charity, Justice, Reason, Prudence, Temperance, Fortitude, Truth, Generosity, Diligence, Hope, and Valour. *Et toutes enfin commencèrent à danser en guise de mommeries, et à faire bonne chère pour remplir et rachever plus joyeusement la fête.*" One of the most singular of these fantastic scenes is the Vow of the Heron, which forms the subject of an ancient poem, printed also by St. Palaye. The Count D'Artois being banished from France, took refuge in London. One day his falcon caught a heron. The Count was at first indignant at so vile a capture, but afterwards gave orders to his "officiers de la bouche" to pluck and dress it. At night, when Edward the Third was at supper with his nobles, his Queen and her damsels, he entered, attended by minstrels and two noble ladies, bearing the heron between two silver plates, and advancing with great state to Edward, presented to him this most cowardly of birds (which is said even to fear its own shadow), as the reward of his indifference for a crown which he allowed to remain in the hands of his rival. Stung with this taunt, the enraged King swore that the year should not pass before Philip should see him in France, bearing fire and sword, to avenge this affront, were the French army ten times greater than his own. The Count D'Artois then went round to the nobles, and all hastened to bind themselves by some wild condition. The gallant Sir Walter Manny, whose ancestor accompanied RICHARD to the third crusade, engaged to take a certain town defended by Godemar du Fay. The Earl of Salisbury declared, in honour of the lady of his heart (the daughter of the Count D'Erby), that he would not uncover his right eye during the war. It is impossible to read the vow made by Queen Philippa without shuddering, for she called heaven to witness that she would destroy herself and her unborn infant, if the period of its birth should arrive before her husband had taken her across the seas, in acquittal of her oath. Edward was filled with horror at her words, and forbade the vows to be continued. The heron was cut up and eaten.

Froissart mentions, that at the battle of Poitiers there were many young knights who had one eye covered with cloth, and that they had sworn to their ladies not to restore it to its use till they had signalized their prowess in France. But most of these conceits were the refinements of a later age of chivalry than that in which the poem is placed.

Note (p), page 105, line 481.

Next sate D'Arselles, and high St. Valery's heir.

Louis D'Arselles and Bernard de St. Valery, two noble Normans, who are mentioned in the annals of that country among the "Preux Chevaliers" of the third crusade.

Notes (q) and (r), page 105, line 482.

And stout St. John, and Arnulph of St. Clair.

Roger de St. John, descended from the family of Ports, Lords of Basing, in Southampton, from the time of the Conquest, and maternally from William de St. John, of St. John, near Rouen, who came to England with William the Conqueror, as grand-master of the artillery, and supervisor of the waggons and carriages; whence the horses' hemes, or collar, was borne as his cognizance. One of his descendants was second wife of Bernard de St. Valery, Lord of

Ambroseden, in Oxfordshire, and who took his name from the castle and town of St. Valery, in France, whence the Conqueror sailed to England. This Bernard was, I believe, the grandfather of the Bernard already mentioned.

(r) Another Norman, who appears, in the history of that country, as one of its bravest crusaders.

Note (s), page 105, line 483.

Harvey, whose axe was never rais'd in vain.

The Harveys, anciently Fitz-Harveys, descended from Robert Fitz-Harvey, younger son of Harvey Duke of Orleans, who came over to England with William. Harvey de Yuon, in the reign of Henry the Second, died on his way to the Holy Land. His son, Henry de Harvey, accompanied RICHARD. Of this family come the Earls of Bristol.

Note (t), page 105, line 484.

And Nevile, skilful on the troubled main.

Henry de Nevile, descended from Gilbert de Nevile, who was admiral to William the Conqueror. Henry died without issue, but his sister, Isabel, was the maternal ancestor of the Earls of Abergavenny, who thence bear the name of Nevile, and the motto *Ne vile velis*.

Note (u), page 105, line 485.

Spencer, whose name was to his office due.

Hugh, fourth son of Thurstan le Despencer, steward to Henry the First. The office had been hereditary from the days of William the Conqueror, and gave its name to the family. The *de* was afterwards omitted by some branches, hence Spencer.

Note (x), page 105, line 486.

And Ferrars' valiant Earl, and Fortescue.

Henry, Earl of Ferrars, in Normandy, was rewarded by

the Conqueror with the lands of Etingdon, in Warwickshire, which had belonged to the family of Sewell from the time of Edward the Confessor. Sewell, however, still held the manor under Count Ferrars, whom he acknowledged as his feudal lord; and one of his descendants married the heiress of the Norman Earls, and thus regained his ancient honours. A similar fortune attended the representatives of many of the dispossessed Saxons.

Note (y), page 105, line 489.

Grosvenor, whose house held kindred with the Dane.

The ancestors of this family came from Denmark with Rollo, and settled in Normandy, where they took their name from the office of master of the royal buck-hounds. Gilbert le Grosvenor, who accompanied William to England, was nephew to Hugh Lupus, Count of Avranches, and first Earl of Chester, himself nephew to the Conqueror. The ample posssssions of this family in Cheshire and the adjacent parts of Wales are well known.

Note (z), page 106, line 501.

The brave De Vaux, in arms a mighty name.

Ranulph, or Robert de Vallibus, corrupted into De Vaux, one of the ancestors of the family of Dacre: that Barony having originally belonged to the family of De Vaux, of whom three brothers settled in England after the Conquest.

Note (aa), page 106, line 502.

And Roland, who from stout Belasius came.

Belasius (now Belasyse, Earls Fauconberg) was a Norman knight, who accompanied the Conqueror to England. I have ventured to substitute the family name of Roland for that of Robert, which belonged to his descendant under RICHARD the First.

Note (bb), page 107, line 522.

With Dædalean art for beauty's fairest flower.

Patric, Earl of Salisbury, being the King's lieutenant in Acquitaine, was slain by Guy de Lusignan (afterwards King of Jerusalem), on his return from a pilgrimage to St. James, in Galicia, leaving Ela his sole daughter and heir, of whom, says Dugdale, it is reported, that being so great an inheritrix, one William Talbot, an Englishman and an eminent soldier, took on him the habit of a pilgrim, and went into Normandy, where wandering up and down for two months, he at length found her out. He then disguised himself as a harper, and being practised in mirth and jesting, became well accepted at the court where she resided. Here becoming acquainted with her, he after a while took her to England, where he presented her to King RICHARD, who received her courteously, and bestowed her in marriage on William Long Espee, one of his father's sons by the Fair Rosamond, at the same time surrendering to William the Earldoms of Rosmar and Salisbury as her inheritance. Ela was descended from Walter de Eurus, Earl of Rosmar, who came to England with the Conqueror, and whose surname still lives in the noble house of Devereux.

Note (cc), page 107, line 426.

And Curzon's pride, the youthful Giraline.

Properly Robert or Richard, but Giraline is a family name.

Note (dd), page 108, line 533.

And Harley, sprung from that victorious Thane.

The family of Harley is so ancient, that that of Harlai, one of the most eminent in France, is believed to be descended from it. One of this house, in 1013, commanded an army under King Ethelred, and defeated Swane, King of

Denmark, near Pershore, thus saving the town. Sir William de Harley was distinguished under Godfrey of Bouillon, and was one of the first Knights of the Holy Sepulchre. He was buried in the Abbey of Pershore, where his tomb still remains, and was the only one which escaped in the time of Henry the Eighth.

Note (ee), page 108, line 537.
The noble Harcourt next, in whom combine.
The house of Harcourt is descended from Bernard, of the blood royal of Saxony, who being born in Denmark, was surnamed the Dane. He was chief counsellor to Rollo, and second in command in his descent on Normandy in 876. He was afterwards minister to William Longsword, Rollo's son and successor, and guardian to his child during his minority. He married a lady of the royal family of Burgundy; from his eldest son descended the ancient Earls of Leicester, while the offspring of the second took the name of Harcourt, and were renowned both in England and France. The Sir Robert Harcourt mentioned in the poem was the son of Ivo, and inherited his father's English possessions, leaving those in Normandy as the portion of his brothers; but it was properly his descendant William, the same that took so distinguished a part in the siege of Damietta in 1218, that acquired the surname of the Englishman. The Harcourts seem to have been particularly stricken with the mania of crusading, and there is scarcely a single expedition to the Holy Land of any importance, in which they were not conspicuous.

Note (ff), page 108, line 542.
The conquer'd spoils, and fame of Erin's war.
William Marshall, Earl of Pembroke, Strigulph Strongbow, Earl of Clare, and Robert Fitz-Harding, Lord of Berkeley

castle, were the three warriors most distinguished in the conquest of Ireland under Henry the Second. The Fitz-Hardings were descended from the Kings of Denmark, and came to England with the Conqueror. In 1168 Robert Fitz-Harding entertained, at Bristol, Dermot Mac Murrough, King of Leinster, with a company of sixty followers, when he came to England to solicit aid from Henry: which event brought on the war with Ireland.

Note (gg), page 108, line 546.

The silver stags upon an azure bend.

Lydulph, of Audleigh in Staffordshire, eldest son of Adam de Audley, bore his father's arms, Gules, a fret Or, and was progenitor of the Lords Audley. Adam, the second son, bore the same arms, with a label of three points Azure in chief, for difference. It was his son, William de Audley, who becoming possessed of the manor of Stanley in Staffordshire (so called from its rough and stony soil), took the surname of Stanley. The arms of this branch (now Earls of Derby) are, on a bend Azure, three stags heads Argent.

Note (hh), page 110, line 579.

His name renown'd on earth, his " Hope in Heaven."

The name of Percy comes from a town in Lower Normandy, near to Villedieu, and not, as some have supposed, from the accident of *piercing* a King of Scotland's *eye*, at the siege of Alnwick Castle: for though that accident is said to have befallen Malcolm the Third (who was contemporary with William Rufus), the officer that slew him was named Hammond, and had no connexion with the Percy family, who did not possess lands in Northumberland till the time of Edward the Second. Its progenitor was Mainfred, a Danish chieftain, who made irruptions on France prior to the expedition of Rollo. Two of his descendants, William and Serlo, assisted

William of Normandy in his conquest of England. William was much beloved by the Monarch, and obtained large grants of land in Hampshire and Lincolnshire. He was also in habits of close friendship with Hugh Lupus, who bestowed on him the lordship of Whitby, where he restored or rather founded the abbey of St. Hilda. His brother Serlo became the first Prior, and his nephew William, who was at Serlo's death chosen Abbot, was of such high renown for sanctity, as to be afterwards canonized. This first Lord William de Percy was surnamed Alsgernons (aux Moustaches); he went with Duke Robert and other Normans to Palestine in 1096, and died at Mount Joy, so named by the pilgrims who usually had the first view of the holy city from that eminence. Here his followers interred his body, but brought over his heart, according to the practice of those ages, to be deposited in Whitby Abbey. His wife was Emma de Port, for the Conqueror having bestowed on him Semar, near Scarborough, and other lands, " he wedded her that was very heir to them, in discharging of his conscience." Emma outlived her husband, and was herself a benefactor to Whitby.

Their son, Alan, called the great Alan, was also so beneficent to the Abbey, as to acquire the title of its second founder; but his warlike achievements are wrapped in oblivion. He had seven sons, and the eldest of these had four children, but they died early, and he and his brothers passed away and left no heir. Maud, the eldest daughter, had married William de Plesset, Earl of Warwick: but he also died childless in Palestine, and the only hope of succession remained with the youngest daughter Agnes. She married Josceline de Lovain, son of Geoffrey Barbatus, Duke of Nether Lorrain, Count of Brabant and Lovain, and brother to Adelicia, second wife of Henry the First of England. He took the name of Percy, but was permitted to retain his hereditary device, *Or, a lion rampant, azure,* which with a change of colour only, is still the arms of Brabant and Hainault. Josceline was of one of the noblest families in Europe, being descended from Charlemagne, and from the illustrious Duke Regnier, who was taken prisoner by Rollo the Dane.

Henry de Percy was the true representative of this illustrious line at the time of RICHARD's Crusade; but to avoid confusion, from the endless repetition of the same familiar name, I have changed it to one frequent in the family annals. In 1234 his younger brother Richard had contrived to get possession both of lands and honours, and it was not till after a solemn trial before Henry the Third, that his nephew William (son of Henry de Percy) obtained justice.

The motto alluded to in the text is, " Espérance en Dieu."

Note (ii), page 110, line 593.

His look appall'd, and death was in his blow.

The elder Percevals seem to have been remarkable at once for talent and cruelty. They are sprung from Robert, younger son of Eudes, sovereign Duke of Brittany; but were thence transplanted into Normandy, and at the time of the Conqueror possessed the castle of Yvery, with great estates and power, and the hereditary office of chief butler. Some of the family came to England with William; but Roger de Yvery, faithfully adhering to Robert, his eldest son, against William Rufus, was by the latter dispossessed of many of his lands, and particularly the castle of Yvery in Oxfordshire, which was bestowed on Guy de St. Valery, and was thenceforward called St. Valeria.

In the meantime the main stem of the family reigned at the castle of Yvery in Normandy, which was built by Albreda, wife of Ralph, Earl of Yvery and Baieux, who had more of the lioness than the dove in her composition, for when the castle was finished, she ordered the architect's head to be struck off, that he might not build another like it; and afterwards, attempting to retain possession of it against her own husband, was killed by him in the attempt. Their son Ascelin (sometimes called Gouel de Perceval) inherited all his mother's ferocity, and acquired the surname of Lupus from his violent character. He was a great warrior, and commanded the Norman forces at Mantes, where William the Conqueror received his death-wound. But one of the most remarkable features of Ascelin's life, was his war with the Earl of Bretevil, on account of a woman which his (Ascelin's) youngest brother had ravished. He defeated the Earl, took him prisoner, and confined him three months in the castle of Breherval, where he was treated with the utmost severity, and exposed at the upper windows of the fortress to the frost in the depth of winter, covered only by his shirt, which was previously dipped in water, and in this situation was he compelled to remain till it froze to his back. Nor could he escape *ex ore Lupi*, from the jaws of the wolf, till he agreed to give three thousand dreux pounds for his ransom: and, what must have been more galling than all the rest, to yield his only daughter in marriage to Ascelin. Nevertheless the war revived, till in three years the Earl was nearly ruined, but he found means to interest Philip King of France and Robert Duke of Normandy in his cause, and also the clergy, who were incensed against Asceline for the little reverence he had shewn them. In Lent, 1095, the Earl, with the forces which all these allies could raise, assisted by Robert de Belesme, a very expert officer, and an inveterate enemy to Ascelin, and by the engines which had lately been used at the siege of Jerusalem (they having been invented about that time by a famous engineer in the first crusade), attacked Asceline, in Breherval; but he defended it two months against them all, and at last made a treaty, by which he remained in possession of all his honours, only allowing the Earl of Bretevil to retain quietly his castle of Yvery, the suzerainty of which Duke Robert had bestowed on him, and which was one cause of quarrel. Ascelin not liking to pay to the Earl the homage he had formerly paid to the Duke.

The second son of Ascelin, William, surnamed *Lupellus*, or *the little wolf*, rebelled against Henry the First. After an unsuccessful battle, he was taken prisoner by a peasant, but bribed him with his arms to let him escape. The peasant shaved him in the manner of an Esquire, and carrying a staff in his hand he reached the Seine, where he was forced to give his shoes to the boatman for his passage, and so go barefoot home.

William took part with Matilda against Stephen. After his death the surname of Lupellus seems to have become general among his descendants.—Richard his fifth son continued the line, and being nearly related to Earl Strigulph whose mother was like his, a daughter of the Earl of Mellent, he accompanied him in his Irish expedition—and was with RICHARD in the Holy Land.

I ought to apologize for the length of this note, but the history of this family seemed to me to present so good a view of the darker manners of the times, of the discourteous Barons against whom knight errantry was really useful, that I felt unwilling to curtail it.—Ascelin must certainly have been one of the greatest as well as one of the worst men of his time.

Note (kk), page 115, line 688.

And wondering wisdom warbled from his tongue.

Pierre Vidal was one of those strange contrasts, so often met with in the history of the middle ages. The character of his muse was different, or he might perhaps bear a comparison with Alfieri, for while good sense and sound feeling reigned in his poetry, his life was marked by an eccentricity little short of madness. St. Palaye calls him the Don Quixote of Troubadours. The professed admirer of every beautiful woman, he believed himself equally the object of regard, and often boasted of imaginary favours. Having once indulged his vanity at the expense of a Provençal lady, her husband punished him by slitting his tongue. Hugues, the Lord of Baux, took compassion on him, and had him cured. He remained attached to the family, and soon became enamoured of Adelaide wife to Barral de Baux, the head of the house. His whimsical passion was a source of great amusement to this lady and her husband; and the latter, far from being jealous of his extravagancies, gave him arms and habits like his own, and allowed him the freest access to his wife. Adelaide on her part pretended to return his love: but being soon disgusted with the presumption which her affected smiles inspired, she forced her husband to dismiss the unhappy minstrel, who while exhaling his sorrow in verses which are yet remarkable for their sweetness, sought consolation in war, and went with Cœur de Lion to Palestine.

The bravadoes in which he announced his prowess were not less extravagant than the complaints in which he breathed his love. "My enemies," said he, "tremble at my name, and the earth shakes beneath my steps. All that oppose me I cut to pieces."

It may well be believed that such a character was a source of great amusement to the young Knights who accompanied our Lion-hearted Monarch, and they alternately amused themselves with feeding and exposing his follies. During the King's residence in Cyprus, they contrived to marry him to a lady, who appears to have been distantly related to some one of the families which had sate on the throne of Constantinople. They persuaded him that she was niece to the Emperor, and was to have the diadem transferred to her. No more was needful to heighten Vidal's eccentricity to madness. He usurped the Imperial state and title, gave that of Empress to his wife, had a throne carried before him, and expended all his earnings in support of his Utopian dignity. Nay, so incurable was this fancy, that five and twenty years after, he succeeded in collecting a little troop as mad as himself, and made a crusade to Constantinople, in the hope of recovering his empire.

But perhaps the most ridiculous proof of his wildness, was that elicited by his passion for Louve de Penautier, a lady of Carcassonne. As her name signified a female wolf, he thought himself bound not only to assume in her honour the name of *Loup*, but to wear the *wolf*-skin also, and in this disguise to be hunted by his own dogs, whom he would not permit to be called off till he was at the point of death. The lady's compassion prompted her to dress his wounds, but she laughed with her husband at his folly.

This folly, however, scarcely ever touches his writings, and the moment that the muse possessed his fancy, she seems to have inspired him with a discrimination and prudence, which it would have been well if he could have carried into the affairs of life. His tale of the Jongleur not only gives admirable lessons to the young Troubadour for his conduct in the world, but some hints by which his patrons might be benefited. He also composed a treatise on the government of the tongue, an invective against Philip Augustus for not redeeming the Holy Sepulchre; another against the King of Spain, for buying peace from the Moors instead of subduing them. He complains of the conduct of the priesthood, and the encouragement given to heresy by their bad lives. And, finally, he launches into invective against the Emperor Henry the Sixth, for detaining RICHARD in prison, against the faith of nations and the privileges of Crusaders. In short, his themes were various, and generally handled with power.

Note (ll), page 119, line 792.

This zeal in age is fed with Christian blood.

One of the first exploits of Saladine was the overthrow of the Egyptian or Fatimite Caliph, who had his residence in Cairo, and was of course the determined enemy of the orthodox caliph, or Caliph of Bagdad. Saladine was through life remarkable for his strict adherence to the doctrines and observances of Islam; and though the Crusaders often forced his noble mind to respect individuals, his hatred of their religion seems to have been not less virulent than theirs for Mohammedanism.

Note (mm), page 120, line 804.

And Mosul's lord was vassal of his hand.

Yemen, or Arabia Felix, was conquered for Saladine by his brother Touranschah, a man whose bloody and violent disposition formed a strong contrast to that of the Soldan. Saladine was long engaged in war with the Sultans of Mosul, whom after a violent contest he subdued.

Note (nn), page 120, line 806.

My fatal reign, my sorrow, and my shame.

There is little temptation to enlarge on the melancholy picture presented by the last years of the kingdom of Jerusalem. Amalric was a brave soldier, and might have made his power respectable, but his avarice and inconsistency ruined his cause. The blind passion with which he sought to obtain the wealthy dominion of Egypt led him into long and useless wars, while at the same time he had the inconceivable folly to sell some of his strongest fortresses to the Saracens and the next moment to break the peace formed with them, if the slightest prospect of advantage was held out from another quarter. His son Baldwin the fourth was only thirteen when Amalric died, and was afflicted with leprosy. Raymond of Tripoli became Regent during his minority, but his reign from the first hour of its commencement was disturbed by the dissensions of his nobles. As Baldwin grew up to manhood he took the reins of government into his own hands and signalized his brief authority by the complete defeat of Saladine near Ascalon. But his spirit and activity gave

BOOK XIII.

Note (a), page 174, line 50.

Dark was Count Maynard, and his scowling look.

Maynard de Gortz, distinguished by Hoveden as a satellite of Leopold and enemy to RICHARD. He was nephew to Conrad.

Notes (b) and (c), page 175, line 95.

Soft Marie's tales, Alphonso's princely lays.

Those who have perused Mr. Ellis's agreeable abstract of our old English Romances of Chivalry, can scarcely fail to remember with pleasure the twelve lays of Marie of France, said to have been composed at the court of our Henry the Second, and which appear to contain more novelty and elegance of invention than is usual in the Fabliaux of that age.

Alphonzo the Second, King of Arragon, was himself a Troubadour and the patron of Troubadours, in whose eyes his bounty covered his numerous vices and his notorious want of public faith. The songs of Bertrand de Born, prove, however, that there were others of the tuneful brotherhood, whose hatred painted in the darkest colours the Prince whom their flattery adorned with every virtue. Beatrix, the sister of Alphonso, was married to Raymond Berenger, Count of Provence. They were both votaries of the Muses.

Note (d), page 176, line 99.

Arnaud, whose strains the female heart allure.

Arnaud Daniel has been celebrated both by Petrarch and Dante. The former calls him the " Great Master of Love," and in a poem, where he begins each stanza with a line from some celebrated poet, he has borrowed one from him, the only Provençal on whom he confers that honour. Nevertheless, the taste of modern critics has agreed to prefer what remains to us of Arnaud de Marveil, whom Petrarch calls " the less famous Arnaud." Arnaud de Marveil was long attached to Adelaide, daughter of Raymond of Toulouse, married to the Viscount de Beziers; but Alphonso of Arragon was also an admirer of this lady; and the unhappy Troubadour was at last dismissed, to appease the jealousy of his royal rival.

Note (e), page 176, line 108.

When Princes sought, and Queens adjudged the prize.

Eleanor of Guyenne presided for some time over the Courts of Love, which her son RICHARD, then only Count of Poitou, held at Avignon. At these meetings questions in the science of Love were frequently debated; some favourite Knight took the name of " the Nightingale, the counsellor of Love," and sustained his side of the argument against other Cavaliers under the names of the Goldfinch, the Chaffinch, &c. It was always understood that the nightingale was to be victorious. One specimen of these questions or *tensons d'amour* will probably be sufficient:

One lady being beloved by a very valiant knight, commanded him to abstain from a tournament, and the prize was in consequence obtained by his rival.

Another lady, whose cavalier was a coward, urged him to enter the lists;—he did so, and was victorious.

Which of these knights gave the strongest proof of love?

Note (f), page 177, line 128.

And knightly youth to deathless deeds inspire.

The reader is requested to bear in mind the distinction between the Langue d'Oc, or Provençal dialect, now preserved only in the songs of the Troubadours and the Patois of some regions of France, and the Langue d'Oil, or Romanse language, the parent of the modern French, in which the Trouvères composed their Fabliaux, and the early romances of chivalry.

Note (g), page 177, line 139.
Such Pierre has framed.

Pierre Cardinal, who lived nearly a century, and died about the year 1200, is called by Sismondi the Juvenal of Provençal poetry. His numbers seem to have been as harmonious as his satire was severe, and he spared neither the highest clergy, the military orders, the monks, nobles, nor even the ladies. Of the clergy he says (with a boldness which in those days is almost inconceivable): "Indulgences, pardons, God and the Devil; they make use of all. To some they grant Paradise by their pardons, and others they send to hell by their excommunication. There is no crime which the monks will not absolve, and they sell to renegades and usurers the sepulture which they refuse to the poor. To live in idleness, to buy good fish, the whitest bread, the most exquisite wine: this is their whole employment. Would to Heaven I belonged to their order, if this be the way of salvation!"

In another place he says:—" Du levant au couchant, je fais cette proposition à tout le monde : je promets un besant d'or à tout homme loyal, pourvu que chaque homme déloyal me donne un clou. D'un petit gâteau je nourrirais tout ce qu'il y a d'honnêtes gens ; mais, si je voulais donner à manger aux méchans, j'irais sans regarder, criant partout : Messieurs, venez manger chez moi." The contrast between this Troubadour and his contemporaries, who devoted the charms of " la gaie science" exclusively to arms and love, induces me to make one more quotation from Pierre Cardinal:—" Once on a time a storm of rain fell on a city, which struck with madness every person whom it wetted; and all but one individual, who was asleep and did not leave his house, shared this fate. When he waked, the rain had ceased, and he went forth to pay visits to his fellow citizens, whom he found indulging in every species of extravagance; one was dressed, another naked; one spit up into the air, another was flinging stones; one was tearing his clothes, another was dressed in royal robes, and believed himself to be a king. The one rational being was astonished to find that all had lost their senses, and sought on every side for a sensible person, but sought in vain. The more he was amazed, the more they too were surprised at his orderly deportment, and they did not hesitate to affirm that *he* had lost his reason, because they perceived that his actions bore no resemblance to their own. Then arose an emulation between them, each striving to inflict on him the greatest number of blows; they push, tear, shake, and overwhelm him; now they knock him down, now they raise him up; and with difficulty he saves himself by gaining his own lodging, covered with mud and half dead.— This fable is a representation of the world, and of those who compose it. The world is the city filled with frantic people; covetousness is the rain with which it is inundated; and pride and depravity have enveloped all men. If any one has been preserved from them by the assistance of God, he is considered as a fool, tormented, and persecuted, because he thinks not like others."

Note (h), page 184, line 291.

On three huge crags, with horrid depths between.

It would be little amusing to the reader to enter into the various etymologies of the name of Trivallis, or even the different opinions respecting its locality. Mr. Sharon Turner and Mr. Mills read it Tyrolis, and consign the lion-hearted King to a castle in the Tyrol. The description in the poem is partly taken from some notes on the subject with which I have been furnished by the kindness of M. Schweighæuser, Jun., Professor of Greek philosophy at Strasbourg; though the vicinity to Landau agrees but ill with the relation that RICHARD was confined in that castle while in the power of the Duke of Austria, and before his fate was generally known. But there are other places which assert the name of Trivallis, and I am inclined to think, that as RICHARD was not only immured by Leopold, but afterwards compelled to follow the motions of the Imperial Diet to Haguenau, Worms, Spires, and Mayence, every castle which can pretend to the honour of having sheltered the heroic monarch is anxious to claim a title so illustrious. I subjoin a portion of M. Schweighæuser's letter:

"Le mention de nos monumens me conduit au château de *Trivallis*, que nous appellons *Trifels (fels* signifie roche, et *Tri* paraît designer le nombre de trois, quoiqu'on ait trouvé aussi d'autres étymologies). Mais je l'ai aussi vu moi-même, et je viens encore de recueillir quelques renseignemens à ce sujet auprès d'un habitant des environs. Vous trouverez quelques indications intéressantes sur les circonstances historiques qui se rattachent à ce château, dans le t. ii. p. 188, de l'*Alsatia Illustrata* de Schœpflin, qui se trouve sans doute dans quelque Bibliothèque de Londres. Outre votre RICHARD, Henri VI. y avait fait garder d'autres prisonniers illustres, et des trésors immenses, et déjà Henri cinq en avait fait un usage pareil. Quant à la position, ce château, flanqué de deux autres plus petits et séparés du château principal par des vallées, est situé à environ trois lieues à l'ouest de la ville de Landau, sur une montagne sauvage, couvert de forêts ténébreuses, mais dominant la riante vallée, où se trouve la petite ville d'Anweiler. Le hazard d'une promenade solitaire, et qui n'avoit d'autre but que de gravir, avec l'impétuosité de la jeunesse, les hauteurs et les rochers, m'y conduisit il y a plus de vingt-cinq ans, et je fus singulièrement frappé par les beautés sauvages de ce site, par les murs imposants du château que je découvris tout-à-coup et dont une tour formidable existe encore, ainsi que par les cris des oiseaux de proie que mon approche troubloit dans leur repos."

Note (i), page 186, line 337.

And steal his accents as I steal his song.

The following lines are nearly a translation of the original song, which is preserved both in the French and Provençal dialects.

Note (k), page 188, line 370.

Th' Imperial Eagle claims the prey.

Leopold sold his royal prisoner to the Emperor Henry VI. for 60,000 *pounds* of silver, of the standard weight of Cologne. With this sum Leopold *built the walls of Vienna*, purchased the duchies of Styria and Neuburg, the counties or earldoms of Linz and Wells, and the bishoprics of Passau and Wurtzbourg.

Note (l), page 195, line 533.

Or roam as wolves, to feast on human blood.

The belief that those who deal in magic are compelled annually to wear for a certain period the form of ravenous animals, and that they are then the most ferocious beasts of the forest, seems to have been a favourite superstition in many parts of the world. America has its wizard tigers; the forests of Germany their weir-wolves, and those of Armorica their loups-garoux, or bisclaverets. In the Lays of Marie of France (mentioned in a preceding note on this book), there is a pleasing fable under the name of Bisclaveret, and the German tale of The Three Sisters, with perhaps many others, have their origin in the same superstition.

Note (m), page 200 line 667.

By vows on Sylvia's conquer'd ramparts made.

Sancho, son of Alphonso, the first king of Portugal, was

assisted in his conquest of Sylvia from the Moors by a party of RICHARD's Crusaders, then repairing to the rendezvous at Messina. The Germans and French, on their way to the second Crusade, had in like manner aided his father in the reduction of Lisbon.

BOOK XIV.

Note (a), page 223, line 121,

Who mourn'd by Henry's craft a brother slain.

The Archbishops of Cologne and Mayence, the Dukes of Louvain, Lembourg, and Saxony, and many other Magnates, were at this time indignant against the Emperor on account of the murder of the Bishop of Liege, brother to the Duke of Louvain, which he was believed to have brought about. This circumstance strengthened their exertions on behalf of RICHARD.

Note (b), page 224, line 158.

And the black soul in lingering tortures fled.

Otho of Burgundy died at Acre on his homeward voyage.

Note (c), page 226, line 186.

Resume thy Seals, and be thyself again.

At this interview, RICHARD not only forgave Longchamp for all the mischief which his intemperate conduct had excited, but restored him to his dignity as Chancellor of England.

Note (d), page 227, line 218.

His form majestic, and commanding air.

In the church of Haguenau, which is ancient enough to have been the scene of this conference, the stone pulpit is covered with bas reliefs, representing the whole story of St.

George and the Dragon, his deliverance of Sabra, and her restoration to her parents. The legend of St. George appears to be popular in Alsace and the neighbouring cantons of Switzerland, where it is frequent on the fountains and in the churches.

Note (e), page 230, line 300.

Of my Constantia's claims, and well-known right.

Constantia, Empress of Germany, sister to King William of Sicily, was certainly his legitimate heir, if a female succession were allowed. Those who are interested to see how far the poem adheres to history, in the relation of this memorable trial, the seven charges, and the celebrated reply of RICHARD, may consult Matthew Paris, Hoveden, or the concise but very clear account of Hume.

Note (f), page 233, line 366.

And give this demon back to power again.

The opinion entertained of RICHARD's talents is shewn by the epithet with which his enemies honoured him. Philip Augustus apprized John of his liberation in these words. "Take heed to yourself, the devil is unchained."

Note (g), page 235, line 398.

Th' Armoric Peers or Paladins of old.

RICHARD's object at Messina was not only to demand his sister's freedom, she having been thrown into prison by Tancred for opposing his elevation, but to secure repayment of her dower, and those treasures which William had bequeathed to Henry the Second, and which RICHARD claimed as his father's heir. Among these was a chair of state of massy gold, belonging to the Queen; and a table formed of one piece of native gold, large enough for twelve persons to dine at. These claims were commuted for a certain quantity of ships and money.

Note (h), page 239, line 496.

And tears are glistening in unwonted eyes.

RICHARD's defence moved the assembly to tears. The heroes of the Crusades were almost as much given to weeping as those of Homer and Virgil: but the eloquence and arguments of the English Monarch seem to have produced no common sensation on the Magnates of Germany. His liberation was certainly due to their conviction of his innocence and injuries.

Note (i), page 239, line 504.

Of Cologne weight, and of the purest gold.

More accurately one hundred thousand marks of the standard weight of Cologne, half to be paid before his liberation and half on his arrival in England; and fifty thousand marks to assist the Emperor in the acquisition of Sicily.

Note (k), page 240, line 530.

Or yield allegiance to his crown no more.

For the honour of the Magnates of Germany, this fact is historical. If the Emperor had been susceptible of shame, he ought to have felt it at that moment.

Note (l), page 241, line 542.

To Arab lutes the merry Christians dance.

This is no ideal picture. In the suspensions of hostility which occurred during the third Crusade, it was often realized. Since the time of Godfrey the spirit of bigotry was evidently much softened on both sides, and the virtues of Saladine and the prowess of the European kings, had conciliated a mutual esteem, which communicated itself to their followers. Gibbon observes, " that on the whole of this war there is a marvellous agreement between the Christian and Mahometan writers, who mutually praise the virtues of their enemies."

Note (m), page 241, line 552.

Who may contend with foes whose sports are these?
This is reported to have been the speech of Saladine, at one of the Christian tournaments to which he was invited.

Note, page 252, line 790.

(Turenne's fair daughter) lured him from my arms.
Maenz, or Amanda de Montagnac, was daughter to the Viscount of Turenne.

Note (o), page 253, line 811.
The letter from his grasp and ran it o'er.
The following lines are much condensed from the original "Sirvente" of Bertrand de Born.

Note (p), page 257, line 900.

And in his hand his sever'd head he bore.
See Dante, Inferno, canto 28.—But Henry, not John, was the name of the "young King."

  I vidi certo; et anchor par ch'io 'l veggia
   Un busto sanza capo andar; si come
   Andavan gli altri de la trista greggia.
  El capo tronco tenea per le chiome
   Pesol con mano, a guisa di lanterna
    * * * * * * * * * * * * *
  Sappi, ch'i son Bertran dal Bornio, quelli,
   Che diedi al re Giovann'i mai conforti—
  I feci 'l padre e 'l figlio in se ribelli:
   Achitophel non fe piu d' Absalone
   Et di David co i malvagi punzelli.
  Perch 'i parti cosi giunte persone,
   Partito porto il mi cerebro lasso
   Dal suo pricipio, ch'e in questo troncone:
  Cosi s'osserva in me lo contrapasso.

BOOK XV.

Note (a), page 268, line 11.

The poor his mite, untax'd the Abbot yields.

Among the ecclesiastical contributors to their Monarch's ransom, Hoveden names the Abbot of Semplingham, of the Cistercian order, who gave his year's wool. But RICHARD directed memoranda to be kept of all the money received from the Church, that it might be faithfully repaid.

Note (b), page 269, line 37.

We guard our captive; so may discord cease.

Fifty thousand marks of silver on the part of the King, and thirty thousand from John, if Henry would detain RICHARD in prison till the Michaelmas following; or one thousand pounds of silver for every month of his captivity; or, finally, one hundred thousand marks of silver from Philip, and fifty thousand from John, if he would confine him another year, or betray him into their hands. " Behold in what manner he loved him !" observes Hoveden, in relating this fraternal proposal. Henry in consequence deferred the liberation of his prisoner, and shewed him the letters. " RICHARD then despaired of his liberty."

Note (c), page 269, line 47.

Have we not sworn? a voice of thunder says.

The Archbishops of Mentz, Cologne, and Saxeburg, the Bishops of Worms, Spires, and Liege, the Duke of Suabia, brother to the Emperor, the Dukes of Austria and Louvain, the Count Palatine of the Rhine, and other Magnates, who were partners in the oath before alluded to respecting RICHARD's safety, reproached the Emperor with his avarice, and compelled him to be faithful.—*Hoveden, fol.* 413.

It is curious to find Leopold in this list.

Note (d), page 271, line 89.

True to thy cause, though late he seem'd thy foe.

The Archbishops of Mentz and Cologne were particularly active in the deliverance of the King. RICHARD promised to assist the empire against France, and received the homage of all the Magnates, " saving their fidelity to the Emperor."

Note (e), page 272, line 124.

Received the King, nor England known his doom.

Perhaps of all the disgraceful circumstances which attended the captivity of RICHARD, this last is the most scandalous. Henry repented that he had let him go, and wished to recover his captive, that he might either obtain the promised gold of John and Philip, or a larger ransom—but RICHARD had just sailed when the pursuers reached Antwerp, " and they dared not follow him by sea."—*Walter of Hemingford*, p. 539.

Note (f), page 273, line 127.

Now Trenchemer joys to steer his long-lost lord.

Alain de Trenchemer, the favourite pilot of RICHARD, is celebrated both in history and romance. His surname was probably derived from his skill. Many ships met the King on his voyage, and his people wept for joy at his return.

Note (g), page 274, line 154.

Not twice thy ransom would have brought thee here.

" The citizens having changed their tears into the oil of gladness, the face of the whole city was adorned, so that the German nobles that accompanied RICHARD, and who believed that England had been drained for the ransom of the King, were astonished at the greatness of its wealth, and one of them said to RICHARD, ' I admire, oh King! the prudence of thy people. Now that thou art returned, they shew their riches in safety; but a short time since, when thou wert in the custody of our Emperor, they deplored their poverty. Verily, O King, if the Emperor could have foreseen the wealth of the English, he would not have believed that England could be easily exhausted; nor have dismissed thee without thou hadst given an intolerable sum for thy redemption.'"—*Walter of Hemingford*, p. 539.

Such speeches are frequently recorded to have been made by foreigners on their visits to England. The latest is perhaps that of the Emperor Alexander.

Note (h), page 275, line 169.

Till RICHARD's might is felt—beneath his power.

The besieged heard the clamour of the multitude, and the sound of the trumpets, but thought it a trick of the generals to delude them. An arrow from the walls killed a man at the King's feet; he afterwards assaulted and took the town.—*Hoveden*.

Note (i), page 276, line 192.

And John's stout rebels fled from Robin Hood.

Mr. Ritson, in his collection of songs, &c. relating to the adventures of Robin Hood, seems to think the popular belief of his having been Earl of Huntingdon, not inconsistent with the manners of the times. Most of the ballads describe him as not being on good terms with John, which countenances the idea that "the King," with whom he had a friendly meeting, was probably RICHARD, especially as Hoveden mentions that after the siege of Nottingham, that Monarch visited Clipstone, and Sherwood Forest, and was much pleased with that part of the country, which he had never seen before. Such an adventure is sufficiently in harmony with RICHARD's character.

Note (k), page 277, line 217.

But a new day rose brighter than the last.

Hoveden records it as a saying, on the death of Henry the Second and accession of RICHARD:

" Mira canam, sol occubuit, nox nulla secuta est. Vere nulla nox secuta est post occasum solis. Nam radius solis solium solis tenens, sole suo jubar lucidius ac latius spargit."

He continues his play of words many lines farther:

" Sol pater, et radius filius cius erat."

Note (l), page 277, line 226.

Used the best means to human wisdom given.

The cross-bow was for some time laid aside, in obedience to the second Lateran Council, which proscribed its use, as an instrument of destruction so powerful and so hateful to God, that he who exercised it against Christians and Catholics should be held accursed. The anathema appears to have occasioned its entire disuse. It had been employed in the first crusade, but does not appear again, even in the Holy Land, till Richard the First, interpreting the prohibition literally, revived it against the Infidels—whose destruction must be equally pleasing to God and man. He afterwards used it in his European battles; and when he fell by the " quarrel" at the siege of Chaluz, it was considered by his enemies as an instance of heavenly retribution.

Note (m), page 280, line 299.

Almighty vengeance shuts the gates of heaven.

Alluding to the Oriental belief that the fall of the Angels was occasioned by their refusal, as creatures formed of the element of fire, to worship Adam, whom God had created of the dust of the earth, and whom their pride considered as inferior.

Note (n), page 288, line 478.

Sole living thing, that seems to live on air.

A small spider, called the naga-t' allah, or " she camel of God," is sometimes the only animal to be seen for many days, and has no visible source of subsistence.

Note, page 288, line 492.

And from their loves the sainted Martyr sprung.

This incident, since so often fabled, seems to have been historically true of the parents of St. Thomas à Becket.

Note (p), page 288, line 496.

Beheld the generous Moor restore his crown.

The adventures of Sancho, brother to Berengaria, and his Moorish mistress, with the assistance afforded him by the Mirammolin in the recovery of his crown, are related at some length by Hoveden, and might furnish materials for three or four romances.

Note (q), page 289, line 517.

Ebbs from each burning limb and bursting vein.

Some travellers assert that the dryness occasioned by the simoom is such as to cause the flesh to crack; so that the sufferer sometimes expires from the consequent loss of blood. Others give a much milder account of its operation, which is probably very various. The most dreadful which I have met with, relates to the Red Desert of Persia.

Note (r), page 291, line 548.

Their lips are yellow with the crust of death.

In the case of persons perishing by thirst in the desert, shortly before death the lips, and all the inside of the mouth, become covered with a yellow crust resembling wax.

Note (s), page 292, line 572.

The juicy melon's sweet and copious draught.

The water-melon, in such regions truly the most precious of fruits, is occasionally found growing in the sand, in the dryest parts of the desert, where its appearance seems little less than miraculous.

Note (s), page 294, line 616.

What seeks the Prince who spurns a friend like me?

The particulars of this revolt, and the two letters of Saladine, are historical.

Note (t), page 311, line 1020.

He spoke, and sunk exhausted in the wave.

The monarch had seen the yellow flags of Saladine on the ramparts, and turned his vessels from a port which he believed already in the hands of his enemies. Jaffa would have been lost, but for the presence of mind and intrepidity of the swimmer. The historical account of the events of this siege have perhaps a stronger interest than can easily be given to a poetical narration.

Note (u), page 315, line 1119.

Led for his use—cried generous Saladine.

See the " Histoire de Saladine."

BOOK XVI.

Note (a), page 330, line 159.

In Sejjin, record of the wrath divine.

Sejjin is the name of the general register, in which are inscribed the actions of the wicked; as Illiyyun is of that which contains the actions of the good. Tasnim is the highest fountain of Paradise; those who are privileged to drink its waters unmixed, shall approach near to the throne of God, and be incessantly employed in the contemplation of the Divinity.—*Koran*.

Note (b), page 330, line 167.

Confusion, Death, upon his impious head.

In the memorable battle of Beder, the first victory of the Faithful, in which Mahommed demanded the succour of Gabriel and three thousand angels; his little troop was beginning to yield before the numbers of the Koreish, when the Prophet, starting from the throne on which he viewed the battle, cast a handful of sand into the air, and exclaimed, " let their faces be covered with confusion." The effect was instantaneous and decisive; both armies in fancy beheld the angelic warriors; the Koreish trembled and fled.—*Gibbon, Decline and Fall*, vol. 9.

Note (c), page 345, line 502.

Meet sin and judgment—I, by birth a Queen!

At the time when the monarchs of France pretended to the title of King of Kings, its Princesses affected that of Queen, which was sometimes given to Alasia; but whether in compliment to her birth, or to her contract with RICHARD, I am uncertain.

Note (d), page 345, line 503.

And if I cannot, like some Sovereigns, kneel.

An allusion to the penance of Henry the Second, after the murder of Becket; and to some of the effects of RICHARD's remorse on the loss of his father, to whose death he accused himself of having at least contributed by his rebellious conduct.

Note (e), page 354, line 713.

The easy price of that triumphant day.

Only two persons of any note are said to have perished on the Christian side in the double battle of Jaffa, which may certainly be reckoned among the most extraordinary in history.

Those who may be desirous of perusing its details, will find many interesting particulars in the Histoire de Saladin, and the Histories of the Crusades; but Gibbon's short account is perhaps more flattering to the fame of RICHARD CŒUR DE LION, than any thing else which has been written respecting him; unless it be Mr. Sharon Turner's admirable sketch of his reign, in his History of England.

The terms of the treaty between RICHARD and Saladine, and the facts on which the concluding pages of the poem are founded, are in the histories of the Crusades. Some liberties have been taken, especially in condensing into one scene the solemn swearing of the peace at Ramla, the accomplishment of the vows of the Crusaders, the celebration of mass in the church of the Holy Sepulchre, and the behaviour of Saladine on witnessing the descent of the Sacred Fire; but almost all the circumstances are historical.

THE END.

LONDON:
PRINTED BY COX AND BAYLIS, GREAT QUEEN STREET,
LINCOLN'S-INN-FIELDS.

PRESERVATION SERVICE

SHELFMARK 994.H.25

THIS BOOK HAS BEEN
MICROFILMED (2004   )
          N.S.T.C.

MICROFILM NO *SEE RPM*

CPSIA information can be obtained
at www.ICGtesting.com
Printed in the USA
LVHW060747230222
711783LV00002B/6